Communicating
EFFECTIVELY

ELEVENTH EDITION

Saundra Hybels

Richard L. Weaver II

Mc
Graw
Hill
Education

COMMUNICATING EFFECTIVELY, ELEVENTH EDITION

Published by McGraw-Hill Education, 2 Penn Plaza, New York, NY 10121. Copyright © 2015 by The McGraw-Hill Education, Inc. All rights reserved. Printed in the United States of America. Previous editions © 2012, 2009, and 2007. No part of this publication may be reproduced or distributed in any form or by any means, or stored in a database or retrieval system, without the prior written consent of The McGraw-Hill Education, Inc., including, but not limited to, in any network or other electronic storage or transmission, or broadcast for distance learning.

Some ancillaries, including electronic and print components, may not be available to customers outside the United States.

This book is printed on acid-free paper.

1 2 3 4 5 6 7 8 9 0 DOW/DOW 1 0 9 8 7 6 5 4

ISBN 978-0-07-352387-3
MHID 0-07-352387-9

Senior Vice President, Products & Services: *Kurt L. Strand*
Vice President, General Manager, Products & Services: *Michael Ryan*
Vice President, Content Production & Technology Services: *Kimberly Meriwether David*
Managing Development Editor: *Penina Braffman*
Marketing Specialist: *Alexandra Schultz*
Director, Content Production: *Terri Schiesl*
Senior Content Project Manager: *Joyce Watters*
Buyer: *Susan K. Culbertson*
Cover Designer: *Studio Montage, St. Louis, MO*
Cover Image: *(left to right) Hill Street Studios/Getty Images, Alberto Pomares/Getty Images, Photodisc Red/Getty Images, Tetra Images/Getty Images, Juice Images/Getty Images, franckreporter/Getty Images*
Media Project Manager: *Jennifer Bartell*
Compositor: *MPS Limited*
Typeface: *10/12 Kepler Std*
Printer: *R.R. Donnelley*

All credits appearing on page or at the end of the book are considered to be an extension of the copyright page.

Library of Congress Cataloging-in-Publication Data

Hybels, Saundra.
   Communicating effectively / Saundra Hybels.—Eleventh edition.
      pages cm
   ISBN 978-0-07-352387-3 (pbk.)
   1. Oral communication.   I. Weaver, Richard L., 1941 - II. Title.
   P95.H9 2014
   302.2'242—dc23

2013039344

The Internet addresses listed in the text were accurate at the time of publication. The inclusion of a website does not indicate an endorsement by the authors or McGraw-Hill Education, and McGraw-Hill Education does not guarantee the accuracy of the information presented at these sites.

www.mhhe.com

Brief Contents

Contents

Preface xi

PART ONE

Basic Principles of Communication

PART THREE

Other Forms of Communication

PART FOUR

Communicating in Public

Chapter 12
Getting Started and Finding Speech Material   310

Chapter 13
Organizing and Outlining the Speech   338

Chapter 14
Delivering the Speech   362

Chapter 15
Informative and Persuasive Speeches   *390*

Preface

Communicating Effectively, Eleventh Edition, is written for students taking speech communication classes for the first time. The book covers the theory and practice of communication, first by examining the communication process, second by discussing interpersonal communication, third by looking at other forms of communication including group and intercultural, Professional communication is discussed in an online chapter. Communication that occurs on the Internet is covered in Chapter 8, "Communication and Technology" in the section on interpersonal communication. The theory and practice of communication is covered, fourth, through a thorough examination of public communication. The overall approach of the book is pragmatic, so that students can not only see but also appreciate the practical application of the ideas, concepts, and theories in their own lives and in the lives of people who are close to them. The pragmatic approach is balanced with a discussion of a number of important theories: Expectancy Violation Theory, Optional Distinctiveness Theory, Relational Dialectics, Social Penetration Theory, Social Exchange Theory, Symbolic Convergence Theory, Leader-Member Exchange Theory, and The Functional Perspective. These theories are important not just for better understanding communication but for analyzing our own communication and the communication of others as well.

Approach

The five specific approaches that appeared throughout the tenth edition have not changed in the eleventh edition. The first approach, Active Open-Mindedness (AOM) boxes, is located in most chapters and is designed to encourage readers to digest, master, and use the knowledge of the textbook by offering practice opportunities in critical examination, analysis, and thought.

The second approach offers readers an opportunity to draw together theory and practice. In each chapter there is an Attention! Reality Check feature, the sole purpose of which is to challenge students to think more deeply and yet more practically about the ideas, concepts, or approaches *and to apply them to their lives.* It is our purpose to get students to take the concepts they are just learning about and bring them into their own real-world experience. We repeatedly ask the questions: (1) Does this make sense? (2) Does this appear logical? (3) Can this happen, or how has this happened in your life? and (4) In what ways might this help you communicate more effectively?

The third approach is simply an answer to the question, "Why study this?" This approach begins in Chapter 1 in the opening section entitled "Everyone Needs Communication Skills," but it continues in the following chapters with sections such as, "The Role of Self and Perception in Communicating Effectively and Strategic Flexibility," "The Role of Verbal Communication in Communicating Effectively and Strategic Flexibility," "The Role of Nonverbal Communication in Communicating Effectively and Achieving Strategic Flexibility," and "The Role of Listening in Communicating Effectively and Strategic Flexibility." The hope is that by the time readers have finished Chapter 5, "Listening," they will not just understand the importance of communicating effectively but recognize, too, how communicating effectively depends on strategic flexibility.

The fourth approach is introduced in Chapter 1, integrated into each of the following chapters, and then added as marginal comments wherever appropriate throughout every chapter. It is called Attention! Strategic Flexibility (SF) which is a value-added system students can use to add to, improve on, and increase their communication skills. SF means expanding your communication repertoire (your collection or stock of communication behaviors that can readily be brought into use) to enable you to use the best skill or behavior available for a particular situation. It is a "value-added" concept because students can use it to build on the skills they already possess. The six-step program for applying SF to real-life situations includes the steps—(1) anticipate, (2) assess, (3) evaluate, (4) select, (5) apply, and (6) reassess and reevaluate. The importance of SF is that most people believe they already communicate well enough, perhaps even very well; thus, they don't need a course in or a book on speech communication. SF is a concept that honors those beliefs and yet suggests that communication repertoires can be expanded, and the more expansion that occurs, the more likely people can "use the best skill or behavior available for particular situations." Simply put, they have more tools in their toolbox.

The fifth approach has to do with the influence of the Internet. Many of the twenty-five sections throughout the tenth edition that focused on the Internet have been moved to Chapter 8, "Communication and Technology," which appears in the section on interpersonal communication. Some, for example, the section on using the Internet to research speeches, remain in the eleventh edition where they were in the tenth edition because of their relevance with particular topics. Also, the section "Resolving Conflict Online" remains in its previous location.

There is an applied, problem-solution orientation that has been evident throughout all the previous editions of this book. This could be viewed as an approach, however, it is woven tightly into the core and fabric of each chapter. That is, it is precisely what this book is about. It can be seen in the use of the Active Open-Mindedness (AOM) boxes, in the use of the Strategic Flexibility (SF) paradigm, as well as in the "Attention! Reality Check" feature which, as noted above, challenges students to think more deeply and practically about the ideas, concepts, and approaches as they apply them to their own lives.

The applied, problem-solution orientation can be seen, too, in the overall approach of your authors as they encourage readers with suggestions for improving their self-concept, adjusting to the perceptual influences in their lives, working on their communication skills, improving their nonverbal communication, talking so others will listen to them, demonstrating the elements of good relationships and improving their relationships using communication strategies, resolving conflicts, improving intercultural communication, communicating effectively online, participating in and leading groups, as well as researching, organizing, and delivering informative and persuasive speeches. For this edition, the chapter on communicating professionally has been moved online.

Each of these approaches—and, certainly, the applied, problem-solution orientation—has the same purpose: to make the book readable, interesting, and challenging. Most important, however, is that they make the book immediate, significant, and relevant: they bring communication into the day-to-day lives of students.

Organization and Coverage

The chapters will again be ordered in a logical way that increases flexibility for users of the book.

A. Basic Principles of Communication

The first four chapters are basic and provide the essential foundation. Chapter 5 on listening can either be part of the foundation or part of the interpersonal unit. We have placed it as part of the interpersonal unit simply to balance the number of chapters in the first and second parts.

1. The Communication Process
2. Self, Perception, and Communication
3. Verbal Communication
4. Nonverbal Communication

B. Interpersonal Communication

The next five chapters are part of the interpersonal unit, although Chapter 9 on "Conflict and Conflict Management" can be tied to the interpersonal chapters, to the online professional communication chapter, to discussions Communication and Technology, or to the small-group chapter, or it can be a transitional chapter used whenever needed to cover the time it takes to run activities. It includes a discussion of conflict in interpersonal, Internet, professional, and group situations.

5. Listening
6. Interpersonal Relationships
7. Evaluating and Improving Relationships

8. Communication and Technology

9. Conflict and Conflict Management

C. Other Forms of Communication

The next two chapters offer great flexibility of use. The chapter on intercultural communication and the online chapter on professional communication may or may not be used. They can be used before, during, or after the small-group chapter to allow time to run exercises and activities.

10. Intercultural Communication

11. Small-Group Participation and Leadership

D. Communicating in Public

The final four chapters remain unchanged (with respect to their order) from previous editions. We have combined the tenth edition's two separate chapters on informative and persuasive speeches into one. There is no loss of content, however, it makes the amount of content assigned while speeches take place less of an apparent burden on students.

12. Getting Started and Finding Speech Material

13. Organizing and Outlining the Speech

14. Delivering the Speech

15. Informative and Persuasive Speeches

New to This Edition

The eleventh edition includes a significant number of changes, and we continue in our desire to effectively meet the needs of both instructors and students as well as to make the book practical, current, and relevant. There are new additions or changes to each chapter; however, there are three large ones that may affect the way a syllabus is constructed:

1. Chapter 8, "Communication and Technology" is an entirely new chapter. Many of the references to technology within other chapters have either been deleted or updated in this new chapter. Those references to technology that remain in other chapters are areas not covered in this new chapter.

2. All three speeches have been moved online.

3. The final two chapters, "The Informative Speech," and "The Persuasive Speech," have been combined to form a single Chapter 15, "Informative and Persuasive Speeches."

- *Consider This sections.* There is one Consider This box in each chapter. All chapters, with the exception of just one, have a new Consider This box.

- *Another Point of View sections.* There is one Another Point of View box in each chapter. All chapters, with the exception of just one, have a new Another Point of View box.

- *Active Open-Mindedness (AOM) sections and marginal boxes* have been retained in their entirety because of their popularity and their positive review by critics.

- *Chapter 1, "The Communication Process."* The opening example that includes references to current technology has been expanded and updated. In the section, "Everyone Needs Communication Skills, the results of a 2010 national survey of employers has been included, which, according to a report in *Spectra*,

"Communication Departments Hold Vital Role," states that "The ability to communicate effectively, orally and in writing," is the first "Select Learning Outcome" that employers want colleges to place greater emphasis on. Also included is the sentence, "But have no doubt about it, whether you are a male or female, your success in this world depends on effective communication skills." The new "Another Point of View" box emphasizes "How sharing in the digital age improves the way we work and live," the subtitle of a book, *Public Parts,* by Jeff Jarvis. To the section, "The Internet and the Model of Communication," we added a quotation by Thomas L. Friedman about globalization and the information technology revolution, in which he says, "to get into the middle class now, you have to study harder, work smarter, and adapt quicker than ever before. There are two new supporting quotations for strategic flexibility, from Kelly McGonigal's book *The Willpower Instinct* and from Newberg and Waldman's book *Words Can Change Your Brain.* There is greater support for how to increase your everyday creativity from Tina Seelig's book *inGenius: A Crash Course on Creativity.* Finally, the new "Consider This" box focuses on the work of Carol Dweck and promotes a belief in growth and improvement—an idea that effectively leads readers to the textbook information that follows.

- *Chapter 2, "Self Perception and Communication."* To the section, "The Role of Self and Perception in Communicating Effectively and Strategic Flexibility," we added a Nathaniel Branden quotation, "No factor is more important in people's psychological development and motivation than the value judgments they make about themselves." The new "Consider This" box focuses on a study by Carol Dweck and Lisa Sorich Blackwell which "demonstrates that your mind-set and attitude are within your own control." There are two quotations by experts that will affect readers' work on their self-concepts. The first involves "letting go of what other people think and making choices that are *right for you . . . ,*" and the other supports the importance of trusting your intuition. There is a new quotation in the section "Social Comparisons" that encourages readers to be realistic, look on the bright side, and determine to try harder, be better, and improve your lot in life. The section, "Where Should Change Begin?," now begins with the quotation, "One of the most defining choices you can make in your entire life," writes Brendon Burchard in his book *The Charge,* "is deciding to control the quality of person you will be on an everyday basis." A new paragraph of clarification and explanation has been added to the section, "The Map Is Not the Territory," by Henry Hitchings, from his book *The Language Wars.* The new "Another Point of View" box from David M. Eagleman's book *Incognito,* is designed to challenge readers regarding the way they perceive reality. In the section, "Deletions, Distortions, and Generalizations," the quotation from Art Markman, from his book *Smart Thinking,* explains why very little of the information in the world makes it into our heads."

- *Chapter 3, "Verbal Communication."* At the end of the opening section of this chapter there is information on the predominance of English in the world, and the section ends with a challenge to readers drawn from the work of Andrew Newberg and Mark Robert Waldman, in their book *Words Can Change Your Brain,* "that we are surprisingly unskilled when it comes to communicating with others": Anything at all that we can do to promote enhancement in this area (the use of language) will obviously have positive benefits for us now and in the future. "The story of the Turtle and the Fish" has been added as a marginal "Attention!" box. To the section, "People Determine Meanings," Newberg and Waldman, from their book *Words Can Change Your Brain,* emphasize the neurological fact that the language we use to convey our feelings, thoughts, and beliefs is a very personal and unique experience. Lexicographer Joan Houston Hall emphasizes the uniqueness of the "quite normal English" that each of us speaks. Roy F. Baumeister and John Tierney, in *Willpower,* write about the use of "appropriate" language. The section, "Gender and Language," has been completely rewritten to include the four basic beliefs that underlie any examination of the relationship of gender and language, the five reasons why sensitivity to gender and language is important, why no single interactional style characterizes either men or women, and why gender in language is more than just differences. The "Another Point of View" box by Newberg and Waldman, from *Words Can Change Your Brain,* supports their contention that "Men and women think, feel, and speak in essentially the same way." The "Consider This" box by Henry Hitchings, from his book *The Language Wars,* underscores why clarity in language is so important. Seth S. Horowitz, from his book *The Universal Sense,* offers a practical example of metamessages.

- *Chapter 4, "Nonverbal Communication."* In her book, *Why You're Not Married,* Tracy McMillan offers an interesting (and provocative) insight regarding what nonverbal cues men look for in women in the "Another Point of View" box. Under the heading, "Types of Nonverbal Communication," there is information on which nonverbal features first catch a person's eye. In the section, "Eye Messages," the effect of the size of the pupil is discussed. There is more material on the advantages of attractiveness in the section of the same name. Dahlia Lithwick cites Deborah Rhode who discusses the discrimination against unattractive women and short men and the disadvantages of being unattractive. In the "Consider This" box, Barbara L. Fredrickson, in her book *Love 2.0,* explains the unique nonverbal fingerprint of love. Karen Elliott House discusses the abaya, worn by women throughout the Middle East to shield their bodies from view. Gad Saad examines the use of tattoos and optimal distinctiveness theory. The research of Matthew Hertenstein regarding our "innate ability to decode emotions via touch alone" is explained in the section, "Touch," and the distinct emotions communicated are listed as well as the conclusion, "touch is a much more nuanced, sophisticated, and precise way to communicate emotions." There is an additional comment about the role smell has in mate seeking. The first paragraph under "Functions of Nonverbal Communication" was deleted and Robert Leonard's explanation of "schema" as an umbrella concept designed as a better way to understand each of the functions discussed in this section, was offered.

- *Chapter 5, "Listening."* At the end of the opening example about Jahmelia Jackson, the two characteristics of dialogue—which Jackson exhibited—are provided. The "Consider This" box quotes J. Keith Murnighan, from his book *Do Nothing!,* about the values of active listening. Under the heading, "The Difficulty of Listening," the new opening paragraph cites Newberg and Waldman, from their book *Words Can Change Your Brain*, about the great gift of listening deeply and fully to someone as "the most commonly cited deep relationship or communication value." Under the same heading, Conant and Norgaard, from their book *Touch Points*, discuss the problem technology contributes and label it "attention deficit traits" (ADT). Sara Konrath's research, in the section, "Empathic Listening," reveals that college students today show 40 percent less empathy than students in the 1980s and 1990s. The "Another Point of View" box quotes Seth S. Horowitz saying that "Listening is a skill that we're in danger of losing in a world of digital distraction and information overload." In the section, "Talking So Others Will Listen," Henry Hitchings, from his book *The Language Wars*, mentions the desire to shape and emphasize the engagement with another as crucial, and Newberg and Waldman, in *Words Can Change Your Brain*, offer twelve strategies that will enhance the dynamics of any conversation. Finally, as a seventh technique for "Talking So Others Will Listen," Rich Kirschner, in his book *How to Click With People*, suggests that people look like they understand, even when they don't in order to give others "a respectful space in which to express [themselves]."

- *Chapter 6, "Interpersonal Relationships."* The opening example has new research support from the *UC Berkeley Wellness Letter* that reveals the three major health benefits from having social relationships. Under the heading "Physical Attraction," the top four characteristics men say they look for in a mate are listed, and good looks are nowhere near the top. The new "Consider This" by Rebecca Webber discusses relationship compatibility. The "Another Point of View" box quotes neuroscientist Gary Small, who suggests that not having conversations or looking others in the eye—human contact skills—the neural circuits that control that mental experience will weaken. In the section, "Beginning Conversations: The Art of Small Talk," Bernardo Carducci's five cardinal rules for making small talk are listed. At the end of this same section, Ian Yarett's offers the five most informative and least personal questions to ask a person on a first date. Two paragraphs have been added to the section, "Social Penetration Theory," to provide clarity and an explanation of what happens when relationships fall apart. There is, too, a further development of one of the important aspects of social penetration theory: reciprocity. The introduction to the section, "Essential Elements of Good Relationships," has been expanded to include what it takes for men with unhealthy behavioral patterns to make the personal changes necessary to improve their relationships. There is more information under the heading "Commitment," that suggests people in relationships need to consider and regularly assess their commitment. The section on "Social Exchange Theory" has been expanded to further explain the practical value of the theory and summarize the assumptions upon which the theory is based as well as state the guiding force in interpersonal relationships: the advancement of both parties' self-interest.

- *Chapter 7, "Evaluating and Improving Relationships."* Under the headings, "Coming Together," "Stage 1: Initiating," research is reported that shatters long-held beliefs about what have been considered "deal breakers" in relationships, and the top five deal breakers from the new survey are presented in the order of their importance. New statistics on marriage are presented in the section, "Stage 5: Bonding." The "Another Point of View" box offers strong encouragement to educated women for satisfying marriages and help with housework. The "Coming Apart" section has been expanded to include the necessity of accepting responsibility for relationship termination as well as the twelve rules for better breakups. The "Consider This" box, from an article by Rebecca Webber, challenges readers to discover who they are and what they really want before choosing someone capable of understanding them, meeting their emotional needs, and possessing compatible values. Under the heading, "Ask Yourself Questions," there is a fourth one discussed by Lundy and Patrissi in their book, *Should I Stay or Should I Go?* which includes the need to love yourself. The traits that best predict relationship satisfaction, offered by Jeffry H. Larson, are listed under the heading, "Improving Relationships: Using Communication Strategies."

- *Chapter 8, "Communication and Technology."* The objectives of this new chapter offer a convenient overview of the chapter's contents. We explain how the use of technology can improve our connections with others, describe how technology can have a detrimental effect on face-to-face (FtF) interaction skills, explain the reasons why text messaging has become so important in romantic and sexual correspondence, describe recommendations for making texting a more rewarding experience, explain the disadvantages of using technology, and end by offering guidelines for using it. Our "Consider This" box, from the book *Smarter Than You Think* by Clive Thompson, quotes Andrea Lunsford, who claims that texting is close to FtF conversation when it comes to pacing. We write about the effect of technology on communication, on our connection to others, on self-concept, interaction skills, self-disclosure, conversation skills, and on relationships. The Another Point of View box, from Tony Dokoupil's *Newsweek* article, "Is the Onslaught Making Us Crazy?" suggests that the computer is like electronic cocaine fueling cycles of mania followed by depressive stretches." All uses of technology should be guided by common sense and good manners.

- *Chapter 9, "Conflict and Conflict Management."* To the end of the introductory material, there is new information from Newberg and Waldman, from their book *Words Can Change Your Brain,* about the importance of intuition in dealing with conflict as well as a paragraph that reinforces and underscores the value and importance of strategic flexibility and its role in dealing effectively with conflict. The "Another Point of View" box by Brendon Burchard, from his book *The Charge,* talks about how to deal with relationship conflict using the ratio of five to one—giving five times as much praise as you give criticism. A last paragraph has been added to the section, "Resolving Conflict," that carefully explains the single, most important element that will determine a couple's happiness. The section, "The Bottom Line," now begins with an explanation of the two questions that will determine whether or not couples stay together: Are my needs being met? and "Can you admit you're wrong?" The section, "Resolving Conflict Online," has been retained because 1) it is a common occurrence online, 2) the tips are helpful in any conflict situation, 3) the tips are practical, and 4) it is not covered in Chapter 8, "Communication and Technology." At the end of the section, "Dealing With Conflict at Work," research that reveals the harmful effects of emotionally charged discussions is discussed. The "Consider This" box, "Personality Characteristics of Those Best at Managing Conflict," has been retained in this new edition by popular demand—instructors like it and students love it.

- *Chapter 10, "Intercultural Communication."* To the opening section of this chapter, "The Role of Intercultural Communication in Communicating Effectively and in Strategic Flexibility," a paragraph is added that includes close to fifteen additional possible careers that require some intercultural expertise. Statistics on the rise of the United States' minority population (it now makes up 35 percent of the country) are presented in this section as well. The "Another Point of View" box details the multicultural nature of Mariane Pearl—the widow of Daniel Pearl who was beheaded by his Al-Qaeda captors. Under the heading "Enhancing and Enriching the Quality of Civilization," the statistics on interracial marriages has been updated. The section

"Intercultural Communication and the Internet," has been retained because 1) it is not contained in the Chapter 8, "Communication and Technology," and 2) it contains a terrific example of how the Internet is viewed in a conservative society such as Iraq. Conant and Norgaard, in their book *Touch Points*, offer a new example of "Power Distance." Gad Saad offers an additional example of "Individualism versus Collectivism." The "Consider This" box offers advice from Lindsey Pollak, *Getting from College to Career*, on how to familiarize yourself with any country or culture. In the section "Improving Intercultural Communication," Gary Stoller discusses five areas where etiquette tips for Americans going abroad are useful. Then Ann Marie Sabath, from her book *Business Etiquette, 3rd ed.*, offers the best bottom line to minding your manners abroad—"have a humble and sincere desire to learn more about their culture. . . ." The two final paragraphs of the chapter, under the heading, "Improving Intercultural Communication," come from Paul Theroux, from his book *The Tao of Travel*, and underscores the importance of nonverbal communication—"People's features, particularly their eyes, are wonderfully eloquent."

- *Online Chapter, "Communicating Professionally."* The material in the section, "Gender Differences in the Workplace," has been updated and brought into line with the information on gender in Chapter 3, "Verbal Communication." The section "Communicating Within a Professional Atmosphere," now ends with a quotation from Brendon Burchard, from his book *The Charge*, in which he emphasizes the importance of creative input and collaborations for success in the workplace. A new section, "Telephone Conversations," has been added with the overall admonition: be polite and respectful. Six appropriate procedures are listed when contacting others by phone. The section "Employment Interviews," begins with two new paragraphs. The first lists the various kinds of employment interviews and underscores the importance of preparation for whatever interview type you will face. The second discusses an important point made by John Hoover in his book *How to Work for an Idiot*. "Because there are bad bosses everywhere," he writes, "You might as well master the art of working with them right where you are." The "Another Point of View" box is from the book, *What Color is Your Parachute?*, in which Richard N. Bolles explains that the employment-interview mechanisms by which a person is selected for a job "are often impulsive, intuitive, nonrational, unfathomable, and made on the spur of the moment." The statistics on how to write a resume, electronic resumes, cover letters, and application letters have all been updated. In the "Consider This" box, Lindsey Pollak, from her book *Getting from College to Career*, writes about the importance of networking. Gad Saad ends the section on "Employment Interviews," and reinforces what Bolles said in the "Another Point of View" box by offering a specific example of how illogical and irrational the employment interview can be. The chapter ends with a section, "Presentations," which covers the need for thorough preparation, a natural style of delivery, and effective visuals.

- *Chapter 11, "Small-Group Participation and Leadership."* A discussion of Social Exchange Theory—introduced in Chapter 6, "Interpersonal Communication,"—is offered as a way to examine power inequalities and how power is governed as well as to understand the various ways that rewards and costs are negotiated. Under the topic, "Groupthink," there is new information on why it occurs: the need for conformity. The "Another Point of View" box cites an article by Jonah Lehrer that discusses the results of a study that showed that individual decision making is superior to the decision making of brainstorming groups. The section "Finding and Evaluating Solutions" now ends with a discussion of an "implementation intention" and the three qualities that characterize a good implementation intention. A new section has been added on "Symbolic Convergence Theory" and its contribution to small-group work. There is a new section, too, on "Leader-Member Exchange Theory," which explains how the relationship between a leader and a subordinate can develop in a unique way and how the quality of leader-subordinate exchanges may make a difference in a group's success. A new section, "The Functional Perspective," delineates the four functions that group discussion must accomplish for the group decision to be wise. The section "Leading the Group" begins with a list of responsibilities for leaders to be effective if they want to inspire group members. In the "Consider This" box, Rick Kirschner states that the best way leaders have to get a group of people to click with one another is to invite them to contribute information and ideas and to welcome their input. Under the heading "Seeking Consensus" there is a new paragraph that supports the importance of open debate and criticism.

- *Chapter 12, "Getting Started and Finding Speech Material."* A new "Consider This" box is located near the beginning of this chapter in which Lindsey Pollak, in her book *Getting from College to Career,* writes about the importance of public speaking—"one of the best skills you can develop for a successful job search and career. . . ." The section "Using the Internet" remains simply because the Internet is the biggest and most available resource for those preparing speeches; however, the section begins with new information: 1) the three kinds of information available on the Internet, 2) the importance of becoming proficient in the language of data—marshalling the facts so that others can lean on them, and 3) the importance of Wikipedia (at one time the scourge of scholars) and, according to LiAnna Davis, in her SPECTRA article, "Bringing Wikipedia Into Your Classroom by Choice," "it is the site people all over the world see when they research topics, including communication studies." The "Another Point of View" box by Sean Gresh not only explains the values of stories but also promotes them as "The best place to start and to finish."

- *Chapter 13, "Organizing and Outlining the Speech."* The "Consider This" box by Art Markman, from his book *Smart Thinking,* uses a terrific analogy to describe the value of transitions. Markman is quoted, too, in the new "Another Point of View" box where he discusses the "advance organizer"—a review for listeners of what is to come in the speech. The speech "Fearless Public Speaking" has been moved online (and remains as an outstanding example of a well-organized speech).

- *Chapter 14, "Delivering the Speech."* Under the heading "Coping with Public-Speaking Anxiety," the first full section of the chapter, statistics regarding what activity most people dread are presented—46 percent had public speaking at the top of the list. The section just mentioned ends with a quotation from Alice Park, who says, "In just the right amounts, the hormones that drive anxiety can be powerful stimulants, arousing the senses to function at their sharpest." In the "Another Point of View" box, Glenn Croston, a research biologist, offers a personal example of performance anxiety she experienced as a child. At the end of the section "A Good Place to Begin," Jay Dixit cites Jessica Hayden who gives readers the advice: "Focus less on what's going on in your mind and more on what's going on in the room, less on your mental chatter and more on yourself as *part* of something." Within the section "Visualize," Newberg and Waldman, in their book *Words Can Change Your Brain,* cite the research studies that support their statement, "positive imagery can reduce a negative mood," and that you can "arbitrarily create an optimistic attitude by manipulating your own thoughts." The "Consider This" box explains the effective oral style of Steve Jobs. At the end of the section "Impromptu Speaking," Howard Schultz, president and CEO of Starbucks, presents readers with his own justification for speaking impromptu. The section "Rehearsing Your Speech," includes a quotation from Susan Cain and her bestselling book, *Quiet,* in which she offers an important suggestion about rehearsing: "do it alone because it takes intense concentration, others can be distracting, it requires deep motivation, and it is often difficult working on a most challenging task." The chapter ends with a quotation from Newberg and Waldman, from their book *Words Can Change Your Brain,* with a plea to readers who want to excel at communicating: "You have to immerse yourself fully in the experience of speaking and listening, and you have to practice, practice, practice."

- *Chapter 15, "Informative and Persuasive Speeches."* The biggest change is the assimilation of chapters 15 and 16 of the tenth edition into a single chapter. Also, the sample informative speech ("Forgetting Everything You Ever Learned") and the sample persuasive speech ("Giving Something Back") have been placed online. The "Another Point of View" box offers a quotation from Kevin Dutton, from his book *Split-Second Persuasion,* that emphasizes the fact that successful persuasion is contingent on a complex combination of factors, what Dutton says is "a nervy cocktail of compromise, enterprise, and negotiation."

Supplements to Accompany *Communicating Effectively, Eleventh Edition*

Communicating Effectively is accompanied by a comprehensive package of resources designed to facilitate both teaching and learning. These include:

Online Learning Center www.mhhe.com/hybels11e

The book's website provides students with creative and effective tools that make learning easier and more engaging. These tools are integrated with the text through the use of Online Learning Center (OLC) icons in the text margins that direct students to the appropriate tools. These include:

Self-Quizzes: There are fifteen multiple-choice and five true/false questions for each chapter.

Assess Yourself: Provide scaled responses to the end-of-chapter questionnaires and surveys that challenge students to assess themselves.

PowerPoint Slides: Provide helpful tips and outlines for each chapter.

Instructor's Manual/Test Bank

This manual, available on the book's website, is a source of both daily plans and activities for the classroom. Every chapter of the *Instructor's Manual* contains Learning Objectives, Tips for Teaching, Chapter Highlights, Activities, and Essay Questions. Additionally, the *Instructor's Manual* includes sample course outlines, annotated sample speeches, and a user's guide to the videos. The Test Bank includes true/false, multiple choice, and short answer questions.

Acknowledgments

We would first like to thank all the instructors, teachers, course directors, and department heads who have chosen to use this textbook from among many possible texts. We appreciate your choice, and we consider it both a responsibility and a privilege to be working for you. Likewise, we wish to thank all the students. Although we know it wasn't your choice to read this textbook, we recognize your commitment—especially when you read the book—and we have worked hard on your behalf. Feel free to forward any comments and suggestions directly to the author at weaverii@sbcglobal.net.

My coauthor, Saundra Hybels, died unexpectedly on September 18, 1999. A dedication to her is printed in the sixth edition. Although I (Richard) did the work on the seventh through eleventh editions, I continue to write as if Saundra is present, and we are writing as a team. That is one reason why I use the third person ("we")—as noted in the first paragraph of this "Acknowledgments" section—instead of the first person ("I").

I would like to thank my colleague and friend of more than 38 years, Howard W. Cotrell. When I met Howard he was a faculty facilitator at Bowling Green State University (Ohio), who worked with a variety of professionals to help them improve their teaching and research. We have coauthored more than 50 articles, and he has been a contributor to my thoughts, feelings, and ruminations on almost every project undertaken.

A special thanks to my mother, Florence (Grow) Weaver, who died in 1998. My mother was always interested, encouraging, and supportive. She was the one for whom I delivered my first public speech (there were no words, just a cry (or rejoicing) at birth!), and I credit her with sparking my initial interest in writing. I dedicated my first book on public speaking, *Understanding Public Communication* (1983), to her with the following words: To **Florence B. Weaver** with whom I first publicly communicated."

Thank you to my sisters Marge Norris and Marilyn Hulett and to Marge's husband, Jim Norris. My sisters have been wonderfully supportive, interested, and inquisitive. Thanks to Edgar E. and the late Zella Willis, my in-laws. Working with Edgar on his books: *How to Be Funny on Purpose* (2005)—for which I wrote the final chapter, "Using the Internet to Find or Develop Jokes"—*Civilian In an Ill-Fitting Uniform: A Memoir of World War II* (2010), and *Moss On the Ivory Tower: A Novel of Mystery and Intrigue* (2012), has provided me opportunities to grow, develop, and change in my own writing ability. Edgar celebrated his 100th birthday on July 12, 2013.

Thank you to Sheila Murray Bethel and her husband, Bill, for their continuing support. A "Consider This" box by Sheila, a professional public speaker, appears in Chapter 15, "Informative and Persuasive Speeches," that reveals the way she prepares her speeches.

Also, I want to thank my immediate family: Andrea, my wife, and Scott, Jacquie, Anthony, and Joanna have been inspirations to both my writing and life. Thanks to my eleven grandchildren: (in birth order) Madison, Mckenzie, Morgan, Amanda, Lindsay, Austin, Grant, Bryce, Rylee (named after me!), Kerrigan, and Dawson, each a unique jewel in the treasure chest of my heart.

A special thank you to Andrea for her comfort, encouragement, strength, contributions, and love. She has always been there for me. There is no way this book could have reached its eleventh edition without the aid and assistance of my wonderful wife. I am fortunate to have an incredibly valuable support system, and I know and appreciate it.

I would like to thank the following reviewers for their detailed and insightful comments. It is their observations, suggestions, and criticisms that have assisted me the most in fashioning and molding this new edition.

Todd Allen, Geneva College
James Allen Brady III, Georgia Military College - Augusta Campus
Perita Carpenter, Trinity Washington University
Ritch Galvan, North Platte Community College
Matt Girton, Lock Haven University
Lara K. Smith, Tyler Junior College
Yunqiu Song, University of Arkansas Community College at Hope
Heather Wilson, Pratt Community College

Communicating
EFFECTIVELY

The Communication Process

Objectives

After reading this chapter, you should be able to:

- Define communication and explain it as a process.

- Explain communication as a transaction and how the three principles relate to effective communication.

- Describe the types of communication.

- Explain the elements of communication competence.

- Discuss the principles of ethical communication and the foundation out of which ethical conduct is most likely to grow.

, CHIP ARMSTRONG, LOVE MY COMPUTER, AND I HAVE LOVED IT AND used it ever since my parents bought one for me when I was young. I used it for staying in touch with my friends (and family while I was away at school), and I remember well using various technology (e.g., email, Facebook, IMs, and texts), in addition to preparing assignments for submission, studying and reviewing materials for class, satisfying my personal curiosity with computer searches (e.g., sports scores, news, and gossip), and, of course, playing games. Although not considered a "computer geek," I was up-to-date and knowledgeable when it came to technology—being an active user of Facebook, online forums, Twitter, and YouTube. I used Facebook to coordinate meetings with fellow classmates, and I used Facebook, online forums, and YouTube to create new studying and learning practices such as my attempts to grasp course material I did not fully understand or pursue additional course material because of my own intellectual curiosity. Also, I took all my class notes on my laptop, read all my textbooks on it, and used it when preparing presentations.

I used broadband, was always on a wireless connection, and I had a "smart phone" (my all-in-one communications and personal data assistant). I made use of streaming video, course management software, and with my use of Facebook, email, websites, message boards, and Blackboard, as well as other social networking sites that I used to connect with professors and peers, I would guess that I easily spent 40 hours a week on the Internet.

I have always thought of myself as someone who could communicate, although I have had few opportunities to speak in public, and I have had no classes in it. My friends have told me I communicate effectively.

I had never thought about taking a course in speech communication because I felt I was an effective communicator. Texting, using the phone and e-mail, conversing fluently with my friends, and giving occasional book reports in high school convinced me.

What I didn't realize was that although speaking fluently was an important aspect of communicating, it wasn't the only requirement. It was a basic, required course that taught me about the importance of listening effectively, the role of verbal and nonverbal communication, how communication influences relationships, groups, and leadership effectiveness, and how to overcome the barriers to effective communication.

When it came to public-speaking skills, I was totally overwhelmed. I had not only felt comfortable speaking to others, but I thought I was very good at it. Why did I even need a course in public speaking? However, undertaking an audience analysis, assembling an outline, and gathering valid and credible information were new activities for me—as were practicing and then delivering a carefully planned, well-rehearsed speech.

What I really discovered—my bottom line, as it were—was that the skills I developed online and in my informal relationships were valuable basics, but not only did I need additional communication skills, but even more important, I needed to learn the fundamentals, then continually practice and polish my skills. The speech-communication class became a laboratory for self-development and acquiring more confidence and poise.

I am now a buyer for a large department store, and the understandings and skills I developed in college—especially in my speech-communication courses—have been invaluable and essential to my successes and advancements.

What is amazing to me as I look back, is how much my understandings and skills in speech communication helped me in all my college courses, in finding and interviewing for jobs, and in dealing with all kinds of different people on the job—including those from other cultures—now that I am fully and happily employed. If I were to make an assessment of its value, I would have to say that communicating effectively is the most important of all the skills I developed in college, with writing coming in as a close second.

Everyone Needs Communication Skills

Everyone reading this book already knows and accepts the value of a college education. Clearly, it is *not* simply to obtain a high-paying job and to guarantee a promising career. You will be better equipped to live a fulfilling life, more likely to contribute the ideas and values necessary to sustaining a democratic society, less likely to fall victim to the "smoke and mirrors" of disinformation spread by those seeking to seize and maintain power, and more likely to maintain a middle-class lifestyle in our global, knowledge-based economy that demands some form of high-quality, postsecondary degree or credential. Paul Taylor, executive vice president of the Pew Research Center, as reported in *USA Today* (Sept. 3, 2009, p. 3B), reaffirms this in his comment, "there is a growing consensus that Americans need a college education to advance in life." It's when you combine your high-quality, postsecondary degree or credential with effective communication skills that you will be fully equipped for effectiveness in this world.

According to a report in *SPECTRA* by Terrel Rhodes that is subtitled, "Communication Departments Hold Vital Role," (November 2012, p. 12), "In a 2010 national survey of employers, the Association of American Colleges and Universities (AAC&U) found that a majority of employers believe colleges should place greater emphasis on a variety of learning outcomes developed through a liberal education." The first "Select Learning Outcome" that employers want colleges to increase their focus on is, "The ability to communicate effectively, orally and in writing (89 percent)." And, just for your interest, the second outcome was "Critical thinking and analytical reasoning skills (81 percent)." I mention the second outcome because in a course that focuses on communicating effectively, the first and second outcomes are closely and inherently linked.

In her book *The Body Language of Dating* (NY: Gallery Books, 2012), Tonya Reiman writes:

> *The human species' finest communicators are its female members, by far. In the early years of the human species, they were the organizing communicators, the planners, the equivalents of today's personal assistants, life coaches, and meddling mothers-in-law. When speech replaced grunts and whistles, women were the majorettes of linguistics parades, leading their gender to today's daily spoken average of twenty thousand words (men speak roughly one-third of that amount per day) p. 82.*

But, have no doubt about it, whether you are a male or female, your success in this world depends on effective communication skills. The problem isn't a lack of ability to communicate; the problem is simply that you have never mastered the skill. Even the very top students from highly competitive schools frequently are unable to write clearly or make persuasive presentations.[1] This is true for two reasons: (1) We take communication for granted. After all, we've been communicating since we were born;

with that much practice, why wouldn't we be good at it? (2) We often think we are better at it than we really are.

If you were told that there were skills that are *more important* to your success than a knowledge of computers, more important than any job-specific skills, and more important than your knowledge of any content area or major, would you want to pursue those skills and improve your ability to perform them? Those skills—basic oral and written communication skills—are the most frequently cited factors in aiding graduating college students to both obtain and sustain employment. The list of studies that support this conclusion goes on and on.[2]

What are the benefits? Why should you take a speech communication course seriously? As a result of a speech communication course you will feel more confident about yourself, you will feel more comfortable with others' perceptions of you, you will experience greater ease in reasoning with people, you will use language more appropriately, and you will have improved critical thinking skills.[3]

This author (Richard) decided on a career in medicine in junior high school. All the courses I took focused in that direction. In high school I focused primarily on math and science courses—taking all the school offered. During my first two years at the University of Michigan, as a premedicine major, I did the same. Then came the university's required speech course. Not only did I do well in the course, I decided to use my last free elective slot to schedule a second speech course, and I was hooked. I found out what I could do with a speech major, how it both complemented and supplemented any other major, and I pursued it for the rest of my college career—at both the undergraduate and graduate levels.

Here is what I discovered that made me switch from a premed major to speech. First, I discovered that speech communication is the ultimate people-oriented discipline. I had pursued premed because I wanted to be in a people-oriented business. I loved the idea that here was a discipline that would develop my thinking and speaking skills. In speech I could apply my imagination, solve practical problems, and articulate my ideas. I was truly free to be human.

The second factor that made me switch majors was that I wanted to be a leader. I knew what skills were important to this goal. Ask yourself, what skills should leaders possess? They are the very same skills every college graduate should have, and they are the same as those that more than 1,000 faculty members from a cross section of academic disciplines selected: skills in writing, speaking, reading, and listening; interpersonal skills, working in and leading groups; an appreciation of cultural diversity; and the ability to adapt to innovation and change.[4] These are all skills that are developed, discussed, emphasized, and refined in a basic speech communication course. They are the central focus of this textbook.

The third and final ingredient that made me switch majors resulted from my study and experience. I recognized the importance of communication skills to my success. Whether it was oral presentations, time spent in meetings, interpersonal skills, interactions with other employees, or use of multimedia technologies, developing effective communication skills was going to be vital in all areas of my life.

Here, then, is the conclusion I discovered. Just as in everyone's life, the need for significance was an emotional force that was driving my judgment. Life is driven by the desire for success. I wanted my life to count for something, I had my own idea of what it meant to be significant, and I was willing to work hard to reach my goals.

In their investigation of the basic speech communication course at two- and four-year colleges and universities, published in *Communication Education* (2006),[5] Morreale, Hugenberg, and Worley—citing supporting research—outline the numerous benefits to students. First, students report that basic interpersonal and public speaking courses are useful and relevant for their future career. Second, students with high and moderate communication apprehension (CA) experience both a reduction in CA and improved grades after completing the course. Third, students demonstrate the positive impact basic speech communication courses have on their behavioral competence, self-esteem, and willingness to communicate (p. 416). As Patrick Combs wrote in capital letters in his book, *Major in Success,* "THE ABILITY TO COMMUNICATE EFFECTIVELY HAS BEEN CONSISTENTLY RANKED THE NUMBER ONE PERFORMANCE FACTOR FOR PROFESSIONAL SUCCESS."[6]

Characteristics of Communication

In this section we look at the process of communication first, then we examine communication as a transaction. Last, we discuss the different types of communication.

Communication Is a Process

A Definition of Communication

Communication is any process in which people, through the use of symbols, verbally and/or nonverbally, consciously or not consciously, intentionally or unintentionally, generate meanings (information, ideas, feelings, and perceptions) within and across various contexts, cultures, channels, and media.

When we say communication is a process, we mean that it is always changing.[7]

Knowing that communication is a process contributes positively to strategic flexibility and creativity because it provides a foundation for growth, development, and change. Basically, it supports the kind of changes likely to occur as you read, experience, criticize, and put into practice the ideas, theories, and knowledge gained from a textbook and course in speech communication.

The Elements of Communication

The communication process is made up of various elements; sender-receivers, messages, channels, noise, feedback, and setting. Figure 1-1 shows how all these elements work together. The amoebalike shape of the sender-receiver indicates how this person changes depending on what he or she is hearing or reacting to.

Sender-Receivers. People get involved in communication because they have information, ideas, and feelings they want to share. This sharing, however, is not a one-way process in which one person sends ideas and the other receives them, and then the process is reversed. First, in most communication situations, people are **sender-receivers**—both sending and receiving at the same time. When you are discussing a problem with a close friend, your friend may be talking, but by listening closely, you are acting as a receiver. By paying careful attention, putting your hand on his or her arm, and showing genuine concern you are sending as many messages as you get, even though you may not say a word. Second, in all situations, sender-receivers share meaning. In your discussion with a close friend, both of you share the language and also share understanding of the situation.

Messages. The **message** is made up of the ideas and feelings that sender-receivers want to share. In the preceding situation, your close friend's message dealt with what had happened to him or her and how he or she was dealing with it, while your message

Figure 1-1
The Elements of
Communication

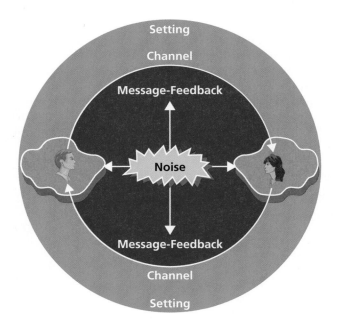

was one of comfort and support. Meaning, however, is *jointly created* between sender and receiver. That is, it isn't just a sender sending a message to a receiver. There is no message at all if there aren't common symbols, like an understanding of each other's language. There is no message—or, perhaps, a very weak one—if there are no common referents, like understanding what the other person is talking about. How often, for example, do you "tune out" teachers if you have no idea where they are coming from?

Notice in Figure 1-1 that the message-feedback circle is exposed behind the sender-receiver. This reveals that your "presence" within a message-feedback situation influences you. More than common symbols and common referents, presence can have powerful emotional, intellectual, physical, and, perhaps, spiritual effects. Think of being in the presence of a message-feedback occurrence between you and the president of the United States; an actor you admire; a priest, rabbi, or minister; or your professor. In these cases, it may not be the setting (to be discussed in a later section), or any other aspect of the message that influences you. It is simply being present within that message-feedback situation.

Ideas and feelings can be communicated only if they are represented by symbols. A **symbol** is something that stands for something else. Our daily lives are full of symbols. We all know that the eagle stands for the United States, the Statue of Liberty equals freedom, and roses express love. Two people walking close and holding hands reveals romance, books represent knowledge, and teachers stand for instruction.

All our communication messages are made up of two kinds of symbols: verbal and nonverbal. The words in a language are **verbal symbols** that stand for particular things or ideas. Verbal symbols are limited and complicated. For example, when we use the word *chair*, we agree we are talking about something we sit on. Thus, *chair* is a **concrete symbol,** a symbol that represents an object. However, when we hear the word *chair*, we all might have a different impression: A chair could be a recliner, an easy chair, a beanbag, a lawn chair—the variety is great.

Even more complicated are **abstract symbols,** which stand for ideas. Consider the vast differences in our understanding of words such as *home, hungry,* or *hurt.* You may recall that as a 2008 presidential candidate, Barack Obama campaigned without wearing a lapel pin depicting the American flag. He began wearing one when some questioned his patriotism. The pins had become an abstract symbol representing true patriotism. How we understand the words *home, hungry, hurt,* or even how we understand the wearing (or not wearing) of the pin, is determined by our experiences. Since people's experiences differ, individuals assign different meanings to abstract symbols.

Nonverbal symbols are ways we communicate without using words; they include facial expressions, gestures, posture, vocal tones, appearance, and so on. As with verbal symbols, we all attach certain meanings to nonverbal symbols. A yawn means we are bored or tired; a furrowed brow indicates confusion; not looking someone in the eye may mean we have something to hide. Like verbal symbols, nonverbal symbols can be misleading. We cannot control most of our non-

Feedback and nonverbal communication are important when we communicate with others.

verbal behavior, and we often send out information of which we are not even aware.

Many nonverbal messages differ from one culture to another just as symbols differ from culture to culture. Black is the color for funerals in Western cultures; in Eastern cultures, that color is white. The crescent moon of male-oriented Islam used to be the symbol for female-oriented worship of the moon mother in ancient Arabia.[8] In one culture, showing the sole of your foot when you cross your legs is an insult. In another culture, respectful behavior is shown with a bow; while in still another, deep respect is shown by touching the other person's feet. Whether or not you are aware of nonverbal messages, they are extremely important in all cultures. Albert Mehrabian, a scholar of nonverbal communication, believes that over 90 percent of the messages sent and received by Americans are nonverbal.[9]

Channels. The **channel** is the route traveled by a message; it is the means a message uses to reach the sender-receivers. In face-to-face communication, the primary channels are sound and sight: We listen to and look at each other. We are familiar with the channels of radio, television, CDs, newspapers, and magazines in the mass media. Other channels communicate nonverbal messages. For example, when DeVon goes to apply for a job, she uses several nonverbal signals to send out a positive message: a firm handshake (touch), appropriate clothing (sight), and respectful voice (sound). The senses are the channels through which she is sending a message.

Feedback. **Feedback** is the response of the receiver-senders to each other. You tell me a joke and I smile. That's feedback. You make a comment about the weather, and I make another one. More feedback.

Strategic flexibility (SF) is an important aspect of jointly created messages. The ability to change messages in ways that will increase your chances of obtaining your desired result is exactly what SF is all about, and the need to change underscores the importance of SF in communication. People are infinitely varied in their individual traits, and even though you think you have created a message with common symbols and referents, it may not be true. Using SF, you can adapt, change, adjust, correct, or do whatever is needed to get the result you wish.

Feedback is vital to communication because it lets the participants see whether ideas and feelings have been shared in the way they were intended. For example, when Deletha and Jordan decide to meet on the corner of 45th and Broadway in New York City, it would be good feedback for one of them to ask, "Which corner?" since the four corners at that particular intersection are among the busiest and most crowded in the city.

Sender-receivers who meet face-to-face have the greatest opportunity for feedback, especially if there are no distractions—or little noise. But, often in these situations a limited amount of feedback occurs because rather than being sensitive to the feedback, communicators are busy planning what they are going to say next. **Sensory acuity** means paying attention to all elements in the communication environment. Are you paying attention to what others are saying? Are you aware of how they are saying it? Do their nonverbal messages support or contradict their verbal messages? Are you gaining or losing rapport with the other person? Is your communication bringing you closer to achieving your objective? Are you aware of distractions or noise that can derail your communication? You begin to notice at once the contribution that sensory acuity can play in all six steps of SF (discussed later in this chapter).

Noise. **Noise** is interference that keeps a message from being understood or accurately interpreted. Noise occurs between the sender-receivers, and it comes in three forms: external, internal, and semantic.

External noise comes from the environment and keeps the message from being heard or understood. Your heart-to-heart talk with your roommate can be interrupted by a group of people yelling in the hall, a helicopter passing overhead, or a lawn mower outside the window. External noise does not always come from sound. You could be standing and talking to someone in the hot sun and become so uncomfortable that you can't concentrate. Conversation might also falter at a picnic when you discover you are sitting on an anthill and ants are crawling all over your blanket.

Internal noise occurs in the minds of the sender-receivers when their thoughts or feelings are focused on something other than the communication at hand. A student doesn't hear the lecture because he is thinking about lunch; a wife can't pay attention to her husband because she is upset by a problem at the office. Internal noise may also stem from beliefs or prejudices. Doug, for example, doesn't believe that women should be managers, so when his female boss asks him to do something, he often misses part of her message.

Semantic noise is caused by people's emotional reactions to words. Many people tune out a speaker who uses profanity because the words are offensive to them. Others have negative reactions to people who make ethnic or sexist remarks. Semantic noise, like external noise and internal noise, can interfere with all or part of the message.

Setting. The **setting** is the environment in which the communication occurs. Settings can have a significant influence on communication. Formal settings lend themselves to formal presentations. An auditorium, for example, is good for giving speeches and presentations but not very good for conversation. If people want to converse on a more intimate basis, they will be better off in a smaller, more comfortable room where they can sit facing each other.

In many situations the communication will change when the setting changes. For example, in the town where one of your authors lives there was an ice cream stand just outside the city limits. People parked in front, got out of their cars, and walked up to a window to order their ice cream. On warm evenings, the place attracted many of the area's teenagers. After years of great success, the owner retired and sold the stand. The new owners decided to enclose it and make it more restaurantlike. You still had to order at the window, but because of the new addition at the front of the building, no one could see you anymore. Once you had your ice cream, you could take it to your car or eat it in the restaurant at one of the tables.

The new restaurant was certainly comfortable. You no longer had to stand in the rain, the place was open year-round, and you could sit down at a table and have dinner. However, comfort wasn't the issue: Every teenager deserted the place and headed for the Dairy Queen down the road. Why? So that they could be seen. For them, eating ice cream was secondary to participating in the social ritual of interacting with or being seen by their peers. In other words, the setting was an important part of their communication.

Setting often shows who has power in a relationship. The question "Your place or mine?" implies an equal relationship. However, when the dean asks a faculty member to come to her office, the dean has more power than the faculty member. When a couple meet to work out a divorce agreement, they meet in a lawyer's office, a place that provides a somewhat neutral setting.

Setting can have a significant influence on communication.

The arrangement of furniture in a setting can also affect the communication that takes place. For example, at one college, the library was one of the noisiest places on campus. Changing the furniture solved the problem. Instead of having sofas and chairs arranged so that students could sit and talk, the library used study desks—thus creating a quiet place to concentrate.

All communication is made up of sender-receivers, messages, channels, feedback, noise, and setting. Every time people communicate, these elements are somewhat different. They are not the only factors that influence communication, however. Communication is also influenced by what you bring to it. That is the subject of our next section.

The Internet and the Model of Communication

Thomas L. Friedman, a columnist for the *New York Times,* writes about the single most important trend in the world today—globalization and the information technology revolution—and says, "Thanks to cloud computing, robotics, 3G wireless connectivity, Skype, Facebook, Google, LinkedIn, Twitter, the iPad, and cheap Internet-enabled

In his book *Public Parts: How Sharing in the Digital Age Improves the Way We Work and Live*, Jeff Jarvis, associate professor and director of the Tow-Knight Center for Entrepreneurial Journalism at the City University of New York's Graduate School of Journalism, writes that the chief technology officer of the U.S. Veterans Administration calls the Internet "the eighth continent." Another writer Jarvis cites called the Internet "an international space." A third called the Internet a new and parallel universe. Jarvis said, "I'm coming around to that point of view, that the Internet is a new layer on the world, perhaps a new society, or a path to a different and more public future" (p. 8). He writes,

> Young people live in that public future—often to the horror of their elders—because they see the rewards that come from being open. They interact in public. That is how they share and connect with one another, how they build their reputations, careers, and brands. They are savvy about the benefits and risks and . . . are learning to act accordingly, protecting their privacy with more skill and intelligence than we assume. We should learn from them, for the future is theirs (p. 8).

Source: Jarvis, Jeff. (2011). *Public parts: How sharing in the digital age improves the way we work and live.* New York: Simon & Schuster.

Questions

1. Do you believe that by its size and use the Internet could ever be considered "the eighth continent"—or, even a "new and parallel universe"?

2. What difference do you think it makes that young people today are building their reputations, careers, and brands online instead of offline—in a world that does not include the use of the Internet?

3. What are some of the characteristics of communication conducted over the Internet when compared with communication conducted face-to-face? When it comes to building reputations, careers, and brands, which do you think is more effective and why?

4. What are some of the benefits and some of the risks of being open when it comes to using the Internet?

---

smart phones, the world has gone from connected to hyper-connected." Friedman adds an important addendum to his comment: "And it is a critical reason why, to get into the middle class now, you have to study harder, work smarter, and adapt quicker than ever before" (p. A7, *The* (Toledo) *Blade*, August 20, 2011).

Although the Internet is related to the communication model, it contains many different configurations because of its many uses. For example, **synchronous communication** means talk that occurs at the same time with no time delay. With respect to senders and receivers, it could be one-to-one, one-to-a-few, one-to-many, or even many-to-one. The best examples of synchronous communication are instant messaging (IM) and chat rooms. **Asynchronous communication** does not occur at the same time; examples include email messages or seeking information from websites. Usenet, electronic bulletin boards, and Listservers are asynchronous. Most of the exchanges between people on the Internet (such as most uses of Facebook and MySpace) consist of asynchronous communication. The words *synchronous* and *asynchronous* help categorize Internet communication, but they also reveal some of the problems in trying to categorize it.

The fact that the Internet is two-way is important. Media such as radio, television, and newspapers are one-way, with restricted access, meaning that not everyone owns a radio station, television station, or newspaper with which to communicate his or her ideas. But on the Internet you can communicate with many senders, and they with you.

An Internet model of communication must have an active receiver who emits information, interacts with—or has the potential of interacting with—the sender or website, and selects his or her own information and decodes it according to personal interests.

Messages can be as simple as conversations between two people, but they can also be traditional journalistic news stories created by a reporter or editor, stories placed on blogs by people with unknown or uncertain credentials, stories created over a long period by many people, or outdated stories that have been stored on a website and never updated since their creation years ago—the latter is called Web rot.

The Internet is represented in the communication model by the word *channel*—the route a message travels or the means it uses to reach sender-receivers. Many differences between the channels of communication in face-to-face communication (FtFC) and those over the Internet are obvious, but the differences in the social cues to communication—especially the social leveling and the differences in turn taking—are important. The computer could easily be labeled "the great leveler" because many of the cues to social status are removed. It is precisely because of this that source validation for information gained from the Internet becomes so important. *Anyone can be a publisher on the Internet.*

Another aspect of leveling, too, is that often in FtFC the assertive, highly confident individual may have an edge with respect to credibility or gaining an audience for his or her ideas—even, perhaps, at having greater opportunities (turns) for talking. On the Internet, assertiveness traits are often not detected, so shy, nonassertive people have an equal opportunity for self-expression and for initiating and taking turns.

One final thought about a similarity between FtFC and the communication that takes place on the Internet. On the Internet, it is obvious that facial expression, eye contact, gestures, and body movement are missing, but the mind plays a role in completing the interpersonal picture. That is, we mentally supply the vocal tone and emphasis because of what we know of others' uses of words, phrases, and expressions.

Finally, some people may believe that the "setting" on the Internet is static and unchanging; however, just a quick examination reveals that the number of mediated environments on the Web is startling. From emails to blogs and chat rooms to websites, in addition to all the social-networking possibilities (e.g., Facebook, MySpace, and hundreds more), the number of different settings becomes nearly as plentiful as in the real world, and each carries with it, of course, its own sets of characteristics, parameters, and guidelines for usage.

Communication Is a Transaction

A communication transaction involves not only the physical act of communicating but also a psychological act: Impressions are being formed in the minds of the people who are communicating.[10] What people think and know about one another directly affects their communication.

The Three Principles of Transactional Communication

Communication as a transaction—**transactional communication**—involves three important principles. First, people engaged in communication are sending messages continuously and simultaneously. Second, communication events have a past, present, and future. Third, participants in communication play certain roles. Let's consider each of these principles in turn.

Reality Check

We have defined communication as a transaction, and we have discussed the three main principles involved. Does this make sense? Does it appear logical? Do the facts you know support this? Take any communication situation that you have been part of recently. Are each of the main principles involved? What implications does this have for future communication situations? That is, when you know communication involves more than just a physical act—that a psychological act is involved as well—what might you think, act, or do differently? How might this help you communicate more effectively?

Participation Is Continuous and Simultaneous. Whether or not you are actually talking in a communication situation, you are actively involved in sending and receiving messages. Let's say you are lost, walking in a big city that is not familiar to you. You show others you are confused when you hesitate, look around you, or pull out a map. When you realize you have to ask for directions, you look for someone who might help you. You dismiss two people because they look as if they're in a hurry; you don't ask another one because she looks as though she might be lost too. Finally you see a person who looks helpful, and you ask for information. As you listen, you give feedback, through both words and body language, as to whether you understand.

As this person talks, you think about how long it will take to walk to your destination, you make note of what landmarks to look for, and you may even create a visual image of what you will see when you get there. You are participating continuously and simultaneously in a communication that is quite complicated.

All Communications Have a Past, a Present, and a Future. You respond to every situation from your own experiences, your own moods, and your own expectations. Such factors complicate the communication situation. When you know someone well, you can make predictions about what to do in the future on the basis of what you know about the past. For example, without having to ask him, Lee knows that his friend Jason will not be willing to try the new Indian restaurant in town. Lee has been out to eat with Jason many times, and Jason always eats the same kind of food, burgers and fries. Lee also knows that Jason doesn't like changes of any kind, so he knows better than to suggest that they go out of town for a concert because he knows that Jason will respond that they should wait until the group comes to their town.

Even when you are meeting someone for the first time, you respond to that person on the basis of your experience. You might respond to physical traits (short, tall, bearded, bald), to occupation (accountant, gym teacher), or even to a name (remember how a boy named Eugene always tormented you and you've mistrusted all Eugenes ever since?). Any of these things you call up from your past might influence how you respond to someone—at least at the beginning.

The future also influences communication. If you want a relationship to continue, you will say and do things in the present to make sure it does ("Thanks for dinner. I always enjoy your cooking"). If you think you will never see a person again, or if you want to limit the nature of your interactions, this also might affect your communication. You might be more businesslike and thus leave the personal aspects of your life out of the communication.

All Communicators Play Roles. **Roles** are parts you play or ways you behave with others. Defined by society and affected by individual relationships, roles control everything from word choice to body language. For example, one of the roles you play is that of student. Your teachers may consider you to be bright and serious; your peers, who see you in the same role, may think you are too serious. Outside the classroom you play other roles. Your parents might see you as a considerate daughter or son; your best friend might see the fun-loving side of you; and your boss might see you as hardworking and dependable.

Roles do not always stay the same in a relationship. They vary with others' moods or with one's own, the setting, and the noise factor. Communication changes to meet the needs of each of your relationships and situations. For example, even though Eduardo and Heidi have been married for 10 years and have three children, they still try to reserve Saturday night for a romantic date. While they are out, they try not to talk about children and family issues. Instead, they focus on each other and what the other is thinking and feeling. On Sunday morning, their roles change. Eduardo fixes breakfast while Heidi gets the children ready to go to church. Now their roles are children and family centered.

The roles you play—whether established by individual relationships or by society—may be perceived differently by different people. These perceptions affect the communication that results. For example, Tom, in his role of youth director, is well organized and maintains tight control over the activities he directs. The kids who play the games he coaches know they have to behave or they'll be in big trouble. Therefore they speak to him in a respectful voice and stay quiet when they're supposed to. To some kids, however, Tom's discipline seems rigid and inflexible. These kids avoid the youth center; they choose not to communicate with him at all.

Types of Communication

As you can see in Figure 1-2, there are different kinds of communication. The figure shows four of the kinds most often used: intrapersonal, interpersonal, small-group, and public communication. In this section we will also discuss intercultural communication.

Intrapersonal Communication

Intrapersonal communication *is language use and/or thought that occurs within you, the communicator.* It involves your active internal involvement in the symbolic processing of messages. You become your own sender and receiver and provide feedback to yourself in an ongoing internal process (see Figure 1-3). It occurs in your mind in a communication model that contains a sender, receiver, and feedback loop.

Intrapersonal communication can encompass daydreaming, talking to oneself, and reading aloud. In her article "Being Civil with Ourselves" (*SPECTRA*, September 2011), Valerie Manusoc writes, "For many of us, the things we say in our minds to and about ourselves—often over and over—are rarely ever subject to rebuke, perhaps because the audience (us) to such communication (ours) is also the critic (us). Moreover, that dialogue often goes unnoticed; we may not even be aware of the cacophony at work within us" (p. 17). Speaking and hearing what one thinks and reads can increase concentration and retention. Using gestures while thinking can assist concentration, retention, and problem solving as well. Another aspect of intrapersonal communication that has the potential of increasing self-understanding and concentration is writing one's thoughts and observations. Some people use such writing to assist them in ordering their thoughts and producing a record that can be used at a later time.

Interpersonal Communication

Interpersonal communication occurs when you communicate on a one-to-one basis—usually in an informal, unstructured setting. This kind of communication occurs mostly between two people, though it may include more than two.

Interpersonal communication uses all the elements of the communication process. In a conversation between friends, for example, each brings his or her background and experience to the conversation. During the conversation each functions as a sender-receiver: Their messages consist of both verbal and nonverbal symbols. The channels they use the most are sight and sound. Because interpersonal communication is between two (or among a few) people, it offers the greatest opportunity for feedback.

Figure 1-2
Types of
Communication

Intrapersonal Communication

Interpersonal Communication and Interviewing

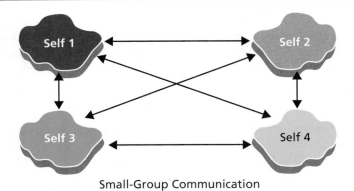

Small-Group Communication

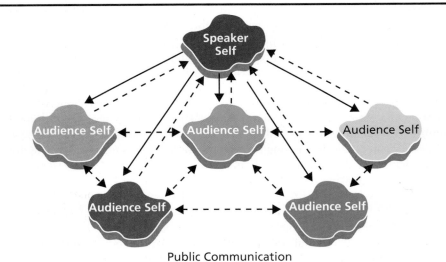

Public Communication

Primary Messages
Secondary Messages

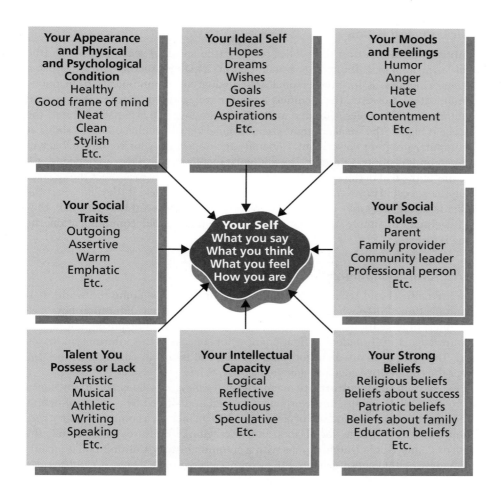

Figure 1-3
Intrapersonal
Communication

Internal noise is likely to be minimal because each person can see whether the other is distracted. The persons involved in the conversation have many chances to check that the message is being perceived correctly. People who want to engage in interpersonal communication usually look for informal and comfortable settings.

Small-Group Communication

Small-group communication occurs when a small number of people meet to solve a problem. The group must be small enough so that each member has a chance to interact with all the other members.

Because small groups are made up of several sender-receivers, the communication process is more complicated than in interpersonal communication. With so many more people sending messages, there are more chances for confusion. Messages are also more structured in small groups because the group is meeting for a specific purpose. Small groups use the same channels as are used in interpersonal communication, however, and there is also a good deal of opportunity for feedback. In keeping with their problem-solving nature, small groups usually meet in a more formal setting than people involved in interpersonal communication.

Public Communication

In **public communication** the sender-receiver (the speaker) sends a message (the speech) to an audience. The speaker usually delivers a highly structured message, using the same channels as in interpersonal and small-group communication. In public communication, however, the channels are more exaggerated than in interpersonal communication. The voice is louder and the gestures are more expansive because the audience is bigger. The speaker might use additional visual channels, such as slides or the computer program PowerPoint. Generally, the opportunity for verbal feedback in public communication is limited. The audience members may have a chance to ask questions at the end of the speech, but usually they are not free to address the speaker during the speech. However, they can send nonverbal feedback. If they like what the speaker is saying, they may interrupt the speech with applause. If they dislike it, they may fidget a lot or simply stop paying attention. In most public communication, the setting is formal.

Intercultural Communication

There are cultural and technological forces that are now reshaping the world. It is communication skills—whether of senders or receivers—that determine how well individuals, organizations, industries, and even nations do in acquiring and applying knowledge, thus broadening their chances for success in this information-driven world. The better you are at negotiating the cultural issues in communication, the greater the competitive edge you gain in a global society.

When we talk about **culture,** we mean "the ever-changing values, traditions, social and political relationships, and worldview created and shared by a group of people bound together by a combination of factors (which can include a common history, geographic location, language, social class, and/or religion)."[11] Cultures could include the Amish or Pennsylvania Dutch, groups with a common history. Cultures could include the Japanese or Taiwanese, groups with a common geographic location. Cultures also could include those who speak the French or Islamic languages.

To help people understand one another better, scholars, teachers, and worldwide business leaders have developed the field of **intercultural communication**—the communication that occurs whenever two or more people from different cultures interact. This field studies how differences between people affect their perceptions of the world and, thus, their communication. Of course, there is no way to understand all cultures. There are, however, certain characteristics that occur again and again, and the study of intercultural communication rests on these characteristics.

Why should you be concerned about intercultural communication? What if your job involved coordinating international student services and exchange programs at your university or college campus? What if you were the manager of a biotech company responsible for leading a diverse team of scientists doing innovative research? What if you were a member of a campus group interested in gathering the support of diverse groups on campus to extend an invitation to a controversial speaker? In each case, to overlook the different cultural backgrounds of those receivers might mean your communication would be less constructive and might result in misunderstandings and breakdowns as well. There are inherent cultural issues associated with any form of communication.

Although people throughout the world have many characteristics in common, there are also many differences. Thus, if people from different cultural groups want to communicate, they must be aware that they may have different systems of knowledge, values, beliefs, customs, and behaviors. For example, crossing your legs in the United

Every year the United States becomes more culturally diverse.

States reveals a relaxed attitude, but in Korea it is a social faux pas. In West Africa, the comment "You've put on weight" means you look healthy and prosperous and is a great compliment; in America, it is an insult. In Japan, they put business cards in safe places and handle them with great care, because they view them as an extension of the person; in America, they are viewed as a business formality and convenience, and Americans are quick to put them away, a behavior insulting to the Japanese.[12] Understanding differences and then utilizing them in the preparation, development, and presentation of your ideas can only help you become a more effective communicator.

Communication Competence

What is **competent communication?** It is the ability to communicate in a personally effective and socially appropriate manner. In their book, *Interpersonal Communication Competence,* Spitzberg and Cupach outlined three components: (1) knowledge, (2) skill, and (3) motivation. First, communicators must recognize what communication practice is appropriate. Second, they must have the ability to perform that practice; and third, they must want to communicate in an effective and appropriate manner.[13]

What is effective and appropriate? It varies according to the situation. However, if communicators display the following elements, regardless of the situation, it is more likely their communication will be considered competent. The first element is *respect,* which suggests communicators must be courteous, polite, and civil. The second element is *empathy,* which means identifying with, sharing the feelings of, or being on the same wavelength as the other person or persons. *Tolerance* is the third element, and this means communicators must be open minded, understanding, and patient. Given differences between people and the potential for misunderstanding, communicators must recognize that ambiguity and error are inherent, automatic parts of almost any communication. Along with tolerance, the fourth element is *flexibility*. Communicators must be willing to adjust and compromise. The fifth element is *interaction management,* and this includes how they participate or involve themselves in any communication situation: their posture, comfort, appropriate role, and willingness to self-disclose.

Strategic Flexibility (SF)

Strategic flexibility (SF) means expanding your communication repertoire (your collection or stock of communication behaviors that can readily be brought into use) to enable you to use the best skill or behavior available for a particular situation. Let's say you're caught in an unfamiliar situation, but you realize that if you can communicate your position effectively, you will free yourself from this uncomfortable position. You suddenly need all of the best skills and behaviors you can call upon. SF is a primary characteristic of successful people, a vital component of excellent relationships at work and at home, a trait of effective group leaders and participants, and the attribute of public speakers who can adapt to changing circumstances or unexpected occurrences.

Kelly McGonigal, PhD, a health psychologist and lecturer at Stanford University, writing in her book *The Willpower Instinct* (NY: Penguin, 2012), and borrowing an idea suggested by Suzanne Segerstrom, a psychologist at the University of Kentucky, says that self-control requires a "pause-and-plan response"—a response pattern (much like strategic flexibility) that gives you freedom. McGonigal writes: "By keeping you from immediately following your impulses, the pause-and-plan response give you time for more flexible, thoughtful action" (p. 37). That is precisely the purpose of using strategic flexibility. It is, indeed, a perfect "pause-and-plan" response.

People who possess SF are happier and more fulfilled because they are not only aware of their own communication skills and deficits, but also they can bring to bear on any situation they encounter a broad range of potentially valuable behaviors. Going into a new situation, they don't always know exactly what will be required, but they realize that their own background, experience, and repertoire will be sufficient not just to meet the new circumstances but to succeed in them as well. The knowledge that SF provides yields confidence and security, and helps reduce any unnecessary and unwanted fear.

Those without SF are those who approach every situation with their own limited resources. Often, this results in knee-jerk responses that depend on nothing more than the same set of behaviors used to approach any and every situation that confronts them. The problem with this approach is that there is no single way to behave in the world. The world is too complex; problems are too complicated; circumstances are too intricate and involved. It's a little like the leader who applies exactly the same set of solutions to every problem, saying, "You may not like my solutions, but at least you know exactly where I stand." This is discomforting information simply because it shows no recognition of SF. All problems require different sets of solutions that result from study, thought, and the serious application of a wide variety of potential behaviors.

The power of the SF concept is in its application. The six steps of SF make this possible. These steps will allow you to take SF into the world and apply it to the real-life circumstances you encounter daily:

1. **Anticipate** = Think about potential situations and the needs and requirements likely to arise because of them. The key to anticipation is forecasting. Remember Louis Pasteur's famous dictum: "Chance favors only the prepared mind."

2. **Assess** = Take stock of the factors, elements, and conditions of the situations in which you find yourself. The key to assessment is alertness.

3. **Evaluate** = Determine the value and worth of the factors, elements, and conditions to all those involved and how they bear on your own skills and abilities. The key to evaluation is accuracy.

4. **Select** = Carefully select from your repertoire of available skills and behaviors those likely to have the greatest impact on the current (and future) situations. Here, one must also predict and forecast the potential effects of the skills and behaviors that will be used. The key to the selection process is appropriateness.

5. **Apply** = Now, with care, concern, and attention to all the factors that are likely to be affected—including any ethical considerations that may be appropriate— apply the skills and behaviors you have selected. The key to application is relevance.

6. **Reassess and reevaluate** = For every action taken, there is likely to be feedback as well as actions taken by others as a direct result of those taken by you. There will be other effects as well—some immediate that can be observed, some long-range that can only be surmised and anticipated. Reassessment and reevaluation may result in the application of further skills and behaviors needed to clarify, extend, continue, or even terminate the situation. The key to reassessment and reevaluation is accurate, careful observation.

In their book *Words Can Change Your Brain*, Andrew Newberg, a medical doctor, and Mark Waldman, his co-author, talk about the need to disrupt old speaking and listening habits—which explains why strategic flexibility is so important: "To improve our conversational skills," they write, "we have to do several things. First we need to recognize that the way we normally speak is inadequate, filled with habituated patterns that were mostly set in place in adolescence and early childhood. Then we have to consciously interrupt those speaking and listening habits, over and over again. And finally we need to replace those old communication styles with new and effective ones" (p. 122). That is the purpose of SF—to allow us time to think, to respond appropriately, and to bring to situations new and more effective tools for communicating effectively. Our suggestion for using SF is well supported because it works.

Creativity

Often when people think of creative endeavors, they immediately think of the arts, and, yet, "just about anything we do can be addressed in a creative manner, from housecleaning to personal hobbies," writes Michele Root-Bernstein, coauthor with Robert Root-Bernstein of *Sparks of Genius: The Thirteen Thinking Tools of the World's Most Creative People* (Wilmington, MA: Mariner Books, 2001).

Creativity is a factor that must be mentioned within the umbrella of SF. It is the capacity to synthesize vast amounts of information and wrestle with complex problems. Creativity is not a rare or special power, and it relates directly to communication because every time you open your mouth, the unique combination of words emitted is a creative extension of who you are. Creativity requires this synthetic ability—this capacity to draw together and make sense of vast amounts of information. The more information you have (from whatever sources you can draw upon, including this instructor, this course, and this textbook), the more you have to bring to or bear on your noticing, remembering, seeing, speaking, hearing, and understanding language and nonverbal communication. Not only are these processes important—a definite understatement—but they also allow you to search and transform the spaces on this earth you occupy. Your creativity frees you to generate possibilities, which of course is the very foundation of SF.

So, what you have is a complementary set of processes that are interwoven and mutually contributing: Creativity offers some of the creative force that drives successful SF, and SF provides the opportunities when you can apply your best creative thinking to a task.

Tina Seelig, who has a PhD in neuroscience from Stanford University Medical School, teaches a course on creativity and innovation at the Hasso Plattner Institute of Design. She writes in her book, *inGenius: A Crash Course on Creativity* (NY: HarperCollins, 2012), about ways to increase your everyday creativity:

> *Essentially, creativity is an endless resource, initiated by your drive to tackle challenges and to seize opportunities. Anything and everything can spark your Innovation Engine [sic]—every word, every object, every decision, and every action. Creativity can be enhanced by honing your ability to observe and learn, by connecting and combining ideas, by reframing problems, and by moving beyond the first right answers. You can boost your creative output by building habitats that foster problem solving, crafting environments that support the generation of new ideas, building teams that are optimized for innovation, and contributing to a culture that encourages experimentation (p. 201).*

To live, then, is to be creative and communicate. To communicate effectively is to enjoy life more fully. Consider this textbook, then, a *guide* for empowering effective communicators—for encouraging both SF and creativity. With this knowledge as a foundation, the next step is knowing how to use it to help you communicate more effectively.

Introduction to Active Open-Mindedness (AOM)

We don't want to claim originality for this term, for we are deeply indebted to the book by Brooks Jackson and Kathleen Hall Jamieson, *un-Spun: Finding Facts in a World of (Disinformation)* (New York: Random House, 2007). We will not be using the label, however, in quite the same way that Jackson and Jamieson did. Their use had to do with detecting "spin"—deception, dishonesty, misrepresentation, and a lack of respect for the facts primarily related to politics and advertising, and their book was aimed specifically at voters and consumers.

Although Jackson and Jamieson's slant on the term **active open-mindedness** is important, we will be using it as a tool for readers with the intent of opening their minds—a tool that they can apply, flexibly, that will help them digest, master, and use knowledge. Our goal is to give readers power over their own faculties, and an AOM

In his book *Do Nothing! How to Stop Overmanaging and Become a Great Leader*, J. Keith Murnighan, a professor at the Kellogg School of Management at Northwestern University, discusses the kind of mind-set that promotes growth, with the obvious assistance of Carol Dweck, a social psychologist at Stanford University:

> *Carol Dweck . . . suggests that people's views of their own skills and abilities are a critical influence on their subsequent behaviors. She focuses on the key difference between having a fixed versus a growth mind-set: people with a fixed mind-set think they were endowed with a certain set of skills and abilities and that they can do little to change them; people with a growth mind-set also think they were endowed with a certain set of skills and abilities but they believe they can grow and improve (p. 144).*

Source: J. Keith Murnighan. (2012). *Do nothing! How to stop overmanaging and become a great leader.* New York: Portfolio/Penguin.

Questions

1. Can you see how a fixed mind-set or a growth mind-set can make such a difference with respect to growth and improvement? How might such a mind-set affect a person's attitude toward improving their ability to communicate effectively?

2. To what extent do you think a person's mind-set may be determined by a person's drive, potential, or outlook on life?

3. Can you see how a person's mind-set can have an important impact on how that person approaches problems and pursues his or her goals?

4. Do you feel that you fall into one of these categories (possessing a fixed mind-set or a growth mind-set)? Do you see the advantages of having a growth mind-set? Are there some specific things you can do to increase your own emphasis on a growth mind-set?

CONSIDER THIS

example in every chapter will give readers practice in critical examination, analysis, and thought.

AOM is especially valuable when you find yourself in baffling or confusing situations or in situations where you are unsure of which option or alternative to select. What it suggests is that rather than "shooting from the hip," or simply guessing what to do, you pull yourself together, gather all your resources, examine the facts, and either render a decision or take action *only* when you are certain which course either makes the most sense or can be supported the best. You will understand better once you begin reading these sections.

Communicating Effectively

Once you understand the process of communication, you can begin to understand why communication does or doesn't work. In an ideal communication situation the message is perceived in the way it was intended. But when messages don't work, it is useful to ask these questions: Was there a problem with the message? Was the best channel used? Did noise occur? Knowing the right questions to ask is essential to building skills in communication.

Most of us already have considerable communication skills. You have been sending and receiving verbal and nonverbal signals all your life. Nevertheless, you have probably had times when you have not communicated as effectively as you should. If you got a lower grade on a paper than you expected, if you unintentionally hurt somebody's feelings, or if the instructor did not understand a question you asked in class, you are not communicating as effectively as you could.

Where to Begin

The information about communication is so vast that most of us could spend a life-time studying the subject and not learn even a fraction of what there is to know. How-ever, as you begin your study of communication, the following five questions are a good starting point.

Which Communication Skills Am I Most Likely to Need? Find out what communication skills are important to you. What do you intend to do in your life? What kind of work do you expect to do? What communication skills are required in this work? Which of these skills do you already have? Which ones need improvement? Which ones do you need to acquire?

For example, a career in business requires almost every communication skill. You need interpersonal skills to get along with the people you work with, intercultural communication skills if you are going to work with people from other countries, and public-speaking skills for making presentations. Although you may use some commu-nication skills more than others, at one time or another you are going to need every one we have discussed in this chapter.

Which Communication Skills Am I Most Lacking? Which kinds of communication are most difficult for you? Intrapersonal? Interpersonal? Intercultural? Small group? Public speaking? What are the symptoms of difficulties in these areas? What problems do you have to overcome before you can perform effectively?

Many people would prefer to avoid, rather than work in, the area that gives them the most trouble. For example, if you are anxious about public speaking, you might feel inclined to avoid any circumstance where you have to give a speech. A better ap-proach, however, would be to get over this fear: You'll be able to offer a wedding toast, give a presentation at a meeting, consider many more job possibilities, and so forth. If you can conquer fear by plunging in and practicing the thing that gives you the most trouble, you will expand the possibilities in your life.

How Can I Get Communication Practice? Are there situations, other than class, where you can practice communication skills that will be useful to you? Are there groups and organizations you can join that will help you develop these skills? It's always a good idea to take what you have learned in class and try it out on the world. Using new skills helps to develop and refine them.

Where Can I Get Help? What people do you know who will help you develop commu-nication skills and give you feedback on how you are doing? Are there people you can ask who will give you support when you are trying something new and threatening? Are you willing to ask them to support you? You can usually count on this kind of sup-port from your friends. Don't you have a friend who would be willing to listen to one of your speeches and tell you whether it works and how you might improve it? Also, don't forget your instructors. Many of them sit in their offices during office hours hop-ing that students will drop by.

What Timetable Should I Set? Have you set a realistic timetable for improvement? Knowing that it is difficult to learn new skills or break bad habits, are you willing to give yourself enough time? Your speech communication class is going to last for a semester or a quarter, and although you will be making steady progress in your interpersonal

Begin to be an astute (keen in discernment) observer of the communication that occurs around you (especially the breakdowns and problems) every day. This will make your journey through this book more rewarding and productive. With a fundamental understanding now of the process of communication, examine all communication situations to which you are exposed for why they do and don't work. Look at each of the elements (Figure 1-1: setting, channel, message-feedback, noise, sender-receivers) and gather the evidence (albeit mostly observational cues) and begin asking questions: (1) Was there something in the setting or channel? (2) Was there a problem with the message or feedback? (3) Did noise occur? (4) Was the problem with the senders-receivers?

It is only when you ask questions and gather relevant facts to back up your observations that you will begin to build a meaningful and useful supply of communication tools. Your communication effectiveness depends on it.

communication and public-speaking skills, change will not happen overnight. The act of communicating—whether with a single person or a classroom audience—takes time and effort. The most realistic timetable is one in which you say, "I'm going to keep working at this until I succeed."

Ethical Communication

Ethical communication, a component of each of the six types of communication, is communication that is honest, fair, and considerate of others' rights. Communication is honest when communicators tell the truth; it is fair and considerate when they consider listeners' feelings. Most people reading this believe that truthfulness, accuracy, honesty, and reason are essential to the integrity of communication, just as it is written in the National Communication Association's (NCA's) Credo for Ethical Communication.[14]

The problem, of course, is neither with what you know to be true nor with what you want to have happen. The problem occurs as you are faced with complex demands (too much being asked of you), limited resources (like time), or the easy access to alternatives to ethical behavior (being handed an exam, paper, or speech)—or what is often likely, the combination of some or all of these. There is always the very human temptation to try to make life easier by nullifying some of your fundamental ethical responsibilities. That, of course, is when your true ethics are revealed.

You have undoubtedly heard numerous excuses for unethical conduct. The most often may be "I didn't know that was considered unethical." Others include "Everyone does it," or "I'm sorry, I just didn't have the time [to be ethical]," "What harm is there in it?" "I've been sick," "I've never done it before," "You know, I'm very busy." It is not surprising that those who engage in unethical behavior have quick and easy excuses for what they do. No excuse, of course, is good enough to justify truly unethical conduct.

Why should you be concerned about ethical communication? It is clearly stated in the NCA's Credo: "Unethical communication threatens the quality of all communication and consequently the well-being of individuals and the society in which we live."[15] As the Credo states in its opening paragraph, ethical communication is "fundamental to responsible thinking, decision making, and the development of relationships and communities within and across contexts, cultures, channels, and media. Ethical communication enhances human worth and respect for self and others."[16]

ATTENTION!

The Seven-Step Path to Better Decisions

1. Stop and Think
2. Clarify Goals
3. Determine Facts
4. Develop Options
5. Consider Consequences
6. Choose
7. Monitor and Modify

In his book *Ethics in Human Communication,* 5th ed. (Prospect Heights, IL: Waveland Press, 2002), Richard L. Johannesen writes, "Potential ethical issues are inherent in any instance of communication between humans to the degree that the communication can be judged on a right-wrong dimension, that it involves possible significant influence on other humans, and that the communicator consciously chooses specific ends [outcomes] sought and communicative means to achieve those ends" (p. 2). The Credo takes Johannesen's comment even further when it states, "Questions of right and wrong arise *whenever* [italics ours] people communicate," thus, it is important to establish a basic code of ethics as you begin a course in speech communication. As you read the following principles of ethical communication, notice the two ethical communication themes of caring and responsibility. These seven principles have been paraphrased from the Credo:

- Protect freedom of expression, diversity of perspective, and tolerance for dissent.
- Strive to understand and respect others' communications before evaluating and responding to their messages.
- Help promote communication climates of caring and mutual understanding that protect the unique needs and characteristics of individual communicators.
- Condemn communication that degrades individuals and humanity through distortions, intolerance, intimidation, coercion, hatred, or violence.
- Commit yourself to the courageous expression of your personal convictions in pursuit of fairness and justice.
- Accept responsibility for the short- and long-term consequences of your own communication, and expect the same of others.
- Avoid plagiarism—presentation of the work of another person in such a way as to give the impression that the other's work is your own, whether it be:
  - the verbatim use of part of a book or article without using quotation marks and without citing the original source.
  - paraphrasing another's words without noting this is a paraphrase essentially taken from another source.
  - using another person's illustrative material without citing the source and, thus, giving credit where credit is due.

The basic idea in avoiding plagiarism is simply to give credit when using someone else's ideas. If you have any doubts, give the credit—using a footnote or a reference *during* (as part of) the communication.[17]

Although most of you reading this book will not pursue a "communication" profession, you will be seen as engaged in the profession of being a communicator. Why? Because, according to Heather E. Canary, in her research article, "Teaching Ethics in Communication Courses," in the journal *Communication Education* (Vol. 56, No. 2, April 2007), it is a fundamental and important "part of personal, professional, and social life" (p. 195). With this in mind, then, if you conduct yourself as an ethical person in your dealings with family, friends, and others, refraining from activities that may be construed as unethical—whether they are governed by written or unwritten codes of personal conduct, rules, or regulations—and if you continue your wholehearted commitment to being a credible, quality person who demonstrates care, consideration, and dedication to values and morals, you will promote ethical thinking and living and be an example to others.

Do You Have Strategic Flexibility?

For each question circle the numerical score that best represents your performance, skill, or ability using the following scale; 7 = Outstanding; 6 = Excellent; 5 = Very good; 4 = Average (good); 3 = Fair; 2 = Poor; 1 = Minimal ability; 0 = No ability demonstrated.

1. Do you try to anticipate situations—think about them *before* they occur—to prepare yourself mentally (and physically) for what is likely to happen? 7 6 5 4 3 2 1 0

2. Do you generally look at new situations with an eye toward determining if communication will be needed or required by you? 7 6 5 4 3 2 1 0

3. From your assessment of a situation, is it easy for you to determine *when* communication is necessary? 7 6 5 4 3 2 1 0

4. Do you find it easy to know—once engaged in communication—what the purpose of the communication is? What people hope to accomplish? 7 6 5 4 3 2 1 0

5. When you are with a group of people, can you—from simple, preliminary observations—determine what their needs and assumptions are? 7 6 5 4 3 2 1 0

6. When you are with a group of people, do you automatically know what their relationship is to you? 7 6 5 4 3 2 1 0

7. Do you also know what your relationship to this group of people is? 7 6 5 4 3 2 1 0

8. Are you able to anticipate how an audience would use any communication you shared with them? 7 6 5 4 3 2 1 0

9. When you are talking with another person or other people, are you able to determine—in advance—what effect your communication *should* have on them? 7 6 5 4 3 2 1 0

10. Can you tell from preliminary assessments what kind of communication might be appropriate in particular situations? 7 6 5 4 3 2 1 0

11. Do you feel you have the breadth of knowledge, experience, and skills to more than effectively meet most of the communication-related situations you encounter? 7 6 5 4 3 2 1 0

12. Do you feel comfortable when you encounter a situation where you know you will have to communicate? 7 6 5 4 3 2 1 0

13. Do you feel confident, secure, and free of nervousness when facing communication situations? 7 6 5 4 3 2 1 0

14. When you have to communicate with others, do you feel as if the behaviors and skills you put into use are the same ones you always use? 7 6 5 4 3 2 1 0

15. When you communicate, do you feel that you use some of the techniques, styles, or behaviors of the other gender? 7 6 5 4 3 2 1 0

16. Do you believe there is a possibility of and value for expanding your range of communication skills and behaviors? 7 6 5 4 3 2 1 0

Go to the Online Learning Center at **www.mhhe.com/hybels11e** to see your results and learn how to evaluate your attitudes and feelings.

www.mhhe.com/hybels11e >

Summary

Everyone needs effective communication skills. They will help you feel more confident about yourself, more comfortable with others' perceptions of you, greater ease in reasoning with others, better at using language, and improve your critical thinking skills. Speech communication is the ultimate people-oriented discipline, fundamental to effective leadership, and a key to professional success.

Communication is any process in which people, through the use of symbols, verbally and/or nonverbally, consciously or not consciously, intentionally or unintentionally, generate meanings (information, ideas, feelings, and perceptions) within and across various contexts, cultures, channels, and media. The elements of communication include senders-receivers, messages, channels, feedback, noise, and setting. The essence of communication is making meaning, and meaning is jointly created between sender and receiver.

The Internet is about communication—people exchanging messages. It can be related to the communication model but has many different configurations when the sender-message-receiver features are examined. It is represented in the communication model by the word *channel*, but there are many differences between the channels of communication in face-to-face communication (FtFC) and those on the Internet. Major differences include both social leveling and the differences in turn taking. Two additional ideas include the role the mind plays in completing the interpersonal picture and the way the number of different settings become nearly as plentiful as in the real world.

Every communication is a transaction. Viewing communication as a transaction focuses on the people who are communicating, the changes that take place in them as they are communicating, and the psychological aspects of the event. It also implies that all participants are involved continuously and simultaneously; that communication events have a past, present, and future; and that the roles the participants play will affect the communication.

Five types of communication are discussed. Intrapersonal communication is language use and/or thought that occurs within you, the communicator. Intercultural communication occurs whenever two or more people from different cultures interact.

Interpersonal communication is informal communication with one or more other persons. Small-group communication occurs when a small group of people get together to solve a problem. Public communication is giving a speech to an audience.

Communication competence is revealed when communicators, using any one of the five types of communication, communicate in a personally effective and socially appropriate manner. Effectiveness and appropriateness are likely when the following five elements characterize your communication: respect, empathy, tolerance, flexibility, and interaction management. Interaction management includes a communicator's posture, comfort, appropriate role, and willingness to self-disclose.

Strategic flexibility (SF) means expanding your communication repertoire to enable you to use the best skill or behavior available for a particular situation. The six steps of SF are anticipate, assess, evaluate, select, apply, and reassess and reevaluate.

Creativity is the capacity to synthesize vast amounts of information and wrestle with complex problems. Your creativity frees you to generate possibilities, which of course is the very foundation of SF.

Active open-mindedness (AOM) is a tool designed to help readers digest, master, and use knowledge. The AOM section added to each chapter offers practice in critical examination, analysis, and thought. With carefully designed situations, suggestions, and questions, it helps readers gather their resources, examine the facts, and render (or refrain from making) a decision or take action when appropriate.

Communication can be improved if you concentrate on several important areas. Find out what communication skills are important to you. Discover the kinds of communication that are most difficult for you and work to improve them. Seek out people who will help you develop these skills and give you support and feedback, and set a realistic timetable for improvement.

Ethical communication, a component of each of the five types of communication, lies at the core of strategic flexibility and should be an important aspect of any program of improvement. Ethical communication is communication that is honest, fair, and considerate of others' rights. Underlying the seven principles of ethical conduct paraphrased from the National Communication Association's Credo are the themes of caring and responsibility. Proper ethical conduct often grows out of an individual's personal commitment to live an ethical life.

Key Terms and Concepts

Use the Online Learning Center at www.mhhe.com/hybels11e to further your understanding of the following terms.

Abstract symbol 9
Active open-mindedness 22
Anticipate 21
Apply 21
Assess 21
Asynchronous communication 12
Channel 9
Communication 7
Competent communication 19
Concrete symbol 8
Creativity 22
Culture 18

Ethical communication 25
Evaluate 21
External noise 10
Feedback 9
Intercultural communication 18
Internal noise 10
Interpersonal communication 15
Intrapersonal communication 15
Message 7
Noise 10
Nonverbal symbol 9
Public communication 18
Reassess and reevaluate 21

Roles 14
Select 21
Semantic noise 10
Sender-receivers 7
Sensory acuity 10
Setting 10
Small-group communication 17
Strategic flexibility (SF) 20
Symbol 8
Synchronous communication 12
Transactional communication 13
Verbal symbol 8

Questions to Review

1. What are the most frequently cited factors important to aiding graduating college students both to obtain and sustain employment?
2. Why is communication called a process?
3. What is the significance in knowing that meaning is jointly created between sender and receiver?
4. What are the differences between the symbols that make up communication messages?
5. Why is communication called a transaction? What are the three principles of transactional communication?
6. How do intrapersonal and interpersonal communication differ from each other?
7. What are the four characteristics that distinguish Internet communication from face-to-face communication?
8. What are the elements communicators need to display to be considered competent?
9. Why should you be concerned about intercultural communication?
10. What is the meaning of strategic flexibility (SF)?
11. What are the six steps of SF, and what is the key to each step?
12. What is the role of creativity in communication?
13. What are the principles of ethical communication, and what is likely to be the foundation for ethical conduct?

Go to the self-quizzes on the Online Learning Center at www.mhhe.com/hybels11e to test your knowledge of the chapter concepts.

CHAPTER TWO

Self, Perception, and Communication

Objectives

After reading this chapter, you should be able to:

- Explain the role of self and perception in communication.

- Describe self-concept and how to improve a weak or poor self-concept.

- Discuss the perceptual steps of selecting, organizing, and interpreting and how each step differs from the others.

- Explain perceptual filters and how they influence perceptions.

- Describe the different ways of adjusting to perceptual influences.

LEANDRA GONZALEZ SPENT HER CHILDHOOD IN MIGRANT CAMPS in Texas and spoke only Spanish. Her parents took jobs weeding cotton so their children could stay in school. Throughout her life, she had a dream of graduating from college—the only one in her family to do so. Throughout her life, too, she had to battle racial, cultural, and gender prejudice as well as teacher "put-downs" and derision from the wealthier White students. In high school she loved math, because in math courses she could study the rules and predict the results. Thus, she avoided having to second-guess teachers' likes and dislikes. Although her self-concept took a beating when teachers would mispronounce her name or students laughed when she missed or couldn't answer a teacher's question, her parents continued to stress education, told her she could be whatever she wanted to be, gave her unconditional love, and stayed in close contact with her because of the Internet while she was away at school. With convincing results in her college classes, an incredible work ethic, a supportive and encouraging group of college friends, support from high school friends with whom she stayed in touch through social networking, as well as powerful, personal motivation to exceed, Leandra Gonzalez bypassed prejudice, achieved beyond expectations, and successfully fulfilled her dreams, and then some.

The Role of Self and Perception in Communicating Effectively and Strategic Flexibility

An obvious question when beginning a chapter titled "Self, Perception, and Communication" is "What does this have to do with communication?" Or, perhaps, "Why do I need to know this?" Both self and perception are foundations for effective communication. Your **self-concept** is how you think and feel about yourself. Self-concept and perception are so closely related that they are often difficult to separate. **Perception** is how you look at others and the world around you. Now, here's the connection: How you look at the world depends on what you think of yourself, and what you think of yourself will influence how you look at the world. Thus, your communication—the words and nonverbal cues you use when you talk with others—will be a direct and obvious result of both your self-concept and perceptions. As noted in Chapter 1, your communication is always changing because, in part, your self-concept and perceptions are always changing.

It will be helpful to keep in mind as you read this chapter what Nathaniel Branden, a psychiatrist and expert on the subject of self-esteem, said: "No factor is more important in people's psychological development and motivation than the value judgments they make about themselves. Every aspect of their lives is impacted by the way they see themselves." Consider your communication—whether it is intrapersonal, interpersonal, group, or public—as an aspect of your life that will be directly impacted.

Realize that your self-concept can set limits on your behavioral possibilities. Because of your self-concept, you may consider yourself unlovable, irrational, inadequate, incompetent, worthless, or inferior. If you think of yourself as unlovable, this may cause you to believe you are ineligible for the love of another person. If you think of yourself as irrational, this may cause you to believe that you are ineligible to render logical, well-grounded judgments and decisions.

Another limitation imposed by your self-concept has to do with risk taking. Being who you take yourself to be, some action or experience becomes unthinkable. To take *that* action or have *that* experience would so violate who you are that, should you do it, you could no longer take yourself to be the same person. You would be forced to see yourself as someone different. Think of what it might take, for example, to leave a destructive relationship, defend your rights in an assertive and forceful manner, or take the initiative to lead a group in a dramatic new direction.

A third limitation imposed by your self-concept relates directly to perception, but because of its importance, needs to be restated. You will perceive the world in ways that are in keeping with your self-concept. For you, that will be "just the way the world is." If you, for example, think of yourself as "world's greatest failure," then you might read anyone else's positive comments about you as cases of misunderstanding or praise as ill-motivated, deceitful flattery. To have a self-concept, then, is not just to have a certain appraisal of yourself, it is to live in a certain world.

Imagine, for a moment, the Leandra situation. Undoubtedly, how she thinks and feels about herself is determined in part by the role and perception of women in Texas migrant camps, by the way she was raised by her parents, and by the perceptions and reactions of her friends and teachers. It will take her a while to understand the place that women hold in society and how she fits into those roles, the function of students at a university and how active they must be to impact their own education, and the perceptions and reactions of her new friends and instructors.

Because Leandra has defined the differences as challenges, and has used her situation to motivate personal growth, development, and change, you can see how readily both her self-concept and perceptions will change and how her communication will change as well. Improvements are likely to be observed in her readiness to ask and answer questions, speak out on her observations and perceptions, and take a more active, assertive role in her relationships with others. If you could stand back and observe as Leandra changes, you would likely see a much stronger, more certain, and—definitely—more effective communicator emerge.

How do self-concept and perception fit into the six steps of strategic flexibility? First, with stronger self-confidence, you will have a sturdy base of operations—more strength and confidence in your ability to anticipate, assess, and evaluate communication situations. Second, with more accurate perceptions, you will increase your repertoire of available skills and behaviors, thus you will have more from which to select and, likely, more accuracy and precision in their application. Reassessment and reevaluation become more effective as well because the context for all your actions will be broader, more immediate, and relevant.

What is important to know is that it doesn't take much change in your self-concept or in your perceptions to influence your communication. The starting point can be just as soon as you want it to be. Nothing is likely to change if you are close-minded, reluctant, and hesitant or full of fear, doubt, and concern. Nothing is likely to change either if you think you know everything you need to know, or if you think there is no need or room for improvement. You must be open to change, since change is going to happen. You must be open to new findings and understandings. And you must be open to options, alternatives, and possible new choices. It can be a great journey, but without a commitment from you, there's likely to be no journey at all—just words on a page or ideas that travel in one ear and out the other—if, indeed, they get that far. "Can we will ourselves to change?" Joann Ellison Rodgers asks, then answers her own question in her article "Altered Ego: The New View of Personality Change." "Yes," says Rodgers, "especially if we think we can. . . . The power of belief is the key."[1]

In her book *inGenius: A Crash Course on Creativity*, Tina Seelig (introduced in Chapter 1), executive director of the Stanford Technology Ventures Program and the director of the National Center for Engineering Pathways to Innovation, writes in Chapter 11, "Inside Out and Outside In" about the importance of attitude with respect to nurturing the brain:

> It is important to note that our mind-sets are malleable [susceptible to the shaping power of surrounding influences]. Carol Dweck of the Stanford School of Education has done a tremendous amount of work on this topic and has shown how the messages that others tell us and that we tell ourselves dramatically influence how we see our place in the world. Compelling proof comes from a study by Dweck and Lisa Sorich Blackwell on low-achieving seventh graders. All of the students had a study skills workshop. Half of the group attended a general session on memory, while the other half learned that the brain, like a muscle, grows stronger through exercise. The group that was told that the brain is like a muscle showed much more motivation and had significantly improved grades in math, while the control group showed no improvement.* This study is supported by extensive research and demonstrates that your mind-set and attitude are within your own control" (p. 189).

*Krakovsky, Marina. (March/April, 2007). The effort effect. *Stanford Magazine*.

Source: Seelig, Tina. (2012). *inGenius: A crash course on creativity*. HarperCollins, New York.

Questions

1. Do you believe that your intelligence (your ability to exercise the higher mental functions as well as your readiness of comprehension) is basically fixed at birth—and, thus, unchangeable throughout life?
2. When the going gets tough, are you one who says, "I am going to have to put in more effort"? Or, when you make an error, are you one who says, "I'm going to learn from this and grow stronger"? These are the kind of people who have a different level of activity in their brains and who believe that intelligence is malleable.
3. Do you believe that your mind-set and attitude are within your own control? What specific actions do you take (or have you taken) that would show this to be true?
4. Do you see how important this concept is as you begin a new course in communicating effectively? Do you understand how it can make a positive and beneficial contribution to not just how much you learn in a course like this but also how much you are likely to grow, change, and develop?

Self-Concept

The case of Leandra Gonzalez reveals that the self is mobile, personal, self-reflexive (causing one to think and reflect), and subject to change. Although she was raised in Texas, worked as a migrant, and spoke only Spanish, she became freer to create her own identity. (The words *self* and *identity* are being used synonymously.) How she thinks and feels about herself is socially constructed as she assumes different roles throughout her lifetime. Her identity is established as a result of mutual recognition from others combined with self-validation. For example, those who had contact with Leandra discovered a soft-spoken, intelligent, witty, and incredibly perceptive individual who was more than willing to share her background, history, and insights—mutual recognition. Because of what they discovered and the respect and admiration they revealed, Leandra became more outspoken, charming, and humorous—self-validation. Her thoughts of being a second-class citizen (how many migrant women are viewed in rural Texas) changed, and she emerged from a self- and culture-imposed shell to become more self-confident, self-assured, and self-reliant.

Just as in Leandra's case, your self-concept is based on the values of the culture and the community you come from. Your culture tells you what is competent and moral by defining attitudes and beliefs; the community you belong to tells you what is expected of you. The extent to which you reflect the attitudes and beliefs of your culture and live up to the expectations of your community will determine how you see yourself. If Leandra were to spend her life in the town where she grew up, her self-concept would be formed by a very limited (and limiting) group of people.

There are at least two elements likely to affect your work on your self-concept. The first element, discussed by Tracy McMillan in her book *Why You're Not Married . . . Yet* (NY: Ballantine Books, 2012), involves "letting go of what other people think and making choices that are *right for you* even if other people don't approve of or understand them" (p. 29).

The second element is discussed by Andrew Newberg, a medical doctor and neuroscientist, with Mark Robert Waldman, in their book *Words Can Change Your Brain* (NY: Hudson Street Press, 2012). It involves trusting your intuition. Newberg writes, "Every person is unique, every interaction is unique, and every conversation is unique. Some strategies will work for some people at certain times while other strategies will be called for with other people at other times. So we have to trust our intuition which . . . contains a vast reservoir of insight that is rarely expressed. . . ." (p. 145). It is strategic flexibility, as you will recall, that gives you time to pause and allow your intuition to determine which strategy is best for each situation you encounter.

Self-concept, which is not a single impression that remains static and unchanging, but rather an array of often conflicting impressions, sensations, and behaviors, is made up of three distinct elements: reflected appraisals, social comparisons, and self-perception. Let's look at each of them.

Reflected Appraisals

In his article, "Mixed Signals" (*Psychology Today* [September/October 2009], pp. 63–71), Sam Gosling, a psychologist at the University of Texas at Austin, writes, "How you're seen does matter. Social judgment forms the basis for social interaction itself. Almost every decision others make about you, from promotions to friendships to marriage, is based on how people see you. So even if you never learn what you're really like, learning how others perceive you is a worthwhile goal" (p. 68). Your parents, your friends, and your teachers all tell you who you are through **reflected appraisals:** messages you get about yourself from others. Most reflected appraisals come from things people say about you. Your college speech communication instructor may say you are a good speaker, your peers may say you are a good friend, and your coach may tell you that you must work harder. All such messages from others help create your self-concept.

Besides being given messages about yourself, you are also given lines to speak.[2] These lines are often so specific that some people refer to them as **scripts.** Some scripts are given to you by your parents, and they contain directions that are just as explicit as any script intended for the stage. You are given your lines ("Say thank you to the nice woman"), your gestures ("Point to the horsie"), and your characterizations ("You're a good girl/boy"). The scripts tell you how to play future scenes ("Everyone in your family has gone to college") and what is expected of you ("I will be so happy when you make us grandparents"). People outside your family also contribute to your scripts. Teachers, coaches, religious leaders, friends, the media, and the Internet all tell you what they expect from you, how you should look, how you should behave, and how you should say your lines. Sometimes you receive the messages directly, and sometimes you get them by observing and then imitating others' behavior.

Writer and radio personality Garrison Keillor gives a list of scripts we get as we are growing up. Have you heard any of them or used them on your own children?

I. *I don't know what's wrong with you.*
  A.   *I never saw a person like you.*
    1. *I wasn't like that.*
    2. *Your cousins don't pull stuff like that.*
  B.   *It doesn't make sense.*
    1. *You have no sense of responsibility at all.*
    2. *We've given you everything we possibly could.*
      a. *Food on the table and a roof over your head.*
      b. *Things we never had when we were your age.*
    3. *And you treat us like dirt under your feet.*
  C.   *You act as if*
    1. *The world owes you a living.*
    2. *You've got a chip on your shoulder.*
    3. *The rules don't apply to you.*

II. *Something has got to change and change fast.*
  A.   *You're driving your mother to a nervous breakdown.*
  B.   *I'm not going to put up with this for another minute.*
    1. *You're crazy if you think I am.*
    2. *If you think I am, just try me.*
  C.   *You're setting a terrible example for your younger brothers and sisters.*

III. *I'm your father and as long as you live in this house, you'll—*
  A.   *Do as you're told, and when I say "now" I mean "now."*
  B.   *Pull your own weight.*
    1. *Don't expect other people to pick up after you.*
    2. *Don't expect breakfast when you get up at noon.*
    3. *Don't come around asking your mother for spending money.*
  C.   *Do something about your disposition.*

IV. *If you don't change your tune pretty quick, then you're out of here.*
  A.   *I mean it.*
  B.   *Is that understood?*
    1. *I can't hear you. Don't mumble.*
    2. *Look at me.*
  C.   *I'm not going to tell you this again.*[3]

If you were given positive reflected appraisals when you were young, you probably have a good self-concept; if the appraisals were largely negative, your self-concept may suffer. The messages you receive about yourself can become **self-fulfilling prophecies**—events or actions that occur because you (and other people) have expected them. For example, at the beginning of the semester Professor Farley said to Kevin, "You're going to be a very good student." Because of this expectation, Kevin wanted to be a good student and worked hard to live up to Professor Farley's prophecy. Similarly, negative prophecies can have a negative impact. If someone tells a child that he or she will "never amount to much," there is a good chance the child will not.

Social Comparisons

When you compare yourself with others to see how you measure up, you are making a **social comparison.** Social comparisons are not just important, they are necessary in helping develop an accurate self-perception. An accurate self-perception is crucial for navigating and responding to the social world through effective communication.

If you think about it, you can't evaluate yourself without some form of comparison. You may, for example, compare yourself with your peers. You might ask, "Do I look as good as she does?" or "What grade did you get on your midterm?" or "What kind of car do you drive?" If you are a parent, you might compare your child with your friend's child. "Can he talk yet?" "Did she get a position on the softball team?" In your job, you are likely to ask yourself if you are doing as well as your co-workers. Did you get as big a raise as your colleague got? Does the boss ever notice you and praise your work? The answers to these social comparison questions all contribute to your self-concept.

Social comparisons are pivotal to self-evaluations. They depend less on objective circumstances than on how you judge yourself in relation to others on particular attributes. You prefer to compare yourself with others who are similar for the attribute of concern. For example, the first question in the paragraph above, "Do I look as good as she does?" may refer to body image. Social comparisons also can be employed to gather information about highly valued attributes (personality, money, or success), social expectations (appropriate attire and expected behavior), and norms (rules, laws, and acceptable practices). That is why comparisons are likely to be made to a variety of targets—there is such a broad range of information needed.

Let's focus on a single attribute of concern: body image evaluation. The repeated media images of thin females and muscular males make these forms seemingly the standard of attractiveness. The gender differences in the attributes associated with body image are those that would be expected. Weight is the primary feature predicting body dissatisfaction among women. Height and shoulders—or muscular shape—is

ATTENTION!

Some Social Comparisons Students Make

- How am I doing compared with other students I know?
- When it comes to schoolwork, am I as good as I think I am?
- Am I as hardworking as other students I know?
- Am I better-than-average scholastically?
- Are the barriers that hold me back (i.e., significant other, work, personal commitments, etc.) more severe than those of others?
- Are my grades better than those of other students I know?
- Can I expect a better return from my college experience than other students will get?

The way we see ourselves is often a reflection of how we compare ourselves with others.

the attractiveness concern of males. From where do the standards come? Pressures for the proper body image come from parents, peers, and dating partners, as well as the media. They can be direct, such as a parent encouraging a daughter to diet or a son to lift weights, or indirect, such as a peer voicing admiration of a particular model who reveals the attributes. Constant exposure is likely to make both men and women self-conscious about their bodies and make them obsess over and consider their physical appearance a measure of their worth. Of course, this is both a narrow and a limited measure.

In a single day, you see many images of how people should look and behave. In a lifetime, you may receive 40 to 50 million commercial messages. Magazines, movies, and videos all contribute to what the "ideal you" should be. Even if you can discount these images as being unrealistic, many of the people around you believe them and judge you and others by what they see and hear. Kristin Neff, a professor of educational psychology at the University of Texas at Austin, is quoted here by Harriet Brown in her article, "The Boom and Bust Ego" (*Psychology Today,* January/February 2012): "Social comparison is inevitable, looking for our place in the social universe we inhabit. And we all do it. But it's not exactly a recipe for self-confidence, because there are always people who do what you do both better and worse than you" (p. 73).[4] The best advice is to be realistic, look on the bright side (as best you can), and determine to try harder, be better, and improve your lot in life.

Self-Perception

You think, feel, speak, and act in accordance with your self-image. The way you see yourself is called **self-perception.** The process of accumulating views of your self is both complex and ongoing. Consciously and subconsciously you weigh whether others' thoughts, attitudes, actions, and reactions will work for you. It is a little like putting pieces of a puzzle together; however, not only does the puzzle picture constantly change, but seldom does anyone have all the pieces that make up the picture. Even when you may have a puzzle piece in your hand, the piece may not fit where you think it goes, or it may not fit the picture you thought it would. Why is this process so confusing?

First, self-perception is made up of so many variables. They include physical, social, intellectual, and spiritual elements such as convictions about principles; basic personal wants and desires; moral, religious, and political feelings; as well as responses to personal freedom, social controls, and oppression of one kind or another. They include, too, how you respond to failings and difficulties (or achievements and successes) as well as mental stress and self-deception.

Second, self-perception depends on the phase of your development, which is constantly changing as well. Often, as one ages, one becomes more open to the ideas of others, okay with being wrong, less attached to particular outcomes, and a better listener.[5] When all is said and done, self-perception is a little like what a state trooper told a woman when he stopped her for speeding: "My measure of your speed is but a momentary picture of what occurs in a fraction of a second. That's all it can be."

Jean Twenge, of San Diego State University, and W. Keith Campbell, of the University of Georgia, compared data from 1975 through 2006. These are yearly surveys given to thousands of high school seniors by the University of Michigan's Institute for Social Research. They found that "today's teenagers and young adults are far more likely than their parents to believe they are great people, destined for maximum success as workers, spouses, and parents."[6] Such feelings can foster great expectations, protect them against depression, and lead them to do better. Twenge says, "American culture seems to be teaching young people to be overly confident."[7]

Numbers of variables and constant change don't deny the importance or application of self-perception. Accept your self-perception as a momentary picture. What can you do to make it positive? First, make certain you have a positive attitude, because how you think about what you do will affect your persistence, attitudes, and achievements. Second, keep your focus objective. For example, look specifically at what is required to achieve success—the steps, resources, or abilities—and not at subjective elements such as your feelings, reactions, and interpretations of the events, people, or situations. Third, try to focus on small achievements because your ability to perform successfully will have a direct effect on your actual performance. Your state of mind clearly impacts your ultimate performance.[8]

Gender, Sex, and Self-Concept

Several research studies show that men and women gain their self-concept in different ways.[9] Two researchers found that when forming self-concept, men give the most importance to social comparisons, whereas women attach more importance to reflected appraisals. Men put more value on reflected appraisals from their parents, while women give more importance to reflected appraisals from their friends.

Other studies have shown that female self-confidence comes primarily from connections and attachments, while male self-confidence comes primarily from achievement.[10] This relates to research findings about gender and language. (In Chapter 3, Verbal Communication, we discuss how women's language is tied to social networks, while men's language is tied to competition and achievement.)

Although your family and peers may influence how you act as a male or female, there is some evidence that your sexual identity is established when you are born. Researchers know this because of a terrible accident that occurred to an infant boy when he was eight months old. A surgeon was trying to repair a fused foreskin and accidentally cut off the boy's penis. Because the doctor thought the child could never live as a boy, he recommended to the parents that they rear him as a girl. When the parents agreed, the boy's testicles were removed and a vagina was constructed.

From this point on, the parents treated the child as a girl. They got her feminine clothes, gave her toys that girls liked, and even put her in the care of a female psychiatrist to help her adjust.

The child, however, never accepted her female identity. She tore off the dresses, refused the dolls, and looked for male friends. Instead of using makeup like her mother, she imitated her father by shaving and urinating standing up.

When she was 12, the doctors began estrogen treatments that enabled her to grow breasts. She did not like the feminizing effects of the drug and refused to take it. When she was 14, she refused any more treatment to feminize her. By this time she was so unhappy that her father told her what had happened to her, and her first feeling was that of relief.

At this point she went back to being a male. The youth took male hormone shots and had a mastectomy (an operation to remove breasts), and a surgeon began to reconstruct male genitals. Although the surgery was only partially successful, the young man married and he and his wife adopted children.

From this and other cases involving ambiguous genitals in newborns, many scientists have concluded that an infant with a Y chromosome will be a boy, regardless of his genitalia, and that nothing will ever change this.

One reason gender is important is that it "helps us organize the world into two boxes, his and hers, and gives us a way of quickly sizing up every person we see on the street."[11] Judith Butler, a rhetoric professor at University of California, Berkeley, says, "Gender is a way of making the world secure."[12] When it comes to social comparisons or reflected appraisals, these distinctions have an enormous bearing on both self-development and self-confidence.

Can You Improve Your Self-concept?

Because self-esteem—the way you view yourself—is the single most significant key to your behavior, it is understandable why you might want to improve. But, to make any change in your self-concept requires hard work—"great determination," says Rodgers, cited earlier when discussing one's will to change. In a landmark study published in the *Journal of Personality and Social Psychology*, a team of researchers surveyed more than 132,000 adults ages 21 to 60 over the Internet to determine if one's self-concept is set by the age of 30 or whether change is ongoing. They discovered that well into adulthood people change to meet their needs. Experiences such as education, courtship and marriage, parenting, the need to make a living, and exposure to an expanding network of social, family, and business connections will alter your self-concept for the good.[13] Conscientiousness—being organized, self-disciplined, and goal-directed—will rise over time, but the biggest increases occur during the 20s. This is good news and answers directly the question posed at the head of this section.

According to Annie Paul, in her review article on "Self-Help," "The only way to change the final product—your self-esteem—is to change what goes into making it—feedback from other people." Then, she quotes Swann, who says, "If you find yourself in bad relationships where your negative self-view is getting reinforced, then either change the way those people treat you by being more assertive, or change who you interact with."[14] In one of the most succinct, profound, and instructive summaries, she writes, "Stand up for yourself. Surround yourself with people who think you're great, and tell you so. Do your best to live up to their high opinions. And be patient. Self-esteem is the sum of your interactions with others over a lifetime, and it's not going to change overnight."[15]

The point here is that change *can* occur, and those who believe their self-concept and abilities can change will be more resilient, more open to experience, and more likely to take risks.[16] If your goals include being more skilled, more effective, more resilient, more extroverted, more nurturing, and more tolerant, your first step, according to Stanford University developmental psychologist Carol Dweck, author of *Mindset*, should be to assume a "growth mindset"—defined as a desire to change.[17]

Where Should Change Begin?

"One of the most defining choices you can make in your entire life," writes Brendon Burchard in *The Charge* (NY: Free Press, 2012), "is deciding to control the quality of person you will be on an everyday basis. What will you stand for? What kind of positive values, standards, and beliefs will you demonstrate each day? How much honesty, integrity, fairness, and kindness will you insist upon when meeting the world? This is the stuff of character" (p. 43).

What is important to understand as you begin any kind of improvement program is that a poor self-concept is part of many human problems. For example, it could be part of a lack of purpose, inadequate motivation, lack of confidence, sadness and pessimism, lack of assertiveness, self-put-down games, and even the lack of wisdom and equality in selecting a mate. When it is related to sadness, just one of these human problems, it could relate to self-criticism, anger turned inward, guilt, shame, feeling inferior, low self-concept, and pessimism. That is why a poor self-concept isn't an easy problem to overcome. Wouldn't it be great if you could just erect a mental wall that would block out all your previous problems, and begin anew?

Andrew Cox, in an article entitled, "Success Depends on our Self-Talk," at the website *Self-help Online,* begins his essay saying, "What we tell ourselves about ourselves—our self talk, will create success—or not. Our success depends so much on the messages we constantly send ourselves. We can be our best friends—or we can be our own worst enemies. Each of us is capable of affirming ourselves—or of sabotaging our own belief in ourselves. And the difference between constructive self criticism and destructive criticism is so small—yet the difference in effect is huge!"[18]

Cox suggests using the powerful statement, "I am capable and worthy and here's what I have to do to make it happen the next time." He suggests creating positive messages (intrapersonal communication) about what makes you special, what unique contributions you have made, what you do well, and how you can use your experiences, education, skills, interests and aptitudes today. To destroy a habit of negative self-criticism requires replacing it with effective positive behaviors. This is not easy to do, but if you are intent on and dedicated to change, it's a good place to begin. Self-talk is also beneficial in motivation, self-improvement, overcoming difficulties, and facing troublesome situations. In addition, it can serve as a mental guide—a positive approach—for implementing the following suggestions.

Where would you start if you could erect a solid barrier between where you are today and where you were yesterday (see Figure 2-1)? First, silence your internal critic,

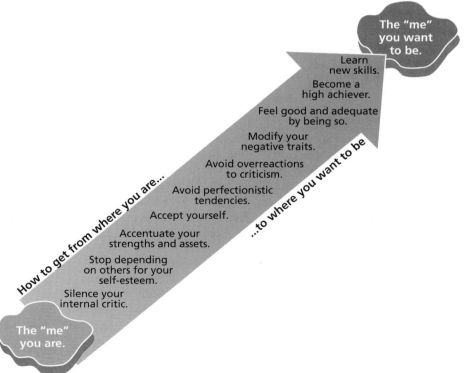

Figure 2-1
How to Begin a Program of Change

Reality Check

We have defined self-concept as how you think and feel about yourself. Let's say—for the purposes of discussion here—that what you have discovered in coming to college is how smart all the other students are. It's as if you don't measure up, but you don't want it to be this way. Study the section, "Can You Improve Your Self-Concept?" What specific suggestions can you begin to apply in your life, right now, that will make a difference in your self-esteem? Do the suggestions given here make sense? Do they appear logical? Do the facts you know right now support the possibility of change? What implications might change in your self-esteem hold for you? How might positive changes in your self-esteem help you communicate more effectively?

nip negative thoughts in the bud, and stop bullying yourself. Replace criticism with encouragement and treat yourself kindly. Second, stop depending on others for your self-esteem; do your own self-evaluation. Stop letting others dominate your life. Take responsibility for your feelings. Just as you can't make others feel happy, don't expect others to make you feel happy or good about yourself. Third, accentuate your strengths and assets. Fourth, accept yourself—warts and all. Give yourself permission to decide that you're doing the best you can. Fifth, avoid your perfectionistic tendencies—the tyranny of all the "shoulds" in your life. Accept flaws, mistakes, and imperfections as part of being human. Sixth, avoid your overreactions to criticism. You needn't feel guilty about things beyond your control.

There are other areas, too, where you can begin to change. A seventh way to get to where you want to be is to modify your negative traits. Focus on what you *can* do, not on what you can't. Eighth, feel good and adequate by being good and adequate—behave morally. Ninth, become a high achiever. It is more about doing what is expected of you, and then some, than it is about high intelligence or excessive brilliance. Tenth, learn new skills. Open yourself to new possibilities, areas for potential growth, and new ways to develop positive attributes. Eleventh, don't feel responsible for everything. Don't try to be all things (and do all things) for people. Twelfth, forgive and forget. Avoid hanging on to painful memories and bad feelings. Your past can control you if you don't control it. What all of this boils down to is developing **self-awareness,** which means knowledge of and trust in your own motives, emotions, preferences, and abilities.[19] To develop self-awareness means evaluating your strengths and weaknesses, acknowledging and taking responsibility for your errors, and acting in ways congruent with your values and needs (even at the risk of criticism or rejection).[20] Finally, begin a program of personal change in specific desired areas by working through the following steps.

What Do You Want to Change about Yourself?

Pick one area in which you would like to improve yourself. See if you can figure out why you have had problems in this area. Were you given a script saying you were inadequate in this area? Are you living out a self-fulfilling prophecy?

Are Your Circumstances Keeping You from Changing?

Are you living in circumstances that are holding you back? Do the people around you support you if you want to do something differently, especially if it involves taking a risk? Sometimes the people you live with try to hold you back—even though they might not be conscious of doing so. For example, one spouse says to the other, "Why do you want to go to Europe? We haven't seen all of the United States yet."

Sometimes you are locked into roles that are uncomfortable for you. Many women feel trapped when their children are small; some people hate their jobs; some students hate school. Are you in a role that you have chosen for yourself, or has someone else chosen it for you? Has someone else defined how you should play this role? Can you play this role in a way that will make it more comfortable for you? Can you change the role so that you can be more like the person you want to be?

Are You Willing to Take Some Chances?

Colleges and universities offer great chances to take some risks. Take a course from a professor who is rumored to be hard but fair. Study a subject you know nothing about. Join a club that sounds interesting—even if you don't know any of its members. Many colleges and universities also offer opportunities to study abroad or to take an internship. Going abroad is especially helpful in building self-confidence.

What Would Be a Realistic Goal?

Too often, people decide they are going to change their behavior overnight. Students who habitually get poor grades will often announce that this semester they are going to get all A's. This is an unrealistic goal. If you are going to try to change your behavior, see if you can break down the problem into steps you can handle. Let's say that you are shy but would like to speak up more in class because you often know the answers. Why not set a goal to speak up once a week in one class? That is probably a goal you can manage. Once you feel comfortable with that, you might increase your goal to speaking up two or even three times a week. Joann Rodgers, again citing the work of Carol Dweck, says, "Shy people who are determined to develop their social skills can force themselves to interact despite the nervousness it provokes, and end up garnering great satisfaction from the effort even if the bashfulness remains. 'Our studies show others rate these people highly nonshy when they interact, despite their feeling of anxiety, says Dweck.' "[21]

Can You Discipline Yourself?

The old saying "Nothing succeeds like success" applies to a positive self-concept: As soon as you experience success, you start feeling better about yourself. Sometimes people think they are unsuccessful because they are not motivated enough. Typical thinking might be, "If only I could motivate myself, I would get better grades." People who think this way confuse motivation with discipline. There's no way to motivate yourself to take out the garbage, do the dishes, or study your class notes. These jobs can be done only through discipline: You say, "I am going to do this job for one hour— whether or not I want to do it is irrelevant." This sort of discipline is what leads to success, which, in turn, helps you feel better about yourself.

Are There People Who Will Support You?

Whenever we try to bring about a change in ourselves, we need to surround ourselves with people who will support us. As Annie Paul said in her review article on "Self-Help," "Surround yourself with people who think you're great, and tell you so."[22] These are people who understand how difficult it is to change and who understand our desire to do so. Take the example of speaking up in class. If you are very apprehensive about doing this, you might consider discussing the problem with an instructor you like and trust. Tell him or her that you are occasionally going to try to say something, and ask for his or her support. Also tell a couple of friends in your class what you plan to do. Just having other people know what you are trying to accomplish often provides good moral support. Not all people will support you, and some may even consciously try to defeat you. For them, the possibility that you might change is too threatening.

When you have found some people to support you, it's important that you tell them what you want to do and give them some direction as to how they can help you.

Can You Be More Other-Centered?

People who lack self-esteem often spend a lot of time looking inward at their miseries, while people who seem happy and content with themselves seem to spend their time interacting with others. If you look inward all the time, you are probably making yourself more miserable. For a few days, experiment with relating more to the people around you. Just asking someone "How was your day?" or "How is your semester (or quarter) going?" shows that you are interested.

If you have an opportunity to bestow some praise, do it. Look for situations around you in which you can praise people, and express your praise with genuine feeling. Tell your mother that her meatloaf tastes great, tell a professor that her class was really helpful on an internship, tell a friend that she looks wonderful in green. When you act positively toward others, they will act positively toward you, and this, in turn, will make you feel better about yourself.

The Map Is Not the Territory

It was the father of general semantics, Alford Korzybski, who stated, "A map is not the territory it represents, but if correct, it has a similar structure to the territory, which accounts for its usefulness." You have maps inside your head that describe the things outside your head. The maps inside your head represent the territory outside your head. The more accurate your maps are, the better equipped you are to function within society. The accuracy of your maps is a measure of your sanity. But, remember that nobody has completely accurate maps.

"It makes more sense," writes Henry Hitchings in his book *The Language Wars* (NY: Farrar, Straus, and Giroux, 2011), "to say that language enables us to construct an *image* of reality. Sensory experience is like a stream, which we channel using language. To put this another way, language organizes our fluid impressions of the world. But it is not the world that we are arranging; rather, we are arranging our experience of the world. When we use language we are translating and interpreting our sensuous responses to things outside us. Language frames our experiences. It breaks experience up into pieces—a digital packaging of analogue reality. Different languages do this in different ways. We could say that each language is like a map and manifests distinct conventions about mapping. The geography of the mental territory being mapped is a constant, but it gets represented in a variety of ways" (p. 310).

What this means for you is simply that your perception of reality is not reality itself, but it is your own version of it—your "maps." In Figure 2-2, the person is bewildered

Figure 2-2
The Map Is Not the Territory

because from the map being held there was no way to know that the mountains on the horizon even existed. Even a road map doesn't accurately depict the territory it is supposed to represent. Your maps, likewise, are distorted because you jump to conclusions with little or no evidence, ignore parts of the territory, see only what you want to see, see things as black and white rather than in shades of gray, and apply labels to people and situations and then refuse to see beyond the labels.

There are some important understandings that Korzybski's theory clarifies for both self-concept and perception. The first has to do with how your maps are created. There is so much information in the world that you can't take it all in, let alone make sense of it all. So what you do is create internal maps of reality that you can refer to as you navigate through life. Your maps contain countless beliefs, values, generalizations, decisions, and numerous other mental aspects about how you see yourself and your relationship to the world around you. Just like a road map, it is a scaled-down version of reality. And just like a road map, maps don't show everything. As you get more information, your maps change.

The second understanding is that you react to the maps inside your head, not the territory outside your head. You react to the maps and not to what the maps represent. For example, if your maps tell you that a certain piece of music is pleasant, you will listen to it. If your maps tell you that the same piece of music is unpleasant, you will not listen to it. It is not the music that you are drawn to, it is your maps of the music. The same occurs in elections. You look not to the candidates when you choose how to vote, you look instead to your maps of the candidates.

The third understanding is that no two people can have exactly the same maps. Problems in communication occur when you try to impose your maps on another person—or other people. Empathizing with others requires learning to recognize the structure of others' maps—seeing the world through their eyes—thus being able to understand and relate to them respectfully and accurately. It helps to know that their maps are likely to be just as jaundiced by their own interpretations as yours are.

The fourth understanding is that to create personal change requires changing maps. There is a natural and understandable desire to protect old maps. That is because they become comfortable. You know how to navigate with these maps, and replacing them with new ones is a little like trying to find your way around a new supermarket. Not only are maps comfortable, they are habit forming. Even when they may not be as useful as they could be, you depend on them because they are what you have. You know where the bread, milk, and cereal are supposed to be in the supermarket. Letting maps go causes temporary chaos, but reconfiguring, reconstituting, or reorganizing maps at a higher level can result in relief from the problems and limitations of the old maps—new abilities to deal with what was previously stressful, perplexing, or overwhelming. You learn where things are located in the new supermarket, and your trips there become efficient, effective, and satisfying.

The fifth understanding is that your maps of reality are *not* who you are—the map is *not* the territory. Rather, your maps are simply a convenient tool you use to navigate through life. To understand that your maps are not who you are but simply a navigation tool will help you understand that maps need to go through the chaos and reorganization process for personal growth to occur. It will help you understand that map "changes" do not represent you in the process of falling apart. The **map is not the territory.** Trying to hold old maps together creates dysfunctional feelings and behaviors such as fear, depression, anger, anxiety, substance abuse, many physical diseases, and numerous other more serious mental problems.

ATTENTION!

What If the Map *Was* the Territory?
Alfred Korzybski, father of general semantics, said, "There are two ways to slice easily through life: to believe everything or to doubt everything. Both ways save us from thinking."

- I would believe my view of reality is the *only* right one.
- Everyone who does not share *my* view of reality is wrong.
- All the images (maps) my brain can concoct become real (accurately represent the world/ territory).
- I would dwell in a make-believe world constructed from my own visions, dreams, delusions, and fanciful notions.

Knowing that the map is not the territory will help you look forward to map changes. Why? Because new maps are likely to work better. New maps will allow you to be a happier, more peaceful person. New maps are likely to produce positive change. And because of the relationship between self-concept and perception, new maps will allow you to come at the world more accurately, see things with greater clarity, and understand events, others, and ideas with increased precision.

STRATEGIC FLEXIBILITY

When you permit changes in your maps of reality, you increase your strategic flexibility because new maps are likely to work better than old maps.

Perception

Perception, you will recall, is how you look at others and the world around you. Acts of perception are more than simply capturing incoming stimuli. These acts require a form of expectation, of knowing what is about to confront you and preparing for it. These expectations or predispositions to respond are a type of perceptual filter called **psychological sets,** and they have a profound effect on your perceptions. "Without expectations, or constructs through which you perceive your world," writes John Ratey, associate clinical professor of psychiatry at Harvard Medical School, "your surroundings would be what William James called a 'booming, buzzing confusion,' and each experience truly would be a new one, rapidly overwhelming you. You automatically and unconsciously fit your sensations into categories that you have learned, often distorting them in the process."[23]

For example, how you view a new instructor depends on your views of all the instructors you have had in the past. How you think about forming a new romantic relationship depends on the romantic relationships you have had in the past. Your knowledge, background, and experiences form the psychological sets and, thus, provide the matrix—that which gives shape or form to anything—into which any new idea or event is placed.

The Perceptual Process

Your perceptions affect more than your direct interactions with people. They also influence your response to all the information around you. This means that before the perceptual process begins, you receive information through your senses: touch, taste, smell, hearing, and sight. Then, whenever you encounter new information, whether it's from a television program, a newspaper, the Internet, or another person, you go through a three-step perceptual process: You select the information, you organize it, and you interpret it. These three steps of the perceptual process repeat themselves in an ongoing and continual process—sometimes even overlapping one another—that directly influences communication behaviors.

Research indicates that what you perceive is influenced by where your attention is directed. Also, your judgments about people are affected by your selective perceptions, that is, by what you choose to perceive.[24]

Whenever you encounter new information you go through a three-step perceptual process: You select the information, you organize it, and you interpret it.

In David M. Eagleman's book *Incognito: The Secret Lives of the Brain*, he gives readers a changed view of how people perceive reality:

> In the traditionally taught view of perception, data from the sensorium [the sensory nerve center of the body] pours into the brain, works its way up the sensory hierarchy, and makes itself seen, heard, smelled, tasted, felt—"perceived." But a closer examination of the data suggests this is incorrect. The brain is properly thought of as a mostly closed system that runs on its own internally generated activity.* We already have many examples of this sort of activity: for example, breathing, digestion, and walking are controlled by autonomously running activity generators in your brain stem and spinal cord. During dream sleep the brain is isolated from its normal input, so internal activation is the only source of cortical stimulation. In the awake state, internal activity is the basis for imagination and hallucinations (p. 44).

*Llinas, R. 2002. *I of the Vortex*. Boston: MIT Press.

Source: Eagleman, David M. (2011). *Incognito: The secret lives of the brain*. NY: Pantheon Books.

Questions

1. This view suggests that seeing has very little to do with the eyes. This means that internal data (all of our sensory information) is not *generated* by external sensory data but merely *modulated* (regulated, adjusted, and changed) by it. Does this point of view make sense?

2. To advance this concept one step forward, different senses influence one another and change the story of what is "really" out there. That is, "what comes in through the eyes is not just the business of the visual system—the rest of the brain is invested as well" (p. 47). How might a view of perception like this contribute to the deletions, distortions, and generalizations that people are prone to make?

3. Given this information, could you make a case supporting the fact that individuals create internal models of the outside world and then act as if those models are accurate depictions of reality? Can you cite any examples that would support this idea?

4. Accepting this information as fact, what could you do as you express your ideas—or your interpretations of reality—so that others would be aware that your observations are unique or, at the very least, unique constructions based on your models of reality?

We do not all perceive information in the same way. Even when several people have access to the same information, they are likely to select, organize, and interpret it in different ways. Let's say, for example, that three different people read the same newspaper: Omar is a Syrian who is studying in the United States; Caroline is an American who has been an exchange student in Syria; and Jim is an American who has never traveled.

When Omar reads the paper, he looks for (selects) news about Syria. In his mind he organizes the information on the basis of what he already knows. He may interpret it by asking the meaning of certain government actions or by thinking that the reporter has the wrong slant on the story. Caroline goes through a similar process. She has a high interest in stories about Syria because she has been there. She, too, organizes what she reads according to what she knows about the country. However, she may interpret the news stories differently because she doesn't have as much information as Omar. Also, her interpretation will probably be from an American point of view. When Jim reads the newspaper, he skips all the stories about Omar's country. He has never been there and has no immediate plans to go there. In fact, he skips all the news about the world and goes directly to the sports section. These three people are all exposed to the same information, but they all perceive it differently.

Just a few additional notes on the three processes. In *selecting* information, it should be clear that you select which cues you choose to pay attention to. Sure, it could be that you respond to the cue that is the brightest, loudest, or most easily seen, but you select cues according to your past experiences or judgments as well. Since you cannot perceive all the available sensory cues, you must be selective, and which cues you select affect both how you understand and respond.

Not only do you actively select the cues, but you actively *organize* those cues, too. Why? Because your collection of sensory cues requires structure and stability to be understood. It's as if you sense a vague form through mist or fog, but you continue to focus on it until it finally makes sense (the mist or fog lift, you get closer to it, or you finally recognize it). You do this by arranging and rearranging patterns until the form finally becomes clear.

Research clearly supports the human need to organize sensory cues. As early as 1932, Frederic C. Bartlett used the simple game of Telephone (in which a story is passed around a circle and changes with each retelling) to show that all incoming stimuli are *not* stored in our memory. Rather, according to Bartlett, our brains use mental guidelines that supply impressions of the whole[25]—the whole story, the whole event, or the whole person. These guidelines are referred to as **cognitive schemata.**

In 1992, Richard E. Mayer, in his book, *Thinking, Problem-Solving, Cognition,*[26] showed that people will change information to fit what they know. When we organize it into previously existing ways of thinking, deletions, distortions, and generalizations (the subject of the next section) occur.

A common concern at this point is what happens when the incoming sensory cues do not fit with any other sensory cues that you know or any structure that you currently possess. Leon Festinger, a researcher,[27] labeled this feeling of imbalance **cognitive dissonance,** and he argued that dissonance is an uncomfortable feeling that will motivate you to reduce it. In the following section, some of the ways for reducing the imbalance—or, striving for consonance (a state of equilibrium)—are discussed.

Finally, you *interpret* your sensory cues by drawing conclusions or judging, and this final step—often occurring instantly and simultaneously with the previous steps—depends on your past experiences, goals, expectations, beliefs, values, needs, world-view (to be discussed in the chapter on intercultural communication), gender, or feelings at the moment. Interpretations, too, vary from culture to culture. The point to understand here is simply that we go beyond the sensory cues—even beyond the "hard facts"—to arrive at our own conclusions and judgments. This will be discussed in greater detail in the following sections on generalizations and perceptual filters.

Deletions, Distortions, and Generalizations

In his book *Smart Thinking* (NY: Perigee, 2012), Dr. Art Markman, the Annabel Irion Worsham Centerrial Professor of Psychology and Marketing at the University of Texas, explains why very little of the information in the world makes it into our heads: "the construction of our sensory systems (like our eyes, ears, nose, and skin) that allows us to perceive the world limits what we can take in" (p. 62).

Any perceptions you have are less than perfect also because of deletions, distortions, and generalizations.[28] **Deletions**—blotting out, erasing, or canceling information—must occur first because your physical senses are limited. Your sight, hearing, touch, taste, and smell are the means you use to get information, but those senses focus only on those aspects of the environment that are most important for your survival. Your senses are not capable of perceiving everything in your external environment.

Deletions occur, too, because of your beliefs. If you believe something to be true, you have an almost infinite capacity to delete information that contradicts that belief. In addition, if you believe something to be true, you will go through your life searching for information that supports that belief and ignore information that does not.

In addition to deleting information, you also distort much of the information from your environment. **Distortions** involve twisting or bending information out of shape. You distort information, first because you observe only a small part of your external environment. Since what you observe is such a small part of the whole, you must fill in the blanks—specifically add information—to make your information make sense. The other reason you distort information is so that it will support your existing beliefs and values—fit into your psychological sets.

In addition to deleting and distorting information, you draw generalizations based on little substantial information. **Generalizations** involve drawing principles or conclusions from particular evidence or facts. Once you have observed something a few times, you conclude that what has proven true in the past will prove true in the future as well. Generalizations are important to your survival. Getting burned by putting a hand on a hot stove will give you a conclusion about the consequences of putting your hand on a hot stove in the future. If you had several bad experiences with members of the opposite sex, of a different race, of a different culture, or of a particular organization, you might generalize that *all* members of the opposite sex, a different race, a different culture, or a particular organization are bad. Then, all future experiences are filtered through that belief, information that contradicts the belief is deleted, and you distort other information so it will support the belief.

There are two perceptual theories closely related to and dependent on generalizations. The first, called **implicit personality theory,** occurs when you construct a picture (theory) of what people's personalities are, based on qualities or characteristics revealed by their behavior. When I (Richard) give talks to fifth graders about writing, I ask them what kinds of characteristics they think of when they hear that a person is a writer. They never hesitate in constructing a picture of a writer as smart, intelligent, and educated, if not open, and communicative as well.

Closely related to implicit personality theory (and sometimes difficult to separate from it), is **attribution.** This occurs when you devise explanations (theories) about other people's behavior so that you can understand whatever is taking place.[29] It can involve attributing causes or intentions as well, and you do it not just to better understand, but you do it to better predict future behavior, too. For example, you observe a fellow student coming out of a local bar and attribute a cause or intention: The student is a "heavy drinker" or is an "alcoholic." Seen at a party, you might expect this student to get drunk. You observe a student coming late to class, and you devise an explanation that the student is lazy or irresponsible. Given choices of whom to work with in a group, you might not select this student.

Keep these three activities in mind as you read the next section on perceptual filters. Realize that even before perceptual filters come into play and certainly while they are operating as well, deletion, distortion, and generalization are also influencing the information.[30]

Perceptual Filters

Deletions, distortions, and generalizations are important and affect your perceptions, but perceptual filters can be even more important. **Perceptual filters** are limitations that result from the narrowed lens through which you view the world. For example,

The purpose of AOM, as it was originally conceived, was to detect dishonesty, misrepresentation, and lack of respect for the facts in the communication of others. In this application, the purpose is to detect it in yourself, that is, to observe how you twist or bend information out of shape. The idea here is to become more self-aware of your own perceptual processes.

The very next time you make an observation—one that you share with another person—stop in the midst of the observation or immediately after making it, and ask yourself the following questions:

1. Have I blotted out, erased, or canceled information? Why did this happen?

2. Have I distorted information because I only observed a portion of the whole and filled in information to make my observations make more sense?

3. Did I distort information to make my observation support my existing beliefs and values?

4. Did I draw generalizations based on little substantial information?

5. Can I clearly identify factors that would narrow the lens through which I view the world? (e.g., biology, culture, values, beliefs, location or setting, physical limitations, etc.)

your biologic makeup has a significant influence. If your biologic makeup differs from that of the predominant society—if you are obese, short, or unattractive, for example—you may have difficulty securing and maintaining a positive self-concept because of the distortions your senses cause. You automatically see things differently from members of the predominant society.

Other significant influences on your perceptions include your culture, values, and beliefs. You, like most people, find it easier to communicate with members of your own culture. Many of your customs (e.g., Halloween), values (e.g., everything should be clean), and beliefs (all humans are created equal)—as well as your manners, ceremonies, rituals, laws, language, religious beliefs, myths and legends, knowledge, ideals, accepted ways of behaving, and even your concept of self—are culturally determined.

There are numerous other influences, such as the ways you have for coping with and tolerating stress as well as your conflict resolution strategies.[31] If through your upbringing you have developed inadequate coping patterns to adapt to stress or resolve conflict, you narrow your lens, and your perceptions will be distorted. One major influence would be the familial patterns you observed between your parents and between your parents and you or other siblings. For example, some of the patterns you may have observed could include the excessive use of denial, projection of blame and responsibility, hypersensitivity to criticism, and rationalizing of failures. Destructive behaviors may have included overeating, excessive smoking or drinking, the overuse of over-the-counter medications, or illicit drug use. Even high rates of illness as a result of high blood pressure, ulcers, irritable bowel syndrome, frequent headaches or neck aches may also have been influential.

Other influences on your perceptions could include your previous experiences. Many failures rather than successes may create difficulty. If you attribute your successes to luck, chance, or the influence of powerful others rather than to your own personal behavior, this could be a factor. If you have suffered stressful life events such as financial difficulties, problems on a job, change or loss of a job, relationship concerns, sexuality concerns, divorce, or moving, particularly if they have been cumulative, your perceptions could be affected. Illnesses, traumas, and surgery, too, can create alterations in self-esteem, body image, and personal identity and can influence

your perceptions. Even your current physiological state can influence your perceptions. Insufficient nutritional food, lack of sleep, or a serious night of drinking and the
consequential hangover can be influential.

Our purpose here has not been to cast a negative light on the role of your perceptions in creating and maintaining your self-concept; rather, it is to show how many factors are likely to filter your perceptions. Any changes from the norm—the perceptions
of those who make up your predominant society—will influence your perceptions in
some manner. Because there are so many influences, and because these influences are
likely to combine in unknown ways and even have some cumulative effect, there is no
way to predict or know how much effect the influences on your perceptions have nor
how your self-concept is altered. What is interesting is that even self-assessments are
likely to be distorted, since the self doing the assessing is also subject to the distortions!

Adjusting to Perceptual Influences

George A. Miller, the psychologist, said, "Most of our failures in understanding one
another have less to do with what is heard than with what is intended and what is in-
ferred." It would be great to believe that there were no such thing as perceptual filters.
It would be great to believe that you come at the world straight on and that objective
reality is, indeed, your reality. It would be great to believe, because of the truthfulness
and honesty with which you conduct your life, that any observation you make is accurate, precise, and correct—that the conclusions you draw conform exactly to truth
or to the standard set by the norm of others in your culture. Unfortunately, this is
never the case. The fact is, your perceptions and the conclusions you draw from them
represent, as noted in Figure 2-3, your reality, your subjective view, or the world as it
appears to you.

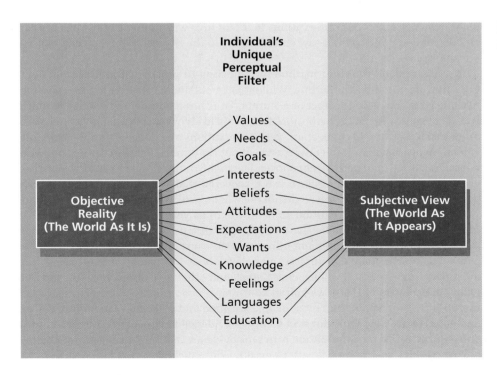

Figure 2-3
Perception

Perceptual Blocks
- Stereotyping and labeling
- Inability to isolate real problem from other problems
- Problem has been narrowed too much
- Inability to define terms
- Failure to use all the senses when observing
- Inability to fully understand problem from various angles
- Sensory overload (too much going on)
- Inability to see all ramifications and connections
- Inability to distinguish between cause and effect
- Failure to investigate the obvious
- Sensory deprivation (too little sensory involvement)
- Failure to investigate sufficiently
- Failure to separate fact from fiction

The difference between **objective reality**—the actual territory or external reality everyone experiences—and a **subjective view**—your personal mental maps of the world—is easy to demonstrate. It is the difference between an examination, or the actual written document that contains the questions (objective reality), and your maps of that examination (subjective reality), which are constructed from your beliefs about the need for examinations, your attitudes toward examinations, your expectations regarding this particular examination, your knowledge about what is likely to be on the examination, and your related thoughts regarding your preparation, as well as your feelings (anxiety or apprehension).

If you think about it, if you were affected by any one of the perceptual influences listed in the section on perceptual filters—lack of sleep, for example—you would experience some distortion from the norm. Whether or not you knew the distortion was occurring might depend on the severity of the influence (three nights without sleep), the circumstances in which you found yourself (taking a final exam), or whether you had other comparisons to make; that is, you had a way to compare your sensory data (observations) with that of others. (Others thought the exam was fair; you thought it unfair.) You have drawn a conclusion that is true based on your perceptions.

Stay healthy, get rest, and exercise. Make every effort to come at the world as healthy, well rested, and sufficiently exercised as possible. Because perception depends on your senses, the better condition your senses are in, the more likely they will respond in proper ways. It is more likely that you will be aware of and adjust to perceptual influences when you have a proper state of mind and body. For example, can you imagine getting physically and emotionally upset with an instructor because of an exam you felt was unfair after three days of no sleep, living on Mountain Dew, isolated in your room, and trying to study a semester's worth of notes in a day and a half?

Avoid hasty conclusions. If you feel it is necessary to announce a conclusion publicly, then state it tentatively rather than as a conclusion. For example, rather than stating that you know that flying saucers exist because you saw strange lights in the sky last night, why not offer your observations in a tentative way that will allow exploration and discussion: "You know, I saw strange lights in the sky last night. Did anyone else see any strange lights?"

Take more time. The third method for adjusting to perceptual influences follows from the last one. Take more time. While it is an old maxim that patience is a virtue, nothing could be more succinct or accurate. Time has a number of benefits. It allows you to gather more facts. With more facts, it is likely your conclusions will change. Time also allows you to think about your observations and conclusions. For example, you might overhear another conversation about the strange lights in the sky, or read a newspaper article about a meteor shower last night, or the glow from locally launched weather balloons. How often have you discovered that your first impressions were wrong—that, for example, you could not tell what a book was about by its cover alone?

There is an important caution to be aware of as you search for information. As noted previously, when you believe something to be true, you will find information to support that belief. That statement introduces the caution. Your external environment contains ample evidence to support all beliefs about a subject.[32] If you believe that most people are bad and will lie, cheat, steal, and otherwise injure you, you can find plenty of evidence in the news and in your daily encounters with others to support that belief. If you believe that most people are good and will behave in honest, caring, and courageous ways, you can find plenty of evidence to support this belief as well. The point of gathering information is to seek evidence that might suggest your beliefs are in error or that other explanations exist for the conclusions you have reached.

Be available. A fourth method for adjusting to perceptual influences follows from the previous methods. Be available to see the other person's viewpoint. Availability, here, means both physical and psychological openness. How often in the heat of an argument could you not stop long enough to really listen to another person's side? Rather, you were so upset you were framing your own ideas, choosing your own words, defending yourself from attack, and trying to outdo, outmaneuver, and outwit the other person. The advantage of counting to 10 to allow your emotions to calm, or stepping back and taking more time, or just trying to put yourself in the other person's shoes helps you become more available. The question "Did anyone else see strange lights?" reveals availability and openness.

There are two other ways you have to adjust to perceptual influences.

Be committed. Commit yourself to seeking more information. Commit yourself to having additional information before making any judgment. Commit yourself to being as fully informed as you would expect others to be with you before sharing their conclusions. Buy a local paper, for example, and examine it for possible explanations of strange lights in the sky. Listen to a local newscast for information. Go ask or make a call to a local expert who might have an answer. It is this kind of climate—the kind of climate in which educated and informed conversation and dialogue can take place—that is likely to produce additional perspectives, alternatives, and conclusions.

Be prepared to change. If everything has worked thus far, you are likely to get information, hear viewpoints, or gain perspectives, alternatives, or conclusions that you did not originally have. If this is true, you must be prepared to change accordingly. Whatever adjustments are necessary, you must be ready to make them. This is why it is important to avoid making hasty conclusions at the outset. In that way, changes at this point will be unnecessary. You simply adjust internally. If you expressed a hasty conclusion, now you must admit the error or openly reveal the adjustment necessary to accommodate the new information, viewpoint, perspective, alternative, or conclusion, and you can't save face, or protect yourself from embarrassment. Publicly admitting an error is difficult for anyone. As it turned out, the strange lights in the sky were a number of planes returning to the local airport at the same time, having all been at the same air show in another state. From the ground, at night, depending on your position or location, the planes lit up the night sky.

As you take steps to reduce the effect of perceptual influences on you, you will notice changes simply because the information you will get is likely to be more accurate and dependable. It will be better information for use in building a stronger self-concept.

STRATEGIC FLEXIBILITY

When you anticipate, assess, evaluate, and select, be ready to change instantaneously and adjust accordingly because of new viewpoints, perspectives, alternatives, or conclusions.

What Do You Think of Yourself?

Please mark each statement in the following way: If the statement describes how you usually feel, put a check in the column *Like Me*. If the statement does *not* describe how you usually feel, put a check in the column *Unlike Me*. For this inventory, there are no right or wrong answers.

	Like Me	Unlike Me
1. I'm pretty sure of myself.	_____	_____
2. I often wish I were someone else.	_____	_____
3. I'm easy to like.	_____	_____
4. I never worry about anything.	_____	_____
5. I find it very hard to talk in front of a class.	_____	_____
6. There are lots of things about myself I'd change if I could.	_____	_____
7. I can make up my mind without too much trouble.	_____	_____
8. I'm a lot of fun to be with.	_____	_____
9. I always do the right thing.	_____	_____
10. I'm proud of the college work that I do.	_____	_____
11. Someone always has to tell me what to do.	_____	_____
12. It takes me a long time to get used to anything new.	_____	_____
13. I'm often sorry for the things I do.	_____	_____
14. I'm never unhappy.	_____	_____
15. I'm doing the best work that I can.	_____	_____
16. I give in very easily.	_____	_____
17. I'm pretty happy.	_____	_____
18. I like everyone I know.	_____	_____
19. I like to be called on in class.	_____	_____
20. I understand myself.	_____	_____
21. Things are all mixed up in my life.	_____	_____
22. I'm not doing as well in college as I'd like to.	_____	_____
23. I can make up my mind and stick to it.	_____	_____
24. I have a low opinion of myself.	_____	_____
25. I don't like to be with other people.	_____	_____
26. I'm never shy.	_____	_____
27. I often feel upset in college.	_____	_____
28. If I have something to say, I usually say it.	_____	_____
29. I always tell the truth.	_____	_____
30. Most people are better liked than I am.	_____	_____
31. I always know what to say to people.	_____	_____
32. I often get discouraged in college.	_____	_____
33. Things usually don't bother me.	_____	_____

Go to the Online Learning Center at **www.mhhe.com/hybels11e** to see your results and learn how to evaluate your attitudes and feelings.

www.mhhe.com/hybels11e ›

Source: In *Measures of Personality and Social Psychological Attitudes* by J. P. Robinson, P. R. Shaver, & L. S. Wrightsman, 1991, San Diego: Academic Press (p. 127–31). Adapted from *The Antecedents of Self-Esteem* by S. Coopersmith, 1967, San Francisco: W. H. Freeman and Company. Used by permission of W. H. Freeman.

Summary

Both self and perception are foundations for effective communication. Self-concept is how you think about and value yourself. Perception is how you look at others and the world around you. How you look at the world depends on what you think of yourself, and what you think of yourself will influence how you look at the world.

Self-concept comes from three sources: reflected appraisals, social comparisons, and self-perception. Scripts and self-fulfilling prophecies also influence your self-concept. If people are willing to give up some of their psychological safety and take some risks, their self-concepts will become more positive.

Although being accepted by others may be more important than it should be, is a fleeting and temporal circumstance, and is based on their viewpoint alone, the fundamental components start with accepting your self. It also means accepting who everyone else is and changing your attitude.

Improving your self-concept is not easy because a poor self-concept is part of many human problems. To start, you must silence your internal critic. Then, stop depending on others for your self-esteem, accentuate your strengths and assets, accept yourself, avoid your perfectionistic tendencies, avoid your overreactions to criticism, modify your negative traits, behave morally, become a high achiever, learn new skills, don't feel responsible for everything, and forgive and forget.

To focus on a single area for improving your self-concept, decide what you want to change, consider your circumstances, take some chances, set reasonable goals, use a program of self-discipline, find people who will support you, and act positively toward others.

Alford Korzybski's theory that the map is not the territory means that your perception of reality is not reality itself but only your version of it—your map. Problems in communication occur when you try to impose your map on another person. To create personal change requires changing your map. Map changes do not represent you in the process of falling apart; often, they work better, create greater happiness, produce positive change, and increase the accuracy and clarity of perceptions.

The perceptual process includes the steps of selecting, organizing, and interpreting information. Perceptions are less than perfect because of deletions, distortions, and generalizations. Closely related to and dependent on generalizations are two related theories. The first, implicit personality theory, occurs when you construct a picture (theory) of what people's personalities are, based on qualities or characteristics revealed by their behavior. Attribution takes place when you devise explanations (theories) about other people's behavior so that you can understand whatever is taking place. Also, numerous perceptual filters will have an effect on your perceptions. Because there are so many influences, and because these influences are likely to combine in unknown ways and even have some cumulative effect, there is no way to predict or know the effect of the influences on your perceptions nor on how your self-concept is altered.

Adjusting to perceptual influences requires that you stay healthy, avoid hasty conclusions, take more time, be available and committed, and be prepared to change. Strategic flexibility—especially the steps of anticipating, assessing, evaluating, and selecting—requires a readiness to change instantaneously and adjust appropriately not just because of new viewpoints, perspectives, alternatives, and conclusions, but because people often come to wrong conclusions. Your interpretations of reality—your mental maps—need to be checked continually to see how accurately they represent the territory, and being prepared to change is part of that process.

Key Terms and Concepts

Use the Online Learning Center at www.mhhe.com/hybels11e to further your understanding of the following terms.

Attribution 49

Cognitive dissonance 48

Cognitive schemata 48

Deletions 48

Distortions 49

Generalizations 49

Implicit personality theory 49

Map is not the territory 45

Objective reality 52

Perception 32

Perceptual filters 49

Psychological sets 46

Reflected appraisals 35

Scripts 35

Self-awareness 42

Self-concept 32

Self-fulfilling prophecies 36

Self-perception 38

Social comparisons 37

Subjective view 52

Questions to Review

1. What is the role of self and perception in communication?

2. How is the self-concept formed?

3. What are the differences among reflected appraisals, social comparisons, and self-perception? Which one is likely to have the most influence on self-formation?

4. In what specific ways can you make your self-perception more positive?

5. What are the fundamental components of being accepted?

6. What are the ways you can improve a weak or poor self-concept?

7. What is the value of Alford Korzybski's theory (The map is not the territory), and how does it contribute to strategic flexibility?

8. What are the three steps of the perceptual process?

9. What role do deletions, distortions, and generalizations play in perception? Can you give an example of each?

10. What are the two perceptual theories related to and dependent on generalizations?

11. What are some of the perceptual filters that narrow the lens through which you view the world?

12. What is the difference between objective reality and a subjective view, and why is this important in communication?

13. What are some of the ways you can adjust to perceptual influences, and which aspect of adjustment contributes most to strategic flexibility?

Go to the Online Learning Center at www.mhhe.com/hybels11e to test your knowledge of the chapter concepts.

CHAPTER THREE

Verbal Communication

Objectives

After reading this chapter, you should be able to:

- Describe how words work, Hayakawa's "ladder of abstraction," and how this knowledge contributes to effective communication.

- Explain how language contributes to the development of credibility and what guidelines can be followed to improve credibility through language.

- Clarify the distinctions among racist, sexist, and ableist language and the concerns raised regarding their use.

- Describe verbal style, explain its importance, and offer specific steps for developing a verbal style.

- Explain the specific stages where communication can be ineffective and how communicators can take steps to prevent this from happening while working on their language skills.

WESLEY COLEMAN DIDN'T KNOW HOW LUCKY HE WAS. He had two parents who cared deeply about him and who were determined to give him a better life. His parents knew that people who communicate clearly, respond quickly, tell interesting stories, and make compelling arguments have a distinct advantage. Those who can't are put at a distinct disadvantage. Even while Wesley was in the womb, his mother would read him stories of adventure, challenge, and risk. In his early years, Wesley loved to be read to, and whenever he visited his grandparents, he would beg to have them sit with him and read. His parents created a ritual of reading Wesley stories before going to bed, and these stories always stimulated his imagination. Soon he was reading to them, and always he was learning new words—building his vocabulary. Wesley loved to write, and he would keep a journal just to record his thoughts. He would write short stories and read them to anyone who would listen. Wesley's was a world of words. His friends admired him because he was so verbal and eloquent. Teachers appreciated his class contributions because he had a way with words. It was his verbal acumen, his success in school, and his desire to help others that led him to law school. Wesley went on to become a successful trial lawyer, but he credits his success to parents who took an active interest in his development of language skills.

The flip side to Wesley Coleman's ability in acquiring and using proper languaging skills, as his parents were well aware, can be devastating. In his book *A User's Guide to the Brain,* John Ratey, a clinical professor of psychiatry at Harvard Medical School, states it succinctly: "When people . . . fail to make proper language connections, or do not stop and consider what they are saying, they wind up not only with speaking, reading, or writing problems—which are bad enough—but with difficulty sustaining social relationships, making moral decisions, controlling anger, and even feeling emotions."[1] The potential repercussions of poor language acquisition and use are enormous, to say the least. There is even evidence that a poor command of language may inhibit your ability to imagine and think up new ideas.[2]

Protests and demonstrations have a lot of connotative language.

So, when you learned to use language in the elementary grades, you did more than master the basic skills. You learned to express feelings and opinions, and, as you matured, to support your opinions with sound arguments and research. You became aware of the many purposes for which language is used and the diversity of forms it can take to appropriately serve these purposes and a variety of audiences. You learned to use the language and forms appropriate for different formal and informal situations—for example, the formal language of debate, the figurative language of poetry, the technical language and formal structures used in report writing. In sum, through your mastery of language, you have experienced expressive and communicative powers, and you appreciate language as both a source of pleasure and an important medium for recording and communicating ideas and information.

"Few languages in world history have been spoken by more people as a second language than as a first," writes Gwynne Dyer, a London-based independent journalist, in a column entitled, "English: The New Latin" (*The* (Toledo) *Blade*, May 22, 2012, p. 6A). "English has had that distinction for several decades." Never before has any language had more people learning it in a given year than it has native speakers; English has probably broken that record as well."

Dyer continues: "The amount of effort invested in learning English is so great that it virtually guarantees that this reality will persist for generations to come." He finishes this thought saying, "No other language is threatened by this predominance of English" (p. 6A).

Although it is spoken by more people, there are more people learning it, and this reality is likely to persist for generations. In their book *Words Can Change Your Brain* (NY: Hudson Street Press, 2012), Andrew Newberg and Mark Robert Waldman claim that, "Although we are born with the gift of language, research shows that we are surprisingly unskilled when it comes to communicating with others. We often choose our words without thought, oblivious of the emotional effects they can have on others" (pp. 3–4). Thus, with the use of our own language of global discourse, commerce, science, entertainment, and communication, there is a great deal of room for improvement—whether that means development or refinement. Anything at all that we can do to promote enhancement in this area (the use of language) will obviously have positive benefits for us now and in the future.

The Role of Verbal Communication in Communicating Effectively and Strategic Flexibility

Communicating Effectively

When you look at the model of communication presented in Chapter 1, it may be too obvious to say that the verbal communication component takes place in the message-feedback element of the model—the words that make up both message and feedback. It may be obvious, but that is far more simplistic than what actually occurs. It overlooks the importance of the senders and receivers. For example, how *you* acquired your ability to use words depended on three factors: (1) native architecture, (2) cognitive development, and (3) environmental influences. See Figure 3-1 for some of the elements involved.

With respect to your native architecture, you can thank the presence of the FOXP2 gene—among others—which enabled the emergence of behaviorally modern humans

Figure 3-1
Verbal
Communication and
the Communication
Model

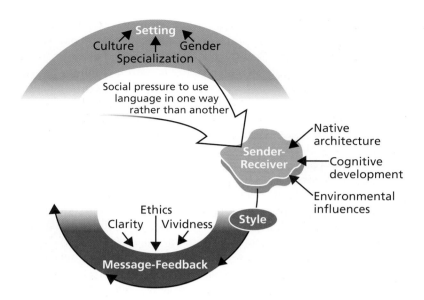

(those with the ability to use language) somewhere between 120,000 and 200,000 years ago. The fact that the FOXP2 gene makes clear is that as a human being, you have in-born language-transmission and language-acquisition devices—native architecture. This native architecture transforms the surface structure of language, which appears in the model as message-feedback, into an internal deep structure, which appears in the model as sender-receiver, that you readily understand.

Cognitive development is the development of the thinking and organizing systems of your brain. It involves not only language but also mental imagery, reasoning, problem solving, and memory development. It began well before your birth as your brain took in information and created paths to a storage area for each bit of information.

Much of your brain "wiring" resulted from environmental influences that took place as your parents and siblings played with and had conversations with you, explained what was happening as you went through your days, introduced you to new activities and environments, encouraged you to explore and experiment, gave you choices, read to you, were interested in your interests, let you know it was okay to make mistakes, and loved and were proud of you. This was your language-acquisition support system. You were analyzing language content long before you were discovering and under-standing grammatical structures.

Just as your communication with others is directly affected by other senders and receivers, the messages and feedback that take place, and the setting and cultural environment in which they occur, these are also the precise elements that affect its development in you, as noted earlier.

Strategic Flexibility

Verbal communication is a key component in strategic flexibility as well. Edward Sapir (1884–1936)[3] and Benjamin Lee Whorf (1897–1941),[4] Sapir's pupil, proposed a theory, the **Sapir-Whorf hypothesis,** that suggests that the language you use to some ex-tent determines or at least influences the way in which you view and think about the world around you. This simply means that your thoughts are affected by or influenced by your language. When you want to talk about how you feel, you are at the mercy of the language you possess. When you are thinking about something that you have perceived, your linguistic habits predispose certain choices of interpretation. When you see automobiles at an intersection, it is what you know about the red, yellow, and green lights that helps you understand what is happening and what the choices are.

It is important to underscore the vital connection that exists between oral language and reading, writing, and critical thinking.[5] An increase in any one area results in a direct and proportional increase in ability and skills in the others. The bottom line is this: The better understanding you have of verbal communication, and the more words you have at your disposal, the more complete will be your ability to think about and view the world around you.

One understanding that the Sapir-Whorf hypothesis instills is that it is a two-way process. That is, the kind of language you use is also influenced by the way you see the world. In the strategic flexibility framework, the more you know about verbal communication, and the more words you have at your disposal, the better you will be at thinking about potential situations and the needs and requirements likely to arise (anticipate)—your view of the world and its possibilities; the better you will be at taking stock of the factors, elements, and conditions of situations in which you find yourself (assessment); the better you will be at determining the value and worth of the factors, elements, and conditions (evaluation); the better you will be at selecting from your repertoire of available skills and behaviors those likely to have the greatest impact (selection); the better you will be at applying the skills and behaviors you have selected (application); and, finally, the better you will be at reassessment and reevaluation.

Here, then, is one fascinating interrelationship, and you can see it in Figure 3-1 in the large arrow from setting to sender-receiver labeled "social pressure." The language of a culture and co-culture together with the unique language of a sender-receiver represent a subtly selective view of the world. This combination of languages and pressures tends to support certain kinds of observations and interpretations and to restrict others. Such transformative power—with the strength of being able to alter your very nature—goes largely unnoticed and, often, even when manifest, retreats to transparency. Thus, the influence of language on strategic flexibility is always present, but is likely to be subtle, difficult to perceive, and often transparent.

How Words Work

One way to understand how words work is to use the **Semantic Triangle**, which was proposed by Charles K. Ogden and Ivor Armstrong Richards, in their book *Meaning of Meaning* (1929). Theirs is a simplistic model that is not without its flaws; however, it gives us a basic understanding. To indicate the direct relationship between symbols (words) and thoughts, they created their model. Just picture a triangle with the word *symbol* at one peak, *thought* at "the second", and *referent* at the third peak. *Thought* refers to the words we use as we think about the symbol, and the word *referent* refers to the image we create in our minds as a result of the symbol. The authors state, "Whenever we hear anything said, we spring spontaneously to an immediate conclusion, namely, that the speaker is referring to what we should be referring to were we speaking the words ourselves" (p. 15).[6] See Figures 3-2 and 3-3.

When you say a word, you are vocally representing something—whether that thing is a physical object, such as your biology textbook, or an abstract concept, such as peace. The word is, as noted in Chapter 1, a symbol: It stands for the object or concept that it names. This is what distinguishes a word from a random sound. The sounds that are represented in our language by the letters *c a t* constitute a word because we have agreed that these sounds will stand for a particular domestic animal. The sounds represented

ATTENTION!

The Story of the Turtle and the Fish

There was once a turtle that lived in a lake with a group of fish. One day the turtle went for a walk on dry land. He was away from the lake for a few weeks. When he returned he met some of the fish. The fish asked him, "Mister turtle, hello! How are you? We have not seen you for a few weeks. Where have you been?" The turtle said, "I was spending some time on dry land."

The fish were a little puzzled and they said, "Up on dry land? What are you talking about? What is this dry land? Is it wet?" The turtle said, "No, it is not." "Is it cool and refreshing?" "No, it is not," "Does it have waves and ripples?" "No, it does not have waves and ripples." "Can you swim in it?" "No, you can't." The fish said, "It is not wet, it is not cool, there are no waves, you can't swim in it.

Don't tell us what it is not, tell us what it is." "I can't," said the turtle. *"I don't have any language to describe it."*

Figure 3-2
Semantic Triangle

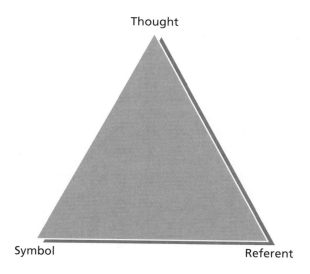

Figure 3-3
The Semantic Triangle
Explained

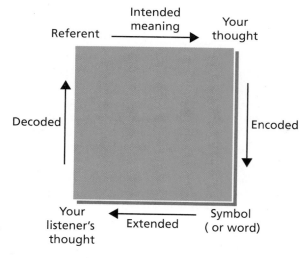

1. The matter (referent) evokes your thought (intended meaning).
2. You encode your thought by choosing a word or words to represent it.
3. That word or words are conveyed (extended) to your listener.
4. Your listener decodes the word and arrives at his or her interpretation of the matter (referent).

by the letters *z a t* do not make up a word because these sounds do not stand for anything. A word that stands for a concrete and emotionally neutral thing—such as the word *mailbox*—can usually be interpreted with good fidelity because most people respond primarily to its **denotative meaning**—that is, its dictionary definition.

Other words stand for abstract concepts that evoke strong feelings. Words such as *freedom* and *love* are easily misunderstood because they carry a lot of **connotative meaning**—the feelings or associations each individual has about a word. For example,

Figure 3-4
The Difference
Between Connotation
and Denotation

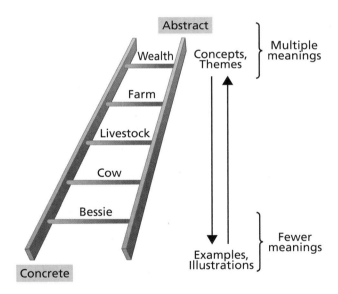

Figure 3-5
The Ladder of
Abstraction

when you hear the word *love,* you don't just think about the word; you probably associate it with a person or an experience you have had. The connotative aspect of words may cause problems in communication because a single word may evoke strong and varied feelings in listeners. Think of the many different reactions people have to the phrases *ravishing sexiness* and *hot-tempered rival.* Figure 3-4 illustrates the difference between connotation and denotation. Notice, too, that your thoughts about the tree are influenced by your language, as discussed in the previous section on strategic flexibility.

Although you need abstract connotative words to express ideas, precise denotative words work best when you want to convey information or get things done—like giving directions or following a recipe. Figure 3-5 shows S. I. Hayakawa's "ladder of

The ladder of abstraction is a tool for developing AOM. In Jackson and Jamieson's book *un-Spun*, they offer readers nine rules to guide them in recognizing and avoiding "spin." For example, rule 1 is, "You can't be completely certain," and rule 2 is, "You can be certain enough." There isn't enough room here to go through each rule, but rule 8 is, "Cross-check everything that matters," and rule 9 is, "Be skeptical, but not cynical." Jackson and Jamieson's advice boils down to two words:

RESPECT FACTS. Now, look at the ladder of abstraction, and notice that the higher the level of abstraction, the farther things move away from the facts. This is how the level of abstraction contributes to AOM. Beyond analysis, the "[ladder] will help you immunize yourself against political propaganda, advertising, and vacant rhetoric (talk that has no substance behind it)." Look at the ladder of abstraction as a tool for developing AOM.

abstraction" from his book *Language in Thought and Action*.[7] The **ladder of abstraction** is a diagram of how we abstract through language, classifications, types, categories, and so on. It assists communicators in finding the right rung on the ladder with enough detail (e.g., examples and illustrations) for clarity, yet not so much that the detail gets in the way of the communication. It has been adopted and adapted in hundreds of ways to help people think clearly and express meaning.

At the bottom of the ladder in Figure 3-5 are examples and illustrations. Farmer Jones's Bessie is a single example, and because of language, you can classify, categorize, and label Bessie—based on her similarities and dissimilarities in features compared with other organisms—as a cow. Such a label raises the level of abstraction from a specific example (Bessie) one rung up on the ladder to a category of animals called cows.

You can observe this particular cow in an environment with other animals such as horses and pigs. One step up on the ladder, in a broader, more abstract, less restrictive classification, you can say this cow is part of Farmer Jones's livestock. His livestock exists within an environment with Farmer Jones's buildings and equipment. Taken together, you move one rung up the ladder of abstraction, and you group his livestock, buildings, and equipment using a new category or label that is even more abstract—farm. Finally, this farm contributes to an even more abstract classification that you can call Farmer Jones's wealth.

A level 5 abstraction might be people of the world. Level 4 could be U.S. society; level 3 could be people who are dominant in that society; level 2 could be spoiled children; and level 1 could be your brother Tim. The more level 1 abstraction you use in your communication, the more likely you will be understood by your listeners. For example, if you are trying to describe a woman and you mention that she wore Birkenstocks and a jean skirt, you have evoked a specific image in your listener's mind. If, on the other hand, you said the woman was dressed in casual attire—a level 2 abstraction—the listener's impression is not as specific, and he or she is free to interpret your meaning in ways that you may not intend. The woman could be wearing a bathrobe and slippers because that, for some people, is casual attire. Using the levels of abstraction carefully will help convey meaning to your listeners.

Why else is the ladder of abstraction useful? First, it will help you better analyze your communications, understandings, and misunderstandings. If a friend down the hall shouted to you "Hey, your econ book is on the floor at your door," that says something more specific and meaningful to you than if the friend said, "Hey, part of your education is sitting out in the hallway." Notice in this example the words *econ book* were substituted for *Bessie* in Figure 3-5, and *education* was substituted for wealth.

Second, it will help you immunize yourself against political propaganda, advertising, and vacant rhetoric (talk that has no substance behind it). If a politician visiting campus said, "And, if elected, I will centralize educational opportunity and expedite a new system of open access," you would quickly notice his or her operation at a high level of abstraction because the politician's words contain no specifics, only generalized, highly abstract references. Recognizing this, you might inquire, "What exactly do you mean? What do you plan to do?" What the candidate might mean is that he or she plans to eliminate the major you are pursuing (centralize educational opportunity) by moving it to another state campus, and lower standards (expedite a new system of open access) by making the state system open to anyone who wishes to attend college—with no prerequisites and no standardized admission tests. This could, you might quickly discover—once the level of abstracted language is reduced—drastically alter the value of your college diploma.

Third, you will make a number of personal adjustments as you become more aware of your own abstracting. You will better differentiate between what happens, what you sense of what happens, what you describe of what your senses sense, and what you infer (a much higher level of abstraction) from what you describe. Think about it this way: What actually happens (e.g., a car accident) to you is concrete and specific—low on the ladder of abstraction. What you sense of what happens (e.g., an interference in your life) depends on your background and experiences and is likely to be high on the ladder of abstraction (abstract) because of all the multiple meanings you use to make meaning of what actually happens (the concrete). Knowing this, to describe what happens, you must make a switch from the interference (abstract) to the accident itself (concrete). What you infer, at an even higher level of abstraction, could include the interference of alcohol, cell phone usage, young, inexperienced drivers, or lousy road signs. Once you realize this, you begin to respond more conditionally to what happens in your life because things are not always what they seem to be. A simple car accident can be road rage, a way to collect on an insurance policy, a mechanical malfunction, or any of a dozen possibilities. You will delay more of your responses, leap to fewer conclusions, snap to fewer judgments, and make fewer inappropriate assumptions.

There are situations when abstract language works best, for example, when you want others to know some general information (such as about a dying parent, or a crash that killed a close friend), but details would not be necessary. Here is a story that circulated via the Internet, with just the sender's name attached, that reveals the power of abstract over concrete language:

> *The Smiths were proud of their family tradition. Their ancestors had come to America on the* Mayflower. *They had included senators and Wall Street wizards. They decided to compile a family history, a legacy for their children and grandchildren. They hired a fine author. Only one problem arose—how to handle that great-uncle George, who was executed in the electric chair. The author said he could handle the story tactfully. The book appeared. It said, "Great-uncle George occupied a chair of applied electronics at an important government institution, was attached to his position by the strongest of ties, and his death came as a great shock."*[8]

STRATEGIC FLEXIBILITY

Here, then, are a number of adjustments you need to make as you anticipate, assess, evaluate, and select. Delay your responses, leap to fewer conclusions, snap to fewer judgments, and make fewer inappropriate assumptions, and the care, concern, and attention required as you apply your skills and behaviors will not just increase, but the entire application step will be more accurate and relevant.

When you study a language, whether it is your native tongue or a foreign one, you must learn what the words stand for; that is, you have to know both their denotative and their connotative meanings. You must also know how to put the words together to make the phrases and sentences that express relationships between the words. This is the *grammar* of a language.

Because the United States has been a one-language nation, many Americans do not understand how language and perception of the world are connected. Americans sometimes complain that immigrants to the United States do not learn and use English. However, if you accept the theory that language influences your world and your perception of it, you see that learning a language is not just a matter of learning a sign system: It is also learning a different way of looking at the world. For example, one of your authors taught a student who had immigrated to the United States when she was a child. Although she was fluent in English, she said she always prayed in Polish; if she used English, the prayer didn't seem real to her.

In *Words Can Change Your Brain,* cited earlier, Newberg and Waldman provide a useful, practical conclusion to this section on "How Words Work," when they write,

> *Naturally, when we speak we make the erroneous assumption that other people relate to our words in the same way we do. They don't. Thus we have to expand our consciousness about language to include the fact that everyone hears something different, even when we are using the same words. Words are needed to create our own inner reality and map of the world, but everyone creates a different map. To put it another way, consciousness—and the language we use to convey our feelings, thoughts, and beliefs—is a very personal and unique experience. When we recognize this neurological fact, we become better communicators because we don't assume that other people understand what we say (p. 58).*

People Determine Meanings

That people determine meanings is precisely what Ogden and Richards' Semantic Triangle (discussed in a previous section) emphasized. The link between any word and the image we create in our minds as a result of it is our thoughts (what we think about the word)—and every person's thoughts about any word are likely to be different from everyone else's. Thus, the final images we create will be different from the images others create, even when the words are the same. It is a "people factor," and it is people who determine meanings.

For the listener to understand what you intend, you should have something definite in mind. If an idea or impression is vague, the resulting message will be confused and ambiguous. Understanding is the core of meaning, and understanding is a two-way process; that is, you are responsible for presenting the idea clearly, and the listener is responsible for trying to understand it accurately. Meanings are ultimately determined by people, not by words. According to Paul Ekman in his book *Telling Lies* (New York: W. W. Norton, 2009), "Surprisingly, many liars are betrayed by their words because of carelessness. It is not that they couldn't disguise what they said, or that they tried to and failed, but simply that they neglected to fabricate carefully" (p. 87).[9]

Lexicographer Joan Houston Hall, chief editor of the *Dictionary of American Regional English* (DARE), as cited by Abigail Tucker in an essay, "Speaking American"

(*Smithsonian*, March 2012, p. 22), writes that "Most people perceive themselves as speaking quite normal English. Sometimes it's quite a surprise to realize that the words they use every day and assume everybody knows wouldn't be understood in other parts of the country."

Tucker offers some examples. "Those fluffy bits beneath the bed, for instance, are dust kitties (Notheast), dust bunnies (Midwest), house moss (South) or woolies (Pennsylvania). A potluck is a tureen dinner in upstate New York or, in the Midwest, a pitch-in or scramble dinner" (p. 22).

You have undoubtedly had the experience of going home from college and talking with friends or family members who did not go to college. Often, the difference can be detected in vocabulary alone. But, good communication requires effective adaptation, and if you know friends and family members will be put off with your use of words, then save their use for the college campus—at least for now. You gain little by "showing off." Your use of newly acquired words is healthy because it is only through use that new vocabulary is obtained and exact meanings for those words is applied. Your new vocabulary also will help you access an even greater amount of information, for it makes both reading and listening more comfortable and enjoyable.

New meanings are continually created by all of us as we change our ideas, our feelings, and our activities. As we think, read, travel, make friends, and experience life, the associations and connections that words have for us are changed.

The Language Environment

All language takes place within a particular environment. A minister speaks in the environment of a church; two friends have a conversation in the student center; an instructor gives a lecture in a classroom. Language that is appropriate to one environment might appear meaningless or foolish in another. The language you use in a dormitory, for example, might be completely inappropriate in a classroom or at home.

People, Purposes, and Rules

According to Neil Postman, who writes about language and education, the **language environment** is made up of four elements: people, their purpose, the rules of communication by which they achieve their purpose, and the actual talk used in the situation.[10] To illustrate these elements, let's take the simple example of John and Mary, who greet each other:

Mary: Hi. How are you?

John: Fine. How are you?

Mary: Good.

The rules for this sort of conversation are known to you, since you often participate in it yourself. If John had failed to follow the rules, however, and had stopped to talk for five minutes about how miserable he felt, Mary might have been annoyed. John would have gone beyond the limits of that sort of conversation.

The kind of conversation Mary and John had illustrates language as a ritual. **Ritual language** takes place in environments where a conventionalized response is expected of you.[11] Greetings are a ritual; you briefly respond to someone—usually only half listening to what the other person has said—and then go about your business.

The rituals you use are determined by the language environment. If you are at a baptism or *bris,* you are expected to say how good-looking the child is or how well he or she behaved during the service. At a wedding you wish the couple happiness and tell the bride she looks beautiful.

Every society's language rituals are determined by the cultural values of that society. In rural East Africa, it would be rude to pass a man you know well with a brief "Hello." You are expected to stop and inquire about the person, his home, his livestock, and his health. In some cultures it is appropriate to tell a couple at their wedding that you hope they will have many sons; in American society, such a comment would be considered inappropriate.

You learn ritualized language when you are very young, from your parents or other adults around you. Researchers have found that young children do not automatically make the conventional responses of "Hi," "Good-bye," or "Thanks"—even though they hear adults doing so. If children are going to use these conventional terms, they must be taught.[12]

As children grow older, they begin to learn and use ritual language. Anyone who has handed out candy on Halloween can tell you that although the younger children may have to be prompted, this is no longer necessary with the older children; they offer their thanks spontaneously.

Appropriate Language

For any society to function it must have some sort of understanding about which words are inappropriate. As children grow up, they try out the new words they hear and, from the reactions of the adults around them, learn the words they shouldn't use. Generally, Americans (and probably most cultures) would agree that the following are inappropriate: First are racial or ethnic epithets against members of groups to which you do not belong. For example a white person should never use the word *nigger* to describe an African American. African Americans, however, can use this word within their own culture because in that context it has a different emotional meaning. Second are words that insult others' appearance or behavior. These words may range from *stupid* or *ugly* to *clumsy* or *incompetent.* Third are words that are blasphemous (religious words) or obscene (body-function words). Fourth are aggressive words intended to control others, such as *shut up* or *drop dead.* Words in any of these categories are highly loaded, emotional words that can do serious damage to human relationships.

Sometimes you have to refer to something for which it would be impolite to use the direct word. To do this you use a **euphemism**—an inoffensive word or phrase that is substituted for other words that might be perceived as unpleasant. For example, you ask "Where's your bathroom?" even when you don't intend to take a bath. If somebody has died, you might use the phrase "passed away." In one instance, when a restaurant in Taiwan wanted to serve dog meat, the owners knew that it would offend some people, and so rather than admit what it was, they called it "fragrant meat." Closer to home, you call your own meat "beef," "veal," and "pork" to veil that it is really dead cow, calf, and pig.

Whereas euphemisms are substitutions for unpleasant words, **doublespeak** refers to words deliberately constructed for political purposes—words specifically intended to impose a desirable mental attitude on those using them. Doublespeak and euphemisms are identical except for two things: (1) Doublespeak does not always have to do with unpleasant words, and (2) doublespeak always relates to a political agenda.

In their book *Willpower* (NY: Penguin, 2011), Roy F. Baumeister and John Tierney write about appropriate language saying, "You could . . . try avoiding those traditionally taboo words: curses. Today this taboo strikes many people as outdated, maybe even nonsensical: Why should society produce a set of words that everybody knows but nobody is allowed to say out loud? But the value of having forbidden words may lie precisely in the exercise of resisting the impulse to say them" (pp. 132–133).

You learn appropriate language as you become more sophisticated and mature. By the time you reach late adolescence, you probably know what language to use for a particular language environment. Whether you want to use the prescribed words is largely irrelevant. The language environment dictates the language that is expected of you. If you violate these expectations, you run the risk of having people respond to you negatively.

Racist, Sexist, and Ableist Language

Any language that is offensive, vulgar, and impolite is unacceptable wherever it occurs. This kind of language should be a zero-tolerance issue—especially if it is expressed at school, work, or in any public location. It can be a form of abuse and bullying. You may use a different vocabulary at home, but realize that the easier such language comes to you, the more likely you will make an unacceptable, unwanted, or inappropriate comment at a time or place when you should not. When you repeat things you've always repeated, you may be hurting someone without even knowing it.

Racist Language

The primary distinction of **racist language** is the tendency to describe the majority group, its actions and its members, in positive terms, whereas minority groups, their actions and members, are portrayed overwhelmingly in negative terms. Racism, then, is discrimination or prejudice based on race.

"A University of Dayton sociologist who analyzed journals kept by 626 white college students found the students behaved substantially differently when they were in the company of other whites than when they were with other races," the Associated Press reported, according to Carmen Van Kerckhove in her essay, "Study: Racist language common among white college students."

"Part of the culture?" she asks. "When the students, who were asked to record their interactions with other people, were alone with other white students, racial stereotypes and racist language were surprisingly common," researcher [Dr.] Leslie [H.] Picca [University of Dayton] found. One student reported hearing the "n-word" among white students 27 times in a single day.

"The results suggest white students have little sense of shame about racial insults and stereotyping and treat them as simply a part of the culture."[13]

Sexist Language

"By the typical definition, **sexist language** is considered to be any language that is supposed to include all people, but, unintentionally (or not) excludes a gender—this can be either males or females," according to the website, *Sexist Language*. "Sexist language is especially common in situations that describe jobs—common assumptions include that all doctors are men, all nurses are women, all coaches are men, or

ATTENTION!

Examples of Doublespeak

Corporate examples:
  Downsizing = firing many employees
  Job flexibility = lack of job security
  Outsourcing = sending jobs to where labor costs are cheaper

Military
  Neutralize = kill or disable
  Secure an area = kill remaining enemy soldiers
  Area denial munitions = landmines
  Engage = attack or fire on the enemy

Politics
  Freedom fighters = armed political rebels
  Internment facility = prison
  Protective custody = imprisonment without due process
  Public donation = taxes

all teachers are women. Most people would agree that these assumptions are largely untrue today, though the language used often perpetuates the stereotypes."[14]

Ableist Language

Words or phrases that express gender, ethnic, or racial bias, either intentionally or unintentionally are inappropriate. The same is true of **ableist language:** language referring to persons with disabilities. In many instances, those words, too, express negative and disparaging attitudes. "The guiding principle for non-handicapping language is to maintain the integrity of individuals as whole human beings by avoiding language that (a) implies that a person as a whole is disabled (e.g., disabled person), (b) equates persons with their condition (e.g., epileptics), (c) has superfluous, negative overtones (e.g., stroke victim), or (d) is regarded as a slur (e.g., cripple)."[15]

If you feel strongly about inappropriate language being used in any of your classes, raise the issue with your instructor. If it occurs at work, raise it at a staff meeting. Although you may think it wise to confront the offensive person immediately and directly, it is best *not* to do so, because it will be an awkward situation for both of you, can lead to a physical altercation, and is likely to have serious and permanent effects on any future contact between you.

If you feel the offending person was unaware of the racist, sexist, or ableist language used, then allow the person to finish his or her opening narrative, then explain that the words he or she used are considered offensive and ask him or her not to use them again. How you deliver this information, however, is important. Be polite but clear. For example, you might say, "Some people find the words you use to describe the . . . as offensive. Perhaps it would be more effective if you rephrased your ideas in this way . . ."

If you end up raising the issue with an instructor, supervisor, or another person in a superior position, there is no need to use specific examples. If you highlight how colleagues should respectfully interact with one another, you may just be surprised at how many people will feel the same way.

The bottom line for you regarding racist, sexist, or ableist language is: watch what words escape your lips. Becoming an effective communicator requires responsibility: Monitor your own behavior.

Specialization

Most language environments have words that are specialized and are used only in those environments. If your plumber tells you that your toilet needs a new sleeve gasket, you probably won't know what that means. You would understand if the plumber told you that the toilet needs a new seal at the bottom to keep the water from leaking out onto the floor. Most professions and occupations have a language that only its practitioners understand. Professional cooks make a *roux,* teachers write up their *behavioral objectives,* and contractors install *I-beams.* Members of an occupational group must learn their specialized language to master their field.

Some language environments can be specialized even if the communicators are trying to reach a mass audience. For example, if you watch a jewelry show on a home shopping network on television, you soon discover that there are many words for describing jewelry. For example, the clasp used to keep the jewelry on your body may be a *lobster claw clasp,* a *box closure,* or a *snap bar* closure. Do you want a *faceted stone,* an *emerald cut,* or a *diamond cut?* You can't make choices until you learn this language. The language of the Internet is an excellent example of specialization.

ATTENTION!

Specialized Language of Digital Cameras
Megapixels = highest resolution photo a camera can take
Optical Zoom = determined by the physical movement of a lens
Dual Image Stabilization = correction for unsteady hands and moving subjects

Other groups develop a language that is never intended to be understood by outsiders. Car salespersons, for example, have many words for describing customers who are out of earshot. A *tire-kicker* is a person who pretends expertise but has none. A *roach, flake,* or *stoker* is a person with a bad credit rating, while a *be-back* is a customer who promises to return but probably won't.[16] Sometimes people create a special language when they feel they don't have as much power as the people around them. Quite often it is a language that those in power do not understand, and it is deliberately used to keep information from them. Students, especially those in high school and college, are one example of special-language groups. They use slang or a special meaning to exclude outsiders or members of the adult establishment. When away from adults, they may also use some of the language the culture considers inappropriate.

When a group has created a special language, you usually cannot step into that group and use its language unless you have some legitimate claim to membership. Students, for example, might secretly make fun of a teacher who tries to talk as they do. How you are expected to speak in a language environment depends on the role you are playing.

Whenever you shift roles, you shift your language environment and your speech as well. Let's say that in a single day you talk to your roommate, you go to class, and you speak to your mother on your cell phone. Your role has shifted three times: from peer relating to peer, to student relating to instructor, to child relating to parent. Each circumstance has entailed a different language environment, and you have probably changed your speech accordingly—perhaps without even realizing it.

The important thing to remember about a language environment is that you must choose language that is appropriate to it. The language used in one environment usually does not work in another. When you think about the environment, you need to ask yourself who it is you are going to be talking with and in what context your language is going to be used. If you don't adapt to the environment, your language will not work, and you will lose the chance for effective communication.

Style, Roles, and Group Memberships

The words you use are determined by all your past experiences, by everything in your individual history. Stephen King, in his book *On Writing,* says it this way: "You undoubtedly have your own thoughts, interests, and concerns, and they have arisen, as mine have, from your experiences and adventures as a human being."[18] You learn words to express thoughts, and thought and language develop together, as discussed in the section on cognitive development at the beginning of this chapter. The way you think and the way you talk are unique; they form a distinctive pattern. In a sense, you are what you say because language is the chief means of conveying your thoughts. Neither language nor thought can be viewed in isolation because they are so interrelated. Together, they determine your verbal style.

Sheryl Perlmutter Bowen, a teacher of communication and women's studies at Villanova University, describes her own language and verbal style in this way: "My own speech . . . is often marked by a preference for personal topics, abrupt topic shifts, storytelling (in which the preferred point is the teller's emotional experience), a fast rate of speech, avoidance of inter-turn pauses, quick turn-taking, expressive phonology, pitch and amplitude shifts, marked voice quality, and strategic within-turn pauses. Given these characteristics," she adds, "my complaining and teasing should both be seen as normal interaction strategies."[19]

ATTENTION!

Tips for Developing a Verbal Style

- Understand your material before you start.
- Say ideas out loud first, and listen to your words, voice, and inflection.
- Write out your ideas in a natural way.
- Let your words flow from you uninterrupted
- Use the active voice.
- Talk to your readers/listeners, and tell them what they need to know.
- Now focus, refine, develop, organize, and further support your ideas.[17]

Style is the result of the way you select and arrange words and sentences. People choose different words to express their thoughts, and every individual has a unique verbal style. Not only do styles vary among people, but each person uses different styles to suit different situations. In the pulpit, a minister usually has a scholarly and formal style. At a church dinner, however, his or her style is likely to be informal and casual. When a football player signs autographs for fans, he speaks to them in the role of athlete—even though he might drop this role when he is with friends and family.

Sometimes style can negate a communicator's other good qualities. You probably know someone who is extremely shy and speaks in a faltering manner. You might also know some people who can never seem to get to the point. If you are critical of these people, it is probably because of their style.

Style, because of its power and influence, is just as important to the acceptance of ideas as all the other aspects of communication. Even if you have the proper information, the right occasion, and a listener interested in your message, what you have to say may be lost if your style is inappropriate.

Impressions of personality are often related to verbal style. When you characterize a person as formal and aloof, your impression is due in part to the way that person talks. Since your style partially determines whether others accept or reject you, it also influences how others receive your messages. Style is so important that it can influence people's opinion of you, win their friendship, lose their respect, or sway them to your ideas.

Like language environment, verbal style is often connected with the roles you play. Professionals, for example, are expected to speak grammatically correct English—both in private and in professional life. A college student is also expected to use correct grammar. Yet if he takes a factory job during summer vacation, using correct grammar might get him into trouble with his fellow workers, for his verbal style could identify him as a "college kid."

Gender and Language

There are four basic beliefs that underlie any examination of the relationship of gender and language. The first is that language is the key instrument and medium by which our views on and assumptions about gender are constructed, perpetuated, and propagated (spread from person to person). The second is that gender is embedded in all institutions, actions, beliefs, and desires that are represented by or through communication, interaction, and the establishment of the social order. What this means is simply that the two are intimately connected and automatically bound to each other.

The third basic belief is that gender *does* make a difference in your language choices. For example, men who sleep around are affectionately titled legends, heroes, and players. Women who have multiple sexual partners are known as sluts or skanky hos. When males turn up at females' doorsteps unexpectedly, they're romantic. If women do the same they may be labeled stalkers, crazy, or desperate. When men are upset, they have a right to be, they're angry. If women have a bad day, they are just hormonal, irrational, or PMS'ing. Words matter, and your language choices have consequences.

Clearly related to this third basic belief is a fourth. The difference between the genders is *not* universal. There are men who exhibit "feminine" conversational qualities just as there are women who follow the conversational styles associated with men.

In a chapter entitled, "Compassionate Communication with Loved Ones," Andrew Newberg, a medical doctor and neuroscientist, and Mark Robert Waldman (authors of *Words Can Change Your Brain)*, have added a section at the end of the chapter entitled, "Who Are Better Communicators, Women or Men?" This is the information contained in the box:

> Men and women process language differently, they have different sized brains and different neurochemical balances, but none of these differences translate into vast differences in behavior, memory, cognition, or verbal skills.* Men and women think, feel, and speak in essentially the same way.** The differences we see are superficial, culturally conditioned, or shaped by childhood experiences and adult biases. In reality, every person, whether male or female, has a unique style of thinking and feeling because no two human brains are wired the same way.
>
> "As the Smithsonian Institution reports, the differences we think exist are massively exaggerated: When it comes to most of what our brains do most of the time—perceive the world, direct attention, learn new skills, encode memories, communicate (no, women don't speak more than men do), judge other people's emotions (no, men aren't inept at this)—men and women have almost entirely overlapping and fully Earth-bound abilities"*** (p. 181).

*"Evolving knowledge of sex differences in brain structure, function, and chemistry." Cosgrove, K. P., Mazure, C. M., Staley, J. K. *Biological Psychiatry,* 2007, Oct. 15; 62(8): 847–55. "Gender differences in cognitive functions." Weiss, E. M., Deisenhammer, E. A., Hinterhuber, H. Marksteiner, J., *Fortschr Neurol Psychiatr.* 2005, Oct; 73(10): 587–95.

**"No gender differences in brain activation during the N-back task: An fMRI study in healthy individuals." Schmidt, H., Jogia, J., Fast, K., Christodoulou, T., Haldane, M., Kumari, V., Frangou, S. *Human Brain Mapping,* 2009, Nov; 30(11): 3609–15. "On sex/gender related similarities and differences in fMRI language research." Kaiser, A., Haller, S., Schmitz, S., Nitsch, C. *Brain Research Reviews,* 2009, Oct: 61(2): 49–59. Epub 2009 May 4.

***"Top 10 myths about the brain." Helmuth L. Smithsonian.com, May 20, 2011.

Source: Newberg, Andrew, and Mark Robert Waldman. (2012). *Words can change your brain: 12 conversation strategies to build trust, resolve conflict, and increase intimacy.* New York: Hudson Street Press.

Questions

1. Do you have any personal examples that prove to you that women and men communicate differently?

2. Do you think the differences in the communication between men and women are truly "superficial"? Or, do you believe the differences are deep, meaningful, and can make the difference between successful communication and failure?

3. Have you noticed examples that would support James W. Pennebaker's (cited earlier) conclusion that, "The stereotypes we hold about women and men are deeply ingrained"?

ANOTHER POINT OF VIEW

In his book *The Secret Life of Pronouns* (NY: Bloomsbury Press, 2011), James W. Pennebaker expresses the problem well:

> The stereotypes we hold about women and men are deeply ingrained. Even within the scientific community, the study of gender differences in language is highly politicized. One group of scientists passionately believes that men and women are essentially the same; another believes that they are profoundly different. Yet others simply don't want to think about it. But the stereotypes persist (p. 45).

Why is a sensitivity to gender and language important?

There are five reasons. Although you may be unaware of some of the influences—simply because they may be subtle, culturally pervasive (and sometimes accepted because of their wide use), or deeply entrenched over generations (with deep historical roots)—they have a direct effect on you.

This sensitivity has a profound effect on your thought and actions. You will see this in all the examples, but just one quick example here: What do you think of when someone says "doctor" or "nurse"? If your answer is "male" for the word "doctor" and "female" for the word "nurse," your thoughts are being affected by gender-related, linguistic choices.

Gender oppositions reflect the potential for conflict. In society today, awareness of gender differences is common. Just the careless use of or reference to roles such as the use of spouse instead of wife or husband, person instead of man, chairperson instead of chairman is, in many quarters, cause for alarm. Look at the use of the words "pretty" and "handsome." One denotes female- and the other male-associated properties. To invert the referents could have unforeseen consequences. For example, perceiving the "pretty" man as a weakling or less man, or the "handsome" woman as masculine and unusually built, offers colorations stimulated by language but influenced by gender.

This sensitivity has an effect on other people's impressions of you. Whether expressed or not, others' opinions and judgments are often based on the language you use. Those more sensitive to gender-loaded language, for example, may render a harsher verdict than those less sensitive, it is true, but with your own developed sensitivity, you are less likely to have a negative effect on anyone. If your goal is to influence others—whether interpersonally or publicly—you should take every opportunity to reduce *any* potentially negative perception.

This sensitivity has a direct effect on your social reality. Because words matter and your language choices have consequences, as previously noted, if you believe that men and women deserve social equality, then your language use should reflect that belief. Another quick example will demonstrate what is meant here. Because both men and women work for the U.S. Postal Service, it makes more sense to say "mail carrier" or "letter carrier" than to say "mailman." Since women also work for the police department, "police officer" is preferable to "policeman." More and more men work as a "flight attendant," thus, these words are preferable to "stewardess." Using gender-neutral language eliminates stereotypes about what jobs are the exclusive domain of women and what jobs men stereotypically hold.

Language use that stereotypes genders can lower self-esteem. It can negatively affect people's self-image, aspirations, and motivations. Language that stereotypes genders can limit both genders with respect to courses of study pursued and career choices made; thus, it can prevent people from realizing their full potential.

It requires little thought to extend this fifth reason to its effect on the empowerment of women. When it comes to achieving equal power and equal opportunities, using gender-neutral language and eliminating stereotypes will increase women's sense of self-worth, their decision-making power, their access to opportunities and resources, and their power and control over their lives, as well as their ability to affect change.

You may think from the examples here that gender inequality is limited to women. It affects men, too. For example, it is often believed that men have, by virtue of being male, the dominant and forceful influence on society. When this role is reinforced and encouraged by our language choices, men are forced into macho, aggressive stereotypes that restrict their freedom and expression. Pressure to be the main breadwinner may leave them with an inability to play the parental role of primary caregiver. Gender stereotyping can lead some to be sexually single minded and to have no control over their hormones—an excuse, whether used or not, for some to be wild, carefree, and sexually irresponsible.

Although there may be an expectation that men will embody male dominance and control, this constraint on men (often reinforced in the media, cartoons, video games, and by peer pressure), is unlike the constraints that femininity imposes on women. For men to be the embodiments of dominance is hardly as restrictive as the expectation that women will *not* be dominant.

Why not tell readers what to do?

The area of gender and language has received a great deal of research attention, and it would be impossible to list all the findings and conclusions in the short space of this section. As demonstrated above, it has enormous importance, and the implications can be far-reaching, to say the least. It would be just as difficult to list all the "right" or "proper" ways to act since context often governs many of these actions. Such a catalog would lose its effect by its length alone, but such a list of differences, too, does not help in understanding why, how, when, and for whom these differences exist or their social meaning or significance.

It is important to understand—and underscore—that increasing your sensitivity to gender as it manifests itself in language does *not* mean learning a laundry list of dos and don'ts. Such action would be meaningless, too, because patterns of gender-related behavior vary across different cultures, and in different contexts within cultures. It is likely to vary as well in schools and at home.

What interactional style characterizes each gender?

It should be clear that there is no single interactional style that characterizes either men or women. For example, sociolinguist Deborah Tannen found that men and women have almost completely different styles of speaking.[20] In fact, she maintains that their languages are so different that they might as well come from different worlds. According to Tannen, when women have conversations, they use the language of *rapport-talk*. This language is designed to lead to intimacy with others, to match experiences, and to establish relationships. Men, however, speak *report-talk*. In this type of speech the speaker's goal is to maintain status, to demonstrate knowledge and skills, and to keep the center-stage position.[21]

Taking Tannen at her word, it would be easy to agree that males and females have distinctive interactional styles. The point here is simply that *both* genders can use both rapport and report talk. *Both* males and females are perfectly capable of using the other gender's interactional style when it suits them. To deny this would be to deny the ability of people to be flexible, spontaneous, and adaptive to others or to circumstances. After all, both styles are equally valid. As Pennebaker writes in *The Secret Life of Pronouns* (cited above), "All people change their language depending on the situations that they are in" (p. 47).

Gender in language is more than just differences.

One important thing to note is that an emphasis on gender differences in language (e.g., women are cooperative, men are competitive) tends to confirm rather than challenge these differences. When gender in language is displayed as differences, the gender categories are treated as bipolar, fixed, and static (e.g., language that suggests women are weak while men are strong, women are timid while men are brave, woman are passive while men are aggressive, women are relationship driven while men are sex driven, women are irrational while men are rational, women are indirect while men are direct, women are nurturing while men are practical, or women are gentle while men are rough). Such bipolar categories offer solutions to gender problems without making a problem of gender itself. A preoccupation with differences such as these simply reinforces stereotypes.

Sensitivity to gender and language offers a challenge to everyone—including contemporary researchers. How do you think about or conceptualize gender without polarization? How are you and our society gendered (e.g., unequal expectations, opportunities, power)? How do individuals, especially the disenfranchised, cope with or negotiate inequality? As an individual, you cannot only affect your environment, but you are also constrained and shaped by social situations and structures.

Powerful Talk

Powerful talk is talk that comes directly to the point—talk that does not use hesitation or qualifications. People who engage in powerful talk are found to be more credible, more attractive, and more persuasive than those who do not.[22] In the college classroom, teachers who used powerful language are considered by their students to be more believable and to have more status.[23]

Powerful talk is characterized by the *nonexistence* of certain communication behaviors. First, hedges and qualifiers—expressions such as "I guess" and "kind of"—weaken the power of speech. Hesitation forms such as "uh" and "you know" make speakers sound too uncertain. Third, tag questions—comments that start out as statements but end as questions ("It would be nice to go on a picnic, wouldn't it?") make speakers seem less assertive. Finally, disclaimers—words and expressions that excuse or ask listeners to bear with the speaker—weaken communications. Examples are "I know you probably don't agree with me, but . . . " or "I'm really not prepared to speak today."[24]

The number of women in powerful positions is increasing steadily, but it has been a struggle for them. Why has there been a struggle? Supreme Court Justice Sandra Day O'Connor says that "In the past there was a widespread belief—declining today, but certainly still there—that women are unfit for power positions." Whether it has to do with powerful talk or assertiveness, O'Connor says "The image of the aggressive leader does not lie easily with traditional notions of femininity."[25]

Research conducted by Dr. Sally D. Farley, social psychologist and principal author of the Albright College study (Reading, Pennsylvania) relates directly to power. "Researchers asked 129 working adults to think of a frequent female gossiper and rare female gossiper, and their perceptions of need for power, inclusion, and affection. Research shows gossips are equally men and women," although their study focused on women. The study concluded: "Compared with rare gossipers, frequent gossipers were perceived as significantly more powerful, and possessed more masculine, or dominant and aggressive, traits and fewer feminine, or soft-spoken and submissive traits" (p. 8B).[26]

Culture and Language

The number of U.S. residents age five and older speaking a language other than English at home jumped from 32 million in 1990 to 47 million in 2000. That means that nearly one in five Americans speak a language other than English at home and the top five languages, excluding English, are Spanish, Chinese, French, German, and Tagalog (Philippines). The estimated Hispanic population of the United States as of July 1, 2006 was 44.3 million, making people of Hispanic origin the nation's largest ethnic or race minority. Hispanics constituted 17 percent of the nation's population. (This estimate does not include the 3.9 million residents of Puerto Rico.)[27] The difference between those speaking Spanish (28.1 million) and those speaking Chinese (2 million) is enormous. School districts are scrambling to find bilingual instructors, governments are looking for ways to help those who don't speak English well, and more and more companies are diversifying their advertising and marketing campaigns to reach people who speak other languages.[28] Why wouldn't companies want to diversify? African Americans and Latinos/Latinas account for one-quarter of department store sales, according to strategic marketing communications agency Meridian.[29]

Although English is unlikely to become the world's dominant language, it will remain one of its most important languages. For routine language, people will probably switch between two or more languages, but, according to British language expert David Graddol, "English-only speakers may find it difficult to participate in a multilingual society."[30] "In 1995, English trailed Chinese as the most common native language. Native English speakers were 9% of the world. That is expected to fall to 5% by 2050," Graddol said, "as Arabic and Hindi-Urdu overtake English."[31]

Why is an understanding of the impact of culture on language important? The following are stories cited by Marilyn Carlson Nelson, chair and CEO of the Carlson Companies, in her speech "On the Path." She says that Chevrolet tried to launch its Nova car in Latin America where *Nova* in Spanish actually means "no go." The successful "Got Milk?" campaign was almost trashed when the translation for "Got Milk?" was discovered to mean "Are You Lactating?" When the phrase "Pepsi, the choice of a new generation" was translated into Chinese, it came out as "Pepsi, the drink that will awaken your ancestors from the dead." Buick planned to launch its new Lacrosse in Quebec, until it learned that the name was Quebec slang for sexual self-gratification. These examples simply underscore the importance of understanding how culture affects language and language choices.[32]

When languages disappear, millennia of human knowledge disappear with them. There are approximately 7,000 languages spoken today, and "one vanishes every 14 days when its last speaker dies."[33] According to K. David Harrison, co-director of National Geographic's Enduring Voices project and a professor of linguistics at Swarthmore College in Pennsylvania, "The rate of language extinction is increasing, proceeding much faster than that of animal or plant species."[34] As an example of the information lost when a language disappears, consider the 4,000 people in Brazil who speak Kayapo. "Their language distinguishes between 56 types of bees—information that will be lost to biologists if the language dies" (p. 7D).[35]

The relationship of language and culture is underscored in a speech by Allan Goodman, President and CEO, Institute of International Education, in a speech, "American Provincialism: Another Inconvenient Truth," delivered to Chatham University in Pittsburgh, Pennsylvania, May 23, 2009. He said, at the conclusion of his speech, "Languages convey much more than facts. Since they are the repositories of culture, knowing them enables us to gain perspective. It has never been more important for Americans to have that degree of understanding and access to different ways of thinking" (p. 368).[36]

Dialect

Toward the end of the summer in central Pennsylvania, many cooks begin to fry or preserve "mangoes." Outsiders are always surprised that Pennsylvania cooks are so interested in this tropical fruit. What they don't know is that in that part of the country a mango isn't a fruit at all; it's what everyone else calls a green pepper or a bell pepper. The central Pennsylvanians' use of the word *mango* is an example of dialect.

A **dialect** is the habitual language of a community. It is distinguished by unique grammatical structures, words, and figures of speech. The community members who use the dialect may be identified by region or by such diverse factors as education, social class, or cultural background. Many people will hold on to their dialects because they are a tie to their own community. See Figure 3-6 for some examples of dialects.

Figure 3-6
Some Examples of
Dialect in the United
States

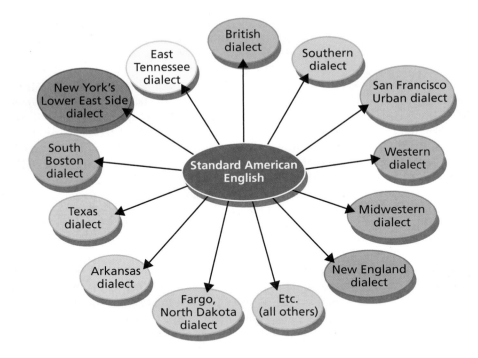

When radio and television became widespread, linguists predicted that their popularity might herald the end of dialect because people would imitate the standard American speech they heard on these media. However, it didn't work that way. Linguists have found that dialect is growing stronger, especially in many urban areas.[37]

It is important to understand what a dialect is and is not. Clearly it is *not* Mexican-Americans living in a Mexican-American neighborhood in Dallas, Texas, using a dialect when they speak Spanish to each other. But, what if an American from the south, who learned Spanish in high school, went into this Mexican-American neighborhood in Dallas, Texas, and talked with the Mexican-Americans living there? This American would likely speak his or her high school–learned Spanish using his or her Southern dialect of American English. True to his or her background, this American would *not* have the variations of idiom, vocabulary (or phonemes [units of sound] and morphemes [meaningful units]) peculiar to the Mexican-Americans from the neighborhood. He or she could not. His or her language would quickly reveal itself to the Mexican-Americans from the neighborhood as "off their standard"—an imperfect use of the standard language used by those Mexican-Americans from the neighborhood for whom Spanish is their native language.

Any language (French, German, Spanish, etc.) learned solely in the classroom will retain recognizable elements of the parent language, but it will have distinctive vocabulary, pronunciation, forms, and idiom that will quickly distinguish it as a linguistic branch of—and not the same as—the parent language. It is exactly the same as when the person, above, speaking Spanish using his or her Southern dialect of American English, traveled north in the United States and found him- or herself anywhere in the north using the Southern dialect of American English. The Southern dialect would have similar distinctions to his or her Spanish, from people in the north who speak American English.

Although there are no clear-cut rules for where and when it is appropriate to use a dialect, it is possible to make some generalizations. A dialect is appropriate in a group with a strong ethnic identity, but it may be inappropriate in situations where standard English is used. Linguistic scholars agree that some dialects have more prestige than others and that prestige is determined by both the people who speak the dialect and those who hear it. Thus, if you want to be accepted by and identified with people who use a dialect or who use a standard English different from your own, you might have to adapt to their way of speaking. Many people in America have discovered that it is not difficult to speak two "languages," a dialect and standard English. By so doing, they find it possible to keep their ethnic identity as well as function in a world where expectations are different.

Speaking and Writing

We use language in both speaking and writing, but the transactional nature of speaking makes it very different from writing.

When two people are engaged in conversation, they interact continuously and simultaneously. Both get and give information, form impressions, and respond to each other. On the basis of each other's responses, both can change their comments to explain, backtrack, hurry up, slow down, or do whatever is necessary to be understood.

Sometimes conversation reflects the participants' past knowledge of each other. They can use a kind of shorthand because of the experiences they've had together. If you are in a close relationship or desire one, you know that the words you speak may affect your present and future relationship. If the relationship is more impersonal, the choice of words might not be so important.

You also are able to change your language to reflect the circumstances. When you get negative feedback, you can change language to appease your listeners. You can use simpler words or concepts if listeners don't seem to understand. Spoken language is also accompanied by **paralanguage**—vocal cues, or the way you say your words. Paralanguage is a nonverbal component, and it will be discussed in the next chapter. Here, it is important to understand that your meaning can be influenced by your pitch and rate (high and fast if you are excited), your volume, and how often you pause. This kind of adaptation occurs in every conversation. Whether you are talking to your father, a professor, or a friend, your language will reflect your impression of this person, the kinds of experiences you have had together, and the role you are playing.

In contrast, it's not so easy to change your written language. In fact, writers have an entirely different set of problems from speakers. When you are speaking, people are reacting to you as the message occurs. For writers, reaction from their audience is unusual, and they have no way of knowing if they have pleased or offended someone, or if they have even communicated their ideas. This means that their words must be chosen very carefully. Also, they have time to go over their words, polish their phrases, and check their grammar. Their readers have more time too. They can always reread the words if they're not clear the first time. Writers are more likely to use a larger vocabulary than speakers do, and readers can look up the words if they don't understand them. Writers do not have the paralanguage of speakers to add to their meaning. If the words they choose don't work, their attempt at communication fails.

In her "AskMarilyn" column, Marilyn vos Savant answered a question from Tim O'Connor of Tucson, Arizona, who asked, "Which is more effective, an oral lesson or a written one?" She wrote, "Let's assume that the lessons are equivalent: They have the same content, they can be heard or read only once, and neither is interactive, etc.

If so, the oral lesson should be more efficient because the brain doesn't need to work at decoding the written material."[38]

Two final comments on writing as it relates to the Internet. First, Dr. Gary Small, a psychiatrist at UCLA, "argues that daily exposure to digital technologies such as the Internet and smart phones can alter how the brain works."[39] The Associated Press report, citing Small, states, "So brain circuits involved in face-to-face contact can become weaker . . . That may lead to social awkwardness, an inability to interpret non-verbal messages, isolation, and less interest in traditional classroom learning."[40] This was a theory that has not been supported in more recent studies (to be cited in Chapter 6, "Interpersonal Relationships")—especially with respect to "isolation."

The second final comment on writing as it relates to the Internet is the concern of teachers that the language used in texting and IM (instant messaging) would find its way into classroom language has not taken place to a large degree. In her book *Always On: Language in an Online and Mobile World,* Naomi Baron, a linguistics professor at American University, from her research on college students, "found that IM abbreviations were rare, contractions were less common than expected, and that when it came to emoticons, students seemed to have a stunted vocabulary."[41] What appeared clear to Baron is that "students consider the two types of communication to be distinct from each other—even if they occasionally slip a word from one language into the other."[42]

Working on Your Communication

Frank Luntz, advisor to CEOs of Fortune 100 companies, political candidates, public advocacy groups, and world leaders, in his book *Words That Work* (Hyperion 2007), writes, "You can have the best message in the world, but the person on the receiving end will always understand it through the prism of his or her own emotions, preconceptions, prejudices, and preexisting beliefs. It's not enough," Luntz writes, "to be correct or reasonable or even brilliant. The key to successful communication is to take the imaginative leap of stuffing yourself right into your listeners' shoes to know what they are thinking and feeling in the deepest recesses of their mind and heart."[43]

When you set out to communicate verbally, you are more likely to be successful if you use words and ideas that have the same meaning to the person with whom you are communicating as they do to you. Sometimes, although you think you are being clear, the other person might not perceive what you think you have communicated.

Communication can go awry at various stages. Let's look at some of the places where this might happen.

What Do You Want to Say?

In 1938, Orson Welles broadcast *The War of the Worlds,* a radio play about Martians invading the United States. You can assume that in writing this play, Welles intended to entertain his audience. Although Welles's intent was clear to him, at least one million people misunderstood it and believed that the play was real. They believed that Martians really had landed and that their lives were in peril. By the time the network announced that the broadcast was only a play, many people had already reacted to it by fleeing their homes to find a place of safety.

Although this is an extreme example of intent going astray, most of us have had times when people's responses were different from those we intended. You intend to

ATTENTION!

How to Answer the Question: What Do You Want to Say?[44]

- Why I am writing this piece?
- What is the focus of the piece?
- Why is this important?
- What group is my primary audience?
- Why would the audience be interested?
- How would it benefit the audience?
- How can the audience use this information?

tell your roommate to meet you at 7:00, but she thinks you said 7:30. You intend to make a joke, but you end up insulting someone. When you are involved in one-to-one communication, you often have a chance to clear up misunderstandings. If you see that the other person looks confused or annoyed or if the response you get indicates that you have not communicated something as precisely as you had intended, you can attempt to clarify what you said.

When you are talking to an audience, however, it is not so easy to clear up misunderstandings. In a public-speaking or mass-communication setting, you may not have a chance to respond to feedback or you may not be able to respond until the communication is over. Therefore, when you are going to communicate to a large audience, you must prepare your words much more carefully than you do in an interpersonal setting.

The first thing you must consider is, What exactly do you want to say? Frank Luntz writes, "the *people* are the true end; language is just a *tool* to reach and teach them, a means to an end."[45] Students who are new to public speaking often do not think through this step clearly enough. Speakers who do not know precisely what they want to say frequently end up confusing their audience. The same may happen if they have not clearly thought out their words.

How Do You Want to Say It?

Although you are often told that you should make careful language choices, you might not know how to go about doing so. Command of language requires years of practice and study. Since it is impossible to lay down strict rules that govern the choice of language for all occasions and for all circumstances, the discussion here is limited to three important aspects of language choice: clarity, vividness, and ethics.

Clarity

A pilot died in the crash of a private jet because the instructions on how to open the emergency door were so unclear that she could not get it open. Although a lack of clarity is usually not a matter of life or death, it can lead to frustration and misunderstanding. In most situations, you have to speak as clearly as possible if you want to be understood. **Clarity** is that aspect or characteristic of style by means of which a thought is so presented that it is immediately understood, depending on the precision and simplicity of the language. Clarity is especially important when there is little opportunity for feedback. For example, if you are saying something of special importance, making a formal speech, or being interviewed by the media, clarity is essential since you will probably not get another chance.

Jargon is language that can be so specialized that it is inappropriate to use outside the field where it originated. Emanuel Rosen, in his book *The Anatomy of Buzz*, writes this about the use of jargon: "From ancient fortified cities to current gated communities, people have always put walls and other barriers around themselves to keep intruders away to differentiate themselves from others. Networks have their own walls and fences, but instead of wire or bricks, people use dialect, jargon, and acronyms to keep strangers out."[46] Physicians often use a highly specialized language to describe illnesses and injuries. Although doctors can communicate with one another, sometimes they have problems communicating with patients because of the walls and fences. Many newspapers carry a column in which a physician answers questions from readers who do not understand what their own doctors told them—a way to break down the walls and add gates to the fences.

How to Be Clear

1. Keep focused on your listener.
2. Organize your ideas carefully.
3. Use the active voice.
4. Use "you" and other pronouns.
5. Use common, everyday words (plain language).
6. Use short sentences.
7. Include only information your listener needs.
8. Lead your listeners slowly using numerous transitions.
9. Avoid jargon, slang, and complicated words.
10. Use common sense.

You may wonder why clarity is so important. In his book *The Language Wars: A History of Proper English* (NY: Farrar, Straus, and Giroux, 2011), Henry Hitchings—also author of *The Secret Life of Words* (2008), answers the question of why it's important in Chapter 2, "The Survival Machine: The Power of Language and the Fight for English":

> As I have suggested, the conventions of usage result from a sense of responsibility towards other users of our language. There are cogent reasons for trying to use language lucidly [clearly]. In many everyday settings we are irritated by language that misleads us, unbalances us or needlessly and fruitlessly diverts our concentration. It is no fun to have to read twice a sentence which, on that second reading, we find we didn't even want to read once. Skillful handling of language will tend to reduce the amount of cognitive effort one's audience has to expend in getting at one's meaning. If my expression is confused and ambiguous, I risk losing your attention (pp. 16–17).

Source: Hitchings, Henry. (2011). The language wars: A history of proper English. New York: Farrar, Straus, and Giroux.

Questions

1. It is easy to see how the proper use of language refers as much to speaking as it does to writing: Audience members should not have to waste cognitive effort on inappropriate language (language that misleads, unbalances, or needlessly and fruitlessly diverts our concentration). Do you have any experiences where this has proven to be true?—that is, examples where a speaker has used inappropriate language that wasted the cognitive effort of listeners?

2. What are some of the ways you have—as a speaker—to make certain that you are being as clear as possible in conveying your ideas?

3. If you wanted to improve your overall clarity in using language—in every aspect of your life—what are some of the techniques you could use to improve it?

Other language that might not be clear to everyone is slang. Slang has its place when you are talking informally with your friends. However, many slang words have such broad and vague meanings that they could apply to almost anything. If you use the word *cool* to compliment someone's shirt and use it again to describe beautiful scenery, you reduce everything to a common element.

Sometimes people feel that if they have taken the trouble to learn long and complicated words, they should use them whenever they can. On a bottle of fluoride solution, the consumer is advised to "hold the solution in the mouth for one minute and then expectorate." In case the consumer doesn't understand the word *expectorate*, the phrase *spit it out* follows in parentheses. Since the purpose of this message is to communicate with the consumer, the simpler words, *spit it out*, should have been used in the first place. Frank Luntz, cited previously, writes, "The most effective language clarifies rather than obscures. It makes ideas clear rather than clouding them. The more simply and plainly an idea is presented, the more understandable it is—and therefore the more credible it will be."[47]

Use more complicated words only when they help make your meaning clearer. For example, if you want your car painted red, you'll be happier with the final results if you use a more precise description than *red*. What shade do you prefer? Burgundy? Crimson? Vermilion? Garnet?

When you increase your vocabulary, you increase your chances of getting your intended meaning across to your listener. The more words you have at your command, the more precise you will be. This does not mean that you should search for big words; on the contrary, familiar words are often the best.

One of the delights of language is that it offers you many subtleties and shades of meaning. Choosing the same words to express all your ideas is like eating a Big Mac for dinner every night. Language is a marvelous banquet providing you with a vast array of choices for anything and everything you want to say.

Vividness

Remember those ghost stories you heard when you were a child? The best ones were those that filled you with terror—the ones laced with bloodcurdling shrieks, mournful moans, mysterious howling. They were usually set in dark places, with only an occasional eerie light or a streak of lightning. If any smells were mentioned, they were sure to be dank and musty.

The teller of a ghost story usually speaks in the first person. Any narrative told from the point of view of "I was there" or "It happened to me" is particularly vivid. By recreating an experience for your listeners, you can often make them feel what you felt. **Vividness** is the aspect or characteristic of style by which a thought is so presented that it evokes lifelike imagery or suggestion.

Vividness also comes from unique forms of speech. Some people would say that a person who talks too much "chatters like a magpie," a phrase that has become a cliché. To one Southern speaker, however, this person "makes a lot of chin music." When we say that language is vivid, we often mean that someone has found a new way of saying old things. Children often charm us with the uniqueness of their language because they are too young to know all the clichés and overused expressions. Another place to look for vivid language is in poetry and song. Although more words have been written about love than any other subject, many songwriters have given us new expressions and therefore new ways of looking at the experience. Their unique perspectives make an old idea sound original and exciting.

To Whom Are You Talking?

As you talk to people, become conscious of them as particular individuals for whom you need to adapt your message. Note the language environment in which your conversation is taking place, and make the adjustments that are necessary. Also, when you are talking about a particular subject, see if you can find words that are unique to the subject—even if you have to define them. Often, learning about a subject is also learning the vocabulary of the subject. Be conscious of what you are saying. This added consciousness will increase your sensitivity to other people as well as your awareness of language choice and use.

Increasing your sensitivity to other people as well as your awareness of language choice is critical for effectiveness in public speaking. Knowing to whom you are speaking should be the focus of every speaker during each step of the speech preparation process, and that focus continues during the actual process of delivering the speech and in assessing its success as well.

What Metamessages Are You Sending?

You probably choose your words carefully when you are making a public presentation. It might not occur to you, however, to be so careful when you are talking to a friend or conversing with a small group of people. Yet you might occasionally have had a

STRATEGIC FLEXIBILITY

Your success in being strategically flexible rests on this aspect: *Know* to whom you are talking. Your sensitivity to other people—along with your awareness of language choice and use—will largely determine your communication effectiveness.

conversation that made you feel uneasy—the words all sounded right, but there was something else going on.

In such cases, you need to think about the **metamessage** (sometimes called *subtext*)—the meaning apart from what actual words express. For example, when one spouse tells the other, "We need to talk," he or she really might be saying, "I want to complain."

Metamessages take many forms. At a graduation ceremony, the president of the university introduced everyone on the stage except one of the deans. The dean realized that this was more than a simple oversight, that he might be in serious trouble. He was right: he was fired the next term.

Many metamessages don't involve words at all. Deborah Tannen believes that American men refuse to ask directions because it puts them in an inferior position and the person they ask in a superior position.[48]

Sometimes metamessages are recognizable to people within a specific culture but not to outsiders. A Polish professor complained that when she was in the United States, one of her American colleagues kept saying, "Let's have lunch sometime." When she tried to pin him down, he looked annoyed. What she didn't realize until much later was that this is an expression that some Americans use to terminate a conversation.

In his book *The Universal Sense: How Hearing Shapes the Mind* (NY: Bloomsbury, 2012) Seth S. Horowitz offers a practical example of metamessages:

> *For a simple demonstration, just say the word "yes." Now say it as if you had just found out you won the lottery. Now say it as if someone had just asked you a question about something in your past that you thought no one knew about. Now say it as if this is the fortieth time you've answered "yes" in a really boring human resources interview about how much you love your job. Lastly, say it as if you were just forced to agree to a really horrible contract in order to keep from losing your job. Linguistically, you indicated affirmation every time, but each time the emotional meaning differed. What you changed was* how *you said the words: overall pitch, loudness, and timing. And someone listening to you who was also a native speaker of your language would get the subtext, which is sometimes even more important than the ostensible meaning of the utterance. (pp. 129–130)*

Language is filled with metamessages, and you have to listen for this kind of talk and understand its meaning if you are going to have accurate communication. You also should be aware of the metamessages you yourself send. For example, it is not unusual for a student speaker to begin a speech by implying that the speech will not be very good: "I just finished this speech this morning," "I couldn't find any research on this topic," or "You'll have to excuse me because I am feeling sick." If you say anything of this sort, you may be engaging in a metamessage; what you may really be saying is, "I am feeling extremely nervous and anxious about giving this speech."

Ethics

Ray Penn, a communications professor, points out that "a choice of words is a choice of worlds."[49] He reminds us that we can cause considerable damage to others by choosing the wrong words. For example, if you are asked to remember your most painful moment, the response will most likely be something someone said.

Penn asks us to consider whether "our analogies create a self-fulfilling prophecy that will ultimately keep us from relating to others unless we get our way." For example, how often in life do you talk of "winners" and "losers," condemning the losers to

ATTENTION!

Choosing the Right Words

1. Make a commitment to being more mindful of the things you say.
2. Pause, and think before you speak.
3. Ask yourself, "Does what I say have value?"
4. Consider who you are conversing with.
5. Consider the environment.
6. Don't be afraid to reflect back on your words.
7. Pay attention to how others speak.[50]

permanent failure? On the international scene, did calling Osama bin Laden "another Hitler" create a self-fulfilling prophecy? When political figures in the Middle East refer to the United States as "Satan" or "the devil," does such labeling influence the way we, as a country, react to them?

Penn also reminds us that language choices can influence people's perceptions of themselves. Insulting words, he points out, can reduce an individual to a mere trait ("dyke," "queer"); they can reduce someone to less-than-human status ("pig," "chicken"); or they can tell the person "I know all about you and you have no mystery" by means of labels ("hillbilly," "redneck," "geek").[51]

Penn reminds us that we make moral choices when we choose the language we are going to use. Many of the choices you make not only determine how you present yourself to others but also decide the nature of your relationships in the years to come. For this reason, it is important that you choose your words wisely and well.

Frank Luntz, whom we have cited throughout this chapter, writes a reminder that will help everyone when it comes to creating words that work, "The most powerful messages will fall on deaf ears if they aren't spoken by credible messengers. Effective language is more than just the words themselves. There is a style that goes hand-in-hand with the substance. Whether running for higher office," Luntz writes, "or running for a closing elevator, how you speak determines how you are perceived and received. But credibility and authenticity don't just happen."[52]

Verbal Communication Self-Evaluation Form

How effective is your verbal communication? For each question circle the numerical score that best represents your verbal communication. Select an event, a situation, a context, and a time when you recently gave a speech or presentation, and analyze it using the following scale: 7 = Outstanding; 6 = Excellent; 5 = Very good; 4 = Average (good); 3 = Fair; 2 = Poor; 1 = Minimal ability; 0 = No ability demonstrated.

1. *Did you use extended conversation?* That is, did you use language that was not highly formal, that was easy for you to use (not a stretch), that seemed like normal conversation, and that revealed a natural, comfortable, relaxed vocabulary and approach?

7 6 5 4 3 2 1 0

2. *Did you reveal clarity in your word choices?* That is, were your words immediately meaningful? Did they arouse specific and definite meanings? Was there no ambiguity or confusion revealed?

7 6 5 4 3 2 1 0

3. *Did you reveal simplicity in your word choices?* That is, did you use simple words? Was your vocabulary instantly understandable? Did you avoid using vague and confusing words? Were you sensitive to audience knowledge and background?

7 6 5 4 3 2 1 0

4. *Did you reveal accuracy in your word choices?* That is, did your words seem to convey exactly what you meant? Did you give your listeners enough, but not too much, information? In your examples, did you give complete details such as names, places, dates, and other facts? When you used an uncommon or technical word, did you accurately define it for your listeners?

7 6 5 4 3 2 1 0

5. *Did your verbal communication reveal appropriateness?* That is, did the words you chose have a direct relationship to your listeners? Did all your facts, examples, illustrations, opinions, statistics, and personal experiences relate directly to your audience? Did you use personal pronouns such as *you, us, we,* and *our*? Did you ask your listeners questions or use rhetorical questions that did not require an answer but which created the impression of direct audience contact?

7 6 5 4 3 2 1 0

6. *Did you reveal dynamism in your choice of words?* That is, was your language vivid? Was it impressive? Did your language appear planned and prepared—as if you had given it some specific thought? Did your language reveal your own personal imprint?

7 6 5 4 3 2 1 0

TOTAL POINTS: _____

Go to the Online Learning Center at **www.mhhe.com/hybels11e** to see your results and learn how to evaluate your attitudes and feelings.

www.mhhe.com/hybels11e >

Summary

Your ability to use words depends on your native architecture, cognitive development, and environmental influences. It is a key component in strategic flexibility because, as the Sapir-Whorf hypothesis emphasizes, it influences the way you view and think about the world around you.

The Semantic Triangle is a way to understand how words work using symbol, thought, and referent and showing the relationship between a person's intended meaning and the meaning that results in the listener's mind. A word is a symbol; it stands for the object or concept it names. For us to understand one another, we must agree on what the particular word symbol stands for—in both its denotative and its connotative meanings. S. I. Hayakawa's ladder of abstraction helps convey meaning accurately to listeners. It helps analyze communications, understandings, and misunderstandings. It helps immunize against political propaganda, advertising, and vacant rhetoric, and it also helps communicators make personal adjustments as they become aware of their own abstracting.

Language is directly linked to your perception of reality and to your thought processes, which begin in earliest childhood. You create meanings for words as ideas, feelings, and activities change. Because you determine meanings, it is important to present ideas as clearly as possible while your listener tries to understand.

For language to be successful, it must be appropriate to the language environment. The language you should use in a particular environment is determined by the role you are playing in that environment. Certain language rituals are predetermined for you by the values of your society (culture and co-cultures). You learn these and other forms of appropriate language during your childhood. Racist language is the tendency to describe the majority group, its actions and its members, in positive terms, but minority groups in negative terms. Sexist language is any language that is supposed to include all people but unintentionally excludes a gender. Ableist language negatively refers to persons with disabilities. All of these are offensive, vulgar, impolite, and unacceptable wherever they occur. When you become an adult and enter the work world, often you must learn a specialized language used by your occupational or professional group.

Style, the way you express yourself, is an important aspect of language. The style that is expected of you often is determined by the roles you play. If you do not modify your language to fit your role, you may speak in ways that are inappropriate for the occasion.

Four basic beliefs underlie the examination of gender and language: 1) language is the means by which our views of gender are formed and shared, 2) gender is embedded in all institutions, actions, beliefs, and desires represented by communication, 3) gender *does* make a difference in your language choices, and 4) the difference between genders is *not* universal. Sensitivity to gender is important because of its effect on your thoughts and actions, on its potential for creating conflict, on others' impressions of you, on your social reality, and because of its effect on self-esteem. Any preoccupation with specific gender differences in language simply reinforces stereotypes, and learning a laundry list of differences or of dos and don'ts (what to say and what not to say) is meaningless because patterns of gender-related behavior vary across cultures and contexts. Most important is developing a sensitivity to gender and language.

Powerful talk comes directly to the point. It is characterized by the lack of hedges, qualifiers, tag questions, and disclaimers. It is generally perceived as more masculine, dominant, and aggressive as opposed to being less feminine, soft-spoken, or submissive.

English is losing its place as a dominant world language. One in five Americans speak a language other than English at home. If you belong to an ethnic group, you may use a dialect—the habitual language of your community. The advantage of dialect is that it helps a person fit into an ethnic community; the disadvantage is that it might not have prestige in a community where standard American English is spoken.

There are many differences between writing and speaking. Writing is formal and structured; uses words alone; and is nonimmediate, with delayed feedback. Speaking is informal and less structured; uses words along with facial expressions, gestures, and tone of voice; and is immediate with, for the most part, instant feedback. Knowing these and the other differences will help you increase both the clarity and accuracy of your messages.

Oral lessons should be more efficient than written ones. With respect to the Internet, decreases in sociability, inability to interpret nonverbal messages, isolation, and less interest in traditional classroom learning have *not,* for the most part, proven to be true. Also, the use of contractions, emoticons, and stunted vocabulary that characterize Internet communication have not appeared in classroom communication as it was once thought they would.

When you work on your communication, you have to decide what you want to say and how you want to say it. In choosing how you wish to communicate, you should aim for clarity, vividness, and ethical choices. Then you should ask to whom you are speaking and what metamessages—the meaning apart from the actual words—you are sending.

Key Terms and Concepts

Use the Online Learning Center at www.mhhe.com/hybels11e to further your understanding of the following terms.

Ableist language 71	Ladder of abstraction 66	Ritual language 69
Clarity 83	Language environment 69	Sapir-Whorf hypothesis 62
Cognitive development 62	Metamessage 86	Semantic Triangle 63
Connotative meaning 64	Paralanguage 81	Sexist language 71
Denotative meaning 64	Powerful talk 78	Style 73
Dialect 79	Racist language 71	Vividness 85
Doublespeak 70	Rapport-talk 77	
Euphemism 70	Report-talk 77	

Questions to Review

1. How did you acquire your ability to use words?

2. What is the Sapir-Whorf hypothesis? How does it influence strategic flexibility?

3. What is meant when a word is referred to as a symbol?

4. What are the three main elements of the semantic triangle, and how do they relate to each other?

5. What is the difference between denotative meaning and connotative meaning?

6. What is the ladder of abstraction, and why is it useful?

7. What are the four elements that make up a language environment?

8. Define *euphemism* and *doublespeak* and give an example of each.

9. What are the differences between racist, sexist, and ableist language, and why is it considered offensive, vulgar, and impolite?

10. What do you mean when you talk about verbal style? How is it developed?

11. How is powerful talk characterized? When people use it, what impression do they make?

12. What are the four basic beliefs that underlie the relationship of gender and language?

13. Why is a sensitivity to gender and language important?

14. What is the difference between rapport-talk and report-talk?

15. What is the problem with perceiving the differences between genders as represented in language as nothing more than bipolar categories?

16. Why is the connection between language and culture important?

17. What is dialect, and what does it have to do with one's cultural background?

18. How do speaking and writing differ? What is the benefit of knowing the differences?

19. What is the difference between clarity and vividness, and what would be an appropriate example of each that reflects the difference?

20. What is the difference between paralanguage and metamessage?

21. What are some of the moral choices you should make in choosing the words you use?

Go to the Online Learning Center at www.mhhe. com/hybels11e to test your knowledge of the chapter contents.

CHAPTER FOUR

Nonverbal Communication

After reading this chapter, you should be able to:

- Frame a clear definition of nonverbal communication and explain the role it plays in communicating effectively.

- Differentiate between verbal and nonverbal communication and explain how the brain processes information from each.

- Clarify each of the characteristics of nonverbal communication.

- Describe each type of nonverbal communication and provide an example of each one.

- Explain the functions of nonverbal communication.

WAS RAISED IN A HOUSE WHERE ONLY POOR ENGLISH WAS SPOKEN, and because my parents allowed us (my two sisters and three brothers) to eat whatever we wanted, I was slightly overweight. Because of my poor English and weight, I was always teased, taunted, and ridiculed. The sneers and derision caused me to remain silent, even though there were times when I wanted to speak up or shout out. To avoid being called on in classes (to avoid further laughter and put-downs) throughout high school, I sat near the back of the classroom and tried to keep a low profile, but I always did well in school by paying attention, reading the textbook, keeping up with assignments (I loved to study), and taking good notes.

When I got to college things changed dramatically. No longer was I teased, I discovered a whole new group of friends, and I realized that sitting toward the back in classes had no value for me. Most of the changes were things I initiated. For example, sitting in front in my classes changed the distance I was from the instructor, and this change, alone, involved me in class discussions, caused me to be noticed and called on for answers, and allowed me to get to know my instructors, and they me.

Involvement in my classes had its own benefits. My facial expressions improved (engaged and smiling), vocal cues increased (speaking up and speaking louder), body movements and gestures changed (sitting with alert posture and raising my hand), and I even changed my physical attractiveness (lost weight, added makeup, jewelry, and glasses) and dress (dressed for prestige and to convey class).

Because of the nonverbal changes I made, my classroom involvement and interaction strengthened, my grade-point average increased, and I became more positive, self-confident, assertive, and contented.

Nonverbal communication is information communicated without using words. Much of it—like this person's overweight, unpopular, and withdrawn personality— is unintentional. People may not be aware they are sending some nonverbal messages. On the other hand, this student knew that being overweight, unpopular, and withdrawn conveyed negative stereotypes she did not like, and with a great deal of personal effort and commitment she set out to change them.

The Role of Nonverbal Communication in Communicating Effectively and Achieving Strategic Flexibility

As much as 93 percent of communication is nonverbal,[1] with 55 percent sent through facial expressions, posture, and gestures and 38 percent through tone of voice.[2]

Despite how much of communication is nonverbal, it is an overlooked component of communication; thus, it is essential to understand how it works and how you can communicate better when you use it.

Communicating Effectively

If you look closely at the communication model discussed in Chapter 1, The Communication Process, you will *not* find nonverbal communication as one of the elements depicted there. It is, however, embedded in every element in the model. Think about it.

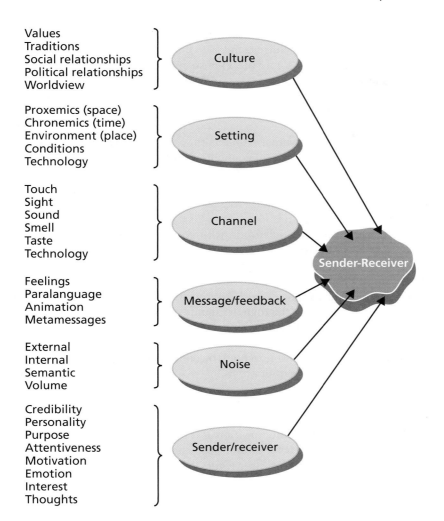

Values
Traditions
Social relationships
Political relationships
Worldview

Culture

Proxemics (space)
Chronemics (time)
Environment (place)
Conditions
Technology

Setting

Touch
Sight
Sound
Smell
Taste
Technology

Channel

Feelings
Paralanguage
Animation
Metamessages

Message/feedback

External
Internal
Semantic
Volume

Noise

Credibility
Personality
Purpose
Attentiveness
Motivation
Emotion
Interest
Thoughts

Sender/receiver

Sender-Receiver

Figure 4-1
Information from
the Elements in the
Communication Model

The size or dress of the sender-receiver is information communicated without using words, just as the pace or loudness of the message or the frown on his or her face is feedback to your message. Information could include noise from others talking too loudly and too close to where you are, or it could be a desperate, clinging handshake—the use of touch as an additional channel—to reinforce the urgency of the meeting. It could be the setting, like a cafeteria, that tells you to moderate what you say so others cannot hear; or, finally, it could be the culture, which may dictate conversational decorum or language choices. Think of the importance of nonverbal communication in the card game of poker where you have to demonstrate tremendous control of your nonverbal communication in order to hide your emotions, lie and bluff, and reveal no sympathy. Now, when you look at the model—see Figure 4-1—you can see information possibilities in every element.

There are four other things you can learn from Figure 4-1. First, nonverbal communication plays an important role in communicating effectively. Second, to be unaware of nonverbal communication is to miss a significant portion of what goes on in any communication situation. Third, as Figure 4-1 indicates, communication is complex;

look at the number of factors you take into consideration—some more important or obvious than others—before, during, and after communicating. Fourth, no two communications can ever be the same. There are so many elements and so many different ways to interpret them.

Strategic Flexibility

You are aware of all the nonverbal elements that are likely to affect any communication you have with others. Now, think about all the processing procedures that your brain engages in (your unique perceptual filter depicted in Figure 2-3 of Chapter 2, Self, Perception, and Communication) as it takes in all or some of these elements. You make use of them as you anticipate, assess, evaluate, select, apply, then reassess and reevaluate each communication.

Part of strategic flexibility has to do with **conversation management**—that is, using nonverbal cues to structure conversations. Think about how you and others signal to indicate it is your time to speak, or how you give the floor to a conversation partner. Think, too, how you gesture to make a point or use your gaze to show you are listening. Cues like the distance you stand from another person, the use of silence in maintaining engagement, or the tone or volume of your voice, all affect the smoothness of an interaction. Conversation management, too, may be associated with power and control. Canary, Cody, and Manusov, in their chapter, "Functions of Nonverbal Behavior," write, "Those who are able to hold the floor the most tend to have more power than others have in a conversation" (p. 187).[3]

If you are attentive to verbal and nonverbal elements, responsive to current usage, and respectful of differential usage, you will probably be able to move into any social setting in your own society. You will be perceptually fluent, rising to all the demands of both verbal and nonverbal communication. It is both language fluency and nonverbal awareness that are most likely to result in strategic flexibility. When you examine the number of nonverbal factors alone (see Figure 4-1), you quickly understand why some people are better communicators than others. They are not just aware of the elements, but they process them and then use them in the strategic flexibility framework. It isn't a mystery; such ability can be learned.

Differences Between Verbal and Nonverbal Communication

Most differences between verbal and nonverbal communication are obvious; however, knowing the differences can help you emphasize the one with which you can be most effective. For example, if you want to make certain that your directions are understood, put your emphasis on verbal communication because it follows specific rules of structure and grammar, because words represent specific things like schools, factories, or stop signs, and because verbal communication has culture- and context-bound meanings. On the other hand, if you want to express your feelings to a spouse who has just lost a close friend, words may be insufficient: Your spontaneous nonverbal signs of sorrow, hurt, and loss may be far more significant.

One of the most important distinctions between verbal and nonverbal communication is the way the brain processes the information. Verbal information is conveyed linearly, one word after another. In nonverbal communication, however, the brain creates a composite of all the signals given off by a new experience. It is "a holistic phenomenon," says Carlin Flora, "in which clues (mellifluous voice, Rolex watch, soggy handshake, hunched shoulders) hit us all at once and form an impression larger than their sum."[4]

According to Jane E. Brody, in an article originally published in the *New York Times,* "Baby Talk: From Birth, Engage Your Child with Words," "society is falling prey to the quick response that our computer generation has become accustomed to."[5] Effective communication skills require both verbal and nonverbal development. Brody says she is alarmed by modern parental behavior, and for support, she relies on Randi Jacoby, a speech and language specialist in New York. Here, she is quoting Jacoby: "Parents have stopped having good communications with their young children, causing them to lose out on the eye contact, facial expression, and overall feedback that is essential for early communication development."[6] Thus, regarding differences between verbal and nonverbal, Brody's point is that young children need "time and one-on-one feedback as they struggle to formulate utterances in order to build their language and cognitive skills."[7]

Finally, there is a common generalization that many people make to distinguish verbal from nonverbal communication. Because verbal language takes place one word after another and we form impressions from nonverbal cues as a composite, it is sometimes said that "one cannot not communicate"—simply because our bodies are *always* emitting nonverbal cues. It can be argued that this is true because one cannot avoid leaking nonverbal signals, and if these are then given meaning by another participant, then the phrase, "one cannot *not* communicate" is true. But here is the point of raising this issue: People are not communicating every waking moment because there is no intentionality involved. Said another way, communication is purposeful, and without purpose, communication becomes random and haphazard—not always without meaning, but definitely arbitrary, aimless, and accidental.

Characteristics of Nonverbal Communication

All forms of nonverbal communication have six characteristics in common. First, much nonverbal communication is unique to the culture or co-culture to which you belong. Second, verbal and nonverbal messages may be in conflict with one another. Third, much nonverbal communication operates at a subconscious level—you are often not aware of it. Fourth, your nonverbal communication shows your feelings and attitudes. Fifth, nonverbal communication varies by gender. Finally, nonverbal communication displays power relationships.

Nonverbal Communication Is Culturally Determined

Your culture affects almost all your communication behaviors. For example, it governs how close you stand while talking with another person, how you use or avoid eye contact, and how you express or suppress powerful emotions such as joy, disapproval, and anger. Your culture determines whether you feel free to express your love of another in public settings by holding hands, hugging, or kissing—what has come to be known as public displays of affection (PDA).

Much nonverbal behavior is learned in childhood, passed on to you by your parents and others with whom you associate. A good deal of it is learned simply through imitation. Growing up in a particular society, you adopt the traits and mannerisms of your cultural group. In Japan bowing shows rank. Slouching is rude in most northern European areas. Putting your hands in your pockets is disrespectful in Turkey.

Your culture governs your body movement. It determines what moves, when it moves, and where it moves, and it imposes restrictions on that movement. For example, your hips may move in sports and dancing, but not in the services of some churches. Children can move their bodies freely in gym class but not in math.

Nonverbal Messages May Conflict with Verbal Messages

Nonverbal communication is so deeply rooted, so unconscious, that you can express a verbal message and directly contradict it with a nonverbal message. For example, Terrence Sejinowski, of the Salk Institute for Biological Studies in La Jolla, California, has developed a computer program that can detect lies by analyzing fleeting facial expressions.[8] The computer is trained to analyze in real time the almost imperceptible expressions like eyelid flutters and strained smiles—the same expressions it used to take Paul Ekman, a psychologist at the University of California–San Francisco, and his team of researchers hours to catalog. With the new computer program, people can be screened for lying without their even knowing it.[9]

Without computer assistance, most people can spot lies little better than half the time. In her study of lying, Maureen O'Sullivan, a University of San Francisco professor, found only 31 people of more than 13,000 who could do better. These so-called wizards read telltale signals such as fidgeting, pressing the lips together, raising the chin, moving the feet, and changing vocal pitch. Researchers warned, however, that such cues are not universal nor even always indicative of a lie.[10]

In **mixed messages** the verbal and the nonverbal contradict each other. The nonverbal communication is often more reliable than the verbal content. You can learn to manipulate words, but you might find it difficult to manipulate your nonverbal communication. You may not be aware of sending it; the message, however, comes through loud and clear.

Nonverbal Messages Are Largely Unconscious

You wake up feeling that you might be getting a cold. It's not yet bad enough to stay home, so you go to classes. The minute one of your classmates sees you, she says, "You look like you aren't feeling very well." She is making a nonverbal assessment: You don't have to say a word for her to know how you're feeling.

When you consider the amount and ordinariness of your nonverbal behavior, it is hardly surprising that you are unaware of much of it. In *The Universal Sense* (NY: Bloomsbury, 2012), Seth S. Horowitz says that our senses of vision, smell, taste, touch, and balance are all limited in range and scope. When you don't know why you are responding to something as you are, however, it could be because of some sound your subconscious picked up. "Your auditory system," writes Horowitz, "is constantly monitoring the background for change . . . It is the only sensory system that is still reliable even while we sleep" (pp. 108–109).

www.mhhe.com/hybels11e >

View "Nonverbal Messages," Video clip on the Online Learning Center.

ATTENTION!

Reality Check
All forms of nonverbal communication have six characteristics in common. These revolve around the fact that nonverbal messages are culturally determined, they may conflict with verbal messages, they operate at an unconscious level, they show feelings and attitudes, they vary by gender, and they display power. Does this make sense? Is it logical? Using a recent communication exchange with someone you know well, analyze just the other person's nonverbal communication in such a way as to confirm all of these six characteristics. What do you gain by knowing these six characteristics? In what ways does knowing the six characteristics help you communicate more effectively?

Nonverbal Communication Shows Your Feelings and Attitudes

The feelings and emotions others can detect in your face include happiness, sadness, surprise, fear, anger, interest, contempt, shame, shyness, and guilt.[11] But research shows that other people are as accurate, if not better, at detecting emotions through vocal cues as through facial expression.[12] As a matter of fact, researchers Planalp and her associates have shown that vocal cues are the most recognizable signs of emotions.[13]

Your body is also quite capable of expressing emotions. In her report on communicating emotion in everyday life, Planalp reports that people easily interpret a person's emotional state from cues such as "being physically energetic, bouncy, jumping up and down, clenching hands or fists, making threatening movements, holding the body rigidly, shuffling, or having a slumped, droopy posture, dancing around, and using hand emblems."[14] If you wanted to demonstrate greater warmth and immediacy to another person, you might reveal a happy facial expression, enthusiastic gestures, closer interpersonal distances, and friendly touches.[15]

Nonverbal Communication Varies by Gender

Men and women use and interpret nonverbal communication differently. North American women not only initiate more eye contact during conversations than men, but they are more comfortable returning eye contact as well. Women maintain a gaze longer, but they are less likely than men to stare at someone—they break eye contact more frequently than men. This is not a contradiction; men are simply less likely to *make* the eye contact, but when they do, they often get "locked in" without realizing their eye contact is being returned.[16]

When surveyed, female students felt that they typically use more gestures than males.[17] Some authorities think women use fewer gestures with other women but more with men. Others think the difference is in the types of gestures used, not in their frequency of use. Although you will automatically return a smile if someone smiles at you first, experts agree that women smile more than men. It is also useful to point out that females are more attracted to others who smile.[18]

Although the experts agree that males use more personal space than females, when students were surveyed, 56 percent of the females felt they required more personal space than males.[19] In Edward T. Hall's book *The Hidden Dimension,* spatial zones are drawn closer for women than for men.[20] Hall notes that women tend to approach others more closely and seem to prefer side-by-side conversations. Men, on the other hand, prefer face-to-face conversations.

Men are more likely to initiate touch with others than are women. Women give and receive more touches than men except when initiating courtship and are more likely to associate touch with personal warmth and expressiveness. When students were surveyed, 57.8 percent of the females agreed that they touch others more than males do.[21] Touch is considered a feminine-appropriate behavior and a masculine-inappropriate one. Mothers touch female infants more than male infants, and female children tend to desire and offer more nonaggressive touch than male children.[22]

Which gender is likely to interpret nonverbal cues better? All experts agree on this one: Females are better interpreters. When students were surveyed, 73.7 percent of the females agreed with the experts. There are two reasons for this. First, women tend to be more sensitive communicators. Second, women use a number of verbal and nonverbal channels to actively communicate to others the importance of relationships.

In her book, *Why You're Not Married . . .Yet* (NY: Ballantine Books, 2012), Tracy McMillan offers an interesting (and provocative) insight regarding what nonverbal cues men look for in women:

> *Evolutionary psychologists at the University of Texas recently published some really interesting findings that may have you reconsidering all those hours spent in the gym. They found that men interested in short-term companionship (like a one-night stand) showed more interest in a woman's body, while men looking for a long-term relationship were more interested in a woman's face.*
>
> *The researchers asked 375 college students to look at a picture of a potential mate. At the beginning of the experiment both face and body were hidden. Researchers then gave them the option of looking at the face or the body, but not both. The results were fascinating. Only one-quarter of the men who were evaluating the image as a potential long-term mate chose to look at the body. But for a short-term mate? Fifty-one percent of men chose to see the body.*
>
> *Researchers theorized that the body showed clues to a woman's fertility—important if you're planning to "hit it and quit it." On the other hand, the face showed clues to a woman's character—something only a man interested in a long-term relationship would care about.*
>
> *Perhaps not surprisingly, women showed no significant difference between faces or bodies when looking for short-term or long-term mates. We'll enjoy sex with a cad just as much as sex with a guy who loves us (p. 31).*

Source: McMillan, Tracy (2012). *Why You're Not Married . . . Yet: The Straight Talk You Need to Get the Relationship You Deserve.* New York: Ballantine Books.

Questions

1. In your experience, would you agree with the results of this study? If so, do you have any personal evidence to support your agreement?

2. When looking for a potential mate, would the face or the body be more important in your assessment? Why is this so?

3. What influence would the results of this study have on the communication between two people who were interested in one another?

Nonverbal Communication Displays Power[23]

Holders of power exert dominance over those with less power. It is one of the most important dimensions of human relationships, and it isn't acquired just through money, social class, education, neighborhood, or family, although all or some of these may contribute. Often it is an individual's subtle behaviors that have an effect on others' perceptions of his or her power. Power is revealed in every nonverbal code. For example, you communicate your status and power through your physical appearance. Your clothes broadcast your sex, rank, and up-to-dateness. Height and physical size are important components of power because tallness and largeness indicate dominance and status. Bodily positions, movements, gestures, and facial expressions convey power and status just like the way you stand and sit. Eye contact, or gaze, can reveal attentiveness, warmth, and intimacy as well as control and power. The distance and spatial arrangements between you and those with whom you are interacting are important indicators of power and status. Touch has the power to repel, disgust, insult, threaten, console, reassure, love, and arouse. The way you use your voice reflects status and dominance just as the possession of time is correlated with power and status and your objects and possessions are often viewed as status symbols. Most perceptions of status and power result from a number of these nonverbal cues working together to convey the impression and not nonverbal cues operating as separate, isolated behaviors.

Expectancy Violation Theory

All of us have expectations about how others should behave nonverbally in particular situations. Think about how you expect people to behave at a funeral, in a movie theater, in class, or even in walking across campus. That is what **expectancy violation theory** (EVT) suggests. When someone violates your expectations, you can perceive the violation either positively or negatively depending, in part, on how much you like the other person. This theory proposes that it is your expectancy that will influence the outcome of the communication as positive or negative. Positive violations are likely to increase the attraction between you and the violator just as negative violations are likely to decrease the attraction between you and the violator.

The value of this theory is in understanding the factors that influence your expectations. There are three factors: (1) interactant variables, (2) environmental variables, and (3) variables related to the nature of the interaction.[24] The traits of the people involved in the communication—interactant variables—include sex, race, culture, status, and age. Environmental variables—what we labeled "setting" in our model of communication—include amount of space available as well as the nature of the territory surrounding the interaction. Social norms, purpose of the interaction, and formality of the situation make up the nature of the interaction. As the theory has evolved, these factors have evolved into communicator characteristics, relational characteristics, and context.

You might say, so what? The bottom line of EVT is simply that when you experience violations, they have a powerful effect on your interaction patterns, on your impressions of the other person, and on the outcomes of your interactions.

Types of Nonverbal Communication

In this section, we will introduce paralanguage, body movement, eye messages, attractiveness, clothing, body adornment, space and distance, touch, smell, time, manners, and silence. If you're curious about which nonverbal features first catch a person's eye, Michelle Healy and Veronica Salazar report the results of a StrategyOne for Listerine survey of 2,024 adults: 1) Overall attractiveness (33%); 2) Smile (23%); 3) Eyes (20%); 4) Body Shape (10%); and 5) Apparel (6%).[25] It is important to remember as you read about the types of nonverbal communication that in most cases no single nonverbal cue operates by itself. Paralanguage is likely to function along with body movement, facial expressions, and eye messages to contribute to the message communicated.[26] It's not just the way the nonverbal components fit together either; words matter as well.

Paralanguage

Verbal communication consists of the words you use to communicate. Nonverbal communication has a **paralanguage**—the way in which you say the words, as noted in the previous chapter on verbal communication. Paralanguage, or paralinguistic cues, exists beside language and interacts with it. For example, a parent tells a child in a mild voice to clean up his room. When the room is still in the same condition two hours later, the parent says, "I thought I told you to clean up your room." This time the parent's voice communicates "If you don't do it soon, you're in big trouble."

One of the pioneers in the study of nonverbal communication, Ray Birdwhistell, shows how important paralanguage can be in its ability to modify everything that is said and place it into context:

> These cross-referencing signals [paralanguage] amplify, emphasize, or modify the formal constructions, and/or make statements about the context of the message situation. In the latter instance, they help to define the context of the interaction by identifying the actor or his audience, and furthermore, they usually convey information about the larger context in which the interaction takes place.[27]

An important aspect of paralanguage—and one noted in the quotation above when Birdwhistell says "by identifying the actor"—paralinguistic cues can create distinct impressions of you, the communicator. For example, what characterizes an attractive, influential voice? Researchers suggest that it is resonant and calm, less monotonous, lower pitched (especially for males), less regionally accented, less nasal, less shrill, and more relaxed.[28]

Albert Mehrabian estimates that 39 percent of the meaning in communication is affected by vocal cues—not the words themselves but the way they are said.[29] In languages other than English, this percentage may be even higher.

Rate

The **rate** (speed) at which one speaks can have an effect on the way a message is received.[30] Faster speakers are seen as more competent, credible, and intelligent.[31] But they are also seen as less honest and trustworthy than slower speakers.[32]

Another aspect of rate is how one person will accommodate or adapt to another's rate. It's called **convergence.** Fast talkers slow down when interacting with slow talkers; slow talkers speed up when talking with fast talkers.[33] People who converge to another's rate are seen as more attractive and persuasive.[34]

Pitch

Pitch is the highness or lowness of the voice. Some people believe that high-pitched voices are not as pleasant as low-pitched voices. However, the same researchers who studied rate of speaking also found that speakers were judged more competent if they used a higher and varied pitch.[35] Lower pitches are more difficult to hear, and people who have low-pitched voices may be perceived as insecure or shy. Pitch can be changed, but it requires working with someone who has had professional training in voice modification.

Volume

The meaning of a message can also be affected by its **volume**—how loudly a person speaks. A loud voice is fine if it's appropriate to the speaker's purpose and is not used all the time. The same is true of a soft voice. Expert teachers know at what points to increase or decrease their volume when they want a class to be quiet.

Quality

The overall **quality** of a voice is made up of all the other vocal characteristics: tempo, resonance, rhythm, and articulation. Voice quality is important because researchers have found that people with attractive voices are seen as more youthful, more competent, and more honest. However, people with immature voices were seen as less competent and powerful but more honest and warm.[36]

Vocal Fillers

A related aspect of paralanguage but not part of it is **vocal fillers**—the sounds you use to fill out your sentences or to cover up or fill pauses. You use many vocal fillers to let others know you are still speaking even though you may not know specifically what to say. They may be nonwords such as *uh, um,* and *er,* or they may be words and phrases such as *you know, like,* or *whatever,* when used to fill a pause. Although fillers are sometimes words, they are used in these instances as if they have no meaning.

Body Movement

Body movement, also called *kinesics,* comes "from the Greek word for 'movement' and refers to all forms of body movement, excluding physical contact with another's body."[37] Researchers Ekman and Friesen divide body movement into five categories: emblems, illustrators, regulators, displays of feelings, and adaptors.[38]

Emblems are body movements that directly translate into words. In Western society the extended thumb of a hitchhiker is an emblem that means "I want a ride." A circle made with the thumb and index finger can be translated into "OK." Emblems often cannot be carried from one culture to another. Shaking your head back and forth in southern India, for example, means "yes."

Emblems are often used when words are inappropriate. It would be impractical for a hitchhiker to stand on the side of the road and shout, "Please give me a ride!" Sometimes emblems can replace talk. You might cover your face with your hands if you are embarrassed, and you hold up your fingers to show how many of something you want. Subgroups in a society often use emblems that members of the group understand but whose meanings are intentionally kept from outsiders—the secret handshake of a fraternity is an example.

Illustrators accent, emphasize, or reinforce words. If someone asks how big your suitcase is, you will probably describe it with words and illustrate the dimensions with your hands. Illustrators can go beyond gestures. When an instructor underlines something she has written on the board, she is telling you that this point is particularly important.

In her book *Executive Charisma,* Debra A. Benton clearly defines the role that posture plays as an illustrator. "Stand tall and straight summons up visions of someone ethical, courageous, awake, alert, and alive. Good posture," Benton says, "shows confidence, vitality, discipline, and youthfulness. Slumped posture," she adds, "implies fright, insecurity, lack of self-acceptance or self-control, lack of discipline, a loser, sheepishness, shame, and guilt. To stand tall and straight is to have a demeanor that says, 'I expect acceptance.'"[39]

Regulators control the back-and-forth flow of speaking and listening. "They are the 'traffic cops' of conversation."[40] They are made up of hand gestures, shifts in posture, and other body movements that signal the beginning and end of interactions. At a very simple level, a teacher uses a regulator when she points to the person she wants to speak next. On a more subtle level, someone might turn away slightly when you are talking, perhaps indicating "I don't want to continue this conversation."

Displays of feelings show, through facial expressions and body movements, how intensely a person is feeling. If you walk into a professor's office and the professor says, "I can see you are really feeling upset," he or she is responding to nonverbal cues you are giving about your feelings. You could also come in with a body posture indicating "I'm really going to argue about this grade"—with your clenched hands or stiff body position showing that you are ready for a confrontation.

Displays of feelings vary in different cultures. For example, many Asian cultures suppress facial expression as much as possible. Mediterranean (Latino/Latina and Arabic) cultures freely express grief or sadness while most American men hide grief or sorrow. Some people see animated expressions as a lack of control. Too much smiling is sometimes viewed as a sign of shallowness.

Adaptors are nonverbal ways of adjusting to a communication situation. They are behaviors that satisfy your physical or psychological needs. What do you do when you feel anxious, relaxed, crowded, or defensive? In general, adaptors are habits and are usually not intended to communicate.[41] However, often they convey a great deal of information.

Because people use such a wide variety of adaptors, and because they are so specific to each person's own needs and the individual communication situation, they are difficult to classify or even to describe generally.

For example, some people use adaptors when they are nervous or uncomfortable in a situation. You might play with jewelry, drum on the table, or move around a lot in your seat. Each of these behaviors is an adaptor—a way of helping you cope with the situation. We all use adaptors, but we are generally not aware of them unless someone points them out.

Facial Expressions

The richest source of emotional information is the face. Paul Ekman analyzed 42 facial muscles that can produce more than 10,000 expressions. He found that seven basic emotions—anger, contempt, disgust, fear, happiness, sadness, and surprise—have clear facial signals.[42] Four of these **facial expressions**—happiness, sadness, fear, and anger—are easily identifiable across cultures.[43] Ekman coined the term "micro-expressions" to describe ultraquick facial movements that signal underlying emotions. Though barely noticeable, these expressions are key to determining whether someone is lying. Ekman, from his original research 40 years ago, found that facial expressions were not cultural but were basically the same from New York City to the remote villages of New Guinea.[44]

Facial expressions, too, play an important role in perceptions of "closeness." Psychologist Albert Mehrabian defined immediacy over 30 years ago as communication behaviors that diminish the physical and psychological distance between people. Teacher immediacy was defined and recognized in 1982 as verbal and nonverbal behaviors that generate perceptions of closeness with students. In a study of teacher nonverbal immediacy, Mary-Jeanette Smythe and Jon A. Hess found that one single item was responsible for students' assessment of teacher immediacy: "Instructor shows a lot of facial expressiveness."[45] Given the importance of facial expressions in displaying emotion, this finding is not surprising; however, the study reveals that students—just like people outside the academic environment—tend to be more attuned to their teacher's (or others') facial movements than to other nonverbal cues like gestures or nodding.

Eye Messages

Eye messages include all information conveyed by the eyes alone. "The many surrounding muscles make eyes a richer source of clues than other parts of the face" writes Annie Murphy Paul in her article, "Mind Reading," "downcast in sadness, wide open in fright, dreamily unfocused, staring hard with jealousy, or glancing around with bored impatience" (p. 76).[46] Jena Pincott adds more insight regarding the important role that the eyes have in her article, "What's in a Face?" "The pupils advertise desire," she writes. "Women's dilate more widely during the hormone surge before ovulation and when looking at attractive men, and men find large-pupiled women more attractive without knowing why. Women prefer men with medium-sized pupils. There are two exceptions: women who are ovulating and those who prefer a 'bad boy.' They both like big pupils" (*Psychology Today,* November/December, 2012, p. 60).

The most important aspect of eye messages is eye contact, and in American culture, meeting another's eyes is a sign of honesty and credibility as well as warmth and involvement. In many cultures, conversing without eye contact can indicate disinterest, inattention, rudeness, shyness, or deception.[47]

When you think about the functions that eye messages can perform, you quickly realize their importance. Eye messages provide turn-taking signals in conversations that regulate interactions. They indicate attentiveness, involvement, immediacy, and connection to others. Prolonged stares, especially with negative facial expressions, can be intimidating. But one of their most delightful and wondrous aspects is their role in flirtation.[48]

Although eye messages have received marginal attention from intercultural scholars,[49] an African proverb says. "The eye is an instrument of aggression."[50] Many Asians and Pacific Islanders would agree. In their countries young people never make eye contact with their elders. In most African countries and many other parts of the world, if a person has more status than you, you should not look him or her in the eye.

Attractiveness

What is attractive to you? **Attractiveness** is having the power or quality of drawing or winning attention.[51] The importance of physical beauty to males is universal; men in all cultures around the world prefer young, nubile (of suitable age to marry) women. More than that, however, men prefer having a physically attractive mate because it is a sign of status.[52] Females, on the other hand, select men with sufficient resources to care for them and have stronger preferences for intelligent, considerate, and outgoing mates. Like men of all cultures, women are attracted to wealth, power, and status.[53]

Sharon Jayson, in her short essay, "The Ugly Truth: Good Looks Make You Richer, Happier" (*USA Today,* March 30, 2012, p. 2B), cites Todd Kashdan, an associate professor of psychology at George Mason University in Fairfax, VA, who studies well-being, as saying, "Think about it [attractiveness] as a gateway to getting what you want from life—job interviews, first dates, making those initial impressions, persuading and influencing other people. Attractiveness gives that slight edge. They're getting the benefit of the doubt at first sight, and unattractive people aren't" (p. 2B). More than just the benefit of the doubt, Abigail Tucker, in her essay, "The Price of Beauty" (*Smithsonian,* November, 2012) says that a "handsome man is poised to make 13 percent more during his career than a 'looks-challenged' peer ... [and] "the net benefit is slightly less for comely women, who may make up the difference by trading on their looks to marry men with higher earning potential" (p. 18).

Physical characteristics you can control are called **elective characteristics** and include clothing, makeup, tattoos, and body piercing. **Nonelective characteristics,** things you cannot change, are height, body proportion, coloring, bone structure, and physical disabilities. Many of the nonelective traits influence how you see the world. A six-foot woman, for example, would see life quite differently from her five-foot sister.[54]

The introduction to the excerpted paragraph below reads, ". . . Scientists have taken a more holistic and dynamic look at the spontaneous nonverbal expressions that flow between two people engaged in ordinary conversations infused with mutual positivity. Widening their approach has enabled scientists to uncover the unique nonverbal fingerprint of love," writes Dr. Barbara L. Fredrickson in her book, *Love 2.0: How Our Supreme Emotion Affects Everything We Feel, Think, Do, and Become* (NY: Hudson Street Press, 2013):

> "Love, this new evidence shows, is characterized by four distinct nonverbal cues. The first cue, not surprisingly, is how often you and the other person each smile at each other, in the genuine, eye-crinkling manner. A second cue is the frequency with which you each use open and friendly hand gestures to refer to each other, like your outstretched palm. (Hostile hand gestures, like pointing or finger-wagging, are by definition, excluded from this category of gestures.) A third cue

> is how often you each lean in toward each other, literally bringing your hearts closer together. The fourth cue is how often you each nod your head, a sign that you affirm and accept each other" (p. 69).

Source: Fredrickson, Barbara L. (2013). Love 2.0: How our supreme emotion affects everything we feel, think, do, and become. New York: Hudson Street Press.

Questions

1. From your experience, do you agree with Fredrickson that these four nonverbal cues "both emanate from a person's inner experiences of love and are read by others as love"?

2. From your experience, are there other nonverbal cues that you send and are read by another person as a fingerprint for "love"?

3. If you accepted these four nonverbal cues as a fingerprint for "love," is there anything you would change if you wanted to communicate your love for another person using nonverbal cues?

Dahlia Lithwick, in her essay, "Our Beauty Bias Is Unfair" (*Newsweek,* June 14, 2010), cites Deborah Rhode, a Stanford law professor who "proposes a legal regime in which discrimination on the basis of looks is as serious as discrimination based on gender or race." Lithwick continues saying, "Rhode is at her most persuasive when arguing that in America, discrimination against unattractive women and short men is as pernicious and widespread as bias based on race, sex, age, ethnicity, religion, and disability . . ." Lithwick writes citing research from Rhode's book, *The Beauty Bias* (NC: Oxford University Press, 2010): "College students tell surveyors they'd rather have a spouse who is an embezzler, drug user, or a shoplifter than one who is obese. The less attractive you are in America," [repeating an observation mentioned above] "the more likely you are to receive a longer prison sentence, a lower damage award, a lower salary, and poorer performance reviews. You are less likely to be married and more likely to be poor" (p. 20).

Clothing

Because clothing gives such a strong and immediate impression of its wearer, it is enormously important to nonverbal communication. Besides communicating, however, clothing may serve as protection; communicate sexual attraction, self-assertion, self-denial, concealment, or group identification; and provide indications of status and role.[55] In addition, think of how much information you can gain from a person's clothing: sex, age, nationality, relation to opposite sex, socioeconomic status, group and occupational identification, mood, personality, attitudes, interests, and values.[56] In his book *You Are What You Wear,* William Thourlby suggests that people make

10 decisions about others based on clothing: (1) economic level, (2) educational level, (3) trustworthiness, (4) social position, (5) level of sophistication, (6) economic background, (7) social background, (8) educational background, (9) level of success, and (10) moral character.[57]

In her article, "The Style Imperative" (*Psychology Today,* September/October, 2008, pp. 79–82), Hara Estroff Marano states that "those who have [style] are distinctive and thus more memorable." "In the end," she writes, "style is fundamentally democratic. It assumes every person has the potential to create a unique identity and express it through grooming and a few well-chosen clothes. Yet style," she also writes, "is also aristocratic. It sets apart those who have it from those whose dress is merely utilitarian. It announces to the world that the wearer has assumed command of herself [or himself]" (p. 82).[58] She ends her article saying that in this "hurry-up world" of fast and frequent communications, it is an important way to transmit information for it "evokes the substance within by way of the surface."[59]

Even though people may appear to dress in similar ways, they don't always see themselves as similar. An Amish woman points out that although Amish women wear dark clothes that cover the body, they are still aware of style. She writes: "Every culture has its own fashion expectations and requirements, and my people are no exception. They are concerned about how they look. They do not all wear black. They have individual color and style preferences. They enjoy shopping. And they talk about styles and fashions among themselves. . . . To these women, high and proper fashion means busy sewing machines, solid-colored, store-bought fabrics, and patterns passed down from generation to generation.[60]

In Saudi Arabia, according to Karen Elliott House, in a *Newsweek* article (October 1 & 8, 2012, pp. 54–58), "I pray my daughters have a life like mine," for women, "anything that reveals the human form is forbidden." On House's abaya—the long, black, shapeless, overgarment worn by women throughout the Middle East to shield their bodies from view—she had a blue and orange braid on its long sleeves. House was told, "This is wrong. Your abaya shows the body, and this decoration attracts men to look at you." In addition to the abaya, "They also cover their faces with a separate black niqab that features a slit for the eyes." Devout ladies "cover even that slit with another black cloth, which can be flipped up or lowered depending on the need to see clearly" (p. 59).

Clothing falls into four categories: uniforms, occupational dress, leisure clothing, and costumes. Each conveys a different nonverbal meaning.

Uniforms identify wearers with particular organizations. They are the most specialized form of clothing. There is little freedom of choice in a uniform. Its wearers are told when to wear it (daytime, summer) and what they can and cannot wear with it (jewelry, medals, hairstyles).

Clothing projects a message; by choosing particular clothing, wearers commit themselves to the statements clothing makes.

By showing rank, military uniforms tell what positions the wearers hold in the hierarchy and what their relationships are to others in the organization. The uniform also implies that its wearer will follow certain norms.[61]

Occupational dress is clothing that employees are expected to wear, but it is not as precise as a uniform. It is designed to present a specific image of the employee.[62] Unlike wearers of uniforms, employees who wear occupational dress have choices. Flight attendants are required to wear specific pieces of clothing, but they can mix items and accessories to their own preferences. What teachers wear affects student perceptions. In a study of teaching assistants, researchers found that those who dressed the most informally were viewed the most positively by students. In this case, informal dress was faded jeans, T-shirts, and flannel shirts.[63]

Leisure clothing is worn when work is over. Because this kind of clothing is chosen by the individual, some people assert their personal identities through it.[64] However, not everyone sees styles of leisure wear as a choice. Many teenagers will wear only a particular brand of jeans because when their group agrees on a brand, everyone wears it. The mass media have had such a great influence on leisure clothing that it's hard to separate media influence from individual preference.

Costumes are a form of highly individualized dress. By putting on a costume like cowboy boots, bandanna, and hat, the wearer announces, "This is who I want to be." Costumes not only require thought regarding the image they convey but also go against many norms. As one student shrewdly observed as he changed his shoes for a job interview at a supermarket in the Northeast, "I better not wear my cowboy boots. They look too aggressive."

Body Adornment

Body adornment includes any addition to the physical body designed to beautify or decorate. Throughout the world people have found ways of changing the body they were born with. Americans are no exception. Hairstyles, facial hair, and makeup undergo conservative changes that are widely accepted. In fact, it's hard to believe that only about 100 years ago people were shocked when women used makeup and cut their hair short, or, more recently, when men began to wear earrings.

In *The Consuming Instinct* (NY: Prometheus Books, 2011), Dr. Gad Saad, a professor of marketing at the John Milson School of Business at Concordia University, talks about one popular current body adornment: tattoos. In "Fashion as Group Identity," Saad writes, "Although one of the motives for getting a tattoo is rooted in the desire to signal group membership, paradoxically a tattoo is also meant to express one's individuality (as a fashion statement). Note that the act of getting a tattoo," he continues, "as an expression of nonconformity to societal norms ends up being a form of belongingness to the 'rebellious others.' The tension between these two universal forces of human identity (conformity and individuality) is well captured by optimal distinctiveness theory,[65] which posits that humans seek an optimal equilibrium between these two opposing pulls" (p. 140).

Space and Distance

The study of **space and distance,** called **proxemics,** examines the way people use the space around them as well as the distance they maintain from others. The minute you enter a classroom, you have to decide where to sit. As you can see in Figure 4-2,

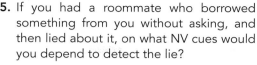

In this AOM all you have to do is raise your awareness level of nonverbal communication (NVC) in order to answer the following questions about the types of NVC:

1. On which type of NVC do *you* depend most in *first* assessing another person's credibility (whether they can be trusted or not)?

2. Which type of NVC would *you* use most to impress a job interviewer in a situation where you really want the job badly?

3. When you are trying to persuade a group of your friends to do something you want them to do badly (above all else), which type of NVC are you likely to depend on most?

4. When you are making an assessment of a potential romantic partner, what is the *set* of NV cues on which you depend the most?

5. If you had a roommate who borrowed something from you without asking, and then lied about it, on what NV cues would you depend to detect the lie?

6. If at work you were seeking a raise or promotion, on what set of NV cues would you depend to impress your supervisor?

7. You have a speech to present to your class on a topic that is important to you, and you want to make a good impression. On what set of NV cues do you depend to make certain your impression is conveyed?

8. You are at a party with a friend of the same sex when a person of the opposite sex to whom you are immediately attracted appears in front of you. What NV cues do you immediately change to make the proper impression?

your choice depends on how much interaction you want to have with the instructor: If you are in the "action zone," you may be indicating that you want to participate in the class.

Territory is the space that a person considers as belonging to him or her—either temporarily or permanently. For example, you would probably be upset if you came into the classroom and found someone sitting in "your" chair.

Sometimes people unwittingly send out a mixed message about their space. Four students who rented a church that had been converted to student housing with four sleeping lofts found that they had little control over their space. Other students dropped in night and day—probably because the building looked more like a public than a private space. The minute their lease ended, they moved into more traditional housing.

Every culture has rules—usually informal—about the use of space and distance. Edward T. Hall, author of two classic books on nonverbal communication, discovered that North Americans use four distance zones when they are communicating with others: intimate distance, personal distance, social distance, and public distance.[66]

Intimate distance, a range of less than 18 inches apart, places people in direct contact with each other. Look at a parent holding a baby. All our senses are alert when we are this close to someone. The parent can touch the baby, smell him, and hear every little gurgle he makes. People also maintain an intimate distance in love relationships and with close friends. Intimate distance exists whenever you feel free to touch the other person with your whole body.

When your intimate distance is violated by people who have no right to be so close, you feel apprehensive. If you are on a crowded bus, subway, or elevator and people are pressed against you, they are in your intimate distance. By not making eye contact you can protect your intimate distance psychologically, if not physically.

Figure 4-2
A Traditional Classroom Arrangement

In such an arrangement, those students occupying the blue seats will account for a large proportion of the total interaction that occurs between teachers and students. Those in the green seats will interact some; those in the white seats will interact very infrequently. The area enclosed in dotted lines has been called the "action zone."

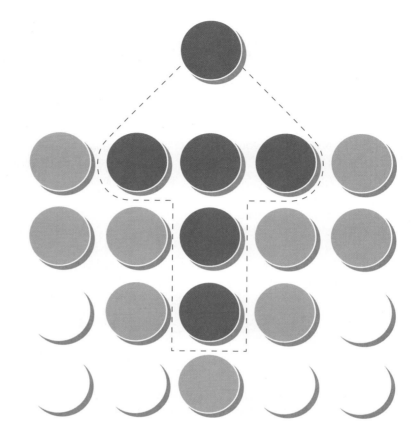

Personal distance, from 18 inches to 4 feet, is the distance you maintain from another person when you are engaged in casual and personal conversations. It is close enough to see the other person's reactions but far enough away not to encroach on intimate distance.

Social distance, from 4 to 12 feet, is the distance you are most likely to maintain when you do not know people very well. Impersonal business, social gatherings, and interviews are examples of situations where you use social distance and interaction becomes more formal.

Public distance, a distance of more than 12 feet, is typically used for public speaking. At this distance, people speak more loudly and use more exaggerated gestures. Communication is even more formal and permits few opportunities for people to be involved with each other.

Figure 4-3 shows the dimensions of the four distance zones. There are wide variations among cultures in the way people handle space and distance in relationships. When visiting another culture, you (as an American) would probably try to keep your "normal" distance between yourself and someone else—a large zone. Your behavior is typical of northern European communities, Scandinavian countries, and Great Britain but could appear "standoffish" in other cultures like Saudi Arabia, Latin America, Italy, France, and Spain, as well as other Middle Eastern countries. People there tend to keep a much closer distance—a small zone. You might view their maintaining nose-to-nose

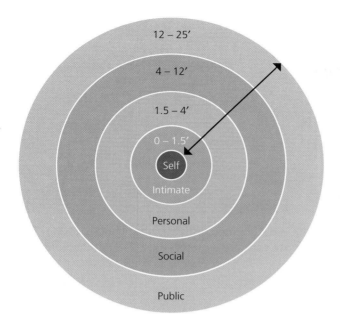

Figure 4-3
The Four Distance
Zones

distance as "pushy" simply because their social space equates to our intimate space. You might find yourself backing away trying to regain your social space while an Arab would be pursuing you across the floor trying to maintain his. If you were visiting a friend in the Netherlands, on the other hand, your roles would be reversed. Their personal space equates to our social space; thus, to maintain your normal distance, you would continue trying to get closer to your friend.

What happens when zone violations occur? This is where expectancy violation theory (discussed previously) comes into play. For example, you know that you have a personal distance you maintain from others, as just discussed. When a person comes too close, it is easy to feel threatened. On the other hand, when a person stands too far away, you wonder if you smell or are socially unattractive in some other way. How you react to violations is often dependent on the reward value related to your relationship with the other person—that is, what you expect to get out of the relationship.[67]

Touch

The closer you stand to someone, the more you increase the likelihood of touching. **Touch** is to be in or come into physical contact with another person, and the study of touch is called **haptics.** Scientists have always thought touch conveyed only a general positive or negative affect, but in a recent article in the journal *Psychology Today* (April, 2013, pp. 52–61) entitled "Louder Than Words," author Rick Chillot described an experiment in which psychologist Matthew Hertenstein of DePauw University demonstrated that "we have an innate ability to decode emotions via touch alone" (p. 54). "Hertenstein" Chillot writes, had volunteers attempt to communicate a list of emotions to a blindfolded stranger solely through touch. Many participants were apprehensive about the experiment. 'This is a touch-phobic society,' [Hertenstein] says, 'We're not used to touching strangers, or even our friends, necessarily.'

The distance people keep from other people is determined both by culture and occasion. The people in the left picture are Americans waiting in line to vote early for a presidential election. Those in the right picture are people from India.

"But touch they did," Hertenstein continues, "it was, after all, for science. The results suggest that for all our caution about touching, we come equipped with an ability to send and receive emotional signals solely by doing so. Participants communicated eight distinct emotions—anger, fear, disgust, love, gratitude, sympathy, happiness, and sadness—with accuracy rates as high as 78 percent. 'I was surprised,' Hertenstein admits. 'I thought the accuracy would be at chance level,' about 25 percent" (p. 54).

Later in the same article, Chillot explains that Hertenstein's research has also shown "that touch can communicate *multiple* positive emotions: joy, love, gratitude, and sympathy" (p. 57). Chillot then clarifies (for our purposes) the most important aspect of Hertenstein's work: "Scientists used to believe touching was simply a means of enhancing messages signaled through speech or body language, 'but it seems instead that touch is a much more nuanced, sophisticated, and precise way to communicate emotions'" (p. 57).

When and where people touch one another is governed by a strict set of societal rules. Richard Heslin has described five different categories of touch behavior.[68] The first is *functional-professional touch,* in which you are touched for a specific reason, as in a physical examination by a doctor or nurse. This kind of touch is impersonal and businesslike. *Social-polite touch* is used to acknowledge someone else. The handshake is the most common form. Although two people move into an intimate distance to shake hands, they move away from each other when the handshake is over. In close relationships people use the *friendship-warmth touch.* This kind of touch involves hugs and casual kisses between friends. Touching is one way to communicate liking.[69] In more intense relationships the *love-intimacy touch* is common. Parents stroke their children; lovers and spouses kiss and fondle each other. The final touch Heslin describes is *sexual arousal touch*—touch used as an expression of physical attraction.[70]

In a newspaper article on work etiquette, entitled, "To Hug or Not to Hug Depends on Business," Patricia Mathews, founder of Workplace Solutions Consultants, a St. Louis-based consultancy, is quoted as saying, "It's truly a gray area. Some people love to be hugged. For others it's 'please don't touch me.'"[71] Ms. Mathews, a member of the Society for Human Resource Management's employee-relations panel, and for 15 years a trainer of workers about illegal harassment in the workplace, claims that three factors have resulted in increased hugging: First, casual dressing in some offices, second, a relaxed work environment, and, third, younger employees. Dianna Johnston, assistant legal counsel with the Equal Employment Opportunity Commission, said, "To be considered unlawful, it would have to be unwelcome."[72] T. Ray Bennett, vice president of human resources with American Bureau of Shipping (ABS) claims, "Hugging is typically not necessary to get the job done, so it's not something we feel is necessary. We suggest that it's usually best to stay professional and stay away from that."[73]

Smell

The study of smell is called **olfactics.** The sense of smell has long remained one of the most baffling of our senses, however, Noam Sobel of the Helen Wills Neuroscience Institute, University of California, Berkeley, and his team of researchers have found evidence of a human smelling ability that experts thought impossible. Contrary to what most scientists have thought, people, just like dogs, mice, and other mammals, compare signals they get from each nostril to get clues about where a smell is coming from.

The sense of smell, being intangible and often ephemeral (transitory or lasting for a very short time), is often ignored and forgotten when the other nonverbal cues are considered. "Without scent, however," writes Molly Birnbaum, in her essay for "The Forum," "Taking Scent for Granted" (*USA Today,* July 1, 2009, p. 13A), "one's experience of the world is dimmed."[74] Brinbaum, having had her olfactory neurons (they run from the nose to the brain) severed when her skull smashed against the windshield in a car accident, writes, "Flavor is reduced to the salty, sweet, bitter and sour of the taste buds. Food, therefore, is nothing but texture and temperature. Coffee is a hot bitter water, milk, thick and gummy. Bakeries are indistinguishable from locker rooms."[75] The complete loss of the sense of smell, known as **anosmia,** often leads to depression.

"Scents can have positive effects on mood, stress reduction, sleep enhancement, self-confidence, and physical and cognitive performance," says Theresa Molnar, executive director of the Sense of Smell Institute, the research and educational arm of the perfume industry's Fragrance Foundation.[76] "A decline in the ability to smell may be an early signal of neurological disorders such as Parkinson's, Alzheimer's, and Huntington's diseases," writes Linda Anderson in her essay, "The Hidden Force of Fragrance." Scents, writes Birnbaum, are closely linked[77] to many aspects of perception. "Olfactory processing is connected to the limbic system of the brain, areas responsible for memory and emotion. Smell ties to recognition: It has been shown that mothers can recognize their newborn babies by scent alone just hours after birth. It ties to sex: Though theories on pheromones are disputed, you'd be hard-pressed to find someone who didn't enjoy the scent of the crook of a lover's neck."[78]

One final note on smell; there is a gender issue involved. "Women consistently outperform men in smell sensitivity tests."[79] "Men are sensitive to smell as well, but because women shoulder a greater reproductive burden, and are therefore choosier about potential mates, researchers are not surprised to find that women are . . . more discriminating in sniffing out . . . compatibility.[80] Writing in "The Underrated Sense" (*Psychology Today,* November/December, 2012), Jonah Comstock underscores the role smell has in mate seeking: ". . . odor-related biochemistry may be part of sexual chemistry—one clue to the mystery of why some people just click" (p. 48).

ATTENTION!

Another Four Senses
"Physiologists largely agree that in addition to the five we all know about, there are four more. The first is our sense of temperature (thermoception). This is different from our sense of touch. We don't need to be touching anything to feel hot or cold. . . . Another is the sense of pain (nociception). Scientists now generally agree that this is a different sensory system from either touch or temperature. . . . Next is vestibular sense (equilibrioception), which includes our sense of balance and acceleration. And there is the kinesthetic sense (proprioception), which gives us our understanding of where our limbs and the rest of our body are in space in relationship to each other. . . . All of these senses contribute to our feelings of being in the world and to our ability to function in it."[81]

Time

The study of time is called **chronemics.** To say that time is very important in American culture is a huge understatement; we are obsessed with time. Our daily life is infused with a sense of urgency driven by the desire to beat the clock. Burgoon, Buller, and Woodall write, "Time is seen as a precious resource, a valuable and tangible commodity. We spend time, save it, make it, fill it, and waste it. It is seen almost as a container with defined boundaries. . . . The way we schedule events also reflects the urgent and precise way we deal with time. We expect classes to start on time (within a minute or so), and when they don't we wait only so long (20 minutes at the most) before leaving."[82]

You can use time for psychological effect. The student who is always late may be communicating considerable negative information. He is really not interested in this class or doesn't respect the instructor. You will probably not arrive too early for a date or party because this might make you appear too eager. If you dent the family car, you might wait for the right time to tell your parents about it. Your control of time, then, is an important form of nonverbal communication. The higher your status, the more control you have over your time. A parent can interrupt children's play to have them eat dinner or to make them go to bed far earlier than they want. Professionals in our society often make others wait for them.

Time differs greatly from one culture to another. People in the United States regard 20 minutes to an hour as being fashionably late, but suppose you were invited to a party in Venezuela, and the host said it would begin about 8 P.M. If you arrived at that time, you would be the only one there—the Venezuelans wouldn't arrive until 9 or 10 P.M. When interacting with people from different cultures, simply assume that their sense of time is different from yours.

Manners

Manners are simply a way of doing anything. You often hear it referred to as one's demeanor, personal carriage, general mode of conduct, or proper etiquette, and attached adjectives may be polite, civil, or well-bred. Businesses had become increasingly informal in dress and attitude as a result of the two-decade influence of Silicon Valley, but the corporate world has changed by desiring more decorum and savoir faire. Etiquette (manners) may not come easily for a generation that wears flip-flops, but that doesn't mean this type of nonverbal communication doesn't matter. More will be discussed on manners in the chapter, "Communicating Professionally and Employment Interviews," available online."

Your manners may be revealed in the way you dress. What is appropriate for a corporation in New York may be very different from what is appropriate for a small office in the Southwest. They may be revealed in your posture, demeanor, conversational mannerisms, or gestures. They may be revealed, too, in your e-mail. E-mail is public communication; thus, don't send private messages, flame a recipient, or let your grievances show. Be careful about your grammar and word choice. Proofread your messages carefully, and avoid digital slang.

Manners vary from business to business just as they do from culture to culture. The point here is not to review the rules of proper manners; there are books that do that. The point, instead, is to call your attention to this type of nonverbal communication and to alert you to what Peter Post, a director of the Emily Post Institute, has said, "Your actions outside of work affect you at work, whether you like it or not. It doesn't turn off at 5 P.M."[83]—just as it doesn't turn off when you sit down at your computer to chat with your friends.

Silence

"In human intercourse," wrote Henry David Thoreau, "the tragedy begins, not when there is misunderstanding about words, but when silence is not understood." You have undoubtedly walked across campus with a relationship partner, not saying a word, but enjoying just being together and appreciating the wonderful silence. Or, you're talking with someone, and you hear a story that is obviously and overtly not true, and instead of responding in any way, you simply say nothing at all. Martin Sawdon, in his essay, "Remaining Silent: Top 10 Reasons for Doing So," offers the following: "1. When words are about to be spoken in anger and might be regretted. 2. When it has been said before and is not worth repeating. 3. To justify one's behavior, of which one is not proud, by citing someone else's. 4. To avoid inflicting unconstructive criticism. 5. When silence resonates and words are empty. 6. When honorable actions are more expressive than words. 7. After indicating graciously that the question oversteps one's boundaries. 8. When the moment is perfect without words. 9. When the heart is full and speaking would be a drain. 10. When to speak would only be to boast."[84] Chris Acheson (2007),[85] based on his scholarly review of research on silence, acknowledges the positive and sometimes powerful uses of silences in certain contexts that U.S. Americans increasingly recognize.

It must be stated, too, as Chris Acheson points out, that there are contexts when silence is seen as completely negative. In law, pleading the Fifth equates silence with guilt, and in politics, silence by politicians is often viewed as hiding something or even lying.[86]

Functions of Nonverbal Communication

In his article "Words on Trial" ("Department of Linguistics," *The New Yorker*, July 23, 2012), Jack Hitt cites Robert Leonard, a forensic linguist who is head of the linguistics program at Hofstra University on Long Island:

> According to Leonard, words serve as catalysts, setting off sparks of potential meaning that the listener organizes into more specific meaning by observing facial expressions, body language, and other redundant cues. We then employ another powerful tool: prior experience and the storehouse of narratives that each of us carries—what linguists call 'schema.' To every exchange we bring unconscious scripts; as any given sentence unspools, we readjust the schema to make better sense of what we are hearing (p. 27).

When you read about the functions of nonverbal communication in this section, keep in mind the way each function feeds into people's prior experience, storehouse of narratives, and matrix of emotions—their "schema."

Nonverbal communication has four functions. Nonverbal cues **complement** a verbal message by adding to its meaning. When you are talking to someone with a problem, for example, you might say, "I'm really sorry," and complement the message with a pat on the shoulder or a hug.

Nonverbal cues also **regulate** verbal communication. How would your boss or one of your teachers tell you that it's time for a meeting to end? He or she might do something obvious, like getting out of the chair, or something more subtle, like arranging papers on the desk, to communicate to you that the conversation is over.

Nonverbal messages can also **substitute** for verbal messages. Your instructor looks up, stares specifically at a couple of class members who are talking, then waits a couple of seconds until everyone is quiet before she begins to speak. Her look says, "All right, everyone be quiet now. It's time to begin."

STRATEGIC FLEXIBILITY

Thinking before acting (or emoting) is the basis for effective strategic flexibility because it requires thinking to anticipate, assess, evaluate, select, and properly apply your skills and behaviors. It is more likely that your strategies will be effective if you can control your initial emotional responses.

Often, nonverbal messages **accent** what you are saying. The instructor's voice is strong and firm when she tells the class she will accept no late papers; the teenager leans forward while she is trying to persuade her parents that she needs a new dress.

The key to controlling and thus improving your nonverbal communication is self-awareness. When you are fully aware of the signals you send, you have a greater opportunity not just for controlling them but for evaluating them as well. When you notice you are sending signals that aren't what you intend, you can either suppress them or change them. It is like using strategic flexibility on a personal—or intrapersonal—level or taking **control** of your life and your behavior.

One way to begin controlling your nonverbal communication is to control your emotions. Emotions often arise spontaneously and quickly—and produce subconscious (or unconscious) responses. But when you are aware of your emotions, you can begin to produce a counterresponse to mask, control, or subdue your actual reaction. For example, when someone asks you at the last minute how he or she looks, rather than express your surprise at what you consider to be an outrageous outfit, you mask your reaction.

Because you produce your emotions, you can control them. Once you are thinking rather than allowing your behavior to be at the mercy of your spontaneous feelings, you can better evaluate situations and consciously provide the responses you consider to be most appropriate.

Judging Honesty by Nonverbal Communication

For some time it has been thought that liars could be detected through their nonverbal communication. For example, it was thought liars would avert their eyes in an interview on average more than people telling the truth, or they would fidget, sweat, or slump in their chairs. Along with some of those cues, it was thought that liars produced distinct, fleeting changes in expression as well. With all of these indicators, a close examination of the nonverbal communication of liars, it was thought, would reveal their deception.[87]

It may come as a surprise as well that brain-imaging machines cannot reliably distinguish a doctored story from a truthful one. The same is true for polygraph tests, which track changes in physiology as an indirect method of detection.[88]

So what, you might ask, is the method for separating truth from fiction? As it turns out, it isn't nonverbal cues at all nor anything that technology has to offer. The key is in the content. According to Benedict Carey's article, "Judging Honesty by Words Not Fidgets," published in the *New York Times* (May 12, 2009), citing Kevin Colwell, a psychologist at Southern Connecticut State University, who advises police departments, Pentagon officials, and child protection workers, "people concocting a story prepare a script that is tight and lacking in detail." Carey goes on to say, "People telling the truth have no script, and tend to recall more extraneous details and may even make mistakes. They are sloppier."[89]

Improving Your Nonverbal Communication

Following are some questions to ask about your nonverbal communication.

How Do People React to You?

www.mhhe.com/hybels11e >

View "Nonverbal Messages,"
Video clip.

Do people ever react to you in a way that surprises you? You may be sending nonverbal messages that are being interpreted differently from the way you intended. For example, you may intend to tease someone but instead hurt his or her feelings. If you see that the person looks upset, you have a chance to explain what you really meant.

Can Videotapes Help Your Nonverbal Communication?

Videotape can tell you a great deal about behaviors you were not aware of and even some that you want to get rid of. Here are just a few items that you might look for when you see your tape.[90]

Eye contact. Since eye contact signals interest in others, increases credibility, and opens the flow of communication by conveying interest, concern, and warmth, make certain yours is comfortable and natural, but direct.

Facial expressions. Your face transmits happiness, friendliness, warmth, liking, and affiliation; thus, it pays to smile frequently. By smiling you will be perceived as more likable, friendly, warm, and approachable.

Gestures. Being lively and animated captures others' attention, makes your information more interesting, and provides conversational positive reinforcement.

Posture and body orientation. Posture and body orientation includes the way you walk, talk, stand, and sit. By standing erect, but not rigid, and by leaning slightly forward, you will communicate that you are approachable, receptive, and friendly.

Proximity. Cultural norms dictate the distances you need to stand for interacting with others. By increasing your proximity to others when in conversation, but not excessively, you not only make better eye contact, but you become more sensitive to the feedback of others.

Paralinguistics. You need to modulate your voice by changing such features as tone, pitch, rhythm, timbre, loudness, and inflection. Make sure you don't use a dull or boring voice.

Humor. When you reveal a willingness to laugh, you foster an inviting, warm, and friendly conversational environment. Laughter also releases stress and tension.

Is Your Nonverbal Communication Appropriate to the Role You Are Playing?

Like your language, your nonverbal communication should change as you play different roles. Observe other people in their roles. How much of their communication is nonverbal? What kind of nonverbal communication does a good teacher show? Who don't you want to be like? Is it their nonverbal behavior that turns you off? Do you do any of the same things? Can you stop doing them?

How Do You Use Your Space?

What messages are you sending out through the posters on your walls? Through the cuddly animals on your dresser? How tidy is your space? How much space do you occupy? Are you a sprawler, or do you keep your arms close to your body and your legs together? Are you conscious of certain space as "belonging" to you? Is it important that you have some spaces that you can call your own? What does the way you regard space tell others about you?

How Do You Use Time?

Are you on time or always late? Are you a procrastinator, leaving everything until the last minute?

If your use of time creates a bad impression, is it possible for you to change your ways?

When you look at all the things you communicate about yourself nonverbally, you will see that you should give nonverbal communication attention and care. Although nonverbal behavior is difficult to change, it can be done, especially if you are aware of how you use it.

Are You Aware of Nonverbal Communication?

How nonverbally aware are you? For each statement circle the numerical score that best represents your nonverbal awareness using the following scale: 7 = Outstanding; 6 = Excellent; 5 = Very good; 4 = Average (good); 3 = Fair; 2 = Poor; 1 = Minimal ability; 0 = No ability demonstrated.

1. I look others directly in the eye when communicating with them.   7 6 5 4 3 2 1 0
2. I gesture with my hands and arms when communicating.   7 6 5 4 3 2 1 0
3. I turn my body fully toward the person with whom I am speaking.   7 6 5 4 3 2 1 0
4. I use a pleasant, appropriate tone of voice when speaking to others.   7 6 5 4 3 2 1 0
5. I use a vocal volume that is appropriate when speaking to others.   7 6 5 4 3 2 1 0
6. When listening to others, I notice and respond to their nonverbal responses to me—their vocal tone, eye contact, facial expressions, posture, gestures, and body movement.   7 6 5 4 3 2 1 0
7. When listening to others, I am quiet when they are talking and allow them to express their ideas without interruption.   7 6 5 4 3 2 1 0
8. When listening to another person, I smile when the person uses humor, and I nod at appropriate times.   7 6 5 4 3 2 1 0
9. When listening to another person, I reveal my full support and attention through my nonverbal cues.   7 6 5 4 3 2 1 0
10. I feel the nonverbal cues I use when speaking, and those I use in responding to others when they are speaking, reveal my comfort, poise, and confidence as an effective communicator.   7 6 5 4 3 2 1 0

TOTAL POINTS: _____

Go to Online Learning Center at **www.mhhe.com/hybels11e** to see your results and learn how to evaluate your attitudes and feelings.

www.mhhe.com/hybels11e >

Summary

Nonverbal communication is information that is communicated without using words. There are nonverbal elements embedded in every element in the communication model. Your degree of fluency in your native language and your level of awareness of nonverbal components are likely to result in greater strategic flexibility.

You send more messages through nonverbal communication than you do through verbal communication, and although they often reinforce each other, there are numerous differences between them. One clear difference is in the way the brain processes the information. In the nonverbal realm, it is a holistic phenomenon in which clues hit you all at once, and you form an impression larger than their sum.

There are six characteristics of nonverbal communication: It is unique to the culture to which you belong; verbal and nonverbal communication may be in conflict with one another; much nonverbal communication operates at a subconscious level; your nonverbal communication shows your feelings and attitudes; nonverbal communication varies by gender; and nonverbal communication displays power.

Expectancy violation theory (EVT) suggests that there are ways of behaving that can be expected, but when someone violates expectations, that violation can be viewed positively or negatively depending, in part, on how much you like the other person. EVT influences the outcome of communications, and the three factors that influence expectations are communicator characteristics, relational characteristics, and context.

There are many different types of nonverbal communication. They include paralanguage, body movement, facial expressions, eye messages, attractiveness (which includes body image as well as elective and nonelective characteristics), clothing, body adornment, space and distance, touch, time, smell, and manners. In the section on "Silence," ten reasons are given for remaining silent, and research on silence acknowledges both the positive and sometimes powerful uses of silence as well as those times when silence is completely negative. In each case, there are cultural variations in what is acceptable and unacceptable practice.

Nonverbal communication serves important functions. It can complement, regulate, substitute for, or accent a verbal message. The key to controlling your nonverbal communication is self-awareness. One way to begin controlling it is to control your emotions. What you need to do is think before you express your feelings. Although it has often been thought that you can detect liars through their nonverbal communication and that brain-imaging machines can detect lying, both have proven inadequate. The key is in the content of what is said. That is, people telling the truth have no script and tend to recall more extraneous details and even make mistakes. Truth tellers are sloppier in the telling of their stories.

One way of evaluating your nonverbal communication is to ask some questions about how you use it: How do people react to you? Can you use videotapes to improve your nonverbal communication? How do you use your space? How do you use time? The answers to these questions will indicate areas in which you can improve.

Key Terms and Concepts

Use the Online Learning Center at www.mhhe.com/hybels11e to further your understanding of the following terms.

Accent 116	Chronemics 114	Displays of feelings 103
Adaptors 104	Complement 115	Elective characteristics 105
Anosmia 113	Control 116	Emblems 103
Attractiveness 105	Convergence 102	Expectancy violation theory 101
Body adornment 108	Conversation management 96	Eye messages 104
Body movement (kinesics) 103	Costumes 108	Facial expressions 104

Questions to Review

1. What are some of the nonverbal components in each of the elements of the model of communication?

2. In what ways does nonverbal communication contribute to your ability to be strategically flexible?

3. In what ways do verbal and nonverbal communication differ, and of what value is knowing these differences?

4. In what ways does one's culture influence his or her nonverbal communication?

5. What is it called when verbal and nonverbal messages conflict? Give an example of this.

6. In what ways does nonverbal communication vary by gender?

7. What is expectancy violation theory, and what is its value?

8. What are the different types of nonverbal communication, and what is an example of each type that clearly distinguishes it as the type it is designed to reveal?

9. What is paralanguage? What are the vocal qualities that contribute to paralanguage?

10. Can you give an example of nonverbal communication in each of the following body movements: Emblems? Illustrators? Regulators? Displays of feeling? Adaptors?

11. What does clothing communicate about you? How do the following kinds of clothing differ: Uniforms? Occupational dress? Leisure clothing? Costumes?

12. What is the study of space and distance called? What are the four distance zones, and how do they differ?

13. What are the eight distinct emotions touch can communicate?

14. What is, perhaps, the most significant research discovery regarding touch?

15. What are the five different categories of touch behavior? Give an example of each.

16. What are the benefits of a sense of smell?

17. Can you give an example of how one's use of time communicates status? How does the use of time differ from culture to culture?

18. What are the reasons for remaining silent, and is it a positive or negative factor in nonverbal communication?

19. What are the functions of nonverbal communication, and how does each one relate to verbal communication?

20. To what extent is nonverbal communication valuable for detecting liars?

21. How would you go about improving your nonverbal communication?

Go to the self-quizzes on the Online Learning Center at www.mhhe.com/hybels11e to test your knowledge of the chapter contents.

CHAPTER FIVE

Listening

After reading this chapter, you should be able to:

- Distinguish among the elements of the Integrative Listening Model (ILM).

- Differentiate and give an example of each of the four listening styles.

- Clarify the elements most likely to have a negative effect on effective listening.

- Distinguish among the six different types of listening and why active listening is a constant characteristic of each.

- Explain how you can talk so others will listen.

THE ASSIGNMENT IN MY SOCIAL WORK CLASS WAS TO WRITE A paper, but the subject for the paper surprised me. Class members were to select someone in their lives who was well-liked and respected, ask their permission to shadow and observe them, then write a report that focused specifically on their listening skills. For my subject, I selected one of my teachers from high school who everyone respected, admired, and liked, and, with her permission, I was allowed to sit in all of her classes for a day, accompany her to lunch, and chat with her at the end of the school day. It was truly an amazing and eye-opening experience. In my paper I discussed both her listening skills and the nonverbal behavior that accompanied those skills.

The qualities that Mrs. Jahmelia Jackson revealed startled me, because I discovered that most of what she did was listen effectively, and if there was one characteristic that stood out above *all* others, it was how she always made others feel important. She did this first and foremost by taking the time to listen carefully and show support for those who shared their story with her. Not only was she open and honest with them, but she was open, too, about learning from them, and she would always express an interest in what they were telling her.

When she responded to others she remained neutral and nonjudgmental, and her empathy appeared both sincere and honest. She gave others genuine acceptance, respect, and encouragement.

Because of her strong, obvious, and supportive qualities, everyone felt they had a bond with her. She always talked less and listened more, limited the advice she gave, validated others' concerns and their willingness to express their feelings, and by asking open-ended questions, clarified what was being said. Thus, she encouraged others to share more information and in greater detail. How self-confirming and self-validating is that for those who spoke with her?

Much of her behavior, as I observed her, was nonverbal, not verbal. That is, she revealed a relaxed body style, maintained excellent eye contact, nodded her head to reaffirm what she was hearing, smiled and expressed that she understood whomever talked with her, and she never crossed her arms or legs, thus avoiding any barrier between her and them.

To me, this was one of *the* most successful, productive, informative, and instructive assignments I have ever been given, and I only hope that I will be able to model the kind of behavior I witnessed. It was easy to see why Mrs. Jahmelia Jackson was considered such an outstanding teacher and human being.

Mrs. Jahmelia Jackson possessed something that Harold H. Saunders, the founder and president of the International Institute for Sustained Dialogue, would call "dialogue." In "We Need to Talk" (*Vital Speeches of the Day*, August 2011, p. 283), he defined it this way: "First, dialogue is not about talking. It's about listening. Dialogue is one person listening carefully and deeply enough to another to be changed by what he or she hears.

"Second, the openness of one person to another makes dialogue the essence of genuine relationship" (p. 283).

Why is this so? Because, writes Rick Kirschner, in his book *How to Click With People* (NY: Hyperion, 2011), "When you help people feel heard and understood, they appreciate you for hearing them out. And when you listen well to what others say, they want to be around you. In this way," as Mrs. Jahmelia Jackson clearly knows, "your influence in their lives will increase" (p. 32).

The **Integrative Listening Model (ILM)** provides a framework for assessing listening both systematically and developmentally. **Listening** includes the processes of listening preparation, receiving, constructing meaning, responding, and remembering.[1] Each of these processes will be discussed in the next sections, as well as how this framework of listening relates to the framework established in Chapter 1 for strategic flexibility. In addition, the process of remembering is discussed more fully in a separate section.

You may think listening is a concept—an abstract notion or idea—but if you think of it instead as a process—a **method** of operating—it will be easier not just to apply it to your life, but for you to visualize and plan, throughout the descriptions, exactly what **you** can do to improve your listening ability. That is, after all, what this chapter is all about—improving your ability to listen as one part of communicating more effectively.

The Role of Listening in Communicating Effectively and Strategic Flexibility (SF)

When you reexamine Figure 1-1, "The Elements of Communication," in Chapter 1, The Communication Process, you will notice that there is no element labeled "listening." It is not mentioned there as one of the elements of communication, and yet, you know intuitively that listening is an essential component of effective communication. Now look at Figure 5-1.

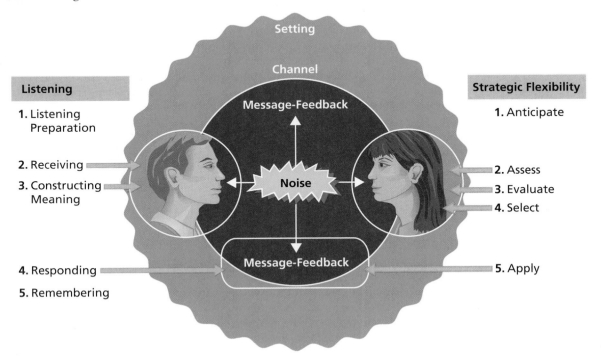

Figure 5-1
Listening, Strategic Flexibility, and the Model of Communication

ATTENTION!

Compare and Contrast

Notice that listening is part of perception, discussed in Chapter 2, "Self, Perception, and Communication." It is one of the five senses (touch, taste, smell, hearing, and sight) and one way we have for gathering sensory cues. What are the differences between the three steps of the process of perception (selecting, organizing, and interpreting) and the five steps of the listening process? Where are they different, and where are they the same?

When you look closely at the ILM framework for listening previously discussed, you realize that listening—just like strategic flexibility—actually begins *before* the elements contained in the model. **Listening preparation** includes all the physical, mental, and behavioral aspects that create a readiness to listen. These are the same aspects that you bring to any communication situation as you **anticipate** (SF) the various needs and requirements likely to arise.

Second, according to the ILM framework, listening involves the element of receiving. This is where the process of listening begins to relate to the elements in the model of communication. **Receiving** is the process of taking in, acquiring, or accepting. It occurs through the various senses (hearing, seeing, smelling, touching, and tasting) and happens within sender-receivers as they receive all the cues, signals, and impulses. Listening is one part of the whole perceptual process discussed in Chapter 2, Self, Perception, and Communication. It is similar to, but not the same as, the **assessment** stage of strategic flexibility in which all the factors, elements, and conditions of situations are considered. Assessment assumes the receiving process has taken place.

There is an important distinction between hearing and listening that takes place at the receiving portion of the framework. You hear sounds—such as words and the way they are spoken—but when you listen, you respond to much more. Hearing is a physiological process involving the various parts of the ear, whereas listening is a more complicated perceptual process involving your total response to others, including verbal as well as nonverbal communication.

Receiving messages is accomplished with your ears in conjunction with your other four senses, and it involves hearing, *not* listening. It is only when you move to the next part of the framework that listening occurs.

Third, according to the framework, listening involves constructing meaning. **Constructing meaning** is the complicated and unique process of making sense of the cues, signals, and impulses received. It goes on in the brains of sender-receivers. A unique aspect of human beings is the ability to make meaning. Although you often think of listening as connected with hearing alone, it usually requires the full and active use of all the senses. For example, let's say that you are at a crowded party with a potential romantic partner. Your partner utters the words "I love you," which you hear quite clearly above the sounds of the people and music around you, but you don't fully understand why those words were said in this context, nor what their full meaning might be. You see that your partner may have had too much to drink, you smell the odor of beer, your partner's touch appears to be suggestive, and the kiss revealed the taste of beer. You heard the words, but you can see that only when all the senses come into play can you construct meaning from those words.

One significant part of constructing meaning involves focusing your attention on particular stimuli. In the "I love you" example, notice how the words rang out loud and clear above the sounds of the people and music around you. **Selective attention** is the ability to focus perception. Although you may be able to focus your attention in specific ways, most people's attention spans are very short. Few people, for example, can give full attention to a message for more than 20 seconds.[2] Something in the message reminds you of something else, or you disagree with the message and let your mind wander. Fortunately, you are able to quickly refocus your attention on the message, but every listener and speaker should be aware of just how easily attention can go astray.

As another part of constructing meaning, you must assign meaning to the cues, signals, and impulses—deciding what in the message is relevant and how it relates to what you already know. As Seth Horowitz, a neuroscientist, said in his book *The Universal Sense* (NY: Bloomsbury, 2012), "If you paid equal attention to everything, with no automatic ability to parse out what was relevant to your needs, you would soon be overwhelmed by trivia both external and internal" (p. 105). Assigning meaning is an important process before responding because you must weigh what the speaker has said against the personal beliefs you hold, question the speaker's motives, wonder what has been omitted, or even challenge the validity of the ideas. As in the "I love you" example, you may understand *what* was said, but do you fully understand *how* it was said? When you assign meaning, you give meaning to the speaker's tone of voice, gestures, and facial expressions as much as you do to his or her words.[3]

Constructing meaning involves two steps in the strategic flexibility process, as you can see in Figure 5-1. There is no way to make sense of cues, signals, and impulses if **evaluation** (SF)—determining the value and worth of the factors, elements, and conditions—fails to occur at the same time. This is the only way to determine how all those cues, signals, and impulses bear on your own skills and abilities. Constructing meaning also involves **selection** (SF): carefully selecting from your repertoire of available skills and behaviors those likely to have the greatest impact on the current (and future) situations.

Fourth, according to the ILM framework, listening involves responding. **Responding** means using spoken or nonverbal messages to exchange ideas or convey information. In strategic flexibility it is the same as **applying**—with the appropriate care, concern, and attention to all the factors that are likely to be affected, including any ethical considerations that may be appropriate—to apply the skills and behaviors you have selected.

From the "I love you" example think about all the potential nonverbal elements that could affect how you might respond: the clothing or dress of the other person; the gestures made while speaking the words; the body movement, posture, and touch; and, perhaps, most important, the way the words were spoken. An additional element might be the setting in which all of this takes place. What would be the appropriate response? What would you say to the other person who has just said, "I love you"?

The fifth stage of the listening process is **remembering**, as shown in Figure 5-2. Remembering is done throughout the listening process and not just as a separate fifth step. A number of strategies that will help ensure that information is being learned well and stored securely in your memory system are discussed in the next section.

In strategic flexibility, the process is complete when the steps of reassessment and reevaluation have taken place. This is just as important in the listening process. You simply need to look back at what has taken place and determine its value, worth, success, effectiveness, or efficiency in light of what you expected.

To review, the listening process has five stages: listening preparation, receiving, constructing meaning, responding, and remembering. Figure 5-2 shows these five stages and offers examples to illustrate how they might occur.

Often, all of these aspects of the framework for listening occur instantaneously, sometimes without conscious effort. Understanding these aspects may help you assess if and where the process breaks down. It may help you slow down the process so that all the information you need can be obtained. Sometimes, for example, patience allows time for more observation and the collection of more information. It may also help you better understand why others may not understand what you say. A pause, for example, may allow time to reflect on what and how you said something but, too, on the full meaning of the other's response.

Figure 5-2
The Listening Process

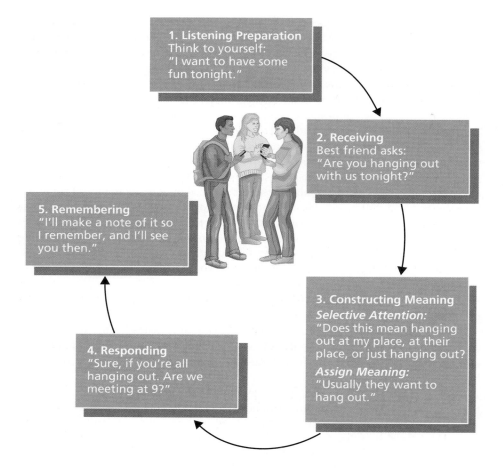

1. **Listening Preparation**
Think to yourself:
"I want to have some
fun tonight."

2. **Receiving**
Best friend asks:
"Are you hanging out
with us tonight?"

3. **Constructing Meaning**
Selective Attention:
"Does this mean hanging
out at my place, at their
place, or just hanging out?
Assign Meaning:
"Usually they want to
hang out."

4. **Responding**
"Sure, if you're all
hanging out. Are we
meeting at 9?"

5. **Remembering**
"I'll make a note of it so
I remember, and I'll see
you then."

Remembering Information

There are a number of techniques useful for remembering information, but there is no single right way or best way to improve your memory. All techniques require your motivation and dedication to the task, because when you are motivated, you concentrate harder, and concentration makes information easier to remember. Motivation is a key; using mnemonic devices (used for remembering information that is to be memorized, but not necessarily understood) is unlikely to create any long-term effect. Information that is simple, clear, and vivid is more easily remembered as is anything that is unusual, funny, or personal.

There are four major techniques. The first is organization. Find a pattern, structure, order, plan, format, or framework. The second is association. Make the things you want to remember relate to one another or to categories you already understand. Group them, if possible. The third technique is visualization. Picturing what you want to remember creates a strong, vivid memory of it. The fourth is repetition. When you repeat ideas, you burn them into your memory. Reading them into a tape recorder, for example, and listening to them repeatedly implants them by sheer repetition. Other techniques often associated with assisting memory include creating rhymes, acronyms, and abbreviations.

Our purpose is not to be unnecessarily redundant, but it is important to remember—as previously noted—that remembering is done throughout the listening process and not just as a separate fifth step. Much of the effectiveness of remembering information will depend on the notes you take, because notes will reduce the amount of information. Also, good notes will make it easier to use the memory techniques just outlined.

Note-Taking Skills

Just as active listening is essential to effective note taking, effective note taking is essential to remembering information. There are those who recommend that you not take notes so you can focus your attention wholly on what the speaker is saying. If you are blessed with a great memory, this method may work for you. There are others who record a lecture so they can give it their full attention while it is occurring, then write notes from the recording. The problem with recording lectures is finding the time to listen to the recording. Taking notes—whenever you do it—has four benefits. First, it will help you remember the information. Second, it will help you organize what the speaker is saying. Third, it may aid in your understanding of the information. Fourth, it is likely to require you to think.

Having been a large-group lecturer for the basic speech communication course for many years, I (Richard) was often asked how to take notes in my lectures. Here is the essence of my advice:

- Sit where you can easily see and hear the lecturer. Also, sit where you can see the board and any computer-generated images that might be shown.

- Do not try to write out everything that is said. Think before you write, but don't get behind. If you get behind, leave a blank where you are (to be filled in later, if possible), and move ahead to where your lecturer is right now.

- Feel free to record the lectures using a small, inconspicuous recorder. If you plan to do this, ask lecturers for their permission before making a recording. If you record, make sure you write down everything on the board or slides in your notes.

- Jot down notes of the main and minor points of the lecture. Often, supporting material can be filled in later.

- Listen carefully for verbal or nonverbal cues that indicate key or essential points.

- Write legibly, and use abbreviations wherever possible. If you cannot write clearly enough so that you can understand your writing later, make certain you allow time to decipher your notes before they grow cold. Reviewing notes later that make no sense can be disheartening.

- If you record the lecture, compare your notes of the main and minor points with the information on the tape, as you listen a second time. Taking notes and recording at the same time will help you remember the information better.

- Fill in any details missed the first time through as you listen to the recording, but do not copy down everything.

- Annotate and highlight any key points or essential information.

- If you did not record the lecture, compare and discuss your comprehension and notes with other students.

ATTENTION!

How to Remember Information

1. Organize the material. Find a pattern, structure, plan, format, or framework.

2. Associate the material with things you already understand.

3. Picture what you want to remember to create a strong, clear, vivid memory of it.

4. Repeat the ideas over and over to implant them in your memory bank.

- Review your notes shortly after the lecture to reinforce both your memory and understanding of the contents.

- Once you have your notes reduced to the essence of the lecture, review them several times just before the examination.

If you find information particularly difficult or challenging, and you must remember it for an examination, once you have reduced your notes to their essence, read them into a recorder, as mentioned in the previous section. Then listen to your notes in your car, at home in your room, or whenever a spare moment occurs. Listening to them over and over will help you learn the material thoroughly. If you think this level of commitment—actually following all these recommendations—is too much for you, it might help you to understand that it all depends on what you want out of college. A college education is what you make of it.

Listening Styles

Most of you have discovered, after being in school for so many years, that there are different ways of learning and different ways of listening. Researchers have identified four different kinds of listening styles.[4] In a **people listening style,** you are concerned with the other person's feelings. You seek out common interests with others and respond to emotions. This listening is common among couples, families, and best friends.

In an **action listening style,** you want precise, error-free presentations, and you are likely to be impatient with disorganization. A boss, for example, might ask for a report from one of the division heads on how the company is doing. She would expect this report to be focused and to the point.

In a **content listening style,** you prefer complex and challenging information. Since this information is generally abstract, you can listen without emotional involvement and then evaluate information before you make a judgment. A doctor might, for example, ask for information from his colleagues on how a particular patient should be treated. Because of his training and experience he will not have difficulty understanding a complex medical explanation.

The final style is **time-style listening.** In this style, you prefer brief and hurried interaction with others and often let others know how much time they have to make the point. Newspeople, getting ready for a television newscast, need to get information quickly and efficiently because they are always working against the clock, so they are likely to be time-style listeners.

For the most part, you do not have just one listening style—although you may prefer one over some of the others. You listen in all the ways discussed here depending on the circumstances. To a roommate, for example, you will use a people style, for a group project you may reveal an action listening style, in a lecture it may be a content listening style, and racing out to run errands in a short amount of time, you may adopt a time-style method of listening before you go.

The most skillful listeners are able to adapt their listening styles to the circumstances. If you haven't learned to do this, you will have a problem in some of your interactions with others. For example, when a person is complaining about a co-worker, she would probably prefer a people-style listener. Yet her boss, who is short of time, wants her to state her problem, listen to his suggestions, and then leave his office—a reaction that will leave her feeling unsatisfied.

STRATEGIC FLEXIBILITY

Because of your quick ability to anticipate, assess, evaluate, and select from your repertoire of available skills and behaviors, you will be able to adapt your listening style to the circumstances.

In his book *Do Nothing! How to Stop Overmanaging and Become a Great Leader*, J. Keith Murnighan, a professor at the Kellogg School of Management at Northwestern University, discusses the value of active listening:

> The beauty of active listening is that it helps overcome the fact that leaders and team members, like any other pair of people, are not always perfect communicators or perfect listeners: either or both of them may be distracted, half listening, or thinking about something else. Also, if there is any tension between them, they may be focused on getting ready for an argument, thinking about how they can win it rather than listening carefully.
>
> Active listening encourages listeners to pay attention so they can repeat, in their own words, what the speaker has just said. It also encourages speakers to be clear and complete so they can limit the number of their back-and-forth exchanges. The two communicators do not need to agree on the importance of a particular job; they just have to understand it and know they both understand it (p. 48).

Source: J. Keith Murnighan. (2012). *Do Nothing! How to Stop Overmanaging and Become a Great Leader.* New York: Portfolio/Penguin.

Questions

1. Murnighan lists three benefits of active listening: 1) It encourages people to think about how their listeners can best hear their ideas, 2) it pushes both people to listen carefully, and 3) it helps avoid misunderstandings. Can you think of additional benefits?

2. In what specific ways does active listening contribute to communicating effectively?

3. If you were talking with a person about critical information, and the other person was not listening actively, what techniques could you use to encourage him or her to engage in active listening?

When you work with people, it's important that you be aware of their listening styles. For example, if you want some critical reaction to a paper you have just written, a content-style listener will be more helpful than a people-style listener because the people listener wouldn't want to hurt your feelings by pointing out your mistakes.

Some research shows that a person's listening style might depend on the culture he or she comes from. One study that compared American, German, and Israeli speakers found that Americans were the most people centered and were likely to pay careful attention to the feelings of the people they were talking to, while Israelis concentrated more on the accuracy of the messages. Germans were the most active listeners and often interspersed questions as they listened.[5]

Culture and Listening

More and more, intercultural encounters will become an important part of your everyday life whether it is in casual encounters, business transactions, interviews, or telephone conversations. Much of the misunderstanding in such encounters can be traced to problems in listening, and when experiencing such problems it is essential that you demonstrate both empathy and sensitivity to cultural differences.

As we will discuss in Chapter 9, intercultural communication often requires that you adjust the ways you approach fundamental aspects of communication—aspects that you may consider normal. For example, you may have to adjust your vocabulary. Both colloquial language and figures of speech often confuse those from other cultures. "The plan was really screwed up," could be restated as "The plan failed completely." Another adjustment might include the elimination of poetic language such as the use of metaphors and literary examples.

There are other adjustments as well. You may need to simplify your grammar. The complex grammar that frequently results from long sentences needs to be altered. Short sentences, for example, and simple grammar can be used instead. Informal communication styles may confuse nonnative speakers who learned more formal English in school; thus, choosing a more formal style may help. Referring to culture-specific rituals and activities may be confusing, too.

Intercultural communication interactions are not always marked by misunderstanding, confusion, and hurt feelings. Often, however, varying degrees of misunderstanding, confusion, and hurt feelings do interfere. For example, the British find it rude and manipulative to be asked their full names. Americans, on the other hand, seek others' full names as a way of showing friendship. To be aware of potential misunderstandings is the first step toward adapting and adjusting your communication.

Lack of knowledge, insufficient language, and even lack of sureness about the conventions that underlie the use of language in intercultural situations create difficulty. For example, a convention the Japanese are known for is gracious apologies, even at the slightest mishap, and even when the fault is not theirs. In a New York supermarket, a member of the Japanese culture had her shopping cart bumped by another shopper's cart, and turned immediately to say "Oh, sorry," even though it wasn't her fault.

Willingness to ask questions, seek clarification, admit errors and difficulties, and reveal empathy will help resolve many intercultural communication problems. Often, you need to understand that using your own cultural rules, even when speaking to someone from a different culture, may not just be inappropriate, but it may offend, too. The more you know and the greater your willingness to achieve accurate, effective communication, the better your chance of being both an effective listener and communicator.

Gender and Listening

Anyone who has had some experience in the world might suspect that men and women listen differently. For example, how often have you heard the complaint, "My boyfriend/husband doesn't listen to me" or "You never listen to me"?

Scholars who have studied communication between men and women have discovered that men and women have different listening styles. In the study of cultural listening styles mentioned earlier, the researchers found that in all three cultures (American, German, and Israeli) women were more likely to be people listeners than were men.[6]

Deborah Tannen, a linguist whose work is discussed in Chapter 3, "Verbal Communication," maintains that men and women come from different communication cultures: Women are interested in relationships and networking, while men are more interested in competitive communication.[7] This theory explains why a husband does not show much interest when his wife tells him about two people who were quarreling at her work. By the same token, the wife pays little attention when her husband talks about the batting averages of some of the players in the major leagues.

Tannen has also found that when men and women talk, women are more likely to be the listeners. Curious about how long this communication behavior has existed, Tannen went back to the literature of earlier times. She found that little has changed over the ages: In Shakespeare's sixteenth-century *Julius Caesar,* Portia begs Brutus to talk to her and not to keep his secrets from her. Tannen says that the culture of boys is based on status and that to maintain their status boys will hold the center of attention by boasting and telling jokes or fascinating stories; the same thing was true of the hero of *Beowulf,* a circa eighth-century saga.[8]

One problem women have to face when they enter the executive or professional world is getting men to listen to them. When Sandra Day O'Connor, the first female Supreme Court justice, was asked what problems she had in her career, she replied that the greatest problem was not being listened to. Finally she found a technique that made people pay attention to her: "I taught myself early on to speak very slowly— enunciating every word—when I wanted someone's undivided attention."[9] Her strategy makes sense: When we find that someone's attention seems to be fading, we are inclined to talk faster.

Another mistake women are likely to make in a business setting is to smile and wait their turn instead of using the male tactic of jumping into the discussion when they have something to say. Men don't follow the female system of taking turns. Patricia O'Brien advises that if women want to be listened to at work they should sit at the middle of the conference table where they can't be ignored, speak with conviction, avoid disclaimers such as "I might not be right but. . . ," and go directly to the main point, omitting the details.[10]

The Difficulty of Listening

Andrew Newberg, a medical doctor and neuroscientist, in his book co-authored with Mark Robert Waldman, *Words Can Change Your Brain* (NY: Hudson Street Press, 2012), writes: "To listen deeply and fully, you must train your mind to stay focused on the person who is speaking their words, tone, gestures, facial cues—everything. It's a great gift to give to someone, since to be fully listened to and understood by others is the most commonly cited deep relationship or communication value" (p. 142).

As discussed in an earlier section, listening preparation includes all the physical, mental, and behavioral aspects that create a readiness to listen. There is far more in that statement than meets the eye. If listening was as natural, easy, and successful as it appears, there would be no need for a whole chapter on the topic. Physically, mentally, and behaviorally, most people are *not* ready to listen well. Figure 5-3 shows some of the factors that have a bearing on senders and receivers.

We take listening for granted, we think we already know what the other person is going to say, our ego gets in the way, we don't take the time to listen, and we exhibit no empathy. "Listening is even more difficult in today's interruption age," write Douglas Conant and Mette Norgaard in their book *Touch Points* (San Francisco: Jossey-Bass, 2011), "when we have become so accustomed to the constant stimulation that many of us have even developed ADT (attention deficit traits). Consequently," these authors continue, "after trying to pay attention for a couple of minutes, your mind starts drifting, your fingers start twitching, and you reach for your PDA" (p. 104). These authors reveal the difficulty of listening, but there is more.

One factor *not* depicted in Figure 5-3 as a barrier to effective listening and yet one that is widely experienced is message/information overload. It can be as simple as a single message carrying too much information at one time when you are prompted to say, "Hold it, hold it, please slow down. I'm not getting everything you're saying." Just as technological innovations such as email, voice mail, text messages, phone calls, meetings, business journals, faxes, memos, manuals, Web research, and more have increased information inundation at an office, information asphyxiation occurs in other arenas as well.

ATTENTION!

How Does Information Glut Affect You?

- You procrastinate.
- You waste your time.
- You delay important decisions.
- You become distracted from your primary responsibilities.
- You become tense.
- You get stressed out.
- There is a loss of job satisfaction.
- You become ill.
- Your personal relationships break down.

Figure 5-3
Some of the Many Factors That Can Be Barriers to Effective Listening

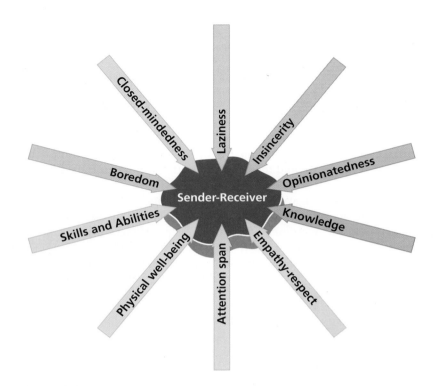

Reality Check
Most people don't think a lot about listening, and if they were asked, most would probably say they are effective listeners. What do you think? Do you have difficulty listening? Research has discovered that the six potentially important factors in listening include laziness, closed-mindedness, opinionatedness, insincerity, boredom, and inattentiveness. From your own personal experience, do these top six factors make sense? Do they seem logical? Overall, which of those six factors generally affects you the most? If you wanted to become a better listener, where would you start? By improving your skill in listening, what bearing do you think your improvement would have on communicating effectively? Would it make a difference? How?

Did you know that today one Sunday edition of the *New York Times* alone carries more information than the average 19th-century citizen accessed in a lifetime?[11] In addition to the Internet, cell phones, text messaging, newspapers, and magazines, there are billboards, advertising on the sides of buses, taxicabs, and some police vehicles, cable and satellite TV with dozens of channels, and an abundance of magazines displayed at the supermarket checkout.

What are the results of information glut? According to a survey published by Reuters (http://www.reuters.com) the results of information glut are procrastination and time wasting, the delaying of important decisions, distraction from primary responsibilities, tension, stress, loss of job satisfaction, illness, and the breakdown of personal relationships. When listening preparation involves physical, mental, and behavioral aspects, it should be clear that any one of these results of information glut can negatively affect listening outcomes—a paralysis of analysis.

There are many factors in addition to message/information overload that affect how effective listening will be. They are listed here in no particular order simply because at any given point in time, any one of them might be the cause (or result) of poor listening. Your attitude (tense, worried, anxious, or troubled), knowledge (comprehension, understanding, or expertise), and abilities or skills (adeptness, talent, or training) will be factors. Your state of mind is also important because listening is hard work. Laziness alone can affect your listening. The setting (environment, location, or position) might have an impact as well as how open-minded (unprejudiced, nonpartisan, neutral, nonjudgmental, nondiscriminatory, objective, broad-minded, or tolerant) you are. Your attention to the stimulus (some people have a very short attention span), empathy with the person or subject being discussed, and respect for the other person could have an effect. Also, your physical well-being matters. Being tired, hung over, or ill might have an effect just as much as if you are rushed, stressed, or tense.

Table 5-1   Factors in and Barriers to Effective Listening

Factors	Barriers
Laziness	Avoid listening if the subject is complex or difficult.
	Avoid listening because it takes too much time.
Closed-mindedness	Refuse to maintain a relaxing and agreeable environment.
	Refuse to relate to and benefit from the speaker's ideas.
Opinionatedness	Disagree or argue outwardly or inwardly with the speaker.
	Become emotional or excited when the speaker's views differ from yours.
Insincerity	Avoid eye contact while listening.
	Pay attention only to the speaker's word rather than the speaker's feelings.
Boredom	Lack interest in the speaker's subject.
	Become impatient with the speaker.
	Daydream or become preoccupied with something else when listening.
Inattentiveness	Concentrate on the speaker's mannerisms or delivery rather than on the message.
	Become distracted by noise from office equipment, telephone, other conversation, etc.

Source: From "A Factor Analysis of Barriers to Effective Listening" by Steven Golen in *Journal of Business Communication*: 27, 25–36 (Winter 1990). Reprinted by permission of the author.

There is an additional factor as well. Speakers speak at approximately 124 to 250 words per minute. Listeners listen at something greater than 600 words per minute. Some researchers have actually suggested that listening may occur at a rate of 1,000 to 3,000 words per minute. The point is, no matter whom you are listening to, they are speaking slower than you are listening. What do you do with the difference? What does anyone do with the difference between speech speed and thought speed? What you do with that difference may determine how effective you are as a listener, and suggestions will be provided in this chapter. Any wonder people don't listen well?

Steven Golen did some research on the factors in and barriers to effective listening.[12] Out of 23 potentially important factors in listening, the 6 listed in Table 5-1 are the ones that stood out. How these factors turn into barriers are listed as well. When you examine each of the barriers in Table 5-1, are they familiar? How many have you actually experienced?

Four other factors cause difficulty in listening: cognitive dissonance, anxiety, control, and passiveness. **Cognitive dissonance** occurs when you feel conflict because you hold two or more attitudes that are in opposition to each other. For example, when Dr. Roman came into the classroom, you knew you would have difficulty listening because you were fearful, scared, and afraid. You were told he had high standards, a fearless attendance policy, and a tendency to humiliate students not prepared for class. It was Dr. Roman's approach to the class, however, that created the cognitive dissonance. Talking casually with you and your classmates, he defended his grading policy, explained the importance of attending class, and clarified the need to be prepared. His genuine warmth and caring made it difficult for you to listen because it didn't conform to what you had been told.

Anxiety is a disturbance that occurs in your mind regarding some uncertain event, misgiving, or worry. Many college courses create anxiety because so much is uncertain, there are so many misgivings, and the nature and structure of courses and examinations cause worry. It cannot be avoided. Just knowing that you have an exam coming up later in the day can cause you not to listen well in classes or lectures earlier the same day.

Control is the desire to have governing influence over a situation and **controlling listeners.** Some people prefer talking to listening. They seek to control their listeners by looking for ways to talk about themselves and their experiences. Often, they do not notice nonverbal signals from others, ignore signs that their listeners are bored, and even overlook overt verbal comments like "I'd better get going" or "I just noticed how late it is."

Passiveness involves the suspension of the rational functions and the reduction of any physical functions to their lowest possible degree. Passive people believe that listening involves no work. If you believe that you don't have to do anything, that you can just sit back and listening will happen, then you are in serious trouble. To learn—especially in situations where the speaker or the subject is not very interesting—requires a serious and concerted effort. So often students put the responsibility on the instructor: "Make it interesting, and I will listen." Education, however, often demands that students actively participate in the learning (acquisition of knowledge) process.

Learning to Listen

You have now read about the role of listening in communicating effectively and in strategic flexibility. You have also read about the effect of culture and gender on the process and the difficulty of listening. Are you aware of how much time you are likely to spend listening? Estimates vary, but some listening researchers estimate that the majority of people spend as much as 60 to 70 percent of their waking hours communicating. About 9 percent is time spent writing, 16 percent is in reading, 30 percent is in speaking, and 45 percent is in listening.[13]

Figure 5-4 shows the average percentage of time people devote to the four communication skills: listening, speaking, reading, and writing. If you spend 70 percent of your waking day engaged in some form of communication, and if you are awake for

Figure 5-4
Percentage of Time Devoted to Various Communication Skills

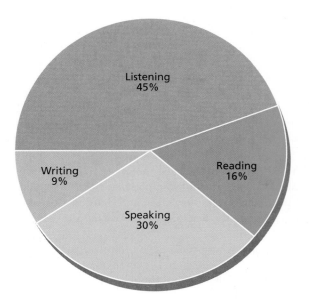

16 hours, then you are communicating in some way during 11 of those hours. Of that time, you spend 7 hours listening. You listen more than you do any other human activity except breathe. Although you spend the greatest amount of time listening, it is the skill that is taught the least.

Listening is a skill that can be learned, but like any skill, it has to be practiced. Listening well is habitual, and if the habit of good listening isn't deeply entrenched through constant practice, you are likely to fall back on your ineffective, unproductive, and unprofitable listening patterns.

Michael Purdy, writer and researcher on listening, conducted a study of 900 college and military students aged 17 to 70 which showed the traits of good and poor listeners:

A good listener:

1. Uses eye contact appropriately.
2. Is attentive and alert to a speaker's verbal and nonverbal behavior.
3. Is patient and doesn't interrupt (waits for the speaker to finish).
4. Is responsive, using verbal and nonverbal expressions.
5. Asks questions in a nonthreatening tone.
6. Paraphrases, restates, or summarizes what the speaker says.
7. Provides constructive (verbal or nonverbal) feedback.
8. Is empathic (works to understand the speaker).
9. Shows interest in the speaker as a person.
10. Demonstrates a caring attitude and is willing to listen.
11. Doesn't criticize, is nonjudgmental.
12. Is open-minded.

A poor listener:

1. Interrupts the speaker (is impatient).
2. Doesn't make eye contact (eyes wander).
3. Is distracted (fidgeting) and does not pay attention to the speaker.
4. Is not interested in the speaker (doesn't care; daydreaming).
5. Gives the speaker little or no (verbal or nonverbal) feedback.
6. Changes the subject.
7. Is judgmental.
8. Is closed-minded.
9. Talks too much.
10. Is self-preoccupied.
11. Gives unwanted advice.
12. Is too busy to listen.[14]

If you wanted to change your listening habits, the Purdy study offers 12 guidelines for change: make good eye contact, be attentive and alert, be patient and don't interrupt, use responsive verbal and nonverbal expressions, ask nonthreatening questions, **paraphrase**, restate and summarize, offer constructive feedback, reveal empathy, show interest, demonstrate a caring attitude that shows you are willing to listen, and

STRATEGIC FLEXIBILITY

Changing your listening habits will give you more insights, ideas, suggestions, and knowledge on which to base all steps in strategic flexibility. Effective listening—like perception—is bedrock (down to fundamentals or the truth of the matter) in strategic flexibility.

For this AOM, you are to take the role of an active, involved observer and detective. From the conversations in which you are involved as well as from the conversations of others, you will identify each of the six kinds of listening (i.e., discriminative, comprehensive, appreciative, critical, informative, and empathic). For each, you are to identify the separate elements of communication by answering the following questions: (1) What was the setting? (2) What was the message? (3) What was the feedback? (4) What were the channels used? (5) Were there any effects of noise? (6) Who were the senders/receivers involved? (7) What are the specific characteristics that led you to characterize this kind of listening in this way?

be nonjudgmental and open-minded. If we were to add one additional guideline, it would be to build your vocabulary. The more words you learn, the better listener you will become.

If you avoid the characteristics of a poor listener, and if you are flexible in your listening style (people-, action-, content-, or time-style listening), you are likely to develop a positive, constructive, and worthwhile listening habit that will, through use, become deeply entrenched. You can speed this entrenchment by challenging your listening ability—seeking out situations many try to avoid rather than experience. You must stretch if you want to grow. Force yourself to listen carefully to sermons, political speeches, lectures, debates, and other material that requires concentration. Given today's movies, television, the Internet, and computer games, seldom is such concentration required. It will, however, be rewarded by your gains in insights, ideas, suggestions, and knowledge in general—let alone your increased ability to listen.

Six Kinds of Listening

You choose a different type of listening based on the situation you are in, and although types of listening and situations vary, there is one constant, unvarying characteristic that must be present no matter what kind of listening is involved—**active listening**. Active listening is *a way of listening*—not a type—*that focuses entirely on what the other person is saying, and it confirms—demonstrates—understanding of both the content of the message and the feelings underlying the message to assure accuracy.*

There are a number of characteristics of active listeners, and these characteristics will be clear to you when you are in the presence of active listeners. First, they look you in the eye. They direct their full and undivided attention at you. Second, they reveal patience. That is, they have slowed down to take the time to value you and your ideas. In this way, active listeners reveal respect for you. Third, they demonstrate empathy—making a serious and obvious attempt at the moment to see what you are seeing and to feel what you are feeling. They are trying to put themselves in your shoes to better understand what you have to say. Fourth, they avoid judgment, which could be revealed in sarcasm, obvious signs of derision, rejection, or contempt. Fifth, they use a concept called **"verify-clarify."** When engaged in listening, active listeners take what they have just heard, re-phrase it, then ask, "Let me see if I understand correctly what you are saying. . . . Is that correct?" This skill will help you verify your understanding, and it will give the other person an opportunity to further "clarify" a point.

Our first experiences of learning to listen usually come from our parents.

There will be some over-lap between these characteristics of active listeners and our definitions of the six types of listening. Allow the overlap to focus greater attention on the characteristic and how it contributes increased effectiveness to the type of listening described.

With this definition of active listening and the characteristics of active listeners, you will see why it is such a valuable and integral part of each of the six types of listening discussed here: discriminative, comprehension, appreciative, critical, informative, and empathic.

Discriminative Listening

This is the most important type, and it is basic to the other five. **Discriminative listening** *is the type that has you being sensitive to both verbal and nonverbal changes— the sounds and sights of communication.* Changes in others' rate, volume, force, pitch, and emphasis allow you to make sense of the meanings or nuances expressed by such differences. For example, subtle emotional variations in a voice allow mothers to know instantly when a child is upset. Changes in others' posture, body movements, gestures, facial expression, or eye contact allow you to understand others' true or intended meaning. Often, muscle and skeletal movements are subdued, understated, and indistinct, but that doesn't make them undetectable.

Comprehension Listening

Just beyond discriminative listening and closely aligned with it is **comprehension listening**—*understanding what others are saying because you are aware of, grasp, and can make sense of the message.* Comprehension is a complex process because it depends first on fundamentals such as your vocabulary as well as the rules of grammar and syntax. On that foundation is built your grasp of how thoughts, ideas, and feelings—knowledge—are assembled. Finally, comprehension listening depends on your ability to extract or synthesize key facts and items from what you hear.

Appreciative Listening

One of the most often used types of listening, **appreciative listening** *means listening for pleasure.* It could include listening to a comedian for fun, a theatrical, movie, television, or Internet presentation for entertainment, a radio program for diversion, music for relaxation, poetry for gratification, a great leader for satisfaction, or a motivational speaker for inspiration.

Critical Listening

Using **critical listening** (sometimes called **evaluative listening**), you *make judgments about what the other person is saying.* For example, you seek to assess the truth of his or her message, and you judge what he or she says against your own values. In this way, you can make a determination of worth: Is what he or she is saying right or wrong, good or bad, beneficial or detrimental, worthy or unworthy?

Ideally, all communication should be listened to critically. When you are receiving new information, however, it is sometimes difficult to evaluate it critically because you do not know much about the subject or, possibly, about the speaker either.

You have five jobs in connection with critical listening. First, *determine the speaker's motives.* What is in it for the other person, or, to rephrase the same question, what is he or she going to get out of it? Another way of saying the same thing is, who benefits? Second, *challenge and question ideas.* Journalists seek answers to six questions: who? what? when? where? why? and how? The first question is above: Who benefits? Then, what happened? When did it happen? Where did it happen? Why did it happen, or why is it important? And how did it happen? The questions can be rephrased in any way that makes sense, but they give you a place to begin challenging and questioning ideas.

The third job you have in critical listening is to distinguish fact from fiction. A **fact** is *something that can be verified in a number of ways,* which might include experiments, direct observation, books, articles, or websites by authorities. Everyone who applies the same test or uses the same sources should be able to get the same information. An **opinion** *is a personal belief.* That cinnamon comes from the bark of a tree is a fact that can be found in any number of places. Wikipedia reveals this information, and it is the first website that occurs when you enter "cinnamon" into the Google search engine. That cinnamon is tasty in foods, especially cookies, is an opinion because some people disagree. Because you hear more opinions than facts, it is important that you make this distinction.

All facts are equally true, but some opinions are more reliable than others. The best ones come from those who have a high degree of authority or credibility. Also, opinions supported by others—especially others who are in positions of authority or who have credibility—are considered reliable.

Your fourth job in critical listening is to *recognize your own biases.* The tendency to interpret information in light of your beliefs can lead you to distort information you hear. As a listener who is aware of your own values and attitudes, you are more likely to hear and less likely to discard information you disagree with. Often it is precisely this information that causes growth, development, and change to occur.

Your fifth job in critical listening is to *assess the message.* To **assess** *is to determine the value of something.* Basically, it is a critical process of chewing over what you have heard before you swallow it. Ideas that may seem acceptable when you first hear them may not be as palatable when you have had time to think about them. Assessment, of course, can take place at any point in the listening process. Remember, too, that reassessment and reevaluation are integral parts of strategic flexibility.

The important thing in assessment is to learn to delay taking a position (or responding) until you receive all the facts and other evidence, until you have had a chance to test them in the marketplace of ideas, and until you have had an opportunity to chew over everything before digestion. Figure 5-5 is a critical listening evaluation checklist for a speech or lecture.

ATTENTION!

The Five Jobs of a Critical Listener

1. Determine the speaker's motives.
2. Challenge and question ideas.
3. Distinguish fact from fiction.
4. Recognize your own biases.
5. Assess the message.

1. Were you able to make any accurate predictions about what the speaker was going to say? What helped you to do so?

2. What was the speaker's central idea? Was it clearly stated?

3. Do you have any ideas of the speaker's motive for giving this speech? If you know the motive, does it make the speech more or less believable?

4. What kinds of supporting points were used to back up the speaker's ideas? Were these points based on evidence you respect?

5. What questions would you like to ask the speaker? Are they questions that clarify what the speaker has said or questions that ask for more information?

6. Think of one or two ways you would like to challenge the speaker.

7. How would you evaluate this speech? What did the speaker do well? Was there anything the speaker could have done to make the speech better?

Figure 5-5
Critical Listening Evaluation Checklist for a Speech or Lecture

Informative Listening

Informative listening *occurs when your primary concern is to understand the message.* It is the most common kind of listening that occurs in college. You use it, too, to obtain directions, understand others, solve problems, and share interests. When your primary concern is to understand someone else's message, your most important mission must be to keep your mind focused, connected, and centered. On the next page we discuss six suggestions specially designed to do that.

First, *identify* the **central idea,** or *the essential thought that runs through the speech or communication.* Once it is identified, look for **main heads** or *the points that reinforce the central idea.* Then, once main heads are located, listen for **supporting points** or *the material, ideas, and evidence that back up the main heads.* This, too, can assist you in remembering the information because when you remember the central idea, the main heads will follow. Main heads without a central idea often look like unrelated points that make no sense, but central ideas tie fragmented ideas together and give them meaning.

The second suggestion designed to keep your mind focused, connected, and centered is to form a **mental outline,** which is *a preliminary sketch that shows the principal features of the speech or lecture.* It gives clues about the way the speaker is thinking, what he or she wants you to know, and how he or she will move through the material. A mental outline offers a picture of the forest and not just a bunch of unrelated trees.

Third, *predict what will come next.* To **predict** is *to forecast or to make something known beforehand.* This helps keep your mind focused. Since attention comes in spurts—as little as 20-second intervals—you must force yourself to concentrate. Prediction is simply a mind game designed to keep you tuned in to what is going on.

Fourth, *relate points to your experience.* This will provide a specific and immediate point of reference, add meaning to the information, and make the information more memorable.

Fifth, *look for similarities and differences.* How is the information similar to or different from what you already know? This is especially important, of course, in intercultural communication since it is the differences that distinguish one culture from another, but you will find this examination of similarities and differences a valuable exercise for keeping your mind focused and alert.

Sixth, *ask questions.* Intrapersonal questions allow you to challenge, test, stretch, and demand more. They are energy producing because they can be exciting, stimulating, and inspiring as well. When you discover questions you can't answer, write them down, and if you cannot ask the speaker or lecturer, seek answers to them on your own.

Empathic Listening

Empathy *is the process of mentally identifying with the character and experiences of another person.* Often, it involves the emotional projection of your self into another's life—or their life as revealed by and through their communication. It is all about feelings. Michael P. Nichols, who has written about listening, points out that when you listen with empathy, you have to suspend your ego and immerse yourself in the other person. Only by doing this will you be able to enter into his or her feelings.[15]

Sara Konrath, a researcher at the University of Michigan's Institute for Social Research, as cited by Stephanie Steinberg in her essay "A Change of Heart for College Students," "found that empathy has been declining—especially since 2000." Steinberg, using Konrath's research, states, "The research finds that college students today show 40% less empathy vs. students in the 1980s and 1990s. The students are less likely to agree with statements such as 'I often have tender, concerned feelings for people less fortunate than me' and 'I sometimes try to understand my friends better by imagining how things look from their perspective'" (p. 7D).[16]

Listening to other people's feelings is not just a way of giving emotional support, but it is a way of creating intimacy as well. To listen empathically, you need to recognize

Empathy works for listening to another's feelings and providing emotional support, but it is a way for creating intimacy as well.

Seth S. Horowitz, an auditory neuroscientist at Brown University and the author of "The Universal Sense: How Hearing Shapes the Mind," ends his essay "The Science and Art of Listening," (*The New York Times*, November 11, 2012, p. 10 SR), saying the following:

Listening is a skill that we're in danger of losing in a world of digital distraction and information overload.

And yet we dare not lose it. Because listening tunes our brain to the patterns of our environment faster than any other sense, and paying attention to the nonvisual parts of our world feeds into everything from our intellectual sharpness to our dance skills. . . .

"You never listen" is not just the complaint of a problematic relationship, it has also become an epidemic in a world that is exchanging convenience for content, speed for meaning. The richness of life doesn't lie in the loudness and the beat, but in the timbres and the variations that you can discern if you simply pay attention (p. 10).

Source: Horowitz, Seth S. (November 11, 2012). "The science and art of listening." *The New York Times*, p. 10.

Questions

1. To what extent do you think effective listening is a skill that can be improved with training?

2. Let's say that you agree with Horowitz that "listening is a skill that we're in danger of losing," and you agree that you are one of the guilty parties (you don't listen well); where would you begin to build up your listening skills? How would you go about it?

3. Would you agree with Horowitz that "the richness of life doesn't lie in the loudness and the beat, but in the timbres and the variations that you can discern if you simply pay attention"? Do you have any personal experiences that would show how this is not only true but also important?

what feelings are involved, let the other person tell you what has happened, then encourage him or her to find the solution to the problem. As simple as the process may sound, it becomes complicated quickly by interwoven feelings, needs for support and encouragement, and confusion about what to do next.

The important thing to remember is that you do *not* have to solve others' problems. If you try to solve every problem that people bring you, you will put a heavy burden on yourself. Think of the person with the problem as "owning" that problem. This attitude will help the other person grow in his or her ability to deal with problems.

When strong emotions are involved, people often need a sounding board. To be there and to utter an occasional, "Oh," "Mmmm," or "I see" is often enough. Much comfort and support is derived from just being listened to.

Talking So Others Will Listen

How important is it to talk so others will listen to you? In his book *The Language Wars* (NY: Farrar, Straus, and Giroux, 2011), Henry Hitchings says,

When we use language, we may be making a social connection, answering a question, enjoying ourselves, passing time, or showing off, but fundamentally we imagine that the interest of the person or people to whom we are speaking is engaged. The desire to shape and emphasize this engagement is crucial. How do I get you to listen to me (p. 20)?

STRATEGIC FLEXIBILITY

When you assess, evaluate, and select from your repertoire of available skills and behaviors, you must appear flexible. As we say in this paragraph: "You must be willing to prepare your ideas and, in turn, listen to the ideas of others."

A large part of getting someone to listen to you involves setting the stage. In *Words Can Change Your Brain* (NY: Hudson Street Press, 2012), Andrew Newberg and Marc Robert Waldman

identified and documented twelve strategies that will enhance the dynamics of any conversation. The twelve strategies are: 1) Relax; 2) Stay present; 3) Cultivate inner silence; 4) Increase positivity; 5) Reflect on your deepest values; 6) Access a pleasant memory; 7) Observe nonverbal cues; 8) Express appreciation; 9) Speak warmly; 10) Speak slowly; 11) Speak briefly; 12) Listen deeply (p. 4).

There are many techniques for reaching out and grasping the attention of others. Often, a combination of techniques works best. We'll briefly discuss assertiveness, getting to the point, being prepared, writing down ideas, being flexible, and changing your vocal style.

First, and perhaps most obvious, you need to be more assertive. In the article "Talking Back to Your Doctor Works," Greider says, "Studies show that doctors remember best the cases of assertive patients. Medical outcomes are also likely to be better."[17] These results are likely to apply across communication contexts. It has long been an established research result that assertive behavior tends to be associated with positive outcomes.

Second, knowing that the other person is likely to be a weak or indifferent listener, avoid idle chit-chat and friendly conversation and get to the point fast. In advance of the conversation, think about what you want to say, how you plan to say it, and what you want from the other person. Then, try to follow your plan. The point isn't to memorize a speech; rather, it is to move rapidly toward your point.

Third, do your homework—that is, know what you are talking about. If some research is necessary to gather facts and relevant information, go to the library or use the Internet to ferret out the facts that will make your case or back up your position. Well-informed people tend to get the ear of others, as opposed to those who either do not know what they are talking about or are simply willing to hear the ideas of others and make no significant contribution of their own.

Fourth, write down your most important points or questions, and prioritize them. A list of ideas has always been associated with a rational, judicious, well-thought-out approach. Even if you do not use your notes, writing them out will assist you in organizing your ideas and phrasing them in the most effective way. When you put your most important ideas first, it is more likely they will be heard or noticed. Otherwise, they may be hidden in the middle or end of your conversation, or they may come too late for the attention span of your listener.

Fifth, have some options in mind, and be willing to listen. You are more likely to get the attention of others when you appear flexible and willing to listen yourself. The old adage "It takes one to know one" suggests that if you want someone to listen to you, you must also be willing to listen to them. But preparation and forethought do not necessarily mean all the alternatives have been considered. Thus, remember that this is a conversation; it is two-way. You must be willing to prepare your ideas and, in turn, listen to the ideas of others.

Sixth, try to change your vocal style. For some people—as indicated earlier in this chapter—this may mean slowing down your rate of delivery. If your pace tends to be slow already, or plodding, speeding up may be a useful approach. Often, it may simply be a need for variety. A change in volume, either louder or softer depending on the circumstances, may also help.

Rich Kirschner, in his book *How to Click With People* (NY: Hyperion, 2011), offers a seventh technique to consider when talking so others will listen: "Whenever speaking with someone, look like you understand, even when you don't. Nod your head when people talk to you as if what they say makes complete sense, even though it may not. Sound like you understand. Utter affirming phrases every once in a while, like *yes, mhmmm, I see, oh, u-huh,* or just grunt affirmatively, as if you know just what they mean. Even if you don't.

"Now, you may be worried that you'll mislead the speaker or that you'll have to proceed as if you understand something you don't," Kirschner continues, "Nothing could be further from the truth. You've merely given the speaker a respectful space in which to express himself. You've given him [or her] a chance" (pp. 34–35).

There are many ways to talk so others will listen. These suggestions will get you started, but overriding any of them are, of course, the courtesy and respect you need to demonstrate. Being assertive, for example, is not an excuse for being aggressive and thoughtless. Avoiding idle chit-chat and friendly conversation is not an excuse for overlooking necessary or important human concerns and connectiveness. You should make all decisions in the context of good judgment, common sense, thoughtfulness, and **propriety**—the character or quality of being proper, especially in accordance with recognized usage, custom, or principles.

Throughout all of this—your use of techniques to get others to listen to you—you need to recognize that there are some people who will not listen to you no matter what you do. Fortunately, these people are likely to be few and far between. You should not be disappointed if the techniques you use fail to work. The bottom line is: Communication involves a large number of factors or variables. No situation is the same as any other. No one has or ever will have control of all the factors or variables; no one has that kind or level of control. The more experience you have, the more practice that you engage in, and the more you believe in yourself and your abilities, the more likely you will be successful. Success is never guaranteed.

Are You a Good Listener?

For each statement circle the numerical score that best represents your listening ability using the following scale: 7 = Outstanding; 6 = Excellent; 5 = Very good; 4 = Average (good); 3 = Fair; 2 = Poor; 1 = Minimal ability; 0 = No ability demonstrated.

1. I listen for the other person's feelings, not just to the words he or she says.   7 6 5 4 3 2 1 0

2. I paraphrase what other people say to me.   7 6 5 4 3 2 1 0

3. I don't interrupt.   7 6 5 4 3 2 1 0

4. I am open-minded to ideas, some with which I may not agree.   7 6 5 4 3 2 1 0

5. I remember what people say.   7 6 5 4 3 2 1 0

6. I am willing to express my feelings.   7 6 5 4 3 2 1 0

7. I don't complete other people's sentences even when I think I know what they are going to say next.   7 6 5 4 3 2 1 0

8. I make eye contact.   7 6 5 4 3 2 1 0

9. I don't think of what I'm going to say next while the other person is talking.   7 6 5 4 3 2 1 0

10. I ask the person questions to get more information and show that I am interested in what he or she is saying.   7 6 5 4 3 2 1 0

11. I am comfortable with silence.   7 6 5 4 3 2 1 0

12. I am aware of a person's body language and my own body language.   7 6 5 4 3 2 1 0

TOTAL POINTS: _____

Go to the Online Learning Center at **www.mhhe.com/hybels11e** to see your results and learn how to evaluate your attitudes and feelings.

www.mhhe.com/hybels11e >

Source: Adapted from www.literacynet.org/icans. Used by permission of Adult Basic Education Office, Professional Development Services, Washington State ABE Literary Resource Center, formerly ABLE Network.

Summary

Of all the communication faults people are accused of, not listening probably ranks as number one. Listening is a skill, and like any other skill it must be learned and practiced.

The Integrative Listening Model (ILM) includes the processes of listening preparation, receiving, constructing meaning, responding, and remembering. It begins before the elements of communication in the model in Chapter 1 with listening preparation, and it continues after the elements depicted there with the process of remembering. Listening, because it is one aspect of the process of perception, is essential to all steps in strategic flexibility.

There are numerous strategies that will help you ensure information is being learned well and stored securely in your memory system. All require conscious effort. Just as active listening is essential to effective note taking, effective note taking is essential to remembering information. Effective note taking requires commitment on your part as well.

Culture has an effect on listening simply because of the potential misunderstandings that can occur. Adjustments in vocabulary, grammar, or informality may need to be made. Gender has an effect because men and women listen differently. Understanding the differences will aid in effective communication.

There are as many factors, or combinations of factors, that cause difficulty in listening as there are listeners. One element is the difference between speech speed and listening speed. In addition to the six factors singled out by Steven Golen, there are the factors of cognitive dissonance, anxiety, control, and passiveness as well.

To be a good listener, you must become actively involved in changing your listening habits. In his study of good and poor listeners, Michael Purdy offers 12 guidelines for change. In addition to building your vocabulary, you need to challenge your listening ability by seeking out situations where concentration and careful listening are required.

Six types of listening are discussed in this book. Active listening plays a significant role in each of them. Active listening is a way of listening—not a type—that focuses entirely on what the other person is saying, and confirms understanding of both the content of the message and the feelings underlying the message to assure accuracy. Five characteristics of active listeners are discussed.

The first of the six types of listening is labeled discriminative listening, where listeners are sensitive to both verbal and nonverbal changes. The second type is comprehension listening, in which listeners understand what others are saying because they are aware of, grasp, and can make sense of the message. The third type is appreciative listening, which means listening for pleasure. Critical listening is when listeners make judgments about what the other person is saying. Informative listening occurs when listeners' primary concern is to understand the message. Finally, empathic listening is the process of mentally identifying with the character and experiences of others.

When you discover that those you want to listen to you are not listening, the techniques of assertiveness, getting to the point, being prepared, writing down ideas, being flexible, and changing your verbal style are ways—or combinations of ways—for reaching out and grasping attention. Whatever techniques you choose, you need to avoid being aggressive and thoughtless and show courtesy and respect. All decisions should be made using good judgment, common sense, thoughtfulness, and propriety.

Key Terms and Concepts

Use the Online Learning Center at www.mhhe.com/hybels11e to further your understanding of the following terms.

Questions to Review

1. What is the role that listening plays in strategic flexibility?

2. What are the elements of the Integrative Listening Model (ILM), and how do each of the elements relate to the model of communication discussed and illustrated in Chapter 1?

3. What is meant by "constructing meaning," and what are its significant parts?

4. What are the techniques discussed for remembering information?

5. What are the four kinds of listening styles, and why is it helpful to know someone's listening style if you are communicating something important?

6. What effects are culture and gender likely to have on listening?

7. What are the factors that make listening difficult?

8. If you want to become a better listener, what are some of the ways you have to improve?

9. What skills are involved in effective note taking?

10. What are the similarities and differences among the six kinds of listening?

11. What contribution does active listening make, and what are its characteristics?

12. What are the five jobs associated with critical listening?

13. What is the most common kind of listening that occurs in college, and what six suggestions will help listeners keep focused, connected, and centered?

14. What is empathic listening, and what are its essential elements?

15. What are some of the techniques you can use to reach out and grasp the attention of others when you must talk so others will listen?

Go to the Online Learning Center at www.mhhe.com/hybels11e to test your knowledge of the chapter contents.

CHAPTER SIX

Interpersonal Relationships

After reading this chapter, you should be able to:

- Explain emotional intelligence and its contribution to communication effectiveness, and clarify the interpersonal needs you are trying to meet when you seek out others.

- Explain how bids and responses to bids contribute to relationship development and your role in both bidding and responding to the bids of others.

- Define self-disclosure, why it's important, and how the Johari Window helps you understand how the self-disclosure process takes place.

- Describe each of the essential elements that draw people together.

- Distinguish among relational dialectics, social exchange theory, and social penetration theory.

ESLIE STEVENS'S ONLINE DATING SERVICE HAD HER RATE HERSELF and her potential mate in categories ranging from sex drive to "socialistic-butterflyosity." An algorithm then calculated her compatibility with a list of matches. Leslie wanted a vegetarian boyfriend who played piano and liked folk music, and she discovered the exact match in Cody Moore—he lived in a dorm on her campus as well. Leslie began sending Cody online messages, and the next thing they knew they were having lunch together and hanging out in real life. Stevens said, "The chances of meeting Moore without the help of an online community were pretty much nil."

Online dating services have changed the way the college crowd interacts. Instead of getting to know classmates over coffee or through mutual friends, students access a goldmine of information about their peers—and potential mates—online.

Interaction with others is called **interpersonal communication,** and it occurs whenever one person interacts with another—usually in an informal setting. You cannot survive in society without interpersonal communication skills. They enable you to function socially and to maintain relationships important to you.

According to the *UC Berkeley Wellness Letter* (December 2010), "Not only do [friends, family, and other social relations] add immensely to your quality of life, research has shown that they also tend to add years to your life. This was clearly seen in a recent review from Brigham Young University in Utah, which looked at 148 studies involving more than 300,000 people. It linked stronger social relationships with a 50% increased chance of survival, on average, over the course of the studies. And the effect was consistent across a number of factors, such as age, sex, and health status" (p. 5).[1] It has been theorized that social relations have a number of health benefits: 1) They provide a buffer against stress by providing emotional and tangible resources to deal with adverse events and illness, 2) they encourage people to take better care of themselves, and 3) they give them meaningful roles that boost their self-esteem and purpose of life.

This chapter begins by examining the big picture—how you understand and get along with others, who are you attracted to and why—and then discusses the specifics in the next two sections: talking to each other and self-disclosure. The final sections examine the essential elements of good relationships and the chapter ends with a discussion of Social Exchange Theory—a perspective which helps partners calculate the overall worth of a relationship.

Emotional Intelligence

Anyone who has taught long enough to see students mature can tell you of some who were smart in the classroom but never went anywhere and others who did not do particularly well in school but went on to have successful careers and relationships. Their success is due to what Daniel Goleman calls "emotional intelligence."[2] Although there isn't unanimous agreement on the validity of the concept of **emotional intelligence,** it provides useful insights into some important aspects of interpersonal relationships. Edwin Locke, for example, argues that the concept is not a form of intelligence and is defined too broadly and inclusively to have intelligible meaning.[3]

Being Self-Aware

Before you can deal with the emotions of others, you need to recognize your own by paying attention to how you feel. Self-awareness requires the ability to get a little distance from the emotion so that you can look at it without being overwhelmed by it or reacting to it too quickly. For example, if you are having an argument with someone and act on your anger, you might tell the other person that you never want to see him or her again. On the other hand, if you can recognize how angry you are feeling, you might be able to say, "Let me think about this some more and talk to you about it later."

Distancing yourself from an emotion does not mean denying it ("I shouldn't feel this way"). Rather, it's a way to articulate to yourself what you are feeling so that you can act on it appropriately.

Managing Emotions

Managing your emotions means expressing them in a manner that is appropriate to the circumstances.[4] You may not be able to do this easily because emotions often come from below the surface of your consciousness. For example, there may have been a time that unexpected tears came to your eyes, or other times when you felt a terrible rage well up inside you.

Another emotion that gets out of control is anxiety.[5] When anxiety is out of control, you feel so worried or so upset that it interferes with the way you function. In a university setting, for instance, most teachers have had students who have been so worried about the right way to do an assignment that they didn't do it at all or did it poorly because they were afraid to take any chances or of doing it wrong.

Managing your emotions does not mean that you should never feel angry, worried, or anxious. These emotions are all part of being human, and if you don't find a way to express them, they can result in depression or antisocial acts. It's important that you control these emotions rather than letting them control you.

One interesting finding about emotions is that women are better than men at detecting them. In a study where men and women were shown video clips in which someone was having an emotional reaction, 80 percent of the time women were better than men at discerning the emotion.[6]

Motivating Yourself

Motivating yourself is setting a goal and then disciplining yourself to do what you have to do to reach it. Whether you are an athlete or a writer, talent is not enough to make you win the race or get your story published. Both writers and athletes will tell you that they worked hard on many boring activities before they mastered their discipline.

Self-motivation requires resisting impulses. If you are studying for a test, for example, it might be tempting to go to the computer and chat with a friend. If you give in to this impulse, you might become so engrossed in the computer that you completely forget the test.

Other influences on motivation, according to Goleman, are positive thinking and optimism. Those who had a strong sense of self could bounce back after they had a negative experience. Rather than dwelling on the failure, they looked at ways in which they could improve.[7]

Recognizing Emotions in Others

Empathy, the ability to recognize and share someone else's feelings, is essential to human relationships. It comes from hearing what people are really saying—both by listening to their words and by reading body language such as gestures and facial

Ten Ways to Become More Empathic

1. Listen attentively.
2. Offer others a pleasant, responsive disposition.
3. Smile often.
4. Use kind words.
5. Be patient, understanding, and supportive.
6. Give of your time.
7. Acquire the empathic attitude, and make it always represent you.
8. Give without expecting a return.
9. Operate by the Golden Rule.
10. Become a role model.

expressions, and recognizing what they mean by a particular tone of voice. When someone has the same feelings or experiences you have had, it's not difficult to feel empathy. You are really put to the test when you haven't had the other person's feelings or experiences. For example, how can you feel empathy with an African student who hasn't been home for three years and stays in the dorm over Christmas? You can feel sorry for him, and you could tell him that you would feel terrible if you couldn't go home for the holidays. However, these emotions are pity (feeling sorry for him) and sympathy (saying that you'd feel bad too), but they are not empathy because you have not shared his experience. You may go in the direction of empathy if you talk to him for a while, look at the pictures of his brothers and sisters, hear about all the delicious things his mother cooks for Christmas, and so on. Empathy is the extent to which you can sit in his place, see what he sees, and taste what he tastes.

Empathy has a strong moral dimension. Being able to recognize and share someone's distress means that you will not want to hurt him or her. Child molesters and socio-paths, for example, are people lacking in empathy. [8] Sharing empathy with others also means that you are able to reach out and help them because when you can feel as they feel, they are no longer alone.

Handling Relationships

When you look at the elements just discussed, and when you recognize all the other factors involved in any interpersonal transaction, you immediately notice the difficulty of trying to keep track of everything that's going on. In her book *Quiet: The Power of Introverts in a World That Can't Stop Talking*, Susan Cain elegantly expresses the problem: "Consider that the simplest social interaction between two people requires performing an astonishing array of tasks: interpreting what the other person is saying; reading body language and facial expressions; smoothly taking turns talking and listening; responding to what the other person said; assessing whether you're being understood; determining whether you're well received, and, if not, figuring out how to improve or remove yourself from the situation. Think of what it takes to juggle all this at once" (p. 217)![9]

The Importance of Emotional Intelligence to Strategic Flexibility

Self-concept is the way you think about and value yourself. The way you look at others and the world around you, and how well you understand and get along with others, have a direct influence on your self-concept, just as the way you think about and value yourself influences both perception and emotional intelligence.

Perception, emotional intelligence, and self-concept have a direct bearing on strategic flexibility simply because they either enhance or impair your ability to anticipate, assess, evaluate, select, and apply your skills and behaviors. The better your perceptive skills, the more likely that your emotional intelligence is high and your self-concept is positive.

Remember the first characteristic of emotional intelligence: self-awareness. Part of maturity is recognizing that just because you have emotions doesn't necessarily mean you must act on them. Not only do you recognize your own emotions, but you understand, too, the triggers that cause them to come to the surface. As you begin to recognize your emotions and their triggers, you will learn how to manage them and to reveal the appropriate ones in given circumstances.

As you become accustomed to using the strategic flexibility framework, you develop self-control through self-discipline. It is as if you are setting mini-goals for yourself. You anticipate situations with the goal of applying the appropriate and relevant skills and behaviors. You achieve success when you maximize your communication, enhance your credibility, and not only support but achieve your intentions.

Listening to others becomes easier when you are secure in your self. Your perceptions become more accurate, and your observations of the nonverbal behavior of others and attempts to really understand them improve. In the end there is a greater chance that you will be able to handle relationships more successfully. Handling relationships is not easy, nor is it automatic. It is learned behavior, and emotional intelligence can help you establish and sustain long-term, meaningful relationships. The problem is simply that emotional intelligence often develops slowly—along with emotional maturity. If you take each of the areas of emotional intelligence, and you make them an issue before thinking about any serious relationship, you are more likely to take the necessary time.

Personal Motivation for Interpersonal Contact

This section is divided into two parts: attractiveness and motives for interpersonal contact. In the first part we examine those elements that cause us to be attracted to others: physical attraction, perceived gain, similarities, differences, and proximity. In the second, motives for interpersonal contact, we look at the interpersonal needs others fulfill: pleasure, affection, inclusion, escape, relaxation, control, and health. There is no doubt that the factors in these two sections can overlap and intermingle.

There are many factors that make up attraction to others. Physical attraction, perceived gain, similarities, differences, and proximity are some of them. What are the likely factors at play here?

For example, one of our needs may be to be seen with people who are attractive, or one of our needs may be to increase our self-esteem by seeking people who will love and support us.

Attractiveness

Helen Fisher, a research anthropologist at Rutgers University, writes, "There is much evidence that people generally fall in love with those of the same socioeconomic and ethnic background, of roughly the same age, with the same degree of intelligence and level of education, and with a similar sense of humor and grade of attractiveness."[10] The point is that we are attracted to people similar to ourselves. From Fisher's vantage point, all it might take is some self-examination to determine what factors would attract you to someone else.

Fisher's research is supported, too, by "researchers from the University of Stirling, Harvard University, and Florida State University [who] published a study that examined standards of beauty on two continents. The results . . . indicated: there is in fact one universal quality that people find attractive, on the plains of Tanzania, in the streets of London, and around the globe: symmetry" (p. 90).[11] "**Symmetry**," Dr. Sharon Moalem, writing in her book, *How Sex Works*, means "exactly that—eyes the same shape, dimples on both cheeks, legs the same length, hands the same size—you name it, left and right sides the same. Across the animal kingdom, males and females find the opposite sex more attractive when their left and right sides match, and humans are no exception (p. 14)."[12] Symmetry means correspondence, consistency, and balance.

"A British study conducted back in 2001 garnered a lot of interest when researchers actually found evidence that looking an attractive person in the eye sparks activity in the *ventral striatum* that looking at less attractive people does not. The ventral striatum is an area of the brain that heats up in anticipation of a reward (p. 97)."[13] "The researchers concluded that the brain may consider the potential for social interaction with an attractive person a reward. Unattractive faces did not produce the same effect. Researcher Knut Kampe of University College London thinks catching the eye of an attractive person might activate the brain's reward center because we associate attraction with social status. 'Meeting a potential good friend or someone who might influence our career might be very rewarding,' he says."[14]

Sometimes our attraction to others can be measured by individual features, but we are more than the sum of our individual parts. What makes you more is not only what others can see, but what goes on inside you as well—your confidence, your belief in yourself, your unwillingness to put yourself down (or up). Even if you are the world's best looking and brightest, you could still ruin another person's feeling of being special in your presence, by either attacking yourself or bragging.[15]

As you read the following ingredients, keep in mind that your brain draws "instantaneous inferences based on tiny nuances of behavior, what psychologists call 'thin slices' of judgment. We form first impressions of another's attractiveness in a tenth of a second, generating a symphonic burst of desire in which everything from voice to wit plays a part," writes Elizabeth Svoboda in her article, "Fast Forces of Attraction" (p. 74).[16] It isn't like spending time weighing the ingredients, like deciding whether or not to buy a car; the conclusion is likely to be based more on emotion than on logic or in-depth analysis.

Every day you encounter scores of people, but most of them recede into a kind of human landscape. Occasionally, however, you think, "Hey, I would really like to get to know this person better." Of the scores of people you meet, how do you pick one whom you want to know better? What are the ingredients that make up your attraction to others?

Physical Attraction

We are often attracted to others because of the way they look; we like their style and want to get to know them better. Physical attraction may be sexual attraction. In most cases, however, it goes beyond that. For adults who have had experience in the world, physical attraction usually recedes into the background as they get to know a person. Physical attraction can be a reason for getting to know someone, but it is usually not the basis for a long-term relationship. According to Lauren F. Friedman, in her article, "Men Are Not the Enemy" (*Psychology Today*, April 2013, p. 20), "The top four characteristics men say they look for in a mate are dependable character, emotional stability, good personality, and love—good looks," Friedman notes, "are nowhere near the top."

Perceived Gain

Often we are attracted to people because we think we have something to gain from associating with them. For example, a man might want a woman willing to subsume herself or to limit her ambitions to make life more congenial for him. Andrew Hacker, a political scientist at Queens College, has predicted a growing divide between the sexes because women are becoming less willing to do this.[17]

Professor Stephanie Coontz, a sociology professor at Evergreen State College in Washington, believes that women "have become more distrustful of marriage and men have been more likely to say marriage is an ideal state."[18] Coontz suggests that the new equality in marriage has caused women to be more cautious—because marriage "comes with a lot of expectations about women doing the comfort-generating work."[19] Because people's behavior about marriage has changed more in the past 30 years than in the last 3,000, according to Coontz, potential gains from relationships—especially marriage—may need to be reassessed and reevaluated.

With respect to perceived gain, "conventional wisdom is that we choose friends because of who *they* are, but it turns out that we actually love them because of the way they support who *we are*."[20] If, indeed, this is the case, then the perceived gain is the increased self-confidence, self-assurance, poise, and composure we gain when we choose the right relationship partner.

Although Americans believe they live in a classless society, this is not true. Even colleges and universities have a social hierarchy: Private schools (especially those in the Ivy League) have the most status, while junior and community colleges have the least. Colleges that are supported by a church are in a category of their own. What does this have to do with attraction? People will usually seek out others in their own class. Sometimes, however, they are motivated to move up, and they try to blend into a higher class because the perceived awards will be greater.

Similarities

You may be attracted to someone who shares your attitudes and beliefs or seems knowledgeable about topics you find interesting and significant. Your **beliefs** are your convictions; your **attitudes** are the deeply felt beliefs that govern how you behave. When it comes to a strongly felt belief, you probably look for people who believe as you do. For example, in today's world it would be difficult for an Albanian and a Serb to be close friends—their politics have put them in opposing camps.

As adults grow older and meet more and more people, they become aware of the kinds of people they like and dislike, and they recognize the importance of compatibility. **Compatibility** means having similar attitudes and personality, and a liking for the same activities.[21] For example, one couple decides to live in the city and focus on their careers rather than have a family. They like drama and excitement in their life—something the city provides. They often attend hockey and basketball games, and they spend their money on trendy clothes and eating out. Because they like the same things, their relationship is likely to last.

Differences

Although two people who have very different beliefs are unlikely to form a strong and lasting relationship, people with different personality characteristics might be attracted to each other. For example, a person who doesn't like making decisions might be attracted to a strong decision maker. Because these characteristics complement each other, they might help strengthen the relationship.

Specific interests may be so similar that they outweigh any differences. An American who runs in the Boston Marathon might have more in common with a runner from Kenya than with someone who spends every Sunday morning reading the newspaper and eating doughnuts. Association with a group might bring people together. Although a Rotary member from Indiana would have a different cultural background from a Rotary member from India, the fact that they both belong to Rotary will create a common ground for some of their interactions.

Proximity

Proximity is the close contact that occurs when people share an experience such as work, play, or school. Even when people might not otherwise have been attracted to each other, they may begin to know and like each other because they are together so much. For example, being in the same study group for a semester, sharing an office, or standing side-by-side on an assembly line are activities that place people in close proximity. Once they begin to share their lives on a day-to-day basis, they may find themselves becoming friends or even forming a romantic relationship.

Sometimes people who are attracted to each other form a strong friendship but lose touch when they no longer have proximity. Typically, friends who move to different cities vow to stay in touch, but it is not unusual for contact to drop to a yearly holiday card. Proximity, then, is important not just for starting relationships but also for keeping them going.

Motives for Interpersonal Communication

In Daniel Goleman's book *Social Intelligence* (Bantam, 2006), he claims that the brain is wired for sociability and connectedness—for altruism, compassion, concern, and rapport. In his words, "We are wired to connect. Neuroscience has discovered that our brain's very design makes it sociable, inexorably drawn into an intimate brain-to-brain linkup whenever we engage with another person."

The point of Goleman's book is that although everyone has needs that will vary with personality and moods, and that when we seek out others, we are trying to meet one or more of our interpersonal needs—pleasure, affection, inclusion, escape, relaxation, control, or health—there is something much deeper—very extensive circuitry—that has established a biological need to interact. Let's briefly examine these other interpersonal needs for seeking out others.

In her article, "Are You with the Right Mate?" Rebecca Webber discusses relationship compatibility:

"There is no such thing as two people meant for each other," says Michelle Givertz (assistant professor of communication studies at California State University, Chico), "It's a matter of adjusting and adapting."

"But you have to know yourself so that you can get your needs for affection, inclusion, and control met in the ways that matter most for you. Even then, successful couples redefine their relationship many times," says [Christine] Meinecke [a clinical psychologist in Des Moines, Iowa]. "Relationships need to continually evolve to fit ever-changing circumstances. They need to incorporate each partner's changes and find ways to meet their new needs."

"If both parties are willing to tackle the hard and vulnerable work of building love and healing conflict, they have a good chance to survive," says [New York psychotherapist Ken] Page. If one party is reluctant, "you might need to say to your partner, 'I need this because I feel like we're losing each other, and I don't want that to happen (p. 65).'"

Source: Webber, Rebecca. (January/February 2012). Are you with the right mate? *Psychology Today*.

Questions

1. Do you agree with the main premise of this excerpt, that "There is no such thing as two people meant for each other?" Why or why not?

2. When it comes to having a successful relationship, why do you think one of the main prerequisites is to know yourself first? Do you think that is important? Do you have any examples of people in your life who exemplify this comment?

3. Is it fair to say that building love and healing conflict is truly hard and vulnerable work? Healing conflict may be obvious, but why would you have to work to build love?

4. If you had a partner who is reluctant to engage in the "hard and vulnerable work" to keep a relationship alive and successful, do you think the author's recommendation for what to say: "I need this because I feel like we're losing each other, and I don't want that to happen," is a realistic suggestion?

Everyone has needs that will vary with personality and moods. When you seek out others, you are trying to meet one or more of the following interpersonal needs: pleasure, affection, inclusion, escape, relaxation, control, and health.[22]

Pleasure

We engage in a lot of interpersonal communication because it's fun. You chat online or gossip or text on your cell phone with your best friend; you sit around and argue about sports teams with your buddies; you stop at the student center to have coffee, but also in the hope of meeting someone you know.

Affection

Whether it is expressed nonverbally (hugging, touching) or verbally ("I'm really glad you called me today"), affection is important to human happiness.

Unlike inclusion, affection is a one-to-one emotion.

Inclusion

Inclusion—involvement with others—is one of the most powerful human needs. Although nearly everyone has had the experience of being excluded, most people have had more experiences of being included. You may eat with a certain group at the cafeteria, go to parties at friends' houses, or join a club at the university. Belonging in this way is important to everyone's sense of well-being.

Escape

At one time or another, we all engage in interpersonal communication to try to avoid the jobs we are supposed to do. For example, before you begin writing your term paper, you decide to wander down the hall of your dorm to talk to a friend. A new form of breaking free is "getting away" by computer. Chat rooms, e-mail, and surfing the Internet are particularly popular and enable you to escape without even going anywhere.

Relaxation

You often talk to your friends or families to relax and unwind from the activities of the day. You might sit with co-workers during a break, spend a few minutes with your spouse after work, or go out with a group of friends on the weekend.

Control

In a broad sense control means being able to make choices.

In the best relationships, the persons try to share control, which may change with the circumstances. For example, a couple we know moved to a new place where the wife had to commute two hours a day. This meant that she was not home to cook the evening meal, so her husband had to do it. He took control by reorganizing the kitchen to his liking—a legitimate action since he was now the main cook.

Researchers have found that people who have control over their own lives are healthier both mentally and physically.[23] Students learn better when teachers give them some independence, and workers feel better about their jobs when they can make some decisions about how their work should be done.[24] People who have the sense that they are in control of their lives are meeting one of their deepest needs.

Health

Research shows that people with strong social ties live longer than those who are isolated.[25] If you have a romantic partner, frequent contact with friends and family, or involvement with volunteer or religious organizations, the social support systems you form assist you in keeping heart rate, hypertension, and stress hormones under control. Lonely people often view the world as threatening, and although they want to be connected, they both expect negative responses and engage in self-protective behaviors that are self-defeating. Experts advise lonely people to join a local club or organization just because of the health-protective effects.

Although the Internet may contribute positively to people's social ties, it, too, can have negative side effects if it rewires their brains as discussed in the Another Point of View box that follows.

Talking to Each Other

Roles, Relationships, and Communication

All relationships are governed by the roles that the participants expect each other to play. Sometimes these roles are tightly defined; other times the participants have the flexibility to define them.

Often the roles you know best are those that are the most traditionally defined, such as teacher and parent. Even though the people who work in these roles might want more flexibility than is allowed by traditional definitions, they often feel social pressure to conform to traditional roles and thus to traditional behavior.

In her *USA Today* essay, "Ever-present devices can push our crazy buttons," Sharon Jayson wonders, after being immersed in technology for a good while, "How much is too much?" Jayson continues, "Our tech saturation has reached such a critical point that some experts say it's rewiring our brains." Quoting neuroscientist Gary Small, a brain researcher at the University of California-Los Angeles:

"Our brains are sensitive to stimuli moment to moment, and if you spend a lot of time with a particular mental experience or stimulus, the neural circuits that control that mental experience will strengthen," he says. "At the same time, if we neglect certain experiences, the circuits that control those will weaken. If we're not having conversations or looking people in the eye—human contact skills—they will weaken" (p. 2D).

Source: Jayson, Sharon. (March 27, 2012). Ever-present devices can push our crazy buttons. *USA Today*.

Questions

1. Do you believe what Gary Small writes about the influence of technology?
2. If interpersonal skills are weakened, what possible ramifications do you foresee?
3. Do you think people can become addicted to various technologies?

Usually at the beginning of a relationship with someone your own age, you can choose the roles you want to play. Friends, for example, often decide on the role they will play within a friendship. Once the relationship is established, role expectations become fixed, and friends expect each other to react in certain ways.

A critical question in a marriage is whether you want to play the role your father or mother played. If you don't, how will you set out to define your own role? Sherod Miller, a psychologist, says that once the partners give up old roles—the ones that were based on gender—they have to work out new ones: a process that leads to negotiating every aspect of their lives, especially when the first baby arrives.[26]

Other psychologists who have studied marriage found that the most successful marriages are ones where the male partners listen to their female partners rather than reacting defensively to complaints and criticism. A husband's willingness to listen shows that he understands and respects his wife's needs, and when this occurs, there is a much better chance of marital stability.[27]

As well as roles for your intimate relationships, there are roles for all aspects of your life and communication that work best in each of them. Your job is to find out which communication works best for all the roles you play. You will see, then, that much of your success in playing a role will depend on how well you communicate in that role.

Beginning Conversations: The Art of Small Talk

Have you ever felt nervous about entering a classroom where you didn't know any of the students? In many new social situations you might feel uneasy. You may wonder whether you will be able to begin a conversation and whether you will find people you like and, just as important, people who like you. The uncertainty you are feeling will probably be shared by other people in the room. How do you go about reducing it?

Figure 6-1
How People Begin
Conversations

If you follow this figure from top to bottom, you will see how conversations begin, progress, and end. In the sections that are numbered, there is some variation: people may speak about one or more of these topics.

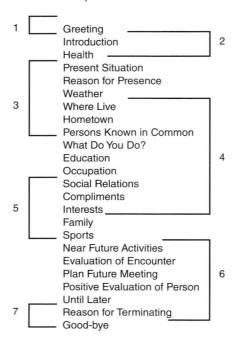

When most people begin conversations, they engage in **small talk**—social conversation about unimportant topics that allows a person to maintain contact without making a deep commitment. There are all sorts of conventions in small talk. Scholars who have studied conversation have found that it follows a routine that varies only slightly. Figure 6-1 shows this conversation pattern.

As you can see in this figure, many of the conversational responses are based on questions, some to find out information, others to establish common ground. Other questions are asked just to fill time or to be sociable. Since most people like answering questions about themselves, they are flattered when someone shows interest in them.

In her article "Smooth Encounters" (*Psychology Today*, April, 2013, pp. 62–69), Mary Loftus includes a section, "How to Thrive at a Cocktail Party," in which she cites Bernardo Carducci, director of the Shyness Research Institute at Indiana University Southeast, who wrote the book, *The Pocket Guide to Making Successful Small Talk* (Pocket Guide Publishing, 1999). Loftus offers Carducci's five cardinal rules for making small talk:

- Be nice, but not necessarily brilliant.

- Keep your opening lines simple, and think about your introduction beforehand (your name, and a little information about yourself that might serve as conversation kindling later).

- Join conversations that are already in progress by extending or elaborating on the topic of discussion or introduce new topics, perhaps from current events.

- End a conversation by saying, "There's someone I have to speak with, but it was really nice meeting you." Then briefly summarize the conversation so they'll know you were listening.

- Don't make the mistake of staying on one subject for too long. It's called "small talk" for a reason. Think conversational hors d'oeuvres, with each topic sampled and savored (p. 69).

Because small-talk topics and questions are socially sanctioned, they create a safe meeting ground. They provide you with a chance to establish who you are with others. They also permit you to find out more about yourself through the eyes of others. Although you don't give away a lot of personal information in small talk, the image you give to others and the image you receive of them will let you know whether you want to see them again.

To offer even further assistance to those in need, Ian Yarett, in a brief essay, "What's the Best Question to Ask on a First Date?" (*Newsweek*, February 7, 2011), begins his piece saying, "The answer [to the title question of his essay] is one that will get you a second night out." Yarett cites the dating site OkCupid, which, according to him, "picked up [its wisdom] from mining its vast cache of user data. These five questions," he writes, "are the most 'informative' . . . and least personal—exactly the kind you want to ask when meeting someone for the first time" (p. 48): (in the order of greatest usefulness) 1) Do you like scary movies? 2) Do you believe in miracles? 3) Do you prefer simplicity or complexity? 4) Have you ever traveled alone around a foreign country? 5) Would it be fun to chuck it all and go live on a sailboat? There you are—armed and ready to meet a new relationship partner for the very first time.

Bids and the Bidding Process

If you knew specifically what it was that holds relationships together, and you knew that it was within your control, would you change the way you conducted yourself in your interpersonal relationships? What holds relationships together are bids and the bidding process. A **bid,** according to John Gottman and his team of relationship researchers, "can be a question, a gesture, a look, a touch—any single expression that says, 'I want to feel connected to you.' A **response to a bid** is just that—a positive or negative answer to somebody's request for emotional connection." See Figure 6-2.[28]

What Determines Your Ability to Bid and to Respond to Bids?

Some people are likely to be better at bids and responses than others. There are three major influences at work. First, it may be a function of the way people's brains process feelings. Second, it may be a function of the way emotions were handled in the homes where people grew up. And third, it may be a function of people's emotional communication skills. These three influences can be complex, interacting variables. Despite their influence, however, sometimes just knowing what ingredients can influence a relationship, or just knowing specifically what you can do to make a relationship you cherish a success, is enough. Placing bids and responding to bids is a skill that can be learned, practiced, and mastered.[29]

How Do Bids Contribute to Relationship Development?

In successful relationships, bids for emotional connection are responded to positively. Bids from either relationship partner are neither ignored nor dismissed, whether they are simple or mundane. It is the simple and mundane bids that weave the fabric that

Figure 6-2
Bids and Responses
to Bids

Questions, gestures, looks, or touches that say, "I want to feel connected to you." — Bid

Response to Bid — A positive or negative answer to someone's request for emotional connection.

ATTENTION!

Reality Check
Based on any meaningful relationship you have had (or are having) recently, analyze a communication event that has taken place (or is taking place) with respect to bids and responses to bids. Does the bidding process make sense to you? Is it logical that it could be so important in holding relationships together? What are some specific things you can do in your relationships that would capitalize on what is known regarding the importance of bidding and the bidding process? Can you see how this would contribute to greater effectiveness in communication?

forms the backdrop for all future bids. Many come nonverbally and include vocalizing, affiliating gestures (like opening a door or offering a place to sit), playful touching, facial expressions, or affectionate touching.[30] Sure, some bids may be unseen, unheard, or overlooked just as some may be sent in a subtle, camouflaged, confused, or nonspecific manner. It is the overall pattern of behavior that is important, not necessarily any single, solitary bid. Remember, in most positive relationships thousands of bids take place daily.

Each encounter in a relationship is made up of many smaller exchanges—bids and responses to those bids. These exchanges of emotional information will either strengthen or weaken the connections between people, and these connections form the fabric we referred to earlier. Here, in the first example, the response to the bid is negative. In the next, the response is positive:

Hey, Chris. Did you get that class report finished?
Would you stop nagging at me? You sound just like my mother!

Would you get me a soda while you're up?
No problem. Do you want anything else?

The point is not the content, and the point has nothing to do with timing or circumstances. The point is that a positive response to a bid typically leads to continued interaction, and the chances for a successful relationship become better and better. And the reverse is just as clear. Negative responses to bids will shut down communication. Bids cease, and the relationship terminates.

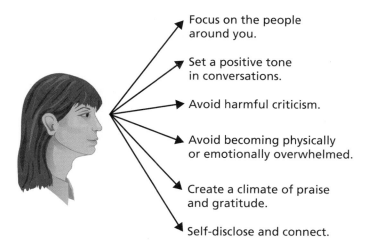

Focus on the people around you.

Set a positive tone in conversations.

Avoid harmful criticism.

Avoid becoming physically or emotionally overwhelmed.

Create a climate of praise and gratitude.

Self-disclose and connect.

Figure 6-3
How to Encourage Bids

How Can You Encourage Bids?

How can you make certain you respond positively to the bids of others if you choose to do so? Gottman and his researchers discuss six common sense ways to encourage and reinforce the bids of others. These are outlined in Figure 6-3.

Owned Messages

An **owned message** (also known as an I-message, as coined by Thomas Gordon[31]) is "*an acknowledgment of subjectivity by a message-sender through the use of first-person-singular terms* (I, me, my, mine). 'Responsible' communicators are those who 'own' their thoughts and feelings by employing these pronouns."[32]

Owned messages tend to provoke less interpersonal defensiveness than you-messages, and they are useful for conveying negative information. Some simple examples of owned and unowned messages will demonstrate the difference. To say "You make me mad" is an example of an unowned message (a you-message) and, as is obvious, has the potential for creating defensiveness in another person. To say "I'm feeling angry" is an example of owning a message and is less likely to create defensiveness.

Gordon said owned messages can be called "responsibility messages" because those who send them are taking responsibility for their own inner condition (listening to *themselves*) and assuming responsibility for being open enough to share their assessment of themselves with others. In addition, they leave the responsibility for the other person's behavior with them.[33]

What does an I-message look like? Gordon suggests a behavior/feelings/effects formula for constructing I-messages.

1. A description by the one concerned of the other's unacceptable (disruptive) behavior.

2. The feelings of the one concerned in reaction to the other's unacceptable behavior.

3. An explanation of how the other's behavior interferes with the one concerned's ability to answer his or her own needs.

ATTENTION!

Benefits of Owned Messages
They demonstrate *your* willingness to take responsibility for:

- Yourself
- Your thoughts
- Your feelings
- Your knowledge claims
- Your actions

and . . .
They reduce defensiveness in others, and they leave the responsibility for others' behavior with them.

Example: "Jennifer, when you leave things everywhere (1) I get frustrated (2) because I cannot do what I have to do (3)."

Remember as you use owned messages, any given behavior can be an asset or a liability, depending on the goal or situation. Interpersonal skills are competent when communicators employ them sensitively and sensibly according to the requirements of a particular social setting. Using owned messages is a skill that is generally perceived to be competent across contexts. It can increase your sense of control and responsibility, and control and responsibility are issues that are basic and paramount to interpersonal competence.[34]

Relational Dialectics

When presenting information on interpersonal relationships, it could easily appear to readers that things in relationships tend to be static and unchanging—much like the words on this page. Instead, things are constantly changing. **Relational dialectics** describes some of the patterns that occur in relationships as a result of the tensions that take place because of conflicting emotional needs.[35] That is, communication partners experience internal, conflicting pulls that cause their relationship to be in a constant state of flux.

There are three primary relational dialectics or patterns that take place in relationships. The first, connectedness and separateness, describes the tension between establishing a close and personal bond with another person and the desire to spend some time alone, away from your partner. There is no question that too much connection results in the loss of individual identity. The second relational dialectic that creates tensions, certainty and uncertainty describes the need for predictability and a sense of assurance in the relationship and the need for the variety and spontaneity that comes from novelty, mystery, and lack of predictability. Too much predictability results in relationships that are bland and monotonous. The third relational dialectic, openness and closedness, occurs when partners feel the pressure to be transparent and to reveal extensive personal information along with the natural individual desire for privacy. Too much transparency and sharing of personal information can steal from one's need to remain undisclosed, exclusive, secluded, and protected.

Self-Disclosure: Important Talk

To communicate who you are to other people, you have to engage in **self-disclosure**—a process in which one person tells another person something he or she would not reveal to just anyone.

The Importance of Self-Disclosure

Social penetration is the process of increasing both disclosure and intimacy in a relationship, and it is one of the most widely studied processes in relational development.[36] The theory is that relationships become more intimate over time as partners disclose more and more information about themselves. When partners in a relationship are motivated, and when they exert the extra effort necessary not just to continue their relationship but to permit its growth, the relationship necessarily undergoes certain qualitative changes. Partners experience an additional sense of connectedness. At the same time, writes one researcher, "communicative transactions become increasingly interpersonal."[37]

Whether you want to encourage a relationship, hold it at the same level, or back off often depends on the information you get during the process of self-disclosure. Gerald Miller and his communication-research colleagues state that there are three kinds of information.[38] The first kind is **cultural information,** which tells us about a person's most generally shared cultural attributes such as language, shared values, beliefs, and ideologies. Information at this level is as shallow and impersonal as is a greeting or good-bye. Knowing it allows you to perform acceptably in most social situations, but it is not very helpful when it comes to relationships.

The second kind of information is **sociological** and tells you something about others' social groups and roles. This level of communication allows you to be successful communicating with your doctor, dentist, lawyer, or hair stylist. You know something about their roles and affiliations, but you know relatively little about the person separate from his or her role.

The third kind of information is **psychological,** which is the most specific and intimate because it allows you to know individual traits, feelings, attitudes, and important personal data. This is the type of information on which most of your predictions about relationships will be based.

It is through self-disclosure, then, that you meet someone who believes the way you do—that you discover a common interest, for example, which you can pursue in greater depth because both of you have some background and information to share. Such a partner is likely to react to situations and events the way you would, and you trust him or her enough to reveal even more about yourself. The Assess Yourself box at the end of this chapter is on trusting others, because trust is an important part of the self-disclosure process.

Self-disclosure is important to relationships in other ways as well. You use it in the process of reciprocity: When someone discloses with you, your tendency is to self-disclose in return. You use self-disclosure for self-clarification—to clarify beliefs, opinions, thoughts, attitudes, and problems: "I thought you understood I was only kidding." You use it for identity management in attempts to make yourself more attractive: "I'm using a new fragrance; did you notice?" You use it for social control when revealing information may increase your control over the situation or a person: "I was given the authority to lead this group, and I think we should all stick to our agenda."

The Process of Self-Disclosure

One way to look at how the self-disclosure process operates was developed by Joseph Luft and Harry Ingham. Combining their first names, they labeled their model the **Johari Window** (see Figure 6-4).[39] It is through the feedback process that you see yourself as others see you and others learn, too, how you see them. For example, giving and receiving feedback tells others how their behavior affects you, how you feel, and what you perceive just as it is a reaction by others, usually in terms of their feelings and perceptions, telling you how your behavior affects them. Because of the importance of

Telling a secret might be one form of self-disclosure.

ATTENTION!

Guidelines for Self-Disclosure

1. Think before proceeding.
2. Examine and evaluate your intentions. Is your motivation to:
   —enhance a relationship?
   —get revenge?
   —cause hurt?
3. Think about the appropriate amount of self-disclosure.
4. Pick your time, place, and person. (Don't self-disclose indiscriminately.)
5. Pay attention to others' self-disclosure: It's a two-way street.
6. Be prepared to live with what you reveal; you can't take it back.[40]

Figure 6-4
The Johari Window

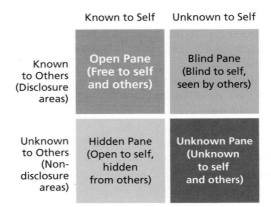

this concept—self-disclosure—understanding the panes in the Johari Window offers a way to picture the entire process of giving and receiving feedback and, as necessary, make adjustments when relationships call for it.

The "Free to self and others" area—the **open pane**—includes information about yourself that you are willing to communicate, as well as information you are unable to hide (such as a blush when you are embarrassed). When students meet for the first time in a class, they follow the instructor's suggestion and introduce themselves. Most of them stick to bare essentials: their names, where they come from, and their majors. When people do not know one another very well, the open pane is smaller than when they have become better acquainted.

The area labeled "Blind to self, seen by others"—the **blind pane**—is a kind of accidental disclosure area: There are certain things you do not know about yourself that others know about you. For example, when you interact in a group, group members will learn about you from your verbal cues, mannerisms, the way you say things, or the style in which you relate to others. They may know that you always look away from people when you talk to them, or they may find out that you always clear your throat before you speak.

The **hidden pane**—self-knowledge hidden from others—is a deliberate nondisclosure area; there are certain things you know about yourself that you do not want known, so you deliberately conceal them from others. Most people hide things that might evoke disapproval from those they love and admire: "I was a teenage shoplifter"; "I don't know how to read very well." Others keep certain areas hidden from one person but open to another: A young woman tells her best friend, but not her mother, that her grades are low because she seldom studies.

The **unknown pane** is a nondisclosure area; it provides no possibility of disclosure because it is unknown to the self and to others. This pane represents all the parts of you that are not yet revealed, such as your intrapersonal dynamics, childhood memories, latent potentialities, and unrecognized resources.

The disclosure and nondisclosure areas vary from one relationship to another, and they change all the time in the same relationship. Figure 6-5 shows how the Johari Window might look in a close relationship. The open pane becomes much larger because a person is likely to disclose more. When disclosure increases, people not only reveal more information about themselves but also are likely to discover things about themselves that they had not known before. If you apply the Johari Window to each of your relationships, you will find that the panes are different sizes in each one. In other words, you are likely to be more self-disclosing in some relationships than you are in others.

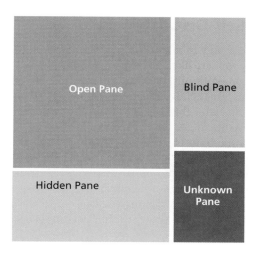

Figure 6-5
The Johari Window
after a Relationship
Has Developed

Source: From Group
Processes: An Introduction
to Group Dynamics by
J. Luft © 1970. Reprinted
by permission of The
McGraw-Hill Companies.

Self-Disclosure and Intimacy: Rewards and Fears

Self-disclosure is the most rewarding when it leads to greater intimacy. Only intimate relationships give you a chance to really be yourself, to share who you are with another person. This kind of intimacy can be found in romantic relationships and among family members and close friends. One study has found that both men and women are willing to self-disclose to about the same degree.[41]

Although in this chapter we take the position that self-disclosure is very important if you are going to have deep and satisfying relationships, we also acknowledge that many people fear the consequences of revealing themselves to another.

Fear of Having Your Faults Exposed

Self-disclosure in a relationship may lead to communicating that you are not perfect and exposing things from your past that you would rather keep hidden. Once your fears, anxieties, or weaknesses are known to another person, that person could tell them to others or use them against you.

Fear That Your Partner Will Become Your Critic

By telling someone you are vulnerable, you open yourself to attack. A wife, for example, tells her husband how bad she felt when she wasn't invited to the senior prom. One day when they are having a fight, he says, "Don't tell me how much people like you. You didn't even get invited to the prom!"

Fear of Losing Your Individuality

Some people feel that if they reveal too much, they lose their sense of self, that there are private things that only they should know. This might be especially true during the years when teenagers are trying to gain autonomy from their families. Part of being autonomous is making decisions on your own and not telling everything to your parents.

Fear of Being Abandoned

Sometimes one partner is afraid that if the other knows something about him or her, he or she will be abandoned. For example, someone might not want to tell another about his struggle with alcoholism for fear that the other person will no longer love, accept, or want him.

ATTENTION!

**Risks of
Self-Disclosure**

- It exposes you.
- It lets others know how to hurt you.
- It may result in rejection.
- It may result in a loss of support.
- It projects an image of you that you may not like (subject to another's interpretation).
- It doesn't always lead to favorable impressions.
- If it comes too early, it can damage a relationship.[42]

When Should Self-Disclosure Occur?

STRATEGIC

FLEXIBILITY

Because of the risks, knowing when to self-disclose requires that you think about potential situations (anticipate); take stock of the factors, elements, and conditions of the situation (assess); determine the value and worth of the factors, elements, and conditions (evaluate); and carefully select the skills and behaviors that are likely to be appropriate (select) before engaging in self-disclosure.

Disclosure should occur only in relationships that are important to you. People who do not know you very well are likely to feel uncomfortable if you tell them too much about yourself too soon. Wait until you have some signs that a relationship has the possibility of developing further. For example, if someone seeks you out to invite you to go out with him or her, after three or four times this is a sign that the person wants the relationship to develop.

For disclosure to work, both parties must be involved in it. If one person does all the disclosing and the other party just sits back and listens, disclosure is not likely to continue. Remember that disclosure means taking a risk. You will never know how another person will respond to your openness until you give it a try. To avoid getting hurt, try testing the water before you plunge in. One way of doing this is to talk about a subject in general terms and see how the other person reacts before you talk about your own experience with it.

Finally, examine your own motives for self-disclosure. Why do you want the other person to know this information? Will it really enhance the relationship, or can it do harm? All of us have some secrets that we should probably keep to ourselves. Sharing them may cause injury or make the other person lose trust in us. Although some secrets are a burden to keep, it may serve the interest of the relationship to do so. Those in relationships who believe in full and complete disclosure with partners risk the possibility of damage and even loss.

Remember the discussion about EVT (expectancy violation theory) in Chapter 4, Nonverbal Communication. It suggests that when someone violates your expectations, you can perceive the violation either positively or negatively depending, in part, on how much you like the other person. This theory proposes that it is your expectancy that will influence the outcome of the communication as positive or negative. Positive violations are likely to increase the attraction between you and the violator just as negative violations are likely to decrease the attraction between you and the violator. The process of self-disclosure offers a great example of EVT in action. Too much disclosure, disclosure that is too rapid for the progress of the relationship, no disclosure at all, or the lack of reciprocity of the disclosure, can all be perceived as violations and, thus, raise red flags regarding further pursuit of a relationship.

Social Penetration Theory

Irwin Altman and Dalmas Taylor, psychologists, describe the dynamics of relational closeness through **social penetration theory,** which suggests that closeness occurs through a gradual process of self-disclosure. You have probably discovered that closeness with another person develops if you proceed in a gradual and orderly fashion. Your relationship will move from superficial to intimate levels of exchange as a function of the self-disclosure that occurs. Altman and Taylor believe that it is only by becoming vulnerable to another person by opening oneself to that person—social penetration through self-disclosure—that we can develop a close relationship.[43]

It may appear from reading the above paragraph that "closeness" is something you desire in all relationships, and this is clearly *not* the case. Relationships cannot all be categorized as intimate or non-intimate. Most relationships, for example, fall somewhere in between these two poles. Sometimes we seek a moderately close relationship such as that with a co-worker or with a new acquaintance about whom we have heard some negative information (e.g., they talk too much, they are a gossip, they have some values we don't share, or they have an unacceptable past)—or, we seek no relationship at all.

Another aspect of social penetration theory is that relationships can and do fall apart—labeled depenetration or dissolution. Just as communication moves relationships forward toward intimacy, it can also move relationships back toward non-intimacy—in some systematic fashion. Continuing destructive conflict that is unresolved can have this effect. But, it should be clear as well, relationships that experience depenetration do not necessarily or automatically dissolve or terminate. Just as some relationships experience violations of relational rules, practices, and expectations, some, too, recover from them and go on to not just exist but thrive.

Perhaps the most memorable portion of social penetration theory is the onion metaphor used to describe self-disclosure. The idea is simply that the depth of self-disclosure is illustrated by removing layers of an onion as if they were portions of your personality. The outer layer of the onion is the public self—similar to the open pane of the Johari Window—and carries information like your height, weight, race, and gender. Below that outer layer lies more private information such as your beliefs, faith, prejudices, and information about your relationships. Beneath this second layer is the inner core of the onion—similar to the hidden pane of the Johari Window. It is within this core that your values, feelings about yourself, and deep emotions lie.

If you were having a discussion with a new acquaintance—one in whom you have some interest—you would no doubt begin to reveal different layers of your personalities—beginning with small talk and progressing to more important topics. With respect to the onion, you would begin to peel off portions. But, one of the important aspects of social penetration theory is that such penetration requires *reciprocity*—the process whereby one's willingness to be open leads to the other person's openness. You are experiencing, along with this new acquaintance, mutual levels of self-disclosure. It is Altman and Taylor's belief that intimacy cannot be achieved without such reciprocity.

The point of discussing social penetration theory is simply that it is another way to understand human behavior, interpersonal relationships, and, more specifically, the gradual and orderly way in which self-disclosure takes place.

Essential Elements of Good Relationships

Once you have begun using bids, owned messages, and self-disclosure, a relationship has truly begun and you need to "grow" it. "When asked the three most important factors for a successful marriage, most adults said trust . . ." (63 percent of the 1,001 adults surveyed). The next answer was time spent together (52 percent), and then compatibility, resolving differences, ability to forgive, and, finally, physical displays of affection.[44] Here, we will look at elements that draw people together: verbal skills, emotional expressiveness, conversational focus, nonverbal analysis, conversational encouragement, care and appreciation, commitment, and adaptation.

When you examine each of the following "essential elements," you will notice there is a strong emphasis on the need for male partners to make changes. Lundy Bancroft, for fifteen years in a career specializing in domestic abuse and the behavior of abusive men, and JAC Patrissi, for twenty years specializing in creative responses for survivors of abuse, in their book designed for women, *Should I Stay or Should I Go?* (NY: Berkley Books, 2011), write in the introduction to their book: "You can't make your partner change, you can ask him to, you can even demand it, but you can't do the work for him." Later in their book, they clarify their statement:

> *A man with unhealthy behavioral patterns (including self-destructive ones) does not change from magical awakenings, or promises, or waking up in a better mood, or deciding one day to be a nicer person. Your partner's transformation can only be brought about by hard work over a long period of time, serious self-reflection, development of empathy, and overcoming self-centeredness. Mystery and poetry do not play a big role here, we're talking about hands-in-the-mud, no-nonsense, committed work that is not much fun, but that can carry great rewards over the long haul (p. 260).*

Verbal Skills

Partners in good relationships must have ongoing conversations, or dialogues, about the relationship itself. They must be able to search together for ways of reducing conflict, to discuss expectations they have of each other, and to explore anything else that might affect the relationship. In her article "Finding Real Love," Cary Barbor ends by saying, "Learning how best to communicate with each other and treat one another will help us enjoy loving, lasting relationships."[45]

Not only do females begin talking earlier than males, on most national assessment tests they score well ahead of males in reading and writing, and many more major in English, comparative literature, and foreign languages than men.[46] To make certain the playing field remains level, males may need to apply themselves more when it comes to verbal skills, because for partners to continue in a relationship, they must find mutually beneficial ways of communicating. Also, males need to alter their perception of relationships as stable, static commodities that never need discussion or reexamination.

Emotional Expressiveness

Gottman noted that your ability to bid and to respond to bids depends on the way your brain processes feelings, the way emotions were handled in your home, and your emotional communication skills.[47] Christina Hoff Sommers claims that females' verbal skills "may be responsible for their superior emotional expressiveness."[48] Her claim is supported by Daniel Goleman in *Emotional Intelligence* who says, "Because girls develop language more quickly than do boys, this leads them to be more experienced at articulating their feelings and more skilled than boys at using words to explore and substitute for emotional reactions such as physical fights."[49] Not only are females more expressive and responsive to others, they "invite others into conversations."[50] Once again, to level the playing field, males need to improve their ability at emotional expressiveness.

Achieving emotional expressiveness may require discussing points of conflict. This is particularly important if relationships are to be successful. Some people are conditioned to stay away from conflict. Childhood messages such as "Hold your tongue" and "I don't ever want to hear you talk that way again" lead us to believe that it's wrong to say words that other people do not want to hear. As adults, however, we have to recondition ourselves to discuss areas of conflict: Withdrawing from or avoiding conflict is too harmful to relationships.

Conversational Focus

A third factor likely to affect your ability to handle relationships is what you choose to talk about. Sommers claims that "Males, whether young or old, are less interested

This AOM asks you to be open-minded about your own strengths and weaknesses as they relate to interpersonal relationship maintenance, and it has two parts.

First, of the essential elements of good relationships (i.e., verbal skills, emotional expressiveness, conversational focus, nonverbal analysis, conversational encouragement, care and appreciation, commitment, and adaptation), with which of the elements do you feel most comfortable and why? That is, projecting yourself into a relationship that you would like to last, which of the elements or which combination of elements would you most likely display? List them in order of priority for yourself.

Second, taking the elements at the bottom of your list (or *not* listed at all), which could you work on for improvement? Here, offer a brief set of steps you could follow that would assist you in giving more attention to, developing, and displaying these weaker (or nonexistent) elements.

than females in talking about feelings and personal relationships."[51] Researchers at Northwestern University analyzed the conversational focus of college students gathered around a cafeteria table.[52] They discovered that 56 percent of the women's targets were intimates, close friends, boyfriends, and family members, but only 25 percent of the conversational focus of men was friends and relatives.[53] When researchers simultaneously presented male and female college students with two images on a stereoscope, one of an object, the other of a person, male subjects more often saw the object while female subjects more often saw the person.[54] Males need to increase their focus on feelings and relationships—not only to make their feelings known, but to make other people, especially their relationship partners, know how they feel about them and about their relationship.

Nonverbal Analysis

A fourth factor that will affect your ability to handle relationships is your ability to read between the lines, to analyze the nonverbal cues of the other person. Dozens of experiments confirm "that women are much better than men at judging emotions based on the expression on a stranger's face."[55] Not only are women better at observing the nonverbal cues of others, they also "tend to give obvious visual and vocal clues to signal that they are following what others say and are interested in it."[56] Clues might include nodding their heads, smiling, establishing eye contact, and offering responsive gestures.[57] Males need to increase their sensitivity to nonverbal cues. Because they are not conditioned to be as observant in this area, they need to be especially vigilant and aware.

Conversational Encouragement

Often, men listen to others without showing their feelings; they keep their responses and feelings to themselves, as noted in the section on emotional expressiveness. This can be interpreted as an unwillingness to listen or lack of interest.[58] Women, on the other hand, encourage others to continue talking using listening noises such as "um, hmmm," "yes," "that's interesting," "so," "and," and so forth. They are encouragers, and these vocalizations not only reveal they are listening and interested, but they also prompt others to continue talking and to elaborate on their ideas.[59]

What are some of the obvious elements of good relationships being revealed in this group?

Listen and Respond to Others[64]

1. Pay close attention.
2. Suspend judgment.
3. Reflect back what they said.
4. Remember disclosure.
5. Listen with honesty—keep private.
6. Reassure and support.
7. Reciprocate with appropriate disclosure.

Roger Axtell, in his book *Do's and Taboos Around the World for Women in Business*, quotes Kathi Seifert, group president of North American personal care products for the Kimberly-Clark Corporation, who says, "Women are naturally more caring, nurturing, and better listeners. They like to help and to respond to people's needs."[60] Shmuley Boteach, dean of the L'Chaim Society, which hosts world figures and diplomats and concentrates on values-based leadership, says women "when speaking to their husbands, . . . stop talking in midsentence because they know they are not being listened to. They feel like a piece of furniture, and this experience of being ignored is a denial of their value. Their spirit is crushed."[61] Fein and Schneider, in *The Rules for Marriage*, write "Learn how to listen without interrupting or offering advice, so that you can understand your spouse's perspective on things."[62] Men need to open up more, show their feelings, listen better, and reveal their responses. It may help, too, if men view conversations as Mary Boone describes them: "The purpose of a conversation is not to *agree* with each other, it's to learn from each other on both an intellectual and emotional level."[63]

Care and Appreciation

Scholars have found that people consistently use ways to communicate whether they want to have a relationship with a person or whether they want to avoid him or her.[65] The approach people use most often to foster a relationship is expressing *caring and appreciation* for the other person. Typical remarks might be, "We had such a good time last night, I would like to see you again," or "I am so glad that we are friends"—bids expressing "I want to feel connected to you." The second most used technique is giving *compliments*: "That was such a funny joke you told last night," or "You look great today"—more bids seeking connection. The third technique they use is engaging in *self-disclosure*—(also a bid) telling someone something about themselves that they wouldn't tell most people: "I felt so bad when I failed the test," or "I really like her; I wish she would pay some attention to me."

Commitment

All relationships need **commitment**—a strong desire by both parties for the relationship to continue and a willingness of both parties to take responsibility for the problems that occur in the relationship. Trying to force a partner to make a commitment, however, is a waste of time, claims Adrienne Burgess, in an article "I Vow to Thee" in the *Guardian*. She says, "Not only does it (commitment) provide no guarantees, but it also causes resentment and hostility, which undermines any loving feelings. In relationships with a real future, therefore, commitment usually develops at much the same rate on both sides. But promises of commitment are meaningless in the long-term, too—commitment isn't an act of will (while we can promise to stay with someone physically, we can't promise the same emotionally), and isn't something we do in any active sense. Commitment is a spin-off from other things: how satisfied we are with our relationship; whether we see a viable alternative to it; and whether moving on would cause us to lose important investments (time, money, shared property, and children)."[66]

All relationships have some kind of commitment as their foundation, but sometimes the partners to the commitment have different expectations. *Unconditional* commitments are those in which you commit yourself to another regardless of what may happen. Marriage vows are often cited as examples of unconditional commitments; however, with divorce rates hovering around 50 percent, it is clear that nearly one out of every two couples who accept the unconditional commitment do not fulfill it. *Conditional* commitments set forth the conditions of the commitment and carry with them the implication of "only if." "I will commit to you only if I do not find something better in the meantime," or "I will commit to you only if something extraordinary doesn't happen."

Although commitments are important and reassuring, it is perhaps better to accept them for what they are worth, based on the trust and faith in the person making the commitment and with hope for a positive future. However, it is best to prepare for the fact that most commitments are conditional, and it is unlikely that all conditions will be, or even could be, revealed or even known. Of course marriage should be an unconditional commitment, but we live in a transient society where planned obsolescence, endless technological advances, and instant millionaires guarantee a rapid and regular turnover of products, information, and fortunes; why should we expect relationships, including marriages, to be anything other than of short duration? Dreams, faith, optimism, visualizations, and confidence are all fine, but they really don't prepare you for a realistic conditional future. Only you can do that.

Matt Richtel, in his "Sunday Styles" essay, "Till Death, or 20 Years, Do Us Part" (*NY Times*, September 30, 2012), writes that "marriages are . . . more vulnerable than at any time. (Given how long we live, 'Till death do us part' is a much bigger challenge than it used to be.) [Stephanie Coontz, the research director at the Council on Contemporary Families] doesn't think a 20-year contract would make for happier marriages, but she believes there is value in asking people to consider and regularly assess their commitment, not necessarily based on a timetable but around life events: when you have kids, one spouse gets a new job or starts to work more hours, a family member dies, the kids leave home."

"All these moments," [Coontz] said, are when the marriage is most vulnerable.

"My advice would be to suggest a re-up every five years, or before every major transition in life . . . with a new set of vows that reflect what the couple has learned" (p. 10).

STRATEGIC FLEXIBILITY

Adapting and adjusting your behaviors and skills to changing circumstances is the foundation of strategic flexibility. Having all the tools in your toolbox is important, but even more important in strategic flexibility is carefully selecting exactly those tools likely to have the greatest impact and applying them with care and concern.

Adaptation

The time and effort dedicated to supporting, encouraging, and nurturing relationships—even well-established ones—must be spent in both introspection (the act of contemplating one's mental processes and emotional state in the relationship) and communication. Introspection and communication within relationships are foreign to conventional masculinity.[67]

Verbal skills, emotional expressiveness, conversational focus, nonverbal analysis, conversational encouragement, care and appreciation, and commitment are tools that help hold relationships together. You need to speak, listen, negotiate, stay on course, and hold your relationship in warm regard.[68] But if you can't adapt and adjust your skills and behaviors to the changes that occur, as introspection and communication will help you to do, these tools are useless. "After years of research," says one writer, "it turns out that what makes for highly adaptive people is their capacity to adapt."[69]

Social Exchange Theory

After reading about the essential elements of good relationships, you may wonder what you, as part of a relationship—or as a person contemplating the beginning of a relationship—does in relation to these elements? What you do can be framed by **social exchange theory,** which suggests that all human relationships are formed using a subjective cost-benefit analysis as well as a simple comparison of possible alternatives. You weigh the costs of forming or staying in a relationship (e.g., weak verbal skills, inferior emotional expressiveness, and feeble commitment) with the rewards or benefits (e.g., attractiveness, finances, and strong connections with others) and decide whether you want to leave the relationship or avoid forming one with this person.

Using a social exchange theory perspective, you would calculate the overall worth of a relationship by subtracting the costs from the rewards—as noted in the paragraph above. When the rewards are greater than the costs, the result is a positive relationship. Social exchange theory, however, goes further by predicting that what you would consider as those rewards will determine the worth of the relationship, and the worth of a relationship will determine the outcome—that is, whether you will continue the relationship or terminate it. It makes sense, then, to assume if those rewards are strong enough, your relationship is expected to endure, if not, it is unlikely to last.

The assumptions upon which social exchange theory are based, then, are that all of us tend to seek rewards and avoid punishments, that we are all rational, and—this is important—that the standards we use to evaluate costs and rewards will vary from person to person and even over time (revealing that relational life is a process that is continually changing).

Sociologist George Caspar Homans' article, "Social Behavior as Exchange," is cited as the seminal work on this theory.[70] John Thibaut and Harold Kelley, also sociologists, offered the following reasons people engage in a social exchange: (1) anticipated reciprocity, (2) expected gain in reputation and influence on others, (3) altruism and perception of efficacy (power to produce an effect), (4) direct reward.[71]

One of the keys to understanding social exchange theory is that the guiding force in interpersonal relationships is the advancement of both parties' self-interest. When self-interest is recognized—especially as an advantage to both parties (that the parties to a relationship are interdependent)—it can enhance relationships. For example, "two heads are better than one," "the sum of the parts is greater than the individual parts," or "we both bring to this relationship unique qualities that together make each of us stronger."

Trusting Others Scale

Indicate the degree to which you agree or disagree with each statement using the following scale: 1 = Strongly agree; 2 = Mildly agree; 3 = Agree and disagree equally; 4 = Mildly disagree; 5 = Strongly disagree. Circle your response following each statement.

1. Most people in my life are reliable and dependable. 5 4 3 2 1 0
2. In general, when there is a task to be done, I prefer doing it myself rather than asking someone else to do it. 5 4 3 2 1 0
3. Other people, in general, possess what I consider to be core (essential) skills and abilities. 5 4 3 2 1 0
4. In general, people share relevant information with me. 5 4 3 2 1 0
5. I get overly anxious when an important job that directly affects me and that I could do is carried out by someone else. 5 4 3 2 1 0
6. In general, the actions others take live up to the values they claim to live by. 5 4 3 2 1 0
7. Sometimes I feel I am being taken advantage of when someone else is taking actions that directly affect me, and yet I have no control over those actions. 5 4 3 2 1 0
8. In general, other people have a benevolent attitude toward me. 5 4 3 2 1 0
9. When in a group, I prefer working independently rather than as part of the group. 5 4 3 2 1 0
10. People tell white lies. 5 4 3 2 1 0
11. I have confidence in the integrity, ability, character, and truth of most other people. 5 4 3 2 1 0
12. In general, when others promise they will do something, I believe it will be done. 5 4 3 2 1 0
13. When others perform actions that directly affect me, I expect positive outcomes to occur. 5 4 3 2 1 0
14. In general, other people are open and honest with me, sharing all of their information, not just selected facts or opinions. 5 4 3 2 1 0
15. Other people voluntarily share their information with me. 5 4 3 2 1 0
16. I prefer to let those around me work independently, even if their work directly affects me. 5 4 3 2 1 0
17. Other people listen to me and to my ideas. 5 4 3 2 1 0
18. In general, others do not do what they say they will do. 5 4 3 2 1 0
19. I prefer situations where people with whom I am working have full opportunities for mutual influence—me influencing them and they influencing me. 5 4 3 2 1 0
20. In general, people are considerate of the ideas and feelings of others. 5 4 3 2 1 0
21. I prefer to monitor the behavior of others when I know their actions will affect me in some way. 5 4 3 2 1 0
22. I am willing to allow others to take actions that are important to and directly affect me, even though I have no control over how those actions will be done. 5 4 3 2 1 0

23. In general, other people are not as important as I am.   5 4 3 2 1 0

24. In general, I prefer to work with others to obtain a mutually acceptable outcome rather than to work alone.   5 4 3 2 1 0

25. In general most people meet my expectations.   5 4 3 2 1 0

TOTAL POINTS: _____

www.mhhe.com/hybels11e >

Before totaling your score, go to the Online Learning Center at **www.mhhe.com/hybels11e** and follow the directions there.

Source: See "Tools for Personal Growth: Building Trust. **Coping.org** Tools for Coping with Life's Stressors" (provided as a public service), by J. J. Messina and C. M. Messina, 2002. Retrieved October 20, 2005, from **http://www.coping.org/growth/trust.htm**. I have quoted from their Web page, and I have refrained from using quotation marks simply because quotation marks form a minor barrier to the ease of reading the information.

Summary

Interpersonal communication, or one-to-one communication, is necessary for you to function in society. It helps you connect with others and develop empathy, and it contributes to your mental and physical health. Emotional intelligence is made up of being aware of your feelings, managing your emotions, motivating yourself, recognizing emotions in others, and handling relationships. All these have a direct bearing on strategic flexibility.

Strategic flexibility benefits from the contributions of perception, self-concept, and emotional intelligence because together these factors promote self-control, assist in managing emotions, and foster effective listening. They help you maximize your communication, enhance your credibility, and accomplish your intentions—all factors that make your use of the strategic flexibility format both more likely and more effective.

The ingredients that make up your attraction to others include physical attraction, perceived gain, similarities, differences, and proximity.

The motives for seeking out interpersonal relationships are pleasure, affection (warm emotional attachments with others), inclusion (involvement with others), escape, relaxation, control (getting others to do as you want them to or being able to make choices in your life), and health.

Relationships with others are governed by the roles you are expected to play. Small talk is an instrument of communication that renders people attractive. To engage in small talk plan ahead, ask open-ended questions, share feelings and information, and reconnect via your past.

Bids and the bidding process are the glue that holds relationships together. Bids can be questions, gestures, looks, or touches, and responses to bids are positive or negative answers to somebody's request for emotional connection. Owned messages are acknowledgments of subjectivity by message senders through the use of first-person singular terms. Their value is that they provoke less interpersonal defensiveness than you-messages.

Relational dialectics describe some of the patterns that occur in relationships as a result of the tensions that take place because of the conflicting emotional needs of partners in relationships. The three primary relational dialectics are connectedness and separateness, certainty and uncertainty, and openness and closedness. There are clear advantages and disadvantages to each.

Self-disclosure is the process of communicating oneself to another person, telling another who you are and what you are feeling. It can be understood through the Johari Window, which has four panes: open, blind, hidden, and unknown. As relationships develop and disclosure increases, the open pane gets larger.

Social penetration theory suggests that closeness occurs through a gradual process of self-disclosure, and it is only through self-disclosure that a close relationship can develop. Social penetration theory is often remembered because of the onion metaphor by which self-disclosure is illustrated by removing layers of an onion as if they are portions of your personality: an outer layer or public self, a second layer that includes more private information, and an inner core that includes your values, feelings about yourself, and deep emotions.

The essential elements of good relationships include verbal skills, emotional expressiveness, conversational focus, nonverbal analysis, conversational encouragement, care and appreciation, commitment, and adaptation.

Social exchange theory suggests that all human relationships are formed using a subjective cost-benefit analysis and a comparison of possible alternatives. You weigh the costs of forming or staying in a relationship with the rewards or benefits. The reasons people engage in a social exchange are briefly mentioned.

Key Terms and Concepts

Use the Online Learning Center at www.mhhe.com/hybels11e to further your understanding of the following terms.

Attitudes 157	Hidden pane 168	Response to a bid 163
Beliefs 157	Interpersonal	Self-disclosure 166
Bid 163	communication 152	Small talk 162
Blind pane 168	Johari Window 167	Social exchange theory 176
Commitment 175	Open pane 168	Social penetration 166
Compatibility 158	Owned message 165	Social penetration theory 170
Cultural information 167	Proximity 158	Sociological information 167
Emotional intelligence 152	Psychological information 167	Symmetry 156
Empathy 153	Relational dialectics 166	Unknown pane 168

Questions to Review

1. How is *interpersonal communication* defined, and when do you use it?

2. What role does emotional intelligence play in strategic flexibility?

3. How and why are you attracted to other people?

4. In what ways do your roles and relationships influence your communication? Provide specific examples to support your explanation.

5. What specific health benefits are likely to occur because of interpersonal relationships?

6. Why is small talk important, and what kind of environment supports small talk?

7. What is a bid, what is the bidding process, and how do bids contribute to interpersonal relationships?

8. What are the parts of an owned message, and how do they support both the bidding process and conflict reduction?

9. What is relational dialectics, and what are the three primary relational dialectics?

10. What contribution does self-disclosure make to nurturing and developing relationships?

11. What is the Johari Window, what are its four panes, and which pane is likely to grow in size along with a developing relationship? Why?

12. What is social penetration theory, and what relation does it have to an onion metaphor?

13. What are the essential elements of good relationships that tend to draw people together?

14. What is the essence of social exchange theory, and why do people engage in it?

Go to the self-quizzes on the Online Learning Center at www.mhhe.com/hybels11e to test your knowledge of the chapter contents.

CHAPTER SEVEN

Evaluating and Improving Relationships

After reading this chapter, you should be able to:

- Describe the stages of relationships coming together and coming apart.

- Explain the essential, broad questions that need to be resolved before embarking on a serious relationship.

- Clarify the different negative influences (six big issues) likely to come your way in an interpersonal relationship and how you might approach them.

- Distinguish among extrinsic, intrinsic, and instrumental rewards and costs.

- Explain how to improve relationships by using communication strategies.

SABELLA MET JAYDEN DURING COLLEGE ORIENTATION, BUT IT WASN'T serious, just a mild interest. They were paired up in a couple of "get-to-know-you" activities, and things just seemed to click. They exchanged cell-phone numbers and email addresses, but Isabella never really thought she'd hear from Jayden, and yet on the very night of the day they met, Jayden called, and they both discovered talk came easily. When Isabella checked her computer, too, she found ten messages from Jayden, all lighthearted, playful, and cheerful.

After talking until early in the morning, they decided to meet for lunch. Living on different sides of campus, they texted each other in the morning to change plans to make it dinner, not lunch, because of a scheduling conflict Isabella had.

Dinner talk proved compatibility (at least superficially), and they followed it with a trip to the mall where they purchased ice cream cones, played video games, walked, and talked even more, and they ended the night kissing each other—kisses that suggested to Isabella that Jayden wanted to move to the next stage.

Things were progressing rapidly, and Isabella began to worry that they didn't know each other well enough. Text messages during the day, instant messaging at night (when each went home after orientation), email messages, and long cell-phone conversations simply served to promote exactly what Isabella feared: too much closeness, self-disclosure, and intimacy too fast. Things were happening so fast she could hardly catch her breath, and she decided to back off, take a break, try to relax, and take some time to think.

It wasn't that Isabella didn't like Jayden, it was simply that she was *not* looking for exclusivity, *not* wanting a serious relationship right now, and *not* willing to sacrifice her newfound freedom and independence when her coursework, major, and other interests required her time and attention.

Although Isabella's decision was sudden, she was certain it was the right one and chose to talk to Jayden face-to-face. He didn't take it well, but she remained firm, and she explained her decision further in email messages she composed especially to try to soften the blow. She wanted to maintain a friendship, but she worried that Jayden wanted (was looking for) much more and, thus, decided to terminate the relationship entirely.

"Popular wisdom would have it," writes Sharon Jayson in an article, "Proof's in the brain scan: Romance can last," (*USA Today,* November 17, 2008, p. 6D), "that romance fades over time." Jayson reports on a study by Arthur Aron, one of the researchers, of the State University of New York–Stony Brook, who says research "always suggested romantic love is over by 12 to 15 months." Jayson says, "Scientists used functional Magnetic Resonance Imaging (fMRI) to scan the brains of 10 women and seven men who said they were still intensely in love after an average 21 years of marriage. When they viewed photos of their partners, their brains reacted."[1] Helen Fisher of Rutgers University, and a coauthor on this study, says, in Jayson's words, "Findings show long-term relationships don't have the obsession and anxiety of new love; instead, they show increased calm and attachment.... Couples view partners as central to their lives; they continue to want connection and engagement and maintain a sexual liveliness"—a conclusion derived because "brain scans of people who say they are still in love after decades of marriage are similar to scans of those who have just fallen in love."[2]

Partners often cite a number of reasons for their failed marriages, and these relate to failed relationships of any kind: poor communication, financial problems, lack of commitment, a dramatic change in priorities, and infidelity. Other reasons include failed expectations or unmet needs; addictions and substance abuse; physical, sexual, or emotional abuse; and lack of conflict resolution skills.

Five factors destroy relationships between young people:

1. The partners fail to anticipate differences resulting from diverse cultural backgrounds, family experiences, and gender.

2. They buy into the notion of a "fifty-fifty" relationship, honestly expecting their partner to meet them halfway.

3. They have been taught that humankind is basically good; therefore they fail to anticipate the conflict that will occur when either of two self-centered partners demands his or her own way.

4. They fail to cope with life's trials. Instead of standing together through hard times, they blame each other or think something is wrong with their partner and the way he or she handles difficulties.

5. They have a fantasy view of love. They quickly feel stuck with an unloving partner and become deceived into believing the next one will be better.

You'll notice that none of these five factors directly affected the destruction of Isabella and Jayden's relationship. Instead, Isabella took it entirely upon herself to end it before it became too serious, before it drained time and energy from what she wanted to pursue in college, and before, too, their personalities began to merge (see information on stage 4: integrating, which follows in this chapter).

The purpose of this chapter is to discuss some of the ways to evaluate and improve relationships. We will first look at the stages of a relationship—both coming together and coming apart—which will help you better understand where a relationship is, especially if it is in one of the declining stages. We discuss some of the questions that need to be asked in evaluating relationships: questions to ask about yourself, your partner, rewards and costs, and relationship roles. In the final section titled "Improving Relationships," we look at aggressive talk, regrettable talk, criticism and complaints, avoidance, defensive communication, and the communication strategies you can use in each case.

Not all relationships are positive and should be saved. Some are highly resistant to any kind of alteration; thus, sometimes any kind of change that either partner attempts will fail. Also, it should be noted that the weaker person in a relationship *always* pulls the stronger one down; it's *never* the opposite, that the stronger one pulls the weaker one up.

Just one clarifying comment on the notion of a fifty-fifty relationship mentioned earlier: Often, couples honestly expect their relationship partner to meet them halfway. This is a fantasy. If you have no intention of committing yourself 100 percent to a relationship—on both an initial and an ongoing level—it is unlikely you will be successful. Fifty-fifty is unrealistic simply because when either partner cannot or fails to hold up his or her end of the bargain—which often happens when *any* other commitments come into play (like work or children)—the relationship fails. In Isabella and Jayden's relationship, Isabella knew that a serious relationship with Jayden would take away from the time and energy required by her coursework, major, and other interests. She could tell from their conversations that Jayden wanted an exclusive, committed relationship, but Isabella knew she would never be able to deliver anything close to fifty-fifty for several years.

The Stages of a Relationship

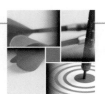

All relationships go through predictable stages as they grow and develop whether they are between romantic couples, friends, business partners, or roommates. Identifying the stages of a relationship and the attributes, stumbling blocks, and joys of each stage can help you negotiate it and the future with more success. The information is useful both to evaluation—do you like where you are, and is it bringing the rewards you want?—and to improvement—what can I do differently to achieve the goals I want?

Most relationships begin with superficial communication; then, if the people like each other, they take steps to see each other again. Mark L. Knapp, a writer and researcher who focuses on relationships, has found that relationships develop along rather predictable lines. He describes five stages in which relationships come together and another five in which they fall apart. Each stage is characterized by certain kinds of communication.[3] Let's begin with a relationship that is coming together, using the example of Isabella and Jayden.

Coming Together

Stage 1: Initiating

There are numerous stumbling blocks when people want to initiate a relationship. The *initiating* stage is characterized by nervousness, caution, and a degree of hesitation,[4] but these are healthy stumbling blocks since engaging in the initiating stage bears some risks, the primary one being rejection. The specific suggestions in Chapter 6, Interpersonal Relationships, regarding small talk, conversation starters, and bids and responses to bids should be of some help at this early stage.

The joys of entering the initiating stage are enormous. It is like beginning any new adventure where the outcome is unknown, but the trip can make it all worthwhile. Joys, of course, include happiness or just finding a friend (companion, soulmate, intimate, confidante, playmate, kindred spirit, buddy, pal, chum, homeboy, homegirl, or colleague). Sometimes just the boost to your self-esteem is sufficient.

In the article "Singles in America" (*USA Today*, February 2, 2012), Sharon Jayson discusses the results of the "second annual Singles in America study," conducted online and completed in December [2011] by market research firm MarketTools for the Dallas-based dating website Match.com: "The results do shatter some long-held beliefs about what have been considered 'deal breakers' in relationships. Only until the very recent past, a potential partner's religion, race or ethnicity, or financial status (especially for a man) often stood in the way of a romance blossoming, says anthropologist Helen Fisher of Rutgers University in New Brunswick, NJ. But no more. Singles today, she says, look at 'those profoundly basic things a person needs for a sound partnership.'"

"The survey found," Jayson writes, "that the top five deal breakers in order of importance are having a disheveled or unclean appearance (67%); being lazy (66%); being too needy (63%); lacking a sense of humor (54%); and distance—living more than three hours apart (49%)" (p. 4D).

Isabella and Jayden were paired in orientation-session activities, and it was small talk as well as bids and responses to bids that led to their attraction to each other. Their first impressions told them the other person was interesting enough for them to pursue further contact, and an extensive cell-phone conversation, then dinner, and a night at the local mall with ice cream, video games, and a chance to walk and talk drew them even closer together. Their first impressions would have predicted movement to the next stage.

STRATEGIC FLEXIBILITY

It is precisely when you find yourself in the initiating and experimenting stages of coming together that you can really flex your strategic muscles. The environment is right, the stage is set, and everything depends on your ability to be alert and make the accurate, appropriate, and relevant moves.

Stage 2: Experimenting

In the *experimenting stage,* people make a conscious effort to seek out common interests and experiences. They experiment by expressing their ideas, attitudes, and values and seeing how the other person reacts. For example, someone with strong feelings about the equality of all races might express an opinion to see whether the other person agrees or disagrees.

The stumbling blocks in stage 2 are fewer. Perhaps the biggest one is the length of time experimenting can take. Talking with someone superficially at school, work, church, or in a chat room can last for years. This is healthy because so many people do not take the time to get to really know another person, and decisions about moving to the next stage often occur without sufficient knowledge and understanding. Thus, it is good to draw out this stage. Most relationships never go beyond this stage and, it seems, many that did perhaps should not have—especially when no foundation for proceeding had been established.

The joy of stage 2 is that everything is generally pleasant, relaxed, and uncritical, although still a bit uncertain.[5] Stage 2 is rewarding, too, if you like getting to know someone else: seeking common ground, testing the waters with self-disclosure, and providing personal histories. Isabella went through this stage with Jayden, and it went on for several days because they had a chance to talk extensively, having dinner together, eating ice cream, playing video games, and walking around the mall. They told each other about their family, upbringing, interests, and hobbies, and both self-disclosed openly.

Isabella and Jayden engaged in an equal amount of self-disclosure. The connectedness and comfort they experienced early on the cell phone, in text messages, instant messages while at home, and their email messages led them to going to dinner and to the mall. If stage 1, initiating, was defined and completed at the end of the orientation activities, then stage 2, experimenting, was completed when Isabella and Jayden finished dinner, ate ice cream, played video games, and walked around the mall. It was a short stage, but it was clear to Isabella that Jayden had every intention of moving their relationship to stage 3, intensifying, and moving it quickly, too.

Many relationships stay at this stage—the participants enjoy the level of the relationship but show no desire to pursue it further.

Stage 3: Intensifying

There are many joys associated with the *intensifying stage.* By this stage many couples have discovered that they like each other quite a lot. They spend more time with each other because they are happy, loving, and warm. They listen to each other's iPods and take pictures of each other with their iPads and cell phones. Not only do they enjoy each other's company, but closeness is both wanted and needed, so they hold hands, kiss, and hug. They start to open up to each other—telling each other private things about their families and friends. They talk about their moral values. They also begin to share their frustrations, imperfections, and prejudices.

For relationships that have progressed to stage 3, other things happen. Partners will call each other by nicknames; they develop a "shorthand" way of speaking; they have jokes that no one else understands. Their conversations begin to reveal shared assumptions and expectations. Trust becomes important. They believe that if either one tells the other a secret, it will stay between them. They start to make expressions of commitment such as making plans together: "Let's go to Ocean City to work next summer." Expressions of commitment include buying gifts for each other or doing favors without being asked.[6] They also start engaging in some gentle challenges of each

ATTENTION!

Reality Check
You are reading the stages of relationships according to Mark L. Knapp, who suggests that all relationships go through predictable stages as they grow and develop. Can you apply his stages to your own life? Have you experienced some of the joy and pain that come with the various stages? Do these stages make sense? Are they logical? How does having this information about the "coming together" and "coming apart" stages contribute to communication effectiveness? Does having a way to conceptualize what is taking place in relationships help you communicate better? How?

STRATEGIC **FLEXIBILITY**

If you are going to use strategic flexibility effectively—especially with respect to the coming-together stages—it requires great sensitivity. One measure that can be used to help you know what to do is your comfort level. When you evaluate factors, elements, and conditions, how comfortable are you with your assessment?

other: "Do you really believe that, or are you just saying it?" Openness has its risks in the intensifying stage. Self-disclosure makes the relationship strong, but it also makes the participants more vulnerable to each other.

This is likely to be the only stumbling block—vulnerability. The key here is trust, and it underscores the value of the "getting-to-know-you" stages of initiating and experimenting. Trust often takes time to develop. When trust is secure, there is less chance of being wounded, injured, or attacked because of a breach of trust. Lack of fidelity, lying, or the sharing of personal information with others outside the relationship are breaches of trust and can cause deep wounds that are difficult to overcome.

Isabella and Jayden witnessed the movement of their relationship to stage 3, intensifying. Jayden loved it that things had progressed so quickly because he saw in Isabella a person with whom he would love to spend the rest of his life. Isabella sensed the intensity of his desires in his conversation, in his unconditional positive regard, and in his touches and kisses, too. Things had moved far too quickly for her, and it was the dissonance she experienced between her interest in Jayden and her interest in her coursework, major, and other interests (e.g., sports, sorority, honor societies, etc.) that caused her to sense a problem and immediately back off. What she knew was that Jayden was already mentally in stage 3, intensifying, and wanting to quickly move the relationship to stage 4, integrating. Isabella, on the other hand, had moved from stage 2, experimenting, but wanted to prevent any further movement of the relationship within or from stage 3.

Stage 4: Integrating

Isabella and Jayden never reached the *integrating stage*—the point at which their individual personalities are beginning to merge. When relationships reach this stage people expect to see partners together, and they are unhappy when apart.[7] If people see just one of them, they ask about the other. The friendship has taken on a specialness. They do most things together and reflect about their common experiences—the things they do together. They go to the same parties and have a lot of the same friends; their friends assume that if they invite one, they should invite the other. Each of them is able to predict and explain the behavior of the other. They feel like one person.

Isabella and Jayden did not reach stage 4: integrating, because Isabella saw it heading in this direction, knew Jayden wanted badly for it to progress, and stopped it dead in its tracks. Those who do reach this stage, however, are usually best friends, couples, or parents and children. It is at this stage—if it hasn't happened before—that partners meet one another's family and friends.

Stage 5: Bonding

The last coming-together stage of a relationship is *bonding*. At this point, the participants make some sort of commitment that announces their relationship to those around them. An announcement of an engagement or marriage would be an example of bonding. In other cases, such as those between friends, the bonding agreement might be less formal—for example, agreeing to room together. Whatever form it takes, bonding makes it more difficult for either party to break away from the relationship. Therefore, it is a step taken when the participants have some sort of long-term commitment to their relationship. "Census Data Analysis" by the Associated Press, as reported in an article, "Weddings March in Reverse in U.S." (*The* (Toledo) *Blade*, December 21, 2011), "Barely half of all adults in the United States are married, and the median age at the time of a first marriage has never been higher—slightly more than 26 years old for women and nearly 29 for men" (p. A1).

In her essay "The M.R.S. and the Ph.D." for *The New York Times* in the Sunday Review section (February 12, 2012, p. 1, 6–7), Stephanie Coontz writes that "Even for women who don't marry, it's better to be educated; a 2002 study found that never-married white women with more education than average lived, 'the longest, healthiest lives of all groups'" (p. 7). She continues:

> One of the dire predictions about educated women is true: today, more of them are 'marrying down.' Almost 30 percent of wives today have more education than their husbands, while less than 20 percent of husbands have more education than their wives, almost the exact reverse of the percentages in 1970.
>
> But there is not a shred of evidence that such marriages are any less satisfying than marriages in which men have equal or higher education than their wives. Indeed, they have many benefits for women.
>
> In a forthcoming paper from the Council on Contemporary Families, Oriel Sullivan, a researcher at Oxford University, reports that the higher a woman's human capital in relation to her husband—measured by her educational resources and earnings potential—the more help with housework she actually gets from her mate. The degree to which housework is shared is now one of the two most important predictors of a woman's marital satisfaction. And husbands benefit too, since studies show that women feel more sexually attracted to partners who pitch in (p. 7).

Source: Coontz, Stephanie. (February 12, 2012). "The M.R.S. and the Ph.D." Sunday Review. *The New York Times*, p. 1, 6–7.

Questions

1. Do you think it's true, as Kate Bolick wrote in an article in *The Atlantic*, that "American women face 'a radically shrinking pool of what are traditionally considered to be 'marriageable' men—those who are better educated and earn more than they do'"?

2. What is the message being conveyed when you hear what Coontz writes: [Marriage rates] "have slipped less for educated women than for anyone else. Furthermore, college-educated women, once they do marry, are much less likely to divorce"?

3. Why do you suppose that "the degree to which housework is shared is now one of the two most important predictors of a woman's marital satisfaction"?

Bonding occurs in nonromantic relationships as well. For example, good friends become best friends often because of some especially meaningful (good or bad) "bonding" experience. Dorm roommates are often randomly assigned, but nonromantic apartment mates, who must depend on each other for bill paying, housekeeping, amenities, and the like, are more likely to be successful if they've reached a bonded relationship before moving in together. Partners in business, in the police, or in the military—where success, reputation, and even survival depend on close bonding with and trusting of each other—each know exactly what to expect from the other in critical situations. This same kind of bonding can occur between dancers and ice skaters as well. Although there are times when you may want to believe it isn't so, sex on its own, or a "one-night stand" with a virtual stranger, is not bonding.

Advancing from Stage 1 to Stage 5

The five coming-together stages build on one another (see Figure 7-1). For a relationship to advance to the next stage, both parties must want the change to occur. Because most of us have only limited time and energy for intense relationships, we are willing to let most of our relationships remain at the second or third stage. The first three stages permit us to become involved in friendships and to carry out normal social

At the bonding stage, participants make a formal commitment that announces their relationship to those around them.

activities. The fourth and fifth stages, integrating and bonding, demand much more energy and commitment—they are reserved for very special relationships.

Notice that, for the most part, in the coming-together stages, the joys both partners experience outweigh the stumbling blocks that occur. In all stages you have five choices: to continue moving forward, to stagnate, to slow down, to go backward, or to exit.[8] Since stage 3 is the first in which there is self-disclosure, moving from stage 2 to stage 3 is particularly sensitive. If one person opens up too quickly, the other might feel so uncomfortable that he or she will be unwilling to go on to a new stage in the relationship.

Figure 7-1
The Stages of a Relationship

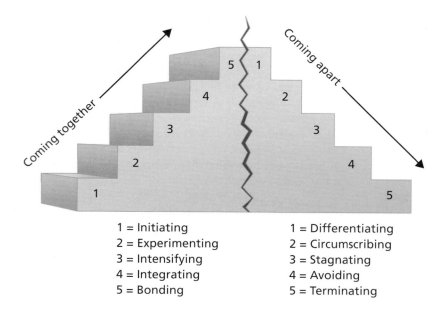

Coming together

Coming apart

1 = Initiating
2 = Experimenting
3 = Intensifying
4 = Integrating
5 = Bonding

1 = Differentiating
2 = Circumscribing
3 = Stagnating
4 = Avoiding
5 = Terminating

It may be impossible to prevent relationships from coming apart; however, social psychologist Steven Scher of Eastern Illinois University, as cited by Mary Loftus in her article, "Smooth Encounters" (*Psychology Today*, April, 2013, pp. 62–69), identified five main elements of apologies:

1. a simple expression of regret ("I'm sorry," "I apologize"),
2. an explanation or account of the cause that brought about the violation ("I forgot to call you"),
3. an expression of the speaker's responsibility for the offense ("What I did was wrong"),
4. a promise of forbearance ("I promise nothing like this will happen again"), and
5. an offer of repair ("What can I do to make this up to you?").

Of course, it depends on the context, prior offenses, the seriousness of the current offense, and other factors; however, an apology right now—providing you mean it—may be of assistance.

Coming Apart

For a relationship to continue, the participants must grow and change together. If they cannot do this in ways that are satisfying to both of them, the relationship will come apart. Although it is more satisfying to look at relationships coming together, we all know that relationships also fail. Relationships that are failing can also be described in five stages—stages that reverse the process of coming together. Notice as you read about each stage that stumbling blocks have eliminated any joy that was there.

Remember as you read the following three paragraphs, that this information is for those who want to break up with their relationship partner. The stages of "Coming Apart" are what normally occur when partners are not growing and changing together.

Carolyn Hax, in her column entitled, "It Can Take Courage to End a Relationship" (*The* (Toledo) *Blade*, July 1, 2012), has great advice for anyone who wants to end a relationship: "The task is to accept responsibility for being utterly, cluelessly, head-smackingly wrong.

"Most of us hate to be wrong," Hax writes, "It is drilled into us as children that there is no worse fate than wrongness. But we are all wrong sometimes. Part of growing up is learning how to be wrong and to make right any damage we may have caused others" (p. 3). Admitting that *you're* wrong has three advantages: 1) You are standing up for what you know is right, 2) You are setting yourself and the other person free, and 3) You are ending the hurt you have already caused and avoiding far more hurt that awaits if your relationship continues.

The following information does not preclude the stages that follow, but it dovetails with what Hax has said above. Elizabeth Svoboda, in "Cognitive Breakups" (*Psychology Today*, January/February, 2011) offers readers her "12 Rules of Better Breakups" (pp. 66–69). Her first corresponds with what Carolyn Hax says (above), "1) Take full responsibility for initiating the breakup; 2) Do it only face-to-face; 3) Act with dignity; 4) Be honest; 5) Avoid big, bad clichés like 'It's not you, it's me'; 6) Avoid point-by-point dissection of where things fell apart; 7) Make it a clean break; 8) Communicate ongoing appreciation of the good times you shared; 9) Don't protest a partner's decision; 10) Don't demonize your ex-partner; 11) Don't try to blot out the pain you're feeling, either; 12) Resist thinking you've lost your one true soul mate."

ATTENTION!

Perk Up Your Relationship

1. Be grateful.
2. Poke fun at each other.
3. Capitalize on good news.
4. Use your illusions.
5. Find your ideal self—in your partner.
6. Notice what's new about your partner.
7. Put it in writing.
8. Provide support in secret.
9. Get back in touch.
10. Look after yourself.[11]

Stage 1: Differentiating

It is at this stage when serious problems begin to emerge in relationships. Often—especially when couples progressed rapidly through the coming-together stages of relationship development without really getting to know each other very well—things can begin to get rocky when partners discover that they have few mutual interests and their personal interests, when pursued, take them further apart rather than draw them together. For example, one partner may like to go out several nights each week while the other wants to stay home. One may like to cook new and exotic food while the other wants to eat meat and potatoes. Their choices in movies, music, video games, even their desire for time alone and away from the other may cause conflict.

When couples enter the *differentiating stage,* the interdependence of their courting stage is no longer so attractive. Now they are beginning to focus on how different they are, and much of their conversation is about their differences rather than their similarities. There is noticeable arguing with talk about being incompatible.[9]

To some extent, the differentiating stage is a healthy phase that most couples experience. Many work out their differences by being autonomous sometimes and interdependent other times. For example, partners may go together to family gatherings and to parties. However, when one partner goes hunting, the other may go shopping or to see other family members.

The differences the two recognized and tolerated during the stages of coming together become focal points for discussion and argument. They can be worked out if they are not too great.

The most visible sign of differentiating is conflict. But differentiating can take place without conflict. Even if nothing specific is bothering the couple, they may discover, as they mature and find new interests, that they have less and less to talk about. One partner, for example, may need time to read the news online every day and follow world events while the other partner may have no interest at all in following the news. Each partner experiences slight loneliness because the two of them are no longer as close as a couple, and regarding the relationship itself, there is some confusion and inadequacy creeping in.[10] "Where is the relationship going? How long can it go on like this? Am I at fault?" are all questions relationship partners may ask themselves. Usually these questions are internalized and never expressed at this stage.

Stage 2: Circumscribing

When a relationship begins to fall apart, less and less information is exchanged. It seems better to stay away from points of conflict in the relationship in order to avoid a full-scale fight. Thus this is called the *circumscribing stage.*

Now conversation is superficial; everyday matters are discussed: "Your mail is on the desk." "Did I get any telephone calls?" "Do you want some popcorn?" The number of interactions is decreased, the depth of discussions is reduced, and the duration of each conversation is shortened. Because communication is constricted, the relationship is constricted.

Most people who find themselves in this stage try to resolve their problems by discussing the relationship itself. In response, the negative turn in the relationship might change. For example, one partner could go out to a movie with the other person, and the other person could agree to try some different food. In other cases, discussion about the relationship might reveal greater differences between the participants. In such cases, discussion about the relationship leads to even more conflict, so the participants limit discussion to "safe" topics. Partners, for instance, may stay away from the topic of having children because they know they will fight about it.

Often, people at this stage pursue different activities. Sometimes, too, they act aloof from each other. These experiences reveal coldness and distance. With respect to each other, partners are uncaring, and one or the other may become depressed or frustrated, feeling unloved and misunderstood.[12]

Persons who are in this stage often cover up their relationship problems. Although they might reveal problems to very close friends, in social situations they give the appearance of being committed to each other. They create a social or public face—in essence, a mask.

Stage 3: Stagnating

The *stagnating stage* is a time of inactivity. The relationship has no chance to grow, and when the partners communicate, they talk like strangers. The subject of the relationship itself is now off limits. Rather than try to resolve the conflict, the partners are more likely to think, "Why bother to talk? We'll just fight, and things will get even worse"; thus, for self-protection, they give short answers to questions.

How long this stage lasts depends on many things. If partners lead busy lives, for example, and just come home to sleep, they might go on in this stage for months or even years. However, if one partner stays home and broods about the relationship, that partner may look for some kind of resolution to the conflict. Most couples whose relationship reaches this stage feel a lot of pain. The partners may find it hard to separate and may hold on to the hope that they can still works things out. Either partner at this stage may feel unwanted, scared, bored, and sentimental.[13]

Stage 4: Avoiding

The *avoiding stage* involves physical separation. The parties avoid face-to-face interaction. They are not interested in spending time together, in building any kind of relationship, or in establishing any communication channels.

This stage is usually characterized by unfriendliness, hostility, and antagonism. Sometimes the cues are subtle: "I only have a minute. I have an appointment." They can also be direct and forceful: "Don't call me anymore" or "I'm sorry, I just don't want to see you." Often, responses are "I don't care" and "I don't know." If communication occurs, it covers general matters only; there is no talk about the relationship.

In relationships where physical separation is impossible, the participants may act as if the other person does not exist. Partners eat in silence, stay busy, and, if possible, spend a lot of time away.[14] Each one carries on his or her activities in a separate room and avoids any kind of interaction. In some cases, partners might choose to sleep in separate rooms. Often, too, partners feel some sense of nervousness, as well as helplessness and annoyance.[15]

Stage 5: Terminating

In the *terminating stage,* the participants find a way to bring the relationship to an end. Differences are emphasized, and communication is difficult and awkward. Each party is preparing for life without the other. They may talk about staying in touch and discuss what went wrong. A goal at this stage may be to divide up their belongings. There are feelings of unhappiness, but these are accompanied by a sense of relief. Often one partner is lonely or scared because of having to face life alone again.[16]

ATTENTION!

Ending a Romantic Relationship Without Being Negative

Make certain you really want the relationship to end.

Do *not* just stop calling, returning phone calls, emails, or text messages.

Do *not* behave so badly the other person initiates the breakup.

Do *not* be caught with a new romantic partner.

Do *not* be hurtful or behave harshly.

Do *not* blame the other person.

Do *not* send mixed signals.

Do *not* avoid giving a clear reason.

Do *not* allow it to turn into a fight.

It is useful to know how to evaluate relationships. However, writing in an article entitled "Are You With the Right Mate?" (*Psychology Today*, January/February, 2012, pp. 57–65), Rebecca Webber offers readers a valuable insight that should precede any process of evaluation:

> One of the most common reasons we choose the wrong partner is that we do not know who we are or what we really want. It's hard to choose someone capable of understanding you and meeting your most guarded emotional needs and with whom your values are compatible when you don't know what your needs or values are or haven't developed the confidence to voice them unabashedly (p. 64).

Source: Webber, Rebecca. (2012, January/February). Are you with the right mate? *Psychology Today*, pp. 57–65.

Questions

1. Do you have any personal experiences—or experiences of people who are close to you, that Webber is correct: we choose the wrong partner because "we do not know who we are or what we really want"?

2. Is your goal in choosing a relationship partner, to find "someone capable of understanding you and meeting your most guarded emotional needs"?

3. If you agreed entirely with the point Webber is making in the above excerpt, what would be your next move? That is, what would you do at this point (before proceeding to the process of evaluating a relationship that was important to you), to know for certain what your needs and values were?

Some relationships cannot be entirely terminated. Partners who have children might terminate their relationship with each other as marriage partners but decide to continue in some kind of relationship as parents to the children. The more amicably this can be done, the better it is for the children involved. Partners might set down a list of rules that will govern the new relationship.[17] When the termination is a divorce, the court is the one that establishes the rules.

Sociologist Diane Vaughan has studied the patterns that occur when a relationship is about to end. She says that one member of the couple, realizing he or she is unhappy, begins the process of ending the relationship. This person typically begins by finding alternatives—often in the form of a transitional person. Although the transitional person might be a romantic interest, the person could also be a minister, a therapist, or a good friend. When one partner begins to find satisfaction elsewhere, the couple's relationship becomes less endurable. At this point the dissatisfied person lets the other know of his or her discontent through body language and words.[18]

Finally the time comes when the dissatisfied person lets the partner know that he or she wants to end the relationship. The partner typically feels betrayed, hurt, and shocked—and is often unprepared. Vaughan says that during the breakup, both partners suffer emotional pain and go through the same stages of disengagement: the process just happens at different times for each of them.[19]

There is an important note regarding terminating a relationship that all partners must recognize and accomplish. Full closure of the relationship is essential. "Memories are 'open,'" writes Carlin Flora, "when recollected with great feeling and 'closed' when they don't conjure up much passion, however dramatic the original event may have been. Open memories are the ones we still struggle to understand. We think about them often, and see them as relevant to our current lives. Closed memories, on the other hand, don't haunt us. They are truly past" (p. 72).[20]

Evaluating Relationships: Asking the Right Questions

One reason many relationships fail is simply that people seldom take the time to ask the essential questions—especially the questions that should be asked *before* embarking on a serious relationship. It is true, of course, that some of us begin a relationship with no intention of its becoming serious and then discover it has evolved to that level without a decision ever being made. Perhaps some of the questions in this section will help you if this happens.

Our purpose is not to destroy spontaneity, surprise, and discovery, but to deal with some of the broad issues that often lead relationships to fail. When these are resolved to your satisfaction, and you have taken all the necessary precautions that would predict a satisfactory future partner, there will be plenty of room for spontaneity, surprise, and discovery.

Ask Yourself Questions

There are four questions to ask yourself.[21] The first has to do with fear of commitment. Are you concerned about the idea of forever? Do you fear you could make a mistake in the person you choose? Do you fear a loss of your freedom or autonomy? Are you afraid of a bad marriage—like your parents, for instance? Do you fear you would be a bad mate?

Antoinette Coleman, in her online newsletter *The Art of Intimacy,* states that "If you answered yes to any of these, it would be a good idea to begin working to understand where these feelings come from. Once you understand them better, you can choose to address them."[22] It may simply be that you are not ready to make any long-term commitment, and you know at this point in your life that you just need more time, or more emotional growth.

The second question is about fear of forming a relationship with another person. How many dating experiences have you had? Do you tend to rush into relationships, or do you move them along with thought and careful decision making? Can you live without a partner? Can you envision yourself in the immediate future with a partner? Do you really know and like yourself? Do you believe you could have a successful relationship?

The third question asks about making a commitment to *this* particular relationship and to *this* particular person. Is there a genuine connection? Do you have a vague feeling that something is missing? What is the quality of your intimate relating—*not* how often or how good the sex is, but how open, sharing, and real your interactions are with each other. Does it seem that the two of you are just killing time? Does your partner want what you want? Do you seem to be inconsistent in your level of contact and affection? Is your partner still not over a past relationship? Do you (and does your partner) really know what you want?

The fourth question is about a loss of self, and it is discussed by Lundy Bancroft and JAC Patrissi in their book *Should I Stay or Should I Go?* (NY: Berkley Books, 2011). The question is easy to ask but sometimes difficult to answer: Is this relationship causing you to lose your sense of who you are? The authors write, "When you have lost track of your values, your humor, and your hopes to the degree that standing back and looking at yourself, you do not recognize the person you know yourself to be inside, it's time to go. . . . If you have become that much of a stranger to yourself, it's okay to choose to go. You are choosing to love yourself. Loving yourself helps everyone, not just you" (p. 324).

Ask Questions about Your Partner

Let's say that through frequent contact and increased levels of self-disclosure you have discovered a potential relationship partner, but you don't know whether this partner is even ready for a relationship. What questions should you ask yourself to determine a partner's readiness? Six are absolutely essential:

1. Is this person able to communicate with you openly and honestly?
2. Does this person appear to have a strong self-concept?
3. Is this person aware of the time and effort required to have a long-term, loving relationship?
4. Is this person willing to put forth the necessary time and effort along with you to make a long-term, loving relationship possible?
5. Does this person see the commitment necessary for a long-term, loving relationship as *more than simply fifty-fifty?*
6. Is this person prepared—as you are—to make a relationship partner his or her *first* priority, after himself or herself, in life?[23]

If the answer to any of these questions is "no," then this partner is probably not for you.

Here is a key point: Entering into a relationship hoping that the other person will change, or thinking that you will change the other person, "is not a solid foundation for a loving, committed relationship. In most cases, with rare exceptions, you are wasting your time."[24] Instead, get into the habit of looking for what you can love and appreciate about your partner, rather than how he or she needs to change or be fixed, and it will change the whole dynamic of your relationship.

Ask Questions about Rewards and Costs

In Chapter 6, Interpersonal Relationships, we introduced a small portion of Altman and Taylor's social penetration theory. Their theory is based on social exchange—the idea that relationships are sustained when they are relatively rewarding and discontinued when they are relatively costly.[25] **Rewards** are the pleasures that result from being in a relationship. **Costs** are the problems. The essential question is, "Do the rewards outweigh the costs?" or, phrased a bit differently, "Are you willing to live with the costs considering the strength of the rewards?" When you know your relationship partner well it is easier to weigh rewards and costs.

Altman and Taylor listed three types of rewards and costs: extrinsic, intrinsic, and instrumental. **Extrinsic** means outside the relationship. **Intrinsic** means within the relationship. **Instrumental** refers to the basic exchange of goods and services. To make sense of these, let's put them into the context of a relationship you have that has not yet progressed to the level of sexual intimacy. Whether or not you want to take it to that level depends on weighing the rewards and costs.

Extrinsic rewards: You like the people your partner has introduced you to and the friends he or she hangs out with.

Intrinsic rewards: You appreciate the attention, warmth, and affection you gain from being in the relationship.

Instrumental rewards: You know that if you decide to raise the current level of intimacy, one of the rewards when you move in with your partner (which you have already discussed) is that you will share both the rent and the furniture.

Extrinsic costs: You are not going to have as much time for your friends, and you are going to have to share them with your partner.

Intrinsic costs: Not only will you feel obligated to return the attention, warmth, and affection you are receiving—probably at an increased level if the level of intimacy increases—but you will also spend time listening, communicating, and self-disclosing.

Instrumental costs: You will have to share your belongings.

Now it is up to you. Often, it is good to actually list the rewards and costs honestly not just so you can compare them but so that you can think about them specifically and over time.

Mira Kirshenbaum, a therapist who works with families and couples, holds that since the dynamics of a relationship are constantly shifting, it is better to ask questions about the relationship that go right to the heart of it. For example, she maintains that the answer to a question like the following will tell a lot about a relationship: "Does it seem to you that your partner generally and consistently blocks your attempts to bring up topics or raise questions, particularly about things you care about?"[26]

Ask Questions about Roles

Roles are important simply because to be happy and content in a relationship, both parties must be satisfied with the roles and expectations. Roles may evolve naturally and spontaneously for males, but for females, they must be discussed and negotiated.

One of the questions we asked students in interpersonal-communication classes had to do with relationship expectations: "What role do you expect to play in any future intimate relationship you have?" Sometimes students referred to the roles their parents played, sometimes they offered a politically correct response such as, "That would have to be worked out with my future partner," and sometimes a few would take the traditional stance that males were the breadwinners and females the homemaker raising the kids. Most female students wanted to play a role equal to that of their partner and have an equal say in how roles would be determined.

In successful relationships, the participants have usually worked out their roles and expectations. But circumstances change through the course of a relationship, and if the communication channels are not available and open, unexpected problems can occur down the road.

Consider an example. Doug and Rita had never directly discussed roles; things were essentially equal. Then unexpectedly Rita found herself pregnant, but Doug and Rita never stopped to talk about how their roles would change once the baby was born. Who was going to take care of the baby during the day? Were there going to be any changes in school commitments or workloads, and who was going to make changes if necessary? Who was going to get up at night when the baby cried? Who would adjust his or her schedule if the baby became sick?

There is no way to ask all the questions that will prepare you for changes likely to occur in relationships. There are, however, some questions you could ask while dating that might give you important information about how your partner views relationship roles. For example, "What do you want in a wife (or husband)?"[27] Many women think males want a maid—a wife who stays home, cooks, cleans, and isn't too smart; however, many males *say* they want, more than anything else, a capable, assertive, happy partner, not just a housekeeper. On the other hand, some men think women want a

Using a recent relationship or one in which you are currently involved as your reference for this AOM, write out the relevant questions, the questions about your partner, questions about rewards and costs, and the questions about roles. Know that all these questions are designed simply to create an awareness of some of the broad issues that often lead relationships to fail. Having examined the questions and thought about their answers, does this provide a better foundation that would likely lead to better relationships in the future? What are some of the barriers or intrusions that might interfere with the establishment of an ideal relationship?

partner who is a big, burly, hairy, handsome "he-man" with money. Most women, however, want a loving, gentle, warm, caring, intelligent, capable, self-confident man who is willing to stand up for his beliefs.

Some other key questions might be, "Who do you think should be responsible for financially supporting the family?" or, a related question, "Who do you think should be responsible for caring for the house and family?" "If you were the husband of a working woman, would you be willing to do an equal share of the housework and child care?" "What determines who will be the boss in a marriage?" "Do you think it's necessary for a couple to be roughly equal in ability in love, in neediness, and in education to have an egalitarian [equal] relationship?"[28]

Both men and women are likely to know how their partner would want them to respond. In the period of infatuation and, often in the early stages of a loving relationship, partners want to please each other. That is sufficient grounds for observing the behaviors of possible future partners to see whether what they say is supported by activities with which you agree—that is, that there are no mixed messages.

Can you ask "too many questions"? Never. Just don't act as though it's an interview. Spread them out over a sufficient amount of time, work them in among other thoughts and feelings, and remember a key point: Often men do not want to open up, share feelings, or even communicate. Accept this as a signal. Do you want to have a long-term relationship in which there is little or no communication?

Improving Relationships: Using Communication Strategies

Negative influences are a natural and expected part of relationships. It is *not* the frequency of their occurrence; it is how carefully, delicately, and respectfully they are resolved to *both* partners' satisfaction that is important. All the motivation and willingness to communicate, assertiveness training, owned messages, and listening and communication skills in the world cannot prevent relationships from becoming fertile ground for silence and stonewalling, for anger and frustration, or for just plain hard times. No speech, article, book, or expert can protect you from the range of painful emotions that make you human.[29]

Jeffry H. Larson, Professor of Marriage and Family Therapy, School of Family Life, Brigham Young University, in his online article "Important Factors to Consider Before Taking the Marriage Plunge" (*Forever Families*, http://foreverfamilies.byu.edu/Article. aspx?a=36, downloaded February 13, 2012) lists the following traits that he considers best predict relationship satisfaction: extroversion, flexibility, good self-esteem, and good interpersonal skills. Certainly, just from examining these four traits alone, it would seem that they would not only assist in improving relationships but, too, offer a firm foundation for handling difficulties.

The greater the number of skills and behaviors you have in your toolbox, however, the greater the likelihood that you will be able to face and resolve all the negative influences that come your way. This is where your ability in and use of strategic flexibility has its real payoffs—not just in holding your relationships together (the big picture), but in satisfactorily resolving all those daily, nuisance-type issues that seem to provoke and keep you in a negative frame of mind.

In this section we will look at six of the big issues: aggressive talk and aggression, regrettable talk, criticism and complaints, and avoidance.

Aggressive Talk and Aggression

Aggressive talk is talk that attacks a person's self-concept with the intent of inflicting psychological pain.[30] This kind of talk includes disparaging words such as *nigger, faggot,* and *slut,* and phrases such as "You are so stupid," or "You are an inconsiderate idiot." Aggressive talk makes recipients feel inadequate, embarrassed, or angry, and because of the impact it has on receivers, it is seldom justified. Not only does aggression breed aggression, but it can escalate, and verbal aggression can quickly lead to physical aggression. People who can control verbal aggression are those who can recognize their anger and control it when it occurs—usually by giving themselves a cooling-off period.

When aggressive talk leads to aggression—an unprovoked attack—in relationships, often the relationship is doomed. People tempted to use verbal aggression should be aware that such actions can destroy relationships.

A more subtle act, and one we are often not aware of committing, is **indirect aggression** (sometimes called *passive aggression*)—when aggression is a mental act (usually characterized by manipulation, scheming, cunning, deviousness, or conniving). People who use this form of communication often feel powerless, and they respond in the only way they can, by doing something to thwart the person in power. For example, if your mother asked you to clean the kitchen, and you did a poor job so that she would never ask you again, you are using passive aggression. Or, if you were forced to go to college, and you flunked all your courses just to show your parents their decision was wrong.

It is difficult to deal with those who are aggressive, and if the acts of aggression are excessive, uncontrolled, or frequent, it may be necessary to seek professional assistance—for you, your partner, or the two of you together.

If your goal is to deal with the aggressive talk of a partner, your first step is to make every effort to see the situation *from his or her point of view:* with empathy. When the time is appropriate—usually *not* immediately after the aggressive talk has occurred because emotions have been triggered and normal conversation may not take place— you might begin a conversation by asking your partner to explain his or her point of view. Encourage him or her to talk about underlying assumptions, beliefs, or background factors that may have led to the behavior you are upset about. Summarize the person's words and *emotions* from his or her point of view (so that he or she agrees

ATTENTION!

Words and Attitudes that May Provoke Aggression

negativity
sarcasm
indifference
manipulation
indirectness
avoidance
obstructionism
ambivalence
procrastination
conceit/egotism
silence
doublespeak
contrariness
elusiveness/
   evasiveness
control
lack of empathy
rejection
disrespect
arrogance
insensitivity

ATTENTION!

Regrettable Words Fall into Five Categories

1. The blunder
2. Direct attack
3. Negative group references
4. Direct and specific criticism
5. Revealing or explaining too much

you understand it). Understanding the other's situation, point of view, and reasons for beliefs and behavior is usually the major task to accomplish.

If it is impossible to have this kind of conversation, it might be helpful for you to imagine a scenario that will allow you to defuse your anger. Or you may interpret your partner's aggressive talk as a legitimate need to take care of himself or herself. If you can focus on evidence from the present or past that proves he or she loves you and is not trying to hurt you, it is easier to forgive the behavior, forget about it, and move on.

Regrettable Talk

Regrettable talk is talk you regretted after saying it. You invited someone to help you move into a new place, and he tells you he has just been diagnosed with cancer and will be in the hospital. Of course you couldn't have known that, but you are now embarrassed for having asked him. Regrettable talk might have hurt someone, or it may have shared a secret you were not supposed to tell.

Mark Knapp, Laura Stafford, and John Daly, all communication researchers, studied regrettable words. They discovered that 75 percent of regrettable words fell into five categories. The most common was the blunder—forgetting someone's name or getting it wrong, or asking "How's your mother?" and hearing the reply "She died." The next category was direct attack—a generalized criticism of the other person or of his or her family or friends. The third was negative group references, which often contained racial or ethnic slurs. The fourth involved direct and specific criticism, such as "You never clean house," or "Don't go out with that guy; he's a sleazeball!" The fifth category—revealing or explaining too much—included telling secrets or reporting hurtful things said by others.

When people were asked why they had made the remark in the first place, the most common response was, "I was stupid. I just wasn't thinking." Some said their remarks were selfish—intended to meet their own needs rather than the other person's. Others admitted to having bad intentions. They deliberately set out to harm the other person. On a less negative level, people said that they were trying to be nice but the words just slipped out. Some people said that they were trying to be funny or to tease the other person, and the words were taken in the wrong way.

How did the people who were the objects of the regrettable words respond? Most often they felt hurt. Many got angry or made a sarcastic reply. Some hung up the phone, walked away, or changed the subject. Others were able to dismiss the statement or to laugh about it. When the speaker acknowledged the error, the listener often helped to "cover" the incident by offering an explanation or justification.

One of the most interesting aspects of this study addressed whether regrettable words had a negative impact on the relationship. Of the respondents, 30 percent said there was a long-term negative change, 39 percent said there was no change in the relationship at all, and 16 percent said that the change was positive—for example, "In the long run. I think our relationship is stronger since it happened."

Criticism and Complaints

Most people experience anger from time to time in close relationships. Anger does not have to destroy a relationship: University of Michigan researchers found that the average couple has one serious fight a month and several small ones.[31] John Gottman, psychologist at the University of Washington, found that anger is not the most destructive emotion in a marriage, since both happy and miserable couples fight. He calls the real demons "the Four Horsemen of the Apocalypse"—criticism, contempt, defensiveness, and stonewalling.[32]

Experts agree that it's *how* partners fight that makes the difference. The most effective kind of anger is that which expresses one's own feelings while conveying concern for one's partner.[33] Since most anger begins with a complaint or criticism, let's look at the most effective way to express it.

Criticism is a negative evaluation of a person for something he or she has done or the way he or she is. In more distant relationships, criticism usually originates from a higher status person and is directed toward one with lower status.[34] If the participants are equals, such as friends or a couple, criticism could come from either partner.

Researchers have discovered that criticism has five targets: appearance (body, clothing, smell, posture, and accessories); performance (carrying out a motor, intellectual, or creative skill); personhood (personality, goodness, or general ability); relationship style (dealing with others); and decisions and attitudes (opinions, plans, or lifestyle). They found that the target of most criticism is performance, followed by relationship style, appearance, and general personhood.[35]

Most people experience anger from time to time in close relationships. Anger doesn't have to destroy relationships. It is *how* people fight that makes the difference.

The researchers also looked at what the recipients perceived as "good" and "bad" criticism. Most of the study's respondents believed that those who did not know them very well didn't have the right to criticize them. They were much more likely to identify criticism as bad if it was given in front of others rather than privately.

Criticism was labeled "bad" if it contained negative language (profanity or judgmental labels such as "stupid jerk") or if it was stated harshly by screaming or yelling. It was better received if it was specific and gave details on how to improve ("If you are going to be home after midnight, please call and let me know where you are"). Criticism was considered good if the person who made it also offered to assist in making the change or if its receiver could see how it would be in his or her best interest to change ("If you called me when you are going to be late, I wouldn't be so upset once you got home"). Finally, good criticism places negative remarks into a broad positive context ("If you called, it would reduce a lot of tension and anxiety in our relationship").

A **complaint** is an expression of dissatisfaction with some behavior, attitude, belief, or characteristic of a partner or of someone else. A complaint differs from criticism in that it is not necessarily directed at any specific person.

In studies of complaints between partners, researchers found that, as with criticism, some responses to complaints were more useful than others.[36] First, when complaints are trivial, they can probably be ignored. "This spaghetti is overcooked," or "Why do I have to be the only one to shovel the snow?" are trivial complaints. Second, a complaint should not be directed at anyone specifically. When you say, "Why doesn't anyone ever close doors?" you are not pointing to any one person, so the guilty party can change his or her behavior without losing face. Third, a complaint should be softened or toned down so that the complainer can express his or her frustration or dissatisfaction without provoking a big argument. Fourth, if the complaint is serious, the partners should discuss it and try to arrive at a solution or a compromise before the complaint turns into a serious conflict.

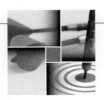

STRATEGIC

FLEXIBILITY

Plan what you want to say before you say it! This is exactly what strategic flexibility demands: To anticipate, assess, evaluate, and select *requires advanced thought*, so that when you assert yourself you do it with care, concern, and attention.

The most useful communication strategy for dealing with criticism is to use owned messages, as discussed in Chapter 6, Interpersonal Relationships. Rebecca Cline and Bonnie Johnson's research emphasized the importance of making the careful language choices that owned messages require.[37] People react negatively and defensively when conversation is filled with you-messages such as "You always blame others for your problems," or "You always need to have the last word, don't you?"

Avoidance

Many people who are in unsatisfying relationships try to dodge any discussion of their problems. Some people use silence; others change the subject if their partners try to begin a discussion. Often people who refrain from discussing relationships are trying to avoid any kind of conflict. The downside of **avoidance**—refusing to deal with conflict or painful issues—is that unless the problem is discussed, it probably will not go away.

The best communication strategy to use with respect to avoidance is a combination of owned messages—"I need to deal with the conflict we're having. I cannot continue avoiding talking about it, because it eats away at me and makes me angry"—and assertiveness. **Assertiveness** is taking the responsibility of expressing needs, thoughts, and feelings in a direct, clear manner. "I know you think that if we don't talk about it, it will just go away, but I know it's going to come up again. I want to talk about it right now [assertiveness]."

Relationship Survey

The following statements refer to people in a close relationship (e.g., a relationship between two partners in an intimate relationship). For each statement decide to what extent it is characteristic of your feelings and behaviors using the following scale: A = Not at all characteristic of me; B = Slightly characteristic of me; C = Somewhat characteristic of me; D = Moderately characteristic of me; E = Very characteristic of me. Write the letter for the answer in each blank.

_____ **1.** I am a good partner for an intimate relationship.

_____ **2.** I am depressed about the relationship aspects of my life.

_____ **3.** I am better at intimate relationships than most other people.

_____ **4.** I feel good about myself as an intimate partner.

_____ **5.** I sometimes have doubts about my relationship competence.

_____ **6.** I am disappointed about the quality of my close relationship.

_____ **7.** I am not very sure of myself in close relationships.

_____ **8.** I cannot seem to be happy in intimate relationships.

_____ **9.** I tend to be preoccupied with close relationships.

_____ **10.** I think of myself as an excellent intimate partner.

_____ **11.** I am less than happy with my ability to sustain an intimate relationship.

_____ **12.** I would rate myself as a "poor" partner for a close relationship.

_____ **13.** I feel down about myself as an intimate partner.

_____ **14.** I am confident about myself as a relationship partner.

_____ **15.** I feel unhappy about my interpersonal relationships.

_____ **16.** I am not very confident about my potential as an intimate partner.

_____ **17.** I feel pleased with my love relationships.

_____ **18.** I sometimes doubt my ability to maintain a close relationship.

_____ **19.** I feel sad when I think about my intimate experiences.

_____ **20.** I have few doubts about my capacity to relate to an intimate partner.

_____ **21.** I am not discouraged about myself as a loving partner.

Go to Online Learning Center at **www.mhhe.com/hybels11e** to see your results and learn how to evaluate your attitudes and feelings.

www.mhhe.com/hybels11e >

Source: The Relationship Assessment Questionnaire, adapted from W. E. Snell Jr., 1999. Used by permission of William Snell.

Summary

The most important relationships in our lives go through five stages as they are coming together: initiating, experimenting, intensifying, integrating, and bonding. Relationships that remain superficial go through only the first or second stage. When relationships come apart, they also go through five stages: differentiating, circumscribing, stagnating, avoiding, and terminating.

In evaluating relationships, ask yourself questions about commitment, forming a relationship with another person, and making a commitment to a specific relationship and particular person. Next, you need to ask yourself questions about your partner. Following that, ask yourself questions about rewards and costs and, finally, ask yourself questions about roles.

To improve relationships you are likely to have to deal with aggressive talk and aggression, regrettable talk, criticism and complaints, and avoidance. There are no universal, all-encompassing, always successful ways for dealing with each of these areas; however, it should be clear that the better you are at applying the strategic flexibility framework, the better you will be at revealing empathy, using owned messages, and displaying assertiveness when necessary.

Key Terms and Concepts

Use the Online Learning Center at www.mhhe.com/hybels11e to further your understanding of the following terms.

Aggressive talk 199	Differentiating 192	Intensifying 187
Assertiveness 202	Experimenting 187	Intrinsic costs 197
Avoidance 202	Extrinsic costs 197	Intrinsic rewards 196
Avoiding 193	Extrinsic rewards 196	Regrettable talk 200
Bonding 189	Indirect aggression 199	Rewards 196
Circumscribing 192	Initiating 186	Stagnating 193
Complaint 201	Instrumental costs 197	Terminating 193
Costs 196	Instrumental rewards 196	
Criticism 201	Integrating 188	

Questions to Review

1. When a relationship comes together, it goes through five stages: initiating, experimenting, intensifying, integrating, and bonding. What happens in each stage?

2. When a relationship is in the process of breaking down, it goes through the following stages: differentiating, circumscribing, stagnating, avoiding, and terminating. What happens in each of these stages?

3. When engaged in the process of evaluating relationships, what are the categories of questions you need to ask? Provide a sample question for each category.

4. What are the differences among extrinsic, intrinsic, and instrumental rewards and costs? Give an example of each.

5. What is the purpose of asking questions about roles?

6. What characterizes aggressive talk, and what are the steps in dealing with it?

7. How do you characterize regrettable talk, and what effect is it likely to have on relationships?

8. What are the real demons of relationships?

9. What are the guidelines tor delivering criticism?

10. What is the difference between complaints and criticism, which responses to complaints are most useful, and what is the best communication strategy for dealing with complaints and criticism?

11. What is the best communication strategy for dealing with avoidance?

Go to the self-quizzes on the Online Learning Center at www.mhhe.com/hybels11e to test your knowledge of the chapter contents.

CHAPTER EIGHT

Communication and Technology

After reading this chapter, you should be able to:

- Explain how the use of technology can improve our connections with others.

- Describe how (in what ways) the use of technology can have a detrimental effect on FtF (face-to-face) interaction skills.

- List the reasons why text messaging has become so important in romantic and sexual correspondence.

- Describe the recommendations for making texting a more rewarding experience.

- Explain the disadvantages of using technology as well as some of the guidelines for using it.

HAVE NEVER REALLY KEPT TRACK OF THE AMOUNT OF TIME I SPEND using various forms of technology, I just use whatever I need at the time I need it. It is all so natural, routine, commonplace, and comfortable. All together, I probably spend three-to-four hours a day using technology—some of my friends spend more, and some spend less—but everyone I know is a fairly heavy user—if not a heavy, definitely too regular. I am online every day, and when I miss a day because of illness or travel or anything else, I feel as if I am out of touch. There is a hollow space in me that only technology can fill—like when I'm really hungry. Without it, I feel alone and isolated. It is, indeed, a need for communication—a need for connection.

My iPhone and iPad are my lifelines to the world, and I reach for them every morning, even before I get out of bed. They are not only my alarm clock, but also my CD player, email device, game player, newspaper, shopping guide, banking assistant, conduit to Facebook and Twitter, and my resource to any question I have or any question I am asked when I don't know the answer. I may even search the same topic multiple times a day because the flow of information is so great and ever-changing. Without them, I would not survive.

Since all my teachers use email to stay in touch with their students, I always check for messages at night before going to bed and in the morning just before going to class. I feel that is part of being a responsible student. My teachers post their syllabi, all class assignments, lecture notes, and quizzes online. I read many of my assignments online as well, post responses when requested, and engage in small-group chats when arranged by my teachers. Of course, before checking for email messages, I check Facebook, MySpace, and Twitter to see if there are any additional messages—including being "friended" on MySpace or "Facebooked." My days begin and end with the use of technology.

Instead of passing notes in the hallway, I text. It is casual, quick, and direct—with no interference or interruption. Socializing in person—when I was in high school—proved difficult because of parental restrictions, overscheduling (I was involved in so many activities), and transportation options.

Even when I am confined to my bedroom, I leave Facebook open while I study—often, late into the night. Why? Because I love seeing the names of my friends pop up in chat windows. Even without talking with them, I feel less lonely just knowing they are out there.

While away at college, I use a combination of email and Skype to stay in touch with my parents. Occasionally, we use our cell phones for a call, but email works well when we are not available at the same time, and Skype is so much better than a phone call. We arrange a time we can both meet to Skype once every week.

To keep in touch with all my friends, especially my two closest friends, Samantha and Sophia, I use text messaging and instagram, but we keep up with each others' activities on Twitter and Facebook, too. I think I have over 300 friends on Facebook, and I send messages to my friends several times a day. I realize, however, that my Facebook account is less like a collection of friends and more like a town hall meeting. Writing on Facebook is like shouting into a crowd, whereas writing on Twitter is like speaking into a room. Nonetheless, it makes me feel connected and important. I post pictures that I take with my iPhone and iPad on a regular basis, and I change my profile at least once a week—usually, just for the fun of it—and I use Facebook to learn the latest gossip, catch up with my friends, publicly reinforce relationships, and turn my acquaintances into friends.

My friends and I often chat about how many "friends" we have on Facebook; however, I am fully aware that the abundant number of relationships available through technology may still leave people feeling isolated. The quantity of the associations available leaves them feeling qualitatively empty. I know it because I experience it as well.

On my Facebook personal profile I have photos of my family, posts about things I enjoy, updates on my personal hobbies and activities including things I am doing or plan to do. By others' reactions to my profile, I know that the kinds of details I share help those who visit my page to get to know me better and relate better to me as well.

What keeps me feeling connected, however, is that on my social-network sites, I regularly (several times a day) make comments on my friends' walls, post reactions to my friends' pictures, send private messages to my friends, use these sites to send instagram and text messages, and even send group messages sometimes.

Speaking of feeling connected, I use the instant messaging tools not just for posting my personal profile but for posting "away" messages, too. I have found it to be useful when I can't get to the computer—like when I'm working on a big school project—but it helps me to always remain connected to my network.

When my friends and I were just hanging out at one of my friend's apartments, we just sat there and watched each other talk online. Sometimes we would even text another person who was sitting right there in the same room with us. Occasionally, we would make plans to do something in person, like going to a movie or a party, but mostly, my friendships were online. And what were we all doing? The same things people used to do in person: flirting, boasting, gossiping, teasing, confessing. With technology you can do it all—all different kinds of communication—at breakneck speed, and it is easy, convenient, and fun.

Not only do I use my iPhone for texting, talking, and taking pictures, I use it to share pictures with others, play music, and play games, too. Because I am active in drama, my drama teacher uses the iPhone to announce the results of tryouts for school plays as well as rehearsal times and places or changes in those times and places when necessary. It is a quick and easy tool for him to maintain contact with all of his actors and actresses.

When I was very young—in elementary school, I think—my grandparents bought me a laptop computer. Up to that point, I had used my mothers's computer, so she was happy when I received my own as a gift. Although I am a heavy user of mobile technology—so that I can keep connected wherever I am and whenever I choose—when I get back to my room, I enjoy lying on my bed and using my laptop instead. I write all of my reports on it; I do all of my research for my papers and other class assignments on it; and I use it to keep up with sports, news, and current events—although I would rather be keeping in contact with my friends, or even playing games, than reading about sports, news, or current events. Those tend to be accidental discoveries rather than purposeful pursuits—although it is all available to me at the touch of a key. When one of the celebrities whose career I follow begins dating someone new, gets into trouble, or is involved in a new concert tour, I can get instant updates when I need to.

I realize how difficult it would be for someone else to try to measure where my offline life begins and where my online life ends. To me, it's not a problem, and my answer to someone who wanted to know would be simple: My offline and online lives are closely integrated and weave comfortably and easily in and out of each

In his book Smarter Than You Think: How Technology Is Changing Our Minds for the Better, Clive Thompson quotes Andrea Lunsford, "one of America's leading researchers into how young people write." Lunsford conducted a five-year Stanford Study of Writing and one of her discoveries is that "the writing strategies of today's students have a lot in common with the Greek ideal of being a smart rhetorician: knowing how to debate, to marshal evidence, to listen to others, and to concede points. Their writing was constantly in dialogue with others" (p. 67).

"I think we are in the midst of a literacy revolution the likes of which we have not seen since Greek civilization," Lunsford tells me [Thompson]. "The Greek oral period was defined by knowledge that was formed face-to-face, in debate with others. Today's online writing is like a merging of that culture and the Gutenberg print one. [Mechanical printing technology is credited to the German printer Johannes Gutenberg in 1450.] We're doing more jousting that takes place in text but is closer in pacing to a face-to-face conversation. No sooner does someone assert something than the audience is reacting—agreeing, challenging, hysterically criticizing, flattering, or being abusive" (pp. 67–68).

Source: Thompson, C. (2013). Smarter than you think: How technology is changing our minds for the better. (New York: The Penguin Press), pp. 67–68.

Questions

1. Have you noticed that your online messages are similar to what takes place in face-to-face conversations—as Lunsford has noted? What are the characteristics that are similar?

2. In what ways have you discovered that your online behavior is preferable to your face-to-face behavior?

3. Do you believe that there truly is—as Lunsford has explained—a merging of face-to-face culture with what takes place in writing? Is this a positive or negative situation?

---

other. Where one ends and the other begins has no meaning since they are fused, and if you followed my life closely, you would see how perfectly assimilated they are. When technology is woven so deeply into the patterns of my everyday life, I don't have a choice about whether to use it or not. It simply provides additional tools—in addition to the face-to-face (FtF) communicating I do—that I *must* use (it's the way things are) in communication. To give up technology would not only make my life logistically difficult, it would significantly change my ability to connect with others.

The Effect of Technology on Communication

The youth of today—from their very early years through the years well beyond college—are really into communication. The college student above, Leah, is not atypical when it comes to her use of technology. Digital communications make up most of the lives of youth today—whether it be mobile phones or social networking, the predominant current forms. In this section we will look at the effect of technology on our connection to others, self-concept, interaction skills, self-disclosure, conversation skills, and on relationships.

The Effect of Technology on Our Connection to Others

The obvious question, perhaps, is why do they do it? From reading the example of Leah, the answer, too, seems obvious. It is quick, easy, and ubiquitous—seeming to exist everywhere. It is what comprises the life of youth today. Some young people suggest that talking on the phone takes too much time—especially when their schedule is packed full—just as Leah's was.

We think, however, that the answer to the question, "why do they do it," is even more basic than the features of the technological instruments themselves (i.e., quick, easy, and ubiquitous). The answer lies in connectivity. What technology has provided—and created an addiction for, in many cases—is being connected to others. Leah felt it when she talked about being alone and isolated without that connection.

Looking at the effect of technology on communication, however, is a bit more difficult. The amount of time spent with technology means that the amount of time spent in other endeavors will be shortened. For example, there will be

The bottom line regarding what technology has provided us is being connected to others: connectivity.

less energy spent exercising, less time relaxing with family and enjoying one-on-one with friends. In addition, there will be less time spent doing classroom assignments and less hours practicing creative pursuits. Are the gains made in "connectivity" equal to, or more important than, any of these? For many people today, the answer is clearly, "Yes"—even an emphatic "Yes!"

Some people may claim that the gains made in "connectivity" offset what is lost in pursuing other endeavors, and, for some, this may be true. Some may say, too, that people have learned how to multitask, and they can now handle all those endeavors mentioned above along with the addition of whatever technology brings, with no problem, and this may be true as well. For some, we are certain, technology simply fills a void that was already present in their lives, and, thus, it adds substance (maybe even importance, richness, and significance) to a previously lackluster life, and that may be true, too. It is really hard to know what the short-term or, perhaps, more important, the long-term effects of technology use will be.

In his *Atlantic* article "Is Facebook Making Us Lonely" (May 2012, pp. 60–69), Stephen Marche writes about connectivity in this way, "What Facebook has revealed about human nature—and this is not a minor revelation—is that a connection is not the same thing as a bond, and that instant and total connection is no salvation, no ticket to a happier, better world or a more liberated version of humanity" (p. 69).

The Effect of Technology on Self-Concept

There is an additional concern that can also be phrased as a subsidiary question to the main one (What is the effect of technology on communication?) which is, to what extent can people develop an autonomous sense of self? That is, constant connectivity tends to support the development of an outward-looking self (a self that is externally manufactured) where people look to others for affirmation. How, then, do they develop a sense of self-worth (an internally developed self) and efficacy (their belief in their own power and ability to affect change and to influence)? An outward-looking self tends to be relatively fragile when compared with a self-governing, independent self. Of course, it is impossible to know the answers, and, as always, answers will vary among individuals and their circumstances.

No matter how the self-concept is affected, one thing is certain. Technology changes the way people think of themselves and how they communicate. When people know they can get attention, always be heard, and never have to be alone, it is easy to understand how addiction to technology can occur. But, it is also easy to understand how different people will be affected in different ways. Obviously, some people depend on technology for fulfilling these needs more than others, but the effects of technology on the self-concept is an important factor to be considered when analyzing the relationship of technology and communication.

The Effect of Technology on Interaction Skills

Regarding long-term effects, one wonders if those youth hooked so securely (one might say "joined at the hip") to their technology will suffer when it comes to learning how to make eye contact, how to engage others in social banter, or how to develop and perfect the art of conversation? These are skills needed to negotiate the workplace and the world, much less their interpersonal relationships. Speaking of relationships, can always-plugged-in youth ever form intimate ties with others? Is intimacy on the Internet sufficient to fulfill their needs for the warmth, affection, and attachment of real-life, intimate relationships? Are youth losing natural, human, instinctive skills needed to navigate through life and to be successful? We think the answer is that some are, some are not.

There is a possibility that technology can affect self-concept development, self-disclosure skills, as well as interaction and conversation ability.

There are people who are naturally skilled at interacting with others, and technology is likely to have no effect on them. It might even hone and polish those skills. There are others, too, who find interacting with others—because of shyness, introversion, or other inhibitions—difficult or challenging. For those people, technology—because it is *not* FtF, because it allows them to take on a different, less inhibited persona, and because it allows them time to think before responding—is a liberating opportunity.

The Effect of Technology on Self-Disclosure

There is an additional positive or negative effect—depending on how you view it—of technology on willingness to self-disclose. If people believe that online communications are less personal than FtF, when they want to talk about sensitive issues or concerns, they are more likely to do it online than FtF simply because FtF discussions open up feelings, thoughts, and related ideas to probing and challenge. An electronic connection allows people to hide from others. By escaping vulnerability they protect their comfort and their feelings of control.

The Effect of Technology on Conversational Skills

Let's look at just one feature, referred to briefly above, that technology allows that is not available in FtF encounters: the ability to read, then read again, messages from others. This occurs in email messages, text messaging, and in IM as well. Think how many times people can read a message before responding. There is no limit. But when people can read messages before writing back, there is no practice of listening; no exercise in improvisation, no use of spontaneity, no training in small talk, and no performance of natural, uninhibited, involuntary, genuine, and, sometimes, creative reactions or feedback. Some of what we will call "conversational surprise" will automatically be missing.

Most youth who own a cell phone communicate with their friends using written messages. Trillions of text messages are sent annually.

Is there any wonder why people who would be considered "high-tech" (heavily dependent on various technology) would begin to lose some of their FtF conversational skills? And, as a direct corollary, is there any wonder why some of these same people may find diminished public-speaking abilities as well? This seems to operate against the very findings we reported in the first chapter of this textbook: One of the top skills that employers look for in potential employees is their ability to listen and communicate—especially speak effectively.

Our contention is simple. Yes, there will be some alterations in people's behavior, but, overall, they are likely to be minimal. Just as there are always those who will yell, "the sky is falling," when any new technology is introduced. People always adapt their behavior and actions as new tools are introduced and become universally available. Fundamentally, however, communication practices and the various ways we relate to each other will stay the same.

The Effect of Technology on Relationships

We don't think the conclusion above, "Fundamentally, however, communication practices and the various ways we relate to each other will stay the same," relates to the effects of technology on relationships. In this case (the effect of technology on relationships), the change is fundamental, important, and pervasive. Text messaging and mobile technology have become the primary methods used in romantic and sexual correspondence and, as a result, other forms of relational communication—the written word, the cell phone, or even FtF communication—are no longer as important. Some people characterize phone conversations as long, slow-paced, and unpleasant. Texting is the new means of courting, bonding, creating emotional connections, and planning dates and activities.

If there was a bottom line to why texting has become so important, it can be captured in this single line said by one user, "I get to say exactly what I want exactly when I want to say it." If there were a second bottom line, it would be, "No matter what I am doing, I can be in touch with and connected to those I care about."

Technology plays an important—make that *essential*—role in relationship formation, maintenance, and dissolution.

Trillions of text messages are exchanged, and a disproportionately large percentage of those are exchanged by teenagers—especially teenage girls. On a daily basis, adults exchange about 10 text messages; boys from 14–17 exchange 30, while girls average 100.

The reasons why text messaging has become so important in romantic and sexual correspondence help explain why it has exploded in popularity since it began around 1995. Obvious reasons are that it is a quick, easy, and convenient way to get messages across. Closely aligned with these reasons, too, is the use of texting as a tool to maintain relationships, whether to stay in contact or express emotions.

According to a survey commissioned by ChristianMingle.com and Jdate.com but conducted by an independent research firm (reported in *USA Today*, July 19, 2013, p. 2A)—one third of all the people surveyed (both men and women) said it was less intimidating to ask for a date via text versus a phone call. Also, 44 percent of the men and 37 percent of the women say that text messaging makes it easier to flirt and get acquainted.

An additional advantage of texting is that users do not need to respond at once—although response time is an important element in texting. In an era of high energy, over-scheduling, great personal responsibility, and stress, users can not only choose to respond (or not respond) in their own time, but they can multitask at the same time, handling relationships by not investing too much time or effort in case they don't click, want out, or prefer making a minimum commitment.

Another important advantage to texting rather than talking is that texting keeps relationships casual. You can ask questions, get answers, and, thus, find out a great deal about the other person before even meeting them. FtF, one-on-one, often makes young adults feel like there is too much of a commitment involved. Think about it. Sitting down for a dinner date or seeing a movie together not only requires time, but there is some risk involved since nobody knows how it's going to go. Some young adults would prefer having a drink together since the time commitment is small, the financial investment is low, and it is a quick hour if things don't work out.

A major reason for texting, especially in the early stages of relationship development, is that it can reduce uncertainty and lessen anxiety. It isn't that facial expression and vocal inflection—richer forms of communication—aren't important, but with texting, a relationship can develop slowly and additional forms of communication such as FtF meetings can be introduced as appropriate. It should be clear that texting is a lesser alternative form of communication for a significant exchange. Planning a place to meet is easy to do when texting. Physical contact, human interaction, and high-quality conversations are important, however, to maintaining relationships, and texting alone cannot supply these ingredients.

There is yet another important reason for the popularity of texting with respect to relationships, according to clinical psychologist Beverly Palmer, a professor at California State University-Dominguez Hills. It is that relationships can be ended much quicker (*USA Today*, July 19, 2013, p. 2A). Text messaging, as opposed to FtF communication, avoids confrontation, discomfort, and interruption. It allows users to shape and mold their communication by choosing their language carefully, organizing it, and using a well-thought-out approach if they choose. FtF communication is spontaneous, requires participants to think quickly on their feet, respond to interruptions during the back-and-forth exchanges, and actually listen to the other person, as well as reason and self-reflect. Technology gives people far more control over their relationships and, too, the way they come to an end.

There are a number of qualities of texting, however, that are not present in normal FtF communication. Texting encourages rapid-fire, single-sentence thoughts—not generally conducive to FtF communication. Relating to this is the compulsion in texting to respond immediately via text. It reinforces instant gratification and can lead to incredible impatience. Texting increases the frequency of small talk, which makes it ideal when beginning relationships, but it can be characterized as superficial as opposed to in-depth. In-depth conversations can take place, but they are much less likely to occur. Texting displays improper grammar and other language shortcuts that add to its speed and efficiency. In some cases, for those who have grown up texting, it can result in weak writing skills, a loss of tone and style when they talk, and an inability to communicate appropriately.

Text messages, too, are not necessarily true reflections of users' instinctive thoughts. They are often edited, re-read, and even written by other people. That is precisely why they cannot be relied upon and why FtF meetings, at some point in serious relationship development, are essential. It is important to note that texting allows users to present themselves as they want to be. This ability to craft and mold one's work has been labeled "the Goldilocks effect."

Texting avoids the complexity and messiness of human communication, but these are precisely the things that lead to better relationships. Remember, the ability to notice, comprehend, and respond to the subtlety and complexity comes with time and a lot of experience. Texting gives the illusion of companionship without the demands of friendship. Without FtF conversational skills, the real world of real people can be a frightening experience. Even looking another person in the eye can be scary. It makes one wonder, at what point will habitual texters become conversation-phobic or, at a greater extreme, conversation-avoidant? After all, texting is easier.

Especially for introverted users, texting can offer positive benefits. For example, according to Alissa Fleck, in an online article, "Texting & Its Positive Impact on Teens," (Retrieved July 24, 2013, from http://everydaylife.globalpost.com/texting-its-positive-impact-teens-6902.html) it can enhance reading ability (greater literacy) by encouraging the interaction and engagement with the written word. Because of the anonymity involved in texting, some feel more comfortable self-disclosing with others. Self-disclosing, or opening up with friends about everything, helps introverts reach out to others and express themselves.

To make a texting experience more rewarding, the following are recommendations. First, use it to reach out and follow up with a first acquaintance. Second, keep your texts short and on point. That is, don't run on about irrelevant things. Third, avoid over-texting. This can be interpreted as "smothering," or "overzealousness." As a relationship develops, the frequency of texting can be increased as relationship partners plan things, gain emotional support and advice, and, perhaps, send love messages. Fourth, never text during a date. Fifth, texting should become a supplement to FtF conversations, not a replacement for them. Straight, truthful, in-person talk is essential to having whole, lasting relationships.

There are four more recommendations. Sixth, avoid texting about anything lewd, overly sexual, or embarrassing. Seventh, avoid late-night texts. Eighth, be careful about how much you self-disclose and how soon. Steamy, romantic texts will appear as desperate, needy, and intrusive if delivered early in a relationship. It is best to wait for a partner's response—self-disclosure reciprocity—before proceeding. Ninth, never use texting to break up with someone. Not only is this a clear sign of cowardice, but it is, too, a sign of disrespect toward yourself and the other person. Ending a relationship should be done in person, and at the very least (as a last resort), over the phone.

The Technology of Connection

Your authors have been reluctant from the outset to define and describe the various tools of technology or the instruments of social networking (aside from the extended, opening example of Leah) for four reasons. First, most are so well known and so heavily used that they are common knowledge—not just familiar, but routine as well. Second, technology changes so rapidly, new tools come into vogue so quickly, and the shifting and lurching although interesting becomes outdated—perhaps, even, outmoded—almost as quickly as the descriptions are written. Third, information about the tools of connection, their popularity, and the number of users is readily available and, too, becomes the focus of news stories and articles—especially, of course, when new milestones are achieved or significant events occur. Fourth, the tools themselves are not what make a difference when it comes to technology and communication. The questions, "How is communication affected by technology?," or the reverse, "In what ways does technology impact communication?" are the important ones for a book called *Communicating Effectively.* This is less a book about the mechanics (tools) and more a book on communication.

Not only are there millions using social networking sites such as FaceBook, MySpace, and Twitter and many others, too, but there are hundreds of those sites available; thus, if communication is affected in any manner, it should be of interest, significance, and an appropriate matter for analysis and evaluation. It isn't the technology of communication, it is the effects of technology on communication.

Disadvantages of Using Technology

No technology comes without problems or disadvantages. The automobile may have offered us freedom and autonomy, but think about its downsides. It costs billions in accidents, roads, petroleum dependence, suburban sprawl, pollution, and traffic jams. These are negative effects that come with the technology.

There is no doubt that smartphones, cell phones, and personal computers have made our lives better and our jobs easier, but they are an intrusive force into our private lives. They can increase stress and make it difficult to concentrate. Some claim that wasting time using various forms of technology can make people lazy. Also, they can so occupy our time that we forget about other things in our life. Think about how much fun it is to keep playing games, continue chatting, persist in surfing the Internet, or carry on with interchanges of short messages. Even watching pornography can be addictive.

If you have listened to others about their use of technology or if you have done any reading about it at all, we are sure that you are aware of other disadvantages, too. For example, there are lack of privacy issues, the unintentional anti-social behavior that may result from overuse, the possibility of being misled by deceptive information, the influence of false rumors, and even the incredible bombardment of information.

Technology can increase stress and make it difficult to concentrate.

Tony Dokoupil, a Ph.D. candidate in communications in Columbia's Graduate School of Journalism as well as senior writer for *Newsweek* and *The Daily Beast*, in the article "Is the Onslaught Making Us Crazy?" (*Newsweek*, July 16, 2012, pp. 24–30) answers the question posed in the title of his article, but first says that it isn't the technology itself or the content. He notes that "a *Newsweek* review of findings from more than a dozen countries finds the answers pointing in a similar direction."

> *Peter Whybrow, the director of the Semel Institute for Neuroscience and Human Behavior at UCLA, argues that "the computer is like electronic cocaine," fueling cycles of mania followed by depressive stretches. The Internet "leads to behavior that people are conscious is not in their best interest and does leave them anxious and does make them act compulsively," says Nicholas Carr, whose book,* The Shallows, *about the Web's effect on cognition, was nominated for a Pulitzer Prize. It "fosters our obsessions, dependence, and stress reactions," adds Larry Rosen, a California psychologist who has researched the Net's effect for decades. It "encourages—and even promotes—insanity" (p. 27).*

Source: Dokoupil, Tony. (2012, July 16). Is the onslaught making us crazy? *Newsweek*, pp. 24–30.

Questions

1. Have you discovered in your own use of the computer—or in the use of computers by your friends—that it "fuels cycles of mania followed by depressive stretches"? Do you think this is an extreme characterization?

2. Are you aware of anxiousness or any actions that could be labeled "compulsive" as a result of extensive computer use?

3. Have you experienced times when your computer use fosters your obsessions, dependence, and stress reactions? —more so than you experience normally?

4. Do you think excessive computer use encourages or promotes insanity? Do you think the characterizations of computer use in the excerpt cited above are extreme? Is there cause for concern?

5. Considering how many youth use computers—and use them extensively—don't you think that you would see far more evidence of these extreme forms of behavior, if, indeed, they were occurring, in society today?

In an online *New York Times* article, "An Ugly Toll of Technology: Impatience and Forgetfulness" (June 7, 2010—downloaded February 6, 2013), Tara Parker-Pope claims that exposure to technology may be reshaping your personality. "Some experts believe," she writes, "excessive use of the Internet, cellphones and other technologies can cause us to become more impatient, impulsive, forgetful and even more narcissistic."

Some Guidelines for Using Technology

We hesitate to offer guidelines simply because most of them are common knowledge. Also, because most people are aware of them (as common knowledge) many people are likely to do as they please—as they have been doing all along anyway—despite any set of guidelines, directives, or warnings. However, you should be aware that with the ability to use technology comes responsibility, and there are some guidelines specific to the use of technology.

Some of the guidelines have to do with prohibiting the transmission of any material in violation of any federal or state law. For example, transmitting any threatening, harassing, defamatory, or obscene material, copyrighted material, plagiarized material, material protected by trade secret, blog posts, Web posts, or discussion forums or replies that are posted to the Internet which violate federal or state law. You are not expected to understand all the federal or state laws that apply, but you should be aware that they exist, you are responsible for what you transmit, and that ignorance of the law does not mean you are exempt from the law. It's a little like getting a ticket for parking your car too close to a street corner. You can tell the officer giving you the ticket that you did not know you couldn't park there (that you are ignorant of that law), but you are still going to get the ticket.

Communicating by using any form of technology should be considered public *not* private communication. You may think that your posts on Facebook, your tweets on Twitter, your texts on your iPhone, or your email messages are a private, personal form of communication: They are *not*. Thus—because they are public, *not* private—private information such as home addresses, phone numbers, last names, pictures, or mail addresses should not be divulged.

No matter what language you choose to use in your everyday life, using obscene, profane, lewd, vulgar, rude, inflammatory, threatening, or disrespectful language in emails, blogs, texts, tweets, or when using other communication tools is prohibited. Sending any message that could cause danger or disruption, personal attacks, including prejudicial or discriminatory attacks, is also prohibited.

Forgery (the act of falsely making or materially altering, with the intent to defraud, any writing) or attempted forgery is prohibited. Attempts to read, delete, copy, or modify the messages of others, deliberate interference with the ability of others to send and receive messages, or the use of another person's user ID or password is prohibited.

Illegal copying—including copying software, downloading copyrighted files, or loading such files onto your computer without permission—and using the printed material and graphics of others is considered plagiarism and is prohibited.

In addition to these guidelines there are others that, to us, appear to be even more obvious; however, there are people new to technology who need to know these. For example, people online are not always who they say they are and, thus, do not automatically deserve your respect or trust. You should not impersonate others in chat sessions, online discussions, or in email messages. Never agree to meet anyone you've met online, unless you are accompanied by someone else and you agree to meet in a public location. Because anyone is free to post information online, it is your responsibility to evaluate the quality of the sources you discover and the value of the content you find. Just because information is posted in a public place (such as on the Internet) does *not* make it valid or reliable.

Use common sense and good manners. Those are overall guidelines that should prove useful and effective in most situations encountered when using technology.

Measure Your Awareness of Texting Etiquette

For each statement circle the answer that best represents your actions when it comes to texting.

1. Do you keep your text messages short (under 160 characters)?   True   False
2. Do you allow your texting to substitute for FtF conversations?   True   False
3. Do you text while you are in the presence of other people?   True   False
4. Do you text while in the movies, at church, in meetings, in class, or while at someone's house?   True   False
5. Do you convey personal information (e.g., important family news) in your text messages?   True   False
6. Do you send text messages during the nighttime sleeping hours?   True   False
7. Do you send text messages while driving?   True   False
8. Do you ever text while in a FtF conversation with someone (others)?   True   False
9. Do you ever use texting for formal invitations?   True   False
10. Do you ever use text messages to dump on your girlfriend or boyfriend?   True   False
11. Do you ever get upset because you don't get an immediate reply to a text message you have sent?   True   False
12. Are you careful of the tone you use in your text messages?   True   False
13. Are you conscientious of other people's schedules when you send them text messages?   True   False
14. Do you use texting to convey immediate, important messages?   True   False
15. Do you keep your abbreviations to a minimum?   True   False
16. Do you make up your own abbreviations?   True   False
17. Do you avoid using sarcasm in your text messages?   True   False
18. Do you avoid sending risky messages that should better be handled FtF?   True   False
19. Do you send messages to which you are unwilling to reply when a reply to your message is made?   True   False
20. Do you only send text messages that you mean?   True   False
21. Do you respond to others' text messages as soon as possible?   True   False
22. Do you use emoticons wisely (avoid using them excessively)?   True   False
23. Do you avoid using one-word responses?   True   False
24. Do you keep texting until you get a reply (sending multiple text messages)?   True   False
25. Do you use texting to confirm plans?   True   False
26. Do you use proper grammar and punctuation?   True   False

Go to Online Learning Center at **www.mhhe.com/hybels11e** to see your results and learn how to measure your awareness of texting etiquette.

Summary

Technology has become so pervasive that it is difficult to discern where people's online life begins and ends and where their offline life begins and ends. Both lives, today, are closely integrated.

When considering the effects of technology on communication, we looked first at its effect on our connection to others, and we concluded that the basic reason people use technology lies in connectivity—being connected to others, although we noted that the time spent with technology means a shortening of time spent in other endeavors.

Second, we looked at the effect of technology on self-concept, and we concluded that technology changes the way people think of themselves and how they communicate.

Third, we looked at the effect of technology on interaction skills, and in this section, we simply raised a number of questions regarding its effects.

In the fourth and fifth sections under the heading "The Effects of Technology on Communication," we looked at the effect of technology on self-disclosure and its effect on conversation skills. Excessive texting has the potential of limiting people's ability to listen well, improvise, be spontaneous, engage in FtF small talk, or perform natural, uninhibited, involuntary, genuine, and sometimes creative reactions, and feedback.

Perhaps the most important section under the heading "The Effects of Technology on Communication" is its effect on relationships because text messaging and mobile technology have become the primary methods used in romantic and sexual correspondence. Numerous reasons are explained why text messaging has become so important beyond the obvious: it is quick, easy, and convenient. Some reasons include the delayed response time, keeping relationships casual, reducing uncertainty, lessening anxiety, and ending relationships more quickly.

In the section on the effect of technology on relationships, the qualities of texting not present in normal FtF communication are listed and the warning that text messages are not necessarily true reflections of users' instinctive thoughts is explained.

The most important paragraph in this section, however, has to do with the complexity and messiness of human communication—the very things that lead to better relationships. Without conversational skills—because of a commitment to texting—the real world beyond texting can be a frightening experience.

The section on the effect of technology on relationships ends by offering recommendations for making the text-messaging experience more rewarding.

At the end of the chapter, we discuss some of the disadvantages of using technology such as wasting our time, lack of privacy, unintentional anti-social behavior, being misled by deceptive information, the influence of false rumors, and the incredible bombardment of information. There are, too, numerous guidelines offered for using technology, but the bottom line is using common sense and good manners.

Key Terms and Concepts

FtF Interaction Skills 210, 212   FtF 206   The Goldilocks effect 214

Questions to Review

1. How close does your use of technology compare with Leah's (in the opening example)? What effects (positive or negative) have you discovered regarding your use of various technology?

2. If you had to select just one answer to the question, "Why do you use technology?," what would your answer be?

3. What trade-offs have you discovered when people are heavy-technology users? That is, what are the areas that get less attention?

4. To what extent do you think technology changes the way people think of themselves and how they communicate?

5. Do you believe that a heavy dependence on technology affects interaction skills? In what ways?

6. Do you believe that using technology promotes greater self-disclosure? Why or why not?

7. What sacrifices are made in FtF conversational interactions when people choose to use technology instead of interacting FtF? That is, to what extent does a dependence on technology affect FtF conversations?

8. What are the reasons why text messaging has become so important in romantic and sexual correspondence?

9. What are the qualities of texting not present in FtF communication?

10. What is "the Goldilocks effect," and how does it affect relationship development? What are the ways people have to offset or see through "the Goldilocks effect"?

11. What are the recommendations for making texting in relationship development more rewarding?

12. What are the disadvantages of using technology?

13. What are the guidelines for using technology?

CHAPTER NINE

Conflict and Conflict Management

Objectives

After reading this chapter, you should be able to:

- Define conflict and conflict resolution, and offer a useful model for resolving conflict.

- Define defensive communication, explain how to avoid it, and distinguish between good and bad criticism.

- Explain what can be done to handle conflict online.

- Explain the key to dealing with conflict at work and the steps for productive problem solving.

- Describe Blake and Mouton's conflict management approaches, objectives, rationales, and outcomes.

IT WAS EMMA'S FIRST TIME LIVING IN A DORMITORY. IT WAS HER FIRST TIME living away from home, too. With respect to a roommate, she had no idea what to expect; however, she knew her new roommate would be there sometime later in the day—at least that's what she was told. When Chloe appeared, she was accompanied by her brother, Ethan, and her father, who helped her move in and get settled. Since Emma had nothing else to do, she helped them carry Chloe's things from their car. Emma's first impressions of Chloe were that she was clean, neat, attractive, pleasant, and easy to get along with; however, once Ethan and her father had gone, Emma's impressions began to change. The difference wasn't like night and day, but as Emma watched and listened, she sensed that Chloe had some problems that were stressing her out.

First, Chloe told Emma that she and her father never got along, and if she had her way, it would have been Ethan, not her father, who drove her to campus. Second, she told her that nothing in her life right now was going well for her. She did not get her first choice when it came to colleges; her boyfriend had recently left her and was dating her best friend; and the company she had worked for throughout high school had gone "belly-up" just before summer, and without summer employment, she was very short of cash.

This was a lot of information for Emma to digest all at one time, and she attributed Chloe's negative attitude and obvious cynicism to all Chloe had going on in her life. When Emma asked her if there was anything she could do to help out, she received an abrupt, "No. The best thing you can do is to not ask questions, and stay out of my business."

Emma felt horrible, and being the open, understanding, and giving person she was, she fell silent, asked Chloe no questions, and sought to avoid any further contact, although that was difficult because they were roommates. Emma would leave the room before Chloe was out of bed, left short notes about her whereabouts on her bed, and kept all her belongings on her side of the room (so there was no dispute or possible argument about who owned what). Emma knew conflict was not inherently bad. She knew, too, that it resulted from differing viewpoints, and she clearly saw vast differences between Chloe's and hers. She realized they viewed the world in nearly opposite ways, and trying to resolve differences—because of vastly differing viewpoints—would not just be impossible but may even spark a physical reaction.

Unfortunately, this continued through most of the term when suddenly, and without explanation, Chloe left campus. Someone came to pick up her things while Emma was in class one day, so Emma never received any answer as to why Chloe left.

It wasn't long before another roommate, Ava, was assigned to her, and this time she and Ava became the best of friends and remained that way throughout their four years of college. They even chose each other as roommates when they moved to an apartment off campus. Emma shared her adventure with Chloe with Ava, and from then on, it became a humorous aside when anything went wrong: "Remember Chloe!" they would say.

In their book *Words Can Change Your Brain* (NY: Hudson Street Press, 2012), Andrew Newberg, a medical doctor, and Mark Robert Waldman offer some valuable introductory advice regarding how to deal with conflict in this helter-skelter, always-on-the-go, up-tempo, caffeine-inspired life many of us lead. They talk about the value of intuition (intrapersonal communication) and its role in communication. "If we want to have more productive and meaningful outer dialogues, both the speaker and listener need to slow down enough to allow the inner wisdom of the observing self—one's intuition—to emerge in the brief periods of silence we create. . . . In that improved state of consciousness, we'll choose our words more wisely.

"As a shrewd Hasidic rabbi once said," Newberg and Waldman write, "Before you speak, ask yourself this question, will your words improve the silence" (p. 75).

It should be noted—as a reminder—that slowing "down enough to allow the inner wisdom of the observing self—one's intuition—to emerge in the brief periods of silence we create," reinforces and underscores the value and importance of strategic flexibility. Having built a collection of communication behaviors—and this chapter should add to your toolbox—this period of silence permits you to more accurately access and evaluate the situation, select the best skills or behaviors available that are likely to have the greatest impact on the current situation, and then apply those. The reason we mention this up front in this chapter is that engaging in strategic flexibility has the potential of dealing effectively with conflict. Conflict can not only have a significantly negative effect on relationships but just as important, maybe even more so, it can have a devastating effect on the human psyche.

Resolving Conflict

In *Interpersonal Conflict* (McGraw-Hill, 2007), authors William Wilmot and Joyce Hocker define **conflict** as "an expressed struggle between at least two parties who perceive incompatible goals, scarce resources, and interference from others in achieving their goals."[1] Conflict is expressed through your communication when you feel your goals and those of another are contradictory, you are both competing for similar and yet scarce resources, or you perceive interference from the other person in trying to get what you want.

When you are in conflict and have decided that nothing will be served by avoidance or aggression, the option left open to you is **conflict resolution**—negotiation, to find a solution to the conflict. If the conflict has occurred because of a perception of incompatible goals, you negotiate to determine how you can both reach your goals. For the negotiation to be considered successful, both you and the other person must be satisfied and feel that you have come out ahead. This is referred to as *win-win negotiating*.

Culture, gender, and power play roles in conflict. Culture plays a role because perceptions, expectations, behaviors, and communication patterns are rooted in culture. Often, when cultures are better understood, conflict prevention and resolution become more effective. Gender is framed in a cultural context, and research shows that in some circumstances there are gender differences to conflict. For example, in laboratory exercises, "men will often exhibit dominating and competitive behavior and women exhibit avoidant and compromising behavior."[2] Wilmot and Hocker cite Deborah Tannen's research when they write, "Women are more likely to avoid conflict. Men are more likely than women to take control of the conversation to lead it in the direction they want. However, they expect their (female) conversational partners to mount some resistance to this effort, as men would be likely to do. Women often remain in the 'listening' role rather than 'lecturing,' which puts them at a disadvantage in having their voices heard."[3]

Power plays a major role in conflict as well. Perceived differences in power can lead to antagonism. "People feel passionately about power—who has it, who ought to have more or less, how people misuse power, and how justified they feel in trying to gain more power for themselves."[5] Conflicts involving power do not have to be destructive. Constructive conflict management almost always depends on a search for power with others.

ATTENTION!

Six Steps for Resolving Conflicts[4]

1. Cool off.
2. Tell what's bothering you using owned messages.
3. Restate what you heard the other person say.
4. Take responsibility.
5. Brainstorm solutions looking for one that satisfies both parties.
6. Affirm, forgive, or thank.

In his book *The Charge: Activating the 10 Human Drives That Make You Feel Alive* (NY: Free Press, 2012), in Chapter 6, "The Drive for Connection," Brendon Burchard talks about how to deal with relationship conflict:

> Naturally, conflict happens, and it's hard to always positively project the best upon our loved ones, so here's a parting study for you to consider. Marriage researchers have found a powerful equation you should be aware of. Happily married couples who end up staying together for life have in common the ratio in which they share positive versus negative input. That ratio is five to one. So you should aspire to give five times as much praise in your relationships as criticism. Be the cheerleader, not the cynic. Coupled together, your intention to positively project onto others and also praise them five times *more than complain will change your relationships forever (p. 125).*

Source: Burchard, Brendon. (2012). The Charge: Activating the 10 Human Drives That Make You Feel Alive. New York: Free Press (a division of Simon & Schuster).

Questions

1. Does the ratio of five to one—five times as much praise as criticism—sound reasonable?

2. Do you think it makes sense to be a cheerleader in your relationships? What do you think are the barriers to being a cheerleader?

3. Does it seem like such a goal—giving five times as much praise as criticism—could change a relationship forever? Are there other changes that must occur in relationships, in addition to the change from criticism to praise, to legitimately change relationships forever?

Deborah Wieder-Hatfield, a researcher in this area, has suggested a useful model for resolving conflict. In this model, each individual looks at the conflict intrapersonally. Then the partners get together to work out the problem.[6]

In the first stage, **intrapersonal evaluation,** each person analyzes the problem alone. This analysis is accomplished through a series of questions: How do I feel about this problem? How can I describe the other person's behavior? What are the facts?

In the second stage, the parties in the conflict get together to work out an **interpersonal definition** of the problem. It is important that both parties believe there is a problem and can define what it is. In this stage, it is important that each person listen carefully and check the accuracy of what he or she has heard by paraphrasing what was said. The same is true for feelings. At the end of this stage, both partners should agree on the facts of the problem.

In the third stage, the partners should discuss **shared goals.** Still focusing on the problem, the individuals should ask, "What are my needs and desires?" and "What are your needs and desires?" Then they should work to see whether their needs and goals overlap.

At the fourth stage, the partners must come up with **possible solutions** to the problem. Here it is useful to create as long a list as possible. Then each individual can eliminate solutions he or she considers unacceptable.

In the fifth stage, the partners move on to **weighing goals against solutions.** Some compromises are inevitable at this stage. The solutions may not be entirely satisfactory to either party, but they are a compromise that both hope they can live with. Negotiators would label this a win-win solution.

Since all resolutions are easier to make than to keep, the last stage of the process is to **evaluate the solution** after some time has passed. Did the solution work? Does it need to be changed? Should it be discussed again at a later date? As we mentioned earlier, it is not easy to change human behavior. When partners work to resolve conflict, even when they come up with good solutions there is likely to be some backsliding. It therefore makes good sense to give partners a chance to live up to their resolutions. Letting time pass before both negotiators are held accountable helps achieve this goal.

John Gottman, from all of his research on couples, says that happy couples have a different way of relating to each other during disputes. Partners make frequent "repair attempts," reaching out to each other in an effort to prevent negativity from getting out of control in the midst of conflict. Humor, too, is often part of a successful repair attempt. If partners can work together and appreciate the best in each other, they learn to cope with the problems that are part of every relationship. Partners must learn to love each other not just for what they have in common but for things that make them complementary as well.[7]

Eric V. Copage, in an article, "Love You! Now, the Difficult Stuff . . ." (*The New York Times*, February 12, 2012), cites Dr. Gregory A. Kuhlman, a psychologist who directs the master's program in mental health counseling at Brooklyn College: "In the end it is not going to be any of these items that determines a couple's happiness. It's going to be whether they can maintain an overall positive atmosphere and sense of teamwork in their [relationship]. It's inevitable that friction produced by their normal differences will challenge this, and they must be intent on managing these positively and cooperatively" (p. 20).

The Bottom Line

There are two major questions that will help you assess your relationship with respect to "The Bottom Line." Lundy Bancroft, who for 15 years has specialized in domestic abuse and the behavior of abusive men, and JAC Patrissi, who for 20 years has specialized in creative responses for survivors of abuse, write in their book *Should I Stay or Should I Go?* (NY: Berkley Books, 2011), "If your challenges are the ordinary ones, the solutions are mutual ones [—the bottom line—]. Each partner needs to work on improving communication, and to develop awareness of where their 'buttons get pushed.' The decision of whether to stay in the relationship is not based on the question 'Is this relationship doing me harm?'; instead, it's about issues along the lines of 'Is this relationship giving me what I need?' Do we have enough in common? Are our feelings for each other strong enough?" (p. 3) So the first question is simply, "Are my needs being met?"

The second question, "Can you admit you're wrong?" is discussed by Carolyn Hax in her column on conflict (*The* (Toledo) *Blade*, October 7, 2012). "In an intimate relationship," Hax writes, "there are steep costs to an unwillingness to admit you're wrong: It damages your credibility, because everyone's wrong sometimes, usually often; it diminishes your partner, since you're more invested in your victory than his truth; it's defensive, which will keep you from ever being truly close; it paralyzes problem-solving" (p. 8D).

Keeping these ideas in mind, the Institute for American Values conducted a study and the results of which bear directly on the discussions in this chapter.[8] Their research countered what they labeled the "divorce assumption"—that most people assume that a person stuck in a bad marriage has two choices: stay married and miserable or get a divorce and become happier. The study found no evidence that unhappily married adults who divorced were typically any happier than unhappily married people who stayed married.[9]

Two-thirds of unhappily married spouses who stayed married reported that their marriages were happy five years later. Those in the most unhappy marriages reported the most dramatic turnarounds. These unhappy partners had endured serious problems, including alcoholism, infidelity, verbal abuse, emotional neglect, depression, illness, and work and money troubles. The study found three principal techniques for their recovery; those in unhappy unions of any kind can learn something about what it takes to improve relationships.

The first technique is **endurance.** Many couples, the study found, did not so much solve their problems as transcend them—they simply and stubbornly outlasted their problems. By taking one day at a time and pushing through their difficulties, the unhappy spouses said in their focus groups, many sources of conflict and distress eased—whether it was financial problems, job reversals, depression, child problems, even infidelity.

The second technique is **work ethic.** Unhappy spouses actively worked to solve problems, change behavior, and improve communication. They tackled their problems by arranging for more private time with each other, seeking counseling, receiving help from in-laws or other relatives, consulting clergy or secular counselors, and even by threatening divorce and consulting divorce attorneys.

The third technique was **personal happiness.** In these cases, the unhappy partners found other ways to improve their overall contentment, even if they could not markedly improve their marital happiness. That is, they improved their own happiness and built, for themselves, a good and happy life, despite a mediocre marriage.

The bottom line to improving relationship happiness proved to be **commitment**—having a positive attitude toward the relationship. Unhappy partners minimized the importance of difficulties they couldn't resolve, and they actively worked to belittle and downplay the attractiveness of alternatives to their current relationship.

Resolving Conflict Online

Kali Munro, a psychotherapist, writes, "Have you ever noticed how conflict can get blown out of proportion online? What may begin as a small difference of opinion, or misunderstanding, becomes a major issue very quickly. Conflict can be difficult at the best of times, but what is it about online communication that seems to ignite 'flaming' and make conflicts more difficult to resolve?"[10] "What can be done to prevent unnecessary conflict in cyberspace?" Munro asks. "The following are tips for handling conflict online with respect, sensitivity, and care." We have abbreviated or eliminated the discussion of each point for space considerations.

1. Don't respond right away. When you feel hurt or angry about an email or post, it's best not to respond right away.

2. Read the post again later. Sometimes, your first reaction to a post is a lot about how you're feeling at the time. Reading it later, and sometimes a few times, can bring a new perspective.

3. Discuss the situation with others who know you. Ask them what they think about the post and the response you plan to send.

4. Choose whether or not you want to respond. You do have a choice, and you don't have to respond. You may be too upset to respond in the way that you would like, or it may not be worthy of a response.

5. Assume that people mean well, unless they have a history or pattern of aggression. Everyone has bad days, gets triggered, reacts insensitively, and

writes an email without thinking it through completely. It doesn't mean that he or she doesn't have good intentions.

On the other hand, some people pick fights no matter how kind and patient you are with them. They distort what you say, quote you out of context, and make all sorts of accusations, all to vilify and antagonize you. Don't take the bait by engaging in a struggle with them—they'll never stop. Sometimes, the best strategy is to have nothing more to do with someone.

6. Clarify what was meant. We all misinterpret what we hear and read, particularly when we feel hurt or upset. It's a good idea to check out that you understood them correctly.

7. Think about what you want to accomplish by your communication. Are you trying to connect with this person? Are you trying to understand him or her and be understood? What is the message you hope to convey? What is the tone you want to communicate? Consider how you can convey that.

8. Verbalize what you want to accomplish. Here are some examples, "I want to understand what you're saying." "I feel hurt by some stuff that you said. I want to talk about it in a way that we both feel heard and understood." "I want to find a way to work this out. I know we don't agree about everything and that's okay. I'd like to talk with you about how I felt reading your post." "I hope we can talk this through because I really like you. I don't want to be argumentative or blaming."

9. Use "I" statements when sharing your feelings or thoughts. For example, "I feel . . ." versus "You made me feel. . . ."

10. Use strictly feeling statements. Feeling statements include saying you felt hurt, sad, scared, angry, happy, guilty, remorseful, and so on.

11. Choose your words carefully and thoughtfully, particularly when you're upset. Do your best to keep in mind that the person will read your post alone. You are not physically or virtually present with him or her to clarify what you meant, and he or she can't see the kindness in your eyes. He or she must rely entirely on your words to interpret your meaning, intent, and tone.

12. Place yourself in the other person's shoes. How might he or she hear your message? To avoid unnecessary conflict or a lot of hurt feelings, it helps to take into account who you're writing to. Use emoticons to express your tone.

In online communication, visual and auditory cues are replaced by emoticons, for example, smiles, winks, and laughter. It helps to use emoticons to convey your tone. In addition, if you like the person, tell them! Having a conflict or misunderstanding doesn't mean you don't like the person any more, but people often forget that reality, or don't think to say it. It may be most needed during a tense interaction.

13. Start and end your post with positive, affirming, and validating statements. Say what you agree with, what you understand about how they feel, and any other positive statements at the beginning of your email. This helps set a positive tone. End on a positive note as well.[11]

Defensive Communication

Defensive communication occurs when one partner tries to defend himself or herself against the remarks or behavior of the other. The problem with defensive communication is that we are so busy defending ourselves that we cannot listen to what the

Table 9-1   Categories of Defensive and Supportive Behavior

Defensive Climate	Supportive Climate
1. Evaluation	1. Description
2. Control	2. Problem solving
3. Strategy	3. Spontaneity
4. Neutrality	4. Empathy
5. Superiority	5. Equality
6. Certainty	6. Provisionalism

www.mhhe.com/hybels11e >

For an example of defensive communication view clip, "Defensive Communication."

other person is saying. Also, defending ourselves is dealing with past behavior; it gives us no chance to think about resolving the problem.

How can we avoid defensive communication? A researcher, in a classic article, came up with six categories of defensive communication and supportive strategies to counter each of them[12] (see Table 9-1). Consider the supportive response in each instance, as communication strategies.

Evaluation versus Description

Evaluative statements involve a judgment. If the judgment is negative, the person you are speaking to is likely to react defensively. If you tell your roommate, "It is inconsiderate of you to slam the door when I am trying to sleep," he might respond, "It's inconsiderate of you to snore every night when I am trying to sleep." On the other hand, if you tell your roommate, "I had trouble sleeping last night because I woke up when I heard the door slam," he is much more likely to do something about the problem. Since you have merely described the problem, the message is not as threatening. Notice that the second statement is an owned message.

Control versus Problem Solving

People who consistently attempt to exert **control** believe that they are always right and that no other opinion (or even fact) is worth listening to.

Others tend to respond negatively if they think someone is trying to control them. For example, if you are working on a class project with a classmate and you begin by taking charge and telling him or her what to do, you will probably be resented. A better approach is for you and your classmate to engage in **problem solving** together. The same applies to close relationships. If conflict arises and you decide what should be done ("I'll take the car, and you take the bicycle"), your partner is not likely to respond positively. It is better to discuss the options together.

Strategy versus Spontaneity

Often **strategy** is little more than manipulation. Rather than openly asking people to do something, you try to manipulate them into doing what you want by using strategies such as making them feel guilty or ashamed. A statement that begins "If you love me, you will . . ." is always manipulative. A better approach is to express your honest feelings **spontaneously:** "I am feeling overwhelmed with all the planning I have to do for the party. Will you help me out today?"

Neutrality versus Empathy

If you receive a low grade on a paper and are feeling bad about it, you don't want your friend to say, "Maybe the teacher was right. Let's look at both sides." When feelings are high, no one wants **neutrality**—an objective response. What is needed is for the other person to show **empathy**—the ability to recognize and identify with our feelings. An empathic response to a poor grade in a course might be, "You must feel bad. You studied hard for that class." Or, as an owned message, you can say, "I understand why you feel bad since I know you studied so hard."

Superiority versus Equality

People who always take charge of situations seem to imply that they are the only ones qualified to do so—they exhibit **superiority.** Even if we have a position that is superior to someone else's, people will react less defensively if we do not communicate this superiority. An attitude of **equality**—"Let's tackle this problem together"—produces much less defensive behavior.

Certainty versus Provisionalism

Don't confuse people who are confident and secure with people who think they are always right. Be skeptical of those who constantly exhibit **certainty.** Confident and secure people may hold strong opinions; they are likely, however, to demonstrate **provisionalism,** to make many statements that permit another point of view to be expressed. For example, someone might say, "I feel strongly on this subject, but I would be interested in hearing what you have to say."

Avoiding Defensive Communication: A Practical Example

Although we have discussed each of the six defensive categories separately, in most communication situations several of them appear simultaneously. You can see how this works in the following situations:

A Defensive Dialogue

> *Boss:*   You're an hour late. If you're going to work here, you have to be on time. (superiority, control)
>
> *Employee:*   My car wouldn't start.
>
> *Boss:*   That's no reason to be late. (certainty, evaluation) You should have called. (evaluation)
>
> *Employee:*   I tried, but . . .
>
> *Boss:*   When work starts at 8 A.M., you must be here at 8 A.M. (superiority, control) If you can't make it, you should look for another job. (superiority, control, certainty) If you're late again, don't bother coming to work. (superiority, control, strategy)

This dialogue leaves the employee feeling defensive, angry, and unable to say anything. Let's take a look at how it might have gone if the boss had been more willing to listen:

A Supportive Dialogue

> *Boss:*   You're an hour late. What happened? (description, equality)
>
> *Employee:*   My car wouldn't start.
>
> *Boss:*   Weren't you carrying your cell phone? (still no evaluation)
>
> *Employee:*   Every time I tried to call, the line was busy. I finally decided that it would be faster to walk here while trying to call.

ATTENTION!

How to Deal with Rejection

1. Avoid self-defeating assumptions.
2. Don't magnify its impact.
3. Don't let it compromise or derail your dreams.
4. Learn from it.

> **Boss:** When people don't get here on time, I always worry that we're going to fall behind schedule. (spontaneity) Wasn't there any way of letting me know what happened? (problem solving)
>
> **Employee:** Yes, maybe there was. I panicked. I should have called my sister and asked her to keep calling too to let you know what happened. If it ever happens again, that's what I'll do.
>
> **Boss:** Good. Now let's get to work. There's a lot of catching up to do.

Dealing with Rejection

It is because your drive to connect with others is so deeply embedded in your DNA that disappointment when you fail to connect or from the departure of a loved one is among the most stressful of all experiences. Research has shown that being ditched by your best friend is as threatening to your well-being as touching a hot stove.

How can you successfully cope with rejection? The first technique for successfully coping with rejection is to **avoid self-defeating assumptions.** Often, the first response to rejection is to let it become an indictment of your life. It may cause you to believe it is an indication of a basic flaw or shortcoming in your personality. Rejection by a partner, for example, may make you feel unlovable by anyone.

The second technique for successfully coping with rejection is **don't magnify its impact.** Rejection often triggers a negative mindset that suggests it is a forecast of your future. The point isn't to minimize its impact, it is to assess it realistically within the perspective of your life. Look, for example, where you have been, where you are, and where you hope to go in the future. Perhaps your rejection isn't as significant as it currently seems without this broader perspective.

Rejection can create a self-fulfilling prophecy if, indeed, you believe you are a reject and then behave in ways that prove your prophecy. If you enter future relationships believing that you are not good enough, incapable of sustaining a relationship, or unworthy of another's love and affection, your attitude is likely to stimulate behaviors that may prompt another rejection. Just remember that a rejection in the past is not a predictor of rejection in the future.

Rejections hurt, but the third technique for dealing with them successfully is **don't let them compromise or derail your dreams.** It is true that you can retreat from the possibility of future rejections, but by doing so you may miss new opportunities and challenges. These new opportunities and challenges may yield pleasure, great happiness, and tremendous success. Think how you might look back and regret your behavior if retreating from the possibility of future rejections was the course of action you decided on.

The fourth and final technique for successfully dealing with rejection is to **learn from it.** If there is helpful feedback, listen to it. If you have time for self-reflection, engage in it. If you see little to change, persevere. Your best course of action may be to deal with it, learn from it, forgive, if necessary, forget about it, and move on. Move on to improving future relationships that matter and have consequence.

Dealing with Conflict at Work

Effective communication is the key to dealing with conflict at work. You can support effective communication with a well-thought-out, reasoned approach. This suggests that your emotions will not be engaged. How can you keep control in a potentially volatile situation? It isn't easy, of course, but the key is "emotional disengaging," according to Florence M. Stone of the American Management Association (AMA).[13] Stone says "it entails turning off your emotions to a situation and examining it as a scenario in a play or plot in a book—that is, objectively."

Some people, when facing conflict on the job, will put on gloves and come out swinging. Some will put on blinders and ignore the problem. But others will seek productive solutions, and the following steps will guide you through that process.

First, *plan, prepare, and rehearse.* You must have a clear idea of your message, and to obtain this clear idea, you must do your homework and review the facts. It may even help to write out the problem. The better command you have of all the facts, the stronger your foundation throughout the process.

Second, *set an appropriate climate.* Anticipate your meeting with the other person by scheduling an uninterrupted time to work through the issues. Make your meeting private so nobody else will witness or overhear your conversation. Set the tone for the entire process by treating the other person as respectfully as you yourself would want to be treated.

Third, *adopt a constructive attitude.* Examine your motives and feelings carefully before delivering difficult or critical feedback. Emotions that reflect anger, frustration, and lack of respect will be quickly detected, as will awkwardness and discomfort. People will more likely be open to critical feedback if they are confident in, feel respected by, and trust the messenger.

Fourth, *assertively state the message.* Assertiveness is neither pushy, obnoxious, aggressive, nor confrontational. It means being open and straightforward about a situation, speaking calmly about what happened and keeping your emotions under control. This is where owned messages come into play. Instead of saying "You did this . . ." say "I was surprised when I heard . . ."

Fifth, *allow your message to sink in.* Stay quiet while your receiver processes your remarks. You do not need to elaborate, justify, or expand on your message at this point. You will have a better discussion if your receiver is allowed time to think and compose himself or herself.

Sixth, *listen carefully to the response.* Do *not* interrupt. Give your receiver an opportunity to express his or her reaction and response, even if this means some emotion is shown. Reveal your understanding and empathy by paraphrasing the remarks, if appropriate, and acknowledge his or her feelings.

Seventh, *restate, clarify, and recycle.* Work with your receiver until he or she has a clear understanding of your position. Encourage discussion to explore the issues, but stay on track. This is not an opportunity to debate and argue the issues. You may elaborate now in response to questions for clarification, but actively acknowledge both the reactions and viewpoints of your receiver as you do. Your active listening skills, accurate paraphrasing skills, and obvious respect for your receiver will help build the trust that forms the foundation for constructive problem solving.

Eighth, *focus on solutions,* not personalities. This is when you both need to offer solutions. It may require a compromise—not a complete adoption of one solution or another—to ensure there is closure to the conflict. It is not about one person winning and another losing; but rather, about both parties finding a way to resolve the conflict.

Ninth, *plan to evaluate solutions.* Schedule a time to meet after a solution has been put into practice, when both parties should be free to discuss it. Did it work? Can we make changes so it will work better?

Some people will never be able to get along with one another no matter what efforts are made. Rather than looking for issues to be upset about, you are more likely to work with such co-workers if you resolve to take the high road. You will be able to work

ATTENTION!

Nine Steps for Seeking Productive Solutions (A Summary)

1. Plan, prepare, and rehearse.
2. Set an appropriate climate.
3. Adopt a constructive attitude.
4. Assertively state the message.
5. Allow your message to sink in.
6. Listen carefully to the response.
7. Restate, clarify, and recycle.
8. Focus on solutions, not personalities.
9. Plan to evaluate solutions.

STRATEGIC FLEXIBILITY

Dealing with conflict requires a thoughtful, rational approach. If you apply the strategic flexibility framework, you are more likely to select just the right set of skills and behaviors that, when applied, will help move the problem toward a solution.

in a more positive manner and environment if you think about the purpose of the work, the long-range goals of the company, and your individual contribution rather than co-worker problems and personality clashes.

If you need more incentive for constructively dealing with conflict at work, protecting your health may be it. In *Words Can Change Your Brain,* introduced earlier in this chapter, Newberg and Waldman say that "In a recent study reported in *Health Psychology* . . . [researchers discovered that] Emotionally charged discussions caused the release of cytokines, proteins that are linked to cardiovascular disease, diabetes, arthritis, and various cancers. When people used words reflecting reason, understanding, and insight, the release of these stress chemicals went down" (p. 179).

Conflict in Groups

When individuals meet in groups to solve problems, conflicts are likely to occur. By *conflict* we mean the expressed struggle between at least two individuals who perceive incompatible goals or interference from others in achieving their goals. One reason there is likely to be conflict has to do with perceptual differences that influence people's responses to any situation. Let's examine some of the obvious perceptual differences.

Culture, race, and ethnicity create perceptual differences because our varying cultural backgrounds influence us to hold certain beliefs about the social structure of our world and the role of conflict in that experience.

Gender and sexuality create differences in perception as a result of different experiences in the world that relate to power and privilege.

Knowledge influences approaches to conflict because it forms the base from which you operate. Whether or not you understand what is going on in *this* case (situation-specific knowledge), and whether or not you have read about or heard about this type of situation before (general knowledge) will influence your willingness to engage in and manage conflict.

In addition to perceptual differences, group conflict generally occurs because of procedure, power, or work distribution.

- *Procedure.* The first source of conflict, and perhaps the easiest to eliminate, is differing views on procedure. How often should the group meet? What form should the minutes take? To keep such conflict from occurring, the group members should discuss and resolve issues of procedure at the first meeting.

- *Power.* Research has found that in business and corporate settings a group often becomes a focal point for power struggles.[14] However, power struggles are not as common in classroom groups. If one person wants power, the problem is often solved by making him or her the chair. If this doesn't solve the problem and members continue their power struggle, the group will probably not work very efficiently.

- *Work distribution.* The third source of conflict, and one of the greatest in classroom groups, is that some members work harder than others. Like power struggles, this kind of conflict is difficult to resolve. Since few students are willing to tell the instructor about such inequality, the harder workers' only hope is to confront the group members who are not working and use peer pressure to persuade them to change.

Although these three kinds of conflict can interfere with group work, not all conflict is harmful. According to Charlan Nemeth, a professor of psychology at the University of California at Berkeley, "dissent stimulates new ideas because it encourages us to engage more fully with the work of others and to reassess our viewpoints" (as cited by

ATTENTION!

Tips for Dealing with Substantive Conflict

1. Determine if there is a problem.
2. If so, set up a private face-to-face meeting to discuss it.
3. In a nonconfrontational manner, ask if there is a problem. If the answer is "No," then say you think there is and gently explain your viewpoint.
4. As you talk, ask for feedback, and take responsibility when you can.
5. Listen to each other with open minds.
6. Respect each other's opinions.
7. Pause to fully digest the other person's opinions.
8. Determine why the other person feels the way he or she does.
9. Avoid blame, accusations, put-downs, and finger pointing.
10. Work out a compromise that pleases both of you.[15]

Personality Characteristics of Those Best at Managing Conflict

The question we wanted answered was: What are the personality characteristics of those who are best at managing conflict situations? In social situations we observed those who seemed most confident and successful, and although we didn't formally survey them, we made mental notes. Then we went to the Internet, and implementing an informal selection of different searches using the Google search engine, we came up with a variety of characteristics. We make no claim to reliability nor validity; however, giving the characteristics that follow the "eyeball test" (just looking over the list to see if they make sense), they appear to be relevant and valuable. That is, if you possessed these characteristics, it would seem to improve your chances at more effective and competent conflict management.

The first, and, perhaps, most important characteristic is maturity. Side-by-side with maturity, we place wisdom—which often comes with maturity. It is mature people who can own up to their mistakes and take responsibility for things that were under their control, and many mature people, too, have a history of dealing with conflict situations. The greater the history (or track record), the greater the likelihood of good decisions (based on the assumption that people learn from their mistakes rather than repeat them). Wise people often have higher intelligence, as well as greater common sense, judgment, and levelheadedness. (We want it to be clear that intelligence guarantees nothing. Many intelligent people cannot effectively deal with conflict.) Maturity and wisdom are strong characteristics when accompanied by a consideration of others—especially the ability to empathize with them. People who empathize often listen well. A tough characteristic (especially when ensconced in conflict) but one that accompanies maturity and wisdom is the ability to keep your emotions in check. Closely related to maturity and wisdom, too, is the ability to remain open-minded, objective, tolerant, and flexible.

If we were to suggest characteristics that do not directly relate to those above, we would add the ability to see things in shades of gray, rather than black or white, a positive attitude toward conflict and its benefits, and the ability to offer options, choices, and alternatives.

Questions

1. Do you know of anyone who is good at resolving conflicts? Which of the preceding characteristics do they possess? Are there characteristics missing from the preceding list that they demonstrated?

2. Have you had opportunities to deal with conflict situations? Do you consider yourself "good at it" or not? Do you think you are better than others? Why or why not?

3. Do you know people who are afraid of conflict? Any conflict? Do you think it's because they lack some of the characteristics listed above? Could it be an unsuccessful background of dealing with conflict situations?

4. If you wanted to become better at dealing with conflict, which characteristics would you want to work on?

Jonah Lehrer, "Groupthink, " *The New Yorker*, January 30, 2012, p. 24). The fourth kind of conflict, conflict about substantive issues, can be rewarding.

The Value of Substantive Conflict

Substantive conflict occurs when people have different reactions to an idea. It is likely to occur when any important and controversial idea is being discussed. As in all exchanges of ideas, people's opinions and perceptions are influenced by their culture, upbringing, education, and experience. These perceptions cause them to react differently to ideas and can create conflict in a group.

Many people believe that conflict is abnormal or bad. There is no doubt that conflict can (and often does) have negative effects. Conflict is destructive when it diverts energy from more important issues and tasks. It is destructive when it deepens differences in values, polarizes groups so that cooperation is reduced, destroys the morale of people or reinforces their already poor self-concepts.

Conflict can, however, be constructive.[16] It is essential for both healthy relationships and groups if it allows people to grow and change, adapt to new situations, or invent new approaches to problems. There is value in conflict when it opens up issues of importance and, therefore, results in issue clarification—a heightened awareness that a problem exists that needs to be solved.

There is value in conflict, too, when it causes reassessment by allowing for the examination of procedures or actions. Other values include greater quantity and quality of achievement, and creative problem solving. Constructive conflict results, too, in healthier cognitive, social, and psychological development, which means those involved are better able to deal with stress and cope with unforeseen adversities. When conflict is avoided or suppressed, all these positive results cannot take place.

The difference between productive and destructive conflict can be seen in their focus. Productive conflict focuses on substantive issues of disagreement, and the goal is to resolve the disagreement. Destructive conflict focuses on the defeat or destruction of the opponent, and it is often characterized by force, aggression, and coercion. Inflexibility is a mark of destructive conflict.

Ron Brownstein, in his book *The Second Civil War,* says, "Conflict is part of politics because conflict is part of American life, and has been forever, and will be forever, and usually is a good thing—taken to a point."[17] Whether sought after or incidental, in groups it is often a good thing.

Managing Group Conflict

There are times when conflict can slow down a group or even bring it to a screeching halt. When conflict arises, the group leader has to step in and try to help group members resolve it. The approach the leader takes should depend on the seriousness of the conflict. Robert Blake and Jane Mouton, who have written about ways to resolve conflict, suggest five ways of managing it.[18] Table 9-2 explains the objectives, supporting rationale, and likely outcomes for each of the following approaches.

Conflict in groups can occur over perceptual differences such as culture, race, ethnicity, gender, sexuality, knowledge, or previous experiences. Although conflict can be destructive, there can be great value in it as well.

Avoidance

Sometimes groups argue over points that are so minor they are not worth the time they take up. If the leader sees this happening, she or he should use **avoidance**—suggest that the issue doesn't seem very important and that the group should move to another topic.

Accommodation

Accommodation occurs when people on one side of an issue give in to those on the other side. If a leader sees accommodation as a possibility, he or she should attempt to find out how strongly people feel about the sides they have taken. If the issue is not really important to one side, the leader might suggest that that side give in.

Table 9-2 Conflict Management Approaches, Objectives, Rationales, and Outcomes

Approach	Objective and Typical Responses	Supporting Rationale	Likely Outcome
Avoiding	Avoid having to deal with conflict. "I'm neutral on that issue. Let me think about it."	Disagreements are inherently bad because they create tension.	Interpersonal problems don't get resolved. They can cause long-term frustration which will be manifested in a variety of ways.
Accommodating	Don't upset the other person. "How can I help you feel good about this? My position isn't important enough to risk bad feelings between us."	Maintaining harmonious relationships should be our top priority.	Other person is likely to take advantage of you.
Competing	Get your way. "I know what's right. Don't question my judgment or authority."	Better to risk causing a few hard feelings than to abandon a position you're committed to.	You will feel vindicated, and the other party will feel defeated and possibly humiliated.
Collaborating	Solve the problem together. "This is my position. What's yours? I'm committed to finding the best possible solution."	Positions of both parties are equally important. Equal emphasis should be placed on quality of outcome and fairness of decision-making process.	The problem will most likely be resolved. Both parties will be committed to the solution and satisfied that they have been treated fairly.
Compromising	Reach an agreement quickly. "Let's search for a mutually agreeable solution."	Prolonged conflicts distract people from their work, take time, and engender bitter feelings.	Participants become conditioned to seek expedient rather than effective long-term solutions.

Source: Adapted from *Inls 180: Communication Processes: Notes on Conflict Management.* Spring 1998. Retrieved November 15, 2010 from www.ils.unc.edu/daniel/180/conflict.html. The chart is based on the work of Kenneth W. Thomas and Ralph H. Kilmann. See Thomas, K. W., & Kilmann, R. H. (1974). Thomas-Kilmann Conflict Mode Instrument. Mountain View, CA: Xicom, a subsidiary of CPP, Inc. The Thomas-Kilmann conflict management instrument is based on theoretical refinements by Kenneth Thomas of the model of management styles proposed by Robert Blake and Jane Mouton.

Competition

Competition occurs when members on one side care more about winning than about the other members' feelings. When a leader sees competition rising, she or he should try to deflect it before members get entrenched in their positions. Sometimes individual members feel competitive with one another, and they use the group sessions to work out their feelings. If this is happening, the leader might point out to each member privately that the conflict is keeping the group from working together.

Collaboration

In **collaboration,** conflicting parties try to work together to meet each other's needs. Collaborators do not attack one another; instead, they try to understand opposing points of view and work hard to stay away from anything that might harm the group's relationships.

For this AOM exercise you will need—once again—to put on your thinking cap and engage your imagination. You have now received a great deal of advice about various strategies for managing conflict. Remember, every conflict includes different variables, and approaching it requires both flexibility and adaptation. Now, using the advice you've gained, your own experience, and any other information you have acquired, put together a step-by-step process that *you* can follow, that conforms to *your* own standards, values, personality, and abilities that *you* can use when facing most of the kinds of conflict *you* have or are likely to have in *your* life. Like any strategically flexible approach, you will need to be open-minded as you adapt to each new conflict situation, but with a variety of approaches and steps, you are increasing the chances for effective strategic flexibility.

Compromise

In **compromise** each side has to give up something to get what it wants. Compromise will work only when each side believes that what it gets is fair and that it has gained at least a partial victory.

How Are You Likely to Handle Conflict?

For each statement circle the answer that best represents your feelings about yourself. If you want to verify your evaluation, give this survey to a friend, and have him or her fill it out on you.

1. Do you listen well? — True — False
2. Do you empathize with others? (Empathize = put yourself in their shoes.) — True — False
3. Do you get angry easily? — True — False
4. Are you generally thought of as a reasonable person? — True — False
5. Do you find compromising with others easy? — True — False
6. Are you a confident person? — True — False
7. Are you someone who always wants to win? — True — False
8. Can you argue about a topic without attacking the other person? — True — False
9. Do you take criticism personally? — True — False
10. Are you someone who is resistant to change? — True — False
11. Are you thought of as a team player? — True — False
12. Are you selfish? — True — False
13. Do you share your feelings openly? — True — False
14. When you disagree with others, do you let them know? — True — False
15. Are you an open-minded person? — True — False
16. Are you a fair person? — True — False
17. Are you rigid in your beliefs? — True — False
18. Are you willing to openly challenge the ideas of superiors, clients, friends, spouses, or family members? — True — False
19. Do you take negatively any disagreement with your ideas? — True — False
20. Are you regarded by others as negative and argumentative? — True — False
21. Are you mindful and respectful of the ideas of others? — True — False
22. Do you have a negative view of conflict? — True — False
23. Do you look at conflict as a way to learn, develop, and change? — True — False
24. Are you a person who always enjoys being the center of attention? — True — False
25. Do conflicts, in general, have positive outcomes? — True — False

Summary

Conflict, as defined by Wilmot and Hocker, is "an expressed struggle between at least two parties who perceive incompatible goals, scarce resources, and interference from others in achieving their goals." Conflict resolution includes negotiation designed to find a solution to the conflict. Culture, gender, and power play roles in conflict. Weider and Hatfield have offered a six-stage model for resolving conflict: (1) intrapersonal evaluation, (2) interpersonal definition, (3) shared goals, (4) possible solutions, (5) weighing goals against solutions, and (6) evaluating the solution.

Defensive communication occurs when one partner tries to defend himself or herself against the remarks or behavior of the other. It relates to conflict management because partners become so preoccupied with defending themselves that they can't listen to what the other person is saying. Fortunately, for each behavior that creates a defensive climate, there is a positive behavior that helps foster a supportive one. For example, description defuses evaluation; problem solving helps deactivate control; empathy lessens neutrality; equality relieves superiority; and provisionalism moderates certainty.

Often, conflict results in being ditched, breaking up, separation, or divorce. The section "Dealing with Rejection" offers four techniques for successfully dealing with rejection. The first is to avoid self-defeating assumptions. The second is don't magnify its impact. The third is not to let it compromise or derail your dreams. Finally, the fourth technique is to learn from rejection. If there is helpful feedback, listen to it.

Conflicts often get blown out of proportion online, thus, in the section "Resolving Conflict Online," Kali Munro, a psychotherapist, offers 13 tips for handling online conflicts including pause, read the post later, discuss the situation with others, choose if you want to respond, assume the best, clarify what was meant, think about what you want to accomplish and verbalize it, use "I" statements when sharing your feelings, use feeling statements, choose your words carefully, empathize, and start and end your post with positive, affirming, and validating statements.

In the section "Dealing with Conflict at Work," we clarify the key to dealing with conflict at work—effective communication. Keeping control in volatile situations is "emotional disengaging"—turning off your emotions and viewing it objectively. In this section, there are nine suggestions for dealing with conflict at work: (1) Plan, prepare, and rehearse. (2) Set an appropriate climate. (3) Adopt a constructive attitude. (4) Assertively state the message. (5) Allow your message to sink in. (6) Listen carefully to the response. (7) Restate, clarify, and recycle. (8) Focus on solutions, not personalities. (9) Plan to evaluate solutions.

In the chapter's final section, we discuss conflict in groups. In the first part of this final section, we discuss all the influences likely to result in conflict. We discuss perceptual differences, procedure, power, and work distribution, as well as conflict about substantive issues. Regarding the value of substantive conflict, we suggest that there are numerous benefits. For example, it promotes healthy relationships and allows people to grow and change, adapt to new situations, and invent new approaches to problems. It opens up issues of importance and results in issue clarification and heightened awareness of problems. Also it causes reassessment, greater quantity and quality of achievement, and creative problem solving. Finally, constructive conflict results in healthier cognitive, social, and psychological development. Conflict is destructive when it deepens differences in values, polarizes members, destroys morale, or reinforces already poor self-concepts.

Robert Blake and Jane Mouton suggest five ways for managing conflict. For each of the five ways—avoidance, accommodation, competition, collaboration, and compromise—the originators of this approach offer objectives, supporting rationales, and likely outcomes. Collaboration is considered ideal because conflicting parties try to work together to meet each other's needs. Collaborators, too, do not attack one another; instead, they try to understand opposing points of view and work hard to stay away from anything that might harm the group's relationships.

Key Terms and Concepts

Use the Online Learning Center at www.mhhe.com/hybels11e to further your understanding of the following terms:

Accommodation 236
Avoidance 236
Certainty 231
Collaboration 237
Commitment 228
Competition 237
Compromise 238
Conflict 225
Conflict resolution 225
Control 230

Defensive communication 229
Empathy 230
Endurance 228
Equality 231
Evaluative statements 230
Interpersonal definition 226
Intrapersonal evaluation 226
Neutrality 230
Personal happiness 228
Problem solving 230

Provisionalism 231
Self-defeating assumptions 232
Shared goals 226
Spontaneity 232
Strategy 230
Substantive conflict 235
Superiority 231
Work ethic 228

Questions to Review

1. What are some of the gender differences that have an effect on conflict?

2. What are the stages in Deborah Wieder-Hatfield's model for resolving conflict, and what role does intrapersonal communication play in this model?

3. What are the ingredients/techniques that relate directly to improving relationships?

4. What is "the bottom line" regarding improving relationship happiness?

5. What specific methods can be used to resolve conflicts online?

6. How does defensive communication relate to conflict and conflict management?

7. What specific supportive behaviors are designed to defuse which specific defensive behaviors?

8. How does intrapersonal evaluation assist in resolving conflict?

9. What do endurance, work ethic, personal happiness, and commitment have to do with relationship happiness?

10. What is the key to dealing with conflict at work?

11. What are some specific suggestions for approaching conflict situations at work?

12. What are the perceptual differences likely to lead to conflict in groups?

13. Describe and discuss procedure, power, and work distribution as potential forces likely to create conflict in groups.

14. What is the value of substantive conflict?

15. What are the objectives, supporting rationale, and likely outcomes for each of Blake and Mouton's five ways—avoidance, accommodation, competition, collaboration, and compromise—for managing conflicts in groups?

CHAPTER TEN

Intercultural Communication

Objectives

After reading this chapter, you should be able to:

- Define and explain the importance of intercultural communication.

- Describe the role intercultural communication plays in communicating effectively.

- Define culture and what it means to possess a cultural identity.

- Explain the six dimensions or frameworks for studying cultural differences.

- Distinguish among assimilation, accommodation, and separation strategies and their purposes.

FROM THE WEBSITE "POCKET CULTURES" COMES THIS STORY ABOUT Carol, from the United States and Abdullah, from Saudi Arabia, who met when Carol was an American diplomat and posted to Islamabad, Pakistan. Abdullah was also in Pakistan with his employer. Their courtship ended up spanning several years and five different countries before they made the decision to marry. Here, Carol writes about how theirs is "a learning experience in communication, [and] cultural distinctions": "We look out for each other and are constant teachers and examples to each other when it comes to any cultural differences or distinctions. We are both cognizant and always want to step with the right foot forward with each other and with our families. Of course we had to face the usual 'What? You're marrying an American?? Are you going to become an American citizen now?' Or, 'How can you think of marrying a Saudi? He's going to put you in a burka in a palace somewhere and we'll never see you again!' We've learned when to overlook or ignore the skeptics and troublemakers and how best to reassure family members on both sides of customs and cultures that are new and different to them. I've learned when it is prudent to be more 'Saudi' and in turn he knows when it's best to be more 'American.' Daily we make that transition between East and West and feel like we have adopted the best of each other's cultures and customs.[1]

In this chapter we first look at the role of intercultural communication in communicating effectively and in strategic flexibility. Then we look at the word *culture* and the importance of understanding your role as a cultural being. In the next section, we discuss the importance of intercultural communication. Then we relate this topic to the model of communication discussed in Chapter 1. We present six dimensions or frameworks for studying cultural differences. There are four barriers to intercultural communication, and we examine how to deal with the barriers—which includes a discussion of dominant and nondominant cultures. Finally, we look at ways for improving intercultural communication.

The Role of Intercultural Communication in Communicating Effectively and in Strategic Flexibility

In Communicating Effectively

What does intercultural communication have to do with communicating effectively? First, we must all agree that it is communication skills—both sending and receiving abilities—that determine how well individuals, organizations, industries, and nations do in both acquiring and applying knowledge. The better the communication, the greater the likelihood of success. Second, we must all agree that because of globalization and the importance of information, there is a rising new category in the world known as the **knowledge class.** It is a class supported solely by its participation in the new information industries with little, if any, reliance on traditional manufacturing, production, or agriculture. The ability of members of this knowledge class to effectively negotiate the inherent cultural issues in communication will give them a competitive edge in a global world.

Closer to where you live, perhaps, the relevance of intercultural communication is no less important. What if it were your job to coordinate international student services and exchange programs on your college campus? What if you were the manager in a biotech company, responsible for leading a diverse team of scientists doing innovative research?

You could be asked to be the social and human services professional or the equal opportunity/affirmative action officer for your company. You might end up as a mediator, arbitrator, reconciliation specialist, or conflict resolution specialist. You might be an immigration or refugee counselor. An employer or supervisor might ask you to be a project development coordinator or workforce developer. Your employment could become more community oriented if you were asked to be the community liaison or public housing specialist, or you might find a job in the area of community and human services. With the growing diversity in this country, such jobs will become not just more available but more needed and necessary as well.

The world today is characterized by an ever-growing number of communications between people with different linguistic and cultural backgrounds. It is likely that you will make such contacts because they occur in the areas of business, military cooperation, science, education, mass media, entertainment, and tourism, and because of immigration brought about by labor shortages and political conflicts— as well as informally in Internet chat rooms and on Internet bulletin boards. Just a quick example will make this point.

"Record levels of births among minorities in the past decade are moving the USA a step closer to a demographic milestone in which no group commands a majority," write Haya El Nasser and Paul Overberg, in their article "Diversity Grows as Majority Dwindles" (*USA Today*, June 11–13, 2010, p. A1). "Much of the rapid growth in diversity," these authors write, "is driven by an influx of young Hispanic immigrants whose birthrates are higher than those of non-Hispanic whites, creating a race and ethnic chasm and a widening age gap" (p. A1). "The nation's minority population is steadily rising and now makes up 35 percent of the United States, advancing an unmistakable trend that could make minorities the new American majority by midcentury" (*The* (Toledo) *Blade*, June 11, 2010, p. A3). And one more thing, "the nation's growing racial and ethnic diversity has spread far beyond large metropolitan centers into smaller towns and rural areas . . . those where [whites] dominate are gradually disappearing, according to an analysis of census data by Penn State's Population Research Institute" (*USA Today*, September 7–9, 2012, p. A1).

In Strategic Flexibility

Intercultural communication has a direct and noticeable effect on each step of strategic flexibility. In the first step (anticipate), you will have a new slant or angle from which to think about potential communication situations. The needs and requirements will be different than without this new knowledge, and forecasting may require the introduction of new or different skills and abilities.

In the second step (assess), the factors, elements, and conditions of situations in which you find yourself will be different. Becoming alert to the introduction of these new ingredients will become easier as your experience broadens. In the third step (evaluate), you will more accurately be able to determine the value and worth of the factors, elements, and conditions and how they bear on your own skills and abilities. Because you will have developed more skills and abilities, in the fourth step (select) you will find it easier to select those most likely to affect the situation.

In the fifth step (apply), you will take greater care and concern and give greater attention to the factors that are likely to be affected. You will understand how to judge their relevance with greater accuracy, and when you reassess and reevaluate your actions you will have increased sensitivity to the intercultural demands of communication situations and how you can enhance, nourish, and encourage further communication efforts.

What Is Culture?

Culture is not a box but a fluid concept that is an ever-changing, living part of you, reflecting your learned, socially acquired traditions and lifestyles. The following is a useful definition. As you read it, recognize that there are no hard edges; rather, there are phenomena that tend to overlap and mingle. **Culture** is:

> *The ever-changing values, traditions, social and political relationships, and worldview created and shared by a group of people bound together by a combination of factors (which can include a common history, geographic location, language, social class, and/or religion).[2]*

The word **worldview** means an all-encompassing set of moral, ethical, and philosophical principles and beliefs that govern the way people live their lives and interact with others. Your worldview governs the way you think, feel, and behave, whether you realize it or not, and affects in a major way how you view every aspect of life—physical, spiritual, emotional, moral, sociological, and mental.

Culture is significant in your life because it is part of you. It includes your patterned, repetitive ways of thinking, feeling, and acting.[3] Thus, it is not only maintained but often expressed through your communication. When Jonathan left a prominent position at a prestigious company, his best friend, Adam, explained his departure this way: "Voicing concern and choked with emotion, Jonathan was no longer able to step up his efforts, as his American dream turned into a nightmare, his emotional roller coaster came to a full stop. Sending shock waves through family and friends, he said his final good-byes, and called it quits." Not only was Adam's communication full of cliches, but each one—eight in two sentences—was uniquely American. Where do the words you choose come from? They reflect your culture because that is where you learned them, that is where they originated, and they are likely to be all you know!

The words you choose reflect your culture because that is where you learned them, and that is where they originated.

Because it is part of you, culture not only influences your perception of your self and your perception of others (discussed in Chapter 2, "Self, Perception, and Communication") but your perception of everything in life with which you have contact. Think about what might be considered true American values: things like democracy, individualism, property, equality, freedom, community, and justice. The degree to which you accept these as your own values is also the degree to which you measure your sense of self on those same values. For example, you would feel better about yourself if you were actively involved in your democracy (being informed of the positions of political candidates and voting), expressing your individualism (being assertive and sticking up for your rights), and owning property (having a nice car).

You Are a Cultural Being

One desired outcome from reading about *culture* is that you will recognize and accept *yourself* as a cultural being. **Cultural identity**—composed of ethnicity, culture, gender, age, life stage, beliefs, values, and assumptions—is the degree to which you identify with your culture, and it is determined by the values you support. If you were born and raised in the United States, your cultural identity involves the degree to which you identify with being American. But it doesn't stop there. You have a number of cultural identities—being a member of the student body, a particular race, a specific age group, a religion, and so on.

There are three things that you need to understand about possessing a cultural identity. First, cultural identities are learned. You learn the ways of thinking, acting, and feeling from your family first, then from your friends and communities. Second, cultural identities vary in strength. Morgan, for example, had all the speech and language patterns, all the actions and reactions of a typical American student. All were so deeply embedded within her that she wasn't even aware of it until she visited Australia with her debate team.

Third, cultural identities vary in their content. For example, not everyone would define what it means to be an American in the same way, just as students have different ways of defining what it means to be a student. The importance of this point becomes evident when you begin to generalize about cultures. To what extent do you value freedom, pleasure, social recognition, and independence? These are values often ascribed to members of the U.S. culture. What if you were a Japanese American and you held cultural identities for both these cultures? The Japanese culture values self-sacrifice, harmony, and accepting traditions—values that, in part, directly contradict those of the U.S. culture.

When you realize all the cultural identities people possess, you also can see the perplexities associated with the *intersection* of issues of race and ethnicity, language, religion, gender and sexual orientation, generation and age, and so forth, as they operate within individuals. These factors interact and come out differently in different people. Understanding cultural identities offers insights into how individuals relate to the many groups to which they belong, but not only that, to understand others, and yourself, you need to realize the variety of groups that create their (and your) cultural identity.[4]

Cultural identity can be a complex issue. For example, a second-generation girl, living in a minority area, whose parents are Korean immigrants, whose friends are Spanish-speaking co-workers, identifies herself as Korean American, a woman, or an American depending on the **context**. In her essay "For Many Latinos, Racial Identity Is More Culture Than Color" (*New York Times*, January 14, 2012), Mireya Navarro notes another complexity. "Many Latinos," writes Navarro, "say they are too racially mixed to settle on one of the government-sanctioned standard races—white, black, American Indian, Alaska native, native Hawaiian, and a collection of Asian, and Pacific Island backgrounds" (p. A9).

Cultural identity can be a simple issue, too. Some groups create their own cultures to isolate themselves from others. In many cities the immigrants still seem to live and work in isolation and resolve to protect their heritage by maintaining all vestiges of their culture and not assimilating. Regarding your perception of others, you might perceive them based on the same set of values—those that you hold dear.

"Culture is a mental set of windows through which all of life is viewed."[5] It is more than an environment or geographical location in which you live, and it is more than any single component of your personality or background, including your race, ethnicity, nationality, language, gender, religion, ability or disability, or socioeconomic status. These components—and certainly the way they combine and interact—affect

ATTENTION!

Cultural Identities
1. Are learned.
2. Vary in strength.
3. Vary in their content.

In *Identity: Your Passport to Success*, Stedman Graham (with Stewart Emery and Russ Hall), offers a "Profile in Success" of Mariane Pearl. Graham writes in the introduction to this profile, "In February 2002, Daniel Pearl, the kidnapped South Asia Bureau Chief of the *Wall Street Journal*, was beheaded by his Al-Qaeda captors. His widow, Mariane, wrote a memoir about his life, *A Mighty Heart*, that was adapted into a film. "Here," writes Graham, "she talks about how her experience affected her own sense of identity" (p. 124). As you read this excerpt, notice the multi-cultural nature of Mariane Pearl:

My identity was strange from the start. My mother is Cuban, my father is Dutch, and I grew up in France in an area that was very, very mixed. Mostly Arabic people lived there. Part of my family is white and part of my family is black. When I was little, in my family, the black people were poor and the white people were rich. And when I was very little, I also thought that everybody had the same circumstances—poor and rich relatives. When I met my first white poor person, I was very confused. I think my interest in this matter of identity started there, because I saw how subjective an identity really is. I also saw that people mostly inherit their identity (p. 134).

Source: Graham, Stedman (with Stewart Emery and Russ Hall). (2012). *Identity: Your Passport to Success.* Pearson Education, Inc.: New Jersey.

Questions

1. Can you imagine what it would be like if this were your own identity? What differences can you see between your current view of the world and what it would be like with an identity like that of Mariane Pearl?

2. What differences do you see between the perspectives people have toward you right now and what those perspectives would be like if you had an identity like that of Mariane Pearl?

3. Do you agree with Mariane Pearl that one's identity is subjective? What does this mean?

4. Do you believe that most people inherit their identity? What implications does this have for individuals?

---

your social and educational status as well as your family, community, and professional interactions. Culture is the way you make sense of your life.[6]

From this brief discussion of culture it is easier to understand intercultural communication. When a message is created by a member of one culture, and this message needs to be processed by a member of another culture, **intercultural communication** takes place.[7]

The Importance of Studying Intercultural Communication

The chances for contacts with people from other cultures have increased dramatically with changes in the workplace; U.S. businesses expanding into world markets in a process of globalization; people now connected—via answering machines, faxes, email, electronic bulletin boards, and the Internet—to other people whom they have never met face-to-face; the ever-increasing mobility of U.S. families; and the changing demographics within the United States and changing immigration patterns as well.[8] It is precisely this increased contact that makes studying intercultural communication so important. (See Figure 10-1.)

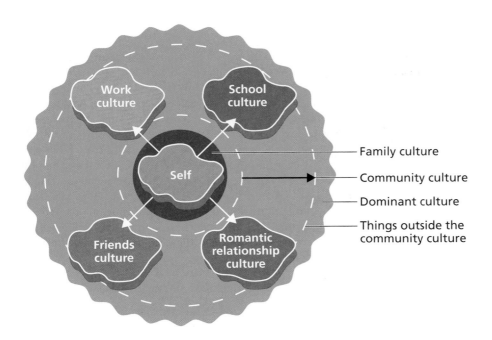

Figure 10-1
The Multicultural Self
A community culture
may include work,
school, friends,
and romantic
relationships, but
these may occur
outside the community
as well.

Family culture

Community culture

Dominant culture

Things outside the
community culture

Understanding Your Own Identity

The first reason for studying intercultural communication is to develop a sensitivity to various cultural heritages and backgrounds to better understand your own identity. In her book *Torn Between Two Cultures,* Maryam Qudrat Aseel says, "It was through the experience of living and being raised in the United States that I came to truly appreciate and understand my own religion, heritage, culture, and language."[9] Your decisions about the values you want to adopt or continue holding, the lifestyles or orientations you wish to pursue, and even the friends you want to have—not to mention the major, occupation, or profession you desire—are affected by racial, cultural, gender, and social-class factors that affect your personal identity, who you are and who you want to be.[10]

Enhancing Personal and Social Interactions

The broader your outlook, the more tolerant and accommodating you become. The chances of having close personal interactions with those different from you—whether in age, physical ability, gender, ethnicity, class, religion, race, or nationality—are increasing daily. Such relationships help you learn about the world, break stereotypes, and acquire new skills.[11]

Solving Misunderstandings, Miscommunications, and Mistrust

Until recently our nation has not learned, nor has it needed to learn, to be multiculturally competent.[12] The study of intercultural communication will not just unlock doors closed for generations; it will open those doors and, thus, resolve misunderstandings, miscommunications, and mistrust through honest, open, positive, healthy communication. People not only fear, but they also distrust the unknown. Trust is gained through knowledge and understanding.

STRATEGIC

FLEXIBILITY

Strategic flexibility requires learning about the world, breaking down stereotypes, and acquiring new skills. Greater tolerance and accommodation will expand your available skills and behaviors as you anticipate, assess, evaluate, and select from your repertoire. In addition, you will reveal greater care, concern, and attention as you apply those skills.

Enhancing and Enriching the Quality of Civilization

Recognizing and respecting ethnic and cultural diversity are important steps on the road to valuing the ways in which diversity enhances and enriches the quality of our civilization. According to Carlos Cortes, "many multiculturalists today seem unwilling to deal with the growing factor of intermarriage. Too much of multicultural education is frozen into a kind of group purity paradigm, when in fact, intermarriage is one of the enormous changes that is taking place in America. For example, one-third of all Latinos born in the United States now marry someone who is not Latino. . . . What will these cultural blends be like?"[13] According to the Pew Research Center (reported by the Associated Press, February 16, 2012) there were 4.8 million interracial marriages in 2012, a record 1 in 12, or 8.4% of all marriages. This results, in part, form a steady flow of new Asian and Hispanic immigrants that has expanded the pool of prospective spouses. When you consider the potential for the new perspectives, cultural insights, and unique wisdom that intermarriages can produce, there is no doubt about the corresponding increase in the quality of our civilization.

Ronald Takaki, writing in his book *A Different Mirror: A History of Multicultural America,* ends Chapter 1, "The Making of Multicultural America," saying:

> Together, "We the" diverse "people of the United States" transformed America into a mighty economy and an amazingly unique society of varied races, ethnicities, and religions. In the process, we transformed ourselves into Americans. Together, we composed "E pluribus unum"—a reality discerned by Herman Melville over one hundred years ago. Our country was settled by "the people of all nations," he wrote. "All nations may claim her for their own. You cannot spill a drop of American blood, without spilling the blood of the whole world." Americans are "not a narrow tribe."[14]

Becoming Effective Citizens of Our National Communities

National communities are co-cultural groupings within the country. National communities were established from the beginning as "our forefathers acquired the lands of Native Americans, 34 percent of the territory of Mexico in 1848, and the island of Puerto Rico in 1898."[15] Prior to the 1960s, most of the immigrants to the United States came from Europe, but of the million or so immigrants who now enter the United States every year, 90 percent are from Latin America and Asia. A study by the Population Reference Bureau suggests that by 2050 the United States will be a global society in which nearly half of all citizens will be from today's racial and ethnic minorities.[16]

Intercultural Communication and the Communication Model

Using our broad definition of *culture,* and with the clear understanding that much of communication is intercultural, you can also see how much influence intercultural communication has had on the model of communication in Chapter 1, The Communication Process.

It Influences Senders and Receivers

If my values, traditions, social and political relationships, and worldview are different from yours, given the same subject to respond to and with everything else in the assignment the same, I will compose a significantly different response. As the differences among communicators become greater, the results in thoughts, feelings, and messages become more divergent as well.

It Influences Messages and Feedback

When my (Richard) parents taught in Pakistan, they were told that raising a question in the classroom is considered an affront to a respected and esteemed authority: the teacher. Instead of interpreting the lack of student response as indifference or lack of understanding, my parents encouraged students to respond among themselves with the teacher as overseer, guide, and outside resource. Jun Liu, in his book *Asian Students' Classroom Communication Patterns in U.S. Universities,* attributes silence in Asian cultures to politeness, the pace of the discussion in U.S. classrooms, fear of wasting class time, and face saving with other international students or with the professor.[17]

Both verbal and nonverbal messages are affected by intercultural communication. Most Americans pay attention and show respect in the classroom by maintaining eye contact with teachers. But Navajo students in the classroom show respect by avoiding eye contact.

It Influences the Setting

Setting can refer to the way communication fits into history: past, present, and future. It also describes how communication fits into a relational setting, such as the influences of power and distance, individualism versus collectivism, or femininity versus masculinity. It can refer to gender, ethnicity, or nationality.

Setting, too, can relate to your own position within a speech community. If you are the only person with a physical disability in an otherwise abled environment, or the only gay man or lesbian in a heterosexual environment, you may face specific expectations or have people project their motivations on your communication.[18]

Intercultural Communication and the Internet

At the website *Educational Portal of the Americas,* it is written: "The rapid spread of computer-mediated communication, such as the Internet, on-line discussions, and e-mail, have great potential for altering the way in which people of other cultures recognize, perceive, and interact with one another. However, in this process of communication as in all, there are both messages to be received and responses to be sent to express the richness of each culture."[19]

Zaid Sabah, writer of an article titled, "Parents disapprove, but Internet romance a big hit,"[20] offers a glimpse of how the Internet is viewed in a conservative society such as Iraq. "Layla Ahmad, retired teacher and mother of three," Sabah begins his essay, "considers the Internet among the most dangerous post-invasion developments in Iraq. . . . We don't accept that our daughters meet boys through the Internet. It's dangerous, and you can't observe your children and what they are talking about."[21] This is an understandable point of view when you consider Iraq is a country where arranged marriages are common, premarital relations of any sort are frowned on, and the Internet represents a threat to the established order—Iraqi traditions. Perhaps it is just this point of view that makes it so popular: It gives young Iraqis a way to meet members of the opposite sex in a society that offers few such opportunities and to set up real dates. Arranging dates online is fine, but finding places to physically meet is difficult because most single Iraqis live with their parents, and it is dangerous to go out at night. University students can meet on campus where it is relatively safe and often walk around or sit together.

For students in the United States, the Internet serves as a vehicle not only for searching for common values and understanding, but also for hearing and seeing in real-time events that take place thousands of miles away. It can bridge the culture gap among nations of the world. For example, it has helped worldwide organizations function by bringing together people from different physical locations with common interests and goals.

Studying Cultural Differences

There are a number of ways to contrast a group of cultures to another group of cultures.[22] Geert Hofstede examined cultural distinctions based on deeply rooted values and derived five dimensions—power distance, individualism versus collectivism, femininity versus masculinity, uncertainty avoidance, long-term orientation.[23] A sixth dimension, Edward T. Hall's high context versus low context, follows our discussion of Hofstede's five dimensions.[24]

Cultural differences are manifest in the cultural identities of the people, as the examples within each category will reveal. Cultural identity influences behavior, including choices of symbols, heroes and heroines, rituals, and even the values one chooses.

The dimensions discussed here are general tendencies only. They are not always true of a culture, nor true of everyone in a culture. Jackie Low is a good example. Raised in Ohio, she has never been to China, never spoken a word of Chinese, and did not know much about China. Anyone who assumed from her looks that Jackie was Chinese would have been incorrect.

Iris Chang, in her book *The Chinese in America,* verifies Jackie Low's experience when she says about the ethnic Chinese in America: "None can truly get past the distinction of race or entirely shake the perception of being seen as foreigners in their own land."[25]

Power Distance

Power distance is a way of contrasting a group of cultures to another group of cultures by measuring social inequality in each. You will notice power differences in family customs, the relationships between students and teachers, the young and the elderly, language systems, and organizational practices. In their book *TouchPoints* (San Francisco: Jossey-Bass, 2011), Douglas Conant and Mette Norgaard offer this example of power distance: "Being one of the most egalitarian tribes in the world, the Danes [the people of the Danish culture] show little overt respect for authority. Consequently, where an American may listen attentively to a boss's proposal, a Dane is likely to raise lots of questions and want to weigh in on every decision before being good to go. To a Danish team leader, this would be normal behavior, but to an American boss, it might be interpreted as a lack of respect" (p. 109).

Continents with high power distance include Africa, Latin America, and Near Eastern countries. Low-power-distance countries include the United States, Germany, China, and Great Britain.

Individualism versus Collectivism

www.mhhe.com/hybels11e >

The degree of integration and orientation of individuals within groups is referred to as **individualism versus collectivism.** When Elaine worked with the Peace Corps in Argentina, she learned about collectivist cultures. Working hand in hand with Eduardo Puerta, a native Argentinian, she realized he had never worked side-by-side with a female and needed to be in control and maintain face. In their discussions, she also came to understand his devotion to his family and preference for government control over the economy and press. Knowing about collectivist cultures helped Elaine not just understand Eduardo, but learn from and respect him as well.

View "Culture and Self" video clip to further understand the value of examining cultural differences.

In his book *The Consuming Instinct* (NY: Prometheus Books, 2011), Dr. Gad Saad (cited earlier in this text), offers an additional example when he writes, "All other things equal, both American and Japanese teenagers have a strong desire to conform to fashion trends, though these pressures to conform might be greater for those hailing from a collectivity society (Japan) as compared to their individualist counterparts (United States)" (p. 195).

You will notice that people in individualistic cultures such as Great Britain, the United States, Canada, France, and Germany value self-expression, view speaking out as a way to solve problems, and use confrontational strategies to deal with interpersonal problems. In collectivist cultures such as many Arab, African, Asian, and Latin American countries, people have unquestioning loyalty to the group, and when in conflict they use avoidance, intermediaries, and other face-saving techniques.

One way to contrast a group of cultures to another group of cultures is to use the dimension of power distance—social inequality. The picture reveals potential power distances between students and teacher as well as between the younger and the elderly.

For this AOM exercise you will need to put on your thinking cap and engage your imagination. Let's pretend that you have just met a foreign student on campus. She is from China, and although she speaks fluent English, she has only recently arrived in your country.

Using the six dimensions discussed for studying cultural differences (e.g., power distance, individualism versus collectivism, femininity versus masculinity, uncertainty avoidance, long-term orientation, and high context versus low context), you are to briefly discuss the likely differences you would experience if you befriended this new acquaintance and were to maintain a long-term friendship.

Use yourself as a representative example of your culture, and mention as you discuss cultural differences the various contexts (e.g., talking with friends, behavior in the classroom, self-disclosing personal information, working on a project together, etc.) in which these differences would most likely occur.

Femininity versus Masculinity

A way of contrasting a group of cultures to another group of cultures that looks at the division of rules between men and women is called **femininity versus masculinity**.

High-feminine cultures believe women should be nurturant, concerned for the quality of life, and reveal sympathy for the unfortunate. In general, feminine cultures allow cross-gender behaviors. High-masculine cultures believe men should be concerned about wealth, achievement, challenge, ambition, promotion, and that they should be assertive, competitive, tough, and recognize achievements. Masculine cultures are more likely to maintain strictly defined gender roles and, thus, have distinct expectations of male and female roles in society. High-feminine cultures include Africa and the Nordic countries of Europe. High-masculine cultures include Latin America, Great Britain, Japan, and the United States.

Uncertainty Avoidance

Uncertainty avoidance compares tolerance for the unknown when contrasting a group of cultures to another group of cultures. When Amelia entered her math classroom on the first day, she was startled to realize her teaching assistant was from Japan. Because Amelia knew Japan was a low-uncertainty-avoidance country, she was able to put into perspective much of what she learned from Junji Akimoto. Junji behaved quietly without showing aggression or strong emotions. Easygoing and relaxed, he ran an open-ended class.

Cultures that feel threatened by ambiguous and uncertain situations and try to avoid them prefer formal rules to control social behaviors. The best example is China. Low-uncertainty-avoidance cultures need few rules and accept and encourage dissenting views and risk taking. Countries with low uncertainty avoidance include Latin America, Africa, and Japan. The United States is considered "medium" on this dimension—neither high nor low.

Long-Term Orientation

Long-term orientation measures the trade-off between long-term and short-term gratification of needs. This dimension was added by Hofstede as a result of his work with Michael Bond.[26] Bond labeled it Confucian dynamism. Elisha's roommate, Mei Li, explained by example that virtuous behavior in China means acquiring skills and education, working hard, and being frugal, patient, and persevering. Knowing what long-term orientation meant helped Elisha understand Mei Li and appreciate her industriousness.

Those at one extreme on this dimension—having long-term orientation—admire persistence, ordering relationships by status, thriftiness, and having a sense of shame that emphasizes care for others and being loyal and trustworthy. China, Japan, and other Asian countries have an extraordinary long-term orientation toward life. At the other extreme—with short-term orientation—are countries like Finland, France, Germany, and the United States where people value personal steadiness and stability but do not have as much respect for tradition because it prevents innovation, nor for saving face, which can hinder the flow of business. These countries, too, favor reciprocation of greetings, favors, and gifts as related to social rituals.

High Context versus Low Context

High context versus low context contrasts how much information is carried in the context (high) and how much in the code or message (low).[27] In high-context communication most of the information is already in the person; very little information is in the coded, explicit, intentionally transmitted part of the message. For example, in the Japanese, African, Mexican, Asian, and Latin American cultures most of the meaning of a message is either implied by the physical setting or is presumed to be part of the individual's beliefs, values, and norms. Often, in long-term relationships communication is high context because the slightest gesture, quickest glance, or briefest comment can be interpreted without explicit statements or extended explanations.

Why? Because most of the information has already been experienced. Few explicit statements or extended explanations are necessary unless new areas of experience or discussion occur. Some people who date a lot tire of it simply because of the time it takes to move from low context to high context—often the preferred mode of communication because it is easier and doesn't require as many explanations and clarifications.

Most Western cultures prefer low-context messages in which the majority of the information is in the communication itself—not in the context. Computer instructions are low context because they require that every space, period, letter, and number be precisely in the right location; there are no exceptions. All the information is in the instruction, or the instruction does not work.

These six dimensions are basic frames of reference to help you appreciate differences. No culture is better than another; no culture is strange; no culture is unusual or foreign. Using these tools will help reduce misunderstandings by encouraging empathy, tolerance, respect, and perhaps, a more accurate interpretation of messages from people of another culture group.

Barriers to Intercultural Communication

Some people do not know about other cultures, and some do not want to know. There is no doubt that both ignorance (lack of knowledge) and naivete (lack of sophistication) can be important barriers to intercultural communication.

In this section, we will briefly consider ethnocentrism, stereotyping, prejudice, and discrimination. These are barriers because each is constructed around a judgment made before any communication takes place that then biases the communication that follows. All communication has a past, present, and future; barriers are part of the past that influence the communication that takes place now and affect all that follows in the future.

Ethnocentrism

When I (Richard) lectured in Australia, I was told never to show arrogance or in any way to reveal condescension or become patronizing. It was wise advice. My hosts had warned me not to be ethnocentric: a common occurrence, they said, when Americans spoke to Australians.

Ethnocentrism is the belief that one's own cultural group's behaviors, norms, ways of thinking, and ways of being are superior to all other cultural groups and, thus, are *the* right ones. Ethnocentrism is not to be confused with *patriotism,* which is devotion to one's country. Ethnocentrism carries devotion to the extreme point where you cannot believe that another culture's behaviors, norms, ways of thinking, and ways of being are as good or as worthy as your own. It becomes a barrier in intercultural communication when it prevents you from even trying to see another's point of view—that is, when it hampers all attempts at empathy.

Stereotyping

Stereotypes are oversimplified or distorted views of another race, another ethnic group, or even another culture. They are simply ways to categorize and generalize from the overwhelming amount of information we receive daily.

The problem with stereotypes is that whether they are positive or negative, once they are established, it is difficult to remove them. Sometimes they exist in our subconscious; these are even more difficult to discard because we are less aware of them. We tend to pick up information from our environment that supports the stereotypes rather than denies them. This simply embeds them more deeply. To remove them, we must first recognize them, then we must obtain individual information that will counteract them.

Prejudice

Prejudice is a negative attitude toward a cultural group based on little or no experience.[28] The difference between stereotypes and prejudice should become clear in this example: When Chris was young, his parents told him never to go into the city because Mexican gangs ruled the city streets at night. Chris, of course, then had the preconceived notion that all Mexicans were bad people. From this stereotype Chris formed a prejudice against Mexicans. The stereotype told him what a group (Mexicans) was like; the prejudice told him how to feel about the group. All this changed when Chris worked for the city to help pay his way through college, and almost all his co-workers were Mexicans. Their attitude toward Chris as well as their behavior quickly changed the stereotype and altered his prejudice.

Discrimination

Discrimination is the overt actions one takes to exclude, avoid, or distance oneself from other groups.[29] Discrimination takes stereotypes and prejudice one step further—to action, whether overt or covert. You can discriminate against someone subtly by slightly turning away your body when in a conversation, or by avoiding eye contact with them. You can discriminate against people by hurling verbal insults at them. You can discriminate, too, by using physical violence, systematically eliminating the group from which the individual comes, or even in extreme cases by using genocide, as when autocratic tyrants exterminate racial or national groups. Yet another form of discrimination occurs when you exclude others from jobs or from other economic opportunities.

Obviously, discrimination can be interpersonal when you do it against another person, collective (when a number of individuals or a group perform the discrimination), or institutional (when a business or industry chooses not to serve a particular group of people).

Dealing with Barriers to Intercultural Communication

For accurate communication to occur, sender-receivers must be operating from the same perceptual point of view. This is usually not a problem when we are interacting with people from our own race or culture; however, when we communicate with someone from a different race or background, we must realize that this person will be operating from an entirely different point of view.

Communication Between Nondominant- and Dominant-Group Members

Much of the literature about communication is written from the point of view of the dominant, or majority, culture. In the United States **dominant culture** includes white people from a European background, while **nondominant culture** includes people of color; women; gays, lesbians, and bisexuals; and those whose socioeconomic background is lower than middle class.

When people are not part of a dominant culture, how do they communicate with people who are? In a tantalizing piece of research, Orbe looked at how people from nondominant groups (people of color; women; gays, lesbians, and bisexuals; and those from lower socioeconomic backgrounds) communicated with people from the dominant group.[30] He found that nondominant members adopted one of three basic strategies when they wanted to confront oppressive dominant structures and achieve success: assimilation, accommodation, and separation.

Assimilation Strategies

When nondominants use **assimilation**, they drop cultural differences and distinctive characteristics that would identify them with the nondominant group. As you can see in Table 10-1, there are three types of **assimilation strategies**.

Table 10-1   Assimilation

Nonassertive	Assertive	Aggressive
Emphasizing what the dominant and nondominant groups have in common	Carefully preparing for meeting dominant-group members	Disassociating from one's own group
Acting positive	Manipulating stereotypes	Copying dominant-group behavior
Censoring remarks that might offend the dominant group	Bargaining	Avoiding interaction with other cultural groups
Avoiding controversy		Ridiculing oneself

Nonassertive Assimilation. In this type of assimilation, minority members want to belong to the majority group, but they do not want to use aggression to get there. In order to achieve acceptance, they emphasize what they have in common with the dominant group and sometimes censor themselves to fit in. However, it often comes at a terrible cost, as you can see in the following passage:

> *I spent the fifties essentially either going to graduate school or beginning my career as a teacher who was very much in the closet—and very much attempting to hide the fact that I was a lesbian. And that meant putting down and holding down a whole part of myself that was really vital to my being. I have these visions of faculty parties or church parties or picnics to which I would oftentimes go with a gay man friend of mine, and we would put on an incredibly good show.[31]*

Assertive Assimilation. In assertive assimilation, people are likely to take a stronger approach to fitting in. They will often carefully prepare for an encounter with the dominant group. They may overcompensate by trying to be twice as smart, twice as witty, and so forth.

African American writer Patricia Raybon, in her book *My First White Friend,* describes her assertive assimilation stage, which occurred when she was a child living in a predominantly white culture:

> *I was reared to smile, to be polite, to say please and thank you and not to act ugly. I was reared to be the cleanest, nicest, smartest, kindest black child I could possibly be. That would make people like me. White people especially.[32]*

Aggressive Assimilation. In this type of assimilation, minority-group members want to fit into the dominant group at any cost. They will imply that there are no differences between the two groups and will be careful to not do or say anything that would indicate their difference, such as speaking in a dialect or making reference to their own group's behavior. They are so eager to be part of the dominant group that they might ridicule the group they belong to.

Accommodation Strategies

The next main category consists of accommodation strategies. **Accommodation** works toward getting the dominant group to reinvent, or at least change, the rules so that they incorporate the life experiences of the nondominant group. The three types of **accommodation strategies** are summarized in Table 10-2.

Table 10-2 Accommodation

Nonassertive	Assertive	Aggressive
Increasing visibility	Letting DG members know who they really are	Confronting members of the DG when they violate the rights of others
Avoiding stereotypes	Identifying and working with DG members who have similar goals	Referring to DG oppression of NG
	Identifying members of the DG who can support, guide, and assist	
	Educating others	

Note: DG = Dominant Group; NG = Nondominant Group.

Nonassertive Accommodation. In nonassertive accommodation, the person does not act in any way that would cause dominant-group members to be defensive or cautious but tries to make people more aware of the group she or he belongs to and tries to change stereotypes they might have. For example, Anna, who is Mexican, often talks to her co-workers about her friends who are professionals, trying to break the stereotype of Mexicans as manual laborers.

Assertive Accommodation. Those who use this strategy try to achieve a balance between their own group and the dominant group. They try to get their own group's members to know the dominant group by sharing something about their lives; they also attempt to educate others about their group's members. Often they will choose a member of the dominant group as a mentor who can guide, support, and assist them.

They also try to educate the dominant group about their group's culture. Maria, for example, persuades some dominant-group members to go to a Mexican restaurant and guides them through the menu.

Aggressive Accommodation. The strategy in this approach is to get into a dominant group and try to change it, although nondominant-group members may confront dominant-group members to gain an advantage. For example, a woman on a committee that brings international scholars to the university may point out that no women have been chosen. Persons using aggressive accommodation may also remind dominant-group members of their history of oppression.

Separation Strategies

In the third category of strategies, nondominant-group members have given up. In **separation,** nondominants do not want to form a common bond with the dominant culture, so they separate into a group that includes only members like themselves. During the 1960s and 1970s, many African Americans and women, unhappy that power structures were not changing quickly enough, formed separate groups that excluded members of the dominant group as well as nondominant-group members who did not share their views (Black Muslims exclude other blacks as well as whites.) Some of these groups still exist today. Table 10-3 outlines the three types of **separation strategies.**

Nonassertive Separation. In this type of separation, the nondominant person avoids the dominant group whenever possible. Although the nondominant person may work with dominant-group members, he or she won't go out to lunch with them or socialize after work. Through verbal and nonverbal cues, the dominant group senses that this person wants to be left alone. For example, when Tom, who is gay, is asked whether he

T a b l e   1 0 - 3   Separation

Nonassertive	Assertive	Aggressive
Maintaining barriers between themselves and the DG	Asserting their voice regardless of the consequences	Making direct attacks on DG members
Keeping away from places where DG members are found	Making references to DG oppression with the goal of gaining advantage	Undermining the DG by not letting its members take advantage of their privileged position

Note: DG = Dominant Group; NG = Nondominant Group.

Reality Check

You may not have experience with some (or any) of the international cultures that are used throughout this chapter for examples, but if you have experience with Americans with Latino, African, or European heritages, the same comments apply. Using specific examples from your own experience, cite instances of assimilation, accommodation, or separation strategies in action. Do the descriptions in this textbook make sense to you? Do the descriptions seem logical? If you were a member of the nondominant culture, which strategy would *you* be likely to use? Why? How might your strategy be implemented? How would its implementation influence how effectively you communicated?

is going to the office Christmas party, he answers no because he knows that the man he lives with would not be welcome.

Some nondominant groups make no attempt to become part of the dominant group. An example is the Hmong people who immigrated to the United States because they were no longer safe in Laos. Anne Fadiman describes them after they had lived for 17 years in the United States:

> *Seventeen years later, Foua and Nao Kao use American appliances but they still speak only Hmong, celebrate only Hmong holidays, practice only Hmong religion, cook only Hmong dishes, sing only Hmong songs, play only Hmong musical instruments, tell only Hmong stories, and know far more about the current political events in Laos and Thailand than about those in the United States. . . . It would be hard to imagine anything further from the vaunted American ideal of assimilation, in which immigrants are expected to submerge their cultural differences in order to embrace a shared national identity.[33]*

Assertive Separation. Persons practicing assertive separation work to form organizations where they can be separate from the dominant group. While in these groups, they work against any dominant-group messages that imply the dominant group is superior and they are inferior. One communication strategy they use is reminding the dominant group of their oppression. Patricia Raybon, whose passage we quoted in the assimilation discussion, describes some of the feelings that led to her assertive separation stage:

> *White people—that relentless, heavy presence. Never benign. Never innocent. "White people" as a category embodied in my view a clear and certain evil—an arrogant malevolence—that had done unspeakable things that I couldn't ignore because I knew the facts of these things. Names and dates and numbers. And the facts haunted me and the numbers justified my hate for all of the evil that I believed white people had done.[34]*

Aggressive Separation. In aggressive separation, people separate from the dominant group and expect their fellow nondominant-group members to do so too. They are very critical of those who practice assimilation or accommodation. It is not uncommon for groups fighting against oppression to separate from the dominant group.

If members of these groups have to have interaction with the dominant group (for example, at work), they will try to undermine the dominants by not letting them take advantage of their privileged positions. For example, an employee would bring legal action against his or her boss for discrimination.

The Consequences of Nondominant- and Dominant-Group Communication

Orbe's research does not lead to a very optimistic picture of American society. If we depict his results on a continuum, as in Figure 10-2, on one end are people who want to belong so much that they are willing to give up or suppress their own cultures, while on the opposite end are people who have decided that they cannot live in the dominant culture of the United States and have gone off on their own. In a country that prides itself on being a place where people from all cultures can live in harmony, nothing on the continuum is acceptable to our vision of what democracy should be.

Belongers |⊢————————————————————⊣ **Separatists**

Nonassertive assimilation | Assertive assimilation | Aggressive assimilation | Nonassertive accommodation | Assertive accommodation | Aggressive accommodation | Nonassertive separation | Assertive separation | Aggressive separation

Figure 10-2
Nondominant Persons'
Communication to
Dominant Groups

Improving Intercultural Communication

Sometimes in an intercultural-communication situation with a person different from us, we may interpret the other person as *abnormal, weird,* or simply *different.* It is important to learn to control the human tendency to translate "different from me" into "less than me."[35] Rather, we need to raise questions. Are there effective ways of dealing with different kinds of people? Can I develop a repertoire of five or six approaches that will help me reach others in real and meaningful ways?[36]

Engage in mindfulness. Mindfulness means paying attention to what is going on in the present moment without judgment.[37] To do this, you must trust your direct and immediate experience. Second, you must show patience—a willingness to observe and describe (perhaps *intra*personally only) what is happening without bias. You simply throw yourself into the present moment and glean wisdom through the trial and error of learning by direct experience. Third, you must accept "what is, as is," in other words, accept whatever it is that the universe serves up. It means accepting life on life's own terms, regardless of *your* feelings about it and (using SF) discovering effective strategies to cope with and eventually appreciate whatever is happening.

Few people live mindfully. They don't meet each moment of life as it presents itself, with full awareness, and allow their judgments to fall away. Not only do they churn out judgments about themselves and others, but they do a number of things at the same time (multitasking); get caught up in feelings about the past or future; avoid any uncomfortable thoughts, feelings, or situations; and disconnect from what is happening right in front of them. If this description fits the way they live, it is easy to see why mindfulness is seldom practiced and is so important. Its value is that because it is an instant of pure awareness *before* they conceptualize, identify, focus their eyes or mind on, objectify, clamp down on it mentally, segregate it from the rest of existence, or think about it in any way, it reminds them of what they should be doing, helps them see things as they really are, and assists them in seeing the deep nature of what it is they are about to examine.

Pay attention to your words and actions. It is only through your thoughtful communication with others that you become aware of your own thinking patterns, assumptions, perceptions, prejudices, and biases.[38] When students come to Cruz-Janzen's classes expecting to learn how to communicate with nonwhites, she tells them they are first going to study themselves, their gender, racial, ethnic, cultural, socioeconomic, and physical (ability, disability, and appearance) socialization. Cruz-Janzen has a very clear motive in this: "As long as whites continue expecting others to explain themselves, whites are

STRATEGIC FLEXIBILITY

To apply the steps of strategic flexibility may require that you ask questions that help you more accurately anticipate, assess, evaluate, select, and apply your abilities and skills. Questions can also help you demonstrate the care, concern, and attention that may reveal true sensitivity—opening the doors to effective intercultural communication.

In *Getting from College to Career* (revised ed., Harper, 2012), Lindsey Pollak, a writer, speaker, and consultant specializing in next generation career and workplace advice, writes about how to familiarize yourself with any country or culture:

Follow international news. *Subscribe to the e-newsletters, websites, or Twitter feeds of such media as CNN International, the BBC, the* Financial Times, *and* The Economist.

Consider language study. *Take classes or download language-learning software such as Rosetta Stone for Mandarin, Russian, Portuguese, or languages from other emerging economics. While English is the primary language of business in many foreign cultures, you'll get much further if you can converse in a colleague's or client's native tongue.*

Complete international coursework. *If you are still in school, consider taking some classes in international relations. Russian literature, Chinese history, international economics, or anything else that will help you build a global perspective. Professors who teach these courses almost always have experience and connections in the countries about which they teach, so be sure to ask them for advice on finding a job or living in the country of their speciality.*

Build your cross-cultural soft skills. *This tip comes from Lingfang Chen, a graduate student from China who is pursuing a master's degree in international business at Hult International Business School in San Francisco. Lingfang says, 'Soft skills, such as cultural sensitivity, cross-cultural communication skills, the ability to apply knowledge to new situations, and the ability to work in team settings, especially with people from diverse backgrounds, are more readily available to people with international experiences.' You can learn such skills through studying abroad, by joining international student clubs on campus or professional associations such as the Asia Pacific-USA Chamber of Commerce (APUCC), and, of course, through friendships with students on your campus who grew up outside the United States (pp. 187–188).*

Source: Pollak, Lindsey. (2012). *Getting from College to Career.* New York: Harper.

Questions

1. Can you add any additional suggestions to those provided by Pollak above?
2. No matter what job or business venture you choose, you are likely to have a global career. Accepting this statement as true, how will you best prepare yourself?
3. What barriers or hurdles do you see that might get in the way of your own, personal preparation for a global career? And, of course, how can these barriers and hurdles be overcome?

setting themselves as the norm, the normal ones, against whom all others must be judged and measured."[39]

Control your assumptions. An **assumption** is a taking for granted or supposition that something is a fact. You can learn from generalizations about other cultures, but those generalizations turn sour when you use them to stereotype or oversimplify.[40]

- Don't assume that there is one right way (yours) to communicate. Question your assumptions about the "right way" to communicate.
- Don't assume that breakdowns in communication occur because others are on the wrong track. The point isn't "who is to blame for the breakdown?" it is "who can make the communication work?"[41] Remember, ineffective communication can occur for a variety of reasons:
  - You may not have transmitted your message in a way that can be understood.
  - Others may misinterpret what you say.[42]

- Don't assume that the preferred rules of interpersonal relationships you have learned in your culture apply universally across all cultures. They do not.
- Don't assume that your cultural definitions and successful criteria of conflict management apply universally across all cultures. They do not.[43]
- Don't assume because another's values and beliefs differ from your own that you are being challenged.
- Don't assume that you can learn about intercultural communication by staying in your comfort zone. Even if it is awkward at first, you need to expose yourself to different cultures.[44]
- Don't assume you know what is best for someone else.

Engage in transpection. Instead of assuming—a process most people begin quickly, naturally, and often subconsciously—take a moment to relax and reflect. **Transpection** is the process of empathizing across cultures.[45] "Achieving transpection, trying to see the world exactly as the other person sees it, is a difficult process. It often involves trying to learn foreign beliefs, foreign assumptions, foreign perspectives, and foreign feelings in a foreign context. Transpection, then, can only be achieved by practice and requires structured experience and self-reflection."[46]

Striving *toward* transpection can help you avoid assumptions and move you closer to tolerance, sensitivity, respect, empathic listening, and effective communication responses. Listen carefully to others, understand their feelings, be interested in what they have to say and sensitive to their needs, and try to understand their points of view.[47]

Gain knowledge. The greater your cultural and linguistic knowledge, and the more your beliefs overlap with those from other cultures, the less likelihood for misunderstandings.[48] You need to read, observe, ask questions, and visit places where there are people from different races and ethnic backgrounds.

When Madison found out her new roommate was from Saudi Arabia, she immediately worried because of what she'd heard in the media about Saudi terrorists. She went online to find out more about the country—customs, traditions, religion, and anything else she could discover. The words *Saudi Arabia* produced over 11 million websites. Using online resources such as The World Factbook, Saudi Arabia Information Resource, Saudi newspapers, and the Lonely Planet World Guide, Madison strove toward transpection to help herself avoid assumptions.

Gain experience. You cannot learn how to be a good communicator just by reading, observing, asking questions, or doing research on the Internet. But gaining experience doesn't require making actual visits to foreign countries or foreign cultures. Find an individual of another culture, and ask if the two of you could have a conversation about intercultural communication. With that as your focus, ask some pointed, specific questions designed to help you better understand him or her and others of the same culture. The following ten questions are designed to get your conversation started:

- How do you, or other members of your culture, cope with and adapt to unfamiliar cultural environments?
- How can members of other cultures begin to communicate with members of your culture?
- What factors can increase our effectiveness in communicating?
- If we had a conflict, what strategies would be successful for managing it?

- What important factors contribute to the development of interpersonal relationships with you or with members of your culture?
- What changes have you noticed in yourself as a consequence of your experiences in a new culture?
- How can I become more *intercultural* as a result of our contact and communication with members of your culture?
- Can we develop community with members of your culture?[49]
- What are some of the worst offenses people outside your culture make in communicating with you or with members of your culture?
- What do you feel are some of the worst offenses you have made as you have become acclimated into this culture?

In his essay "How to Mind Your Manners Abroad" ("Business Travel," *USA Today*, March 29, 2011, p. 3B), Gary Stoller (with the help of the *Lonely Planet* guidebook) put together a list of five areas where etiquette tips for Americans going abroad are useful. Although each area in his essay has several examples, I have selected the best from each one to make the point. First, in the area of table manners, Stoller says that, "In Mexico whenever you catch the eye of someone who's eating—even a stranger—it's good manners to say, '*Provecho*,' which means enjoy."

In the area of Drinking, Stoller writes, "At a pub in Australia, it's customary to buy a round of drinks for everyone in your group." Under Tipping and bargaining, Stoller says that "Tipping is not common in Japan. If you want to show your gratitude to someone, give a gift rather than a tip." For Body Language, Stoller advises that in Brazil, an OK gesture made with the thumb and index finger is "a gesture akin to extending a middle finger in the USA." In Britain, the equivalent of giving someone the finger occurs when you stick up an index finger and a middle finger with the palm of your hand facing you. Finally, in the area of business etiquette, in Brazil it's considered rude *not* to answer a cell phone when it rings, even if it interrupts a business meeting. Also, it is considered rude *not* to bring a gift made in the USA for a first meeting with a client or not to say good morning, good afternoon, or good evening, or *not* to express interest in a country's history and culture.

In her book *Business Etiquette* (Pompton Plains, NJ: Career Press, 2010, 3rd ed.), Ann Marie Sabath offers the best bottom line to minding your manners abroad. "It is remarkable," she writes, "how wonderful people can be when you have a humble and sincere desire to learn more about their culture and are not reticent about doing things their way."

Let's say that you are heading abroad, and you have done *no* homework whatsoever to prepare for your trip. In *The Tao of Travel* (Boston: Houghton Mifflin Harcourt, 2011), Paul Theroux has some reassuring advice. "I've wandered around four continents using only English and a few courtesy phrases of Tibetan, Amharic, Quechua, Albanian, or whatever. Our basic needs," he writes, "sleeping, eating, drinking—can always be indicated by signs or globally understood noises."

And, what's more, he offers a beautiful paragraph on which to end this section:

Even on the emotional level, the language barrier is quite porous. People's features, particularly their eyes, are wonderfully eloquent. In our everyday lives, the extent to which we wordlessly communicate is taken for granted. In 'far-flungery,' where nobody within a hundred miles speaks a word of any European language, one fully appreciates the range of moods and subtle feelings that may be conveyed visually (pp. 45–46).

ATTENTION!

Improve Your Intercultural Communication (A Summary)

1. Pay attention to your words and actions.
2. Control your assumptions.
3. Engage in transpection (that is, improve your ability to empathize across cultures).
4. Gain knowledge.
5. Gain experience.

There are other ways to gain experience in intercultural communication—to obtain a broader worldview. Frequent ethnic restaurants, watch world news in addition to local news, read books written by authors from other countries, learn another language, and when countries with which you are unfamiliar are mentioned, find them on a map. Listen to world music, rent foreign films, and travel—whether in person or through videos. Your local library has dozens of videos on foreign countries. But don't just observe. Converse with people of other cultures. Take part in cultural celebrations that differ from your own. Volunteer to serve on committees, teams, or groups in which members of other cultures will be serving. Listen, engage, and keep asking questions. Take time to understand what people believe about childrearing, educational opportunities, world politics, and life in general.

How you learn about intercultural communication will depend on your willingness to find it out. You will see that the knowledge and understanding you gain is well worth any effort you put forth.

Cultural Awareness Self-Assessment Form

For each statement circle the numerical score that best represents your performance, skill, or ability using the following scale: 7 = Outstanding; 6 = Excellent; 5 = Very good; 4 = Average (good); 3 = Fair; 2 = Poor; 1 = Minimal ability; 0 = No ability demonstrated.

1. I listen to people from other cultures when they tell me how my culture affects them.

7 6 5 4 3 2 1 0

2. I realize that people from other cultures have fresh ideas and different points of view to bring to my life and to the workplace.

7 6 5 4 3 2 1 0

3. I give people from other cultures advice on how to succeed in my culture.

7 6 5 4 3 2 1 0

4. I give people my support even when they are rejected by other members of my culture.

7 6 5 4 3 2 1 0

5. I realize that people outside my culture could be offended by my behavior. I've asked people if I have offended them by things I have done or said and have apologized whenever necessary.

7 6 5 4 3 2 1 0

6. I realize that when I am stressed I am likely to make myself and my culture right and another culture wrong.

7 6 5 4 3 2 1 0

7. I respect my superiors (boss, teacher, supervisor, group leader, etc.) regardless of where they are from. I do not go over their heads to talk to someone from my culture to try to get my way.

7 6 5 4 3 2 1 0

8. When I am in mixed company, I mix with everyone. I don't just stay with people from my culture, or only with people from the dominant culture.

7 6 5 4 3 2 1 0

9. I go out of my way to work with, recruit, select, train, and promote people from outside the dominant culture.

7 6 5 4 3 2 1 0

10. When people in my culture make jokes or talk negatively about other cultural groups, I let them know that I don't like it.

7 6 5 4 3 2 1 0

TOTAL POINTS: _____

Go to the Online Learning Center at **www.mhhe.com/hybels11e** to see your results and learn how to evaluate your attitudes and feelings.

www.mhhe.com/hybels11e >

Source: Adapted from "Leadership Self-Assessment," ICANS (Integrated Curriculum for Achieving Necessary Skills), Washington State Board for Community and Technical Colleges, Washington State Employment Security, Washington Workforce Training and Education Coordinating Board, Adult Basic and Literacy Educators, P.O. Box 42496, 711 Capitol Blvd, Olympia, WA 98504. Retrieved October 25, 2005, from http://www.literacynet.org/icans/chapter05/leadership.html.

Summary

Intercultural understanding increases both sending and receiving abilities, making communication between people with different linguistic and cultural backgrounds as constructive as possible. With broader experience, the care and concern you demonstrate will not just nourish intercultural communication but will encourage further communication efforts as well.

Culture is the ever-changing values, traditions, social and political relationships, and worldview created and shared by a group of people bound together by a combination of factors (which can include a common history, geographic location, language, social class, or religion).

To accept yourself as a cultural being means embracing a cultural identity composed of ethnicity, culture, gender, age, life stage, beliefs, values, and assumptions. A cultural identity is learned, varies in its strength, and varies in its content as well.

Five reasons for studying intercultural communication include (1) better understanding your own identity, (2) enhancing your personal and social interactions, (3) helping solve cultural misunderstandings, miscommunication, and mistrusts, (4) valuing the ways it enriches the quality of our civilization, and (5) becoming effective citizens of our national communities.

Intercultural communication influences the communication model first by its effect on the values, traditions, social and political relationships, and worldview of senders and receivers; second, by its effect on verbal and nonverbal messages; and, third, by the influences it has on the historical setting, relational setting, and a person's position within a speech community.

The Internet offers a vehicle for searching for common values, understandings, and approaches to managing a world of different cultures.

Power distance relates to social inequality. Individualism versus collectivism relates to the degree of integration and orientation of individuals. Femininity versus masculinity pertains to the division of roles between women and men. Uncertainty avoidance describes the degree of tolerance for the unknown. Long-term orientation relates to trade-offs between long-term and short-term gratification of needs. Finally, high versus low context refers to the amount of information already contained in the person or context versus the amount in the coded, explicit, transmitted part of the message.

The four barriers to intercultural communication include ethnocentrism, stereotyping, prejudice, and discrimination. To deal with barriers, nondominant-group members use one or more of three main strategies to get what they want from dominant-group members: assimilation, accommodation, or separation.

Five ways to improve intercultural communication are: (1) pay attention to your own words and actions; (2) control your assumptions; (3) engage in transpection—the process of empathizing across cultures; (4) gain knowledge; and (5) gain experience.

Key Terms and Concepts

Use the Online Learning Center at www.mhhe.com/hybels11e to further your understanding of the following terms.

Accommodation 258
Accommodation strategies 258
Assimilation 257
Assimilation strategies 257
Assumption 262
Context 247
Cultural identity 247
Culture 246
Discrimination 256
Dominant culture 257

Ethnocentrism 256
Femininity versus masculinity 254
High context versus low context 255
Individualism versus collectivism 253
Intercultural communication 248
Knowledge class 244
Long-term orientation 254

National communities 250
Nondominant culture 257
Power distance 252
Prejudice 256
Separation 259
Separation strategies 259
Stereotypes 256
Transpection 263
Uncertainty avoidance 254
Worldview 246

CHAPTER REVIEW

Questions to Review

1. What is the role intercultural communication plays in communicating effectively and in strategic flexibility?

2. What are the strengths and weaknesses of the definition of *culture* offered in this textbook?

3. What does it mean to possess a cultural identity?

4. Can you make a case for the study of intercultural communication?

5. What are the likely components of a multicultural self?

6. How does intercultural communication relate to the model of communication?

7. What is the influence of the Internet on intercultural communication?

8. What are the six dimensions that can be used as a framework for studying cultural differences?

9. What are four barriers to intercultural communication, and how do they work? Why are they considered barriers?

10. What are the three ways members of a non-dominant group work to get what they want from dominant-group members?

11. What are some ways for improving intercultural communication?

12. What is the process of transpection, and why is it important?

Go to the self-quizzes on the Online Learning Center at **www.mhhe.com/hybels11e** to test your knowledge of the chapter concepts.

CHAPTER ELEVEN

Small-Group Participation and Leadership

After reading this chapter, you should be able to:

- Define a small group, describe the characteristics of small groups, characterize the different types of groups, and describe the factors that determine group effectiveness.

- Compare and contrast Social Exchange Theory (SET) and Symbolic Convergence Theory (SCT), and explain their contribution to understanding small groups.

- Explain how groups become cohesive and the weaknesses that can occur when they become too cohesive (e.g., groupthink).

- List and explain the steps in group problem solving.

- Explain the ways in which leaders can influence followers, the three elements likely to make people leaders, and the different approaches to leadership.

- Compare and contrast Leader-Member Exchange Theory (LMX) and The Functional Perspective (TFP), and explain their contribution to understanding the way groups operate.

- Clarify the functions effective leaders must perform in leading groups.

I JUST NEVER MADE MUCH SENSE TO HER. WHEN CHRISTINA WAS IN HIGH school the rage seemed to be gathering in study groups for class tests and in work groups for projects. Christina couldn't escape the work groups for projects, but she tried study groups once or twice and discovered some group members did not do their share of the work, some simply used the groups to "study" for them, and some just used the groups for their own personal entertainment—wasting everyone's time. These experiences turned Christina off to the purpose and value of group work.

When Christina arrived on campus as an incoming freshman, she discovered she had little choice. There were discussion groups during orientation, in her residence hall, in many of her classes, and in her beginning speech-communication class. Not only did she *not* look forward to that portion of the speech-communication class, but she thought it a waste of her time as well. Christina preferred working alone until she was told that research has proved that groups can be far superior for solving many types of problems than individuals acting alone.[1]

When the time came for the group-discussion portion of the speech-communication course, Christina held her breath when her instructor announced which group she was in, but when her instructor said she was the designated leader of the group as well, it nearly knocked her out of her chair.

Fortunately, Christina had faced academic challenges before: enrolling in rigorous courses, meeting nearly impossible deadlines, sometimes several at the same time, and pulling all-nighters for some exams. She knew she could face this one, too, but what she needed most right now was a change in attitude. Rather than considering the group a waste of her time, she needed to look at it as essential for getting a good grade, a new learning experience, and maybe, just maybe, a technique or approach she could use in the future.

Christina paused in her thinking and looked around the classroom at her group members, nodded at each one as she made eye contact, and considered herself lucky that they were all (up to this point and as far as she could tell) active, responsible, and dependable class members.

Finally, she decided she would read closely the textbook information on "Discussion in Groups," "Leading the Group," and the chapter on "Conflict and Managing Conflict." Also she decided to talk to her instructor after class to gain any tips and suggestions that might help her.

A small group is a gathering of 3 to 13 members interacting with one another in such a manner that each person influences and is influenced by each other person.[2] A *small-group discussion* refers to a small group of persons talking with one another with the expressed purpose of achieving some interdependent goal such as solving a shared problem, coordinating member activity, or increasing understanding.[3] To solve problems, coordinate activities, or increase understanding small group members must develop a sense of cooperation, overcome differences, and search for group outcomes that will be satisfactory to all.

Small groups are essential in helping society function efficiently, and many of you—especially those with Internet access—spend several hours each week communicating in such groups. Not only do you participate in chat rooms, mailing lists, newsgroups, Web forums, and other interest groups, you might also take part in a seminar discussion, talk with a group of co-workers about improving job conditions, discuss with family members how to make the household run more efficiently, or discuss a variety of topics and issues with a group of friends. You may even surf the Net looking for a

ATTENTION!

Examples of Small Groups
- tutorials
- discussion
- brainstorming
- focus
- snowballing
- buzz
- paired (or one-on-one)
- clinical teaching
- simulations
- seminars
- plenary sessions
- peer
- study
- cliques
- problem-based
- team-based
- role play
- games
- IT approaches
- conferences
- growth
- task
- clubs
- squads
- team
- community

blog, MySpace, Facebook, or another social-networking site, where you can express yourself on any number of ideas. Many of you, too, belong to service or professional groups. Often these groups involve both the completion of tasks and social life. Some are singularly social. Whatever groups you belong to, you want them to function efficiently if they are task-oriented groups, and you want them to be enjoyable and satisfying if they are social. If a group is task oriented, participation should be pleasurable, but you want to meet, get on with the job, and then spend some time socializing with other group members.

This chapter discusses how groups work. In this chapter, we note the characteristics of small groups, how such groups go about solving problems, and the process of participating in them. We recognize and acknowledge groups such as marriage-encounter workshops, counseling groups, and growth groups that, in general, have no real collective goal. Also, we recognize groups that exist solely to satisfy the social needs of their participants. Most of these—including the social groups formed in online chat rooms—are informal and seldom have an agenda except enjoyment or friendship. Later in this chapter we concentrate on effective leadership.

Why Learn about Small Groups?

You have undoubtedly heard all the stories. As one goes, a camel is just a horse put together by a committee. Another observation is that a committee is a group that keeps minutes but wastes hours. Still a third was reported by a committee member who said, "To be effective, a committee should be made up of three people. But to get anything done, one member should be sick, and another absent."[4] Many people dread group work. Fortunately, there are many who look forward to solving problems, making decisions, and accomplishing tasks while working with others.

Effectiveness in small groups is essential to your career success.[5] Of the nine skills required for career success identified by Whetten and Cameron, more than half of them are either directly related to or can be acquired in small groups. The nine skills are developing self-awareness, managing personal stress, solving problems creatively, establishing supportive communication, gaining power and influence, improving employee performance through motivation, delegating and decision making, managing conflict, and conducting effective group meetings.[6] If we were to add one item it would be achieving strategic flexibility.

Effectiveness in small groups will save you time and money. You are going to spend a significant amount of your time working in groups, whether they involve family, friends, fraternities, sororities, religious groups, work groups, social groups, educational groups, or therapy groups. The better you are at understanding them and developing efficiency in them, the better you will like them and make use of them in developing and obtaining your goals and the goals of the organization. Few leaders can succeed today on their own without the aid of competent, committed team members.

Effectiveness in small groups will help you in college. Students who study in small groups learn more effectively than those who don't, and there is a positive correlation between small-group study experiences and overall satisfaction in college.[7] Sare Rimer, in her article, "Harvard Task Force Calls for New Focus on Teaching and Not Just Research," cites the example of Professor Mazur, a Harvard physicist, who "threw out his lectures in his introductory physics class when he realized his students were not absorbing the underlying principles. . . . His classes," Rimer writes, "now focus on students working in small groups."[8] Small-group work will increase the amount of your participation, the amount you will learn from one another, the motivation you have toward tasks, the responsibility you take for your own learning, and the quality of the solutions you discover.[9]

Effectiveness in groups will help you personally. The better you are in groups, the more likely you will accomplish your own goals and projects, and the more of those goals and projects you complete, the better you will feel about yourself.[10] You will feel better about yourself, too, for the contributions you can make to the success of any group you join. Because of your knowledge, background, and experience, you will be better able to predict what happens when people communicate in small groups and, then, to intervene on behalf of better group decision making and more successful participation by all group members. In addition, because of working closely with others in these contexts, you will expand your understanding of yourself.

It won't take you long as you begin having small-group experiences to understand why the story shared in the first paragraphs of this section is often true. Many groups are not run effectively, skillfully, or diplomatically.[11] With just the knowledge shared in this chapter on small groups, and with experience in applying what you learn, you will quickly stand out as a valuable member of groups to which you belong. You won't need to announce your superior knowledge nor use heavy-handed approaches. Using the strategic flexibility framework—anticipating, assessing, evaluating, selecting, and then applying your skills and behaviors with care, concern, and attention to all the factors that are likely to be affected—you will be able to subtly and helpfully nudge the group into functioning effectively.[12]

The final reason for learning about small groups is the explosion of discussion groups on the Internet. Online discussion groups (ODGs) such as email lists, mailing lists or listservs, Usenet newsgroups, Web-based bulletin-board-style forums, and social networking sites generate a significant portion of online content. They are great places to talk with others interested in whatever you are or just to lurk and learn. These groups provide places to get suggestions and feedback, ask questions, test ideas, or just observe conversations by others around a particular topic. Some consider them to be "the most important and engaging type of content available online."[13]

Characteristics of Small Groups

All small groups have common characteristics. These groups reflect the culture in which they function; they have norms—expectations that group members have of how other members will behave; and they have rules—formal and structured directions for behavior.

Cultural Values

When Americans think they should solve a problem at work or in the community, their first instinct is to form a group. Once the group begins to function, everyone is more or less equal. If someone wants to talk, he or she is given a chance. If all in the group cannot agree on a solution, the group takes a vote and the majority decides.

This kind of group-forming and group-operating behavior seems so natural that we don't think twice about it: It is part of our culture. We should not assume, however, that other cultures work the same way. When one of our authors asked a Polish friend why the Poles didn't organize child care cooperatives, her friend replied, "In Poland, we never work in groups."

Most societies have a dominant problem-solving mechanism, but it may differ greatly from culture to culture. In many countries men are much more likely than women to make decisions about workplace and community issues. In many of these same countries, only elder members of the group can participate in decision making.

Seventy percent of the world lives in a *collectivist* society—a society whose loyalties are to the family or, more broadly, to the clan, the tribe, or the caste.[14] In such groups, problem solving and decision making are most likely to occur within the family or the clan. If a group is formed that includes members from different clans or families, the way the participants work to solve a problem will depend on their perception of how the solution would affect their own families or clans.

Americans who join a group in another country cannot assume that the group will function in the same way that an American group does. In a campus setting, when American students work with international students, they should also be sensitive to the different ways the work of the group may be perceived. In some cases it might be appropriate to explain at the start how American groups work.

Group Norms

Norms are the expectations group members have of how other members will behave, think, and participate. Norms are informal—they are not written down. Members assume that others understand the norms and will follow them.

A daily staff meeting of the editors of a college newspaper shows how norms operate. All the editors (associate, managing, and city editors, as well as editors of the opinion, campus, and sports sections) look to the editor-in-chief not only to set the agenda for the meeting but to begin it, to recognize participants, and to maintain control throughout the meeting. The editor-in-chief assumes that all editors will attend each meeting, be on time, bring the necessary information that pertains to their areas, and generally act in a polite and responsible manner. In other words, they will follow the norms of behavior for their daily staff meeting. The editor's manner and demeanor set the tone for all meetings.

In familiar settings, we take group norms for granted. But if we join a group where the norms are not so obvious, we might sit back and listen until we figure out what the group norms are. For example, a new person joining an online discussion group should sit back and read to try to get a sense of how the group operates before he or she participates. Different chat rooms, user groups, newsgroups, and Web forums each have their own group norms of how people using those interest groups should behave.

Norms are important because they give a group some structure. If members know how to behave, the group will function more efficiently. Also, outsiders can look at the group's norms to see whether they want to join the group. If, for example, you feel comfortable only in informal settings, you will probably not want to join a group that has numerous rituals and ceremonies.

Group norms also govern how participants communicate with one another. This may be especially true in male–female interactions. It is important that group members be treated equally and that all members be given sufficient consideration and concern by all others. Any differences in the way people are treated should be based on their needs or roles in the group and not on gender.

Group Rules

Unlike norms, **rules** are formal and structured directions for behavior. Rules may dictate what jobs group members should do, how meetings should be conducted, how motions should be introduced, and so on. The rules help a meeting to progress and ensure that everyone can be heard but that no one person will monopolize the floor. Sometimes, when order and decorum are especially important, a group will appoint a parliamentarian to see that the rules are properly interpreted and followed.

Not all groups have rules. Informal groups such as book clubs have norms such as meeting at different homes, providing food, and being prepared to discuss a particular book. A community group such as the Junior League, on the other hand, has rules, by-laws, voting, minutes to approve, and even penalties for not attending regularly. These distinctions between groups are likely to be based on the degree of informality or formality or perhaps on size. Formal and large groups generally have both norms and rules. Small and informal groups usually have norms but few rules.

Types of Groups

www.mhhe.com/hybels11e >

View "Small Group Communication," clip to see a task-oriented group in action.

From your own experience, you can probably distinguish several different kinds of groups. For example, you are probably a member of informal social groups. **Social groups** are groups designed to serve the social needs of their participants. When you were young, you went to school with members of a social group of friends, you met and socialized with friends at work, and you frequently saw friends from your place of worship. All these were social groups; all had norms associated with belonging, but there were few, if any, rules. These are informal groups.

Many groups are **task oriented**—that is, they serve to get something specific accomplished. Task-oriented groups often have problem-solving or decision-making goals. *Problem solving* involves using some specific procedure—such as the one we discuss later in this chapter—to resolve the difficulty (problem) under consideration. *Decision making*, of course, occurs within the process of problem solving whenever alternatives emerge and choices must be made. When a group is designated as a "decision-making group," its task is recommending action—making clear choices among several possibilities.

A task-oriented problem-solving group in the workplace might be designated to solve the problem that smoking presents. That is, what should be done to protect nonsmokers and yet protect the rights of smokers as well? A task-oriented decision-making group might be charged with presenting a variety of possible alternatives to management, yet this group does not solve the problem. That is left to management.

Many decision-making groups operate in our society. Juries are one example. Groups can be delegated to decide who is to receive an award, who might be a guest speaker, or what kind of activities the group might like to support. A classroom professor experienced the operation of a decision-making group when students in one class met and recommended to him that the date of an examination be changed from the day after homecoming weekend to any of three possibilities the group presented. He presented the three alternatives to the class, and a vote determined the new date.

There is another important kind of group meeting as well. The **information-sharing group** can be found in corporations, schools, churches, families, and service clubs, in social fraternities and sororities, and among faculty in departments on campus. Whenever people meet to be informed and to inform others, to express themselves and to listen

STRATEGIC

FLEXIBILITY

Determining when and how much social interaction is necessary in task-oriented or information-sharing groups requires strategic flexibility— especially the ability to anticipate, assess, and evaluate the social climate of the group.

to others, to get or give assistance, to clarify or hear clarification of goals, or to establish or maintain working relationships, information sharing becomes the purpose. Such groups are necessary when people plan to do business together over a long period.

In either task-oriented or information-sharing groups, there is a closely interrelated social dimension as well. The degree to which members concern themselves with the task or with information sharing affects the social interaction of the group. Likewise, the degree to which members show concern for relationships within the group has a direct effect on task accomplishment or information sharing. In some faculty meetings, department members converse, tell jokes, and communicate informally before the formal agenda begins. This behavior establishes an effective social climate before the information sharing takes place.

Yet another type of group—not discussed in detail in this chapter—is the **learning group**, in which the purpose is to increase the knowledge or skill of participants. While the most obvious is the study group, reading clubs, the League of Women Voters, and Bible study groups are also learning groups. A group of scuba divers or skiers and an investment club are examples of skill-development learning groups.

Social Exchange Theory (SET)

We won't dwell on this theory here since we discussed it in Chapter 6, "Interpersonal Communication," but we need to mention it because "[John] Thibaut and [Harold] Kelley [psychologists]—the developers of SET—"suggested that people try to predict the outcome of an interaction before it takes place" (Griffin, *A First Look at Communication Theory*, p. 117)—just as you would try to predict the outcome of a small group to which you have been assigned. You realize, first, that your goals (rewards) can be achieved only through interaction with the other group members (costs) and, second, that to achieve your goals (rewards) you will need to adapt the methods you use (costs) to other group members.

Power is an essential theme within SET, and as you examine the leader of and the other members of your small group, you will quickly be able to determine some of the power differentials—some members have greater power than others or, to put it another way, there are inequalities between the members. These power differentials are likely to have an effect on how you achieve your goals (rewards). In SET, power is governed by two variables: 1) how it is structured in the group (e.g., leaders often have greater power than members, assertive members often have greater power than non-assertive members), and 2) how power is used. You have the ability to directly affect other members' behavior, and you can cause other members' behavior to change by changing your own behavior.

Notice when you engage in small-group activities—including in-class small group discussion—how SET operates and the various ways that rewards and costs are negotiated. SET is far more complex than this; however, this will give you a taste of a small portion of what is involved in it.

Small-Group Effectiveness

Why do some groups succeed and others fail? Why do some come up with creative solutions for problems while others fall short? Why do some groups have members who get along and other groups have members who are always fighting?

ATTENTION!

Online Small-Group Effectiveness[15]
- Assume good intent.
- Role model the behavior you wish others to use.
- Practice and encourage active listening/reading.
- Be as explicit as possible in your communication.
- Don't auto-matically assume understanding.
- Build trust by doing what you say you will do.
- Encourage an environment that values trust.
- Use irony and humor with care.
- Think before a post goes up.
- Approach every contribution with curiosity.

ATTENTION!

Reality Check

Why do some groups succeed and others fail? The discussion in the section "Small-Group Effectiveness" covers workable size, an appropriate meeting place, suitable seating arrangements, cohesiveness and commitment, and groupthink. Do these reasons that some groups succeed and others fail make sense? Are they logical? From your own experiences in groups, what do *you* think are the major factors that determine success or failure? If you were in charge of a group and wanted to be certain it would succeed, what specific things would you do to help guarantee the group's success? How are these things likely to aid effective communication?

Research shows that effective small groups have certain characteristics in common: a sense of solidarity, an ability to focus on their task, and a task that is appropriate for their particular group.[16]

Solidarity can come from members' sharing common interests (baseball trivia, exercising), knowing one another at work, or sharing some social time together before and after group meetings.

Focus comes from a leader or member who tries to keep the group directed toward its subject. This is the person who says, "That's an interesting point, but our problem is to . . ."

Appropriateness exists when a group and its task are well matched. For example, a student group cannot solve the problem of a deficit in the university budget. However, it might be able to solve a problem like screening strangers who enter dormitories or finding a better way to publicize elections for student senators.

In addition to having solidarity, focus, and task appropriateness, a truly effective group must be of a workable size, must meet in appropriate surroundings with suitable seating arrangements, and must inspire its members to feel cohesiveness and commitment.

Workable Size

A group works best when all its members can communicate and interact with one another. For a group to be effective, it should have from 3 to 13 members. Research indicates that an ideal size for a group is five members.[17] If a group has too many members, it cannot work effectively to solve problems or do the job at hand. It should be broken up into smaller groups—each with its own job to do. The student government, for example, is usually divided into committees: the social committee, the food advisory committee, the constitutional revision committee, and so on. The committees then study the issues and make recommendations to the larger body.

A group may be too large for all its members to participate in group discussions, decisions, and actions. When this occurs, it is time to break the group into still smaller units. With the student social committee, for example, some members could check out the availability of certain musical groups, while other members could conduct a poll to see which musicians the students would like to have on campus.

Groups can also be too small. When there is a lot of information to gather, or when the task requires specialized skill or knowledge from its members, it is important to have enough members to do the job. For example, if a department is completely computerized, it may be faced with many decisions. Some people might be assigned to find the best kind of computer software—or the best available software for updating what the department already has. Then the question may be how to get everyone to use the system or to check their email. Others might be assigned to establish computerized networks with other departments or programs on campus or to develop instructions for getting onto electronic bulletin boards. If there are enough members to investigate each of these areas, no single person will have too much to do.

An Appropriate Meeting Place

The place where a group meets often influences the general atmosphere of the meeting. A group that meets in a classroom or a conference room will probably be more formal than a group that meets in someone's room or apartment.

The meeting place can be chosen on the basis of who the group members are and what they want to accomplish. Members who know one another well might want to meet in someone's home; when members do not know one another well or if the group wants to attract new participants, it would be better for the group to meet in a public place.

Sometimes the meeting place will be determined by what the group wants to accomplish. A parents' group seeking citywide support for a tax increase in order to add new classrooms to the high school might meet in the high school cafeteria. Travel Abroad, a group of interested citizens who enjoy sharing slides and talks about their travels, might gather in the meeting room of the local public library.

Suitable Seating Arrangements

Seating of group members should not be left to chance, with each member choosing a chair. Donald C. Stone, a professor of public service, believes that a seating plan is important if people are to pay attention at meetings.[18] For small groups, Stone recommends seating people where they can all see one another's faces. A circular table would serve this function, as would classroom desks or small tables placed in a circle. For larger groups, Stone recommends a U-shaped arrangement of tables. In this arrangement people should sit only on the outside of the U. Otherwise, they will have their backs to one another.

Stone also makes recommendations about chairs. The perfect chair, he says, is one that has a little padding on the seat. If the chairs have hard seats, people will not be comfortable in them for very long; if the seats are too soft, group members might be tempted to doze off.

Cohesiveness and Commitment

As a positive force, **cohesiveness** is the feeling of attraction that group members have toward one another.[19] It is the members' ability to stick together, to work together as a group, and to help one another. **Commitment** is the willingness of members to work

Circular tables facilitate discussion because group members can see one another's faces.

together to complete the group's task. When members are committed, the group is likely to be cohesive. There are few more powerful and satisfactory feelings than the feelings of belonging to a group and of being loyal to that group.

Although cohesiveness is often a matter of group chemistry, an effective group leader can help cohesiveness develop the first few times the group meets. A good leader will make certain that all members are introduced and, if appropriate, given a chance to say something about themselves. Cohesiveness will also be helped if members have a chance to do a little socializing before and after the meetings. Finally, during the discussions, a good leader will try to draw out the quieter members. The more everyone participates, the better the chance for group unity to develop.

Groupthink

Workable size, appropriate meeting place, suitable seating arrangements, and cohesiveness and commitment are positive aspects of small-group effectiveness. Groupthink is a negative aspect. Social psychologist Irving Janis, having made a careful study of groups, found that cohesive groups can become victims of **groupthink,** a group dysfunction in which the preservation of harmony becomes more important than the critical examination of ideas.[20] Janis's point is simply that groups can bring out the worst as well as the best in people.[21] Because groupthink can limit group effectiveness, group members need to be sensitive to its operation.

Why does groupthink occur? Gregory Berns, a neuroeconomist at Emory University, as cited by Bryan Walsh, in "The Upside of Being an Introvert" (*Time*, February 6, 2012), "has found that when people oppose group consensus, their amygdalae [the mass of nuclei in the brain involved in many of our emotions and motivations] light up, signaling fear of rejection. The risks of groupthink," says Berns, "are perhaps most apparent in criminal juries, where the desire for social cohesion can sometimes short-circuit justice" (p. 44). The bottom line, according to Walsh, is simply that people want to fit in—conform.

There is a potential cultural element involved in groupthink. In a culturally diverse group, it could be that cultural norms may be silencing dissenters.[22] "For example," writes Leonard Greenhalgh in his book *Managing Strategic Relationships*, "Asian cultures emphasize interpersonal harmony. In such cultures, it's considered impolite to contradict what someone has just said. Saying 'I disagree' risks loss of face for the person you're disagreeing with."[23] The point is that someone who is interculturally insensitive may misinterpret silence in a diverse group for indifference, and the silent person may be ignored. That's why it is so important to draw out the views of all group members in culturally sensitive ways.

The key indicators that groupthink may be occurring include situations when the group is examining few alternatives, not being critical of one another's ideas, not examining early alternatives, not seeking expert opinion, being highly selective in gathering information, and not having any contingency plans. These are likely to occur in groups when they have an illusion of invulnerability, when they rationalize poor decisions, believe in the group's morality, exercise direct pressure on members to go along, maintain the illusion of unanimity, and use mindguards—information control—to protect the group from negative information.[24] Mindguards are similar to what happens when juries are sequestered and forbidden to talk to those not on the jury, read any newspapers, listen to anything on television or radio, and refrain from Internet access.

STRATEGIC FLEXIBILITY

Groupthink—a subjective process—can be detected only when an objective point of view is used. If you think about the situation (anticipate), take stock of the factors, elements, and conditions (assess), and truly weigh and consider the value and worth of those factors, elements, and conditions (evaluate), you are most likely to recognize and expose the key indicators of groupthink.

There are a number of examples in our history when groupthink influenced decisions, and the decisions resulted in disaster. The Vietnam War, the Bay of Pigs, the *Challenger* disaster, and the Iraq War are four. Knowing about groupthink will allow you to see, listen, and evaluate the methods used to sway public opinion on major policies. Watch, for example, as certain words are repeated, specific phrases such as "we're running out of money" or "we're running out of time" are used as a threat, and the coordination of spokespersons who stay focused and "on message" until change occurs are organized and orchestrated until a specific policy or idea is adopted.

Although our society depends on groups to make decisions, and we spend more and more time in groups, not all group decisions are superior. Group decisions can be just or unjust, fair or discriminatory, and sensitive or insensitive to the needs of others; they can be responsible or irresponsible, respectful of or in violation of people's rights. In a dormitory, for example, students on one floor decided unanimously to designate a lounge area as a permanent "no-talk study area" where students could go at any time if they needed total quiet for study. When the ruling was put into effect, students found they had eliminated the meeting place of a number of important campus groups that could find no other convenient place to meet.

Two students on the dorm floor knew beforehand about the groups that met in the lounge. Because of the high cohesiveness, solidarity, and loyalty of the deciding group, however, these students chose not to speak up. Their decision to remain silent was a direct result of groupthink.

The essential point about groupthink is that it helps us understand why some groups do not exhibit the kind of critical thinking essential to ethical and responsible problem solving and decision making. It should be clear, too, that groupthink can occur in groups of all kinds. Although our example is a dormitory group, such actions can occur in clubs, committees, boards, teams, and work units. Groupthink is sometimes hard to detect, but detection is worth the effort. When you are part of a group, you want that group to be the best. Groupthink can hinder a group's best efforts.

Discussion in Groups

Most groups that work efficiently have a process they typically follow for discussing a problem. Different procedures can work equally well; what is important is that the steps help the group focus on the problem. Many groups use a sequence of steps similar to the one shown in Figure 11-1. Let's look at each of these steps in some detail.

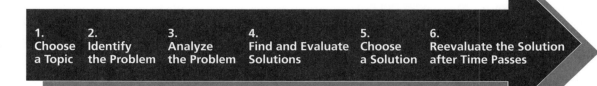

1. Choose a Topic
2. Identify the Problem
3. Analyze the Problem
4. Find and Evaluate Solutions
5. Choose a Solution
6. Reevaluate the Solution after Time Passes

Figure 11-1   Solving a Problem

Choosing a Topic

If you are in a class, you may be required to pick a topic your group can discuss. How do you choose a topic? How do you find a subject that all group members will find interesting enough to work on?

Your first approach might be to look at your own school. Are there any problems or improvements your group might like to tackle? How's the housing? Does registration run smoothly? Does the bookstore have fair prices? Are computers available to all students 24/7? Any of these questions might lead to an interesting discussion.

Take a look at the community. Are there any problems there? How do the students get along with the townspeople? Are students good neighbors? Do the banks cash out-of-town checks without adding a service charge? Do the local merchants realize how important students are to the economy of the town? Are there issues in the city council or county commissioner's office that might affect the school?

If your group is interested in attacking a broader social issue, the supply is almost limitless. World peace, health care, immigration, green house gases, abortion, and attacking the federal deficit are all issues that are hotly debated and will continue to be debated in the future. Discussing one of these topics in your group might be a good way for everyone to become informed about an important issue.

When a group cannot find a topic that all members consider interesting, it should try brainstorming. In **brainstorming** all members of the group suggest ideas—however far out they might seem. The goal of brainstorming is for the group to be as creative as possible. No one should make judgments about the ideas suggested during the brainstorming session. If members fear that their ideas might be condemned, they will be less willing to share some of their wilder thoughts (see Table 11-1).

Once the group runs out of ideas, it's time to stop brainstorming and take a look at the topics that were generated. Sometimes one idea is so good that everyone says, "That's it." More commonly, however, the group will have to evaluate the ideas. Each topic should be assessed in terms of whether all members are willing to work on it and whether it can be narrowed enough to permit comprehensive research. For example, taking on the problems of the country's landfills (garbage dumps) is too big a job. However, the group might be able to research and discuss the problems with the local landfill.

Table 11.1   Brainstorming Guidelines

Have someone record all ideas.
Keep your mind open to all ideas.
Let all ideas flow freely.
Do not belittle any ideas.
Only when your team has exhausted *all* ideas should you stop generating and recording.
Start evaluating which ideas should be discarded.
Consider how even extreme ideas might be interpreted in other ways.
End up with a manageable number (3 to 5) of alternative solutions.
Make sure everyone is encouraged to participate.

Source: *Brainstorming Guidelines,* by J. Fritz, August 2001. Retrieved January 20, 2005, from **http://www.os2cs.unb.ca/profs/fritz/cs3503/storm35.htm**

In an article, in *The New Yorker*, "Group-think," author Jonah Lehrer (January 30, 2012, pp. 22–27) writes that "the first empirical test of [Alex] Osborn's brainstorming technique was performed at Yale University, in 1958." Lehrer continues by explaining that "Forty-eight male undergraduates were divided into twelve groups and given a series of creative puzzles. The groups were instructed to follow Osborn's guidelines. As a control sample, the scientists gave the same puzzles to forty-eight students working by themselves. The results," writes Lehrer, "were a sobering refutation of Osborn."

The solo students came up with roughly twice as many solutions as the brainstorming groups, and a panel of judges deemed their solutions more "feasible" and "effective." Brainstorming didn't unleash the potential of the group, but rather made each individual less creative. Although the findings did nothing to hurt brainstorming's popularity, numerous follow-up studies have come to the same conclusion. Keith Sawyer, a psychologist at Washington University, has summarized the science: "Decades of research have consistently shown that brainstorming groups think of far fewer ideas than the same number of people who work alone and later pool their ideas" (p. 23).

Source: Lehrer, Jonah. (2012, January 30). Groupthink: The Brainstorming Myth. *The New Yorker*, pp. 22–27.

Questions

1. Thinking just about yourself here, do you think that you, working solo, could come up with more solutions to a problem (that you knew something about, of course) than a group using brainstorming?

2. What are the reasons a group using brainstorming are likely to make individuals in the group *less* creative?

3. Given what you know about brainstorming, would you choose brainstorming as your technique in a group for coming up with a large number of ideas quickly? Why or why not?

Identifying the Problem

Once the group has a topic, its members can work toward identifying a specific problem. At this point, much of the work focuses on narrowing the problem so that it can be covered thoroughly. For example, let's say a group of students want to work on reducing crime. They narrow the problem to crime on their campus. They narrow it even further to rape, and they then identify the specific problem: getting the campus administration to accept the need for additional lighting on campus. Notice that through this process of narrowing and focusing, the group has come up with a topic it will be able to handle and discuss in the time it has.

The most important thing the group can do in this stage is identify a problem that is manageable. One of the biggest mistakes groups make is choosing a problem that is so broad that it cannot be adequately covered.

Analyzing the Problem

Asking the First Questions

Groups can take several approaches to analyzing problems. Sometimes it is useful to know what has caused the problem; other times it's enough to acknowledge that the problem exists. For example, a group that wanted to raise student awareness about donating blood did not need to explore why the American Red Cross needs blood. The problem was that students were not donating blood. Another group became interested in establishing a pregnancy crisis center because several local newspaper articles indicated that pregnant students had nowhere on campus to turn for assistance. This group, too, acknowledged that a problem existed.

Before making a final choice of topics, a group might want to find out how extensive the problem is and how many people are affected by it. For instance, citizens in one community wanted to establish an exchange of guns for toys. However, a neighborhood survey discovered that few people owned guns. In checking with the local police, the citizens discovered that few gun-related deaths occurred in their community. The group discovered that guns affected so few people in its area that it did not pursue its plan.

The group should also ask whether anyone else is trying to solve the problem now or has tried to solve it in the past. For example, a group that wants to solve the problem of poor student preparation for college should check with local school administrators to see if someone has been, is, or will be working on this problem—as well as whether or not administrators consider it a problem. Perhaps the group can add to the work that other people have already done or are in the process of doing.

Once the group has gone through this initial analysis, it should decide whether to proceed or to find a new topic. If it decides to proceed, it's ready to begin defining terms.

Defining Terms

The group should define any terms related to its problem that might be vague or ambiguous. For example, a classroom group decided that the campus mailroom took too long to deliver mail. Since individual members in the group defined "too long" in various ways, the group had to arrive at a precise meaning for the term. After some discussion they agreed that "too long" was anything over 24 hours. A community group that wanted to start a program to teach illiterate persons how to read and write first had to define "illiterate." Did it apply only to people who could not read or write? What about a person who could do some reading and writing but not enough to function in ordinary society? From a practical point of view, was this person also illiterate?

Seeking Out Information

To understand a problem fully, a group will need to seek outside information. The kind of information will vary depending on the problem or task. To get information, individual members may each investigate a different aspect of the problem. First they might decide to interview people who have had experience with the problem. For example, if they were trying to find out why library hours had been cut, one group member could interview the director of the library and others could interview students or faculty to see if they were affected by the reduced hours.

Many subjects require research that extends beyond personal experience. A group that is discussing the problem of harmful household products being dumped in landfills would find it useful to interview an expert, such as a chemistry professor. Groups can also find background information on their subjects in the library and on the Internet.

A group will work more efficiently if every member prepares for each meeting. Then when the group meets, all members will be ready for discussion and able to move on to the next task.

Wording the Final Question

Once the problem is analyzed, the next step is to phrase it as a question. A well-worded question should summarize the group's problem; it should be simply and clearly worded; and it should focus on a single central idea. It should use neutral terminology and present a specific problem for the group to solve. Depending on the topic, it should take the form of a question of fact, a question of value, or a question of policy.

Questions of fact deal with what is true and what is false. Examples of these questions are the following: Can we protect the drinking water supplies of our largest cities? Can we reduce gun-related deaths in our nation? Can we make our homeland secure? Does sexism affect our lives? Can we learn effective note-taking skills?

Questions of value are questions of whether something is good or bad, desirable or undesirable: Is recycling a beneficial activity? To what extent is the violence depicted on television and in video games harmful to people in our society? Is fraternity or sorority membership worthwhile?

Questions of policy are questions about actions that might be taken in the future. Such questions are often asked in institutional settings, such as schools, businesses, or organizations, and they usually include the word *should*: Should colleges increase the number of required courses? To what extent should business and industry assume the responsibility for cleaning up the environment? Should all students be required to have real-world work experience as part of their college education? Should businesses be required to be environmentally responsible?

Finding and Evaluating Solutions

Most problems do not have a single easy solution. Sometimes there are a number of alternatives, and the way a group looks at these alternatives is an important factor in the group's effectiveness. Not only must a group suggest alternatives that are realistic and acceptable, but it must also look at both the negative and the positive consequences of all the alternatives.

At other times a group may have difficulty finding appropriate solutions. If members cannot come up with good solutions when they work together, they may find it helpful to work separately for a while, with each member coming up with two or three solutions to present at the next meeting. Some research, as referred to earlier, has shown that when people work alone, they often come up with more innovative ideas than they would in a group.

Sometimes a group can think of several solutions, but some will have to be discarded because they are impractical. In a group that wanted to teach adults to read and write, for example, someone suggested that unemployed elementary schoolteachers should be hired to teach illiterate adults. Although everyone agreed this was a good idea, no one could think of a way to get the money to pay the teachers.

To see if proposed solutions are practical, the group should list each one along with its advantages and disadvantages. Some of the questions a group can ask about proposed solutions include these: Will the solution solve the problem? Is it practical? Is permission necessary to put the solution into effect? Who will implement the solution? How much money will it cost? How much time will it take? If a solution doesn't pass such scrutiny, the group will have to keep working until it finds one that does.

To see if decisions are practical, the group should consider the same types of questions raised regarding solutions. Solutions and decisions are similar because they are both group products or outcomes. Some questions regarding a group's decisions might be the following: What are their relative merits and demerits? What is the best decision the group can support? How will the group's decision be put into effect? To what extent does it satisfy group scrutiny? That is, when the good and bad points in the information are examined, do any need more elaboration? Has some information been left out?

ATTENTION!

Problem-Solving Outline

1. Choose your topic.
2. Identify your problem.
   A. Narrow it.
   B. Make certain group can manage it.
3. Analyze your problem.
   A. Cause? Extensiveness? People affected? Cost?
   B. Define terms.
4. Find and evaluate solutions.
   A. Discard any that are impractical.
   B. List each along with its advantages and disadvantages.
5. Choose a solution.
   A. Get group consensus.
   B. If no consensus, put ideas to a vote.

In his book *Smart Thinking* (NY: A Perigee Book, 2012), Art Markman writes, "To make an idea specific enough to evaluate, it is important to create what New York University psychologist Peter Gollwitzer calls an *implementation intention*. A good implementation intention has three qualities. First, it describes the actions that need to be taken to carry out a plan. Second, it describes when and where those actions will be carried out. Third, it grapples realistically with the obstacles that may arise in trying to carry out the plan" (p. 203). An implementation intention seems to draw together the ideas presented above and offers a practical method for finding and evaluating solutions.

Reevaluating Solutions

It is true that in in-class discussions, it is impossible to reevaluate the solutions groups devise simply because finding and evaluating solutions is the final goal, the solutions are seldom, if ever, implemented, and the discussion groups that originate the solutions are soon terminated, never to meet again. Group members, for the most part, have no long-range, permanent commitment to the solutions. We offer this final step in group discussion work because in business and organizations—as well as in many group discussions that occur in private life—solutions are implemented, and their effectiveness in resolving the problems they are designed to solve becomes not just important but sometimes vital, as when a relationship's survival is dependent on a solution working.

There are two important ideas when it comes to reevaluation. The first is to set a future time when some formal or informal reevaluation can take place. The second is to ask the essential questions that will help guide or frame the future. Because conditions change and new information arises, solutions may need to be honed, polished, or tweaked to add clarity or accuracy. Solutions may be too broad or too limiting; they may need to be redesigned or changed dramatically; or they may not work at all and may need to be dropped. Questions that might be asked include: Is the solution working? What conditions or information have changed that may make alternatives to our solution necessary? Are there things we can do to make the solution work better? As we look down the road now, are there any additional things we can do that will anticipate potential changes that we see occurring in the future? Should we establish another time, now, when we can meet to make another assessment of our solution?

Symbolic Convergence Theory (SCT)

You have undoubtedly been in a group when one of the members cracks a joke, tells a story, or says something that is clearly outside of what's going on right then in the group. In SCT this is called a dramatizing message, if it, in some way, paints a picture or calls to mind an image. According to Em Griffin, in his book *A First Look at Communication Theory* (NY: McGraw-Hill, 2012), it could be classified as dramatizing, too, if it "portrays an event that has happened within the group in the past or might happen to the group in the future" (p. 248).

Most of the comments made in a group refer to what's currently going on in the group, and most bear no imagery. These comments cannot be classified as dramatizing for the purposes of SCT, according to Ernest Bormann, who originated this theory.

You might wonder why this is even important. Because some dramatizing messages have the potential of serving the group well. They can enliven the group by increasing the tempo of the discussion, exciting group members, causing group members to interrupt one another, and by eliciting boisterous, lively, and animated comments. As discussion members become involved—like a chain reaction—words ignite sparks and SCT "predicts that the group will converge around [the] fantasy theme" (Griffin, p. 250).

By painting a picture or calling to mind an image (creating a fantasy theme), dramatizing messages help members make sense out of confusing situations or bring some clarity to the discussion.

It needs to be pointed out, however, that not all jokes, stories, or potential dramatizing messages "get that kind of reaction [painting a picture or calling to mind an image]. They often fall on deaf ears, or group members listen but take a ho-hum attitude toward what was said. Of course," writes Griffin, "an embarrassing silence or a quick change of subject makes it obvious that the dramatizing message has fallen flat" (p. 249).

Let's say, for example, that a group was discussing the topic of gun legislation and some possible federal restrictions on guns, and the atmosphere had become rather tense since members had clearly taken sides on the issue. Suddenly, and for no apparent reason, one of the group members said, "You know, when seconds count, the cops are always just minutes away." Other members laughed, and one added, "If you find yourself in a fair fight, your tactics suck." Notice here that a chain reaction has begun, and a fantasy theme has been created. Tension in the group has dissipated, and a third member pipes up saying, "Don't pick a fight with an old man, 'cause if he's too old to fight, he'll just kill you." Now, with the tension gone, and images about fighting clearly established (irrelevant, obviously, to the discussion topic), the leader enters the discussion, and draws it back to the topic of guns, saying, almost under her breath, "I carry a gun because a cop is too heavy," and then says, "Let's look at some possible restrictions on guns that legislation could cover. . . . "

Other possible dramatizing messages, according to Griffin, include "language such as a pun or other wordplay, double entendre, figure of speech (e.g., metaphor, simile, personification), analogy, anecdote, allegory, fable, narrative, or other creative expression of ideas" (p. 248).

Participating in Group Discussion

www.mhhe.com/hybels11e >

To see an example of the importance of task roles, view the "Small Group Communication" clip.

Groups, like individuals, can be defined as mature or immature. Often an immature group is a new one. It is overly dependent on its leader and, in the beginning, is often passive and unorganized. As the group matures, it is able to function independently of its leader, and its members become actively involved and capable of organizing their discussions.[25]

Although most groups have a specified leader, the leader does not have total responsibility for giving the discussion a direction or for moving the group along. In most groups, an individual member may temporarily take over the leadership from time to time. For example, a member who temporarily leads a group may have more information or experience in a certain area than the usual leader.

Individual group members continue to play the same roles in groups as they do in any other communication. A person who likes to take charge is likely to want the role of group leader, while a person who is shy will be as hesitant in a group as in any other kind of communication. In addition to the roles we play in life, however, some roles are specific to small-group communication. Kenneth Benne and Paul Sheats, pioneers in the classification of functional roles in groups, have identified the various behaviors

Table 11.2   Group Roles

Task Roles	Maintenance Roles	Dysfunctional Roles
Initiator-Expediters	Encouragers	Aggressor
Information Givers and Seekers	Harmonizer-Compromisers	Blocker
Critic-Analyzers	Regulators	Recognition-seeker
	Observers	Self-confessor
		Playboy
		Dominator
		Help-seeker
		Special-interest pleader

associated with leadership in organizations and groups. For people interested in improving their skill in functional leadership, the task and/or maintenance roles Benne and Sheats describe offer a variety of different possibilities.[26]

Task Roles

Task roles are roles that help get the job done. Persons who play these roles help the group come up with new ideas, aid in collecting and organizing information, and analyze the information that exists. Task roles are not limited to any one individual; they may be interchanged among the members as the group goes about its job (see Table 11-2). Following are some of the common task roles.

Initiator-Expediters. Members who act as **initiator-expediters**—by suggesting new ideas, goals, solutions, and approaches—are often the most creative and energetic of the group. When the group gets bogged down, they are likely to make such statements as "What if we tried . . ." or "I wonder if . . . would solve our problem."

Initiator-expediters often can suggest a new direction or can prevent the group from losing sight of its objectives. They are not afraid to jump in and give assistance when the group is in trouble. Often, too, they are the ones who hold the light so that others can see the path.

Information Givers and Seekers. Individual members may both seek information and give it. Since lots of information will lead to better discussion, many members will play the roles of **information givers and seekers.** Information givers are often the best informed members of the group. They might have had more experience with the subject or even be experts on it.

The more complex the subject, the greater the group's need for information seekers. These are people who are willing to go out and research the subject. They might agree to interview experts, go to the library, or initiate an Internet investigation. If the group has very little information on a subject, it might be necessary for several members to play the role of information seeker.

The roles of information giver and seeker are the most important in any group. The information the group gets provides the foundation for the entire discussion. The more group members who play these roles, the better the quality of group discussion.

STRATEGIC FLEXIBILITY

Those whose behaviors exhibit well-honed strategic flexibility skills are likely to be among the best critic-analyzers simply because they often look at the total picture and see how everything fits together. It is part of the process of anticipating, assessing, evaluating, selecting, and applying.

Can you detect those group members who may be playing task, maintenance, and even dysfunctional roles here? Which roles would need to be played to get all members back on a single track?

Critic-Analyzers. *Critic-analyzers* are individuals who look at the good and bad points in the information the group has gathered. These people see the points that need more elaboration, and they discover information that has been left out.

The critic-analyzer is able to look at the total picture and see how everything fits together. People who play this role usually have an excellent sense of organization. Often they can help keep the group on track: "We have mentioned this point twice. Maybe we need to discuss it in more depth." "Maybe we should go back and look at this information again. Something seems to be missing."

Maintenance Roles

People who play **maintenance roles** focus on the emotional tone of the meeting. Since no one wants to spend his or her entire time being logical, gathering information, and doing the job, it is important that some emotional needs be met. People who play maintenance roles meet these needs by encouraging, harmonizing, regulating, and observing.

Encouragers. **Encouragers** praise and commend contributions and group achievements: "You really did a good job of gathering this information. Now we can dig in and work."

The best encouragers are active listeners. They help in rephrasing points to achieve greater clarity. They do not make negative judgments about other members or their opinions. Encouragers make people feel good about themselves and their contributions.

Harmonizer-Compromisers. Members who help to resolve conflict in the group, who settle arguments and disagreements through mediation, are the harmonizer-compromisers. People who play this role are skillful at discovering solutions acceptable to everyone. **Harmonizer-compromisers** are especially effective when they remind group members that group goals are more important than individual needs: "I know you would like the library open on Sunday morning, but we have to find the times that are best for everybody."

Regulators. As their name implies, **regulators** help regulate group discussion by gently reminding members of the agenda or of the point they were discussing when they digressed: "We seem to be wandering a little. Now, we were discussing . . . "

Good regulators also find ways to give everyone a chance to speak: "Vilma, you haven't said anything. Do you have any feelings on this subject?" Sometimes the regulator has to stop someone who has been talking too much: "Roberto, you have made several interesting points. Let's see what some of the others think of them." A regulator who is too authoritarian, however, might find that others resent him or her. In this role, it is important to word statements or questions tactfully.

Observers. **Observers** aid in the group's cohesiveness. They are sensitive to the needs of each member: "I think we have ignored the point that John just made. Maybe we should take some time to discuss it."

Dysfunctional Roles

Occasionally, things in a group do not proceed as planned. There may be many reasons for weak discussions. One may be that a person or persons in the group are playing "individual" or dysfunctional roles. Recognizing these roles will help both leaders and members suppress, control, or compensate for their influence. **Dysfunctional**, or **individual, roles** include the following:

- The **aggressor** may work in many ways—deflating the status of others; expressing disapproval of the values, acts, or feelings of others; attacking the group or the problem it is working on; joking aggressively; showing envy toward another's contribution by trying to take credit for it; and so on.

- The **blocker** tends to be negativistic and stubbornly resistant, disagreeing and opposing without or beyond "reason" and attempting to maintain or bring back an issue after the group has rejected or bypassed it.

- The *recognition-seeker* works in various ways to call attention to himself or herself, whether through boasting, reporting on personal achievements, acting in unusual ways, struggling to prevent his or her being placed in an "inferior" position, and so on.

- The **self-confessor** uses the audience opportunity which the group setting provides to express personal, non–group-oriented, "feeling," "insight," "ideology," and so on.

- The **playboy** makes a display of his or her lack of involvement in the group's processes. This may take the form of cynicism, nonchalance, horseplay, and other more or less studied forms of "out of field" behavior.

- The **dominator** tries to assert authority or superiority by manipulating the group or certain members of the group. This domination may take the form of flattering others, asserting a superior status or right to attention, giving directions authoritatively, interrupting the contributions of others, and so on.

- The **help-seeker** attempts to call forth a "sympathy" response from other group members or from the whole group, whether through expressions of insecurity, personal confusion, or deprecation of himself or herself beyond "reason."

Here is a chance to do some self-analysis for the purpose of instruction and possible future change in behavior.

Most people have performed one or even several of the dysfunctional roles as they participated in a small group.

Read each role carefully and then write down one or two that you are aware that you have displayed/performed. Now, answer the following questions:

1. What was the setting in which this took place?

2. Who were the other members of the group when this occurred?

3. What was your intention in performing this/these dysfunctional role(s)?

4. Did the performance of this role achieve its purpose?

5. Given the same circumstances, would you do it again?

6. Is it clear to you how these dysfunctional roles can negatively influence group behavior?

- The **special-interest pleader** speaks for the "small-business man," the "grassroots" community, the "housewife," "labor," and the like, usually cloaking his or her own prejudices or biases in the stereotype that best fits his or her individual need.[28]

Just one cautionary note regarding a group's move to suppress individuals playing any of these roles: By suppressing such action, a group may also inhibit, restrict, or suppress comments, suggestions, or input from some of the group's best participants. Participants who play a dysfunctional role at one point may play highly constructive, contributing roles at other points.

If members find themselves playing any of these dysfunctional, or individual, roles and they realize such role playing is not in the best interests of the group as a whole, self-discipline is one of the best ways to control the influence. Consider the good of the whole as more important than the good of any individual part of that whole.

Group Leadership

We begin our discussion answering the question, what is a leader? We then look at how leaders influence followers, how people become leaders, and approaches to leadership. Our final section covers leading the group.

What Is a Leader?

Some people hold recognized leadership positions: the president of the United States, a state senator, the principal of our elementary school. Others do not have formal leadership positions but are leaders because a group acknowledges them as such: the student who organizes a study group to prepare for an examination, the employee who puts together a car pool, the friend who gets people together to purchase tickets for a group to attend a rock concert. The characteristic these leaders have in common is that they exert some kind of influence. A **leader**, then, is a person who influences the behavior of one or more people.

Why is one person more influential than another? Why are some people leaders and others followers?

www.mhhe.com/hybels11e >

How Leaders Influence Followers

For an example of
leadership in a group,
view the "Small Group
Communication,"
video clip.

Some leaders influence their followers through sheer force of personality. Others wield influence because they are in a position of power in an organization and the people they lead are their subordinates. Most often, however, leadership is a combination of factors. Researchers have identified five sources of influence for leaders, and we will discuss each source (referred to as "relational power bases") in a moment.[29]

The Internet, and particularly the World Wide Web, is having an enormous influence on leadership as more and more knowledge becomes "common." In this cyberage, the information power wielded by old-style hierarchies is becoming restricted to information about organizations themselves or information that people are either incapable or unwilling to share freely, honestly, and efficiently—a circumstance that portends poorly for the longevity of bureaucracies.

Organizational hierarchies are being "flattened" and are more responsive to internal and external forces (employees as well as stakeholders), and along with this change, the legitimacy of organizational power structures is being reevaluated. Despite these changes—and the fact that all organizations are not or have not changed—the work by French and Raven[30] regarding the seven points of power people have over others may be relevant, especially where clear organizational hierarchies are still in place.

French and Raven suggest that individuals exert influence over others by communicating from five relational power bases.[31] In this section we examine reward power, coercive power, referent power, legitimate power, and expert power. (See Figure 11-2.)

Reward Power

Leaders can have influence through **reward power** if they can provide positive reinforcement for desired behavior. In an organization, rewards can take such forms as promotions or pay raises. In a group discussion, positive reinforcement may take the form of praises, approval, recognition, or giving members attention.

Coercive Power

Reward power and coercive power are not so much different types of power as opposite ends of a continuum. **Coercive power** reflects leaders' potential to inflict

Figure 11-2
Sources of Influence

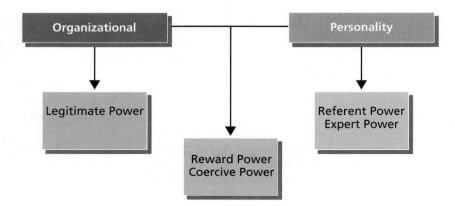

punishment. In an organization leaders can punish followers by demoting them, refusing to raise their pay, or firing them. In group discussion, punishment may take the form of criticism or refusing to pay attention to them.

Referent Power

Referent power is a function of the respect and esteem given to leaders because of the personal attributes with which others identify. It is person-oriented. In a discussion group members may look up to them, want their approval, or emulate them. Also, referent power may occur because members have a personal identification with the leader as evidenced by perceptions of similarity or interpersonal affinity.

Legitimate Power

Legitimate power, in contrast to referent power, is based on a leader's authority because he or she has a *position* in the organizational structure. He or she is "the boss," for example. Referent power is person-oriented while legitimate power is depersonalized. In a discussion group, legitimate power may arise because the leader is designated "leader" by the instructor or other outside authority. "Social norms assign to persons who hold positions of legitimate authority a certain right to oversee or influence others."[32] Just because leaders have legitimate power, however, does *not* mean they must shed personal attributes with which others may identify.

Expert Power

Through **expert power** leaders influence based on their special skills or knowledge. In an organization, just as in discussion groups, these leaders earn respect by their experience and knowledge. It is a form of referent power that results from recognized expertise. It is limited to the topic of expertise and, thus, is more limited than referent power; however, expertise may be the most important form of referent power in the information age. In a discussion group, members may recognize leaders' superior understanding of the subject under discussion as well as the skillful use of the discussion agenda.

   In the case of each of these five power bases, it is the members' observations of the leader's role, demeanor, or behavior that form the basis of their perceptions of leader power. Members may be less or more likely to respond to leaders' suggestions, instructions, and requests based on their observations of the leader's communication.[33] When evaluating the success of group discussions, members' perceptions of power and the way it was used become important criteria to consider. Often members consider referent, expert, and reward power as those positively associated with both learning and motivation, whereas legitimate and coercive power are sometimes negatively associated with learning and motivation.[34]

How People Become Leaders

What makes a person a leader? Some people are truly motivated to serve others. These people are known as **servant leaders,** people who "work for the well-being and growth of all employees and are committed to creating a sense of community and sharing power in decision making."[35]

In this on-site situation, which leadership style is likely to be the best one? On what factor is leadership style likely to depend in this situation?

In this section, however, we will discuss personality, the group situation, and strategic flexibility.

Personality Traits

Leaders are rarely (if ever) born, and no single set of traits consistently distinguishes leaders from followers. Research suggested that leaders would exhibit higher levels of extroversion, agreeableness, and conscientiousness than nonleaders.[36] But in a study of 99 undergraduates (36 leaders and 63 nonleaders), results did not show significant relationships between leadership and either extroversion or agreeableness.

Some traits do increase the probability that certain leaders will lead their followers successfully. Author Warren Bennis lists self-knowledge, openness to feedback, eagerness to improve, curiosity and risk taking, concentration and persistence, readiness to learn from adversity, a regard for tradition and stability as well as the need for revision and change, and openness of style. Leaders also work well with the system and serve as a model or mentor for others.[37]

Situational Factors

In many situations people emerge as leaders because they have the competence and the skill to solve the problem at hand. The person who emerges as leader is the one who is best able to meet a specific group's needs. These characteristics are *external* in that they depend on the situation and on the kind of skill or expertise needed to solve the problem. For example, if a group of students is assigned to make a videotape and only one student knows how to run a video camera, he or she will be the leader—at least until everyone else has learned.

Although a person may become a leader solely on the basis of outstanding personality or skills, most people become leaders when their personalities or skills are appropriate for a particular circumstance or when they can fulfill a need of the group. Hence the name *functional leadership*—suitability of a leader's personality, skills, or knowledge to the needs of a group. We discuss functional leadership in a separate section that follows.

Strategic Flexibility

Those people who are strategically flexible are more likely to become leaders. Why? First, they are likely to be more perceptive since they are accustomed to anticipating and assessing situations already. Second, they are likely to be well adjusted since it requires psychological maturity to deal with anything they are required to face. Third, they have already added bricks and mortar to a solid foundation of communication skills and behaviors; thus, they have more to bring to any situation they face.

Strategically flexible people are also empathic, enthusiastic, and intuitive, all of which supports leaders in reaching their goals. Put into the context of leadership, **strategic flexibility** also will reinforce your self-confidence and help you become more assertive in thinking and dealing with others.

Just as we linked strategic flexibility and creativity in Chapter 1, The Communication Process, they are tightly linked in effective leadership as well. We live in a rapidly changing world, thus, without creativity and innovation, leaders will find it difficult dealing with any of the business realities that require creative solutions: process improvement, problem solving, recruiting, retaining and motivating employees, decision making, dealing with limited resources and rapidly changing technology, and satisfying customers. In small-group discussion, the personality mix of group members, alternative routes to completing tasks, time constraints, and outside influences are sufficient to test the creativity of any leader, but it is creative and innovative leaders—no matter the group context—who are likely to be successful.

Approaches to Leadership

There are many approaches to leadership. First, we examine three traditional but somewhat incomplete styles: authoritarian, democratic, and laissez-faire. **Leadership style** is simply the manner in which a leader exerts control over a group. No one leadership style is best for all situations; that is precisely why strategic flexibility is so important in filling leadership roles.

Traditional Leadership Styles

Traditional leadership styles offer a useful reference point for examining today's leadership needs. Here, we will look briefly at authoritarian, democratic, and laissez-faire leaders.

Authoritarian Leaders

The **authoritarian leader** holds the greatest control over a group. He or she takes charge by deciding what should be talked about and who should talk. This leader approves some ideas and discards others. Most of the discussion in the group is directed to the leader for approval.

Often an authoritarian leader gains the leadership position because he or she is the only group member with expertise. Sometimes a group starts out with an authoritarian leader but later operates more democratically.

An authoritarian leader is often the best type of leader when a group must do a job very quickly. For example, a group is meeting to write a grant proposal that is due in two days. One person takes charge of the project and appoints other members to do various tasks. This is the most efficient way to get the job done in the available time.

Democratic Leaders

A **democratic leader** is one who lets all points of view be heard. Rather than decide things personally, he or she will offer ideas and let the group react to them. The group is never told what to do, though the leader may suggest a direction to take. Leadership in a democratic group is often functional: It may vary with the task and may even move from one individual to another when the group finds this appropriate. Democratic groups work best when members are equal in status and experience and when there is sufficient time to solve the problem.

Laissez-Faire Leaders

The **laissez-faire leader** does very little actual leading. He or she might call the group together, but that's about it. Such a leader neither suggests any direction nor imposes any order on the group. Support groups, such as groups for people with cancer or for people who were abused as children, might feel uncomfortable with an acknowledged leader since the members attend for the purpose of helping one another.

Functional Leadership

We tend to place too much responsibility on the leader of a group and too little on participants. Every member of a group should be a leader in some area. We call this sharing of expertise, when leadership varies with the task of the group and moves from one individual to another as the group finds it suitable, **functional leadership.**

The advantage of functional leadership is that the group's concern is no longer the "property" of any one individual; it belongs to the group as a whole. What matters is whether group needs and goals are being satisfied. This means that leadership is active and changing, that the focus of participants is on the group rather than on an individual leader, and that the importance of sharing and member involvement is emphasized.

To be ready to be leaders at any moment requires that members be persuasive and adaptive; be able to convince the group they can contribute to the direction of the group; foster agreement, cooperation, or understanding; or influence the group's success in any capacity. Functional leaders must be responsive and responsible.

Shared Leadership

The best way to view shared leadership is to contrast it to the command-and-control style of authoritarian leadership. **Shared leadership** occurs when all group or team members assume both decision-making authority and responsibility for the team's results. It is similar to democratic leadership, but it does not reside in a single person.

A supportive and encouraging climate for shared leadership is one in which there is a commitment among group members to one another; a trust level where members take what others say in good faith; respect and mutual regard despite large differences among members; a valuing among members of the unique qualities each brings to the group; mutual empathy in which there is a true attempt to understand and feel with;

STRATEGIC FLEXIBILITY

Effectiveness as a functional leader focuses on your ability to use strategic flexibility—being adaptive, persuasive, aware, sensitive, and responsible. The key may be found in the question, "What skills do I have that will help move the group forward?"

and for those taking part, hope that the conversation holds the possibility that all will gain or learn from the process.[38]

Although shared leadership is an ideal leadership style, there are four potential pitfalls. First, attention to process—maintaining a climate of conversation—can take attention away from the desired product or outcome. The second potential pitfall is the possibility that gifted individuals with unique contributions who might have risen to a leadership role in a functional or emergent situation will not do so in a shared leadership condition.

The third pitfall is that the commitments, understandings, and practices of shared leadership are sophisticated, and for this reason, many may shy away from it. Finally, like all models of leadership, it is culturally specific. What may be viewed as appropriate in one society or group, may not be so in another.[39]

Situational Leadership

In the simplest terms, a **situational leader** can adopt different leadership styles depending on the situation.[40] In his book *E-Leader,* Robert Hargrove recommends a "balanced" leadership style, by which he means one that can be shifted in various situations by asking, "Who do I need to be in this matter?"[41] Leaders may need to be directive, empowering, collaborative, facilitative, or whatever and he makes it clear that there is no one right way to manage. The point of situational leadership is that the talented leader employs the most appropriate style based on the context—which is a combination of task, situation, and group. This is demonstrated in Figure 11-3.

The first situational leadership style (square 1) is labeled **telling** in which the leader is focused more on the task and less on the group (high task–low group). It is similar to the authoritarian style in which the leader states the problem, takes charge of the task, and tells group members what to do. If you are concerned about your grade, placed in a task-oriented group in which other members do not appear willing or able to complete the task if left alone, you might resort to manipulation or even coercion to get the job done.

The second situational leadership style (square 2) is labeled **selling**. In this style, leaders state the problem and decide what to do, but they sell the other group

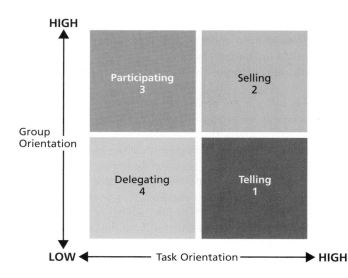

Figure 11-3
Situational Leadership Styles

members on the idea to gain majority support. Selling is high task–high group. Leaders must explain how the idea will benefit the group and then persuade others to go along. The major differences between telling and selling are:

Telling	**Selling**
• One-way communication	• Two-way communication
• Use of manipulation and coercion for control	• Use of persuasion and explanation for group support
• Negative environment	• Positive reinforcement

The third situational leadership style (square 3) is **participating**. Using this style, leaders state the problem but immediately consult with group members. Participating is low task–high group. With all group members participating, leaders offer support and the group determines the best thing to do only after hearing all members' ideas and reactions. Notice in this style the increased focus by the leader on the group and the corresponding diminished focus on the task.

The fourth situational leadership style (square 4) is **delegating**. Delegating is low task–low group. Leaders hang back and let members plan and execute the job. This style of leadership is used in more mature, established groups where members can run their own show—much like the case in shared leadership.

Leader-Member Exchange Theory (LMX)

The purpose of LMX is to explain how the relationship between a leader and a subordinate can develop in a unique way. It is a relationship-oriented theory that suggests that leaders develop an exchange with each subordinate and that the quality of these exchanges (relationships) will determine that subordinate's 1) responsibility, 2) decision-making influence, 3) access to resources, and 4) performance. According to LMX, the way you increase a group's success is by making certain that the exchange between a leader and each group member is positive.

What are the specific outcomes that are likely to result from positive exchanges? Members will work harder, become more committed to the tasks of the group, and share more of the administrative duties of the group. As expected, members who have positive exchanges with leaders (or supervisors) will reveal high satisfaction with their role in the group, be less likely to undermine or leave the group, and will probably get more attention (be called upon more) by the leader of the group. Another product has to do with loyalty. Members with positive member exchanges will be totally committed to their leader.

Additional benefits include the prediction that positive member exchanges will cause members to behave in ways that benefit the group such as helping other group members, supporting any changes that may occur in the group, and revealing common courtesy and respect. Members will exhibit all the traits that promote successful groups; they are empathic, patient, reasonable, sensitive, and good at seeing the viewpoint of other group members—especially their leader. Also, they are less likely to exhibit aggressiveness, sarcasm, or a self-centered viewpoint.

Although LMX is weak in describing specific behaviors that will promote and develop such high-quality relationships with members, it doesn't take an amazing leap in perspective to assume that leaders who show trust, respect, openness, autonomy, and discretion are likely to be most effective in developing positive member exchanges.

The Functional Perspective (TFP)

Randy Hirokawa and Dennis Gouran, speech communication researchers, take the realistic position that the quality of a group's interaction has a direct effect on the group's final decision. Their conclusion is based on the very reasonable assumption that group members not only care about their topic but are also intelligent and willing to discuss it using facts, new ideas, and clear thinking. TFP clearly delineates the four functions that group discussion must accomplish for the group decision to be wise. It includes the following: "(1) problem analysis, (2) goal setting, (3) identification of alternatives, and (4) evaluation of positive and negative characteristics of each alternative" (Griffin, *A First Look at Communication Theory*, p. 234.)

Problem analysis involves finding something that requires improvement or change and then taking a realistic look at current conditions. Goal setting concerns the need for group members to be clear on what they are trying to accomplish by establishing criteria by which to judge the group's proposed solutions. Identifying alternatives means finding a number of alternative solutions from which group members can choose—or, combine to find an entirely new solution. Finally, the evaluation of positive and negative characteristics of each alternative involves testing the merits of each option against the criteria group members think are important. This means a point-by-point comparison of alternatives.

Leading the Group

Sean Gresh, executive communications consultant, delivered a speech to the Ipswich Rotary Club entitled, "Inspiring to Win" (*Vital Speeches of the Day*, November 2012, pp. 356–359). He suggests that effective leaders cannot lead without inspiring group members and asks rhetorically, "And how does one do that?" "By communicating clearly, by living your values, by telling a compelling story about what your [group] stands for, and by showing appreciation for the work of everyone associated with you, no matter what her or his role" (p. 358).

Leaders can help groups work better when they are strategically flexible. That is why we begin this section with listening.

Listening

Many of the functions effective leaders must perform in leading the group depend on effective listening. Effective listening helps create an atmosphere of acceptance and understanding in which others can then explore problems and determine solutions. It helps in managing conflicts, developing employees, and tapping into the key issues that drive others. Good leadership involves modesty, empathy, and reflective listening.[42] Some writers believe that listening is "the most important of all leadership skills."[43]

Listening, as you will recall from Chapter 7, is an essential foundation for strategic flexibility. It is the way to obtain the essential messages and information you need to be able to properly anticipate, assess, evaluate, select, and apply your skills and behaviors. Listening also can counter the natural tendency of leaders to give orders, directions, and provide information and answers. It allows others to contribute their ideas and opinions, permits open dialogue to occur, reveals the trust you have in others to provide valuable input, and gives you time to think about whether you should respond at all, and how.

Maintaining Neutrality and Objectivity

Since the point of view of group leaders can affect all group procedures, if they suspend judgment and encourage full consideration of all viewpoints, they are likely to appear neutral. **Neutrality** means not taking sides but allowing the weight of members' evidence to determine the outcome of group decision making. Members prefer open-mindedness and give high marks to leaders who encourage evaluation, examination, and differing interpretations.

A second point of view of leaders that can affect group procedures is **objectivity**, basing conclusions on facts and evidence rather than on emotion or opinions. If the goal of groups is to investigate problems systematically and realistically, then leaders' objectivity can make a difference.

Neutrality and objectivity are important principles that can guide and direct group activity. Without them, groups cannot achieve their greatest potential.

Establishing Procedures

Every formal small-group meeting should be conducted according to a plan that organizes the group's work. An **agenda** is a list of all the items that will be discussed during the meeting. It is often constructed with the cooperation of key participants. The leader should distribute the agenda a few days in advance of the meeting to remind people of the meeting and allow them to prepare. It also ensures that important business will not be overlooked.

Start and end on time, and stick to the agenda. Get all points of view and ideas. Encourage feedback. Make sure minutes are kept of the meeting for future reference.

Finding Solutions

If you are part of a problem-solving group, you will need to follow the steps in decision making (see Figure 11-4). Begin by defining the problem and making certain there is just one problem to solve. You can do this by clearly defining and separating the issues. With this as a base, ask members for alternatives. As members offer suggestions, make certain they are accepted without criticism from the group. What is important

Figure 11-4
A Brief Problem-Solving Guide

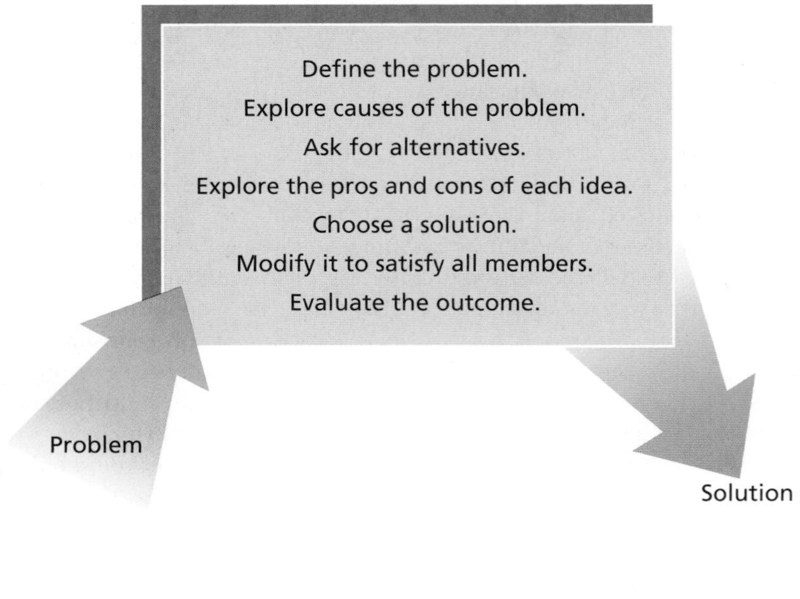

Define the problem.
Explore causes of the problem.
Ask for alternatives.
Explore the pros and cons of each idea.
Choose a solution.
Modify it to satisfy all members.
Evaluate the outcome.

Problem

Solution

is for group members to explore the pros and cons of each idea by asking, in each case, "What are the advantages and disadvantages of this alternative?"

When you have investigated the strengths and weaknesses, you will need to choose a solution. A solution can draw from several alternatives, or it can be one suggested that stands alone. Sometimes solutions need to be modified to satisfy all members. The important part here is to make certain that all members of the group have had the opportunity to participate in the decision making. Once action has been implemented, the outcome will have to be evaluated. This can be done through discussion, or it can be handled through a report by one member.

Helping the Group to Progress

Leaders must be willing to interject themselves and enforce the group's agenda. This requires some discretion and diplomacy because group members do not like to be bossed. A leader might say, for example, "Excuse me for interrupting you, Sabrina, but I wonder if we might hear what some of the others are thinking."

Summarizing is one good way to help the group progress. Doing so alerts the group to where it has been, what it has accomplished, where it is now, and where it is going. A final summary and a statement of goals for the next meeting is also a good way to close each group meeting, "Today we had a disagreement over whether we should lease our equipment to outsiders or permit only our own students to use it. At our next meeting, I think we should work to resolve this issue."

Hidden agendas can interfere with the group's process. **Hidden agendas** are unannounced goals, subjects, or issues that are important to individual members or subgroups but are not on the group's public or stated agenda. For example, in a classroom group one member is more interested in social life than in the topic the group is supposed to be discussing. This person often asks questions about dorm life, football games, or other weekend activities. Most hidden agendas lose their force when recognized by a tactful reminder to the group as a whole to stay on topic.

Seeking Diversity

We've seen that diversity describes the many differences and similarities that exist among people, such as age, race, gender, or ethnicity. Sexual orientation and some physical abilities or qualities may not be apparent. Diversity also includes less obvious differences such as religious and moral values, education, social status, age, political views, or thinking style.

Why should leaders seek diversity? With diversity, group discussions are likely to be livelier, more spirited, and simply more enlightening and interesting.[44] Diversity also promotes broad understanding and knowledge. It prevents minorities from feeling isolated or like spokespersons for their minority, and it creates a vibrant atmosphere that challenges and breaks down stereotypes. When everyone in the group is accepted and feels important, leaders can build a group whose members will work together to learn, interact, and produce better results.

Raising Questions

One of the ways a leader can be most helpful is by raising pertinent questions. Sometimes, during discussion, it is easy for a group to lose sight of its original goal. A group of students, for example, might be discussing the issue of date rape and get diverted

STRATEGIC FLEXIBILITY

Helping the group move along requires strategic flexibility—the ability to anticipate group needs, assess what is going on and where the group needs to go, evaluate the information presented and its value, select from your own skills and behaviors and, with discretion and diplomacy, decide to intervene on behalf of group progress.

to the subject of unfriendly law enforcement officials. If the group leader says, "Is this directly related to the problem?" the group will realize that it is not and will get back on the subject.

Sometimes a group will try to discuss a subject but will lack sufficient information. A group discussing faculty and student parking might realize that it doesn't know how many parking places are assigned to each category. The leader may ask someone to find this information.

Focusing on Answers

Focusing on answers means evaluating alternatives by considering their advantages and disadvantages. A useful leadership role is played by members who ask such questions as these: What consequences are likely to occur? What are the costs going to be? What barriers have to be overcome? How serious are the barriers?

Sometimes solutions call for a plan of action. If your group decides that the only solution to its problem is to demonstrate against the administration, members would be faced with making plans for that demonstration. How are you going to publicize your grievances, get recruits, and carry out the protest? Effective leadership helps a group plan carefully for the action it has decided to take.

Delegating Responsibility

Some people see a leader as the one who does all the work. This should not be true in any group. A good leader should be able to delegate responsibility to the group's members. If a group is going to do research, for example, the leader could assign some members to go to the library, some to interview experts, and others to coordinate and present the information to the group.

Some leaders do not delegate because they believe they are the only ones who can do the job right. If you are one of these people, you should consider taking a risk and letting some of the other people do some of the work. You might be surprised how well they do it. Also, sharing the work makes participants feel more involved and committed.

Encouraging Social Interaction

Social interaction occurs in a group when people feel recognized and accepted by other members. The more friendliness, mutual trust, and respect exhibited, the more likely the members are to find pleasure in the group and work hard to accomplish its goals. Further, group discussions are more likely to be of high quality when group members participate fully in the process. The group leader can also strengthen social interaction by encouraging shy members to speak, by complimenting worthwhile contributions, and by praising the overall accomplishments of the group.

Sharing a Vision

When leaders describe a great leader, the first characteristic on their list is "a creative visionary."[45] Leaders with **vision** are able to anticipate and make provision for future events. They have foresight, insight, and imagination.

Why is having a vision important? First, organizations advance when a clear, widely understood vision creates tension between the real and the ideal; people work

In his book *How to Click with People: The Secret to Better Relationships in Business and in Life*, Dr. Rick Kirschner, educator, professional trainer, speaker, coach, and bestselling author, writes in Chapter 13, "Group Click," in a section titled, "Invite members' contributions":

> To get a group of people to click with one another, seek out ways to increase each one's participation in the group. People are more likely to participate in a group when they feel they are valued members of the group and they know that they are welcome to be themselves, think for themselves, and speak for themselves. One of the best ways to support full participation by implicitly addressing all of these things is to invite people to contribute information and ideas—and to welcome that input when it comes. With this kind of open exchange of ideas and information, group members who have had the chance to personally make a difference in the process feel invested in the group's results (p. 243).

Source: Kirschner, Rick. (2011). *How to Click with People: The Secret to Better Relationships in Business and in Life.* New York, Hyperion.

Questions

1. Is this realistic? Do you think it would work?
2. How can a leader get group members to feel welcome to be themselves, think for themselves, and speak for themselves? What techniques should the leader use?
3. Can you see how these suggestions would help make even a classroom group—one completing a class, group assignment—more effective?

together to reduce the gap. Second, a vision motivates as it draws people together to accomplish a common purpose or reach a common goal. Third, a vision will increase support, inside and outside the group. Here is what Rudolph Giuliani, former mayor of New York City, says about vision in his book *Leadership:* "A leader must not only set direction, but communicate that direction. He usually cannot simply impose his will—and even if he could it's not the best way to lead. He must bring people aboard, excite them about his vision, and earn their support. They in turn will inspire those around them, and soon everyone will be focusing on the same goal."[46]

How do you judge a vision? First, ask yourself how clearly it is articulated. Second, does it address the primary concerns of members? Third, does it translate into practical and specific strategies, methods, and techniques that can be used to attain it?

Seeking Consensus

Consensus means general agreement, and it is a way to make certain all group members—excluding the problem of "groupthink" discussed previously—leave a meeting or discussion feeling every member was in accord. Obtaining consensus may be as simple as asking each member individually if he or she agrees or asking for a show of hands. Sometimes, however, getting consensus may be more challenging. Often it depends on leaders leading the group in an impartial way and having the knowledge to select the most appropriate method. Timing is important too.

Although seeking consensus is important, it is also important to allow open debate and criticism because dissent stimulates new ideas and encourages group members to engage more fully with the work of others. In his article on "Groupthink" (*The New Yorker*, January 30, 2012), Jonah Lehrer writes, "Criticism allows people to dig below the surface of the imagination and come up with collective ideas that aren't predictable" (p. 24).

When things are complicated or difficult in a meeting, a coffee break or a wait until the next day may yield the result desired. Knowing that most members do not like being in the minority, a leader may delay slightly in counting a vote or make certain that all the "agreements" are tallied first. A strong leader who commands respect also can say, "Hearing no objections"—which is an indication that consensus has been reached—and then move on to the next topic. This is an especially good method in large meetings where members do not like holding up the meeting, delaying proceedings, or being perceived as stubborn. When the agenda is long, an efficient leader can look over the members and state, "Then, seeing no objections, we'll move on to the next item." Notice that this is a different tactic—and one more likely to succeed—than asking, "Does anyone object?"

A final method for seeking consensus is to work out the differences. Perhaps those who agree and disagree can be reconciled by some further discussion. Maybe the differences are smaller than at first perceived and with some simple changes in wording, or with the elimination of a superfluous phrase, everyone can agree. Good leaders, too, can serve as mediators, and, perhaps, with some comfortable or easy suggestions can arbitrate the differences and gain consensus.

Do You Have What It Takes to Be a Leader?

Indicate the degree to which you agree or disagree with each statement using the following scale: 5 = Strongly agree; 4 = Mildly agree; 3 = Agree and disagree equally; 2 = Mildly disagree; 1 = Strongly disagree. Circle your response following each statement.

1. I easily and comfortably question others' ideas and opinions. 5 4 3 2 1
2. I strive to find out and meet the needs of other group members. 5 4 3 2 1
3. I feel good when I measure the results of my hard work, rather than counting the time it took. 5 4 3 2 1
4. I feel comfortable thinking of others' needs. 5 4 3 2 1
5. I readily listen to the opinions of others. 5 4 3 2 1
6. I feel comfortable sharing power and control. 5 4 3 2 1
7. I seek out and move on to new opportunities. 5 4 3 2 1
8. I express my feelings easily to others. 5 4 3 2 1
9. I am able to easily share my accomplishments with others. 5 4 3 2 1
10. I am aware of my own strengths and weaknesses. 5 4 3 2 1
11. I feel comfortable with conflict. 5 4 3 2 1
12. I feel comfortable with change and making change. 5 4 3 2 1
13. I make goals. 5 4 3 2 1
14. I am able to motivate others. 5 4 3 2 1
15. I am constantly looking for ways to improve. 5 4 3 2 1
16. I feel comfortable knowing people look at me as a model for what is good. 5 4 3 2 1
17. In general I am a confident person. 5 4 3 2 1

TOTAL POINTS: _____

Before totaling your score, go to the Online Learning Center at **www.mhhe.com/hybels11e** and follow the directions there.

www.mhhe.com/hybels11e >

Source: Adapted from "Leadership Self-Assessment," ICANS (Integrated Curriculum for Achieving Necessary Skills), Washington State Board for Community and Technical Colleges, Washington State Employment Security, Washington Workforce Training and Education Coordinating Board, Adult Basic and Literacy Educators, P.O. Box 42496, 711 Capitol Blvd., Olympia, WA 98504. Retrieved October 25, 2005, from **http://www.literacynet.org/icans/chapter05/leadership.html**

ASSESS YOURSELF

Summary

A small group is made up of 3 to 13 people who get together to do a job, solve a problem, or maintain relationships. Effectiveness in small groups is essential to your career success, will save you time and money, will help you in college, and will help you personally to accomplish your own goals and projects.

Small groups vary from one culture to another, subscribe to norms, and have rules. The different types of groups vary from social groups, to task-oriented, information-sharing, and learning groups.

Using Social Exchange Theory (SET) you try to predict the outcome of a small-group interaction before it takes place. You might realize, first, that your goals (rewards) can be achieved only through interaction with the other group members (costs) and, second, that to achieve your goals (rewards) you will need to adapt the methods you use with respect to other group members. Also, you are likely to note that there are power differentials in the group. In SET, power is governed by two variables: 1) how it is structured in the group and 2) how it is used.

For small groups to be effective, they must have a workable size, an appropriate meeting place, suitable seating arrangements, and cohesiveness and commitment, and they must guard against groupthink—when members start to think too much alike.

Most groups that meet together to solve problems use a problem-solving sequence to structure their work. A common sequence is that the group chooses a topic, identifies the problem, analyzes the problem, finds and evaluates solutions, and chooses the best solution. Small groups beyond those in the speech communication classroom also reevaluate solutions after some time has passed.

Using Symbolic Convergence Theory (SCT), you would recognize a dramatizing message that paints a picture or calls to mind an image. It could be classified as dramatizing, too, if it portrays an event that has happened within the group in the past or might happen to the group in the future. They can enliven the group by increasing the tempo of the discussion, exciting group members, causing group members to interrupt one another, and eliciting boisterous, lively, animated comments. By painting a picture or calling to mind an image dramatizing messages help members make sense out of confusing situations or bring some clarity to the discussion.

Participating in group discussion involves the use of both task and maintenance roles. Recognizing dysfunctional, or individual, roles will help both leaders and members suppress, control, or compensate for their influence.

One characteristic that all leaders have in common is that they exert influence; thus, a leader is a person who influences the behavior of one or more people by rewarding them, threatening to punish them, having a particular personality, using their position of power, or knowing more than anyone else. One theory of leadership is that people become leaders because of their personalities and the situations in which they find themselves. People who are strategically flexible are more likely to become leaders.

The three traditional leadership styles include authoritarian leaders who take charge of a group, democratic leaders who give everyone a chance to participate in decision making, and laissez-faire leaders who do little leading.

Functional leadership occurs when leadership varies with the task of the group and moves from one individual to another as the group finds it suitable. Shared leadership occurs when all group or team members assume both decision-making authority and responsibility for the team's results.

Situational leaders can adopt different leadership styles depending on the situation. Using the telling style, they focus more on the task and less on the group. In the selling style, leaders state the problem and decide what to do, then sell the other group members on the idea. Using the participating style, they state the problem but immediately consult with group members. In the delegating style, they hang back and let members plan and execute the job.

Using Leader-Member Exchange Theory (LMX), you explain the unique way in which a relationship between a leader and a subordinate develops. It is a relationship-oriented theory that suggests that leaders develop an exchange with each member and that the quality of these exchanges determine that member's 1) responsibility, 2) decision-making influence, 3) access to resources, and 4) performance. With positive leader-member exchanges, members work harder, are more committed to the group, reveal high satisfaction with their role in the group, are less likely to undermine or leave the group, and become committed to their leader.

In The Functional Perspective (TFP), researchers predict that the quality of a group's interaction has a direct effect on the group's final decision because group members not only care about their topic but are also intelligent and willing to discuss it using facts, new ideas, and clear thinking. TFP delineates the four functions that group discussion must accomplish and they include (1) problem analysis, (2) goal setting, (3) identification of alternatives, and (4) evaluation of positive and negative characteristics of each alternative.

In leading groups, leaders have a number of responsibilities. These include listening, maintaining neutrality and objectivity, establishing procedures, helping the group to progress, seeking diversity, raising questions, focusing on answers, delegating responsibility, encouraging social interaction, sharing a vision, and seeking consensus.

Key Terms and Concepts

Use the Online Learning Center at www.mhhe.com/hybels11e to further your understanding of the following terms.

Questions to Review

1. Why learn about small groups? How does effectiveness in them affect you?

2. What are the common characteristics that all groups possess?

3. What are the differences among types of groups?

4. What relevance does Social Exchange Theory (SET) have to small-group discussion?

5. From your own experience, what are the traits most likely to contribute to small-group effectiveness?

6. When it comes to an appropriate meeting place and suitable seating arrangements, what are the criteria that contribute the most to a group's success?

7. What is groupthink, what are some key indicators that it may be occurring, and when is it most likely to take place?

8. What is the process most groups follow for discussing a problem?

9. What step or steps are likely to cause the most difficulty in effectively completing the problem-solving outline?

10. What role can Symbolic Convergence Theory (SCT) and dramatizing messages have in a small group?

11. When participating in group discussion, distinguish among task, maintenance, and dysfunctional roles, and explain which behaviors are most associated with progress in problem-solving groups.

12. What are the five sources of influences for leaders?

13. How do people become leaders?

14. What is the contribution strategic flexibility makes in people becoming leaders?

15. What are the strengths and weaknesses of the three traditional approaches to leadership (authoritarian, democratic, and laissez-faire)?

16. What are the differences among functional, shared, and situational approaches to leadership?

17. What are the main differences between classical or authoritarian leadership and shared leadership?

18. What are the distinctions among the four styles of situational leadership: telling, selling, participating, and delegating?

19. What are the differences among leadership factors, group factors, and situational factors when it comes to deciding on a leadership approach? Which are likely to have the greatest influence on deciding which situational leadership style to use?

20. What does Leader-member Exchange Theory (LMX) add to our understanding of the way groups progress? What are the benefits of LMX?

21. Can you see how an understanding of The Functional Perspective (TFP) can make a positive contribution to the success of group discussion?

22. With respect to actually leading a group discussion, what aspects would be the most troublesome for you to accomplish? Why?

23. When it comes to seeking diversity, what would a diverse group look like and what might be its advantages?

24. When it comes to sharing a vision, why is having a vision even important in leadership?

Go to the self-quizzes on the Online Learning Center at **www.mhhe.com/hybels11e** to test your knowledge of the chapter contents.

CHAPTER TWELVE

Getting Started and Finding Speech Material

Objectives

After reading this chapter, you should be able to:

- Develop a procedure for narrowing a topic.

- Distinguish between an informative and a persuasive speech.

- State a specific purpose and a central idea for a speech.

- Describe the process of researching a topic in preparation for giving a speech.

- Distinguish among the various kinds of supporting material and give a hypothetical example of each one.

TRIG HAD SEVERAL OPPORTUNITIES TO GIVE PUBLIC SPEECHES IN high school, church, and a number of groups to which he belonged, but he had no formal training in it, played it "by ear" when involved in it, and knew that his "good enough" really wasn't as good as it could be. The basic speech-communication course gave him numerous chances to improve. Trig wanted to be better. He knew there would be many times when he would be called on to speak, whether it was in his classes, fraternity, sports activities, or at work. The key motivator for him was simple: he wanted to do the best that he could; he wanted to be the very best he could be; he wanted to have every bit of influence he could have; and, he wanted to be in control of his future.

These were not small goals to be sure, but Trig wanted to leave the world a better place because he had inhabited it. It was a philosophy or approach to life instilled by his father as far back as he could remember.

Trig loved the Internet, and he used it for everything. Most important, he found it to be an unbelievable asset in doing research for papers, projects, and reports. To know how to increase its value, use it more efficiently, and incorporate it effectively into his speeches was of great value, but how to best outline and organize his ideas for maximum effect was, perhaps, the most dramatic learning. Trig had little problem with delivering his ideas, but often he let his oral skills carry the day—that is, he never really thought much about organizing and outlining his ideas.

Looking back on what he learned in his speech-communication class, he realizes that the time he spent listening and critiquing the ideas of his classmates, polishing and honing his own ideas, and, especially, reflecting on the entire speech-communication experience (all that goes into a well-constructed, effectively delivered speech) was not only worthwhile, but it may have been the most valuable experience of his entire college experience because of the contribution it made to his other college courses and to his life after college. Trig became an effective, influential, and powerful mover and shaker and was looked to by others for the positive, constructive, and genuine contributions he could make. Strong, well-rehearsed, effective public-speaking abilities gave him the tools he needed to excel.

Why Study Public Speaking?

Public speaking is a vital area of personal development and a crucial factor in your professional success as well. Being able to speak with integrity, in a style that both engages and motivates listeners, is one of the most important traits employers look for in new employees and will allow you to accomplish just about anything you want. It can open doors, reduce barriers, and build connections between you and others.

Knowledge of Public Speaking

If you do not know very much about public speaking, it is easy to believe that success in doing it is simply a knack. But few people who are truly accomplished public speakers would tell you that. As in so many areas, public speaking knowledge is the

In *Getting from College to Career*, Lindsey Pollak, a consultant specializing in next generation career and workplace advice, writes about the importance of public speaking:

> Public speaking is one of the biggest human fears, and most people would do pretty much anything to avoid it. It's also one of the best skills you can develop for a successful job search and career, and a great way to stand out from your peers. Being articulate and confident will get you very, very far. Public speaking is not just for politicians—it's a skill that transfers to virtually every career path. No matter what career you choose, you're going to have to talk (p. 192).

Source: Pollak, Lindsey. (2012). *Getting from College to Career*. New York: Harper.

Questions

1. What do you see as the importance of possessing public speaking skills at this stage of your life?
2. What are some of the specific ways you have—outside of this class—to learn how to be a better public communicator?
3. Do you believe that good speaking skills are a key to getting what you want in life? Can you give some specific personal examples of how and why this is true?

foundation on which skill depends. Then, as your knowledge expands and your skill develops through repeated experiences, and you have opportunities to both test your knowledge and customize and individualize it, your expertise grows along with your confidence and competence.[1]

Public Speaking and the Elements of Communication

Public speaking relies on the same elements as other forms of communication: sender-receivers, a message, a channel, and feedback. The speaker is the main sender-receiver, although audience members also respond as sender-receivers by providing nonverbal feedback or asking questions. The message in public speaking is the most structured of all communication. The speaker works on the message beforehand, planning what he or she will say. The usual channel is the voice and gestures, but some speakers enhance the channel by using graphics such as computer-generated visuals, posters, or slides. Feedback to a speech usually comes from the entire audience rather than from one or a few individuals. Typical feedback would be applause, laughter, or slight verbal or nonverbal expressions of agreement or disagreement.

Preparation for Public Speaking

You have heard the aphorism "If you fail to prepare—you prepare to fail." It is the purpose of this section of the chapter to give you the basics of preparation: finding a topic, narrowing it, selecting a purpose and central idea, analyzing the audience and occasion, doing research, gathering supporting material, and organizing and outlining what you discover.

Finding a Topic

Before you find a topic, be sure to know the purpose of your speech. Is it to inform, to persuade, or to entertain? The general purpose of your speech will help guide you in finding a topic. Any great speech begins with a great topic. One obvious place to begin is by making a personal inventory. A **personal inventory** is an assessment of your own resources. What are you interested in? What are you passionate about? Would your interests make a good speech? See Figure 12-1.

Why is it important that passion drive your search for a topic? In addition to improving your delivery, passion will make it easier for you to do the appropriate research and gather the necessary supporting material. There is no question that passion will buttress the delivery of your speech by eliminating some of your anxiety, creating a sense of desire, generating some of your animation, and framing a sense of purpose and determination. You will feel better at every step in the process.

Beyond the Personal Inventory

In addition to making your personal inventory, begin brainstorming for topics and develop as long a list of ideas as possible. Listen to the radio and television, check the Internet, and read magazines and newspapers extensively to keep up with current news and stories of interest. Remember that your goal will be to present and clarify a subject so that your audience will not only understand and recall the information you share, but use the information as well. If your general purpose is persuasion, in addition to clarifying the subject your goal will be to change the way your listeners think or feel about your topic, or to get them to do something about it. To do that, you need to be informed.

Keep your audience in mind as well as your own interests as you search for a topic. If the topic concerns your health, happiness, or security, it is likely to affect theirs as well. If it offers a solution to an obvious problem that disturbs or unsettles you, it is likely to trouble them as well. If the topic generates controversy or conflict of opinion

Hobbies you enjoy

Teachers who stand out

Things you want to accomplish

Values you cherish

The life you want to lead

Interests you have

Jobs you've held

Experiences you've had

Books you've read

Traveling you've done

Personal concerns

Things to Ponder

Views you hold

What you want to do with your life

Your family life

Things you feel are wrong in this world

Things you feel are right in this world

Friendships you value

The job that you want to hold

Presents you've received

Lessons that you've learned

Personal convictions

Figure 12-1
Making a Personal Inventory

Source: From ANALYZING YOUR TOPIC. Research Tutorial for Freshman and Transfer Seminars, Webster University. Used by permission of Webster University, St. Louis, MO.

when you mention it to others, you can be sure it will generate some disagreement among your listeners. And, if it offers information about a misunderstood, mistaken, or misinterpreted issue, it is likely to have interest for your audience for the same reasons it caught your attention.

If you are still having difficulty locating a topic for your speech, we recommend looking at the *Topic Selection Helper* at the Maui Community College Speech Department–University of Hawaii website, **http://www.hawaii.edu/mauispeech/html/infotopichelp.html**. Entering these keywords into a search engine may produce a similar site.

Narrowing the Topic

A common mistake made by beginning speakers is trying to cover a topic that is too broad. Look at the topic of music in Figure 12-2 and all the possible subtopics there. Each subtopic would include more than enough information for many a speech. On any subtopic in the figure you would discover so much relevant and interesting material that you would not even be able to read it all, let alone cover it in a single speech. But, you can see, too, that if you chose to cover the entire topic—music—your treatment would be so superficial that your speech would not be very meaningful.

How do you narrow a topic? First, for any topic you select, brainstorm some narrower aspects of it. Write down those ideas. Second, choose one of the narrower topics that you find interesting. Third, ask the following four questions about the narrowed topic:

- Will this narrowed topic be of interest to my audience?
- Will this narrowed topic be understood by my listeners?
- What are the specifics of the assignment, and will this topic fit into those specifics?
- How long do I have to cover the topic?

The broader the topic, the more superficial the speech. Remember that your time allotment will have a great deal to do with how much information you can cover.

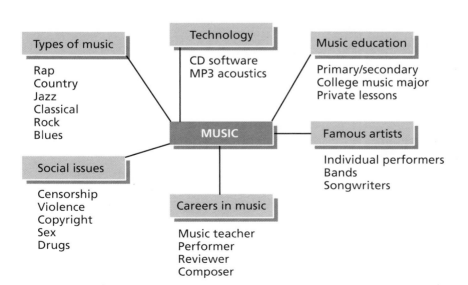

Figure 12-2
Possible Speech Topics under the Heading "Music"

From: *ANALYZING YOUR TOPIC*. Research Tutorial for Freshman and Transfer Seminars, Webster University. Used by permission of Webster University, St. Louis, MO.

Selecting a Purpose

Whenever you give a speech, having a purpose will help you look for materials, organize and outline your speech, and adapt to the needs and interests of your audience.

There are three stages in working out the **purpose** for your speech: (1) selecting the general purpose, (2) selecting the specific purpose, and (3) stating the central idea.

The General Purpose

When you state your **general purpose,** you should determine whether you intend to inform or persuade. **Informative speeches** generally concentrate on explaining—telling how something works, what something means, or how to do something. A speaker who gives an informative speech usually tries to give his or her audience information without taking sides, even when the issue is controversial. For example, if you are giving an informative speech about using animals for research, you will not state whether you are for or against doing so; you will let members of the audience make up their own minds.

In a **persuasive speech** the speaker takes a particular position and tries to get the audience to accept and support that position. For example, student fees should be incorporated into college tuition, or free music downloads should be legal.

Often the same subject can lead to either an informative or a persuasive speech—depending on your wording of the topic and your approach. "Technology has added a whole new dimension to student cheating," is clearly an informative topic. But "The university must take greater strides to prevent student cheating" is persuasive. Even more strongly persuasive, because it places the responsibility on the shoulders of listeners, is, "Each of us has a responsibility to help prevent cheating in college."

Many of the important decisions in speechmaking require that speakers answer questions they ask themselves.

Sometimes it's difficult to fit a speech firmly into an informative or a persuasive slot. In a persuasive speech, informative material often plays an important role. If you are speaking in favor of political candidates, it is natural to use information about their backgrounds and voting records. In an informative speech, even when you try to present both sides, one side might seem more persuasive than the other to some audience members.

The Specific Purpose

After you have decided whether the general purpose of your speech is to inform or persuade, you must then decide on a **specific purpose**—a single phrase that indicates precisely what you expect to achieve in your speech. For example, "To inform my audience of the methods the university uses to protect the safety of its students." Your specific purpose statement is used in the development of your speech; you don't actually say it in your speech. There are five guidelines for constructing your specific purpose:

1. *Make it a clear, complete, infinitive statement,* not a sentence fragment, and not a question:

    To inform listeners of the value of home schooling.

    To persuade listeners to become educated consumers.

2. *Phrase it in terms of the effect you want to have on listeners:*

    To inform listeners of ways they can help people with disabilities.

    To persuade listeners of the negative effects of binge drinking.

    You should also be able to rephrase your specific purpose from a listener's vantage point. At the end of your speech, listeners will refrain from binge drinking or be able to explain specific ways they can help people with disabilities.

3. *Limit the statement to one distinct idea only.* For example, a specific purpose that reads "To inform my audience about the value of daydreams and how to use them to escape and relax" would need to be rephrased to focus on either their value or on how to use them to escape and relax.

4. *Use specific language:*

    To inform listeners of the negative effects of alcohol on the body.

    To persuade listeners that they should help control drunk driving.

5. *Make certain your purpose meets the interests, expectations, and levels of knowledge of your listeners.*

If your audience will be students, use yourself as a gauge: Does your specific purpose meet your own interests, expectations, and levels of knowledge?

Once you have determined your statement of purpose, you should subject it to some tests. Does it meet the assignment? You might discover, for example, that your opinions on a subject are so strong that you are unable to talk about it without favoring one side over the other. This means your subject is better for a persuasive speech than for an informative one. If you have been assigned an informative speech, you should keep this subject for a later time.

Another important test is to ask whether you can accomplish your purpose within the time limits of the speech. If your speech purpose is too broad to fit into

ATTENTION!

Test Your Specific Purpose

1. Does it meet my own interests, expectations, and level of knowledge?
2. Does it meet the assignment?
3. Can I accomplish it within the time limit given?

the allotted time, you will either have to narrow the topic further or find a new topic. One speaker discovered, for example, that her purpose, "to inform my audience about physical fitness," was too broad; too many issues were involved. She rephrased her purpose: "to inform audience members about how low-impact aerobics can improve their health."

The Central Idea

Whereas the specific purpose expresses what you want to accomplish when you give the speech, stating the **central idea** establishes the main thrust of the speech. The central idea is much like the thesis statement you learn about in writing courses. Everything in the speech relates to the central idea. In an informative speech, the central idea contains the information you want the audience to remember; in a persuasive speech, it tells audience members what you want them to do.

The difference between a specific purpose and a central-idea statement is illustrated in the following examples. Notice that the central idea, though a first draft, explains the why or the how of the specific purpose:

Specific purpose: To persuade audience members to protect themselves against unsuccessful and unhappy marriages.

Draft of central idea: Unsuccessful and unhappy marriages occur because people do not take the time to become friends first, communicate honestly with each other, resolve conflicts constructively, learn to work around problems, discover an enduring attraction, contribute equally to the relationship, trust each other, and take their commitment seriously.

When the central idea was stated, it encompassed too many points to cover in a single speech. So the speaker rephrased it in such a way that the ideas could be grouped:

Central idea: Unhappy marriages occur because of poor communication.

The central idea should be stated in a full sentence, should contain one idea, and should use precise language. Sometimes it is not possible to come up with a central-idea statement until you have finished organizing and outlining the speech. When you start working on your speech, you should have a tentative central idea in mind; when you have finished organizing and outlining, you can refine it.

It is important to have a specific purpose and central idea to guide your research and investigation, but you must not let them bind you unnecessarily. Part of the process of research is being flexible and responsive to what you discover. If you are actively engaged in research, you never know what you are going to find.

"The central idea should come at the end of the speech introduction, just before the transition to the body of the speech. The topic of the speech should be clarified and connected to the audience and to the speaker's credibility prior to previewing the main points and moving into the body of the speech," says one of the reviewers of this book. This is an excellent suggestion, especially for beginning speakers. However, as a speaker gains experience, the decision about where the central idea appears in the speech and when it should be revealed might depend on a number of influences. For example, is it important for audience members to have some context (more information) before hearing the central idea? Would it be better to offer audience members a number of examples, illustrations, or facts and statistics to support the point of view, before the central idea is stated? Will the central idea, because it may antagonize some

STRATEGIC   FLEXIBILITY

As you research, think about your potential speech situation and the needs and requirements likely to arise because of it. Take stock of all the factors, elements, and conditions that you are likely to find yourself in. As you select the material you will use, remain open and flexible to the possibility of making changes in your specific purpose and central idea so that they reflect exactly what you plan to accomplish in your speech.

audience members, be more effective if held until near the end of a speech? Could the speech be given in its entirety without ever stating the central idea specifically? The idea of placing the central idea at the end of the speech introduction is a good one and will work in most cases, but for seasoned speakers, there should be possibilities, alternatives, and choices depending on the topic, the audience, and the occasion.

Analyzing the Audience

Audience analysis means finding out what your audience members know about your subject, what they might be interested in, and what their attitudes and beliefs are. The very next step in audience analysis is adapting your speech to their interests, level of understanding, attitudes, and beliefs. Audience analysis has two important benefits: First, it will improve your effectiveness since your presentation will be created and delivered with listeners' specific needs in mind. Second, when you focus on what matters most to your listeners, it will help you accomplish your objectives.

Strategic flexibility is important in audience analysis. What choices are likely to make you the most strategically flexible? First, choose your target audience. A **target audience** is a subgroup of the whole audience that you must reach to accomplish your goal. It is on this subgroup that you are likely to have your greatest impact.

The second choice is to do your homework. Go to the library, work on the Internet, use surveys, interviews, or informal conversations to gain as much information as you can about your target audience. If you are asked to speak before an organization, talk extensively about the group to the person who arranged the speaking engagement or the one who invited you. Doing your homework will also help you avoid stereotyping—using preconceived notions about your listeners and, thus, neglecting individual differences.

The third choice likely to make you the most strategically flexible in audience analysis is to continue to analyze your audience even after you begin speaking. Here is what to look for as you gain feedback from your audience:

- Do your listeners look confused? Have you overestimated their knowledge of the topic? Take the time to clarify terms to offer them the necessary background.

- Do your listeners look bored? Are there ways to spice your speech with more examples, greater audience involvement, more animation, or a higher degree of excitement?

Audience Knowledge

One important aspect of audience analysis is taking into account how much the audience is likely to know about a subject. If you are talking to a lay audience and pick a topic related to a specialized field of knowledge, you will have to explain and define some basic terminology before going into the subject in any depth. For example, when Sam spoke to his class about dietary fat, he had to explain such terms as *saturated, polyunsaturated, hydrogenated,* and *trans fats* before he could talk about anything else.

Speakers should realize that although people have general information about many subjects, they usually don't know the specifics. Most people know, for example, that the Constitution guarantees us the right to free speech. Yet if you were to ask them what *free speech* means, they would probably be a little fuzzy on a definition or on what is encompassed by the term. Would they know, for example, that the courts regard ringing a bell or burning a flag as a form of free speech?

ATTENTION!

Keys to Audience Analysis

- What do they have in common? Age? Interests? Ethnicity? Gender?
- Do they know as much about your topic as you, or will you be introducing them to new ideas?
- Why are these people listening to you? What are they looking for?
- What level of detail will be effective for them?
- What tone will be most effective in conveying your message?
- What might offend or alienate them?[2]

Audience Attitudes and Beliefs

When planning your speech, you also need to consider your audience's attitudes and beliefs about your subject. **Attitudes** are beliefs that cause people to respond in some way to a particular object or situation—like the topic of your speech. **Beliefs** are statements of knowledge, opinion, and faith: convictions about what one thinks is right and wrong or true and false. You will have a much better chance of having an impact on your audience when you already know how they feel about your topic. This is where strategic flexibility can play a major role in your preparation as you anticipate, assess, and evaluate your potential speech situation and the needs and requirements likely to arise because of it.

If you discover—through informal conversation, a show of hands, or even a brief survey—that listeners hold positive views about your topic and your message, you can use your speech to focus chiefly on reinforcing those views.

If you discover that listeners hold negative views, you will have to plan your speech carefully. Anticipate their objections and prepare your responses—even build those responses into your speech. You may have to limit what you ask of them, or you may have to start your speech with points you know will get agreement from them and move to more controversial points only after you have their agreement on acceptable issues. You might even begin your presentation by listing opposing arguments before explaining your own position.

Since people's attitudes and beliefs will affect how your speech is received, it is absolutely essential to consider them when you are planning your speech. You can find important clues to people's attitudes and beliefs through audience demographics.

Audience Demographics

Even if you have no specific information about your audience's knowledge, interest level, and attitude toward your subject, certain factual information about the audience members can tell you a great deal. **Demographic analysis** reveals data about the characteristics of a group of people, including such things as age, gender, education, occupation, race/nationality/ethnic origin, geographic location, and group affiliation.

When you work with demographic information, you generalize about the entire audience; your generalizations might not be true of individual members. For example, on the

Using only the information you have from these pictures, what do you know about these audiences—their interests, attitudes, and beliefs? How might this knowledge help you shape a speech you intend to give them?

So much of the success of speeches depends on how speakers tune, align, or adjust their messages exactly to the needs, wants, and desires they discover through their audience analysis. Just from what you know (without having to do additional research and investigation), what would be your analysis of an audience to which *you* will speak with respect to their knowledge, attitudes and beliefs, and demographics? Be specific.

1. A group of teenagers just ready to graduate from high school
2. A group of parents gathering to hear about your college experience thus far
3. A group of co-workers to whom you want to explain a new concept or approach
4. Your classroom colleagues to whom you will deliver your first speech

basis of demographic data you have gathered, you might generalize that the ages of your speech class audience are between 18 and 27—even though one member is in his 50s. On the basis of such generalizations, you can make some predictions about what might interest the people in this audience and what they might be knowledgeable about.

Age. As a speaker, you need to have a sense of the age range of your audience because interests differ with age. College-age people are usually interested in school, future jobs, music, and interpersonal relationships. Young parents are often interested in subjects that might affect their children, such as school bus safety and school board policy. However, computers, elections, and world and national news have interest for most age groups because they affect everyone.

It is sometimes difficult to generalize with respect to age. Look, for example, at "college-age" people. The average age of college students is no longer about 20. It is now around 26, and it is likely to go higher with more adults going back to school. We need to be sensitive to age differences to avoid stereotyping in our speeches.

Gender. In a speech that's open to the public, you will probably have both men and women in your audience. If you deliver a speech to a mixed audience but do not acknowledge the presence, and appeal to the needs, of both genders, not only will you miss the mark, but your speech may even seem sexist and inappropriate.

Education. The audience's level of education gives you some idea of the group's knowledge and experience. We can assume that the more education people have, the more specialized their knowledge. Lawyers, doctors, and PhDs all have specialized knowledge; however, they might have little information about subjects other than their own. Your main consideration when you prepare a speech is whether your audience has the same knowledge you have or whether you will have to start with the basics.

Occupation. Sometimes occupation indicates an area of specialized knowledge: Paramedics and nurses know about the human body; lawyers know about legal rights; social workers know about social problems. A person's occupation can also indicate interest in a subject. Most professional groups would probably be interested in a speech about ethics in their profession. If you are speaking to an occupational group, try to adapt your speech to that audience's job interests.

Race/Nationality/Ethnic Origin. When politicians speak to whole audiences made up of a single racial or ethnic group, they try to identify with the listeners' goals and aspirations.

Respect Your Audience

1. Don't waste their time.
2. Polish your delivery beforehand.
3. Be knowledgeable about your topic.
4. Present information in an interesting way.
5. Be sincere and enthusiastic about your desire to share your thoughts.
6. Be sure to have analyzed your audience.
7. Be very aware of your time limit.

If you are speaking to a group with members from diverse backgrounds, you should be particularly careful in your use of language. If your audience includes foreign students, they may have problems understanding slang and colloquial expressions. Not everyone has gone to summer camp, and not everyone has eaten *kim chi*.

Geographic Location. Your audience's geographic location may affect the content and approach of your speech. If the federal government is giving money to improve airport runways, find out if some of this money is coming to the local airport. If the nation has been hit with a crime wave (or a heat wave), has this been a problem in your local area? If you have a chance to speak in a town or city other than your own, the audience will be pleased if you know something about its area.

Group Affiliation. Knowing the clubs, organizations, or associations that audience members belong to can be useful because people usually identify with the goals and interests of their own organizations. If you speak to a group, you should be aware of what it stands for and adapt your speech accordingly. Some groups have particular issues or themes for the year, and they look for speakers who can tie their speeches into these themes.

Analyzing the Occasion

Your analysis of the occasion should go hand-in-hand with your assessment of the audience. Let's look at the questions you need to ask about the occasion for speeches outside the classroom.

Time

Three facets of **time** matter: time frame for the speech, time of day, and the length of time of your speech. First, time frame for your speech refers to the events leading up to a speech event—even long-term historical forces. If something recent bears directly on your subject, you need to mention it in your speech to (1) put your topic into the proper framework, (2) let audience members know that you are aware of the event and its relationship to your speech, and (3) help your credibility.

Second, time of day has a direct bearing on speech effectiveness. Audiences are less alert in the early morning and late afternoon. Giving a speech at either of those times requires you to make special efforts to hold their interest. An interesting topic, or a topic handled in an interesting way, can get the attention of even a sluggish audience.

Finally, respect the length of time you have been given for your speech. Stick to the time limit. Listeners will get restless if you go on too long and be disappointed if you run short.

Place

Place refers to the physical stage for the speech and the interaction with the audience. If you are not familiar with the room, make sure you take a look at it before you speak. Is the temperature comfortable? Is the lectern where you want it? Are the chairs arranged the way you want them? How big is the room? Do you need a public address system?

Channel

What **channel** of communication links you and your audience: Is it closed-circuit television? Is the address on the radio? Is the transfer made over an Internet connection? The channel could be the sound system in a large auditorium. When technology is involved in any way, it is important that it works, but you need to know what to do if it doesn't.

ATTENTION!

Using Personal Experience

1. It is *not* research.
2. It should not substitute for research.
3. It should be given *no* weight in proving a point or making an argument.
4. It holds audience attention, lets the audience know why you were interested in the topic, and contributes to your credibility.
5. Use it to guide and direct your research.

A Good Place to Start

If you have chosen a topic in which you have a strong interest, the first thing you should ask yourself is whether you have had any direct experience with the subject. Your own experience can provide interesting and valuable material.

Let your topic be the stimulus for freeing your thoughts and prompting your creativity. **Creativity** is the ability both to have new thoughts *and* to rearrange old ideas in a new way. As your creative juices begin to flow, make certain you record your ideas, whether on notecards, a PDA, a tape recorder, a notepad, on your computer, or the back of an envelope.

Before you discard any ideas, remember that sometimes we do not put enough value on personal experience; we think that if something happened to us, it can't be important. Relating personal experiences to the subject of your speech can provide the most interesting material you use. On the other hand, sometimes we rely on it too much and exclude other sources of information. Reach a balance.

There are several ideas regarding your use of personal experience and observation that need attention. First, you should be aware that personal experience and observation is *not* research, and that is the reason it does *not* appear in the next section, entitled "Researching Your Topic: Where to Look." Not only does it not count as research, it should not substitute for it, nor should it be given weight when it comes to proving a point or making an argument. Second, personal experience and observation may be useful for holding audience attention, letting listeners know why you were interested in the topic and chose to pursue it, its positive contribution to your credibility. Third, allow your personal experience with the topic you have selected to guide and direct your research.

Researching Your Topic: Where to Look

Once you have decided on the topic, specific purpose, and central idea of your speech, it is time to begin looking for useful information. The three most common sources you can draw on for relevant material are interviews, the library, and the Internet. Because there is an enormous amount of information to be obtained from the Internet, it is accessible 24/7, it is a comfortable and easy way to access information, it is cost effective, and it is the resource of choice for finding information, you are likely to devote most of your time to Internet research. Check with your instructor to determine the research expectations for your speeches.

Interviewing

When you can talk directly to decision makers, conducting interviews is one of the best ways to gather up-to-date information from experts. If the subject is complicated, you can ask questions about points you don't understand.

Computer databases put an immense amount of information at your fingertips 24 hours a day, 7 days a week.

One advantage of the Internet is that it provides contact with authorities and others around the world on a 24-hour basis. Using interest groups such as mailing lists, newsgroups, live chat groups, Web forums, and social networks, you can ask questions, share ideas, sound off, and just plain converse with others on almost any topic.

Using the Library

Any library—whether large or small—has millions of pieces of information. Fortunately for users, all libraries organize their information in essentially the same way, so when you learn how to use one library, you can use this skill in any library. Today, most library resources can also be found on the Internet.

Using Computer Databases

Literary, musical, artistic, reference materials, and periodical and newspaper collections are all stored in **computer (or online) databases**—which are collections of information organized for easy access via the computer. Databases vary in their content as well as in their arrangements and protocols. The reason is that there are many database producers and vendors, and each of them has its own corresponding software. For most classroom speeches, computer databases will supply most of the necessary resources.

Using the Internet

There are, basically, three kinds of information available on the Internet according to the Web page of Donnelly College (http://donnelly.edu/htdocs/libraryResearch.html). The first area includes electronic scholarly journals. These are reliable sources of scholarly research papers, written by experts, peer reviewed, and edited by other professionals. "You can feel confident in quoting them." The second kind of information is trade magazines which are published electronically by professional organizations and are reliable sources of information. Although professionally edited, the articles are unlikely to have as high a research base as scholarly journals. The third area is websites where anyone can publish any content they wish. Without professional editors, peer reviewers, or validity checkers, accuracy may be suspect, and the important point: "it is up to the individual viewing the site to determine the validity of the information."

In his book *StandOut* (Nashville: Thomas Nelson, 2011), Marcus Buckingham makes the point that,

> We live in a digital, data-based world where virtually every action and consequence can be measured. Many of the people you seek to persuade are comforted by data and are prepared to make a decision only when supplied with the data that "prove" a particular action will lead to a particular consequence. **Learn to be proficient in the language of data.** Learn how to marshal the facts so that others with a lower tolerance for ambiguity can lean on these facts and find the certainty they need (p. 108).

And while we're discussing a digital, data-based world, let us mention Wikipedia. At one time the scourge of scholars, it is now achieving greater acceptance. In her article "Bringing Wikipedia Into Your Classroom by Choice" (SPECTRA, November 2012), Lianna Davis writes that it "exists in 285 languages and features 23 million articles. An active community of more than 80,000 volunteer editors around the world adds new content and reviews content others have submitted. "The English Wikipedia," Davis continues, "if printed without images, takes up more than 1,600 volumes of a printed encyclopedia. It's the fifth most popular site in the world, according to comScore— behind only Google, Microsoft, Facebook, and Yahoo." Because of its popularity, Davis says, "it is the site people all over the world see when they research topics, including communication studies" (p. 6).

There are a number of useful steps for engaging in research on the Internet. Just as in doing any research, it is best to begin by defining and understanding your problem. Having a general purpose, a specific purpose, and a central idea can be a big help. Here are steps for doing research using the Internet.

1. *Define your goals.* Be specific about the information you need. Breaking a topic into its component parts will make your information search clear and easier to conduct.

2. *Determine the types of information you need.* Knowing the kinds of information you want will help you choose the resources and tools that will best meet your needs. For example, are you looking for statistics, in-depth books, magazine articles, expert comments, or biographies?

3. *Identify keywords, phrases, and subject categories.* Play with your search terms; use synonyms; try distinctive terms; apply alternative spellings. Search by topic, sub-topic, company, product, a person's name, and so on.

4. *Read the instructions, tips, and techniques for using the search tools you have chosen.* If you understand the types of information each tool covers and the kinds of search options you have available, you will expedite your search.

5. *Use more than one source and search tool.* Although there is duplication among sources on sites, queries performed on different search engines usually produce different results.

6. *Practice netiquette.* Be considerate of others in doing your research.

7. *Review your progress.* Look at some of the most promising records, and see if there are other terms that you can use to sharpen or widen your search. Compare what you've learned with what you decided you wanted to learn in step 1. Make adjustments or redirect your focus if necessary.

8. *Practice critical thinking!* Evaluate the information you find. Don't accept what you read as the truth; get confirming sources, ask questions, talk to experts, probe for motivations, and use your intuition. If something just doesn't sound right, check it out further.

Evaluating Information on the Internet. The fact that something is on the Internet does not make it credible, valid, or worthwhile. Just as in any library, along with all the good information there is plenty of bad information as well.

The stature of researchers can be measured not in the quantity of information they amass but in its quality. To ensure that you are gathering material of high quality, use the following six criteria:

1. *Reliability.* What is the source of the information? Did the information come from an academic, government, or commercial site? An educational institution is likely to offer information designed to teach or help learners, whereas a commercial organization is likely to offer information designed to sell or market a product. We would tend to ask about information posted at a commercial site, "What's in it for them?" or "What is their agenda?"; we would be less inclined to ask the same question regarding information posted at an educational site.

ATTENTION!

What Is a Reliable Source?

- Is the information fair, objective, lacking hidden motives, and showing quality control?
- Is the source well-known (an academic, government, or commercial site that has a good reputation)?
- Are there possible conflicts of interest?
- Is the information relevant and useful?
- Is the information subjected to a peer-review procedure or editorial board?
- Does the website have regular updates?
- Does the information include bibliographic citations?
- Does the website allow easy browsing and have a quality design?

ATTENTION!

- Research is another word for gathering information. The more information you gather, the closer you get to making a good impression, convincing audience members, and proving your point(s).
- It is the substance of a speech and what makes it important, significant, and worthy of audience attention and interest.
- It is the key to speaker credibility and believability. It is what makes a speaker worthy of the audience's trust.
- It is how one determines "quality." What makes a speech of high quality? Time, effort, and research are features of distinction and superiority.

The essential question you need to ask to find reliable material is, "What sources are likely to be fair, objective, lacking hidden motives, and showing quality control?" Investigate the source before you print the information. With so many sources to choose from in a typical Internet search, there is no reason to settle for unreliable material.

2. *Authority.* Who sponsors the site, who manages it, and what are their credentials? The sponsors should clearly have some expertise in the subject area of their site or in the subject area being written about.

If no credentials are offered, enter the name of the author into a search engine such as Google. Often, you will find that the author has a home page that can be quickly accessed, and in many cases the necessary credentials appear on that page. If no credentials are available, you need to reserve judgment about the value of the information you have discovered. There is no need to discredit an unknown source, but you should, at the very least, make your listeners aware of the situation.

3. *Currency.* How up-to-date is the site? Has it been updated recently? The most recent date should be clearly listed somewhere on the site. But the fact that a website is recent doesn't mean the information contained there is recent—it could be reprinted from somewhere else. You need to discover, if you can, how old the information is and when it was first published.

4. *Objectivity.* What is the purpose of the organization sponsoring the document or information? Is the purpose purely to collect and publish data? Are there political, ideological, or other agendas? Is the information presented objectively, or does it represent the biases of its author? Is there evidence to support the conclusions? Is the coverage thorough? If you have questions about the data, are you able to call the provider and ask for the identification of the original source of the data? Can you ask about data-collection techniques?[3]

5. *Validity.* Is the information at the site confirmed by information at other sites? One way to make certain that information is sound is to find it repeated at a number of different websites or in other sources. Does the work update other sources or add new information? A goal of researchers is to ensure that their information compels serious attention and acceptance; thus, it must be supported by generally accepted authorities.[4]

6. *Intuition.* Think clearly about the website you have chosen and the information found there. Websites are rarely refereed or reviewed; thus, you must be the judge. Avoid information from sources, for example, that use citations poorly. If sites are unsigned or badly written, this may be a sign that you should not use the information. Is the source too elementary, too technical, too advanced, or just right for your needs? Remember, even children publish on the Web. Does the information strongly or directly contradict other information you have found? Are there relevant and appropriate links to additional sites? Have you checked them out?

There are a number of websites which, for one reason or another, are unacceptable as reliable or valid sources of information for speeches. For example, many instructors still do not accept Wikipedia as a legitimate source for research. As noted above, Wikipedia is now achieving greater acceptance. In its original incarnation, entries could be altered by anyone, sources lacked their creator's name, articles could be vandalized, and articles, too, could be the subject of unchecked information. Because of this, entries could contain inaccurate information." It is always wise to check with your instructor regarding Internet sources that may be deemed unacceptable, and always apply *all* the evaluation criteria to any resource found on the Internet.

Citing Your Sources in Your Speech

Do not waste your research by failing to cite it in your speech. If you have done the research, citing it makes you and your information credible. There are several important ingredients of any verbal citation:

- The name of the person being quoted, or who wrote the article, or who authored the book, or who you interviewed.
- The qualifications of the person or author. What is it that makes him or her an expert? Why did you choose to quote this person in your speech?
- The name of the article, book, magazine, or journal.
- The date of the quotation or the piece being cited, or the date the interview took place.

For example, "Jane Smith, surgeon general of the United States, in her article on "The Health of American Citizens," said in last week's *Time* magazine, ..." If you are citing an Internet website you might say, Teresa Henley, author of the 2014 bestselling book *It's All About Accuracy*, said this on her Web page that is updated daily. . . . " Such citations give your listeners an opportunity to weigh and consider your sources, but probably even more important, they let your listeners know that you have done your homework. Obviously you need to record all relevant information about your sources as you go along.

Supporting Material: What to Look For

Once you know where to look, your next task is to begin searching for useful material. **Supporting material** is information that backs up your main point and provides the essential content of your speech. Four important guidelines should help direct your search. First, return to the specific purpose of your speech, and let that keep you focused and directed in your search. Second, keep your audience in mind. Find supporting material that you know will interest them. Third, try to find material that you know will hold listener attention. The better it is at holding attention, the easier your job of delivering your speech will be. Fourth, consider the short attention spans of your listeners. Use short narratives; much variety; little history; short explanations; clear, uncomplicated information—nothing that requires deep concentration; startling information that holds attention easily; a minimal amount of numbers; and numerous transitions and internal summaries.

Michael Kane, a psychologist at the University of North Carolina at Greensboro, sampled the thoughts of students at eight random times a day for a week, and he found, on average, "they were not thinking about what they were doing 30 percent of the time."[5] Kane said, "We regularly catch people's minds wandering before they've noticed it themselves."[6] The point of Kane's research is simple: Trying to keep your mind on target is quite a task for a lot of people. It reinforces the points made in the paragraph above—find supporting material that will not just interest your audience but will hold their attention as well.

ATTENTION!

Reality Check

It is often hard to believe that some piece of information you discover on the Internet might not be as credible, valid, or worthwhile as it might first appear. There are six major criteria under the section, "Evaluating Information on the Internet." These include reliability, authority, currency, objectivity, validity, and intuition. Do these make sense? Are they logical? Using the recent discovery of a piece of information you found on the Internet as an example, apply each of the six criteria to it. Are there any categories you have difficulty using? Did any of the categories not fit? If the stature of researchers can be measured by the quality of information they amass, do you think these categories truly ensure that you will gather material of high quality? Do you see how this can contribute to communicating effectively? Do you think it can make a significant difference?

Every speech you put together should have supporting material for the main content. In the sections that follow, we discuss types of supporting material: comparison, contrast, definition, examples, statistics, testimony, and polls.

Comparison

Comparisons point out the similarities between two or more things. For example, Kalyani, who spoke about the use of peer evaluation in one of her classes, used this comparison:

> *Think of peer evaluation as a reflection of real life. Like real life, it includes people who take it seriously and those who do not; opportunities to assist friends and hurt enemies; and even a wide range of possible, and often contradictory, viewpoints.*

Sometimes a comparison can show us a new way of looking at something. Mario Cuomo, in a graduation speech at Iona College, used a comparison he borrowed from the president of his alma mater, Father Flynn. Cuomo said he asked Flynn how he should approach his graduation speech:

> *"Commencement speakers," said Father Flynn, "should think of themselves as the body at an old-fashioned Irish wake. They need you in order to have the party, but nobody expects you to say very much."[7]*

Contrast

Contrasts point out the differences between two or more things. A contrast might reveal how using the Internet is different from using the library or how online medical advice is different from medical advice from one's private-practice, real-life doctor. Here, Avery Austin uses contrast in his classroom speech to show how coed dorms are different from single-sex dorms:

> *Students in coed dorms are far more likely than those in single-sex dorms to drink alcohol regularly, have a sexual partner, and engage in high-risk behavior.[8]*

Definition

A **definition** is a brief explanation of what a word or phrase means. Use definitions whenever you suspect that some people in your audience might not know what you are talking about. After you define something, it also might be appropriate to give an example. In the following speech excerpt, the student gives a definition followed by an example:

> *Fatigue is decreased ability of an organism to perform because of prolonged exertion. Have you ever studied and studied for a tough examination only to go into the examination completely tired out and exhausted?*

Examples

An **example** is a short illustration that clarifies a point. Commonly used in speeches, examples can come from personal experience, from research, or from imagination.

Barbara Oakley, a professor of engineering at Oakland University, used a personal example to open her article, "The Killer in the Lecture Hall,"[9] about what to do with deeply disturbed students on campus:

> *The sticky note on my door was wiggling. It was a gift from a student. Glued to the middle of it was a cockroach.*

STRATEGIC FLEXIBILITY

As you use your specific purpose for guidance, keep your audience in mind, find material that will hold listener attention, and realize listeners have short attention spans. Remain strategically flexible because it is your unique combination of material that will make your speech not only unique, but potentially outstanding.

Sean Gresh, executive communications consultant, delivered a speech to the Ipswich Rotary Club (Mass.) on August 30, 2012, entitled, "Inspiring to Win: A Leadership Lesson from a Corporate Speechwriter—A Great Leader Can't Lead Without Inspiring." After telling his audience that he had "been asked to share with [them] a few thoughts on what the Rotary means to me and what drives me personally and professionally," Gresh tells his listeners this:

> The best place to start and to finish is with stories. For when all is said and done, the stories we tell—and those we live—define us individually and collectively.
>
> The Nobel laureate Isaac Bashevis Singer described the essence of storytelling in his famous short story, "Naftali the Storyteller and His Horse, Sus."
>
> Naftali, a peasant, told Reb Zebulun, an old bookseller, "When I grow up, I'll travel to all the cities, towns and villages, and I'll sell storybooks everywhere, whether it pays or not . . . [and I will also] become a writer of storybooks." And Reb Zebulun responded, 'When a day passes, it is no longer there, what remains of it? Nothing more than a story. If stories weren't told or books weren't written, man would live like the beasts, only for the day…Today we live, but by tomorrow, today will be a story. The whole world, all human life is one long story."
>
> When you look back on your life, key themes emerge in the stories making up your life—your biggest challenges, your successes, your passions, your failures, the key persons in your life. Truth to tell, one really doesn't know what one's vocation in life is until his or her last chapter is told (p. 356).

Source: Gresh, Sean. (November, 2012). "Inspiring to win: A leadership lesson from a corporate speechwriter—A great leader can't lead without inspiring." *Vital Speeches of the Day,* LXXVIII: No. 11: 356–359.

Questions

1. What implications might this excerpt from Gresh's speech have for speakers?

2. When you look back on your own life, do you see some key themes that make up your life? Are there stories that truly shape who you are today? (your biggest challenges, your successes, your passions, your failures, or key people in your life?)

3. Do you agree with Isaac Bashevis Singer's essence of storytelling—that "if stories weren't told or books weren't written, man would live like the beasts, only for the day"?

Don't get me wrong. It wasn't that I was an unpopular professor. To the contrary—according to student evaluations, I might as well have had a sign on my forehead that said "Kindly."

I was told later that the cockroach was a symbol of love from—well, let's call him Rick. Rick had recently moved into the lab across the hall from my office, where he spent the night in a sleeping bag under one of the benches.

Rick, who had been a student for more than a decade, sometimes whiled away his time discussing guns and explosives with some of the more munitions-minded faculty members. He admitted that he kept his basement stocked with a variety of "armaments."

Sometimes speakers use **hypothetical examples**—examples that are made up—to illustrate a point. A speaker should always tell the audience if an example is hypothetical. The words *imagine yourself* cue the audience that the example is hypothetical:

Imagine yourself at the beach in the summer—the sand, the glistening water, and the sun beating down on you. As you sit up from your beach towel, you scan the beach and notice a sign that reads "Save the Whales!" That sign should also read

No matter the general or specific purpose of the speech, no matter the subject matter or occasion, and no matter the formality or informality of the presentation, examples are one of the best means for arousing interest and keeping attention.

"Save Your Skin!" Although the effects of tanning may not show up for 10 to 20 years, the health risks and problems that tanning causes can be serious.

Statistics

Statistics—facts in numerical form—have many uses in a speech. Being factual material, they are a convincing form of evidence. Quite often, a speaker who uses statistics is seen as someone who has done his or her homework.

In her speech, Rylee talked about the exploding national debt, and to impress her listeners about how big a trillion is, she used statistics. "It is 1 followed by 12 zeros," she said, "and if you spent a million dollars a day for a million days, it would take you 2,739 years to spend a trillion dollars. You have not lived a trillion seconds; the country has not existed for a trillion seconds, and Western civilization has not been around a trillion seconds. Four hundred fifty-four dollar bills weigh a pound. A trillion dollars weighs 2.2 billion pounds—over a million tons. An average-sized car weighs 2,500 pounds; a trillion dollars weighs the same as 880,000 cars. If you counted normally, 'one, two, three . . . ,' it would take you 95 years to count to one billion, and it would take you 200,000 years to count to one trillion."

Using the Internet, statistics are easy to find. There are numerous statistical sources available and most computer databases supported by your campus library, or libraries that make their information available to the public online, include statistical databases in their lists of reference works. Often, however, you don't have to make a special search for statistics; the sources you use for your speech will have figures you can use.

Rules for Using Statistics. Know Who Generated the Numbers and How. Notice that when you read or hear statistics, the first thing you usually find out is who, or what company, institution, or business, generated the numbers. It is helpful to know not only who produced them but how they were created. For example, results from a sampling of 10 students do not carry as much weight or significance as from a sampling of a thousand. If those thousand students are distributed across the nation, the weight and significance increases again.

Use the Best Possible Sources:	The headline "World's Food Supply Failing to Keep Pace" will be much more believable if it comes from *The New York Times* than from one of the tabloid newspapers by the checkout stand in your local supermarket. Get your statistics from well-respected sources.
Make Sure the Information Is Up to Date:	Figures on military spending in 2008 are useless—unless you want to compare them with figures for the current year. If you do this, you must account for inflation.
Use Statistics That Show Trends:	We can often tell what is happening to an institution or even a country if we have information from one year to another. There is even a Trends Research Institute, based in Rhinebeck, New York, with its own *Trends Journal,* designed to follow major trends in every area of life.[10]

Mia Ashley talked about reducing your portion sizes and the importance of a regular exercise routine to either lose or maintain proper weight. As part of her speech, she discussed foods to fight cancer, and here she quoted Jane Brody writing on personal health in *The New York Times.*[11]

> *Based on 7,000 studies of 17 kinds of cancer, it [the World Cancer Research Fund] concluded that being overweight now ranks second only to smoking as a preventable cause of cancer. "Convincing evidence" of an increased risk resulting from body fatness was found for cancers of the kidney, endometrium, breast, colon and rectum, pancreas and esophagus.*
>
> *Other major findings of increased risk included red and processed meats for colon and rectal cancer, and alcoholic drinks for cancers of the mouth, throat, larynx, esophagus, breast, and colon and rectum.*

Use Concrete Images:	When your numbers are large and may be hard to comprehend, using concrete images is helpful. William Franklin,[12] president of Franklin International, Ltd., speaking to members of the Graduate School of Business at the Japan Business Association and International Business Society in New York, reduced demographic information he had to the following:

> *If we shrink the world's 5.7 billion population to a village of 100 people—with all existing human ratios remaining the same—here is the resulting profile.*
>
> *Of these 100 people, 57 are Asian, 21 European, 14 from North and South America, and 8 from Africa.*

ATTENTION!

Functions of Supporting Material

1. It helps clarify the speaker's point.
2. It emphasizes the important points of the speech.
3. It makes the points of the speech more interesting.
4. It provides the foundation for audience belief in the speaker's point(s).
5. Without supporting material, speeches are strings of assertions (claims without backing).[13]

51 female, 49 male

80 live in substandard housing.

70 cannot read.

Half suffer from malnutrition.

75 have never made a phone call.

Less than 1 is on the Internet.

Half the entire village's wealth would be in the hands of 6 people.

Only 1 of the 100 has a college education.

You are in a very elite group of only 1 percent who have a college education.[14]

Testimony

When you cite **testimony,** you use another person's statements or actions to give authority to what you are saying. Experts are the best sources of testimony. Suppose you are planning to speak about NCAA violations and you get some information from the athletic director of your school. When you use this information in your speech, tell your audience where it came from. Because the information is from an expert, your speech will have more authority and be more convincing than it would be if you presented only your own opinions.

Testimony can also be used to show that people who are prominent and admired believe and support your ideas. For example, if you want to persuade your audience to take up swimming for fitness, it might be useful to mention some famous athletes who swim to stay fit. If you want people to sign your petition to build a new city park, mention other citizens who are also supporting the park.

If you use quotations, keep them short and to the point. If they are too lengthy, your speech could end up sounding like everyone but yourself. If you have quotations that are long and wordy, put them into your own words. Whether you quote or paraphrase, always give credit to your source. In her speech "We, The People: Prize and Embrace What Is America," Farah M. Walters, president and CEO of University Hospitals Health System and University Hospitals of Cleveland, used the words of Eleanor Roosevelt, who said, "As individuals, we live cooperatively and, to the best of our ability, serve the community in which we live. Our own success, to be real, must contribute to the success of others. When you cease to make a contribution, you die."[15]

Polls

Polls are surveys of people's attitudes, beliefs, and behavior. Quite often they are conducted on controversial subjects. If you want to know how the U.S. public feels about Social Security, abortion, or the war on terrorism, you can probably find a poll that tells you. National polls can also provide useful information about what particular segments of the population think or know about an issue.

A single poll may yield far more information than is necessary for a speech. You must decide how much or how little to use. Try to select responses that will appeal precisely to your listeners' ages and socioeconomic circumstances.

When your statistics come from a survey, it is important to find out how many and what kinds of people were questioned. For example, if you discovered survey results saying that 30 percent of the U.S. public eats with chopsticks, you might find the statistic fairly startling and be tempted to use it—until you note that the survey included only 100 people and that many of them were Chinese immigrants.

Spend Time Pondering What You Have Uncovered

At the end of your investigation you are likely to end up with far more material than you can possibly use in a single speech. Using the strategic flexibility framework, you have probably already anticipated, assessed, and evaluated as you moved through the research phase of your preparation. Now comes the selection process.

The more you have to select from, the more precise you can be. Take time to think first, and then decide: (1) What material will best meet your specific purpose? (2) What material do you know for sure will interest listeners? (3) What material will hold their attention? (4) In what ways can you appeal to your stimulation-saturated listeners?

If you have maintained a sharp focus on your audience *throughout* the entire process of framing your specific purpose and central idea, as well as when finding important and relevant information to support your ideas, answering these four questions, as you ponder what you have uncovered, will not only be easy to do, but it will be rewarding as well. It can go a long way in 1) strengthening your confidence in these early stages of speech preparation, 2) reducing any fear or anxiety that may accompany your thoughts about giving a public speech, and 3) providing a clear, distinct, and straightforward path through the remaining stages of speech preparation.

Do You Have Confidence as a Speaker?

For each statement circle the answer that best represents your feelings about your *most recent* speech, either "True" or "False." Work quickly and don't spend much time on any statement. We want your *first impression* on this survey.

1. I look forward to an opportunity to speak in public.	True	False
2. My hands tremble when I try to handle objects on the lectern.	True	False
3. I am in constant fear of forgetting my speech.	True	False
4. Audiences seem friendly when I address them.	True	False
5. While preparing a speech I am in a constant state of anxiety.	True	False
6. At the conclusion of a speech I feel that I have had a pleasant experience.	True	False
7. I dislike using my body and voice expressively.	True	False
8. My thoughts become confused and jumbled when I speak before an audience.	True	False
9. I have no fear of facing an audience.	True	False
10. Although I am nervous just before getting up to speak I soon forget my fears and enjoy the experience.	True	False
11. I face the prospect of making a speech with complete confidence.	True	False
12. I feel that I am in complete possession of myself while speaking.	True	False
13. I prefer to have notes on the platform in case I forget my speech.	True	False
14. I like to observe the reactions of my audience to my speech.	True	False
15. Although I talk fluently with friends I am at a loss for words on the platform.	True	False
16. I feel relaxed and comfortable while speaking.	True	False
17. Although I do not enjoy speaking in public I do not particularly dread it.	True	False
18. I always avoid speaking in public if possible.	True	False
19. The faces of my audience members are blurred when I look at them.	True	False
20. I feel disgusted with myself after trying to address a group of people.	True	False
21. I enjoy preparing a talk.	True	False
22. My mind is clear when I face an audience.	True	False
23. I am fairly fluent.	True	False
24. I perspire and tremble just before getting up to speak.	True	False
25. My posture feels strained and unnatural.	True	False
26. I am fearful and tense all the while I am speaking before a group of people.	True	False
27. I find the prospect of speaking mildly pleasant.	True	False

28. It is difficult for me to search my mind calmly for the right words to express my thoughts.　　　　True　　　False

29. I am terrified at the thought of speaking before a group of people.　　　　True　　　False

30. I have a feeling of alertness in facing an audience.　　　　True　　　False

Go to the Online Learning Center at **www.mhhe.com/hybels11e** to see your results and learn how to evaluate your attitudes and feelings.

Source: Insight vs Desensitization in Psychotherapy by G. L. Paul in *Measures Of Personality And Social Psychological Attitudes*, pp. 188–190 by J. P. Robinson, P. R. Shaver and L. S. Wrightsmen, 1991. Copyright © 1966 by the Board of Trustees of the Leland Stanford Jr. University, renewed 1994. All rights reserved. Used with the permission of Stanford University Press, www.sup.org.

Summary

To be an effective public speaker, you need knowledge, preparation, and delivery. It is important that everything you do as a public speaker is rooted in knowledge because practicing skill without knowledge is a fruitless endeavor.

After knowledge, preparation is the second major component of effective public speaking. Whenever you are scheduled to make a speech it is important to find a topic that interests you. Begin your search by making a personal inventory and consult newspapers, books, magazines, interviews with others, and indices to magazines and journals, along with the Internet.

Narrow your topic by brainstorming narrower aspects, writing down those ideas, then asking which ones will be of interest to and understood by your audience. Consider also what your assignment requires and how long you have to cover your topic.

Every speech should have a general purpose, a specific purpose, and a central idea. The general purpose relates to whether the speech is informative or persuasive. The specific purpose focuses on what you want to inform or persuade your audience about—or what you want your listeners to achieve as a result of your effort. The central idea captures the main idea of the speech—the specific idea you want listeners to retain after your speech.

Audience analysis is the process of finding out what your listeners know about your subject, what they might be interested in, what their attitudes and beliefs are, and what kinds of people are likely to be present. Useful demographic information about your audience includes age, gender, education, occupation, race/nationality/ethnic origin, geographic location, and group affiliations.

Analysis of the occasion should accompany your assessment of the audience. Time involves the time frame for the speech, time of day, and the length of time of your speech. Place refers to the physical stage for your speech and your interaction with your listeners. Channel is the route traveled by your signal as it moves from one location to another. Purpose refers to your specific purpose, that statement that tells precisely what you want to accomplish.

When you are putting together material for your speech, a good place to start is to ask yourself whether you have had any direct experience with the subject; however, personal experience is not research nor should it substitute for it. Put yourself in your listeners' position. Ask yourself how much research your listeners need and what kind of research is likely to be most effective.

When researching your topic, you should use interviews with others, the library, and the Internet. Always evaluate the quality of Internet information on the basis of reliability, authority, currency, objectivity, validity, and your own intuition.

Supporting material includes comparisons, contrasts, definitions, examples, statistics, testimony, and polls. Once you have gathered all your supporting material, you need to spend time pondering what you've uncovered and, too, remember that you need to find supporting material that will not just interest your audience but will hold their attention as well.

Key Terms and Concepts

Use the Online Learning Center at www.mhhe.com/hybels11e to further your understanding of the following terms.

Questions to Review

1. What justifications are there for studying public speaking?

2. Why is having knowledge about public speaking so important to growth, development, and change in expanding public-speaking skills?

3. What are the elements that need to be considered in selecting a topic for a speech?

4. What is it that distinguishes among general purpose, specific purpose, and central idea?

5. What contribution does strategic flexibility make to analyzing the audience?

6. What are the most effective ways to gain knowledge about your listeners?

7. What must be discovered about your audience? Is it clear to you why information about your listeners is so important in the planning and preparation of your speech?

8. When you analyze a speech occasion, what are the most important factors to consider?

9. What are the advantages and cautions of using personal experience and observation?

10. In researching your topic, what are the places you have available to you for looking for information?

11. What are some of the ways you can use to jump-start your creative spirit?

12. What are the specific questions you need to ask to make certain the information you get from the Internet is of high quality?

13. Why should you cite your research sources in your speech? How should you do this?

14. What are the four guidelines that should help direct your search for supporting material for your speech?

15. What are the differences among comparison, contrast, examples, statistics, testimony, and polls? What are the benefits of using a variety of different kinds of supporting material for a speech?

Go to the self-quizzes on the Online Learning Center at www.mhhe.com/hybels11e to test your knowledge of the chapter contents.

CHAPTER THIRTEEN

Organizing and Outlining the Speech

Objectives

After reading this chapter, you should be able to:

- Organize and outline your speech.

- Identify the five patterns of organization for a speech, and choose the best one for your purpose.

- Use both full-sentence and keyword formats to outline a speech.

- Explain the functions of speech introductions and conclusions, and be able to write one of each.

- Explain the function of transitions and be able to write them.

S OFIA DECIDED THAT EACH MAIN HEAD IN THE BODY OF HER speech about reducing test anxiety would be one phase in dealing with anxiety, and within that phase she would mention a number of methods. Although her single bold point would be that there are specific, simple ways for dealing with anxiety, she also knew that one of the best methods was to start early and maintain both your mental and physical health.

Sofia decided to deal with three phases: (1) long-range planning, (2) short-range planning, and (3) the day of the test. Given her time limit (five minutes), she decided she would have to keep the information under each main point brief, but she would try to deal with some methods she could illustrate with a personal experience or an example—to maintain listener interest.

Sofia separated her information into three piles. As she was dividing up the information, she discovered some that would work for the introduction and conclusion to her speech, and she labeled it at once so she wouldn't forget. Because she was working at her computer, Sofia began typing a rough draft of her outline. She knew it was early, but having an outline allowed her to discard information that was not relevant, focus specifically and intently on information she wanted to include, and organize her thinking at this early stage.

I. There is an important long-range approach for dealing with test anxiety.
   A. Maintain your physical health through exercise, diet, and rest.[1]
   B. Sustain your mental health by focusing on past testing successes and engaging in positive self-talk.[2]
   C. Bolster your confidence by believing you will do well, knowing the information backward and forward, taking self-tests, and having another student quiz you.[3] Not one website I visited failed to mention the importance of good study habits.

II. The short-range approach for dealing with test anxiety is more familiar to us all.
   A. "Preparation is the best way to minimize anxiety."[4]
   B. Create a study plan by determining how much time you have and how much you have to study. How much material will you cover in each session? When are the review sessions?[5]
   C. Try to anticipate the test by asking yourself what questions may be asked and answering them by integrating ideas from your lectures, notes, texts, and supplementary readings.[6]
   D. Begin a program of positive self-talk: "I am smart enough." "I am capable." "I am ready and I can perform well." Use such statements to block out negative and self-defeating comments.[7]

III. There are important last-minute activities you can engage in to relieve test anxiety on the day of and at the test.
   A. Be rested and comfortable; you must be psychologically and physically alert to perform well.[8]
   B. Know what to expect. Learn ahead of time the kind of test it will be, where and when it will be held, and what materials to bring. This helps eliminate the element of surprise.[9]

C. Relax as much as you can by using deep-breathing exercises, imagery, visualization, and muscle relaxation techniques to increase your focus and concentration.[10]

D. Avoid contact with others—especially worried test takers. Test anxiety is contagious and unproductive.[11]

E. Read the test instructions carefully; *make sure your copy of the test is complete* (that there are no pages missing); answer the easiest questions first; read each question carefully; review the test questions and your answers to them before you turn in your test.[12]

Sofia filled in the details of her outline, and wrote it out completely for her instructor. She condensed the outline to just keywords and put them on several 3 × 5–inch cards. She began practicing her speech using the cards. Because she had been so thorough in her research, she was so familiar with her material, and she had chosen an important and relevant topic, she could speak on it conversationally and comfortably without having to rely on her note cards (see Figure 13-1).

When the time came to give her speech, her delivery was smooth. Sofia felt strong and in control. The structure of her speech was easy for her to remember and instantly intelligible to her listeners. After the speech, several classmates told her she had done a terrific job.

I. Long-range
   A. Exercise, diet, and rest (Mann & Lash, 2004)
   B. Past testing successes (Probert, 2003)
   C. Believe, know info, take self-tests, be quizzed (Muskingum Center for Advancement of Learning)

II. Short-range
   A. Preparation (SUNY Potsdam Counseling Center)
   B. Study plan (Penn. State University)
   C. Anticipate test (SUNY Potsdam)
   D. Self-talk (Probert, 2003)

III. Last-minute
   A. Psych. & phys. alert (Mann & Lash, 2004)
   B. Elim. surprise. (Academic Services, Southwestern University)
   C. Deep-breathing, imagery, vis. (Mann & Lash, 2004)
   D. Avoid contact (U of IL Counseling Center)
   E. Read inst., copy complete, answer easy ques., read ques., review (U of FL Counseling)

Figure 13-1
Sofia's Keyword Outline

Notice two things: (1) Her entire outline of the body of her speech would fit on three 3 × 5–inch cards, and (2) she has placed her sources on the card too, so she doesn't forget to cite them in the verbal portion of her speech.

Principles of Organization

Relate Points to Your Specific Purpose and Central Idea

< www.mhhe.com/hybels11e

For help in outlining your material, use the computerized "Outline Tutor" on the book's website.

The points you make in your speech should relate directly to your specific purpose and central idea. In this outline of a speech titled "The Challenge to Excel," notice that all the main points do this:

Specific purpose:	To inform my classmates about the four things required to excel.
Central idea:	No matter what people's abilities are, there are four things they can do to excel.
Main ideas:	I. Learn self-discipline.
	II. Build a knowledge base.
	III. Develop special skills.
	IV. Bounce back from defeat.

Distinguish Between Main and Minor Points

When organizing your speech, distinguish between main points and minor points. If you do this, the speech will flow more naturally and will seem logical to your listeners. The **main points** are all the broad, general ideas and information that support your central idea; the **minor points** are the specific ideas and information that support the main points. Say that the purpose of your speech is to persuade audience members to learn to incorporate computer-generated graphics in their research papers. The central idea of your speech is that they can illustrate their ideas better and more efficiently by using a computer. Your main point would have this broad, general idea: "Computers help you draw faster, revise drawings more easily, and produce a better-looking, better-illustrated paper." Your minor points will explain the main point in more specific terms: (1) Most people do not draw very well; (2) a computer enables you to draw like a professional, even if you don't have drawing skills; and (3) revising and changing drawings is easy and efficient. All these minor points help explain the ways in which the computer is more effective and efficient for illustrating ideas.

If you have difficulty distinguishing between major and minor points, write each of the points you want to make on a separate index card. Then spread out all the cards in front of you and organize them by main points, with minor points coming under them. If one arrangement doesn't work, try another.

Phrase All Points in Full Sentences

Writing all your points in full sentences will help you think out your ideas more fully. Once your ideas are set out in this detailed way, you will be able to discover problems in organization that might need more work.

Give All Points a Parallel Structure

Parallel structure means that each of your points will be in the same grammatical form. For example, on a speech about alcohol, the speaker started each suggestion with the words *what alcohol* followed by a verb.

What alcohol is.

What alcohol feels like.

What alcohol does to your body.

In his speech "Sustainability," Richard Lamm, former governor of Colorado, used parallel structure in this manner:

> *Our globe is warming, our forests are shrinking, our water tables are falling, our icecaps are melting, our coral is dying, and our fisheries are collapsing. Our soils are eroding, our wetlands are disappearing, our deserts are encroaching, and our finite water is more and more in demand. I suspect these to be the early warning signs of a world approaching its carrying capacity. We cannot call upon the lessons of history to help us evaluate the seriousness of these problems because it is an entirely new paradigm. Ecologically we are sailing on uncharted waters while moving at unprecedented speed. We have lost our anchor and our navigational instruments are out of date.[13]*

Patterns of Organization

Once you have researched your speech, decided on a specific purpose, and listed the main points, you are ready to choose an organizational pattern. This organizational pattern will mainly affect the **body**—the main part of the speech. (Introductions and conclusions are discussed later in the chapter.)

The body of the speech is made up of your main points. Most classroom speeches should not have more than four or five main points, and many will have no more than two or three. If you want to cover a topic in depth, use fewer main points. If you want to give a broad, general view, you might want to use four or five main points.

In this section we discuss five possible arrangements of main points: time order, spatial order, cause-and-effect order, problem–solution order, and topical order.

Time Order

Time order, or *chronological order,* is used to show development over time. This pattern works particularly well when you want to use a historical approach. For example, in a speech about what to do if you are the victim of a crime, the speaker arranged her main points in chronological order:

Specific purpose:	To inform my audience members about what to do if they are victims of a crime.
Central idea:	If you become a victim of a crime, there are some things you should do.
Main points:	I. Try not to panic.
	II. Attract attention; scream or yell "Fire!"
	III. Protect your own safety; if there is a weapon or you don't know whether there is, don't resist. If there is no weapon, fight back, kick, or run.
	IV. Report all crimes immediately to the police; don't disturb any evidence.

STRATEGIC FLEXIBILITY

Although strategic flexibility is important throughout the organizing and outlining process, there are several key points when it becomes crucial. Selecting the method you use to arrange the main points in your speech is certainly one of them.

The speech topic, the audience, and the amount of time available are factors to consider when determining your pattern of organization.

Spatial Order

When you use **spatial order,** you refer to a physical or geographical layout to help your audience see how the parts make up the whole. To help your audience visualize your subject, you explain it by going from left to right or from top to bottom, or in any direction that best suits your subject.

For example, a student decided that spatial order was the best way to explain how speakers should "stage" their presentations to include the use of visuals such as slides, overheads, movies, or computer displays. She organized her speech around three aspects of a speaker's presentational environment.

Specific purpose:	To inform audience members about how to be fully effective by staging their presentations.
Central idea:	Speakers need to approach their environment from three angles: space, lighting, and mechanics.
Main points:	I. Speakers should control the space as much as possible (location of speaker, screen, and visuals).
	II. Speakers must have control over the lighting, since proper lighting is important to relaxed viewing.
	III. Speakers must have control over the mechanics of how projection systems work and where controls are located.

Notice how the speaker moved from the largest aspect of presentational concern—space—to the next smaller concern—lighting—to the smallest or most defined concern—location of the mechanics of controlling the equipment. This is a well-thought-out spatial order.

Cause-and-Effect Order

A speaker who uses **cause-and-effect order** divides a speech into two major parts: cause (why something is happening) and effect (what impact it is having). Notice the cause-and-effect order revealed in items I and II under "main points" in the following outline:

Specific purpose:	To inform my audience about the possible effects of tattoos and body piercings.
Central idea:	Everyone needs to be aware of the health risks posed by such body modification practices, including physical disfigurement, bacterial and viral infections, along with blood-borne pathogens like HIV and the C and B forms of the hepatitis virus.
Main points:	I. Tattoos and body piercings have become so common that they hardly attract notice. One recent study of 7,960 college students in Texas found that one in five had at least one tattoo or piercing of a body part other than the earlobe.
	II. Dr. Scott Hammer, professor of medicine at Columbia College of Physicians and Surgeons, estimated that 1 piercing in 10 becomes infected. Staphylococcus bacteria, which can live on the skin and in the nose, is a frequent cause.[14]

Problem–Solution Order

Like speakers who use a cause-and-effect arrangement, a speaker who uses a **problem–solution order** also divides a speech into two sections. In this case, one part deals with the problem and the other deals with the solution. For example, look at this outline for a speech titled "Lose Weight Fast":

Specific purpose:	To inform audience members that by eating a high-fiber diet, moving around, and pumping iron, they can lose weight fast.
Central idea:	You don't have to starve yourself, become a competitive athlete, or engage in other extraordinary measures in order to drop unwanted weight.
Main points:	I. When I asked how many in here would like to shed 10 pounds fast, you all raised your hands, but unfortunately there are too many highly hyped, too-good-to-be-true diets and fads that are unsafe. Some diets are safe and reputable; others are not.
	II. You can eat as much as you want of vegetables, fresh fruits, grains, and unrefined starches. Rather than taking special programs in aerobics or dancing, you need to make movement, such as increased walking, a regular and habitual part of your daily activities. You need to change fat into muscle by regular (20-minute) strength-training routines.

This will be a tough AOM to accomplish, but if this chapter on organizing and outlining speeches is to make an indelible impression, you must take the opportunity to apply the information by analyzing the organizing and outlining accomplished by another or other speakers.

For the purposes of this AOM exercise, select one of your lecturers, a teacher in another class, or a student who must give a speech in another of your classes. It is easier to be open-minded when there is no present (or future?) relationship between yourself, the person you are critiquing, and the person to whom you may or may not be submitting your analysis.

Use the following questions to guide your critique:

1. Who spoke, what did he or she speak about, and where did this event occur?

2. Is it clear to you that this speech was a prepared effort as opposed to a spontaneous one? How can you tell?

3. Did the speaker follow an outline, or, if he or she used a manuscript, did the speech appear well organized? In what way(s)?

4. What pattern(s) of organization was followed?

5. Were the introduction, conclusion, and transitions clear? Can you cite an example or two?

6. If you were to give a suggestion or two to this speaker regarding *just* the organization of his or her speech, what would your suggestion(s) be?

The problem-solution order is best for persuasive speeches—although, as just demonstrated, it can be used for informative speeches too. Here is an example of a persuasive speech using the problem-solving approach.

Specific purpose: To persuade audience members that habits of creative thinking, hard work, and an enthusiastic spirit will achieve success.

Central idea: In our fast-paced, highly competitive society, where jobs are scarce, flexibility is essential, and willingness to learn crucial, there are three basic skills necessary.

Main points:
I. Develop your creativity by taking different views, asking searching questions, and being an idea generator.

II. Reveal a solid work ethic by being reliable, having initiative, and maintaining social skills.

III. Convey an enthusiastic spirit by becoming actively involved, reaching realistic goals, and celebrating achievements.

Topical Order

You can use a **topical order** whenever your subject can be grouped logically into subtopics. Here are some examples: four ways to save money for college, inexpensive ways to travel abroad, five foods that help you live longer.

In the next sample, a student uses a topical order in a speech titled "Native Americans."

Specific purpose: To inform my audience about the importance of family in Native American culture.

Central idea: To protect their values, continue their traditions, and maintain their families, Native American tribes are trying to keep children from being adopted by outsiders.

Main points:
   I. Native American tribes have values that are different from those of mainstream American society.

   II. Native Americans believe their traditions will die out if their children are adopted by outsiders.

   III. Native Americans want to maintain their families, for values and traditions must be taught to children while they are young.

Preparing an Outline

An **outline** is a way of organizing material so you can see all the parts and how they relate to the whole. Outlining your speech will help you organize your thoughts and discover where your presentation might cause problems in structure.

The Outline Format

Your speech will be organized into an introduction, a body, and a conclusion (with transitions connecting them). Since the introduction and the conclusion deal with so few points, they are usually not outlined, although some people prefer to outline them. As previously noted, outlining can help you see whether all essential parts are included. This is especially important for beginning speakers. We use Roman numerals to designate the main points of the body of the speech, as demonstrated in the examples of speech organization.

Main and Supporting Points

The outline sets forth the major portion of the speech—the body—and shows the content's organization into main and supporting (minor) points. Remember that the broad, general statements are the main points; the minor points contain the more specific information that elaborates on and supports the main points.

Standard Symbols and Indentation

All outlines use the same system of symbols. The main points are numbered with Roman numerals (I, II, III) and capital letters (A, B, C). Minor, more specific points are numbered with Arabic numerals (1, 2, 3) and lowercase letters (a, b, c). The most important material is always closest to the left-hand margin; as material gets less important, it moves to the right. Note, then, that the outline format moves information from the general to the more specific through the use of numbers, letters, and indentation:

   I. *University*
       A. *College of Arts and Sciences*
         1. *English*
         2. *History*
         3. *Mathematics*

ATTENTION!

Benefits of Outlining

1. To organize ideas without excess verbiage.
2. To keep you from being sidetracked from your intent.
3. Keeps your organization easy to see.
4. Nicely displays the information you have.
5. Let's you see what information you still need.
6. Gives you a quick picture of how your ideas fit together.
7. Tells you in a nutshell whether or not you are achieving your purpose.[15]

Reality Check

You have read information on principles and patterns of organization as well as preparing an outline. Most of the time when you deliver speeches in other classes and in the "real world," you will not need to present an outline. It will be the speech that is more important. Does the information in these three sections make sense? Is it logical? Do you think it contributes significantly to communicating effectively? Knowing what you do now about organizing and outlining, when you are asked to give a speech in another class or in the "real world," what information in these sections is likely to be most valuable for you? What are *you* likely to use in the future? Can you see, specifically, how it will help *you* be a more effective communicator?

    4. *Psychology*
    5. *Science*
  B. *College of Business Administration*
    1. *Accounting*
    2. *Economics*
    3. *Finance*
    4. *General Business*
  C. *College of Education*
    1. *Early Childhood Education*
    2. *Elementary Education*
    3. *Secondary Education*
    4. *Special Education*

Another thing you should note about the outline format is that there should always be at least two points of the same level. That is, you can't have just an A and no B; you can't have just a 1 and no 2. The only exception to this is that in a one-point speech, you would have only one main point.

Full-Sentence and Keyword Outlines

There are two major types of outlines: full-sentence and keyword. A **full-sentence outline** is a complete map of what the speech will look like. All the ideas are stated in full sentences. In a full-sentence outline it is easy to spot problem areas and weaknesses in the structure, support, and flow of ideas. This type of outline is useful as you plan and develop your speech.

Keyword outlines give only the important words and phrases; their main function is to remind the speaker of his or her ideas when delivering the speech. Sometimes speakers will add statistics, quotations, or sources to keyword outlines when such information is too long or too complicated to memorize or they simply need reminders. Some speakers prepare a full-sentence outline on the left and a keyword outline on the right, as in the following example. The keyword outline enables the speaker to avoid having to look at his or her notes all the time.

Produce should be carefully washed before you eat it.	Wash produce
Breads without preservatives should be refrigerated.	Refrigerate bread
Meat should not be eaten raw.	No raw meat

The main points (whether presented in full sentences or by keywords) are sometimes put onto cards—one to a card. We discuss the reasons for this in Chapter 14, Delivering the Speech.

The Speech Introduction

The **introduction** is the opening statement of your speech. It gives the audience members their first impression of you, it introduces them to the topic, and it motivates them to listen. If you don't hook audience members in the beginning, you might never get their attention.

Outlining an introduction would be especially valuable to beginning speakers who want to make certain everything important is included. If you have a wonderful idea

An "advance organizer" is simply a review for listeners of what is to come in the speech. It's simply a sentence about each of the main topics that is just sufficient enough to get listeners thinking. Art Markman, the Annabel Irion Worsham Centerrial Professor of Psychology and Marketing at the University of Texas, in his book, *Smart Thinking*, talks about one of the purposes of the advance organizer:

> One purpose of the advance organizer is to get people prepared to use some of their existing knowledge. It is crucial that people attach new knowledge to things they already know. Giving people information about what will be coming in your presentation gives them the opportunity to activate the knowledge they already have in preparation for learning. In the interests of time, my colleagues often dive into their talks without preparing the audience. So, it takes awhile for people listening to the talk to figure out *how to connect the content to things they already know (p. 82).*

Source: Markman, Art. (2012). *Smart thinking: Three essential keys to solve problems, innovate, and get things done.* New York: A Perigee Book (Published by the Penguin Group).

Questions

1. Can you see the value of an advance organizer to a speech? What would you say is the greatest advantage or benefit of an advance organizer?

2. What is the ideal number of main points you should try to cover in a speech? In what way does this number relate to an advance organizer?

3. What is the role that you, as a speaker, have in focusing listener attention, keeping their attention throughout a speech, and making certain that they understand your main points?

for one, use it. If you need some guidance, try to use some or all of the following techniques in your introduction:

Get attention.

Announce your topic.

Preview your central idea and main points.

Establish your credibility.

Get Attention

In addition to telling your audience what you are going to talk about, your introduction should arouse attention and interest. Gaining attention is not just a matter of getting audience members to listen to your first words—they would probably do that anyway. Rather, it is a matter of creating interest in your subject. You want your listeners to think, "This really sounds like an interesting subject" or "I am going to enjoy listening to this speech."

Notice in the following example how Sofia Mena began her speech "Dealing with Test Anxiety." She designed her introduction to get the attention of her listeners:

> I have heard it over and over again until I am getting sick of it. "It's just not fair. I didn't ask to be here. I don't deserve this kind of treatment." Have you heard students saying things like this? Although my speech today is titled "Dealing with Test Anxiety," it could just as well be called "Taking Responsibility for Your Life." Throughout my speech today, I want you all to keep one thought in the back of your mind: You are responsible for your own learning.

349

STRATEGIC

FLEXIBILITY

Another key point when strategic flexibility becomes crucial in the organizing and outlining of your speech is when you construct your speech introduction. Your introduction sets the tone for your entire speech; thus, you must bring all your skills to the task of carefully planning and preparing it.

Certain techniques are proven attention getters. Let's look at others and at the functions they serve. Note that sometimes a speaker might use more than one of these techniques.

Use Humor

Research shows that speeches with some humor produce a more favorable reaction to the speaker.[16] Often a speaker will use humor in his or her introduction. Notice how Garrison Keillor, no stranger to humor himself as the creator and host of *A Prairie Home Companion*—the radio program centered on the events of the fictional town of Lake Wobegon, Minnesota—began his commencement address to Gettysburg College:

> *I bring you greetings from Lake Wobegon, to all of you in the German branch of the Lutheran Church—we pray for you daily without ceasing. It's a great pleasure for all of us on this platform to be part of your day—the Class of '87. And to be here as witnesses at this grave and solemn moment in your lives.*
>
> *When I graduated from college, I sat about where you are and watched a candidate for summa cum laude honors walk up the stairs to be recognized, and step on the inside hem of his gown. And walk all the way up the inside of it. It was something that we all remembered, who saw it, as an object lesson in how talent and intelligence might fare in this world. And some of us had tears in our eyes as we saw it.[17]*

Use an Example

Short examples often work quite well in introductions. They may be personal examples, or they could have happened to someone else. A student used this example to spark interest in her speech:

> *Gilbert is 42 years old. He has three children, ages 17, 10, and 4. Gilbert never read to his two oldest children or helped them with their schoolwork. If they asked for help with reading, Gilbert's reply was, "Ask your mother." Last week everything changed. Gilbert read* The Cat in the Hat *to his four-year-old. It was the first time Gilbert had ever read to one of his children. In fact, it was the first time Gilbert had read anything aloud at all.*
>
> *Gilbert had been illiterate. For the past four months he has been learning to read through a program in the literacy council. I am Gilbert's teacher.*

Refer to the Occasion

If you are asked to speak for a special occasion or if a special occasion falls on the day you are speaking, make a reference to it, as when a speaker said, "I am very honored to have been asked to give a speech for Founders' Day."

Because the introduction to your speech is so important, it is worthwhile to spend extra time trying to find something unique or unusual. This is especially true when the speech is a traditional one, like a commencement speech, and the attention of audience members is likely to be seriously divided between the speaker and many potential diversions. Here is how Robert L. Dilenschneider, president and CEO, The Dilenschneider Group, chose to face the challenge in his commencement address at Muskingum College, New Concord, Ohio:

> *Thank you very much. Muskingum is a great place. I am privileged to be here. And I am thrilled that you asked me to speak today. Thank you. When I took suggestions on what to say here today, two pieces of advice stuck with me.*

First, my two sons, 15-year-old Geoffrey, and 11-year-old Peter, said, "Keep it short, crisp, and to the point." They reminded me of Robert DeNiro's talk at New York University several years ago when the actor stood up and told several thousand students, faculty, and parents, "Break a leg."

And then DeNiro sat down.

The second thought came from a friend in Ireland who said, "The students have been lectured to for four years. Don't give them another lecture. They want to get on with the day and their lives."[18]

Show the Importance of the Subject

Showing audience members that the subject is important to their own lives is a good way of getting and keeping attention. In the following example, not only does the student let her listeners know how important the subject is to them, but she also keeps their attention by building suspense:

Getting the attention of your audience is a matter of creating interest in your topic.

If I asked you right now, how many of you have done what I am going to talk about today, every one of you would raise your hand. This is a topic that affects everyone. Sometimes it nags at us day in and day out. Often it creates a negative spiral of fear of failure, self-doubt, feelings of inadequacy, anxiety over the expectations others have of us, and even feelings of being overwhelmed—that tasks seem unmanageable and that we are overextended—by trying to manage too much. All this takes a serious toll on us physically, mentally, and emotionally. We even have some wonderful mental self-seductions for tolerating the discomfort: "I'll do it tomorrow," "What's the harm of a half-hour of TV now? I've still got time," or "I deserve some time for myself." What is this thing that makes us feel we have lost control over our day-to-day routine? It is procrastination.

Use Startling Information

Using information that startles or surprises your audience is a good device for gaining attention. The only caution is that you do not overdo it because it will lose its effect.

A student began her speech using startling information in this way:

How often have you said "I'm stressed out," or "I'm under way too much stress"? It really doesn't matter whether it's too much to do, not enough sleep, a poor diet, or having to give a speech. Of course, it could just as easily be about money, a loved one's illness, failing an exam. If any of this fits you, realize that if it is or becomes prolonged, according to Melinda Smith, Ellen Jaffe-Gill, and Dr. Jeanne Segal, at their HelpGuide.org website, updated in July 2013, "Chronic stress disrupts nearly every system in your body. It can raise blood pressure, suppress the immune system, increase the risk of heart attack and stroke, contribute to infertility, and speed up the aging process. Long-term stress can even rewire the brain, leaving you more vulnerable to anxiety and depression." Subjects exposed to stress, according to some websites I'll introduce you to momentarily, showed increases in infection rates from 74 percent to 90 percent, and clinical colds rose from 27 percent to 47 percent.

Use Personal Examples

Don't be afraid to refer to your own life when you can tie examples from it into your subject. Personal examples make a speech stronger because they are a way of showing that you know what you're talking about. In the next example, the speaker used an example from his own experience to begin a speech about dropping out of school:

Seven years ago I was a teenage dropout. I went away to college because my parents wanted me to. I moved into a dorm, made lots of friends, and began to have a wonderful time—a time that was so wonderful that I only occasionally went to class or studied for an exam. The college, realizing that first-year students take time to adjust, put me on probation for the first year. In the second year, however, I had to settle down.

I tried to study, but I didn't have any idea of what I was studying for. I didn't have a major, and I had no idea of what I wanted to do with my life. Finally I asked myself, "What am I doing here?" I could come up with no answer. So after finishing the first semester of my sophomore year, I dropped out. It was the second-best decision I ever made. The first-best was to come back to school—at the grand old age of 27.

Use a Quotation

Sometimes you can find a quotation that will get your speech off to a good start. A well-chosen quotation can also give credibility to your speech. For instance, a political candidate giving a campaign address about the need to raise taxes might begin by quoting Franklin D. Roosevelt:

Taxes, after all, are the dues that we pay for the privileges of membership in an organized society.

State Your Purpose, Central Idea, and Main Points

By the time you reach the end of your introduction, your audience should know what you intend to accomplish and the central idea of your speech. For example:

The physical abuse of children is a serious problem in this country, and today I want to talk about how bad the problem is and some of the things we can do about it.

In your introduction, you might also want to use **initial partition**—to preview your main points at the outset. Not only does this give members of the audience a sense of your direction, but it also helps them to follow your speech more easily. The student speaking on the physical abuse of children previewed her main points this way:

Since this problem covers such a broad expanse, I would like to limit my talk to three areas: parental abuse of children, social agencies that deal with abuse, and what the ordinary citizen can do when he or she suspects a child is being abused.

Additional Tips for Introductions

When writing an introduction to a speech, remember the following points as well:

1. Although you might want to build curiosity about your speech topic, don't draw out the suspense for too long. The audience will get annoyed if it has to wait to find out what you're going to talk about.

2. Keep your introduction short. The body of your speech contains the main content, and you shouldn't wait too long to get there.

3. Be ready to adapt. Was there anything in the situation that you did not anticipate and need to adapt to? For example, did someone introduce you in a particularly flattering way? Do you want to acknowledge this? Did your audience brave bad weather to come and hear you talk? Do you want to thank them?

The Speech Conclusion

A good **conclusion** should tie a speech together and give the audience the feeling that the speech is complete. It should not introduce any new ideas.

If you have not had very much experience in public speaking, it is especially important that you plan your conclusion carefully. No feeling is worse than knowing that you have said all you have to say but do not know how to stop. If you plan your conclusion, this won't happen to you.

In preparing a conclusion, it may be helpful to follow a model. A conclusion should:

- Signal the end of your speech. (You could say, "The last thing I would like to say . . . " or "Finally . . . " Please note that the phrase "In conclusion I would just like to say that . . . " is overused. Try to find an original signal.)

- Summarize your main points.

- Make a memorable final statement.

This model is designed to show beginning students what to work toward as they prepare their conclusions. Try not to let the model stifle your creativity or imagination. Give your conclusion an inspirational quality. Make the audience members feel that the speech was terrific and that they would like to hear you speak again.

Here are some approaches to concluding your speech.

Summarize Your Main Ideas

If you want your audience to remember your main points, it helps to go back and summarize them in the conclusion of your speech. The student whose topic was "Five Tips for Improving Term Papers" concluded her speech this way:

> *Let me briefly summarize what you should do whenever you write a term paper. Use interviews as well as the Internet, show enthusiasm about the subject, paraphrase quotations, don't pad your paper, have your paper printed on a quality printer, and proofread your paper before you hand it in. If you follow these hints, you are certain to do better on the next paper you write.*

Include a Quotation

If you can find a quotation that fits your subject, the conclusion is a good place to use it. A quotation gives added authority to everything you have said, and it can often help sum up your main ideas. In his speech to persuade the audience not to make political choices on the basis of television commercials, the student used a closing quotation to reinforce his point:

> *An executive in the television industry once wrote, "Television programming is designed to be understood by and to appeal to the average 12-year-old." Since*

none of us are 12-year-old viewers, I would suggest that we fight back. There is only one way to do that. Turn off the television set.

Inspire Your Audience to Action

When you give a speech, especially a persuasive one, your goal is often to inspire the audience to some course of action. If this is the goal of your speech, you can use your conclusion to tell audience members precisely what they should do. Notice how Ralph W. Shrader, chairman and chief executive officer, Booz Allen Hamilton, closed his speech, "Don't Tell Me the Future: Resilence, Not Prophecy, Is the Greatest Gift," to the Association for Corporate Growth, McLean, Virginia (October 17, 2008):[19]

> *And that's the thought I'd like to leave you with: While we can't know our destiny (and I've come to believe we shouldn't want to), we do have a large measure of control over our destiny as individuals and as institutions.*
>
> *What gives us this control? Hard work, experience, and resilience.*
>
> *There's no question that hard work, focused on a goal, is never wasted—even if the destination changes. The experience, expertise, and discipline we gain is invaluable and will lead to success, as we have the resilience—the optimistic opportunism—to sense the winds of change and go with them.*
>
> *There's a Japanese proverb that says, "Even the fortune-tellers do not know their own destiny."*
>
> *I'm convinced we have more control over our destiny by not knowing it—as long as we strive for excellence and have the resilience to make the best of the way things turn out. Thank you (p. 45).[20]*

Additional Tips for Conclusions

When writing a conclusion for a speech, keep these additional points in mind:

1. Work on your conclusion until you feel you can deliver it without notes. If you feel confident about your conclusion, you will feel more confident about your speech.

2. If you tell your audience you are going to conclude, do so! Don't set up the expectation that you are finished and then go on talking for several more minutes.

3. Don't let the words "Thank you" or "Are there any questions?" take the place of a conclusion.

4. Give your conclusion and leave the speaking area if appropriate. If you don't do this, you will ruin the impact of your conclusion and perhaps even your entire speech. (Leaving the speaking area may not be appropriate if there is a question period following the speech.)

Speech Transitions

The final element to work into your speech is **transitions**—comments that lead from one point to another to tell your audience where you have been and where you are going. Transitions are a means of smoothing the flow from one point to another. For

Art Markman, a professor at the University of Texas, in his book, *Smart Thinking*, and in a chapter entitled, "Maximizing Memory Effectiveness," discusses the value of transitions using an interesting analogy:

> . . . *Generating information helps solidify the connections across pieces of information. Think of your knowledge as a pile of peanuts. If all of the pieces of your knowledge are independent, then it is like having a bunch of salted peanuts in a bowl. Picking up any one of them will not affect your chances of picking up another. Even if you try to pick up a bunch in your hand, there is always a chance a few will slip through your fingers. But if you pour caramel over the peanuts and let it harden, then you get peanut brittle. Now, picking up one peanut allows you to pick up all of the other ones stuck to it. Generating information provides the connections among ideas that allow them to be drawn out together (p. 166).*

Source: Markman, Art. (2012). *Smart thinking: Three essential keys to solve problems, innovate, and get things done.* New York: A Perigee Book (Published by the Penguin Group).

Questions

1. How important do you think it is for speakers to "solidify the connections across pieces of information"?

2. Do you have any examples from your own experiences of speakers who failed to use transitions in their speeches? What effects did this have on you as a listener?

3. Given the fact that speakers need to have a strong introduction and an effective conclusion, as well as powerful main points, of course, how do you think the connections made across pieces of information are overall? That is, how much do they contribute to communicating effectively?

example, if you are going to show how alcohol and tobacco combine to become more powerful than either acting alone, you might say:

> *We all know, then, that cigarette smoking is hazardous to our health and we all know that alcohol abuse can kill, but do you know what can happen when the two are combined? Let me show you how these two substances act synergistically— each one making the other more powerful and dangerous than either would be alone.*

Now you are set to speak about their combined effect.

Tips for Transitions

In writing transitions, you should pay attention to these points:

1. Use a transition to introduce main heads and to indicate their order: "First . . . Second . . . Third . . . "; "The first matter we shall discuss . . . "; "In the first place . . . "; "The first step . . . "; "Let us first consider . . . "; and the like.

2. Write out your transitions and include them in your speech outline. A transition that is written out and rehearsed is more likely to be used.

3. If in doubt about whether to use a transition, use it. Since a speech is a onetime event, listeners cannot go back and refer to previously mentioned material. Do everything you can to make the job of listening easier and more accurate.

The Reference List

At the end of your outline you should have a **reference list** of all the material you have used—and only that which you have used—in preparing your speech. This reference list should include everything you have employed in your speech (books, newspapers, magazines, and Internet resources) as well as all the people you have interviewed.

There are a couple of things to remember about reference lists. First, adopt a style and be consistent. For example, every book you cite should be recorded using exactly the same style. Every magazine should be recorded using the same style for magazines, and every Internet citation should be consistent as well. Because there are so many different kinds of Internet resources besides websites, if you need reference-list style guidelines for other resources such as email, newsgroups, Internet books (sometimes referred to as ebooks), and online magazines (often referred to as ezines), enter the words "citing Internet resources" in your search engine, and use any of the guides provided. Your instructors may have a preferred style they want you to follow, so check with them first to see what the assignment calls for.

The second point is to keep careful notes along the way. If you look at the style requirements *before* you begin gathering information, you will have all the data necessary when you begin to put together your reference list. Trying to piece together—if not locate—information at the last minute is both frustrating and time consuming.

Rather than viewing the requirement of submitting a reference list as a chore—or, as some students would label it, "busywork"—think of it as a useful, productive exercise. How? Look at your reference list to make sure you have secured information for your speech from a wide range of sources. This not only helps validate the data you are using but lets listeners know, too, that your viewpoints are more credible.

When you have assembled your entire reference list, look at the sources you have accumulated. Do they look like credible sources when you examine the expertise of the authors or the credibility of the websites? Using credible sources, of course, adds to your own credibility. Just as important—and maybe more—using poor material or sites with no credibility can destroy your credibility in an instant.

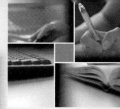

How Much Do You Know about Organizing a Speech?

For each question circle the letter of the best answer.

1. What is the primary reason for organizing a speech? A well-organized speech:
   A. promotes clear communication.
   B. is an easier way to prepare any speech.
   C. provides more of a challenge for listeners.
   D. allows for the preparation of an outline of the speech.

2. What is one of the advantages of organizing your speech? Organizing it will give you:
   A. believability.
   B. a point of view.
   C. total comprehension.
   D. an emotional advantage.

3. Once you have written your general and specific purposes, what are the next three levels on which you can organize your speech?
   A. Main head and first two subpoints.
   B. Introduction, main heads, and conclusion.
   C. Evidence, attention factors, and transitions.
   D. Central idea, main points, and supporting material.

4. Which of the following pieces of advice relates to refining your main points?
   A. Restrict each one to no more than two ideas.
   B. Always limit your number of main heads to three.
   C. Make sure all your main points develop your central idea.
   D. Determine your main points by the quantity and quality of your supporting material.

5. If you arranged your main points in a time sequence—for example, dealing with periods of time in history—you would be using which of the following organizational patterns?
   A. Causal.
   B. Topical.
   C. Spatial.
   D. Chronological.

6. Which of the following is the cardinal rule for using supporting material? They must:
   A. hold attention.
   B. enliven your speech.
   C. be easy to remember.
   D. support, explain, illustrate, or reinforce your central idea.

7. Why is it important to make your organization obvious to your listeners?
   A. This isn't important; you should not make it obvious.
   B. Because organization—whatever the topic—convinces.
   C. Because a listening audience can't stop the speech and go back over it.
   D. If you have spent the time on it, the audience should notice your efforts.

8. Why is it important to time your speech in practice?
   A. Speaking is different from reading.
   B. To help you memorize your words.
   C. So you know where to place your emphasis.
   D. To help you better phrase the main heads of your speech.

9. What is the key to effectiveness in presenting your well-organized ideas to your listeners?
   A. Be conversational.
   B. Elevate your language and approach.
   C. Speak slightly below your audience's level of understanding.
   D. Try to talk to your audience as if you are talking entirely to yourself.

10. In the conclusion of your speech—with respect to the organizational pattern you have selected—you should do what?
    A. Repeat your main heads.
    B. Offer listeners new evidence for your position.
    C. Tell them if it was topical, spatial, causal, or chronological.
    D. Be totally spontaneous, natural, relaxed, and comfortable as you think of any additional ideas that may help them understand your speech better.

Go to the Online Learning Center at **www.mhhe.com/hybels11e** to see your results and learn how to evaluate your attitudes and feelings.

www.mhhe.com/hybels11e >

Summary

The principles of organization include selecting information that relates to the specific purpose and central idea; distinguishing among the introduction, body, and conclusion of the speech; distinguishing between main and minor points; and phrasing all points in full sentences with parallel structure.

A number of patterns of organization work well for organizing speeches: time order, using a chronological sequence; spatial order, moving from left to right, top to bottom, or in any direction that will make the subject clear; cause-and-effect order, showing why something is happening and what impact it is having; problem–solution order, explaining a problem and giving a solution; and topical order, arranging the speech into subtopics.

An outline is a way of organizing material to highlight all the parts and how they relate to the whole. In most cases, the body of the speech is what is outlined—the introduction and conclusion are handled separately.

The outline shows the organization as main and minor points through the use of standard symbols and indentation. Many speakers like to construct two outlines: a full-sentence outline for organizing the speech and a keyword outline to summarize the main ideas and to function as notes during delivery of the speech.

The purpose of the introduction is to set the tone for the speech, introduce the topic, and get the audience's attention. Some attention-getting devices are using humor, giving personal examples, referring to the occasion, showing the importance of the subject, telling startling information, asking questions, and using quotations.

The speech conclusion should signal the audience that the speech is over and should tie all the ideas together. In their conclusions, speakers often summarize main ideas, use quotations, and inspire the audience to take further action.

Speech transitions help an audience follow where a speaker is going. They introduce main heads and may be written into the speech outline.

Your outline should be followed by a bibliography—a list of all the material from other sources that you have used in your speech. All the items should be presented in a standard bibliographical form.

Key Terms and Concepts

Use the Online Learning Center at www.mhhe.com/hybels11e to further your understanding of the following terms.

Body (of speech) 343	Keyword outlines 348	Spatial order 344
Cause-and-effect order 345	Main points 342	Time order 343
Conclusion (of speech) 353	Minor points 342	Topical order 346
Full-sentence outline 348	Outline 347	Transitions 354
Initial partition 352	Problem–solution order 345	
Introduction (of speech) 348	Reference list 356	

Questions to Review

1. Can you tell the difference between an organized speech, presentation, lecture, or report and one that is not organized? What difference does this make in your attentiveness to the speaker? In your understanding of the information? In your overall evaluation of the effort?

2. Is organizing ideas difficult for you? Why or why not?

3. Which pattern of organization was most appealing to you? Why? Which seems to be the most difficult? Why?

4. How important are introductions in speeches? What purposes do they serve?

5. Is it true that if you grab the attention of listeners in the introduction to your speech, you will have their attention throughout the speech? Why or why not?

6. How are transitions used in a speech?

7. Have you ever been moved by a speech? What was it about the speech that moved you?

8. What are the barriers or hindrances that restrain people from organizing their speech efforts as well as they could?

9. Faced with an upcoming speech that you have to prepare, do you ever feel overwhelmed with ideas and suggestions? What do you do in situations like that? Do you just go on and prepare in your own way? Or do you actually take and use as many new ideas and suggestions as you can, given the time you have to prepare your speech?

Go to the self-quizzes on the Online Learning Center at www.mhhe.com/hybels11e to test your knowledge of the chapter contents.

CHAPTER FOURTEEN

Delivering the Speech

Objectives

After reading this chapter, you should be able to:

- Explain specific methods for dealing with public-speaking anxiety.

- Distinguish among the four types of delivery and explain the type considered most effective and why.

- Identify the elements that affect how you look and how you sound, and explain how you adjust to them to improve your delivery.

- Describe various types of visual support and how to use them in your speech.

- Clarify the steps to follow in rehearsing your speech.

I, MICAELA, HAVE BEEN SHY SINCE I WAS BORN. IN CERTAIN SITUATIONS I feel stronger and freer than in others, but in situations where I must perform, I am hesitant, nervous, and tense. I have done a great deal of reading about shyness, and I realize shy people are less likely to get involved in activities and participate in class discussions. My shyness, for example, has led me to being overlooked by teachers who have mistaken my shyness for not understanding the work. I know, too, that in higher education shy people are more likely to choose courses that match their level of shyness. For example, they avoid classes that involve a lot of communication and tend to favor subjects like accounting, computer science, and electrical engineering. It was precisely because shy people have more difficulty in job interviews, and are often passed over for job promotions in favor of more outgoing peers, that I decided to take matters into my own hands. I cannot totally control it, but I can learn to manage it effectively by developing the right skills, gaining confidence, and seeking opportunities that challenge me, stretch me, and offer me leadership experience. My speech-communication course gave me everything I was looking for, because it moved into the public-speaking portion of the course slowly, offered me guidance and suggestions regarding leadership, provided specific ideas for dealing with nervousness, strengthened my abilities in public speaking, and made available gentle and encouraging advice from a knowledgeable instructor.

There is no magic formula for effectively delivering your speech. From your own observations of speakers, you know that the most effective ones often are those who use their natural gestures and idiosyncrasies to their best advantage. Delivery is a highly personal matter, and because there is no standard form, the best advice is for speakers to tailor their speech to their own personal strengths and weaknesses. How do you discover your own personal strengths and weaknesses? Four ways will work: (1) gain experience; (2) engage in self-critiques; (3) listen to the advice, criticism, and suggestions of others; and (4) experiment and be willing to make the changes necessary to increase your effectiveness. Remember, only you control what works and what doesn't; use your control to your best advantage.

The U.S. Marine Corps has a wonderful saying that applies here: "Proper prior planning prevents poor performance." Just because there is no formula and no standard for effectively delivering your speech doesn't mean you shouldn't plan. First, rehearsal will certainly reduce anxiety and improve your performance. Second, there are always things you can do to enhance your message. And, third, don't forget that *how* you present is as important as *what* you present. If you have devoted yourself to the task of preparing an effective speech, as discussed in Chapter 12, Getting Started and Finding Speech Material, then surely you will want to give the same attention to the way you present that information to your listeners.

STRATEGIC FLEXIBILITY

This is an opportunity to turn strategic flexibility toward your own natural talents and abilities and try to forecast, with as much accuracy, alertness, and appropriateness as possible, the skills and behaviors you need to call on, with reference to specific speech occasions, to express yourself in the most advantageous, useful, powerful, and potent manner you can.

Coping with Public-Speaking Anxiety

When asked, what activity do you most dread, a survey of 1,000 adults (*USA Today*, May 14–16, 2010, p. 1A) had public speaking (46 percent) at the top of the list, followed by thoroughly cleaning their home (43 percent), visiting the dentist (41 percent), visiting the DMV (Department of Motor Vehicles) (36 percent), and doing taxes (28 percent). Over-and-over, when it comes to what is most feared, public speaking is at or near the top of the list. No wonder there is so much anxiety associated with it.

In *The Real Story of Risk* (Amherst, NY: Prometheus Books, 2012), Glenn Croston, a research biologist, offers readers the following example in a section labeled, "The Thing We Fear More Than Death":

> *Marjorie Asturias of Dallas, Texas, routinely gives talks as the president and CEO of her budding firm, Blue Volcano Media. Today she even enjoys giving the talks, but as a child she panicked at the thought of performing.* The fear of public speaking manifests itself in many ways, with some freezing while others are nauseous. For Asturias, the fear made her break into hives. "Growing up, I was so terrified of public speaking and public performance that my legs once broke out into massive hives in the days leading up to my first piano recital at the age of ten," said Asturias. "My aunt was so concerned that she took me to the doctor, who examined me extensively and concluded that there was absolutely nothing physically wrong with me, that the hives appeared to be psychosomatic in nature. I ended up wearing knee-high socks to the recital just to cover up the angry rash wrapped around my legs. Sure enough, the day after the recital they disappeared as mysteriously as they came. I even elected to fail a Reading class in the sixth grade just to avoid giving*

> *a five-minute oral book report. And when I had to perform in a school play I suffered such terrible stomach pain right before I was to go onstage that the teacher had to replace me with another student. Lo and behold, the moment I sat in the audience, the pain was gone" (pp. 234–235).*

*Glenn Croston gained this information from personal correspondence with Asturias, March, 2012.

Source: Croston, Glenn. (2012). *The Real Story of Risk: Adventures in a Hazardous World*. Amherst, NY: Prometheus Books.

Questions

1. What do you think people are afraid of? What would you say is the major cause?

2. Does this example ring a bell for you? That is, is it something that could have happened to you—or to somebody you know?

3. If you had a friend like Marjorie Asturias, what specific suggestions might you make to help her deal with the problem? (Feel free to use any of the suggestions in this textbook.)

4. The fear of public speaking is common, and some people feel it more strongly than others. What are some specific kinds of things people can do *leading up to* a public-speaking performance, that would either prevent or lessen the fear?

Public-speaking anxiety is a disturbance of mind regarding a forthcoming public-speaking event for which you are the speaker. Anxiety is often triggered by stress, and some are more vulnerable to it than others. It is the same process no matter whether you fear speaking, snakes, heights, being closed in small spaces, spiders, or getting shots. Experiencing fear is universal, and fear of speaking in public is nearly universal, but it does not prevent successful speeches.

Physiological responses to anxiety vary in both their kind and intensity; however, the most obvious signs include tense muscles, trembling, churning stomach, nausea, diarrhea, headache, backache, heart palpitations, numbness or "pins and needles" in arms, hands, or legs, and sweating or flushing. Avoiding things that make you anxious is only a temporary solution and may make you worry about what will happen next time. Also, every time you avoid something, it is harder the next time you try it. Avoidance, too, sets you on a pattern of avoiding more and more things. For some people, just the thought of having to give a public speech can trigger an adrenaline surge that quickens your pulse, raises your blood pressure, and kick-starts your anxiety. Knowing how to cope with anxiety can help you lessen or, in some cases, avoid the surge.

There are four things to remember when coping with public-speaking anxiety. First, *experienced public speakers get nervous before a presentation.* There are stories of extreme public-speaking anxiety among some of our most successful and experienced politicians, evangelists, and entertainers including Ronald Reagan, Billy Graham, Jane Fonda, Barbra Streisand, Leonardo DiCaprio, Harrison Ford, Julia Roberts, Bruce Willis, Samuel L. Jackson and Donny Osmond. Winston Churchill, one of the most famous diplomats and orators of the twentieth century, fainted the first time he gave a speech.

Nerves do not need to be your enemy. Being nervous can work to your advantage. It can give you the added boost of energy that animates you and helps give your message assurance and enthusiasm.

No matter how nervous you are, you are probably the only one who knows it.

As long as you act as if you are confident and play the role of a secure and knowledgeable speaker, you will be in command of the public-speaking situation.

Remember as you read this section that all anxiety need not be eliminated. "Sometimes," writes Alice Park, in her article "The Two Faces of Anxiety," (*Time*, December 5, 2011), "it should be embraced—even celebrated. In just the right amounts, the hormones that drive anxiety can be powerful stimulants, arousing the senses to function at their sharpest." It is, indeed, what Park writes next that justifies this section. "The key isn't not to feel anxious; it's to learn ways to manage that experience" (pp. 56 & 59).

A Good Place to Begin

An important philosophy to help you deliver your ideas with confidence is to focus on your speech as a communication *task, not* a performance.[1] (See Table 14-1.) "Most speakers with stage fright view speeches as *performances.*"[2]

"The goals, attitudes, and behaviors that make for effective public speaking are in fact more like those of ordinary communication encounters than of public performances."[3] Mentally connecting public speaking with daily communication episodes, *not* performances, has several advantages. First, it means that all those negative past public performances you may have had—from elementary school through high school—can be deleted from your memory.

Second, you do not have to memorize your material. Performances create anxiety because of the fear of forgetting words, thoughts, or your place in the speech. Seldom

Table 14-1   Speaker-Perceived Differences Between a Communication Orientation and a Performance Orientation

Communication Orientation	Performance Orientation
Goal: to share ideas with an audience	Goal: to satisfy an audience of critics
Audience interested in what the speaker has to say	Audience interested in analyzing and criticizing your performance
Similar to everyday conversation	Formal talk
Normal, natural behavior	Put-on, artificial behavior
Common, ordinary, average	Extraordinary, exceptional, unusual
Familiar circumstances	Unfamiliar circumstances
Reveals genuine and true expression of self	Must follow proper behaviors to be correct
Results depend on whether or not you shared your message	Results depend on polish, eloquence, and refinement

do you have memory blocks during conversations with others. Third, you can focus on your *real* purpose in speaking to your audience—getting your listeners to accept and understand your information or change their attitude or actions. "The typical speech audience," says Motley, "is more interested in hearing what you have to say than in evaluating your performance skills."[4] A performance orientation causes an emphasis on put-on, artificial behavior (undue emphasis on self), whereas in conversations, you are seldom looking at yourself at all.

In his article "The Art of Now: Six Steps to Living in the Moment," (*Psychology Today,* November/December, 2008), Jay Dixit writes that "Thinking too hard about what you're doing actually makes you do worse. If you're in a situation that makes you anxious—giving a speech, introducing yourself to a stranger, dancing—focusing on your anxiety tends to heighten it. . . . (Here, Dixit quotes Jessica Hayden who is a dance teacher and owner of Shockra Studio in Manhattan) 'Focus less on what's going on in your mind and more on what's going on in the room, less on your mental chatter and more on yourself as *part* of something'" (p. 66).

Time-Tested Ways for Dealing with Nervousness

Now that you have a philosophy in mind—focusing on your speech as a task and *not* as a performance—let's review the most-often-used methods for dealing with nervousness. Remember throughout this discussion that some nervousness, as explained in the opening portion of this section, can be helpful. The most-often-used methods are: be prepared, be positive, visualize, anticipate, focus, and gain experience.

Be Prepared

If you prepare your speeches so thoroughly and so carefully that you cannot help but be successful, you will have taken the first giant step toward dealing with nervousness. I (Richard) have *never* heard of a speaker being *too* prepared. As a public speaker, I would begin my preparation early. In that way, I could continually work with my ideas in my mind and change information as I would think of new ideas or new ways of saying things. Once I had most of the ideas written down, I called the rest of my preparation "honing, polishing, and perfecting"—the constant process of being flexible and adjusting right up to the time of delivering the speech.

Be Positive

It is easier to be positive when you are engaged in constructive, practical, useful, productive work. If you choose a topic you care about, and if you discover information you *want to* share with your listeners, you are more likely to have an optimistic, confident, and upbeat frame of mind. Start by believing that you can give a successful speech. Dwelling on past disasters, predicting a catastrophe, or forecasting failure is likely to become a self-fulfilling prophecy, and the best way to counter such negativity is to bombard such thoughts with enthusiastic, affirming, supportive, and encouraging work and ideas.

Visualize

Closely related to being positive is using the power of visualization. Positive mental imaging can significantly increase your performance. It is commonly used by musicians, athletes, and actors. The best way to do this is to picture yourself walking up to the lectern, having complete control over your behavior, and delivering a forceful and effective talk to a supportive, approving, responsive, and sympathetic audience. Repeat this process of visualization several times before giving your speech.

ATTENTION!

Before Speaking

- **Visualize.** Picture yourself in the classroom, standing up, taking your notes to the lectern, and speaking. Visualize a successful outcome.
- **Practice.** Practice going through your presentation, over and over again. Rehearse with someone who is supportive, so that you learn to succeed rather than fail.
- **Focus on the little things.** Through visualization speakers can get all the negative stuff out, so when the day of the speech arrives, they can focus on real issues.[5]

In their book *Words Can Change Your Brain*, Newberg and Waldman offer the specific research studies that support their statement that, "positive imagery can reduce a negative state of mind, whereas negative images will maintain or enhance a negative mood," and, what's more, you can "arbitrarily create an optimistic attitude by manipulating your own thoughts . . ." [and they conclude by saying] "So by all means, prime yourself with positive feelings and thoughts before you engage . . ." (p. 131).

Anticipate

There are a number of parts to anticipation—or foreseeing your situation. First, you can anticipate some nervousness. It is common, but most listeners don't detect it. What you are feeling on the inside is seldom noticed on the outside. Second, anticipate role playing. One of the best ways for countering any nervousness you feel is to role-play coolness, calmness, and confidence. Just like an actor on the stage, look as though you are in charge and in control, and your audience will believe it. Third, anticipate something less than perfection. There is no such thing as a perfect speech, but remember that your listeners do not know what you plan to say; they only know what you actually say. Thus, if you make an error, lose your place, or forget to say something, anticipate proceeding as if nothing happened. Nobody but you will know.

Focus

One problem that increases nervousness is when speakers focus on themselves rather than on their listeners. "Will my audience like me?" "Will I look foolish before my audience?" "Will my listeners think I am brilliant?" "Will I lose my place?" "Will they know how nervous I am?" All these thoughts are self-centered and selfish. Worrying about yourself and your image is vanity—and vanity of the worst sort. "Worst sort?" Yes, because this focus puts yourself above both your audience and your message. The entire process of speech preparation should be audience-centered, and to suddenly shift the focus from them to your self demeans and discounts your prior preparation. To counter such changes of focus, you must substitute audience-centered thoughts such as, "I have chosen an important topic that will interest my listeners and hold their attention, and I have information that will be useful to their lives."

Gain Experience

There is, of course, no substitute for experience. This course is a terrific first step in gaining that experience, but you should begin looking for and taking advantage of opportunities in other classes, in clubs and organizations, in churches and family gatherings, and in work situations as well. Begin putting what you learn in this class to use, and you will find that the more you learn about public speaking and the more experiences you have, the less nervousness you will feel. As your experiences continue beyond this class, your fears about public speaking will recede until they are replaced by the healthy nervousness that empowers you not only to do well, but to seek even more such opportunities. You are likely to find, from these experiences, that you will look forward to public speeches with interest, eagerness, and—perhaps—with passion. It happens!

Other Strategies for Reducing Anxiety

There is no single, surefire formula that reduces every person's anxiety before a speech. Here are a few more suggestions.

- *Dress in comfortable clothes.* Wear clothes you feel at ease in—but clothes that show you have made some kind of special effort for the speech. Psychologically, it is important to feel confident and in control.

ATTENTION!

During your speech, deal with nervous symptoms as they occur:

- Dry mouth? Take a little sip of water.
- Knees knocking? Shift your weight and flex your knees.
- Hands trembling? Put them together.
- Voice is quivering? "Pause, take a deep breath or two, and smile. It is amazing what a smile will do."
- Sweating? "Forget it, nobody sees that anyway."[6]

- *If your anxiety is high, ask your instructor if you can speak first or second.* Being among the first to speak means you have less time to worry.

- *Take several deep breaths on the way to the front of the room.* An increased respiratory rate because of nervousness can cause you to feel short of breath. Taking several deep breaths can break this cycle and have a calming effect.

- *Remember that your audience is made up of people just like you.* They want you to do well; they are supportive.

- *If possible, move around.* Moving releases nervous energy and restores a feeling of calm. Try to gesture and move when you use transitions and personal examples.

- *Pick out friendly faces, and make eye contact with these people.* An encouraging, supportive expression on a listener's face can do wonders to promote confidence and reassure speakers.

- *Give yourself a reward after your speech, and congratulate yourself for having succeeded.* Even though your speech may not have been perfect, remind yourself that you were able to do it. Remember, you're human, and humans aren't perfect.

Characteristics of Good Delivery

A good speech can bring even more satisfaction to speakers than to listeners. There is nothing quite like the experience of communicating your ideas effectively, having them understood clearly, and feeling an entire audience respond to you in a positive way. Successful speakers love the "rush" they get from compelling performances.

Speaking to audiences is a skill you can learn if you are willing to discover and develop your personal strengths and weaknesses. Success in delivering a speech, however, cannot be defined as simply getting from the beginning to the end without suffering any major catastrophes. The key question is: "Does your delivery effectively do what it is intended to do?"

- Did you increase your listeners' understanding of your ideas?
- Did you successfully change the way they felt about an idea?
- Did you change their beliefs?
- Did you move them to action?

These are your goals, and all aspects of your delivery should contribute to achieving them.

Some potentially distracting elements can be controlled. For example, speakers who pace, pound the lectern, or jingle coins in their pockets draw the focus onto themselves rather than to their message. When his attention was brought to the strength of his accent and its effect on his Sunday messages, a newly hired interim pastor immediately sought help from a speech and language tutor, and, with the tutor's help, began to speak more slowly and to more carefully articulate his words.

In the following section, the characteristics we will discuss include conversational quality, attentiveness, immediacy, and directness. Sections that follow consider other important elements as well, such as how you look and how you sound. It is important to note at the outset that effective delivery does not rest in a single element. Effective delivery is a composite—a blend, mixture, or synthesis of all the elements combined into one impression.

Conversational Quality

When speakers are attentive, immediate, and direct, in most cases they will sound conversational. When you have a **conversational quality**, you talk to your audience in much the same way that you talk when you are having a conversation with another person. The value of sounding conversational in speaking is that you give the impression that you are talking *with* the audience rather than *at* it. In the next excerpt, notice how the speaker uses conversational language and the word *you* to involve his audience:

> *Have you ever felt embarrassed—I mean really embarrassed—where you never wanted to show your face in public again? Has your face ever turned red when lots of people were watching you? I would guess that you've had this experience once or twice in your life—I know I have. But—don't you ever wonder what happens to our bodies when we're embarrassed?*

How do you achieve a conversational tone in speaking? The most useful way, right from the planning stage, is to imagine giving your speech to one person or to a small group of people. Have a mental picture of this person or persons, and try to talk directly with him, her, or them in a normal, conversational manner. This will help you achieve the right tone.

There is an important caution, however: A conversational tone doesn't mean being casual. A speech occasion is more formal than most conversations. Even though you are aiming for a conversational tone, you shouldn't allow long pauses or use such conversational fillers as "OK," "um," or "you know." "Once you are aware of this habit," says Mark Abramson, an attorney with Robison Curphey & O'Connell, who teaches part-time at the University of Toledo law school and is the former president of the Westgate Toastmasters, "you simply need to stop, pause for a moment, and then clamp your mouth shut before you let one escape."[7] You should also avoid some of the slang and "in" jokes or expressions you would use in casual conversation. Here are a few additional hints on how to achieve a conversational quality:

- Use contractions such as *don't, can't, isn't,* and *weren't.* They are more conversational than their two-word counterparts.
- Use words everyone will understand.
- Use an outline rather than writing out your speech word for word.

Attentiveness

You might wonder how a speaker could be inattentive to his or her own speech. Yet it's quite possible to be present and functioning as a body while not being there in spirit. You are so overcome with the mechanics and anxiety of giving a speech that you forget that doing so is basically a human encounter between a speaker and listeners.

Attentiveness means focusing on the moment, being aware of and responding to your listeners' needs. To ensure that you will be attentive to your audience, you can do a number of things:

1. *Pick a topic that is important to you.* If you are speaking on something of great interest and importance to you, it is likely that you will communicate your interest and enthusiasm to your audience. Also, if you can get involved in your subject, you are likely to feel less anxiety about giving your speech.

Using the characteristics discussed in this section (conversational quality, attentiveness, immediacy, and directness), perform a thorough self-analysis being as objective and open-minded as you can be.

1. Which factors will be easier for you? Which will be more difficult?

2. Which factors, for you, are likely to be most effective or successful (that is, successful in delivering a speech)?

3. What specific steps can you take to improve (develop?) each of these factors to become an even more effective communicator?

2. *Do all the work necessary to prepare the best speech possible.* If you work on your speech—organize and practice it—you will be much more confident about it and will feel less anxious when the time comes to give it. Then you will be able to concentrate on delivering your speech.

3. *Individualize your audience members.* Try to think of your audience as individual human beings rather than as a mass of people. As you give the speech, think: "I am going to talk to Kristen, who sits in the second row. Gabriel always looks like he is going to sleep. I am going to give a speech that will wake him up."

4. *Focus on the audience rather than on yourself.* As you speak, look for audience feedback and try to respond to it. The more you focus on the audience members and their needs, the less likely you are to feel anxiety.

Alberta followed these four guidelines when she gave her speech. She selected a topic, "Foster Care for Problem Kids," that was important to her; she did the work necessary to prepare the best speech she could; she looked at individual audience members as she delivered her speech; and she focused on listeners rather than on herself. At one point, noting some restlessness in her audience, she even added an unplanned anecdote to her speech.

Immediacy

Immediacy occurs when the communicator is completely focused on the communication situation. Assess the difference between the following two excerpts from student speeches. Which one appears more immediate, and why?

> *The way humans express themselves sexually is learned at a very young age, and throughout our lives we use very similar, if not the same, recurring patterns to express ourselves sexually. However, sexual expression is learned behavior, and it may not mean the same for everyone. To improve people's understanding of one another, it will help us to know how we develop sexual knowledge, feelings, and behaviors.*

This is the second excerpt, and it deals with a similar topic:

> *If you and I are like the average population, sexual activity among all of us here has occurred much earlier than ever before. There has been more pressure placed on us to have sex. You know that you and I can blame our peers, and we can blame the*

Communicate Your Ideas Effectively

1. Practice and rehearse your speech beforehand.

2. Maintain eye contact with everyone in the room.

3. Know your material well. Avoid reading your notes.

4. Use variety in your tone of voice. Expressiveness reveals your enthusiasm.

5. Use hand gestures that are natural and appropriate.

6. Speak clearly. Avoid slurring and mumbling.

It is well known that Steve Jobs was a very effective public speaker. Peter Sander, in his book *What Would Steve Jobs Do?* (N.Y.: McGraw-Hill, 2012), explains his effectiveness in this way:

Steve had an oral style that is difficult to describe and best learned by watching it . . . He was calm and confident. He was clear and articulate, using short sentences and simple words, very seldom "techie." There were almost no "ums" or "ahs" or filler words. The cadence and flow were almost ideal, with pauses and silence in the right places to allow the audience to digest his message or to build excitement. He was genuine and credible; it was pretty clear that he was saying what he thought, not what the audience wanted to hear.

The presentation, the accompanying visuals, and the message were crisp, visually simple, and easy to grasp (pp. 185–186).

Source: Sander, Peter. (2012). *What Would Steve Jobs Do? How the Steve Jobs Way Can Inspire Anyone to Think Differently and Win.* New York: McGraw-Hill.

Questions

1. Is Jobs' delivery style so unique that it cannot be (could not be) copied or imitated by anyone else?
2. Is it clear from this limited description why Jobs might have been a successful public speaker?
3. What can you learn from this description of Jobs' delivery style? That is, is there anything in the description that might help you improve your own delivery?

media as well. It doesn't really matter who or what is to blame, the fact is that along with this sexual activity, you and I must accept responsibility for our sexual behavior.

Both excerpts are about the same length, and they both are about a topic that relates to listeners. But the first speaker uses the pronouns *we* and *our* and the word *people*. These choices are removed from listeners and noninvolving. The excerpt is abstract and lacks immediacy. The second speaker began and ended with *you and I* and even included it in the middle of this quotation; this closes the gap between speaker and audience. Notice, too, the second speaker's use of *here,* which reinforces the speaker's sense of the present. From just a casual reading of both excerpts, the second is more immediate, lively, and likely to hold audience attention.

Directness

Closely aligned with both attentiveness and immediacy is directness. **Directness** means being natural and straightforward. Your writing teachers have probably told you that you shouldn't choose big words if a small word says the same thing—that your goal is to communicate with readers, not to dazzle them with your vocabulary and knowledge of complicated grammatical structure. The same is true for a speech, only more so. Your audience is going to hear this speech only one time, so you have to be as specific and direct as possible.

The second goal in trying to achieve directness is to be straightforward. Being straightforward means selecting an effective specific purpose and a strong central idea. Then make all your points and examples relate to them.

Sometimes you come up with a wonderful idea or example, but you find that you can't relate it directly to the main point. One of the hardest things to do in speaking (or in writing) is to get rid of material that is fascinating or wonderful but doesn't work. However, it has to be dropped if it interferes with your directness. (Put it in a file folder and use it for something else another day.)

Types of Delivery

There are essentially four methods of delivery: making impromptu remarks, speaking from a manuscript, memorizing the speech, and speaking extemporaneously from notes.

Impromptu Speaking

Impromptu speaking is giving a speech on the spur of the moment. Usually there is little or no time for preparation. Sometimes your instructor might ask you to give an impromptu speech in class. Other times you might be asked to give a toast or offer a prayer at a gathering, or you may make a few remarks at a meeting.

If you are asked to give an impromptu speech, the most important thing is not to panic. Your main goal is to think of a topic and organize it quickly in your head before you start to speak.

In finding a topic, look around you and consider the occasion. Is there anything you can refer to? Decorations? A friend? A photo that recalls a time together? Formal occasions usually honor someone or something, and the person or thing being honored can provide a focus for your speech: "I am delighted to be at this yearly meeting of documentary filmmakers. Documentary filmmaking is one of the noblest professions." Other times you might want to refer to the place or the people: "I am happy to be here in Akron again. The last time I was here . . ." or "I am very touched by the warm reception you have all given me."

In impromptu speaking it's essential to keep your remarks brief. No one expects you to speak for more than a minute or two. The audience knows that you are in a tight spot, and it doesn't expect a long and well-polished speech.

In his book (with Joanne Gordon) *Onward* (Emmaus, PA: Rodale, 2011), Howard Schultz, president and CEO of Starbucks Coffee Company, justifies his use of impromptu speaking in this way: "My refusal to stick to a script . . . made some of our people nervous—anything that was said onstage could be picked up by journalists and bloggers in the audience and plopped online immediately—but my rationale was simple. I wanted to react naturally, whether I was greeted with contempt or kindness. Letting my words flow according to the mood rather than a teleprompter freed me to connect sincerely with this important constituency in a very delicate period" (p. 130).

STRATEGIC FLEXIBILITY

It is the extemporaneous type of delivery that makes the best use of on-the-spot strategic flexibility when you can use all the immediate, available, and obvious audience and situational cues to assess, evaluate, and select the skills and behaviors likely to have the greatest immediate impact on your listeners and apply them at once as you adjust, tailor, enhance, and fine-tune your communication.

Speaking from a Manuscript

Speaking from a manuscript involves writing out the entire speech and reading it to the audience. When you read a speech, you can get a clear idea of how long it is, so manuscript speaking is a good method when exact timing is necessary. Because a manuscript also offers planned wording, political leaders often favor this method when they speak on sensitive issues and want control over what they say. When Louisa, for example, decided to run for president of the student government, she prepared a five-minute speech in manuscript form for her appearance on the campus television station with the other candidates. Louisa knew that having a manuscript would help her stay within her time limit and would also help her say

If you are asked to give an impromptu speech, the most important thing is not to panic.

exactly what she wanted to say. However, she knew that she had to be very familiar with the manuscript so that she could break away from it to look directly at the camera.

Speakers find that it is difficult to sound spontaneous when using a manuscript; if listeners think they are being read to, they are more likely to lose interest. Experienced speakers who use manuscripts are often so skilled at delivery that the audience is not aware the speech is being read. Beginning speakers, however, have difficulty making a manuscript speech sound spontaneous and natural.

Feedback is another problem in speaking from a manuscript. If the audience becomes bored and inattentive, it is difficult to respond and modify the speech; the speaker is bound to the manuscript. A manuscript also confines a speaker to the lectern—because that's where the manuscript is.

Speaking from Memory

Speaking from memory means writing out the entire speech and then committing it to memory word for word. It has the same advantages for speakers as the manuscript method: Exact wording can be planned, phrases and sentences can be crafted, and potential problems in language can be eliminated. Also, a memorized speech can be adapted to a set, inflexible time limit. Francisco, who was running against Louisa in the student election, decided to memorize his speech. He felt this was a good idea because he wanted exact wording, but he also wanted the freedom to move around. Feedback was not a problem to Francisco because he was speaking to a television audience via the campus's closed-circuit television station. In other situations, however, responding to feedback can be a problem because it is difficult for the speaker to get away from what he or she has memorized. A speaker who gets off track or is distracted may forget parts of the speech or lose his or her place.

A memorized speech can create considerable pressure. Not only does the speaker have to spend the time memorizing the speech, but he or she is also likely to worry about forgetting it. In addition, making a memorized speech sound natural and spontaneous requires considerable acting talent.

Extemporaneous Speaking

In the **extemporaneous speaking** method, a speaker delivers a speech from notes. The speaker might commit the main ideas of the speech to memory—possibly also the introduction and conclusion—but will rely on notes to remember most of the speech.

Extemporaneous speaking has several advantages. It permits flexibility so that a speaker can adjust to the feedback of listeners. For example, if a speaker sees that several audience members do not understand something, he or she can stop and explain. If the audience looks bored, the speaker can try moving around or using visual support earlier than planned. Extemporaneous speaking is the one method of delivery that comes closest to good conversation because a speaker can be natural and responsive to the audience.

One disadvantage of the extemporaneous method is that the speaker may stumble over or grope for words. However, much of this problem can be overcome by rehearsing the speech beforehand. Sometimes speakers want to use exact words or phrases. Although in extemporaneous speaking the speech as a whole is not memorized, there is nothing wrong with memorizing a particularly important sentence or having it written down and reading it from a note card.

Speaking extemporaneously is the best method of delivery. In addition to eliminating heavy burdens for the speaker (writing out or memorizing the speech), it enables a natural and spontaneous style of speaking. It also makes the listeners a central element in the speech, for the speaker is more free to respond to them.

How You Look

Appearance

As you rise from your chair and walk to the lectern to give your speech, the audience's first impression of you will come from how you look. Audience members will notice how you are dressed, if you walk to the lectern with confidence, and whether you look interested in giving this speech.

On days when you are going to make a speech, it is a good idea to look your best. Not only does looking good give the audience a positive impression of you, but it also gives you a psychological boost. Deanna D. Sellnow and Kristen P. Treinen, in a research article, "The Role of Gender in Perceived Speaker Competence," discovered that being sloppily dressed had a greater negative impact on audiences than being casually or formally dressed had a positive one.[8]

Try to stay away from clothing that might distract from your speech. For example, avoid T-shirts with writing on them and accessories you might be tempted to play with.

If it's a formal occasion, wear dress-up clothing; if it's informal, wear what you think everyone else will wear. If you don't know what others will be wearing, ask the person who has invited you to speak.

Body Language

A speaker who uses some movement is likely to attract more attention than a speaker who stands absolutely still. Of course, this does not mean that all movement is good. To be effective, your movement should be carefully coordinated with your speech. For example, if you want to stress your most important point, you might indicate this nonverbally by moving closer to your audience. If you want to create intimacy between you and your audience as you are telling a personal story, you could sit on the edge of the desk for a brief period.

Avoid movement that might be distracting. Probably you have seen a speaker (or teacher) who paces back and forth in front of the room. This movement is not motivated by anything other than habit or nervousness: As a result, it's ineffective.

Eye Contact

In North American culture it is considered extremely important to look into the eyes of the person you are talking to. If you don't, you are at risk of being considered dishonest or of being seen as having something to hide. However, there are sharp differences among cultures. Eye behavior varies according to the environment in which it is learned.

Careful audience analysis may uncover differences in other areas of nonverbal communication, language, rules of social situations, social relationships, and even motivation.[9] Be sensitive to these, and when you are an audience member be careful

What Your Appearance Conveys

- Self-esteem
- Self-respect
- Confidence
- Organizational skills
- Soundness of judgment
- Attention to detail
- Creativity
- Reliability[10]

about judging speakers from other cultures by standards that they have not learned and to which they do not personally subscribe.

Facial Expression

Because speakers are their own most important visual support, listeners have every reason to expect an expressive face and voice. By using a mirror or cell phone or computer camera you have a chance to see your own face and to know what you are expressing. If you don't look like someone you would like to listen to, obviously facial expression is an area you would need to work on. Since facial expressions often mirror attitude, perhaps you need to change your attitude. Rather than thinking of giving the speech as an assignment, a chore, or more busywork, think of it as a legitimate opportunity to share some important information with people who really care. If you think such a change in attitude doesn't matter, you may be surprised by a negative listener reaction.

Gestures

When we speak, we usually use hand and arm gestures to express or emphasize ideas or emotions. The best way to add more gestures to your speech is to practice in front of a mirror or use a video camera. Always aim for gestures that look spontaneous and that feel natural to you.

Posture

The way you sit in your seat, rise and walk to the lectern, and return to your seat after the speech can leave as much of an impression as the posture you use during your speech. Because we don't have a very good sense of how we look to others, a speech class is a great opportunity to get some feedback. Try to listen to critical remarks from your instructor and classmates without feeling defensive. If you can learn from your mistakes, you will improve every time you give a speech.

How You Sound

When members of a speech class have a chance to see themselves on a video recording, most of them react more negatively to the way they sound than to the way they look. Few people really like their own voices.

Our voices reveal things about us that might be far more important than the words we speak.[11] How loud, how fast, how clear and distinct the message—all are part of the information we send about ourselves.

The voice is also a powerful instrument of communication. Because it is so flexible, you can vary it to get the effect you want. You can speak in a loud voice and then drop to a mere whisper. You can go through basic information quickly and then slow down to make a new and important point. You can even use your voice to bring about a change of character. Notice how your favorite actor or comedian uses many different voices.

Volume

You probably need to speak in a louder voice than you feel comfortable with. Always check out the back row to see whether people can hear you. Generally you can tell if they are straining to hear you, and often they will give you some nonverbal sign (like leaning forward or cupping a hand behind an ear) that you need to speak louder. If the place in which you are speaking is unusually large, ask whether people in the back can hear. If people have to strain to hear you, they probably will not make the effort unless you have something extraordinary to say.

Using a Microphone

The rules for using microphones are simple: Make sure they are turned on, and don't blow into them to see if they work. If the microphone is a stationary one, make certain it is adjusted to your height, and stand 8 to 12 inches away from it while you speak. You should not have to lean down or over to speak into it. If you have attached a small microphone to your clothing, you will want to test it first to see whether everyone can hear you. In one auditorium, whenever the speaker moved in front of one of the side speakers, there was a loud reverberation. This is another reason for checking out the facilities and equipment before giving a speech.

Pace

Like volume, pace is easy to vary. **Pace** refers to how fast or how slowly a person speaks. If you speak too fast, you may be difficult to understand. If you speak too slowly, you risk losing the attention of your audience. If audience attention seems to be drifting away, try picking up your pace. Usually speakers don't know that they have been going too fast until someone tells them so after the speech is over.

Ideally a speaker varies his or her pace. Speaking fast and then slowing down helps keep the attention of the audience. Also, don't forget the benefits of pausing. Making a pause before or after a dramatic moment is a highly effective technique. The next time you are watching a comedian on television, notice how he or she uses pauses.

Pitch and Inflection

As we noted in Chapter 4, Nonverbal Communication, pitch is the range of tones used in speaking. **Inflection** is a related concept. It refers to the change in pitch used to emphasize certain words and phrases. A person who never varies his or her speaking voice is said to speak in a **monotone.**

If you listen to professional news readers or sportscasters, you will discover that they use a lot of inflection. By emphasizing certain words and phrases, they help direct listeners' attention to what is important.

Try reading the following sentence, emphasizing a different word each time you read it; you should be able to read it in at least eight different ways:

You mean I have to be there at seven tomorrow?

The best way to get inflection in your voice is to stress certain words deliberately— even to the point of exaggeration. Try recording something in your normal voice and then in your "exaggerated" voice. You might be surprised to find that the exaggerated voice is more interesting.

Enunciation

Enunciation is made up of articulation and pronunciation. **Articulation** is the ability to pronounce the letters in a word correctly; **pronunciation** is the ability to pronounce

ATTENTION!

What Your Voice Conveys
Here is what people think based on how you speak:

- Soft: lacking confidence, weak
- Loud: pushy, aggressive
- High-pitched: girly, inexperienced
- Too fast: anxious, stressed, untrustworthy
- "Ums" and "aws," "like," and "you know": unprepared

How do you gain their trust? Lower your pitch, moderate your tone, speak clearly and slowly, and remove the fillers. If you want to be in charge, then align *what* you say with *how* you say it.[12]

the whole word. Not only does good enunciation enable people to understand us, but it is also the mark of an educated person.

Three common causes of articulation problems are sound substitution, omission of sounds, and slurring. Sound substitution is very common. Many people say "dere," "dem," and "dose" for *there, them,* and *those.* In this case a *d* is substituted for the more difficult *th* sound. The substitution of a *d* for a *t* in the middle of a word is widespread in American English. If you need any proof, try pronouncing these words as you usually do: *water, butter, thirty, bottle.* Unless you have very good articulation, you probably said "wadder," "budder," "thirdy," and "boddle."

Some people believe they have a speech defect that prevents them from producing certain sounds. This can be easily checked. For example, if you always say "dere" for *there,* make a special effort to make the *th* sound. If you are able to make it, you have a bad habit, not a speech defect.

People also commonly omit sounds. For example, some people say "libary" for *library,* and some frequently omit sounds that occur at the ends of words, saying "goin" for *going* and "doin" for *doing.*

Slurring is caused by running words together, as in such phrases as "Yawanna go?" and "I'll meecha there." Slurring, as with other articulation problems, is usually a matter of bad speech habits, and it can be overcome with some effort and practice.

Once you are aware of a particular articulation habit, you can try to change it. Sometimes it helps to drill, using lists of words that give you trouble. It also helps to have a friend remind you when you mispronounce a word. If you are in doubt about how to pronounce a word, look it up in the dictionary. The Internet offers pronunciation dictionaries where you can hear the proper pronunciation.

Using Visual Support

Visual support includes devices such as charts, graphs, slides, and computer-generated images that help illustrate the key points in a speech. Visual support serves four functions: It helps hold the attention of listeners, it provides information in the visual channel, it helps audience members remember what speakers have said, and it helps speakers in several ways. Visual support often helps speakers by:

1. providing another means for supporting or illustrating content.
2. adding an attention-grasping element to the speech.
3. giving them a chance to move around or demonstrate.
4. offering them assistance in remembering their information.

According to one study, if audience members are given only verbal information, after three days they remember a mere 10 percent of what they were told. If they are shown material without verbal communication, they remember 35 percent of what they see. However, if both verbal and visual information is provided, listeners remember 65 percent after three days. But just because you have visual support does not mean that audience members will automatically give you their attention. Poorly designed or inappropriate visual materials will not keep listeners' attention.

Types of Visual Support

Your visual material should help make your topic lively and interesting to the audience. There are numerous types of visual support to choose from. In making your choice, ask yourself which kind of visual material would best illustrate your topic and appeal to your listeners.

In this section we will discuss the chalkboard, the actual object, models, posters, diagrams, and charts, tables and graphs, computer graphics, videos, and handouts. PowerPoint also is a type of visual support; it is simply high-tech. Because presentation software programs—Microsoft's PowerPoint dominates—are so readily available "and 94 percent of professional speakers depend on it,"[13] we have given PowerPoint a section of its own immediately after our discussion of handouts.

The Chalkboard (or Whiteboard)

Since a chalkboard (or whiteboard) exists in every classroom, it is the most accessible visual support. It works particularly well for writing keywords or phrases, drawing very simple diagrams, and giving URLs (Web addresses) for speech material.

When you use the board, it's important that you write quickly to avoid having your back to the audience any longer than necessary. Once you have the word or diagram on the board, turn around, stand next to it, and as you explain, point to it with your hand. Make sure that your writing is large and clear enough for the entire audience to read.

The Actual Object

Sometimes it is useful to use the thing you are talking about as visual support. Audience members like to see what you are talking about, especially if the object is not familiar to them. One student brought a violin and a viola to class to demonstrate the differences in the sounds and the looks of the two instruments. Another, explaining how to make minor adjustments on one's car, brought a carburetor. Still another borrowed a skeleton from the biology department to illustrate a speech on osteoporosis, a bone disease.

Models

A **model** is a replica of an actual object that is used when the object itself is too large to be displayed (a building), too small to be seen (a cell), or inaccessible to the eye (the human heart). A model can be very effective visual support because it shows exactly how something looks. It is better than a picture because it is three-dimensional. A student who was discussing airplanes used in warfare brought in models of planes he had constructed.

Posters, Diagrams, and Charts

A poster consists of lettering or pictures, or both. The purpose of a poster is to enhance the speaker's subject. For example, when speaking about the style of electric cars, a student used a poster showing pictures of one make to show how the batteries had been incorporated into the overall design of the car. A poster may also be used to emphasize the keywords or important thoughts in a speech. A student who spoke on how to save money on clothes used a poster to list the following points:

- Decide on a basic color.
- Buy basics at one store.
- Buy accessories at sales.

Not only did the poster provide the audience with a way to remember the points, but it also gave, in visual form, the general outline of the speech.

A diagram may range from a simple organizational chart to a complex rendering of a three-dimensional object. Diagrams are particularly valuable in showing how

ATTENTION!

Guidelines for Using Visual Support

1. DO use them to summarize or show the sequence of content.

2. DO use them to visually interpret statistics by preparing charts and graphs that illustrate what you will say.

3. DO use them to illustrate and reinforce your support statements.

4. DO use them to add visual clarity to your concepts and ideas.

5. DO use them to focus the attention of the target group on key points.

6. DON'T project copies of printed or written text. Instead, summarize the information and show only the key points on the visual aids.

7. DON'T read the information on your overheads or slides.

8. DON'T use copies of your transparencies as handouts.

9. DON'T use charts, graphs, or tables that contain more information than you want to provide.[14]

Figure 14-1
One Cavern's Size

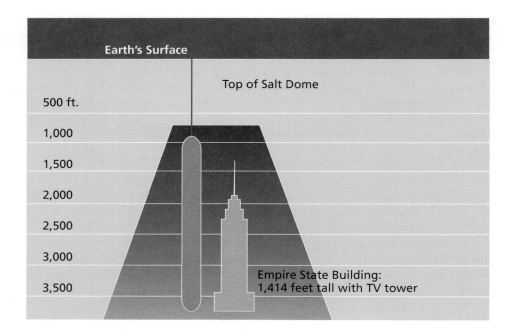

something works. For example, in a speech about storing toxic wastes, a student used the diagram in Figure 14-1 to show how waste can be stored in a salt cavern. Including a drawing of the Empire State Building was particularly useful because it gave the viewer an idea of the depth of the mine.

An **organizational chart** shows the relationships among the elements of an organization, such as the departments of a company, the branches of federal or state government, or the committees of the student government. Note how a speaker used the organizational chart in Figure 14-2 to show how the academic side of a university is organized and how a student wishing to express dissatisfaction should approach people in a specific order, beginning with a faculty member.

A **flip chart** is a series of pictures, words, diagrams, and so forth. It's called a "flip chart" because it is made up of several pages that you flip through. A flip chart is best used when you have a complicated subject that needs several illustrations or when you want to emphasize several points in your speech.

Figure 14-2
Organizational Chart

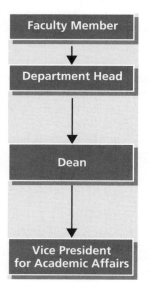

Tables and Graphs

Tables and graphs are easy to prepare and can condense a lot of information into a useful, understandable form. Perhaps most important, anyone can make this visual support because no special skills are required. With the use of a computer, creating tables, putting information into the tables, changing the tables, and creating titles for the tables can be accomplished through the click of a mouse.

Tables are columns of figures arranged in an order that enables the viewer to easily pick out the information needed. For example, when Rosa Amin spoke to her class on the topic "Living Alone," she used a simple table to illustrate problems associated with creating a budget. She said, "My monthly budget is divided into these things" and pointed to the table (see Table 14-2). "This represents costs of $2,000 a month," said Rosa. "I work 30 hours a week at the library for $10 an hour, for which I receive $1,200 a month. I am fortunate to receive an allowance from my parents of $200 a week, or $800 a month—while I am in school—which brings my monthly income to $2,000. So, if I can stick to my very strict budget, I am able to just break even each month. Often, I can cut corners on food, clothing, school supplies, and entertainment—and then I can sometimes realize a monthly savings," Rosa said.

Graphs are used to present statistical material in a visual form that helps viewers see similarities, differences, relationships, or trends. There are three commonly used types of graphs: bar, pie, and line. If you want to see a variety of the graphs available, look in any issue of *USA Today*. The bar graph in Figure 14-3—as the source notes—is from one of these graphs.

A line graph is particularly useful for showing trends over a period of time or for making comparisons. For example, Figure 14-4 shows how many people were online as of June 2010; however, the source notes that "The art of estimating how many are online throughout the world is an inexact one at best. Surveys abound, using all sorts of measurement parameters."[15] So, how did Internet World Stats get its results? In the same way most survey organizations do, "From observing many of the published surveys over the last two years, here is an 'educated guess' as to how many are online worldwide."[16]

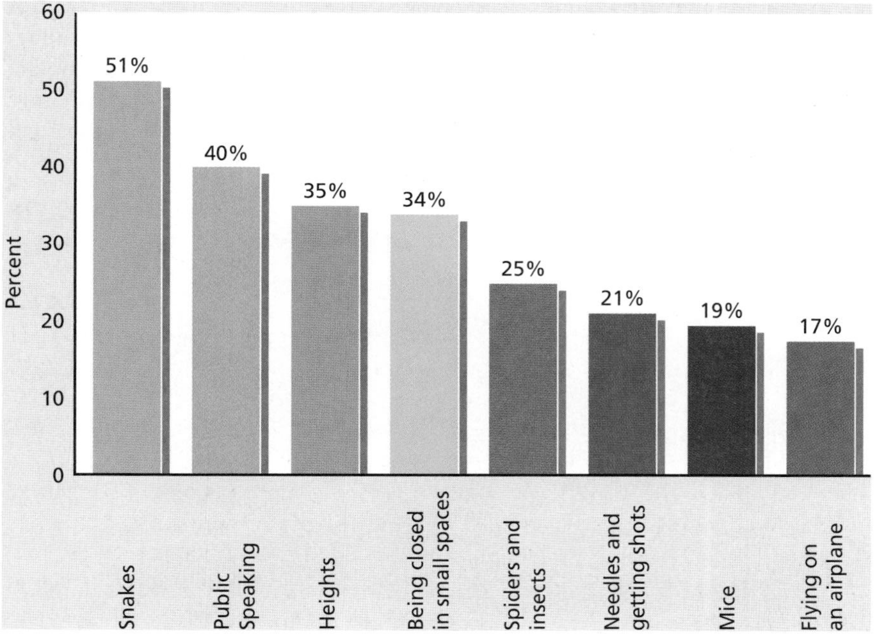

TABLE 14-2 Rosa's Budget: Expenses

Rent	$ 500
Car payment	300
Food	400
Utilities	200
Clothing	150
Books/school supplies	150
Entertainment	150
Savings	75
Miscellaneous	75
Total	$2,000

Figure 14-3
List of Things That People Fear

Source: "Snakes Scarier Than Public Speaking" from *USA Today*, March 26, 2001. Reprinted by permission of USA Today.

Figure 14-4
Internet Users in the World Distribution by World Regions–June 30, 2012.

Source: "Internet Usage Statistics" from Internet World Stats, www.internet-worldstats.com

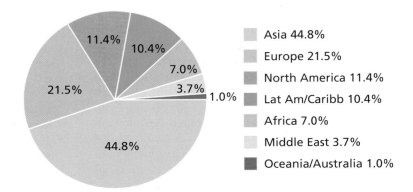

- Asia 44.8%
- Europe 21.5%
- North America 11.4%
- Lat Am/Caribb 10.4%
- Africa 7.0%
- Middle East 3.7%
- Oceania/Australia 1.0%

In a speech titled "Let's All Read," Martin used the pie graph in Figure 14-5 to illustrate the fact that nearly half the nation's population doesn't buy books, much less read them.

Computer Graphics

The computer offers numerous options to speakers. The phrase **computer-generated graphics** refers to any images created or manipulated via computer—art, drawings, representations of objects, pictures, and the like. If you want to create a graph or some other piece of visual support, a computer with a graphics program can generate it. Computers are best for processing numerical data and then converting those data into bar, line, or pie graphs. Having a computer-generated graph enlarged is a relatively simple, inexpensive process; photocopiers can enlarge images, sometimes to 200 percent of the original size.

The average computer user may not yet have the capacity to produce visuals like those seen on television—which often cost thousands of dollars to produce—but well-thought-out visuals, projected on a screen or a computer, can give your presentation a professional and sophisticated look. And the computer software available today can make even the simplest attempt at slide production extremely professional looking.

Perhaps the most important advice regarding your visuals is to make them readable. Follow the "6 × 6 rule." Use no more than six words horizontally, and use no more

Figure 14-5
Pie Graph

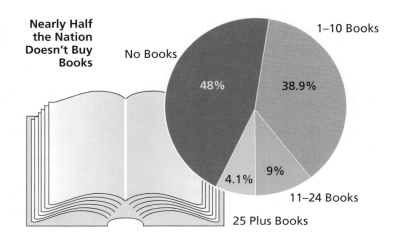

than six items on a page—fewer than that, if possible. This will result in a visual that conveys its meaning readily, and it will help ensure that the slide can be seen by the people farthest away. Here, we'll apply the 6 × 6 rule in a bulleted list:

- Keep text larger than 18 points.
- 44 points = titles; 32 = text; 28 = subtext.
- Use no more than three fonts.
- Use dark background and bright text.
- Overheads need light background, dark text.
- Insert tables and graphs when appropriate.

One essential element in any presentation is visual variety. How do you obtain variety? You can use diagrams, flowcharts, and graphs to illustrate your ideas. Most software packages offer opportunities to obtain variety. There are clip-art packages that allow you to insert professional-quality graphics into your visuals. There are numerous Internet sources from which clip art can be downloaded free. With a scanner, you can add cartoons, magazine and newspaper headlines, and photographs. To keep the focus of listener attention on you, not the visuals, occasionally intersperse a visual without words or pictures to give audience members a chance to refocus their attention, and concentrate on your textual message.

You can get additional visual variety through the use of **multimedia**—various media (sound, graphics, and animation, as well as text) used to deliver information. You can liven up your message with pictures and music, but you need to be cautious, especially if you are a beginner. Aim for just enough graphics, sound, and animation to support, elaborate, and focus the point of your message without risk of obscuring or overwhelming your point.

The techniques combining MP3 player with television and computers and computer-generated graphics with video cameras bring sophisticated capabilities to the nonprofessional as well as the professional speaker: Many of these resources are already being used in high-quality workplace speeches and sales presentations. Check to see if you have access to such technology.

Videos

If you decide to use a video to support your speech, you have two choices: You can use one made by other people, or you can make your own. If you are making a long speech, a preprogrammed video can be a very good visual reinforcement of what you are saying. A student who gave a speech on how applicants are propagandized by college admission recordings followed her speech with the college's own admissions video. The students were amazed at the difference between their perception of the college and the recording's portrayal of it.

With so many easy, inexpensive, and convenient ways to capture moving images, most people can not only make their own recordings but customize them to match their subject and their audience. One student, for example, made a recording illustrating four basic karate moves for his speech. Because recordings are so easy to work with, he was able to stop the recording to talk about each move then go on to the next one.

Handouts

When material is complex or when there is a lot of it, audience members may need a handout. For example, a student who spoke about the calories in fast foods gave audience members a handout showing the caloric values of specific foods. Other times a handout is useful to reinforce the points you are making in your speech. A student who spoke about 10 ways to recycle made a handout of her main points and distributed it at the end of her speech.

If you use handouts, choose the best time to pass them out. If you distribute your handouts too early, the audience will read them and ignore you. Also, most people dislike having a handout read to them. If your handout repeats the points you are making, give it out when your speech is over.

PowerPoint

The most widely used software program is Microsoft's PowerPoint (PP). Its popularity results from three benefits: (1) It provides tools for creative multimedia presentations that combine text, graphics, video, and sound; (2) it lends itself to a wide variety of speech applications; and (3) it is easy to use. PowerPoint is high-tech visual support, and speakers should incorporate PowerPoint into their speeches just as they would any of the other types of visual support previously discussed. The important thing for speakers to remember is this: *Never* turn to read PowerPoint information to listeners. This defeats the effectiveness and use of PowerPoint.

The most important guideline for the successful use of PP is to treat it as an aid, or, as one component of a speech. A great PP presentation should enhance your information, *never* take its place. Thus, when you use PP, you should:

- Use bullets, not numbers. (Never include full paragraphs of text.)
- Put no more than one topic on a slide.
- Use the 6 × 6 rule already discussed.
- Select a readable typeface and size. Use a minimum 36-point font for titles, and 24 points for the other information. Avoid using all caps; it makes it look like you're shouting.
- Use the same colors consistently throughout the presentation. Always choose light letters on a dark background.
- Keep the background simple and allow plenty of space around words and images. Include a combination of words, pictures, and graphics. It is this kind of variety that keeps the presentation interesting.

Remember, computer-generated graphics and multimedia are props that should support and enhance your main ideas, not take their place. It is you—the main actor, speaker, and focus of the speech—who must engage your listeners.

Rules for Using Visual Support

- *Use visual support to supplement, not replace, the speech.* The visual support should not become the whole show. It should be a useful addition to reinforce the speech.
- *Show the visual support only when you are ready for it.* Put the visual in an inconspicuous place; then, when you are ready to use it, take it out. When you are finished with it, put it away. You don't want it to compete with you for attention.
- *Before your speech, check the room to see if your visual support can be easily displayed.* If you are using projection equipment, find the electric outlets and

see if the room has blackout shades or curtains. If you're using your computer, make sure it has sufficient battery power. If you are hanging a chart, decide how to hang it. Are you going to need tape or thumbtacks?

- *Practice with your visual support before the speech.* Practice using equipment until you can operate it quickly and easily. Check to see how much time your visual support takes. If it is going to take too much time, decide how you will cut back.

- *Talk to the audience, not to the visual.* You may need to look at your visual occasionally, but remember to maintain eye contact with the audience.

Rehearsing Your Speech

The next stage is actually to deliver the speech. If possible, practice to one or a few patient, kind friends, or family members after first practicing privately. Ask them if the main points made sense. Could they tell if you were consistently on the topic? Did your speech ramble off in different directions? Make any adjustments in your speech according to the responses and suggestions you receive. Remember, it's not what you say that matters; it is what your listeners hear that makes a difference. Also, practice your speech using your visual support or PowerPoint.

As you practice your delivery, try to imagine the exact location where you will be giving the speech. If you can practice in that location, even better. Imagine your listeners and practice making eye contact with them as you deliver your ideas. The more you can simulate—visualize—the actual situation and audience, the greater the likelihood you will reduce your nervousness when you deliver your final speech. If you record your rehearsal you will be able to evaluate your performance using the Assess Yourself box at the end of this chapter.

As you continue rehearsing, adjust your outline each time you give the speech by continuing to shorten it to key terms. Because you will be using *only* a key-term outline for the actual, final delivery of your speech, the time to arrive at the best selection of keywords to use is during early rehearsals.

The following six-item process can serve as a checklist as you approach your final rehearsals for the speech.

1. Stand against one wall and look over your "audience." Remember to establish eye contact with people in all parts of the room.

2. Check your starting time. In this practice session you want to find out how long your speech is.

3. Deliver the speech all the way through without stopping. As you speak, remember to look at your audience.

4. When the speech is over, check your ending time.

5. Analyze your performance: Did any parts of the speech give you difficulty? Did the speech seem clearly organized? Check your outline: In giving the speech, did you leave anything out? Was your outline clear and easy to follow? How about time? Do you need to add or delete any material to make the speech the proper length?

6. Make the necessary changes and rehearse the speech again. And rehearse again and again until you are completely comfortable with the material, your pace (speed of delivery), and with all aspects of the speech. How many

ATTENTION!

Writing Notes for Your Speech

It is better to know your material so well that you can give it from your heart rather than from cards. Having notes, however, can be a lifesaver. 3 × 5 cards are well suited for speech notes. They can be easily concealed on your body for quick and easy retrieval, then cupped in the hand so they are not as distracting as having an 8.5 × 11-inch piece of paper. If you are going to be behind a lectern, then full-size paper is quite effective. On your notes put down the key ideas for each area of your speech, rather than creating word for word notes. By creating key word or key idea notes you will avoid the temptation of reading your speech from your notes. This will enable you to easily connect to and build a better rapport with your audience.[17]

rehearsal times depends totally on you and your comfort level; there is no exact guideline.

You may be hesitant to rehearse because you feel silly talking to an empty room. Yet if you go into a store to buy a new piece of clothing, you probably spend a lot of time in the dressing room looking at it from several angles. By rehearsing a speech, you are doing the same thing: You are trying it on to see if it fits; if it doesn't, you will have time to make the necessary alterations.

In her book, *Quiet: The Power of Introverts in a World That Can't Stop Talking* (NY: Broadway Books, 2013), Susan Cain offers an important suggestion for rehearsing: "Deliberate Practice [which is the key, she says, to exceptional achievement] is best conducted alone for several reasons. It takes intense concentration, and other people can be distracting. It requires deep motivation, often self-generated. But most important, it involves working on the task that's most challenging to *you* personally" (p. 81).

"We learn the basics [of communication] in grammar school and high school," write Newberg and Waldman in *Words Can Change Your Brain*, "but if you want to excel at communicating, you have to unlearn many bad habits and replace them with advanced skills like empathic listening. You have to study the mechanics of verbal inflection, and you have to learn how to read facial expressions that most people tend to ignore. You have to immerse yourself fully in the experience of speaking and listening, and you have to practice, practice, practice" (p. 20).

Delivery Self-Evaluation Form

How effective is your delivery? For each question write the numerical score that best represents your delivery using the following criteria: 7 = Outstanding; 6 = Excellent; 5 = Very good; 4 = Average (good); 3 = Fair; 2 = Poor; 1 = Minimal ability; 0 = No ability demonstrated. Use this form as you assess, evaluate, and critique the rehearsal you videotape for your speech.

1. Did you demonstrate a conversational quality? _____
2. Did you focus on the moment by being aware of and focusing on your listeners' needs? _____
3. Were you completely focused on the communication situation? _____
4. Were you natural and straightforward? _____
5. Did you deliver your speech extemporaneously—showing your natural responsiveness to your listeners without depending on your notes? _____
6. Did you appear spontaneous and not rehearsed or reading your notes? _____
7. Was your attire appropriate for the occasion? _____
8. Were your body movements appropriate and not distracting? _____
9. Did you look into the eyes of individual audience members? _____
10. Did your face appear expressive and yet natural? _____
11. Did your gestures appear natural, comfortable, and spontaneous? _____
12. Did your posture help reinforce a positive, alert impression? _____
13. Did you speak loudly enough, and yet not too loudly? _____
14. Was your pace or rate of speaking varied and, thus, not monotonous? _____
15. Did your voice and inflection reveal emphasis and variety when needed? _____
16. Did you reveal proper and effective enunciation (both articulation and pronunciation)? _____

TOTAL POINTS: _____

Go to the Online Learning Center at **www.mhhe.com/hybels11e** to see your results and learn how to evaluate your attitudes and feelings.

www.mhhe.com/hybels11e >

Summary

To achieve effective delivery, speakers need to tailor their speech to their own strengths and weaknesses by gaining experience, engaging in self-critiques, listening to the advice of others, and experimenting and making the necessary changes.

Public-speaking anxiety is a disturbance of mind regarding a forthcoming public-speaking event for which you are the speaker. It is triggered by stress, and the physiological responses to anxiety vary in both their kind and intensity. One key to reducing nervousness is to think of delivering your speech as a communication task, *not* as a performance.

There are a number of time-tested ways for dealing with nervousness. They include being prepared and positive. Also, if you visualize, anticipate, focus, and gain experience, you are more likely to look forward to public speeches with interest, eagerness, and even passion. Other ways for reducing nervousness include dressing in comfortable clothes, asking to speak first, taking several deep breaths, remembering your audience is composed of people like you, moving around, picking out friendly faces, and giving yourself a reward after your speech.

Good delivery involves, first and foremost, achieving a conversational quality. But the bottom line is, "Does your delivery effectively do what you intend it to do?"

The four ways of delivering a speech are speaking impromptu, with very little preparation; speaking from a manuscript; speaking from memory; and—the best method of delivery—speaking extemporaneously, from notes.

Speakers should concentrate on what they wear and on their body movement, eye contact, gestures, and posture so that they appear at their very best and, thus, their appearance does not distract in any way from their message. Speakers should also pay special attention to volume, pace, pitch and inflection, and enunciation.

Visuals help hold attention and clarify information. Common types of visual support include the actual object, models, posters, diagrams, charts, tables, graphs, computer graphics, videos, and handouts. Although PowerPoint is high-tech visual support, speakers should incorporate it into their speeches just as they would any of the other types of visual support. When using visual support, make sure that it can be easily seen, enhances the speech rather than overpowers it, and never takes the place of the speaker but reinforces and underscores the content of the message.

Rehearsing your speech involves saying the speech out loud in front of patient, kind friends or family members, imagining the exact location where you will be giving the speech, imagining your listeners, recording your rehearsal if possible, adjusting your outline each time you give the speech for clarity and organization, checking its length, and following the checklist as you approach the final delivery of the speech.

Key Terms and Concepts

Go to the Online Learning Center at **www.mhhe.com/hybels11e** to further your understanding of the following terms.

Questions to Review

1. What is the philosophical approach recommended for reducing public-speaking anxiety, and what are its strengths?

2. What are some time-tested ways that you can see would help those who experience public-speaking anxiety and who need assistance in controlling their nervousness?

3. What are other strategies for reducing anxiety?

4. Which is the most important characteristic of an effective delivery style?

5. Of the different types of delivery (impromptu, manuscript, memory, and extemporaneous), with which style are you most comfortable? Why? Which do you find most difficult? Why?

6. If you were motivated to improve your speaking ability, which of the different types of delivery would you concentrate on, and why?

7. Weigh the value of how you look when it comes to giving speeches. How important is it? How important is the way you sound?

8. What visual support is best for your speech? Why? Will it simplify, clarify, and enhance your speech? In what ways?

9. What is the most important guideline when it comes to PowerPoint presentations? Explain.

10. What is the suggested method for rehearsing speeches?

Go to the self-quizzes on the Online Learning Center at www.mhhe.com/hybels11e to test your knowledge of the chapter contents.

CHAPTER FIFTEEN

Informative and Persuasive Speeches

Objectives

After reading this chapter, you should be able to:

- Distinguish among speeches about objects, speeches about processes, speeches about events, and speeches about concepts.

- Use the strategies for defining ideas, describing ideas, and explaining ideas.

- Clarify how to get audience members interested and involved in your speech.

- Explain the methods for helping listeners remember your main ideas.

- Define persuasion and describe its purpose.

- Clarify the ethical standards persuaders should follow.

- Distinguish among values, beliefs, and attitudes; explain the purpose of each and how each contributes to effective persuasion.

- Describe each of the strategies persuaders can use.

- Build your credibility through the qualities of competence, dynamism, character, and caring.

I N DOING INITIAL RESEARCH FOR A SPEECH THAT HE NEEDED TO WRITE for a speech communication class, Louis discovered some information claiming that half the marriages in the United States fail—that is, that there is a 50 percent chance that a marriage won't make it. The statistic was cited by an infidelity support group, in the promotion for a book on divorce, and by a men's counseling center in California. With further research, however, Louis discovered that pollster Louis Harris wrote, "The idea that half of American marriages are doomed is one of the most specious pieces of statistical nonsense ever perpetuated in modern times."[1] Louis knew that he had a unique angle on a topic that would not just interest the class but teach them something as well, because everyone wants a successful marriage and wants to know how to attain it.

Having developed an informative speech topic, Louis began his research. With the tentative title "Until Death Do Us Part," he talked to two divorce lawyers, consulted a number of online statistical sources for current information and statistics, and examined four books: Jim Smoke's book, *Growing Through Divorce* (Harvest House), Sharon Wegscheider-Cruse's *Life After Divorce* (HCI), Harold H. Bloomfield and Peter McWilliams's *How to Survive the Loss of a Love* (Prelude Press), and Catherine Napolitane's *Living and Loving After Divorce* (Signet). After framing a thesis and devising points that would support it, Louis organized his evidence around each of the points and refined them as he continued. The visual aid he planned to use would *refute* America's most-often-cited statistic: "Fifty percent of marriages will end in divorce." Louis ended his content preparation by writing out his conclusion in full, then, finally, his introduction. As Louis practiced his delivery and presentation skills, he not only visualized his audience before him, but he also kept his goal of creating understanding in his listeners at the forefront of his mind.

The purpose of an informative speech is to provide listeners with information that will help them make decisions as individuals and as citizens. The need for high-quality information demands skill in our ability to produce and deliver it. Although some of this information is delivered in written form, much of it is oral: The teacher before the class, the radio or television reporter broadcasting to an audience, the professional sharing ideas with colleagues, the employer explaining policies to employees, the politician clarifying issues or defining approaches to problems—all of them need oral skills to convey information.

The **informative speech**—one that defines, clarifies, instructs, and explains—is a common phenomenon in our society. If we are going to prosper in the information society, the ability to give an informative speech is a necessary skill. The need to increase understanding is a universal one.

You are likely to encounter informative speeches in a variety of contexts. You're probably familiar with the *lecture*, which is simply an informative talk given before a class audience. One is unlikely to escape college or university without experiencing a number of lectures, since the lecture remains the most common form of class presentation. The next is a *lecture/demonstration*, an informative talk that shows listeners how to do something or how something works. Teachers show how to prepare an assignment; sales representatives show how their products work; supervisors show employees how to do their jobs. The last is an *explanation* of ideas or policies. Most of the examples in this chapter come from speeches of explanation.

How to Excel
To benefit an audience, you need to go beyond just giving an informative speech in the traditional sense, telling them what they already know. Otherwise it would only be a review. As a result, you may lose their attention. To be truly informative, your goal will be to:

- Stimulate thinking ability
- Give a gift of knowledge to the audience
- Leave the audience feeling they have benefitted[2]

Table 15-1   Guidelines for Selecting Your Informative Topic

Audience knowledge	Relate your topic to your audience	Work on your topic
• Be clear. • Maintain their interest. • Keep it simple (not too technical).	• Why does your audience want to hear this? • What does your topic have to do with them? • How can you elicit audience involvement? • What familiar and relevant information can you use?	• Make it real. • Avoid abstractions. • Use detailed descriptions. • Use comparisons, metaphors, similes, and analogies.

Table 15-1 is a useful place to begin work on your informative speech. It draws together valuable information from previous chapters.

Goals of an Informative Speaker

A study by Paul Schrodt, *et. al.* (meaning there were other authors of the study—in this case, five others), with the sophisticated title, "Instructor Credibility as a Mediator of Instructor's Prosocial Communication Behaviors and Students' Learning Outcomes," published in the academic journal *Communication Education*[3] sheds light on how those who have as their goal establishing positive speaker-audience relationships and increasing audience learning, should behave. The results of this study indicate that "instructors seeking to enhance interpersonal relationships with their students, and thus, play a substantial role in facilitating classroom learning" should engage in confirming behaviors such as responding to students' questions, demonstrating an interest in students, and using a variety of teaching methods (p. 366). The advice applies as well to speakers wishing to inform. Speakers can anticipate audience questions, even incorporate them into their speech, tie their speech closely to the interests of their audience members, and use a variety of supporting materials. This is practical, useful, and valuable information to have as you begin the planning and preparation of an informative speech.

With so much information available, it's surprising that listeners don't buckle under from information overload. When listeners are so swamped with information, we face a serious problem as speakers. We have to ask ourselves, "How can I, as an informative speaker, make my information stand out?"

Increasing Understanding

Since the goal of an informative speech is to give the audience new or in-depth information on a subject, it is particularly important that a speaker put together a speech that audience members will understand. Several things will help understanding: language choice, organization, and illustrations and examples.

Language Choice

In our highly technological world, many of us speak a specialized language that is understood only by people in the same field. If you are giving a speech that uses technical or specialized vocabulary, you must take the time to define your terms, or consider whether you can avoid technical terms altogether.

ATTENTION!

Grab Attention and Generate Interest

- Relate the topic to the audience: Let people know how the topic relates to them on a personal level.
- Share the importance of the topic: Tell the audience why the topic is important.
- Startle the audience: Provide an astonishing, interesting, arresting, or intriguing fact or statement.
- Ask a thought-provoking question.
- Open with an appropriate attention-getting quote by a great thinker or famous person.
- Use a narrative: Tell the audience a true story that relates to the topic.[4]

The goal of an informative speech is to give listeners new or in-depth information on a subject.

Organization

A good organizational pattern will show how ideas relate to one another and will help listeners move from one idea to another. As a listener you probably know that your attention will wander if the speaker is rambling or you have trouble finding the main points of the speech.

Illustrations and Examples

If you are going to explain a principle that might be unfamiliar to your audience, use an example to show what it is or how it works. For example, a student who was explaining three basic body types held up pictures to illustrate each type. When he held up a picture of a thin, lightly muscled person, the meaning of the term *ectomorph* was immediately clear.

Getting Attention

The first goal of a speaker is to get the attention of audience members. In most public-speaking situations there are many distractions: People come in late; the air-conditioner fan turns on and off; a fly buzzes around the room; the microphone gives off feedback.

The best way to get and keep attention is to create in your audience a strong desire to listen to your material. Ask yourself whether your material is relevant. Does it apply to the people in your audience? If it doesn't, how can it be adapted to their needs?

If the audience perceives the information as new, it is more likely to pay attention. "New" doesn't necessarily mean a subject no one has ever heard about—you might present a new perspective or a new angle. Certain topics are going to provoke a "ho-hum" reaction from the audience. You don't want your audience to think "Not another speech about jogging" (or dieting and nutrition, or getting organized). When

You are to select an informative speech that you have recently heard or will hear, and you are to analyze it with respect to the goals of an informative speaker (i.e., increasing understanding by language choice, organization, or illustrations and examples, getting attention, and helping retention). Answer the following questions with respect to the informative speech you have selected:

1. What were the various methods the speaker chose to make his or her information stand out?

2. Did his or her choices of methods work effectively? What could he or she do to improve in this area?

3. When it comes to informative speeches, which of the methods discussed are likely to most effectively capture and hold *your* attention?

4. Will you remember the informative speech you heard? What specific methods did the speaker use to help you remember his or her ideas? If you could suggest a way or several additional ways not used, which way(s) would you suggest?

Richard Lamm, from the Center for Public Policy and Contemporary Issues at the University of Denver, was asked to deliver an address to the 1998 World Future Society, he chose a title that might—just from hearing it—put many listeners to sleep: "Unexamined Assumptions: Destiny, Political Institutions, Democracy, and Population." So he planned an introduction that ran counter to both his title and his topic, one that he knew would get the attention of his audience. He began:

> A priest was riding in a subway when a man staggered toward him, smelling like a brewery, with lipstick on his collar. He sat in the seat right next to the priest and started reading the newspaper. After a few minutes, the man turned to the priest and asked "Excuse me, Father, what causes arthritis?"
>
> The priest, tired of smelling the liquor and saddened by the lifestyle, said roughly "Loose living, drink, dissipation, contempt for your fellow man and being with cheap and wicked women!"
>
> "That's amazing," said the drunk and returned to his newspaper. A while later, the priest, feeling a bit guilty, turned to the man and asked nicely, "How long have you had arthritis?"
>
> "Oh," said the man, "I don't have arthritis, I was just reading that the Pope did."
>
> The parable, of course, is a lesson on assumptions.[5]

When you want people to remember certain points, it is useful to give these points special emphasis. Sometimes this can be done with verbal cues: "This is my most important point" or "If you remember only one thing I said today, remember this." Sometimes you can use a cue after a point: "Now let me show you how important what I just said can be to you." A point can be emphasized, too, by repeating it, by changing your rate of speech, or by pausing just before you say it.[6]

Frank Luntz, in his book *Words That Work* (Hyperion, 2007), writes about the power of poignant (severe or sharp) language. He says, "Words that work are catalysts. They spur us to get up off the couch, to leave the house, to *do* something. When communicators pay attention to what people hear rather than to what they are trying to say, they manage not merely to catch people's attention, but to hold it."[7]

Helping Retention

There are other ways to help retention. Whenever possible, use several brief examples and illustrations for each concept you are introducing, and vary them as much as possible. Realize that some of your listeners will respond better to verbal explanations, some to graphs and charts, and some to video and so on. The more variety you supply, the greater the likelihood you will tap into methods your listeners use to stimulate their recall.

Yet another effective way to help retention is by using visual support. "Presentation research shows that really 'a picture is worth a thousand words'—with message retention being increased over words by a factor of five."[8] A study by the Wharton School of Business found that "on average, people retain about 10 percent of a presentation communicated through words alone, whereas the effective use of visual aids increases retention up to 50 percent."[9]

James McGaugh, a neurobiologist at the University of California at Irvine, says that memory and emotion are intimately linked biochemically; thus, "Any kind of emotional experience will create a stronger memory than otherwise would be created."[10] For speakers, it means that if your intent is to aid listeners' retention, sharing *emotional* anecdotes, stories, illustrations, and experiences will help.

Types of Informative Speeches

As you read about the following types of informative speeches, keep in mind that to be successful, you must never overestimate the information your audience has nor underestimate their intelligence.

Objects

Speeches about objects are about things, people, places, animals, and products. Because of the time limits placed on the length of your speech, you cannot discuss any topic completely. This means you must focus your attention on some aspect of your topic. Instead of focusing on body adornment, for example, you might choose tattoos.

Processes

Speeches about processes deal with patterns of action. One type of speech about processes is the **demonstration speech,** a speech that teaches people how to perform a process. A speech on how to research the job market might discuss the process of evaluating online job sites. The important thing to remember is that you need to limit your information to just what can be explained clearly and completely in the time you are allowed.

Events

Speeches about events focus on things that happened, are happening, or will happen. They need to go one step further than mere history and show listeners how they can use the information. One student, who traveled to Washington, DC, to become part of a nationwide protest, talked about the kinds of students she met, but also showed her listeners how they could organize an effective protest movement—things she learned from her trip.

Concepts

Speeches about concepts deal with theories, ideas, beliefs, and other abstract principles. Here it's important to be both clear and understandable. For example, Nadia chose the topic "the empowerment of women." Because her definition and approach were abstract, she then focused on units on her own campus where imbalance was clear: faculty, administration, and female representation on important committees and boards.

Notice how easily Nadia could turn her speech into a persuasive one—especially considering the reason she pursued the topic in the first place: the imbalances she heard about and observed on her campus. Nadia kept her speech informative by doing two things: providing unbiased information and refraining from making arguments.

Overarching Principles

No matter which of the general types of informative speeches you choose, the principles that make a good speech remain the same. Strive for clarity, strong organization, and vivid language.

Don't try to cover too many points, clarify the relationship between your main points, and keep your speech moving forward according to a well-developed plan. Define your terms and use examples. Restate and paraphrase, and use numerous transitions. Involve your audience, offer clear supporting material, and conclude your speech with impact. In all cases, avoid becoming too technical. The test of a good speaker is to communicate even the most complex ideas clearly and simply.

STRATEGIC FLEXIBILITY

The process of determining which type of strategy to use for presenting material in informative speeches is dependent on your effective use of strategic flexibility—thinking about potential situations and the needs and requirements likely to arise because of them. The key for speakers here is forecasting.

Strategies for Informative Speeches

There are different types of strategies for presenting material in informative speeches. Each type requires a special skill. Sometimes all of these types can be found in a single speech; usually at least two will be used.

Defining

A **definition**—an explanation of the meaning of a word or phrase—can often make a critical difference in whether your audience understands your speech. The best source for definitions is to use topic-relevant, credible sources. For example, the definition of *communication* varies greatly between discipline-specific resources and a general dictionary. Sometimes dictionary definitions are sufficient—especially when words have no tie to a discipline—and sometimes a thesaurus offers word variants that will help you clarify and define.

Definition can also go beyond explaining words or phrases. Four useful ways to define concepts in a speech are by etymology, example, comparison and contrast, and function.

Etymology

Etymology, the study of the origin and development of words, can be used as a basis for definition. For example, when discussing romantic love and the intense feelings that occur, one speaker pointed out that the word *ecstasy*, which is a common label

www.mhhe.com/hybels11e

View the video clip from an informative student speech, "Indian Weddings, by Preeti Vilku."

Remember the Principles

However you create your speech include the principles of what makes a good speech:

1. Involve your audience.
2. Keep them involved.
3. Use a clear central idea.
4. Give clear supporting material.
5. Conclude the speech with impact.
6. Avoid becoming too technical in your explanations.[13]

for emotions during the time of romantic love, is derived from a Greek word meaning "deranged"—a state beyond all reason and self-control.[11] She went on to show that the word *deranged* accurately describes the state of mind that exists early in romantic relationships. The *Oxford English Dictionary* is the best source for word etymologies.

Example

An example illustrates a point. When using an example, a speaker often either points to an actual thing or points out something verbally.

In this excerpt, Christina Burton talks to her class about her addiction:

> *I am an addict, and I admit it. But I'm not alone because I know that many of you are too. When my roommate gets out of bed, the first thing she does is turn on her four-cupper for a cup-a-joe to jumpstart her day. She's one of 167 million coffee drinkers in the United States, and together we consumed nearly 6.3 billion gallons last year alone.*[12]

Comparison and Contrast

Comparisons point out the similarities between two or more things. When Dwight Cushenberry, who grew up in a rural farming community, gave his class speech "Auctions, 24/7," he not only had numerous experiences with farm auctions and found them exciting, but in his speech, he could compare those with the excitement and thrill of using eBay:

> *eBay has brought the excitement of participating in an auction to millions. It revved up the old auction spirit in me as well. Just like an old farm auction, you're likely to find almost anything on eBay; just like a farm auction, too, when you use eBay you are part of a community of members. And just like an old farm auction, you are likely to get carried away with the excitement and overpay for something. For me, eBay has been a godsend because it captures all the excitement of an old farm auction, but the real thrill is that you can enjoy the excitement 24/7.*

Contrasts point out the differences between two or more things. In her class speech "Girls Get a Grip," Lenore Ashley used contrast when she talked about the way males and females express their anger:

> *Now, you all know how guys express their anger because first, it's obvious, and second, it's consistent. When that bubbling cauldron of hormone-laden emotion explodes, guys will express their anger physically. They'll shove someone's face into a toilet, or they'll push them up against a car. The reason you don't always see females express their anger is that it's more subtle. That doesn't mean it's less effective, and if you're ever on the receiving end of a female's anger, you already know how effective it can be. Females express their anger in nonphysical, indirect, covert forms: backbiting, exclusion, rumors, name-calling, and manipulation.*

Choices of strategies for presenting material in informative speeches depend on the unique combination of speaker, topic, audience, and situation.

Function

With certain topics it's useful to define by function—showing how a thing performs or how it can be used. Speakers may stress an object's usefulness, advantages, benefits, convenience, or service. Eugene Finerman, a satirist and professional speechwriter, began his speech on humor, "Humor and Speeches: A Stand-Up History," by defining the function of humor:

> *A plumber, a jockey and a rabbi walk into a pet store . . . What a cheap trick to get your attention, but that is the charm—and the power—of humor. Humor can engage, entice, coax and persuade. It can ridicule, vilify, agitate and incite. Humor can warm an audience or inflame it. The effective speaker and the astute speech-writer know the value of and place for humor. It is a natural means of communication, and it has served the public speaker for as long as there have been speeches.[14]*

Describing

To describe is to provide a mental image of something experienced, such as a scene, a person, or a sensation. Many times your audience will be able to visualize what you are talking about if you create a picture for them.

Size or Quantity

Size is the measurement or extent of a thing when compared with some standard. Notice how Kellie, a student, described a spider's web in her speech:

> *Not only did it stretch from the ground to the lower limbs of one tree, close to six feet off the ground, but several dew-covered fibers—only one-millionth of an inch in diameter each—secured the hundreds of other radiating and evenly spaced fibers between trees as well. This spider's strong and elastic web silk—its stretched strength second only to that of fused quartz—was a geometric orb the size of the front door of our house with the spider sitting motionless in the central hub.*

Shape

Shape is the outward form, configuration, or contour of a thing. In a speech on insect control in gardening, one student used the following description of a cabbage worm:

> *It looks like a brilliant yellow-green caterpillar that begins at a length of an inch or so with about the circumference of your little finger. It has antennae coming from its head with numerous short pudgy feet. As it chomps away at garden cabbage throughout the summer, it extends its length from two to three inches, and it grows in circumference to about the size of the large part of your thumb.*

Weight

Weight is the heaviness of a mass, object, or thing. Since people have a hard time visualizing large numbers, speakers need to relate them to something from the listeners' own experience. One speaker was trying to impress her listeners with how much a million was. She said that a class in Des Moines, Iowa, collected 1 million bottle caps. How much did they weigh? According to the speaker, these caps weighed 21½ tons: "They were put into 200 bags and the bags were so heavy it required a moving van to take them away."

ATTENTION!

Strategies for Making Your Informative Presentation Interesting

- Relate to your listeners' interests.
- Use attention-catching supporting material.
- Establish a motive for your audience to listen to you.
- Use word pictures.
- Create interesting presentation aids.
- Use humor.[15]

Color

Color is an obvious component of description and serves quickly to call up mental pictures. Here, Aaron Roberts uses the importance of color in website design in his speech "Color My Web":

> *What do you first think about when you see the color red? How about blue? And yellow? Which of these colors best represents you—who you are? How many of you have websites? Do you realize that your website is the window through which the world can catch its first glimpse of you? Because the Web is for the world, you must take the time and effort to choose colors that best present you to the world.*

Composition

Composition, a description of the makeup of a thing, can be a useful part of description. Notice here how Jeremiah Stamler, in a speech called "Internet Snake Oil," discussed what the composition of a good website is—especially important if you happen to be surfing the Internet for medical sites for information about treatment and rehabilitation:

> *Do you know what the composition of a good website is? Well, no site is perfect, but the best ones share five important qualities. First, they are upfront about who they are and what their mission is. Second, the advertising on reputable websites is always clearly separated from the editorial content. Third, both the original source of the information and the date it was posted or reviewed are marked. Fourth, online experts are identified by name, credentials, and institution. And, fifth, confidentiality is treated as more than a technicality.*

Explaining

We were not born knowing how to do such things as cook or play volleyball—someone told us how to do them. Explaining is the process of making something clear.

For example, in a speech on how to make a toasted cheese sandwich with an iron, the speaker used the following steps:

1. Gather what you need: bread, cheese, margarine, aluminum foil, and an iron.
2. Heat the iron to medium-high.
3. Make a sandwich from the cheese and bread. Butter both sides of the bread on the outside.
4. Wrap the sandwich in aluminum foil.
5. Place the iron on each side for about 20 seconds. (Check to see if you need more time.)

Using Numbers

Few people can visualize large quantities, such as millions or billions. When you work with numbers, follow these suggestions.

- If numbers are unusual or surprising, explain why.
- Round off large numbers.
- If you have a lot of numbers, try to convert them to percentages.
- Look for opportunities to replace numbers with words. For example, it's easier to understand "More than half the people said . . . " or "A majority believed . . . " than "More than 370 people said . . . "

- Try to relate numbers to something familiar. For example, say "The number of people killed in the earthquake was equal to the entire student body of this college."
- If possible, try to compare numbers. For example, "Forty-five percent of the seniors but only 3 percent of the first-year students believed . . ."
- Use graphs and other visual aids to make numbers more concrete.

Connecting the Known with the Unknown

When listeners are unfamiliar with a subject, a speaker can help them understand it by connecting the new idea to something they already know. For example, when a British student wanted to explain the game of cricket to her American classmates, she started by listing the ways that cricket was similar to baseball.

Repeating and Reinforcing Ideas

Repetition in a speech is important because it helps listeners remember key points. However, if it is overdone, speakers run the risk of boring listeners. Let's look at a format that will enable you to spread out the repetition and reinforcement in a speech.

In your introduction, tell your listeners what you plan to tell them in the body of your speech. In the introduction to her speech "Becoming a Smart Buyer," Heather listed her main points: "Today I want to talk about the four steps to becoming a smart buyer. These steps are: find out price, get a receipt, examine service and repair, and read contracts carefully."

In the body of your speech, tell your listeners your full message (explain your points). In Bishetta's speech, she explained each of her steps:

The first step in dealing with difficult bosses is to understand them. To find out what makes them tick will allow you to speak their language.

The second step is to reveal loyalty. Most bosses will give you the freedom to solve problems in your own way as long as they are convinced of your loyalty.

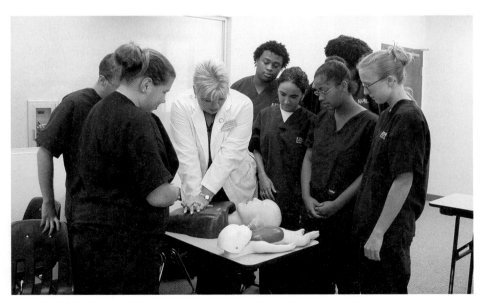

Whether you are using numbers, connecting the known with the unknown, or repeating and reinforcing ideas, when you are explaining, your main goal is making something clear.

The third step in dealing with difficult bosses is to establish strong communication channels. With good rapport, problems can be discussed openly and directly, facts and discoveries can be given, and information that might prove valuable can be shared.

In your conclusion, tell your listeners *what you told them* in the body of the speech. This is the place to summarize your main ideas. Bishetta concluded her speech by saying:

Now you can see how you can go about dealing with difficult bosses. You need to understand them, show loyalty, and establish strong communication channels.

Arousing Interest in Your Topic

Besides arousing curiosity, presenting anecdotes, building anticipation, and building suspense, there are numerous other techniques you can use for holding attention throughout a speech. One of the keys is to think specifically about holding listener attention at every point during your speech preparation.

Arouse Curiosity

One way to make sure that you will be listened to is to create a desire to learn about your subject by stimulating your listeners' curiosity. For example, one speaker began his speech with "Do you know how to stop procrastinating?" Another stated "Before this speech is over, I plan to share with you a message that has the potential of changing your life forever."

Present Anecdotes

An **anecdote** is a short, interesting story based on your own or someone else's experience. Although some speakers use them in their introductions, anecdotes are particularly useful in the body of your speech because they can get audience attention back if it is wandering.

Nicole Gant, a mother who home-schooled both a daughter and a son before returning to school herself, used this anecdote in her speech to her class:

The Internet kept not only me, but both my children as well, connected to the rest of the world—to libraries, research institutes, and other students and families with similar interests. My kids dissected virtual frogs, worked through a set of college-level genetics problems offered by MIT, checked in on a vocabulary-building site that sprinkled their dialogue with SAT–worthy words, and researched the life of Georg Philipp Telemann, who composed the baroque trio that my son, a flutist, plays with friends in an afternoon group. When I look at the moldering set of World Books that formed the intellectual basis for my early education, I just laugh out loud.

Build Anticipation

One way to build anticipation is to preview your points in the introduction. Gwendolyn Haas, for example, said that she was going to talk about what makes Olympic champions. Then she said in a speech titled "Olympic Inspiration":

The qualities I want to talk about not only make Olympic champions; they are invaluable, too, in school, in the home, or on the job. First, champions anticipate. They have a dream of themselves as a champion. They aim high, because often they don't just meet their goals but surpass them. Second, champions motivate. They are driven not just to be the best but to do their best as well. They never quit because they know the satisfaction of completing a difficult task against the odds. Third, champions activate. They make their own luck because they know luck strikes those best prepared to capitalize on it.

The audience is now more likely to listen for each of her points: (1) anticipate, (2) motivate, (3) activate. Notice the way Gwendolyn kept them parallel. Framed in the same way, they were easier for listeners to remember.

Build Suspense

Building suspense is one of the best ways of keeping attention. Esteban Estrada decided to speak on drunk driving, and he began his speech with a personal experience:

> *There was no way I could anticipate what would happen. My girlfriend, Angelica, and I were coming home from dinner out and a movie. We were on State Street, one of the main streets of my hometown, when suddenly we were sideswiped by a car. Not knowing what was going on, and thinking it was inadvertent, we continued driving. Suddenly, the car sideswiped us again. We were about seven blocks from the police station, so we drove there fast. But the car that had been following us disappeared. We waited almost 20 minutes, and thinking it safe, we decided to continue toward Angelica's house. Suddenly, out of nowhere, it was behind us again. We made it to Angelica's and ran inside. The car squealed past, but forgetting the curve leading into the court where Angelica lived, the outlaw car missed the turn, ran one wheel in the gutter and another up a driveway, and broke the front axle. The police were called; all three teenage boys had been drinking.*

Other Techniques for Getting Attention

Most of these ideas have been discussed elsewhere; they are gathered here to highlight the way they can help get attention in informative speeches. Don't forget that it is a combination of elements working together that holds listeners' attention.

Content

When thinking about the *content* of your speech, tie old ideas to new ones. One student talking about food additives (an old idea), for example, tied it to chemicals found naturally in foods that cut the risk of cancer and heart attack (a new idea).

Evidence

Speakers can use *evidence* to hold attention when they select their information with listeners in mind. In his speech, "Forgetting Everything You've Learned," Mauricio Raul Munoz demonstrated this well. He began with a dramatic quotation about college being "one of the worst possible environments in which to retain anything we've learned." Knowing that his listeners would need serious evidence to support his points, he mentioned PhDs and MDs, then researchers at Boston's Beth Israel Deaconess Medical Center under main point one. In addition to personal experience, he used statistics from Tufts University, an opinion from a researcher at Stanford University, and two from the National Institute of Aging for main point number two. He cited the Harvard College Alcohol Study and researchers from the University of North Carolina's Bowles Center for Alcohol Studies for main point three.

ATTENTION!

Reality Check
One of the difficult problems informative speakers face is how to arouse interest in their topic. Here, a number of suggestions are made for arousing audience interest. Do these suggestions make sense? Are they logical? Of the suggestions, which one would most easily arouse *your* interest if you heard it used by a speaker? Of the suggestions, as a public speaker which ones do you think you can use most comfortably and easily? Why? Can you see how these suggestions—if followed and used by public speakers—are likely to increase the possibility of effective communication?

ATTENTION!

S.P.A.R.K. Your Listeners' Attention
The elements of S.P.A.R.K. are:

- Stories
- Pictures
- Analogies
- References, Quotes & Questions
- Keep them laughing

S.P.A.R.K. may be used anywhere within your message.

S.P.A.R.K. will help you:

- Relax and get comfortable with your listeners.
- Grab your listeners' attention.
- Gain listener involvement.
- Remember what you are going to say.
- Increase learner retention.
- Emphasize a key point.[16]

Immediacy

Choosing examples that are immediate is another way to hold attention. *Immediacy* means closeness or nearness in time or space. Shelly gave a speech on the importance of psychological counseling, and she scheduled an interview with an on-campus psychologist before her speech to make her example more immediate. In this way she could talk not only about how to go about making such appointments and where and when the services were provided but also about what topics are of most concern to students on her campus. Thus, the subject of psychological counseling became immediate.

Organization

Organization is so important that we spent a whole chapter discussing it. When speakers use transitions and internal summaries, and relate their material to their central idea, it helps listeners follow the speech. When listeners can't follow a speech, their minds will tend to wander. Making only a few points and using some repetition also help sustain interest throughout a speech.

Style

Content, evidence, and organization are important, but so is *style* or language, as you learned in Chapter 3 on verbal communication. We suggest rereading that chapter before you give your speech.

Delivery

Finally, speakers can get attention through their *delivery*. Take an active role in motivating and getting your audience involved. When you are the fifth speaker in an 8 A.M. class on a Monday, people aren't going to listen to you just because you are there.

Getting Listeners Involved

Before we discuss three external ways to get the audience involved, let's review the methods for getting audience involvement that are within the speech:

1. Choose a topic that is inherently interesting—one that is both significant and relevant and has attention-holding value in and of itself.

2. Select examples, personal experiences, and stories that are interesting and relevant to listeners.

3. Use an organization scheme that is simple, clear, and easy for listeners to follow.

4. Incorporate transitions that guide listeners to what has been said, what is going to be said, and the purpose or central idea of the speech.

5. Make certain that all judgments and decisions regarding speech material are made with listeners in mind.

Now we look at getting the audience to participate, asking rhetorical questions, and soliciting questions from the audience.

Get the Audience to Participate

As every magician knows, choosing someone from the audience to participate in an act is a good technique for keeping attention. In a speech on first aid, the speaker called for a volunteer from the audience so that she could point to pressure points.

Getting everyone to participate works too. In a speech on self-defense, the speaker had the class practice a few simple moves.

Ask Rhetorical Questions

Some speakers use **rhetorical questions**—questions audience members answer mentally rather than out loud. Meredith Carey used rhetorical questions in her speech "Recover, Refocus, Regenerate":

> *I was there when they lowered my grandmother into the ground; I was very close to my grandmother, and it hurt deeply knowing she was gone forever. I knew that the fights between my parents were leading to separation, but their divorce was devastating for me because I loved them both so much, and even the idea of divorce really shocked me. And going away to college—leaving my friends, the town and home where I grew up, and my boyfriend all the way through high school—almost ripped me apart. Have changes like these shaken you to the core? Have there been other changes in your lives that have freaked you out? What do you do with all your feelings of rage? Hurt? Sorrow? What do you do when you feel like you are drowning in a sea of anger? Or in an ocean of despair? Are you a person who likes regularity in your life? Predictability? Can you cope with all these changes? Are you prepared for even more changes in your life?*

Solicit Questions from the Audience

A question-and-answer session encourages listeners to get involved. You might even tell your listeners at the beginning that you will take questions when you finish, which may encourage them to pay attention in preparation for asking questions.

Here are some useful guidelines if you plan to solicit questions from your audience: First, make sure you listen to the full question before answering it. Second, if a question is confusing, ask the questioner to rephrase it. If you are still confused, rephrase it yourself before answering it. For example, say, "Let me make sure I have heard you right; what you are asking is . . . Am I right?" Finally, in responding to questions, try to keep your answers brief and to the point. This is no time for another speech. As a final check, it's also a good idea to ask, "Does that answer your question?"

The Persuasive Speech

In connection with her community service at united way, Lena discovered the Louman Center, a community gathering place on the east side of town. The Louman Center focuses on youth activities, and as term projects for both a sociology and a speech communication class, Lena created a packet of information designed to convince the board of the Louman Center to institute an after-school leadership program. The information packet was buttressed by a persuasive speech designed to outline such a program, convince the board of the need for such a program, and offer specific methods for implementation. Looking forward to her capstone project for the minor she was pursuing, Lena mentioned her availability the following term to actually put such a program in place and get it started.

Because of her persuasive speech, the board of the Louman Center accepted her proposal in its entirety, and Lena looked at it as a great way to pursue her goal to

STRATEGIC FLEXIBILITY

Here, we reinforce the importance of making certain that all judgments and decisions regarding speech material are made with listeners in mind. Once again, if you make it part of the entire strategic flexibility process, it will be one of the factors, elements, or conditions that you continually include in your decision making.

help others. As part of her capstone project, Lena not only gave persuasive speeches about the value of the after-school leadership program to other service organizations around the community; she also gave "recruitment" type speeches in all the schools in the community as well, seeking a wide diversity of students who had an interest in becoming leaders.

Lena is engaged in **persuasion**—the process of trying to get others to change their attitudes or behavior. Most likely, you are involved in some sort of persuasion every day of your life. You try to persuade someone to join you for lunch or to join your study group. Others are involved in trying to persuade you: Radio commercials exhort you to buy, professors try to persuade you to turn in your papers on time, candidates for student and local government try to persuade you to vote for them, and the Internet offers a constant barrage of persuasive messages.

Since persuasion runs through every aspect of our society, you need to study how it works. Understanding persuasion will help you evaluate the persuasive techniques of others and develop your own persuasive messages in the most effective way possible.

Persuasion and the Communication Model

Often when we think of persuasion, we think of a communicator having an influence on a listener or on many listeners, such as a salesperson on a purchaser or a politician on a group of potential voters. This view emphasizes the source of the communication as the main influence in the persuasion process. However, sometimes when we think of persuasion, we think of people buying products ("Okay, I'll buy the larger TV with the clearer picture"), changing their attitudes ("Maybe Paula is the better candidate"), or altering their beliefs ("All right, maybe student demonstrations can make a differ- ence"). This view emphasizes the receivers of persuasive messages as the main part of the persuasion process. When we emphasize the message in a persuasive situation, we might say, "That is a powerful statement" or "What a great speech!"

And yet the focus of persuasion should not be on the sender, the receiver, or the message. All share in the persuasive process, even though one may play a more impor- tant role than the other two. Only when all three combine successfully does effective persuasion occur.

What Is Persuasion, and What Is Its Purpose?

Listing all the persuasive messages that have affected you over the past 12 hours is a difficult task. Advertisers have tried to get you to buy their products; a friend may have asked for a loan; your family may have tried to get you to come home for the weekend; a newspaper editorial may have convinced you to support a charitable cause; your friends may have persuaded you to go downtown with them; an instructor may have told you to keep up with your reading; a partner in a chat room may have asked you to continue conversing.

It is impossible to escape persuasive speaking, and persuasion has consequences. Change can occur when persuasion takes place. *Persuasion* is the process that occurs when a communicator (sender) influences the values, beliefs, attitudes, or behaviors of another person (receiver).

The key to understanding persuasion is influence. **Influence** refers to the power of a person or thing to affect others—to produce effects without the presence of physical force. For example, an instructor could have changed your habits by getting you to read regularly rather than cramming at exam time. Influence implies a degree of control over the thinking, emotions, and actions of others. *Social influence* is what occurs when a person's values, beliefs, attitudes, or behaviors are changed because of the behavior or presence of a person, individuals, a group or groups, or society.

Persuasion thus depends on influence, but you are unlikely to do something just because someone else affects you in some way. That is where motivation comes in. **Motivation** is the stimulation or inducement that causes you to act. For example, let's say you decide to go downtown with your friends to avoid their pestering if you don't go. Maybe you decide to keep up with your reading because doing so will help you do better in a course. Thus, in addition to being open to influence, we must also be motivated to do what we do.

Persuasion, influence, and motivation are closely linked. As persuaders, if we can relate our goals to things that persuade, influence, or motivate our listeners because they lead to desirable outcomes, we are far more likely to be successful. But if persuasion were truly this simple, people would be pulled and pushed so often that a numbing effect might eventually block out persuasive efforts.

Any persuasive effort has ethical implications. Sometimes ethical choices are clear from common knowledge and good judgment alone. Sometimes they are not. When making decisions about persuasion that may be questionable, you should consult other people if possible.

There is no doubt that persuasion plays a significant role in people's lives, and it does have consequences. Before we discuss specific strategies that persuaders can use to influence and motivate others, we need to look at values, beliefs, and attitudes because these are precisely what persuaders are trying to influence.

Ethical Persuasion

Ethics are a matter of conforming to acceptable and fair standards of conduct. Ethics are particularly important to persuasion because you are trying to change people—often in a significant way. If your audience doesn't perceive you as ethical, your speech will fail. Here are some ethical principles that are particularly useful in persuasive speaking:

1. Treat your audience with respect. Assume that audience members are intelligent and mature and will respond to a well-reasoned and well-organized appeal.

2. Take care not to distort or exaggerate your facts. Find the best facts you can, and let them stand on their own.

3. Avoid lying or name calling. Even if you think that the opposing side is stupid or vicious, it's unacceptable to say so. Show that your ideas are better.

4. Avoid suppressing key information. If you discover important information that doesn't support your view, include it but find a way of refuting it.

5. If you have something to gain personally from your persuasive speech, tell your audience what it is.

Values, Beliefs, and Attitudes

When a persuasive message taps into our values, beliefs, and attitudes, not only are we more responsive, but we are more likely to accept the sender. For example, we tend to respond positively to people who share our values. If you believe in the importance of recycling, you are more likely to be receptive to a speaker who advocates recycling. Thus, persuaders who have investigated audience values, beliefs, and attitudes are more likely to be effective if—and this is the big "if"—they can adapt to them and use them effectively in their presentations.

Marcus, as he was thinking about subjects for a persuasive speech, considered talking to his class on the topics of welfare, Medicare, and the graduated income tax. As he used the information he gained from his own classroom audience analysis, he came up with an entirely different set of subjects; topics more closely tied to students' values, beliefs, and attitudes included suicide, racism, and political indifference.

Values

Values are the ideas we have about what is good and what is bad and how things should be. They are general guiding principles, standards, or judgments about how we should behave or about some final goal that may or may not be worth attaining.[17] These general guiding principles divide into two types: (1) *instrumental values,* which guide people's day-to-day behavior, and (2) *terminal values* or final goals that are or are not worth attaining.

Instrumental and terminal values are fairly easy to distinguish. Values that guide day-to-day behavior are loyalty, honesty, friendliness, courage, kindness, cleanliness, thrift, and responsibility. Terminal values may vary, but some are shared by all human beings: freedom, world peace, family security. Other enduring values include inner harmony, happiness, safety, personal security, achievement, progress, enlightenment (the value of the scientific method and rationality), and patriotism.

There are two points to think about when considering terminal values. First, they are not likely to change because of one brief, persuasive speech; they change only over time. Second, the degree to which you can tie your approach or appeal into widely accepted terminal values may help determine whether you achieve your goals. If you can show that your approach is consistent with or reinforces the values your audience members hold, they are more likely to accept it as a natural outgrowth of the values they already support. For example, Marcus chose racism as his topic because he could relate it to so many terminal values his classmates support: freedom, equality, friendship, inner harmony, and happiness.

Beliefs

Often, it is values that determine and anchor beliefs. For example, if one of our values is patriotism, we might believe in a capitalistic economy, a democratic form of government, and a public education system.

Beliefs are statements of knowledge, opinion, and faith. A statement of knowledge is "I believe [know] that if I let go of this book, it will drop to the floor." A statement of opinion is "I believe [have an opinion] that vitamin supplements help keep us healthy." A statement of faith is "I believe [have faith] that there is a God."

Beliefs can come to us from a variety of sources. Besides our own observations, we depend on the observations of our parents, teachers, religious leaders, and friends—especially as we grow up. As adults, we depend more on the observations of professionals, scientists, and journalists. We seldom develop beliefs in isolation. Our interactions have much to do with what we observe, how we observe it, and the conclusions we draw from our observations.

If you compare values with beliefs, you realize that beliefs are, in general, easier to change than values. Values are central; they are more securely anchored. The fact that beliefs are easier to change does not necessarily mean they can and will be changed. While statements of knowledge can be changed with more knowledge and statements of opinion can be changed in the same way, statements of faith are less likely to be changed—at least by a brief persuasive speech.

If a persuasive speaker can tap into our values, beliefs, and attitudes, we are more likely to respond to his or her message.

Attitudes

Attitudes are predispositions to respond favorably or unfavorably toward a person, subject, or situation. A favorable attitude toward honesty in your educational experiences would cause you to respond in some way: to speak out in favor of doing your own work, to discourage friends or classmates from being dishonest, or, depending on the strength of the attitude, to report cheating or plagiarism that you observe.

Why Persuasion Is Challenging

One obvious difficulty is the sheer amount of persuasion that occurs. To say that we are besieged by persuasive messages is an understatement. Your persuasive message is likely to be received as just another persuasive message unless you take special care to make it stand out from others.

A second challenge is that persuasion tends to work slowly, over time. For example, how often have you gone out and bought a product after hearing or seeing just one advertisement for it? Persuasive speakers, however, ordinarily do not have the luxury of repeated efforts.

A third difficulty is that the value, belief, or attitude you are trying to change may be deeply entrenched. It's unusual for a single speech to shake or change our strongest feelings.

Another challenge is laziness. Getting people to do something can be difficult, let alone getting them to change an established way of doing things or of thinking. The routine is easier and perhaps more rewarding.

Finally, a threat to freedom, like a persuasive appeal that seems coercive—"Do things my way"—causes people to react, maybe even to reject, the appeal. Some people respond negatively to a persuasive appeal even when the point of view expressed is similar to their own.

For a persuasive message to stand out, it must be special or unique.

Dr. Sheila Murray Bethel, best-selling author of *Making a Difference*, now in its 21st printing (and translated into five languages), is a professional speaker. She was inducted into the Speaker Hall of Fame in 1986 and has been recognized as one of the "Twenty-One Top Speakers for the 21st Century" by *Successful Meetings* Magazine. She has given over 2,500 presentations to more than two million people in 17 countries. Here, she shares the steps she takes when preparing a speech:

When I prepare for a speech I imagine a blank canvas on which I will paint word pictures to persuade, entertain, and inform my audience. There are several steps I take to begin:

First, determine what the theme of the presentation will be. This is my umbrella. I confer with my client to establish their needs and goals for the event to which I will be speaking. In the professional speaking business we refer to this as a "needs assessment." Without it you will never truly engage the audience.

Second, I ask myself if I have only 30 seconds to leave one vital message on this topic (theme) with the audience, what would it be? I follow that thought pattern until I have six or more central ideas in descending order of importance. This allows me to be flexible with the time frame of the presentation. Many times a speech is cut short because of an event at the venue that is out of my control.

My speeches are hydraulic. If I have the allotted time then I can deliver all of my main points; if not, the most important won't get lost in the cutting. That does not mean that the speech dwindles to a low-key ending.

It means I know where I can cut at the last minute. Each main point then has a story, anecdote, quote, or statistic assigned to it to help paint the picture and persuade.

At this point, I design a powerful opening and closing. Laughter and/or pathos are the quickest way to your listener's heart and mind.

I usually have a short "cheat sheet" of the key points to put near the lectern as I am speaking. When you give several speeches a month to different groups with different agendas, there is no way you can truly "tailor" the presentation and remember all the little important items for each audience. People often think you have to memorize the speech. Not so. Every speech given by a U.S. president, or leader in any field is on a Tele-prompter, monitor, or actual notes.

I do not use PowerPoint or audio/video clips or special effects. I can't compete with the movie makers. Audiences are so sophisticated in their viewing habits that if I try to compete I'll fail. And, I believe a good story told with passion, humor, and conviction will paint a more powerful picture in the listener's mind than all the external resources you can use.

In the end, if I have done all this to the best of my ability, I remind myself that no matter how good I am, 50% of the responsibility of my message being well received lies with the audience. I do my best, and the rest is up to them.

Source: From Dr. Sheila Murray Bethel. She shared these steps with the author (Richard) in a personal e-mail dated May 18, 2004. Her e-mail address is located on the website **http://www.bethelinstitute.com.** Telephone: 760-346-3525. Her lecture topics include leadership, branding, customer service, and communications. A free video is available at **http://www.speakerstreams.com/murraybethel/.**

Many factors can affect the receptiveness of your audience. Time of day may affect how awake or responsive people feel. Educational level could affect how much your listeners understand, how complex your argument can get, or how technical your language can be. Socioeconomic level might affect the kinds of subjects to which your audience responds. For example, you might speak to an audience of young people about how to get a job or how to impress an employer or talk to a group of retirees about investments and exotic travel opportunities.

Speakers can turn such difficulties into strengths by carefully analyzing their audiences and using this information in their research and other preparation—in selecting their organizational schemes, choosing their language, and presenting their messages. Persuasion requires all three elements—sender, message, and receiver—working together.

www.mhhe.com/hybels11e >

View clip #8, an excerpt from a persuasive student speech, "Living Wills, by Susan Hrabar."

Strategies of Persuasion

In persuasion, just as in any other form of communication, there are no guarantees. No strategy is foolproof. The best approach is to use all the available strategies to meet the demands of the audience. Obviously, different audiences will require different approaches, so the more strategies you can use, the better.

Determine Your Purpose

Subtracting a purpose from a persuasive effort is like pulling out the main rod of an umbrella. Without the rod, the whole umbrella collapses. Your purpose should be a highly specific and attainable persuasive goal.

When you begin planning a persuasive speech, one of the first questions you should ask yourself is what you want your audience to think or do. As we have noted in previous chapters, this is called your *specific purpose*. Here are some specific-purpose statements for persuasive speeches:

To Get Audience Members to Believe a Certain Way

- To persuade audience members that state lotteries exploit poor people.
- To persuade audience members that their college theater program is worthwhile.

To Get Audience Members to Act

- To persuade audience members to eat more fresh fruit and vegetables.
- To persuade audience members to write to their congressional representatives in support of stronger gun-control legislation.

If you keep your specific purpose in mind, it will be easier to generate main points for support. As you find support for your purpose, remember that you will want your audience members to respond in one or more of the five following ways:

1. *To change or reinforce beliefs.* A speaker wants to persuade the audience to change a belief or way of thinking or to reinforce a belief and take action. For example, a speaker who wants to convince listeners that state lotteries exploit the poor will provide evidence that poor people are the most likely to spend money on lotteries and that lotteries serve no constructive purpose.

2. *To take action.* For example, a speaker who wants the audience to eat more fresh fruits and vegetables or write to congressional representatives will try to motivate listeners by outlining probable results.

3. *To continue doing what they are already doing.* Some audience members might already be doing what you are asking them to do. For example, if several members of the class are taking theater classes, they might find a speech on supporting the college theater program interesting because it reinforces what they already believe.

STRATEGIC FLEXIBILITY

It is when you face choices—which strategies are likely to be best for this audience?—that your strategic flexibility will be revealed. The more knowledge and experience you have, the larger the repertoire of available skills and behaviors you will have from which to select.

Why Analyze Your Audience?

1. To determine what to talk about
2. To better meet their needs
3. To assure that you are giving the right speech to the right audience
4. To better customize your speech
5. To help organize your ideas
6. To assist in eliminating ideas that do not belong
7. To determine what is acceptable and what is not
8. To determine how long to talk
9. To help assure that you will do well
10. To relax you when giving your speech

4. *To avoid doing something.* The speaker might want audience members to stop buying or wearing fur, to stop watching a particular television program, or to get their legislators to prohibit personal firearms or abolish capital punishment.

5. *To continue not doing something.* This goal is slightly different from the second goal. It works best if audience members are considering taking action that you are against. For example, if they're thinking about playing the lottery (because the payoff has become so large), you might be able to persuade them not to do so.

Any audience is likely to represent every possible point of view on your subject. When you're planning your speech, you should consider all of them.

Analyze Your Audience

Whether you use your own observations, surveys, interviews, or research, you need to get good information about your audience—as we discussed in Chapter 12, Getting Started and Finding Speech Material—in order to appeal to your audience's values, beliefs, and attitudes whenever possible.

The second reason to analyze your audience is to predict its response to your persuasive effort. For example, even when speaking about day care to a group of working mothers—who share a common desire to find good day care for their children—you will find big differences in age, socioeconomic background, and even marital status. It might be helpful to select a target audience.

Your **target audience** is a subgroup of the whole audience that you must persuade in order to reach your goal. You aim your speech mostly at the individuals in this subgroup, knowing that some members of your audience are opposed to your message, some agree with it, some are uncommitted or undecided, and some find it irrelevant.

Politicians always go after a target audience because their success often depends on how many different constituencies they can appeal to. When uncommitted or undecided individuals are targeted, the reason is that they are the ones most likely to be influenced by persuasion.

Appeal to Your Audience Using Logic

One of the most important theorists in the history of the speech communication discipline, Aristotle, thought that effective persuasion consisted of three parts: a source's credibility *(ethos),* emotional appeals *(pathos),* and logical appeals *(logos).* We consider these in reverse order, beginning with logical appeals.

A **logical appeal** is one that addresses listeners' reasoning ability. Evidence in the form of statistics or any other supporting material will help persuade the audience. Chapter 12, Getting Started and Finding Speech Material, explains in detail the kinds of supporting material you can use in a logical appeal.

A logical appeal may be argued in several ways: through deductive reasoning, inductive reasoning, causal reasoning, or reasoning by analogy. These appeals are developed and supported within the body of your speech. Causal reasoning and reasoning by analogy are both forms of inductive reasoning, but because of their importance, we will discuss them briefly in separate sections.

Different types of Deductive Reasoning

Deductive reasoning moves from the general to the specific. Here is a deductive argument used by one student:

Acid rain is a problem throughout the entire northeastern United States.

Pennsylvania is a northeastern state.

Pennsylvania has a problem with acid rain.

Care is needed, however, with this pattern of reasoning. Have you ever heard someone say, "It's dangerous to generalize"? A faulty premise really is faulty deductive thinking, as in this example:

All college students procrastinate.

Mary is a college student.

Therefore, Mary procrastinates.

Deductive reasoning can form the structure for an entire speech, for just a single part, or for several parts. Here, Harvey Mackay, best-selling author and motivational speaker, in a speech, "Postgraduate Life: What You Should Know," delivered to Grand Canyon University in 2008, uses a deductive approach in just a single part of his speech. He has just offered his listeners a definition of teamwork: "My definition of teamwork is: A collection of diverse people who respect each other and are committed to each other's successes."[18] In the quotation, Mackay gives his conclusion—a great example of teamwork—before he cites his example:

> Let me tell you about a great example of teamwork. One rainy day a salesman was driving on a two-lane country road and got stuck in the mud. He asked a farmer for help. The farmer hitched up Elmo, his blind mule, to the salesman's car. The farmer grabbed a whip, snapped it in the air, and yelled: "Pull Sam, pull!" Nothing happened. He snapped it again, "Pull, Jackson, pull." Still nothing. He snapped it again: "Pull, Bessie, pull." Still nothing. Then he flicked Elmo: "Pull, Elmo, pull!" And Elmo ripped the car right out of the ditch. The driver is confused and perplexed. He said: "Hey, why did you have to call out all those names?" "Look, if he didn't think he had any help, he wouldn't even try!" We all need help. Being part of a team is one way to get it. Listen to your team.[19]

Inductive Reasoning

Another logical technique is **inductive reasoning**—reasoning from the specific to the general. Usually when we use inductive reasoning, we move from a number of facts to a conclusion. The facts, in this case, could be developed within the body of the speech, with the conclusion offered at the end, in the speech's conclusion. Here is how a student used inductive reasoning to persuade her audience that the college should require everyone to take a foreign language:

In some parts of the United States, you need to understand Spanish to get by.

Americans are traveling more and more to countries where a language other than English is spoken.

The mark of an educated person is that he or she can speak, write, and read at least one other language.

Conclusion: Everyone should learn another language.

In her speech to her class, "I Lived to Tell about It," Adrienne Bower used inductive reasoning to arrive at the action step of her speech. She believed that her listeners might reject her conclusions if they heard them first, so she built her case slowly with statistics, facts, opinions, and a personal example. Here is some of the information she provided her audience:

1. *According to the Core Institute at Southern Illinois University, cited in an article in USA Today, by Michael P. Haines, the director of the National Social Norms Resource Center at Northern Illinois University, the average number of alcoholic drinks consumed weekly by freshmen in 2000 was 8.5 for males, 3.7 for females. For sophomores, it was 9.1 for males, and 3.8 for females.[20] Yet, at one institution, the Core Institute reported that 58 percent of students surveyed had consumed five or more drinks at one sitting in the previous two weeks.[21] The average, according to the Core Institute, across campuses is 46.5 percent who had consumed five or more drinks at one sitting in the previous two weeks.[22]*

2. *"Half the students age 10 to 24 questioned in a 1999 study by the Centers for Disease Control said they had consumed alcohol in the preceding month," reported Jeffrey Kluger in an article "How to Manage Teen Drinking (The Smart Way)" in* Time *magazine.[23] The Core Institute, which surveys 30,000 to 60,000 college students annually, reports that heaviest drinkers are males in fraternities or on athletic teams followed closely by female students in sororities.[24]*

3. *"College students are young and irresponsible, and drinking is part of their culture," says Rob Waldron in an article "Students Are Dying: Colleges Can Do More," for* Newsweek.[25] *Another article in* Time, *"Women on a Binge," by Jodie Morse includes the line "More college women regularly get drunk," as part of her headline.[26] Morse also includes the statistic, "Since 1993, women's colleges have seen a 125 percent increase in frequent binge drinking."[27]*

4. *Last year, I was drinking hard lemonade and bottled mixed drinks with friends in the parking lot of Burger King. I didn't know how much my friend Stephanie had to drink, and I thought she was being careful, but she crashed the car on the way back to our sorority. The tree hit the driver's side of the car, and Stephanie died in the hospital of her injuries. You probably read about it last year. Three of my sorority sisters and I lived to tell about it, but it was a harrowing experience I never want to relive.*

   Now, my point is not to try to eliminate drinking from college campuses. "Prohibition didn't work for the nation in the 1920s, and it's a failure on college campuses today," says Michael P. Haines.[28] It isn't going to happen. My point, too, isn't to develop terror campaigns designed to scare students about the hazards of drinking too much. This is another approach that hasn't worked well.[29]

   My solution has five parts, and it is based on one common assumption: College-age kids are going to drink: (1) Lower the national drinking age to 18 so that drinking takes place in the open where it can be supervised by police, security guards, and health-care workers.[30] (2) Get out the information that heavy drinkers are not in the majority, that most students who drink "do so responsibly, according to a study funded by the U.S. Department of Education."[31] "When students are armed with the truth about the moderate and responsible drinking habits of the majority of their peers," says Haines, "they tend to consume less themselves."[32] (3) Widely promote a designated-driver program whereby all local bars give free soft drinks to the non-drinker in any group.[33] (4) Establish a university policy whereby all college students are sent a birthday card to arrive the day before they become eligible to drink, which wishes them a happy birthday but reminds them to drink responsibly. (5) Drink responsibly. Take full responsibility for yourselves, knowing that moderate drinking habits are "a powerful way to help create a healthier, safer campus culture." [34]

Sometimes it will work best to give the facts and then draw the conclusion (induction); in other cases you might want to start with the conclusion and then support it with facts (deduction).

Causal Reasoning

Another way to reason is causally. **Causal reasoning** is a logical appeal that pertains to, constitutes, involves, or expresses a cause and therefore uses the word *because*, which is either implicitly or explicitly stated. For example, "I failed the class because I didn't complete the assignments," or "The basketball team is losing because it has an incompetent coach." The latter example points out some of the problems of causal reasoning. That the coach is incompetent may be a matter of opinion. The team might be losing because it doesn't have good players or because the other teams have taller players or because there is no way of recruiting good players. The causal pattern can be used for presenting evidence as well as for organizing an entire speech. The cause-and-effect pattern is one of the ways to organize a speech that is discussed in Chapter 13, Organizing and Outlining the Speech.

Reasoning by Analogy

Finally, you can reason by **analogy.** In this case you compare two similar cases and conclude that if something is true for one, it must also be true for the other. Casey used analogy to try to get his listeners to understand the value of new electronic gadgets. He said, "Think of these as tools to make your life easier. These are just like the tools you've been using all along. The only difference is that these electronic tools are faster, smaller, and more adaptable to your specific needs."

Often speeches of policy use analogy. Advocates of a policy look to see if the policy has succeeded elsewhere. For example, Katrina Paschalis was trying to get her listeners to understand that a better lifestyle will help prevent cancer. Her goal was to get her listeners to take an active part in their own preventive health care:

> *You all know the threat that cancer holds on your life. It is a pervasive threat, but it needn't be scary. It is something you can handle. Think of living a healthy lifestyle as similar to owning a new automobile. Just as you want to keep the inside clean, you want to avoid smoking to keep your own insides clean. Just as you want to make sure all the fuel and other liquids you put into your car are exactly what the manufacturer's warranty requires, you, too, want to make certain you only take in drinks and foods known to be good for you. And just as you want to drive your car with care, you, too, want to use proper physical activity. If you take care of the insides, what you put into it, and how you drive it, you can keep your car in new condition. If you avoid smoking, a poor diet, and physical inactivity, you can prevent half of all the cancers in the USA and, thus, live your life as if in new condition.*

Logical Fallacies in Argument

A **fallacy** is a component of an argument that is flawed in its logic or form, and because of the flaw, it renders the argument invalid. There are many different types of fallacies. In his book, *Attacking Faulty Reasoning* (Wadsworth, 2005)—a book used in courses on logic, critical thinking, argumentation, and philosophy—T. Edward Damer

A List of Some Common Fallacies

Hasty generalization

Missing the point

Post hoc or false cause

Slippery slope

Weak analogy

Appeal to authority

Ad populi

Ad hominem and tu quoque

Appeal to pity

Appeal to ignorance

Straw man

Red herring

False dichotomy

Begging the question

Equivocation[35]

Things People Want

Time

Comfort

Money

Popularity

Praise

Pride of
   accomplishment

Self-confidence

Security

Leisure

Fun

Prestige

Enjoyment

Health

Better appearance

Exclusivity

Envy

Ego gratification

Business
   advancement

Social advancement[39]

explains 60 of the most commonly committed logical fallacies. The ability to identify logical fallacies in the arguments of others, and to avoid them in one's own arguments, is a valuable skill. Fallacious reasoning may keep you from knowing the truth, and the inability to think critically can make you vulnerable to manipulation.

Appeal to Your Audience Using Emotion

In their book *How to Persuade People Who Don't Want to Be Persuaded,* Joel Bauer and Mark Levy report the results of a study published in the *Harvard Business Review* showing messages that caught the attention of executives had four characteristics: (1) they were personalized, (2) they evoked an emotional response, (3) they came from a trustworthy or respected sender, and (4) they were concise. But Thomas Davenport and John Beck, who conducted the study with 60 executives, concluded that "The messages that both evoked emotion and were personalized were more than twice as likely to be attended to as the messages without those attributes."[36] Bauer and Levy summarized the findings by driving the main point home to their readers even more dramatically: "To get attention, to be remembered, to change the moment, you must make your messages personal and evoke emotion in your listener."[37]

An **emotional appeal** focuses on listeners' needs, wants, desires, and wishes. Recent research shows that the people who are most successful at persuasion are those who can understand others' motives and desires—even when these motives and desires are not stated.

In a public-speaking situation it is impossible to appeal to each individual's motives and desires, so it helps to know about basic needs we all have. Psychologist Abraham Maslow proposed a model that arranges people's needs from relatively low-level physical needs to higher-level psychological ones.[38] This model, referred to as a **hierarchy of needs,** is shown in Figure 15-1.

As you can see at the bottom of the figure, the first needs all human beings have are *physiological needs.* Starving people do not care about freedom; their need for food is so great that it outweighs all other needs. Therefore, physiological needs must be taken care of before other needs can be met. Since we usually assume that basic needs are taken care of, they are generally not a basis for a persuasive speech, although politicians, clergy, and educators may try to persuade citizens to address the unmet basic needs of the poor.

Figure 15-1
Maslow's Hierarchy of
Needs

Self-Actualization Needs
(Genuine fulfillment, realization of potential)

Self-Esteem Needs
(Recognition, respect from others, self-respect)

Belongingness and Love Needs
(Friendship, giving and receiving love, affection)

Safety Needs
(Stability, freedom from violence, freedom
from disease, security, structure, order, law)

Physiological Needs
(Food, water, sleep, and physical comfort)

Safety needs are next in the hierarchy. The whole area of safety needs can be useful in persuasion, since all of us have these needs in varying degrees. In the following excerpt, notice how the speaker appeals to the student audience's need for safety:

> *In the last three months there have been six assaults on this campus. Where have they occurred? All in parking lots with no lights. When? At night, after evening classes. Does this mean that you can't take any more evening classes without fearing for your life? Should you leave your car at home so you can avoid the campus parking lots?*

Belongingness and love needs, the next level, also have a potent appeal. If you doubt this, turn on your television set and note how many commercials make a direct pitch to the need to be loved.

Here is how one student used the need to belong to urge new students to join the Campus Fellowship—a student social group on campus:

> *The first year is the hardest year of college. You are in a new environment and are faced with a bewildering array of choices. I felt this way in my first year. Then I met someone from "The Campus Fellowship" who invited me to one of its meetings. The minute I walked in the door several people met me and made me feel welcome. Today some of these people are my best friends.*

Self-esteem needs stem from our need to feel good about ourselves. We see a lot of persuasion based on these needs in self-help books. Typical themes are that you'll feel good about yourself if you change your fashion style, learn how to climb mountains, practice meditation, and so on. One student appealed to self-esteem needs when she gave a speech called "Try Something New:"

> *I have a friend who, at the age of 35, decided to learn how to play the flute. She had never played an instrument before, but she loved music and thought it would be interesting to give it a try. Now that she has been studying for two years, she told me, "I will never be a great player but this has been a wonderful experience. I enjoy my CDs even more because I know what the musicians are doing. I understand so much more about music. It's wonderful to try something new." I am here today to urge you to try something new yourself. To see what you can discover about yourself.*

At the top of his hierarchy, Maslow puts *self-actualization needs*—the need to realize one's potential and attain fulfillment, to do our best with what we have. An admissions director for a community college made this statement in a speech to a group of older students in an attempt to persuade them to go to college:

> *I'm sure that many of you look back at your high school days and think "I was a pretty good writer; I wonder if I still could write," or "I really liked my business courses; I would like to try my hand at bookkeeping again." I believe one of the saddest things that can happen to us is not to be able to try out things that we are good at, things that we have always wanted to do. Our new college program for returning adults will give you a chance to do just that— try out the things you are good at.*

How many different emotions or needs are being tapped to get results like these?

This will be a real test of your active open-mindedness, for it asks you to analyze a persuasive speech with respect to the appeals the speaker made. Answer the following questions as a result of listening to a single, recent, persuasive speech:

1. What was the speech? Who delivered it? Where was it given? When?

2. Was the speech more of one using logic or more of one using emotion? Was this an appropriate choice? Why?

3. From your reading of the section, "Appeal to your Audience Using Logic," analyze all the logical elements in the speech.

4. From your reading of the section, "Appeal to Your Audience Using Emotion," analyze all the emotional elements in the speech.

5. Would this speech have been more effective had the speaker chosen a different emphasis? (logic vs. emotion)

6. Did the speaker use research to prove his or her points?

STRATEGIC FLEXIBILITY

The key to selecting and applying the right emotional appeal is based on strategic flexibility, but how you anticipate, assess, and evaluate the factors, elements, and conditions depends on the foundation you have established as a result of researching your audience.

You have the best chance of choosing the right emotional appeal if you have done a thorough job of researching your audience. For instance, safety needs tend to be important to families, especially those with young children. On the other hand, younger audiences, such as college students, generally focus more on belonging, love, and self-esteem needs. If you focused on safety needs to encourage a college audience to buy savings bonds, the students probably wouldn't find your speech very interesting. Self-actualization needs probably appeal most to older audiences. Adults who are approaching midlife are the most likely to ask themselves whether they have made the right choices for their lives and whether they should make some changes. Age, of course, is only one factor to consider in assessing needs. The more information you have about your audience, the better your chance of selecting the right emotional appeals.

Although emotional appeals can be powerful, they can also be very personal, and if you are faced with a decision of whether to use an appeal to logic or an appeal to emotion—especially with an audience you are not totally familiar with—your best bet is likely to be to use logic and to depend on your listeners' critical thinking skills.

Use Research to Prove Your Points

No matter how you plan to appeal to your listeners—whether by logic or emotion—a crucial element in the persuasion process is your research. Larry Tracy, a professional speaker, in a speech to a chapter of the National Speakers Association titled "Taming Hostile Audiences," said it succinctly: "Emotions do indeed play an important role with any audience, but it is still verifiable, factual data that persuades reasonable people to come to your side."[40]

When doing your research for your speech, look for a variety of sources. An opinion from an expert may be your best piece of evidence, but an additional fact might drive the point home. Don't forget to include your own personal experience with your topic.

A variety of research is more likely to hold the attention of your listeners, too. Just as a series of statistics (numbers) is likely to bore your audience, a series of similar examples or opinions can do the same thing.

There is no overall guide to how much evidence you need to prove a point to your listeners, but ask yourself: "What would it take to convince me?" A second guideline is to ask yourself: "How much time do I have?" For most short, in-class speeches you might want to follow the "rule of three": three main heads, three subpoints for each, and three brief pieces of evidence to support each subpoint. Although the rule of three generally applies to most speeches, some evidence takes time to relate—like examples, illustrations, and personal experience—and some points require more evidence and some less. These are judgment calls, and because you are in charge, you will need to make the decisions.

Choose Your Language Carefully

Remember, people are not inclined to think or act the way you want them to unless they are motivated. Try to keep language in mind as you select supporting material. You want to stimulate the emotions of your listeners with special words. And you want to create emotional pictures that will make people feel what you are talking about.

Look at the images created by the language in Lance R. Odden's speech "Talk to Your Children about the Tough Stuff":

> *Remember that the innocent freshman pledge who died at MIT last year had been told to drink a beer and a bottle of bourbon. Remember the three students who died in the Virginia college system with no one learning from the previous experience. Remember the deaths of the students at LSU. Remember the rape, which was alcohol induced, at a local high school party. Note that just last Tuesday, in Denver, an 18-year-old girl died after having consumed over a liter of tequila.[41]*

Appeal to Your Audience Using Your Credibility

Why are some people more persuasive than others? Research on persuasion says you are more likely to be effective as a persuader if listeners consider you to be credible. **Credibility,** or believability, consists of four qualities: competence, dynamism, character, and caring. Being ethical is essential. We have placed the section on "Ethical Persuasion" toward the opening of this chapter because of its importance. It is part of a person's character, it is true, but we simply want to remind you that being ethical—ethics—is part of listeners' perceptions of your credibility. Aristotle, as you will recall, labeled "credibility" ethos, and in this section we will discuss the qualities: competence, personal experience, commitment, research, dynamism, character, and caring.

Competence

Someone who has **competence** possesses special ability, skill, or knowledge. That is, listeners perceive the speaker as knowledgeable. A speaker who is perceived as knowledgeable on his or her subject gains much credibility. For example, let's say that two classroom speakers have chosen to speak on the same topic, the value of exercise. The first speaks primarily from personal experience and occasionally cites other people but offers no sources and cites no evidence. The second, clearly, has done her homework. She has read books and magazines on exercise, she has worked as a trainer at a local fitness club, and she cites authorities and other evidence to support her point of view. Some of the second speaker's comments, however, contradict some of what you heard the first speaker say. Who will you believe? In this case there isn't much doubt. You believe the speaker who has proven herself to be knowledgeable.

ATTENTION!

The Value of Research (in no particular order)

- establishes the quality or depth of your ideas
- allows listeners insights into the background of your ideas
- establishes or reinforces your credibility
- provides the support necessary for listeners to accept or adopt your ideas
- offers listeners a look at the seriousness of your ideas
- helps move your persuasive approach or argument forward

Reality Check
You are more likely to be effective as a persuader if listeners consider you to be credible. The issue of credibility is so essential to effective persuasion that the "Assess Yourself" section at the end of this chapter deals with it directly. Whether listeners believe you depends on your competence, dynamism, character, caring, and ethics. Do these elements of credibility make sense? Are they logical? Knowing what you do about yourself, which of these areas is likely to give you the greatest problem with respect to building your own credibility with people who do not know you? What specific things will *you* do to build *your* credibility? Is it clear to you how building your credibility will make a significant contribution to communicating effectively? In persuasive situations alone?

Competence Based on Personal Experience. When you are a speaker trying to persuade an audience, it will help your credibility if you can reveal some personal knowledge about your subject. Competence does not depend only on book learning or specialized training; you can be competent because of your personal experience—as noted above in the speech by the second speaker on exercise. Nancy, in another example, speaks of her own experience with alcoholism:

> *One night I went to a party. I remember the early part of the evening, but that's about all. The next thing I remember was waking up in my own bed. I didn't remember the end of the party or how I got home. When I woke up that morning and realized I didn't remember anything, I knew I was in serious trouble.*

You don't always have to relate such a dramatic example as Nancy's. One student who was working as a volunteer at a rest home persuaded other classmates to volunteer there as well.

Competence Based on Commitment. Another way to demonstrate competence is to establish your commitment to your topic. Listeners are more inclined to believe speakers who have taken actions that support their positions. If you can show that you have contributed to a charity, donated blood, or worked in a soup kitchen, you are more likely to persuade others to do the same.

Competence Through Research. You can develop competence through research. By interviewing and by reading articles and books, you can quote acknowledged experts, thereby making your speech more credible. When you are using information derived from experts, make that clear in your speech with such references as:

> *According to Dr. Jessica Smith, a noted authority in this area . . . From Ronald Jones's best-selling book, The Growing Years . . .*

Competence Through Dynamism

Speakers with **dynamism,** another aspect of credibility, show a great deal of enthusiasm and energy for their subjects. For example, when a student tried to get his classmates to become more politically active, he spoke of his own work in a local politician's primary campaign as one of the most exciting times of his life. He described his experience so vividly that the audience was able to feel his excitement.

Much of the dynamism in a speech will be created nonverbally. A speaker who stands up straight, projects his or her voice to the back of the room, and doesn't hesitate will be seen by the audience as more dynamic than one who doesn't do these things. Watch for the most dynamic speakers in your class, and make some mental notes on how they convey their energy and enthusiasm nonverbally.

Competence Through Character

A speaker with **character** is perceived as a person of integrity who is honest, reliable, loyal, and dependable. Sometimes we have no way of assessing speaker's characters unless they do something dishonest, unreliable, disloyal, or undependable. Showing up late for a speech may shed some light on a speaker's character, but there is likely to be a more reliable key in a speech-communication class. After a month or so together, students can identify classmates who have integrity—who are honest, reliable, loyal, and dependable. These are people who come on time for class, are fully prepared, give their speeches on time, pull their weight in groups, give evidence they have spent

Because so much of persuasion depends on the person doing the persuading, compare these two pictures. Make a judgment. Which person is likely to be more persuasive because of expertise, dynamism, trustworthiness, and ethics—and why?

time preparing their speeches, and offer competent responses in their oral evaluations and comments. They are perceived as people of good character and therefore worth listening to.

Competence Through Caring

Caring is the perception by listeners that speakers are concerned about their welfare. You will respond more positively to speakers who appear kind, warmhearted, attentive, considerate, sympathetic, understanding, and compassionate. Although it may seem like a difficult task to make such a determination of speakers quickly, you do it all the time. For example, how long does it take, upon meeting an instructor during the first day of class, to decide whether that instructor is concerned about your well-being? Interested in your success? Sympathetic to your level of comfort? In many cases, these assessments—even though sometimes wrong—are made almost instantaneously, and they are made based on a wide variety of both verbal and nonverbal clues.

The following quotation about the nature of persuasion comes from the Introduction to *Split-Second Persuasion: The Ancient Art and New Science of Changing Minds* (Houghton Mifflin Harcourt, 2011) by Kevin Dutton.

> . . . Minds—just ask any used car salesman— don't change easily. Nine times out of ten, persuasion is contingent on a complex combination of factors, relating not just to what we say but also how we say it. Not to mention, once said, how it's interpreted. In the vast majority of cases, influence is wrought by talking. By a nervy cocktail of compromise, enterprise, and negotiation. By wrapping up whatever it is that we want in an intricate parcel of words . . . (p. 7).

Source: Dutton, Kevin. (2011). *Split-Second Persuasion: The Ancient Art and New Science of Changing Minds.* Boston: Houghton Mifflin.

Questions

1. Do you have any personal experiences with persuasion that would lead you to believe that the quotation is true—that minds don't change easily?

2. Are there positive benefits of or negative issues with the fact that minds don't change easily?

3. What are some of the "complex combination of factors" that make persuasion difficult, that is, that cause minds to change only with difficulty?

4. If you were advising a neophyte in the art of persuasion, what strategies would you suggest that he or she use to speed up the process by which minds change?

Structure Your Material Effectively

How you decide to structure your material may depend on the material itself; it may depend on your own interests or intentions; or it may depend on the situation or assignment. The most important consideration, however, is audience-centered—how you want (or expect) your listeners to react.

Questions of Fact, Value, and Policy

In Chapter 11, "Small-Group Participation and Leadership," we discussed using questions of fact, value, and policy in group discussion. In persuasive speaking, if you can identify the question type, it gives you an idea about how to shape your response. For example, *questions of fact* are those which ask you to answer whether or not something is true or false, and these questions are always answered "Yes" or "No." The approach is to answer the question and construct the body of the speech with a variety of evidence that supports your position.

Questions of value are concerned with the relative merit (goodness or badness) of a thing. In this case you would choose between things, ideas, beliefs, or actions and then explain why you chose in the manner you did. What makes your choice right or wrong, beneficial or detrimental, favorable or unfavorable, and so on? You support your choice with a variety of appropriate evidence.

Finally, questions of policy deal with specific courses of action, and they usually contain such words as *should, ought to, have to,* or *must.* They ask you to explain what you should do, and your response is to create a plan of action to solve some sort of problem. You then use evidence to justify your plan and prove, too, that it fixes the problem.

One-Sided versus Two-Sided Arguments

Should persuaders present one side or both sides of an issue? When you know your listeners basically support your ideas, one side may be sufficient. For example, a student knew that she didn't have to persuade her audience of the pros and cons of speed dating. Instead, she came up with some unique ideas for how her listeners could find dates.

There are occasions, however, when speakers should present both sides of the picture. Often the presentation of both sides will boost credibility: The speaker is likely to be perceived as fairer and more rational. When an issue of public importance is controversial, it's a good idea to present both sides, since most people will probably have heard something about each side. When a student spoke on gun control, he presented both sides because he knew there were strong feelings for and against.

Research results seem to indicate that (1) a two-sided speech is more effective when the listeners have at least a high school education; (2) the two-sided speech is especially effective if the evidence clearly supports the thesis; and (3) the two-sided presentation is more effective when listeners oppose the speaker's position, but the one-sided approach is more effective when listeners already support the thesis.[42]

Ethical considerations should sometimes be taken into account when deciding whether to present two sides. For example, if presenting only one side will suppress key information, then presenting two sides is essential, but you may need to refute the side you don't agree with.

STRATEGIC FLEXIBILITY

As you draw together the information you have discovered on your own interests and intentions, on the situation and assignment, and, of course, on your listeners' attitudes and how you expect them to react, these factors become the foundation for strategic flexibility.

Order of Presentation

The organizational schemes most commonly used in persuasive speeches—covered previously in Chapter 13, Organizing and Outlining the Speech—are the cause-and-effect order and the problem–solution order. The cause-and-effect order has two parts. The first part of the body develops the cause of a problem, and the second discusses its effects. For example, the first part could talk about the time pressures and convenience that drives people to fast food. The second, the effects, could discuss the unhealthy results—including obesity.

In the problem–solution order the first part of the body of the speech develops the problem, and the second part of the body of the speech gives a solution. A speaker, for example, could talk about negative emotions and chronic pessimism as risk factors for heart disease, smoking, excessive drinking, and poor eating habits—the problem. In the solution half, the speaker could support the benefits of optimism—the body of evidence that well-adjusted, socially stable, well-integrated people have a lower risk of disease, premature death, and even lower blood cholesterol levels[43]—and how to develop an optimistic point of view.

A third pattern of organization, the motivated sequence, is a time-tested adaptation of the problem–solution order. The **motivated sequence,** developed by Professor Alan H. Monroe in the 1930s,[44] is a pattern of organization designed to persuade listeners to accept a point of view and then motivate them to take action. The full pattern has five steps:

1. *Attention:* The speaker calls attention to the topic or situation.

2. *Need:* The speaker develops the need for a change and explains related audience needs. This is the problem-development portion of the speech.

3. *Satisfaction:* The speaker presents his or her solution and shows how it meets (satisfies) the needs mentioned.

ATTENTION!

Tips for Using Monroe's Motivated Sequence

1. Be careful of repetition.
2. Do all the steps.
3. Take time to build the need.
4. Use clear "statements" at the beginning of each step.
5. Make your need/want step and action advocated consistent.
6. Make sure all proposals have workability.[45]

4. *Visualization:* The speaker shows what will result when the solution is put into effect.

5. *Action:* The speaker indicates what kind of action is necessary to bring about the desired change.

Any persuasive problem-solving speech can be adapted to the motivated sequence. Notice how the speaker uses this pattern in "To Cheat or Not to Cheat: That Is the Question":

Specific purpose: To persuade my listeners that they should take a strong stand to eliminate academic dishonesty.

Central idea: Unless you are willing to take a strong stand to eliminate academic dishonesty, cheating is likely to continue and will hurt us all.

Main points:

I. *Attention.* The decision to cheat or not can be difficult to make—especially when you are under a lot of pressure.

II. *Need.* Often students face the temptation to be academically dishonest daily, whether it be cheating or helping others to cheat.

III. *Satisfaction.* Students should focus on the value of honesty, the importance of integrity in academic matters, and the privilege of a college education.

IV. *Visualization.* Academic honesty is important to educational growth. Aim for learning, grades that represent solid effort, feelings of self-worth and integrity, and a clear conscience about never having helped others to cheat.

V. *Action.* Think about academic honesty. If you have ever cheated, don't do it again. If you haven't, don't start. Being honest in your work makes you feel better about yourself.

Are You a Credible Speaker?

For each question circle the numerical score that best rates your performance based on the last or most recent speech you have given: 7 = Outstanding; 6 = Excellent; 5 = Very good; 4 = Average (good); 3 = Fair; 2 = Poor; 1 = Minimal ability; 0 = No ability demonstration.

1. Are you generally perceived to be a person of goodwill? 7 6 5 4 3 2 1 0
   A. Do you treat others courteously?
   B. Do you generally display acceptance, approval, and appreciation?
   C. Do you generally consider yourself equal to others?

2. Did you do things prior to your previous speech to develop your credibility? 7 6 5 4 3 2 1 0
   A. Were you aware of your image in all contacts with your audience members prior to your speech?
   B. Did you make your listeners aware of your qualifications?
   C. Did you set a favorable tone prior to your speech?

3. In your past speech, did you build your credibility through quality communication? 7 6 5 4 3 2 1 0
   A. Did you strive for believability in your message?
   B. Were your feelings, meanings, intentions, and consequences clear?
   C. Did you maintain respect for the thoughts and feelings of your listeners?

4. In your past speech did you intentionally raise your perceived competence by doing the things the listeners perceived as competent? 7 6 5 4 3 2 1 0
   A. Did you quote people who are acknowledged experts on your topic?
   B. Did you list facts and issues pertinent to your topic?
   C. Did you use any of the special vocabulary of the experts?

5. Did you pay special attention to the organization of your speech? 7 6 5 4 3 2 1 0
   A. Did you have—and reveal—one clear, powerful central thesis?
   B. Did you reveal the structure of your speech to your listeners?
   C. Did the pattern of organization you followed remain consistent throughout your speech?

6. Did you mention your personal involvement in, your prior commitment or your active current commitment to the topic of your speech? 7 6 5 4 3 2 1 0
   A. Did you specifically let your listeners know your personal experiences with your topic?
   B. Did you specifically let your listeners know the personal actions you have taken in the past which are clearly compatible with your basic orientation?
   C. Did you tell your audience what you are doing or will do as a consequence of your orientation to your topic?

7. Did you reveal a solid knowledge base on your topic? 7 6 5 4 3 2 1 0
   A. Did you appear qualified, informed, and authoritative?
   B. Did you have fresh, clear, relevant, and specific supporting material?
   C. Did you specifically refer to your research effort during your speech?

8. Did you do things during your speech to build your trustworthiness?   7 6 5 4 3 2 1 0
   A. Did you self-disclose—within the limits of interpersonal safety, of course?
   B. Did you compliment your audience?
   C. Did you appear honest, kind, friendly, pleasant, earnest, and sincere?
9. Did you do things deliberately in your speech to appear forceful, bold, and dynamic?   7 6 5 4 3 2 1 0
   A. Were you poised, relaxed, and fluent?
   B. Did you reflect a clear emotional commitment to your ideas? Complete ego involvement?
   C. Were your nonverbal cues (face, voice, gestures, and body movement) completely supportive of your ideas?
10. Was the evidence you used in your speech significant, relevant, and interesting to your listeners?   7 6 5 4 3 2 1 0
   A. Did you objectively evaluate your evidence in terms of its usefulness?
   B. Did you tell your listeners who the authorities of your evidence were, and why those authorities should be respected?

Go to the Online Learning Center at **www.mhhe.com/hybels11e** to see your results and learn how to evaluate your attitudes and feelings.

Summary

The informative speaker should increase understanding through careful language choices, coherent organization, and illustrations and examples. The speaker should hold attention with narratives, select subjects with which listeners can identify, and use visual support to help listeners retain information.

The principles that make a good speech remain the same for all four types of informative speeches: speeches about objects, about processes, about events, and about concepts.

Definitions can use etymology, example, comparison or contrast, or function. Descriptions include size, shape, weight, color, or composition. Explanations can rely on numbers, connecting the known with the unknown, and repeating and reinforcing ideas.

Creating interest in your topic is a matter of presenting anecdotes, building anticipation or suspense, and using a variety of other techniques. A speaker can involve the audience by selecting an interesting topic and examples, choosing a simple and clear organizational pattern, and using transitions. Three other methods are inviting volunteers to participate in the speech, asking rhetorical questions, and soliciting questions from the audience.

Persuasion is the process that occurs when a communicator influences the values, beliefs, attitudes, or behaviors of another person. The focus of persuasion should be on the sender, the receiver, and the message, because all three share in the persuasive process. It is only when all three combine successfully that effective persuasion occurs. As in all speaking, you should be ethical by conforming to acceptable and fair standards of conduct.

The key to understanding persuasion is influence, the power of a person or thing to affect others—to produce effects without the presence of physical force. Persuasion involves motivation as well. Motivation is the stimulation or inducement that causes a person to act. We are motivated to do what we do in order to reduce tension, meet needs, or achieve goals or because we want personal growth, mastery of the environment, and self-understanding. These are useful motivators for persuaders to keep in mind.

We are more likely to respond to persuasive messages that tap into our values, beliefs, and attitudes. Values are the ideas we have about what is good and what is bad and how things should be. Instrumental values guide people's day-to-day behavior, while terminal values are central to our culture. Beliefs are simple propositions, conscious or unconscious, expressed in what people say or do. People often begin statements of belief with the phrase "I believe that . . ." Attitudes are predispositions to respond favorably or unfavorably toward a person, subject, or situation. Persuaders who are sensitive and responsive to the values, beliefs, and attitudes of listeners are more likely to be successful.

Effective persuasion, even though it happens on a daily basis, is challenging. Speakers who understand why it is difficult to change values, beliefs, and attitudes can put the process into perspective and work to create a receptive mental attitude. Challenges include the sheer amount of persuasion that occurs; how slowly persuasion tends to work; how deeply entrenched values, beliefs, and attitudes may be; laziness; and the desire for freedom of action. These difficulties should increase persuaders' willingness to invest time, effort, and care in their preparation for speeches.

There are specific strategies persuaders can use to be effective. In preparing a speech, you must determine your purpose and analyze your audience. In appealing to your audience using logic, you choose to use deductive reasoning, inductive reasoning, causal reasoning, or reasoning by analogy. In appealing to your audience using emotion, insight into others' motives and desires is provided by Maslow's hierarchy of needs. It is important to use research to prove your points and choose your language carefully. Because research on persuasion says you are more likely to be an effective persuader if listeners consider you credible—or believable—you need to develop competence through your personal experience, based on commitment, and through your research, dynamism, character, and caring.

When you structure your material, you need to consider whether or not you are supporting a question of fact, value, or policy, whether to use a one-sided or two-sided argument, and your order of presentation. The three organizational schemes include cause-and-effect, the problem–solution order, and the motivated sequence—a time-tested adaptation of the problem–solution order—that includes the five steps of attention, need, satisfaction, visualization, and action.

Key Terms and Concepts

Use the Online Learning Center at www.mhhe.com/hybels11e to further your understanding of the following terms:

Analogy 415
Anecdote 402
Attitudes 409
Beliefs 408
Caring 421
Causal reasoning 415
Character 420
Comparisons 398
Competence 419
Composition 400

Contrasts 398
Credibility 419
Deductive reasoning 413
Definition 397
Demonstration speech 396
Dynamism 420
Emotional appeal 416
Etymology 397
Fallacy 415
Hierarchy of needs 416

Inductive reasoning 413
Influence 407
Informative speech 392
Logical appeal 412
Motivated sequence 423
Motivation 407
Persuasion 406
Rhetorical questions 405
Target audience 412
Values 408

Questions to Review

1. How many informative speeches have you heard in the past week? In what contexts have most of them been delivered? Were most of them effective? What made them effective or ineffective?

2. What are the biggest challenges that giving an informative speech presents to you?

3. What specific techniques can you use to increase listener understanding? Get the attention of listeners? Assist listener retention?

4. What are the differences among the four types of informative speeches—speeches about objects, processes, events, and concepts?

5. What principles govern the creation of any informative speech?

6. What are the different strategies you can use if you need to define your ideas?

7. What strategies can you select if your goal is to describe your ideas?

8. Of the different strategies for informative speeches, which ones do you feel most comfortable using and why?

9. What are the best methods for arousing your interest in a speaker's topic? What is likely to grab your attention?

10. Think of a recent persuasive message that you have heard. How did the speaker influence and motivate you?

11. What are the differences among values, beliefs, and attitudes?

12. For you, which values, beliefs, or attitudes are the ones most likely to be stable? Most likely to change?

13. For you, which of the challenges of persuasion listed in the chapter would likely make you most resistant to someone else's persuasion? How might you as a speaker overcome (or approach) this particular challenge?

14. Besides those discussed in this chapter, are there other factors that make persuasion challenging?

15. As a persuader, which strategies do you feel most comfortable using when persuading others?

16. As an audience member, which strategies would work best in speeches trying to persuade you? Or which ones would likely hold your attention better than others?

17. When you compare logic, emotion, and credibility (*logos, pathos, and ethos*), on which do persuaders most often depend?

18. How do questions of fact, value, and policy differ?

19. If you were speaking on the value of a college education, what techniques for building your credibility would you use if you were talking to a high school audience?

20. Have you ever heard persuaders who were not ethical? What did they do?

21. For you to be ethical in persuasion, what principles should you follow?

22. On a controversial topic, which would work best: a one-sided or a two-sided argument? Why?

Go to the self-quizzes on the Online Learning Center at **www.mhhe.com/hybels11e** to test your knowledge of the chapter contents.

Glossary

A

ableist language Language referring to persons with disabilities. (ch 3) (72)

abstract symbol A symbol that represents an idea. (ch 1) (9)

accent Nonverbal message designed specifically to place stress on the verbal message. (ch 4) (116)

accommodation An approach that works toward getting the dominant group to reinvent, or at least change, the rules so that they incorporate the life experiences of the nondominant group. Something that occurs in groups when people on one side of an issue give in to the other side. (ch 9, 10) (236, 258)

accommodation strategies When people are not part of a dominant culture, those processes people use to get the dominant group to reinvent or change the rules through the use of nonassertive, assertive, or aggressive accommodation. (ch 10) (258)

action listening style That kind of listening in which the listener wants precise, error-free presentations and is likely to be impatient with disorganization. (ch 5) (130)

active listening Making a mental outline of important points, thinking up questions or challenges to the points that have been made, and becoming mentally involved with the person talking. (ch 5) (138)

active open-mindedness A tool readers can use, flexibly, to help them digest, master, and use knowledge and to give them practice in critical examination, analysis, and thought. (ch 1) (22)

adaptors Nonverbal ways of adjusting to a communication situation. (ch 4) (104)

agenda A list of all the items that will be discussed during a meeting. (ch 11) (300)

aggressor One who commits an aggression or begins quarrels by deflating the status of others, expressing disapproval of others' values, acts, or feelings, or attacking others, joking aggressively, and taking credit for others' contributions. (ch 11) (290)

aggressive talk Talk that attacks a person's self-concept with the intent of inflicting psychological pain. (ch 7) (199)

analogy In reasoning, comparing two similar cases and concluding that if something is true for one, it must also be true for the other. (ch 15) (415)

anecdote A short, interesting story based on an experience. (ch 15) (402)

anosmia The complete loss of the sense of smell. (ch 4) (102)

anticipate The first of six steps of the strategic flexibility format in which users think about potential situations and the needs and requirements likely to arise because of them. (ch 1, 5) (21, 123)

anxiety A disturbance that occurs in your mind regarding some uncertain event, misgiving, or worry. (ch 5) (135)

apply The fifth of six steps of the strategic flexibility format in which users, with care, concern, and attention to all the factors that are likely to be affected—including any ethical considerations that may be appropriate—apply the skills and behaviors they have selected. (ch 1, 5) (21, 127)

appraisal interview A type of information interview in which a supervisor makes a valuation by estimating and judging the quality or worth of an employee's performance and then interviews the employee in connection with the appraisal. (website)

appreciative listening To listen for pleasure. (ch 5) (139)

articulation The ability to pronounce the letters in a word correctly. (ch 14) (377)

assertiveness Taking the responsibility of expressing needs, thoughts, and feelings in a direct, clear manner. (ch 7) (202)

assess The second of the six steps of the strategic flexibility format in which users take stock of the factors, elements, and conditions of the situations in which they find themselves. (ch 1, 5) (21, 138)

assimilation When nondominants use assimilation, they drop cultural differences and distinctive characteristics that would identify them with the nondominant group. (ch 10) (257)

assimilation strategies When people are not part of a dominant culture, those processes they use to drop cultural differences and distinctive characteristics that would identify them with the nondominant group including the use of nonassertive, assertive, and aggressive assimilation strategies. (ch 10) (257)

assumption A taking for granted or supposition that something is a fact. (ch 10) (262)

asynchronous communication Communication in which people are not directly connected with each other at the same time. (ch 1, 11) (12, 274)

attentiveness Focusing on the moment. (ch 14) (370)

attitudes Deeply felt beliefs that govern how we behaves. Also, a group of beliefs that cause us to respond in some way to a particular object or situation. (ch 6, 12, 15) (157, 320, 409)

attractiveness Having the power or quality of drawing, pleasing, or winning. (ch 4) (105)

attribution Devising explanations (theories) about other people's behavior so that they can understand whatever is taking place—which can include attributing causes or intentions. (ch 2) (49)

audience analysis Finding out what one's audience members know about a subject, what they might be interested in, and what their attitudes and beliefs are. (ch 12) (319)

authoritarian leader One who holds great control over a group. (ch 11) (295)

avoidance A refusal to deal with conflict or painful issues. (ch 7, 9) (202, 236)

B

beliefs One's own convictions; what one thinks is right and wrong, true and false. Also, they are classified as statements of knowledge, opinion, and faith. (ch 6, 12, 15) (157, 320, 408)

bid A question, gesture, look, touch, or other single expression that says, "I want to feel connected to you." (ch 6) (163)

blind pane That area in the Johari Window known as an accidental disclosure area. (ch 6) (168)

blocker A dysfunctional small-group role in which a participant tends to be negativistic and stubbornly resistant, disagreeing and opposing without or beyond "reason," and attempting to maintain or bring back an issue after the group has rejected or bypassed it. (ch 11) (290)

body adornment Any addition to the physical body designed to beautify or decorate. (ch 4) (108)

body movement (kinesics) Describes a phenomenon responsible for much of our nonverbal communication. (ch 4) (103)

body (of speech) The main part of the speech. (ch 13) (343)

brainstorming A technique of free association; in groups, when all members spontaneously contribute ideas in a group without judgments being made. The goal of brainstorming is for the group to be as creative as possible. (ch 11) (282)

C

caring The perception by listeners that speakers are concerned about their welfare. (ch 15) (421)

causal reasoning A logical appeal that pertains to, constitutes, involves, or expresses a cause and therefore uses the word *because,* which is either implicitly or explicitly stated. (ch 15) (415)

cause-and-effect order Organization of a speech around why something is happening *(cause)* and what impact it is having *(effect)*. (ch 13) (345)

central idea The essential thought that runs through the speech or communication. (ch 5, 12) (141, 318)

certainty That defensive climate (one aspect of defensive communication) in which people think they are always right. (ch 9) (231)

channel The route traveled by a message; the means it uses to reach the sender-receivers. (ch 1, 12) (9, 322)

character A speaker perceived as a person of integrity who is honest, reliable, loyal, and dependable. (ch 15) (420)

chronemics The study of time. (ch 4) (114)

clarity That property of style by means of which a thought is so presented that it is immediately understood, depending on the precision and simplicity of the language. (ch 3) (83)

coercive power In an organization, the ability of a leader to punish followers (e.g., by criticizing them, refusing to pay attention to them, using power to demote them, refusing to raise their pay, or firing them). (ch 11) (292)

cognitive development The development of the thinking and organizing systems of your brain that involves language, mental imagery, reasoning, problem solving, and memory development. (ch 3) (62)

cognitive dissonance A psychological theory, applied to communication, that states that people seek information that will support their beliefs and ignore information that does not. (ch 2, 5) (48, 135)

cognitive schemata The mental guidelines our brains use that supply impressions of the whole—the whole story, the whole event, or the whole person. (ch 2) (48)

cohesiveness The feeling of attraction that group members have toward one another. It is the group's ability to stick together, to work together as a group, and to help one another as group members. (ch 11) (279)

collaboration In Blake and Mouton's approaches to managing conflict, this occurs when conflicting parties try to work together to meet each other's needs. (ch 9) (237)

commitment A strong desire by both parties for the relationship to continue. In groups, it is the willingness of members to work together to complete the group's task. (ch 6, 9, 11) (175, 228, 279)

communication Any process in which people share information, ideas, and feelings. (ch 1) (7)

comparison Supporting material that points out the similarities between two or more things. (ch 12, 15) (328, 398)

compatibility Similar attitudes, personality, and a liking for the same activities. (ch 6) (158)

competence A person who possesses special ability, skill, or knowledge. (ch 15) (419)

competition Competition occurs when members on one side care more about winning than about the other members' feelings. (ch 9) (237)

competent communication To communicate in a personally effective and socially appropriate manner. (ch 1) (19)

complaint Expression of dissatisfaction with the behavior, attitude, belief, or characteristic of a partner or of someone else. (ch 7) (201)

complement Nonverbal cues designed specifically to add to the meaning of a verbal message. (ch 4) (115)

composition The makeup of a thing. (ch 15) (400)

comprehension listening To understand what others are saying because you are aware of, grasp, and can make sense of their messages. (ch 5) (139)

compromise A conflict-management approach in which conflicting parties try to work together to meet each other's needs. (ch 9) (238)

computer (or online) databases A collection of items of information organized for easy access via a computer. (ch 12) (324)

computer-generated graphics Refers to any images created or manipulated via computer—art, drawings, representations of objects, pictures, and the like. (ch 14) (382)

computer-mediated communication (CMC) A wide range of technologies that facilitate both human communication and the interactive sharing of information through computer networks, including email, discussion group, newsgroups, chat rooms, instant messages, and Web pages. (ch 1) (16)

conclusion (of speech) In a speech, the closing remarks that tie a speech together and give listeners the feeling that the speech is complete. (ch 13) (353)

concrete symbol A symbol that represents an object. (ch 1) (8)

conflict Expressed struggle between at least two individuals who perceive incompatible goals or interference from others in achieving their goals. (ch 9) (225)

conflict resolution Negotiation to find a solution to the conflict. (ch 9) (225)

connotative meaning The feelings or associations that each individual has about a particular word. (ch 3) (64)

consensus General agreement where each group member is in accord. (ch 11) (303)

constructing meaning The complicated and unique process of making sense of the cues, signals, and impulses received. (ch 5) (126)

content listening style That kind of listening in which the listener prefers complex and challenging information. (ch 5) (130)

context High context occurs when most of the meaning of the message is either implied by the physical setting or is presumed to be part of the individual's beliefs, values, and norms. It is considered low context when most of the information is in the code or message. (ch 10) (247)

contrast Supporting material that points out the differences between two or more things. (ch 12, 15) (328, 398)

control The desire to have governing influence over a situation. (ch 4, 5, 8, 9) (113, 116, 133, 136, 230)

controlling listeners People who prefer talking to listening and seek to control their listeners by looking for ways to talk about themselves and their experiences. (ch 5) (136)

convergence An aspect of rate (the speed at which one speaks) demonstrated by how one person will accommodate or adapt to another's rate. (ch 4) (102)

conversational quality When speakers talk to audiences in much the same way they talk when they are having a conversation with another person. (ch 14) (370)

conversation management Using nonverbal cues to structure conversations. (ch 4) (96)

costs The problems associated with relationships. (ch 7) (196)

costumes The type of clothing that is a form of highly individualized dress. (ch 4) (108)

creativity The capacity to synthesize vast amounts of information, wrestle with complex problems, and generate possibilities. (ch 1, 12) (21, 22, 323)

credibility The believability of a speaker based on the speaker's expertise, dynamism, trustworthiness, and ethics. (ch 15) (419)

critical listening Includes all the ingredients for active listening and, in addition, evaluating and challenging what is heard. (ch 5) (140)

criticism A negative evaluation of a person for something he or she has done or the way he or she is. (ch 7) (201)

cultural differences Includes not just obvious differences between people from other countries, but also differences based upon income, regional origins, dress code and grooming standards, music preferences, political affiliation, how long an individual has been in this country, skin tone, language ability, religion, etc. (website)

cultural identity The degree to which you identify with your culture. (ch 10) (247)

cultural information Information used in making predictions based on a person's most generally shared cultural attributes such as language, shared values, beliefs, and ideologies. (ch 6) (167)

culture The ever-changing values, traditions, social and political relationships, and worldview created and shared by a group of people bound together by a combination of factors (which can include a common history, geographic location, language, social class, and/or religion). (ch1, 10) (18, 246)

D

deductive reasoning Reasoning from the general to the specific. (ch 15) (413)

defensive communication When one partner tries to defend himself or herself against the remarks or behavior of the other. (ch 9) (229)

definition Supporting material that is a brief explanation of what a word or phrase means. (ch 12, 15) (328, 397)

delegating That style of situational leadership in which leaders hang back and let members plan and execute the job. (ch 11) (298)

deletions The blotting out, erasing, or canceling of information that makes people's perceptions less than perfect because their physical senses are limited. (ch 2) (48)

democratic leader One who lets all points of view be heard and lets group members participate in the decision-making process. (ch 11) (296)

demographic analysis Reveals data about the characteristics of a group of people, including such things as age, sex, education, occupation, race/nationality/ethnic origin, geographic location, and group affiliation. (ch 12) (320)

demonstration speech A speech that teaches people "how to" perform a process. (ch 15) (396)

denotative meaning The dictionary definition of a particular word. (ch 3) (64)

dialect The habitual language of a community. (ch 3) (79)

directness Being natural and straightforward. (ch 14) (372)

disciplinary interview A type of information interview that concerns a sensitive area, where the employee is notified, and the interview involves hearing the employee's side of the story and, depending on the outcome, instituting disciplinary action. (website)

discrimination The overt actions one takes to exclude, avoid, or distance oneself from other groups. (ch 10) (256)

discriminative listening To listen for both verbal and nonverbal changes in a speaker that allow you to make sense of the meanings and nuances expressed. (ch 5) (139)

displays of feelings Face and body movements that show how intensely we are feeling. (ch 4) (103)

distortions The twisting or bending of information out of shape that makes people's perceptions less than perfect because they observe only a small part of their external environment. (ch 2) (49)

dominant culture Includes white people from a European background. (ch 10) (257)

dominator A dysfunctional group role in which a member tries to assert authority or superiority by manipulating the group or certain members of the group. (ch 11) (290)

doublespeak A term that refers to euphemisms created by an institution, such as government, to cover up the truth. (ch 3) (70)

dynamism For speakers, a great deal of enthusiasm and energy for their subject. (ch 15) (420)

dysfunctional (individual) roles Any role played by a group member that can be characterized as aggressor, blocker, recognition-seeker, self-confessor, playboy or play-girl, dominator, help-seeker, or special-interest pleader. (ch 11) (290)

E

elective characteristics The nonverbal, physical characteristics over which you have control such as clothing, makeup, tattoos, and body piercing. (ch 4) (105)

emblems Body movements that have a direct translation into words. (ch 4) (103)

emotional appeal A persuasive strategy that focuses on listeners' needs, wants, desires, and wishes. (ch 15) (416)

emotional intelligence The ability to understand and get along with others. (ch 6) (152)

empathy The process of mentally identifying with the character and experiences of another person. The ability to recognize and identify with someone's feelings. (ch 5, 9) (142, 230)

employment interview An interview used by an employer to determine whether someone is suitable for a job. (website)

encouragers A person who praises and commends members contributions and group achievement. (ch 11) (289)

endurance To simply and stubbornly outlast relationship problems. (ch 8) (209)

enunciation How one pronounces and articulates words. (ch 14) (377)

Equality Small-group members who offset or counter the defensive climate of superiority with a supportive behavior that encourages others to approach problems together. (ch 9) (231)

ethical communication Communication that is honest, fair, and considerate of others' rights. (ch 1) (25)

ethics Behavior that is in accordance with right principles as defined by a given system of ethics (such as your culture and co-culture), or professional conduct within a specific business environment. (website)

ethnocentrism The belief that one's own cultural group's behaviors, norms, ways of thinking, and ways of being are superior to all other cultural groups. (ch 10) (256)

etymology The study of the origin and development of words. (ch 15) (397)

euphemism Inoffensive words or phrases that are substituted for words that might be perceived as unpleasant. (ch 3) (70)

evaluate The third of the six steps of the strategic flexibility format in which users determine the value and worth of the factors, elements, and conditions to all those involved and how they bear on one's own skills and abilities. (ch 1) (21)

evaluation Determining the value and worth of the factors, elements, and conditions. (ch 5) (127)

evaluative listening (sometimes called critical listening) Occurs when judgments are made about what others are saying. (ch 5) (140)

evaluative statements Expressions that involve a judgment. (ch 9) (230)

example Supporting material that is a short illustration that clarifies a point. (ch 12) (328)

exit interview A type of information interview that occurs at the termination of an employee's employment, and is designed to resolve any outstanding concerns of employers and employees. (website)

expectancy violation theory When others violate your expectations about how they should behave, you can perceive the violation either positively or negatively depending, in part, on how much you like the other person. The theory proposes that it is people's expectancy that will influence the outcome of communication as positive or negative. (ch 4) (101)

expert power The influence and power that an expert has because he or she knows more than anyone else. (ch 11) (293)

extemporaneous speaking Speaking from notes. (ch 14) (374)

external noise Interference with the message that comes from the environment and keeps the message from being heard or understood. (ch 1) (10)

extrinsic Means outside the relationship. (ch 7) (193)

extrinsic costs The sacrifices, losses, or suffering as a result of things that occur outside the relationship (could include not having as much time for your friends or sharing your friends with your partner). (ch 7) (197)

extrinsic rewards The gifts, prizes, and recompenses that occur outside a relationship (could include liking the people your partner has introduced you to or the friends he or she hangs out with). (ch 7) (196)

eye messages As an aspect of nonverbal communication, they include all information conveyed by the eyes alone. (ch 4) (104)

F

facial expressions Facial movements that signal emotions. (ch 4) (104)

fact Something that can be verified in a number of ways. (ch 5) (140)

fallacy An improper conclusion drawn from a premise. (ch 15) (415)

feedback The response of the receiver-senders to each other. (ch 1) (9)

femininity versus masculinity That way of contrasting a group of cultures to another group of cultures that involves the division of roles between women and men. (ch 10) (254)

flip chart A series of pictures, words, diagrams, and so forth. It is made up of several pages that speakers "flip" through. (ch 14) (380)

full-sentence outline A complete map of what a speech will look like. (ch 13) (348)

FtF Face to face as in face-to-face conversation. (ch 8) (206)

functional leadership When leadership varies with the task of the group and moves from one individual to another as the group finds it suitable. (ch 11) (296)

G

general purpose The intention of the speaker to inform or persuade. (ch 12) (316)

generalizations The process of drawing principles or conclusions from particular evidence or facts that makes people's perceptions less than perfect because once people have observed something a few times, they conclude that what has proven true in the past will prove true in the future as well. (ch 2) (49)

groupthink A group dysfunction in which the preservation of harmony becomes more important than the critical examination of ideas. (ch 11) (280)

H

haptics The study of touch. (ch 4) (111)

harmonizer-compromisers Compromisers in small groups are participants who help resolve conflict, settle arguments, discover solutions acceptable to everyone, and remind others that group goals are more important than individual needs. (ch 11) (289)

help-seekers In small groups these participants play the dysfunctional role of calling forth a "sympathy" response from other group members by expressions of insecurity, personal confusion, or deprecation of themselves beyond "reason." (ch 11) (290)

hidden agendas Unannounced goals, subjects, or issues of individual group members or subgroups that differ from the group's public or stated agenda. (ch 11) (301)

hidden pane That area of the Johari Window where self-knowledge is hidden from others—a deliberate non-disclosure area in which there are certain things you know about yourself that you do not want known and deliberately conceal them from others. (ch 6) (168)

hierarchy of needs The relative order of the physical and psychological needs of all human beings. (ch 15) (416)

high context versus low context That way of contrasting a group of cultures to another group of cultures that involves the degree to which most of the information is carried in the context (high) or most of the information is in the code or message (low). (ch 10) (255)

hyperpersonal The quality of Internet relationships that makes them more intimate than romances or friendships would be if partners were physically together. (ch 2) (40)

hypothetical example An example that is made up to illustrate a point. (ch 12) (329)

I

illustrators Gestures or other nonverbal signals that accent, emphasize, or reinforce words. (ch 4) (103)

immediacy It occurs when the communicator is completely focused on the communication situation. (ch 14) (371)

implicit personality theory The theory that we construct a picture of what people's personalities are based on qualities or characteristics revealed by their behavior. (ch 2) (49)

impromptu speaking Speaking on the spur of the moment with little time to prepare. (ch 14) (373)

indirect aggression (also called *passive aggression*) People who use this form of communication often feel powerless and respond by doing something to thwart the person in power. (ch 7) (199)

individualism versus collectivism The way of contrasting a group of cultures to another group of cultures that involves the degree of integration and orientation of individuals within groups. (ch 10) (253)

inductive reasoning Reasoning from the specific to the general. (ch 15) (413)

inflection A change in pitch used to emphasize certain words and phrases. (ch 14) (377)

influence The power of a person or things to affect others—to produce effects without the presence of physical force. (ch 15) (407)

information givers Member of a group who provides critical information. (ch 11) (288)

information interview An interview in which the goal is to gather facts and opinions from someone with expertise and experience in a specific field. (website)

information seekers Member of a group who researches a subject and provides the information to the group. (ch 11) (288)

information-sharing group A type of group that meets to be informed or to inform others, to express themselves and to listen to others, to get or give assistance, to clarify or hear clarification of goals, or to establish or maintain working relationships. (ch 11) (276)

informative listening A type of listening where the primary concern is to understand the message. (ch 5) (141)

informative speech A speech that concentrates on explaining, defining, clarifying, and instructing. (ch 12, 15) (316, 392)

initial partition A preview of the main points of a speech at the outset (often, in the introduction of the speech). (ch 13) (352)

initiator-expediters Member of a group who suggests new ideas, goals, solutions, or approaches to solve problems. (ch 11) (288)

instrumental Refers to the basic exchange of goods and services. (ch 7) (196)

instrumental costs The sacrifices, losses, or suffering as a result of exchanging goods and services (could include sharing your belongings). (ch 7) (193)

instrumental rewards The gifts, prizes, and recompenses that occur as a result of the basic exchange of goods and services (could include raising the current level of relational intimacy with one of the rewards being moving in with your partner and sharing in both the rent and the furniture). (ch 7) (197)

Integrative Listening Model (ILM) A framework for assessing listening both systematically and developmentally. (ch 5) (125)

integrity Uprightness of character and honesty. (website)

intercultural communication When a message is created by a member of one culture, and this message needs to be processed by a member of another culture. (ch 1, 10) (18, 248)

internal noise Interference with the message that occurs in the minds of the sender-receivers when their thoughts or feelings are focused on something other than the communication at hand. (ch 1) (10)

interpersonal communication One person interacting with another on a one-to-one basis, often in an informal, unstructured setting. (ch 1, 6) (15, 152)

interpersonal definition Second Stage of Deborah Wieder-Hatfield's model for resolving conflict when parties to the conflict get together to 1) make certain there is a problem, 2) define what it is, and 3) agree on the facts of the problem. (ch 9) (226)

interview A series of questions and answers, usually exchanged between two people, that has the purpose of getting and understanding information about a particular subject or topic. (website)

intimate distance The distance zone, a range of less than 18 inches apart, that places people in direct contact with each other. (ch 4) (109)

instrumental costs The problems associated with relationships. (ch 7) (197)

instrumental rewards The pleasures that come as a result of being in a relationship. (ch 7) (193)

intrapersonal communication Communication that occurs within you; it involves thoughts, feelings, and the way you look at yourself. (ch 1) (15)

intrapersonal evaluation When each person in a conflict analyzes the problem alone. (ch 9) (226)

intrinsic Means within the relationship. (ch 7) (196)

intrinsic costs The obligation to return the attention, warmth, and affection you receive, and the time you will spend listening, communicating, and self-disclosing. (ch 7) (197)

intrinsic rewards The gifts, prizes, and recompenses that occur within a relationship could include the attention, warmth, and affection you gain from being in a relationship. (ch 7) (196)

introduction (of a speech) In a speech, the opening remarks that aim to get attention and build interest in the subject. (ch 13) (348)

J

Johari Window A model of the process of disclosure in interpersonal relationships, developed by Joseph Luft and Harry Ingham. (ch 6) (167)

K

keyword outline An outline containing only the important words or phrases of a speech that helps remind speakers of the ideas they are presenting. (ch 13) (348)

knowledge class A class of individuals supported solely by its participation in the new information industries with little, if any, reliance upon traditional manufacturing, production, or agriculture. (ch 10) (244)

L

ladder of abstraction A diagram of how we abstract, through language, classifications, types, categories, etc. (ch 3) (66)

laissez-faire leader One who does very little actual leading. This leader suggests no direction for and imposes no order on a group. (ch 11) (296)

language environment The environment in which language takes place (e.g., in a classroom). (ch 3) (69)

leader A person who influences the behavior of one or more people. (ch 11) (290)

leadership style The amount of control a leader exerts over a group. (ch 11) (295)

learning group The purpose is to increase the knowledge or skill of participants. (ch 11) (277)

legitimate power (also called *organizational power*) Leaders in formal organizations who derive their influence because they are "the boss" or because of the organizational hierarchy and its rules. (ch 11) (293)

leisure clothing The type of clothing that is up to the individual and that is worn when work is over. (ch 4) (108)

listening Includes the processes of listening preparation, receiving, constructing meaning, responding, and remembering. (ch 5) (125)

listening preparation Includes all the physical, mental, and behavioral aspects that create a readiness to listen. (ch 5) (126)

logical appeal An appeal that addresses listeners' reasoning ability. (ch 15) (412)

long-term orientation The way of contrasting a group of cultures to another group of cultures that involves the tradeoff between long-term and short-term needs gratification. (ch 10) (254)

M

main heads or main points The points that reinforce the central idea. All the broad, general ideas and information that support your central idea. (ch 5, 13) (141, 342)

maintenance roles Group members who play these roles focus on the emotional tone of the meeting. (ch 11) (289)

manners A way of doing, often used in reference to demeanor, personal carriage, mode of conduct, and etiquette. (ch 4) (114)

manuscript speaking Writing out an entire speech and reading it to the audience from the prepared script. (ch 14) (373)

map is not the territory The map is the personal mental approximation and the territory is the actual land or external reality that people experience. Map versus territory simply contrasts the subjective internal experience with the objective external reality. (ch 2) (45)

memory (speaking from) This type of delivery involves writing out the entire speech and then committing it to memory word for word. (ch 14) (374)

mental outline A preliminary sketch that shows the principal features of the speech or lecture. (ch 5) (141)

message The ideas and feelings that a sender-receiver wants to share. (ch 1) (7)

metamessage The meaning, apart from the words, in a message. (ch 3) (86)

minor points The specific ideas and information that support the main points. (ch 13) (342)

mixed message A message in which the verbal and nonverbal contradict each other. (ch 4) (98)

model A replica of an actual object that is used when the object itself is too large to be displayed (e.g., a building), too small to be seen (e.g., a cell), or inaccessible to the eye (e.g., the human heart). (ch 14) (379)

monotone Little variety of pitch in a speech. (ch 14) (377)

motivated sequence Organization of a speech that involves five steps: attention, need, satisfaction, visualization, and action and works because it follows the normal process of human reasoning. (ch 15) (423)

motivation The stimulation or inducement that causes people to act. (ch 15) (407)

multimedia Refers to various media (e.g., text, graphics, animation, and audio) used to deliver information. (ch 14) (383)

N

national communities Cultural groupings within a country. (ch 10) (250)

natural delivery The collection of speech and actions that best represents your true self—that is, free from artificiality, affectation, and constraint. (website)

neutrality Not taking sides (in a group discussion). (ch 9, 11) (230, 300)

noise Interference that keeps a message from being understood or accurately interpreted. (ch 1) (10)

nondominant culture Includes people of color, women, gays, lesbians, and bisexuals, and those whose socioeconomic background is lower than middle class. (ch 10) (257)

nonelective characteristics The nonverbal physical characteristics over which you have no control and which you cannot change such as height, body proportion, coloring, bone structure, and physical disabilities. (ch 4) (105)

nonverbal communication Information we communicate without using words. (ch 4) (92)

nonverbal symbol Anything communicated without words (e.g., facial expressions or hand gestures). (ch 1) (9)

norms Expectations that group members have of how other members will behave, think, and participate. (ch 11) (275)

O

objective reality The actual territory or external reality everyone experiences. (ch 2) (52)

objectivity Basing conclusions on facts and evidence rather than on emotion or opinions. (ch 11) (300)

observers Group members who are sensitive to the needs of other group members and, thus, aid the group's cohesiveness. (ch 11) (290)

occupational dress The type of clothing that employees are expected to wear, but not as precise as a uniform. (ch 4) (108)

olfactics The study of smell. (ch 4) (113)

openness The free exchange of ideas within the bounds of reasonable behavior. (website)

open pane The area of the Johari Window that involves information about yourself that you are willing to communicate, as well as information you are unable to hide. (ch 6) (168)

opinion A personal belief. (ch 5) (140)

organizational chart A chart that shows the relationships among the elements of an organization, such as the departments of a company, the branches of federal or state government, or the committees of student government. (ch 14) (380)

outline A way of organizing material so all the parts and how they relate to the whole can be seen. (ch 13) (347)

owned message (also known as an I-message) An acknowledgment of subjectivity by a message-sender through the use of first-person singular terms *(I, me, my, mine)*. (ch 6) (165)

P

pace How quickly or slowly a person speaks. (ch 14) (377)

paralanguage The way we say something. (ch 3, 4) (81, 101)

paraphrase When you restate the meaning of another's communication using other words than those used by the other person. (ch 5) (137)

participating That style of situational leadership in which leaders state the problem but immediately consult with group members. (ch 11) (298)

passiveness The suspension of the rational functions and the reduction of any physical functions to their lowest possible degree. (ch 5) (136)

people listening style That kind of listening in which the listener is concerned with the other person's feelings. (ch 5) (130)

perception How people look at themselves and the world around them. (ch 2) (32)

perceptual filters The limitations that result from the narrowed lens through which people view the world. (ch 2) (49)

personal distance The distance zone, a range from 18 inches to 4 feet, that people maintain from others when they are engaged in casual and personal conversations. (ch 4) (110)

personal happiness A technique used in unhappy unions designed to improve relationships by improving a person's overall contentment and happiness (even if they could not markedly improve their marital happiness). (ch 9) (228)

personal inventory Appraising your own resources. (ch 12) (314)

persuasion The process of trying to get others to change their attitudes or behavior; also, the process that occurs when a communicator *(sender)* influences the values, beliefs, attitudes, or behaviors of another person *(receiver)*. (ch 15) (406)

persuasive speech When a speaker takes a particular position and tries to get the audience to accept and support that position. (ch 12) (316)

PETAL In using presentation graphics, (1) develop pertinent materials, (2) choose an engaging format, (3) present your materials in a timely manner, (4) satisfy yourself that they are appropriate to the audience, and (5) ensure that everything is legible. (website)

pitch Highness or lowness of the voice. (ch 4) (102)

place Refers to the physical stage for the speech and the interaction with the audience. (ch 12) (322)

playboys (or playgirls) are group members who make a display of their lack of involvement in a group's processes by being cynical, nonchalant, using horseplay, or other "out of field" behavior. (ch 11) (290)

polls Surveys taken of people's attitudes, feelings, or knowledge. (ch 12) (332)

power distance The way of contrasting a group of cultures to another group of cultures that involves social inequality. (ch 10) (252)

powerful talk Talk that comes directly to the point, that does not use hesitation or qualifications. (ch 3) (78)

PowerPoint One of the most widely used software programs designed for use in presentations. (ch 14) (384)

predict To forecast or to make something known beforehand. (ch 5) (141)

prejudice A negative attitude toward a cultural group based on little or no experience. (ch 10) (256)

problem–solution order Organization of a speech into two sections: one dealing with the problem and the other dealing with the solution. (ch 13) (345)

problem solving Using some specific procedure to resolve the difficulty (problem) under consideration. (ch 9) (230)

professional communication Communication that is connected with, preparing for, engaged in, appropriate for, or conforming to business professions or occupations. (website)

pronunciation The ability to pronounce a word correctly. (ch 14) (377)

propriety The character or quality of being proper, especially in accordance with recognized usage, custom, or principles. (ch 5) (145)

provisionalism In defensive communication it is the supportive climate which is demonstrated when small group participants make statements that permit other member's views to be expressed, and it is designed to offset or counter the defensive climate labeled certainty. (ch 9) (231)

proxemics The study of how people use space. (ch 4) (108)

proximity The close contact that occurs when people share an experience such as work, play, or school. (ch 6) (158)

psychological information The kind of information that is the most specific and intimate because it allows you to know individual traits, feelings, attitudes, and important personal data. (ch 6) (167)

psychological safety Approval and support obtained from familiar people, ideas, and situations. (ch 2) (56)

psychological sets A type of psychological filter that includes your expectations or predispositions to respond. (ch 2) (46)

public communication The sender-receiver *(speaker)* sends a message *(the speech)* to an audience. (ch 1) (18)

public distance The distance zone, a distance of more than 12 feet, typically used for public speaking. (ch 4) (110)

public-speaking anxiety The disturbance of mind regarding the uncertainty surrounding a forthcoming public-speaking event for which you are the speaker. (ch 14) (365)

purpose Determining the intent of a speech. (ch 12) (316)

Q

quality (of voice) Comprised of all voice characteristics: tempo, resonance, rhythm, pitch, and articulation. (ch 4) (102)

questions of fact Questions that deal with what is true and what is false. (ch 11) (285)

questions of policy Questions that are about actions that might be taken in the future. (ch 11) (285)

questions of value Questions of whether something is good or bad, desirable or undesirable. (ch 11) (285)

R

racist language The tendency to describe the majority group, its actions and its members, in positive terms, whereas minority groups, their actions and members, are portrayed overwhelmingly in negative terms. Racism, then, is discrimination or prejudice based on race. (ch 3) (71)

rapport style A style of communication designed to establish connections and negotiate relationships. (website)

rapport-talk Type of language women use in conversation, designed to lead to intimacy with others, to match experiences, and to establish relationships. (ch 3) (77)

rate (of speech) Speed at which one speaks. (ch 4) (102)

RDAT In using slides in a presentation, read the visual, describe its meaning or significance, amplify it with an explanation or illustration, and, finally, transition to the next slide. (website)

reassess and reevaluate The sixth of six steps of the strategic flexibility format in which users closely examine the results of any steps taken or not taken by them. (ch 1) (21)

receiving The process of taking in, acquiring, or accepting information. (ch 5) (126)

reference list A list of all the material you have used—and only that which you have used—in preparing your speech. (ch 13) (356)

referent power When leaders enjoy influence because of their personality. (ch 11) (293)

reflected appraisals Messages we get about ourselves from others. (ch 2) (35)

regrettable talk Saying something embarrassing, hurtful, or private to another person. (ch 7) (200)

regulate Nonverbal cues designed specifically to direct, manage, or control behavior. (ch 4) (115)

regulators (1) Nonverbal signals that control the back-and-forth flow of speaking and listening, such as head nods, hand gestures, and other body movements. (2) Group members who play this role help regulate group discussion by gently reminding members of the agenda or of the point they were discussing when they digressed. (ch 4, 11) (103, 290)

relational dialectics This theory describes some of the patterns that occur in relationships as a result of the tensions that take place because of conflicting emotional needs. (ch 6) (166)

remembering Information that is learned well and stored securely in your memory system. (ch 5) (127)

report style A style of communication designed to preserve independence and negotiate and maintain status. (ch 10) (254)

report-talk Type of language men use in conversation, designed to maintain status, to demonstrate knowledge and skills, and to keep center-stage position. (ch 3) (77)

respect Conveys regard and appreciation of the worth, honor, dignity, and esteem of people. (website)

responding Using spoken and/or nonverbal messages to exchange ideas or convey information. (ch 5) (127)

response to a bid A positive or negative answer to somebody's request for emotional connection. (ch 6) (163)

responsibility Your ability to meet your obligations or to act without superior authority or guidance. (website)

résumé A summary of a person's professional life written for potential employers. (website)

reward power A leader can have an influence if he or she can reward the followers (e.g., through promotions, pay raises, or praise). (ch 11) (292)

rewards The pleasures that come as a result of being in a relationship. (ch 7) (196)

rhetorical question A question that audience members answer mentally rather than aloud. (ch 15) (405)

ritual language Communication that takes place when we are in an environment in which a conventionalized response is expected of us. (ch 3) (69)

roles Parts we play, or ways we behave with others. (ch 1) (14)

rules Formal and structured directions for behavior. (ch 11) (276)

S

Sapir-Whorf hypothesis The language you use to some extent determines—at least influences—the way in which you view and think about the world around you. (ch 3) (62)

scripts Lines and directions given to people by parents, teachers, coaches, religious leaders, friends, and the media that tell them what to say, what they expect, how to look, how to behave, and how to say the lines. (ch 2) (35)

select The fourth of six steps of the strategic flexibility format in which users carefully select from their repertoire of available skills and behaviors those likely to have the greatest impact on the current (and future) situations. (ch 1) (21)

selection A term that refers to one of the steps of constructing meaning. It is the careful choosing from your repertoire of available skills and behaviors those likely to have the greatest impact on current and future situations. (ch 5) (127)

selective attention The ability to focus perception. (ch 5) (126)

self-awareness Knowledge of and trust in your own motives, emotions, preferences, and abilities. (ch 2) (42)

self-concept How a person thinks about and values himself or herself. (ch 2) (32)

self-confessors A dysfunctional small-group role in which participants express personal, non-group oriented "feelings," "insights," "ideology," and so on. (ch 11) (290)

self-defeating assumptions A technique for coping with rejection, which occurs when those faced with rejection let it become an indictment of their life (believing it's a basic flaw or shortcoming in their personality). (ch 9) (232)

self-disclosure Process by which one person tells another something he or she would not tell just anyone. (ch 6) (166)

self-esteem See *self-concept.*

self-fulfilling prophecies Events or actions that occur because a person and those around her or him expected them. (ch 2) (36)

self-improvement Seeking all means available to improve your professionalism and expertise. (website)

self-perception The way in which one sees oneself. (ch 2) (38)

selling That style of situational leadership in which leaders state the problem and decide what to do, but they sell the other group members on the idea to gain majority support. (ch 11) (297)

semantic noise Interference with the message that is caused by people's emotional reactions to words. (ch 1) (10)

semantic triangle A model proposed by Charles K. Ogden and Ivor Armstrong Richards to indicate the direct relationship between symbols (words) and thoughts. (ch 3) (63)

sender-receivers In communication situations, those who simultaneously send and receive messages. (ch 1) (7)

sensory acuity Paying attention to all elements in the communication environment. (ch 1) (10)

separation When nondominants do not want to form a common bond with the dominant culture, they separate into a group that includes only members like themselves. (ch 10) (259)

separation strategies When people are not part of a dominant culture, those processes that people use to get the dominant group to reinvent or change the rules through the use of nonassertive, assertive, or aggressive separation. (ch 10) (259)

servant leader Person who works for the well-being and growth of all employees and is committed to creating a sense of community and sharing power in decision making. (ch 11) (293)

setting Where the communication occurs. (ch 1) (10)

sexist language Any language that is supposed to include all people but unintentionally (or not) excludes a gender. (ch 3) (71)

shared goals Third Stage of Deborah Wieder-Hatfield's model for resolving conflict when partners examine each other's needs and desires to find out where they overlap. (ch 9) (226)

shared leadership It occurs when all group or team members assume both decision-making authority and responsibility for the group or team's results. (ch 11) (296)

situational leadership It occurs when leaders adopt different leadership styles depending on the situation. (ch 11) (297)

small-group communication It occurs when a small number of people meet to solve a problem. The group must be small enough so that each member has a chance to interact with all the other members. (ch 1) (17)

small groups Gatherings of 3 to 13 members who meet to do a job, solve a problem, or maintain relationships. (ch 11) (268)

small-group discussion Refers to a small group of persons talking with each other with the expressed purpose of achieving some interdependent goal such as solving a shared problem, coordinating member activity, or increasing understanding. (ch 11) (272)

small talk Social conversation about unimportant topics that allows a person to maintain contact with a lot of people without making a deep commitment. (ch 6) (162)

social comparisons When people compare themselves with others to see how they measure up. (ch 2) (37)

social distance The distance zone, a range from 4 to 12 feet, that people are most likely to maintain when they do not know people very well. (ch 4) (110)

social exchange theory The theory that all human relationships are formed using a subjective cost-benefit analysis as well as a simple comparison of possible alternatives. (ch 6) (176)

social groups Groups designed to serve the social needs of their participants. (ch 11) (276)

social penetration The process of increasing both disclosure and intimacy in a relationship. (ch 6) (166)

social penetration theory The theory that closeness occurs through a gradual process of self-disclosure; it uses the onion metaphor to describe self-disclosure—as the removal of layers to reveal deeper aspects of a personality. (ch 6) (170)

sociological information Information that tells you something about others' social groups and roles. (ch 6) (167)

space and distance Those distances people maintain between themselves and others that convey degrees of intimacy and status. (ch 4) (108)

spatial order Organization of a speech by something's location in space (e.g., left to right, top to bottom). (ch 13) (344)

special-interest pleaders Small-group members who play a dysfunctional role in which they speak for the "small-business man," the "grassroots" community, the "housewife," "labor," and the like, usually cloaking their prejudices or biases in the stereotypes that best fill their individual needs. (ch 11) (290)

specific purpose A statement for a speech that tells precisely what the speaker wants to accomplish. (ch 12) (317)

spontaneity It is the supportive climate in defensive communication designed to offset or counter the defensive climate of strategy when participants express their honest feelings freely. (ch 9) (230)

statistics Facts in numerical form. (ch 12) (330)

stereotypes Oversimplified or distorted views of another race, ethnic group, or culture. (ch 10) (256)

strategic flexibility Expanding your communication repertoire (your collection or stock of communication behaviors that can readily be brought into use) to enable you to use the best skill or behavior available for a particular situation. (ch 1, 11) (20, 295)

strategy It is the defensive climate in defensive communication that is manipulative (making others feel guilty or ashamed) offset or countered by the supportive climate, spontaneity. (ch 9) (230)

stress interview A type of information interview that is sometimes part of the job search and is designed to see how an interviewee acts under pressure. It is designed to give interviewers a realistic sense of their response to difficult situations. (website)

style The result of the way we select and arrange words and sentences. (ch 3) (74)

subjective view The personal, internal, mental map of the actual territory or external reality that people experience. (ch 2) (52)

substantive conflict Conflict that arises when people have different reactions to an idea. Substantive conflict is likely to occur when any important and controversial idea is being discussed. (ch 9) (235)

substitute Nonverbal message designed specifically to take the place of a verbal message. (ch 4) (115)

superiority It is the defensive climate in defensive communication in which participants take charge of situations in which they feel they are the only ones qualified to do so and is offset or countered by the supportive climate, equality. (ch 9) (231)

supporting material Information that backs up your main points and provides the main content of the speech. (ch 12) (327)

supporting points The material, ideas, and evidence that back up the main heads. (ch 5) (141)

symbol Something that stands for something else. (ch 1) (8)

symmetry When there is a corresponding arrangement or balancing of the parts or elements of a whole in respect to size, shape, and position on opposite sides of an axis or center—sometimes referred to as harmony, congruity, or correspondence. (ch 6) (156)

synchronous communication Online group discussion in which group members communicate at the same time. All participants are virtually present at the same time (e.g., in a telephone conversation, a face-to-face encounter, or a real-time, online group format). (ch 1, 11) (12, 274)

T

target audience A subgroup of the whole audience that you must persuade to reach your goal. (ch 12, 15) (319, 412)

task-oriented group A type of group that serves to get something specific accomplished, often problem-solving or decision-making goals. (ch 11) (276)

task roles Roles that help get the job done. Persons who play these roles help groups come up with new ideas, aid in collecting and organizing information, and assist in analyzing the information that exists. (ch 11) (288)

teamwork The unity of action by a group of workers to further the success of the business or organization. (website)

telling That style of situational leadership in which the leader is focused more on the task and less on the group. (ch 11) (297)

territory Space we consider as belonging to us, either temporarily or permanently. (ch 4) (109)

testimony Another person's statements or actions used to give authority to what the speaker is saying. (ch 12) (332)

texting The common term for the sending of short (160 characters or fewer, including spaces) text messages from mobile phones. It has a special language as well as its own abbreviations and terse messages. (ch 6) (174)

time The three facets of time that matter in analyzing the speech occasion are: time frame for the speech, time of day, and the length of time of your speech. (ch 12) (322)

time order Organization of a speech by chronology or historical occurrence. (ch 13) (343)

time-style listening That kind of listening in which the listener prefers brief and hurried interaction with others and often lets the communicator know how much time he or she has to make the point. (ch 5) (130)

topical order Organization of a speech used when the subject can be grouped logically into subtopics. (ch 13) (346)

touch To be in contact or come into contact with another person. (ch 4) (111)

transactional communication Communication that involves three principles: (1) people sending messages continuously and simultaneously; (2) communication events that have a past, present, and future; and (3) participants playing certain roles. (ch 1) (13)

transitions Comments that lead from one point to another to tell listeners where speakers have been, where they are now, and where they are going. (ch 13) (354)

transpection The process of empathizing across cultures. (ch 10) (263)

Twitter An online communications service that lets people exchange text messages known as tweets, of up to 140 characters. (ch 6) (161)

U

uncertainty avoidance The way of contrasting a group of cultures to another group of cultures that involves tolerance for the unknown. (ch 10) (254)

uniforms The most specialized form of clothing and that type that identifies wearers with particular organizations. (ch 4) (107)

unknown pane Area of the Johari Window that is known as a nondisclosure area and provides no possibility of disclosure because it is unknown to the self and to others. (ch 6) (168)

V

values Beliefs about how we should behave or about some final goal that may or may not be worth attaining. (ch 15) (408)

verbal symbol A word that stands for a particular thing or idea. (ch 1) (8)

verify-clarify When an active listener rephrases what they have just heard from a speaker and asks it as a question in order to understand the speaker's points correctly. (ch 5) (138)

vision Foresight, insight, and imagination. (ch 11) (302)

visual support Visual material that helps illustrate key points in a speech or presentation. Visual support includes devices such as charts, graphs, slides, and computer-generated graphics. (ch 14) (378)

vividness That property of style by which a thought is so presented that it evokes lifelike imagery or suggestion. (ch 3) (85)

vocal fillers Words we use to fill out our sentences or to cover up when we are searching for words. (ch 4) (103)

volume (of vocal sound) How loudly we speak. (ch 4) (102)

W–Z

Web conferencing or Web forums Online group discussions that use text messages (and sometimes images) stored on a computer as the communication medium. Messages are typed into the computer for others to read. (ch 11) (275)

worldview An all-encompassing set of moral, ethical, and philosophical principles and beliefs that governs the way people live their lives and interact with others. (ch 10) (246)

References

Chapter 1

1. Boyer, P. (2003). *College rankings exposed: The art of getting a quality education in the 21st century.* Lawrenceville, NJ: Thomson/Peterson, p. 119.

2. Boyer, *College rankings exposed,* pp. 100 & 119; Haslam, J. (2003). Learning the lessons—Speaking up for communication as an academic discipline too important to be sidelined. *Journal of Communication Management, 7*(1), 14–20; Tucker, M. L., & A. M. McCarthy. (2003). Presentation self-efficacy: Increasing communication skills through service-learning. *Journal of Managerial Issues, 13*(2), 227–245; Winsor, J. L., D. B. Curtis, & R. D. Stephens. (1997). National preferences in business and communication education. *Journal of the Association of Communication Administration, 3,* 170–179; [No author]. (1992). What work requires of schools: A SCANS report for America. U.S. Department of Labor. *Economic Development Review, 10,* 16–19; Rooff-Steffen, K. (1991). The push is on for people skills. *Journal of Career Planning and Employment, 52,* 61–63; [No author]. (1998, December 29). Report of the national association of colleges and employers. *The Wall Street Journal, Work Week,* p. 1A; Maes, J. D., T. G. Weldy, & M. L. Icenogle. (1997). A managerial perspective: Oral communication competency is most important for business students in the workplace. *Journal of Business Communication, 34,* 67–80; Lankard, B. A. (1960). *Employability—The fifth basic skill.* ERIC Clearinghouse on Adult, Career, and Vocational Education, Columbus, OH (ERIC Document Reproduction Service No. ED 325659).

3. Ford, W. S. Z., & D. Wolvin. (1993). The differential impact of a basic communication course on communication competencies in class, work, and social contexts. *Communication Education, 42,* 215–223.

4. Diamond, R. (1997, August 1). Curriculum reform needed if students are to master core skills. *The Chronicle of Higher Education,* p. B7.

5. Morreale, S. L. Hugenberg, & D. Worley. (2006, October). The basic communication course at U.S. colleges and universities in the 21st century: Study VII. *Communication Education, 55*(4), 415–437.

6. Combs, P. (2003). *Major in success: Make college easier, fire up your dreams, and get a very cool job.* Berkely, CA: Ten Speed Press.

7. Berlo, D. K. (1960). *The process of communication: An introduction to theory and practice.* New York: Holt, Rinehart and Winston.

8. Washington, D. (2000). *The language of gifts: The essential guide to meaningful gift giving.* Berkeley, CA: Conari Press.

9. Mehrabian, A. (1981). *Silent messages: Implicit communication of emotions and attitudes* (2nd ed.). Belmont, CA: Wadsworth.

10. Wilder, C. (1979, Winter). The Palo Alto Group: Difficulties and directions of the transactional view for human communication research. *Human Communication Review, 5,* 171–186.

11. Barnes, S. B. (2003). *Computer-mediated communication: Human-to-human communication across the Internet.* Boston: Allyn & Bacon, p. 4.

12. Gilster, P. (1997). *Digital literacy.* New York: John Wiley, p. 15.

13. Nieto, S. (1999, Fall). Affirming diversity: The socio-political context of multicultural education. In F. Yeo, The barriers of diversity: Multicultural education & rural schools. *Multicultural education,* 2–7; also in F. Schultz (ed.). (2001). *Multicultural education* (8th ed.), Guilford, CT: McGraw-Hill/ Dushkin.

14. Griswold, W. (1994). *Cultures and societies in a changing world.* Thousand Oaks, CA: Pine Forge Press.

15. Spitzberg, B. H., & W. R. Cupach. (1984). *Interpersonal communication competence.* Beverly Hills, CA: Sage.

16. [No author]. (1999). *Ethical comm: NCA credo for ethical communication.* National Communication Association (NCA). Retrieved November 9, 2004, from http://www.natcom.org/policies/External/EthicalComm.htm

17. Ibid.

18. Ibid.

19. Ibid.

Chapter 2

1. Rodgers, J. E. (2006, November/December). Altered ego: The new view of personality change. *Psychology Today,* pp. 70–75.

2. Muriel, J., & D. Joneward. (1971). *Born to win: Transactional analysis with gestalt experiments.* Reading, MA: Addison-Wesley, pp. 68–100.

3. Keillor, G. (1985). *Lake Wobegon days.* New York: Penguin/ Viking Press, pp. 304–305.

4. Smalley, Regina, & Jayne, Stake. (1992, August). The gender role/self-concept link: looking beyond the college sophomore." ERIC (Education Resources Information Center) # ED353509. Retrieved October 30, 2009, from http://www.eric.ed.gov/ERICWebPortal/custom/portlets/recordDetails/detailmini.jsp?_nfpb=true&_&ERICExtSearch_SearchValue_0=ED353509&ERICExtSearch_SearchType_0=no&accno=ED353509

5. Boone, M. E. (2001). *Managing inter@ctively: Executing business strategy, improving communication, and creating a knowledge-sharing culture.* New York: McGraw-Hill.

6. As reported by Elias, Marilyn (2008, November 19). Study: Today's youth think quite highly of themselves. *USA Today,* p. 7D.

7. Ruggero, Lorena Nava. (2008, November 17). Teens more confident, less competent. *SDSUniverse* (San Diego State University). Retrieved October 30, 2009, from http://www.sdsuniverse.info/sdsuniverse/news.aspx?s=426

8. Manz, C. C., & H. P. Sims, Jr. (2001). *The new superleadership: Leading others to lead themselves.* San Francisco: Berrett-Koehler, p. 110.

9. Schwalbe, M. L., & C. Staples. (1991). Gender difference in self-esteem. *Social Psychology Quarterly, 54*(2), 158–168.

10. Joseph, R. A., H. R. Markus, & R. W. Tafarodi. (1992, September). Gender and self-esteem. *Journal of Personality and Social Psychology, 63*(3), 391–402.

11. Rosenberg, D. (2007, May 21). (Rethinking) gender. *Newsweek,* p. 53.

12. Ibid.

13. Walther, J. B. (1992). Interpersonal effects in computer-mediated interaction: A relational perspective. *Communication Research,* pp. 52–90. As cited in E. Griffin (2006). *A first look at communication theory,* 6th ed. Boston: McGraw-Hill, p. 143.

14. Walther, J. B., C. L. Slovacek, & L. C. Tidwell. (2001). Is a picture worth a thousand words? Photographic images in long-term and short-term computer-mediated communication. *Communication Research, 28,* 110 and 122. As cited in E. Griffin, *A first look,* p. 149.

15. Ibid.

16. Levy, S., & B. Stone. (2006, April 3). The new wisdom of the Web. *Newsweek,* pp. 47–53.

17. Ratey, J. R. (2001). *A user's guide to the brain: Perception, attention, and the four theaters of the brain.* New York: Pantheon Books, p. 56.

18. Ma, Miranda Lai-yee. (2003). *Unwillingness-to-communicate, perceptions of the Internet and self-disclosure in ICQ.* (A graduation project in partial fulfillment of the requirement for the degree of master of science in New Media, the Chinese University of Hong Kong, Hong Kong.) Retrieved March 20, 2004, from http://216.239.41.104/search?q=cache:jqalB1tqnocJ:www.com.cuhk.edu.hk/courses/msc/Aca p. 5 of 37.

19. Tidewell, L. C., & J. B. Walther. (2002). Computer-mediated communication effects on disclosure, impressions, and interpersonal evaluations—Getting to know one another a bit at a time. *Human Communication Research, 28,* 317–348.

20. Srivastava, S., O. P. John, S. D. Gosling, & J. Potter. (2003). Development of personality in early and middle adulthood: Set like plaster or persistent change? *Journal of Personality and Social Psychology, 85,* 1095–1106.

21. Paul, A. M. (2001, March/April). Self-help: Shattering the myths. *Psychology Today,* 66.

22. Ibid., p. 66.

23. Rodgers, Altered ego, p. 74.

24. Ibid.

25. Cox, Andrew. (No date). Success depends on our self-talk. *Self-help Online.* Retrieved October 30, 2009, from http://www.self-help.co.nz/Articles/Self-development+Articles/Success+Depends+On+Our+Self+Talk.html

26. See Wright, Karen (2008, May/June). In search of the real you. *Psychology Today,* pp. 70–72.

27. Ibid.

28. Rodgers, Altered ego, p. 74

29. Paul, A. M. (2001, March/April). Self-help: Shattering the myths. *Psychology Today,* p. 66.

30. Ma, Miranda Lai-yee, *Unwillingness-to-communicate,* pp. 20–21.

31. Maltz, D. N. & R. A. Borker. (1982). A cultural approach to male female miscommunication. In J. J. Gumperz (Ed.), *Language and Social Identity* (Cambridge: Cambridge University Press), pp. 196–216.

32. Bartlett, F. C. (1932). *Remembering: A study in experimental and social psychology.* London: Cambridge University Press.

33. Mayer, R. E. (1992). *Thinking, problem-solving, cognition* (2nd ed). San Francisco: Freeman.

34. Festinger, L. (1957). *A theory of cognitive dissonance.* Stanford, CA: Stanford University Press.

35. [No author]. (1999, December 28). *External reality and subjective experience.* Western Michigan University. Retrieved November 24, 2004, from http://spider.hcob.wmich.edu/bis/faculty/bowman/erse.html

36. Heider, F. (1958). *The psychology of interpersonal relations.* New York: Wiley. Also, Kelley, H. H. (1973). The process of causal attribution. *American Psychologist, 28,* 10–128.

37. [No author]. (1999, December 28). *External reality and subjective experience.* Western Michigan University. Retrieved November 24, 2004, from http://spider.hcob.wmich.edu/bis/faculty/bowman/erse.html

38. Yeager, S. (2001, January 1). *Lecture notes: Self-concept.* DeSales University. Retrieved November 24, 2004, from http://www4.allencol.edu/˜sey0/selfla.html

39. *External reality and subjective experience.*

Chapter 3

1. Ratey, J. J. (2001). *A user's guide to the brain: Perception, attention, and the four theaters of the brain.* New York: Pantheon Books, p. 253.

2. [No author]. (no date). *Let's talk about it: Fostering the development of language skills and emergent literacy.* The Whole Child, For Early Care Providers, (PBS) Public Broadcasting Service. Retrieved December 18, 2004, from http://www.pbs.org/wholechild/providers/talk.html

3. Payack, P. J. J. (2008). *A million words and counting: How global English is rewriting the world.* New York: Kensington Publishing, p. 3.

4. Ibid.

5. Carey, A. R. & S. Ward. (2009, June 10). USA TODAY Snapshots: How many words are there? *USA Today,* p. 1. (Source: Global Language Monitor)

6. Payack, p. xiv.

7. Sapir, E. (1958). The status of linguistics as a science. In E. Sapir, *Culture, language and personality* (ed. D. G. Mandelbaum). Berkeley: University of California Press.

8. Whorf, B. L. (1940). Science and linguistics. *Technology Review, 42*(6), 229–231, 247–248; Whorf, B. L. (1956). *Language, thought and reality* (ed. J. B. Carroll). Cambridge, MA: MIT Press.

9. Paratore, J., & R. McCormack (eds.). (1997). *Peer talk in the classroom: Learning from research.* Newark, DE: International Reading Association. As reviewed by Hoffman, J. (2004, July). *Communication Education, 53*(3), 297.

10. Ogden, C. K., & I. A. Richards. (1927). *Meaning of meaning.* New York: Harcourt, Brace & Company.

11. Hayakawa, S. I. (1991). *Language in thought and action* (5th ed). New York: Harcourt.

12. Cotrell, H. W. (2001). *Spice up that family history.* Retrieved December 2, 2001, from email.

13. Ekman, Paul. (2009) *Telling lies: Clues to deceit in the marketplace, politics, and marriages.* New York: W. W. Norton & Company, p. 87.

14. Boone, M. E. (2001). *Managing inter@ctively: Executing business strategy, improving communication, and creating a knowledge-sharing culture.* New York: McGraw-Hill, pp. 109–110.

15. [No author]. (2002, April 2). Egg mystery boils down to physics: Mathematicians unravel gyroscope effect. *The* (Toledo) *Blade,* p. 3A.

16. Bennett, Jessica. (2008, April 7). Just go to Helvetica. *Newsweek,* p. 54.

17. Postman, N. (1992). *Technopoly: The surrender of culture to technology.* New York: Vintage Books.

18. Goffman, E. (1971). *Relations in public.* New York: Basic Books, p. 62.

19. Greif, E. B., & J. B. Gleason. (1980). Hi, thanks, and goodbye: More routine information. *Language in Society, 9,* 159–166.

20. Van Kerckhove, Carmen (2007, January). Study: Racist language common among white college students. Racialicious. Retrieved November 3, 2009, from http://www.racialicious.com/2007/02/02/study-racist-language-among-white-college-students/

21. [No author]. (no date). Sexist language. *Sexist Language.* Retrieved November 3, 2009 from http://www.sexistlanguage.com/

22. [No author]. (2005, February 24). Guidelines for non-handicapping language in APA journals. Girl-Mom. Retrieved November 3, 2009, from http://www.girlmom.com/forums/avoiding-ableist-language.

23. Bennet, J. (1995, March 29). A charm school for selling cars. *The New York Times,* pp. D1, D8.

24. Adapted from Toupin, Edward B. (2001, May 7). Natural writing . . . using your verbal style to create your written style. *WebProNews.* Retrieved December 14, 2009, from http://www.webpronews.com/topnews/2001/05/07/natural-writing-using-your-verbal-style-to-create-your-written-style

25. King, S. (2000). *On writing: A memoir of the craft.* New York: Scribner's, p. 208.

26. Tanno, D. V. (2000). Jewish and/or women: Identity and communicative style. In A. Gonzalez, M. Houston, & V. Chen (eds), *Our voices: Essays in culture, ethnicity, and communication.* Los Angeles: Roxbury., p. 33.

27. Luntz, F. (2007). *Words that work: It's not what you say, it's what people hear.* New York: Hyperion, p. 43.

28. Ibid.

29. Tannen, D. (1990). *You just don't understand.* New York: Morrow, pp. 42–43.

30. Ibid., p. 76.

31. Tannen, D. (1990). *You just don't understand.* New York: William Morrow.

32. Nichols, M. P. (2009). *The lost art of listening: How learning to listen can improve relationships,* (2nd ed.). New York: The Guilford Press.

33. Ibid., p. 92.

34. Tannen, *You just don't understand,* pp. 51–52.

35. Mulac, A., J. M. Wiemenn, S. J. Widenmann, & T. W. Gibson. (1988). Male/female language differences and effects in same-sex and mixed-sex dyads: The gender-linked language effect. *Communication Monographs, 55,* 316–332.

36. Tannen, D. (1992, February). How men and women use language differently in their lives and in the classroom. *Education Digest, 57,* 3–6.

37. Turner, L. H. (1992). An analysis of words coined by women and men: Reflections on the muted group theory and Gilligan's model. *Women and Language, 15,* 21–27.

38. Tannen, *You just don't understand,* p. 153.

39. Ibid, p. 245.

40. Ibid., pp. 255–256.

41. Griffin, E. (2006). *A first look at communication theory.* Boston: McGraw-Hill, pp. 479–480.

42. Troemel-Ploetz, S. (1991). Review essay: Selling the apolitical. *Discourse & Society,* Vol. 2, p. 497.

43. Ibid., p. 491.

44. Ibid., p. 495.

45. Herring, S. (2000). Gender differences in CMC: Findings and implications. *The CPSR Newsletter.* Winter. Available at http://www.cpsr.org/publications/newsletters/issues/2000/Winter2000/herring.html

46. As quoted in Baron, N. S. (2008). *Always on: Language in an online and mobile world.* New York: Oxford University Press, pp. 52–53.

47. Herring, Susan. (2003). Gender and power in online communication. In J. Holmes & M. Meyerhoff (Eds.), *The handbook of language and gender* (pp. 202–228). Oxford: Blackwell. As quoted in Baron, N. S. (2008). *Always on: Language in an online and mobile world.* New York: Oxford University Press, pp. 52–53.

48. Ibid.

49. Johnson, C. E. (1987, April). An introduction to powerful talk and powerless talk in the classroom. *Communication Education, 36,* 167–172.

50. Haleta, L. L. (1996, January). Student perceptions of teachers' use of language on impression formation and uncertainty. *Communication Education, 45,* 20–27.

51. Johnson, An introduction to powerful talk, p. 167.

52. O'Connor, S. D. (2003). *The majesty of the law: Reflections of a supreme court justice.* New York: Random House, p. 197.

53. [No author]. (2008, May 5). Gossipers seen as influential, in power. *The* (Toledo) *Blade,* p. 8B.

54. [No author]. (2007, July 16). Facts for features—Hispanic Heritage Month 2007: Sept. 15–Oct. 15. *U.S. Census Bureau: Newsroom.* Retrieved November 3, 2009, from http://www.census.gov/Press-Release/www/releases/archives/facts_for_features_special_editions/010327.html

55. [No author]. (2003, October 9). Foreign languages spoken in U.S. homes on rise. Census Bureau Study. *The* (Toledo) *Blade,* pp. 1, 7.

56. Nelson, M. C. (2004, March 15). On the path: Business's unfinished journey to diversity. *Vital Speeches of the Day, LXX*(11), 337.

57. Whitman, C. T. (2008). Women: Making our presence known. *Vital Speeches of the Day, LXXIV* (11), 515–18.

58. [No author]. (2004, February 27). English declining as world language. *USA Today,* p. 7A.

59. Ibid.

60. Nelson, *On the path,* p. 339.

61. Weise, E. (2007, September 19). Researchers speak out on languages on brink of extinction. *USA Today,* p. 7D.

62. Ibid.

63. Ibid.

64. Goodman, A. (2009, August). American provincialism: Another inconvenient truth. *Vital Speeches of the Day, LXXV* (8), 367–68.

65. Hummel, S. (1999, January 25). Do you speak Bostonian? *U.S. News and World Report,* 56–57.

66. vos Savant, M. (2008, July 10). AskMarilyn. *Parade,* p. 15.

67. (No author). (2008, December 4). Growing up digital affects social skills, psychiatrist theorizes. *The* (Toledo) *Blade,* p. 6A.

68. Ibid.

69. Baron, N. S. (2008). *Always on: Language in an online and mobile world.* New York: Oxford University Press. As cited in Johnson, Carolyn Y. (2008, June 21). Relax, English teachers: Iming is not killing language. *The* (Toledo) *Blade,* p. 2D.

70. Ibid.

71. Luntz, F. (2007). *Words that work,* p. xiii.

72. Adapted from: Toupin. Edward B. (2001, May 7). Natural writing . . . Using your verbal style to create your written style. *WebProNews.* Retrieved December 14, 2009, from http://www.webpronews.com/topnews/2001/05/07/natural-writing-using-your-verbal-style-to-create-your-written-style

73. Ibid., p. 3.

74. Rosen, E. (2000). *The anatomy of buzz: How to create word of mouth marketing.* New York: Doubleday, p. 215.

75. Luntz, F. (2007). *Words that work,* p. 5.

76. Tannen, *You just don't understand,* p. 62.

77. Penn, C. R. (1990, December 1). A choice of words is a choice of worlds. *Vital Speeches of the Day,* 117.

78. Ibid.

79. Luntz, F. (2007). *Words that work,* p. 80.

80. [No author]. (2009). "Choosing the Right Words." *grasscity.com.* Retrieved December 14, 2009, from http://forum.grasscity.com/sex-love-relationships/502722-life-advice-choosing-right-words.html

Chapter 4

1. Mehrabian, A. (1981). *Silent messages: Implicit communication of emotions and attitudes* (2nd ed.). Belmont, CA: Wadsworth.

2. Brody, J. (1992, August 19). Personal health: Helping children overcome rejection. *The New York Times,* p. C12.

3. Canary, D. J., M. J. Cody, & Va. L. Manusov. (1998). Functions of nonverbal behavior. In Canary, D. J., T. M. Emmers-Sommer, & S. Faulkner. (1998). *Sex and gender differences in personal relationships.* New York: The Guilford Press, pp. 1–23. As cited in Stewart, J. (2009). *Bridges not walls: A book about interpersonal communication* (10th ed.). New York: McGraw-Hill, pp. 183–190.

4. Flora, C. (2004, May/June). Snap judgments: The once-over. Can you trust first impressions? *Psychology Today,* 60.

5. Brody, Jane. (2009, October 5). Baby talk: From birth, engage your child with words. *The* (Toledo) *Blade,* p. C1.

6. Ibid.

7. Ibid.

8. Boyce, N. (2001, January 15). Truth and consequences: Scientists are scanning the brain for traces of guilty knowledge. *U.S. News & World Report,* 42.

9. Ibid.

10. [No author]. (2004, November 8). They can't tell a lie—some people just know. *The* (Toledo) *Blade,* p. 1D.

11. Ekman, P., & W. V. Friesen. (1969). The repertoire of nonverbal behavior: Categories, origins, usages, and coding. *Semiotica, 1,* 49–98.

12. Goodman, E. (2002, May 1). Some prefer to smile, furrow brows to Botox. *The* (Toledo) *Blade,* p. 11A.

13. Planalp, Communicating emotion in everyday life; Planalp, S., V. L. DeFrancisco, & D. Rutherford. (1996). Varieties of cues to emotion occurring in naturally occurring situations. *Cognition and emotion, 10,* 137–153.

14. Planalp, Communicating emotion in everyday life.

15. Andersen, P. A., & L. K. Guerrero. (1998). The bright side of relational communication: Interpersonal warmth as a social emotion. In Andersen & Guerrero, *Handbook of communication and emotion,* pp. 303–324.

16. Griffin, M. A., D. McGahee, & J. Slate. (1998). *Gender differences in nonverbal communication.* Valdosta State University, Valdosta, Georgia. Retrieved December 28, 2004, from http://www.bvte.edc.edu/ACBMEC/p1999/Griffin.htm. Throughout this section, Griffin, McGahee, and Slate site three sources: Burgoon, J. K., D. B. Buller, & W. G. Woodall (1996). *Nonverbal communication: The unspoken dialogue* (2nd ed.). New York: McGraw-Hill; Hanna, M. S., & G. L. Wilson (1998). *Communicating in business and professional settings* (4th ed.). New York: McGraw-Hill; Ivy, D. K., & P. Backlund (1994). *Exploring genderspeak.* New York: McGraw-Hill.

17. Griffin, McGahee, & Slate, *Gender differences in nonverbal communication.*

18. Ibid.

19. Ibid.

20. Hall, E. (1966). *The hidden dimension.* Garden City, NY: Doubleday.

21. Griffin, McGahee, & Slate, *Gender differences in nonverbal communication.*

22. Ibid.

23. Andersen, P. A. (1999). *Nonverbal communication: Forms and functions.* Mountain View, CA: Mayfield, pp. 305–333.

24. Burgoon, J. K. & S. B. Jones. (1976). Toward a theory of personal space expectations and their violations. *Human Communication Research, 2,* 131–146.

25. *USA Today,* "Snapshots," August 30, 2011, p. D1.

26. Canary, D. J., M. J. Cody, & Va. L. Manusov. (1998). Functions of nonverbal behavior. In Canary, D. J., T. M. Emmers-Sommer, & S. Faulkner. (1998). *Sex and gender differences in personal relationships.* New York: The Guilford Press, pp. 1–23.

27. Birdwhistell, R. L. (1970). *Kinesics and context.* Philadelphia: University of Pennsylvania Press, p. 117.

28. Addington, D. W. (1968). The relationship of selected vocal characteristics to personality. *Speech Monographs, 35,* 492–505; Pearce, W. B. (1971). The effect of vocal cues on credibility and attitude change. *Western Speech, 35,* 176–184; Zuckerman, M., & R. E. Driver. (1989). What sounds beautiful is good: The vocal attractiveness stereotype. *Journal of Nonverbal Behavior, 13,* 67–82; Zuckerman, M., H. Hodgins, & K. Miyake. (1990). The vocal attractiveness stereotype: Replication and elaboration. *Journal of Nonverbal Behavior, 14,* 97–112.

29. Mehrabian, A. (1968, September). Communication without words. *Psychology Today,* 53; Mehrabian, A. (1981). *Silent messages: Implicit communication of emotions and attitudes* (2nd ed.). Belmont, CA: Wadsworth, pp. 42–47.

30. MacLachlan, J. (1979, November). What people really think of fast talkers. *Psychology Today,* 113–117.

31. Ray, G. B. (1986). Vocally cued personality prototypes: An implicit personality theory approach. *Communication Monographs, 53,* 272; Buller, D. B., & R. K. Aune. (1988). The effects of vocalics and nonverbal sensitivity on compliance: A speech accommodation theory explanation. *Human Communication Research, 14,* 301–332; Street, R. L., & R. M. Brady. (1982). Speech rate acceptance ranges as a function of evaluative domain, listener speech rate and communication context. *Communication Monographs, 49,* 290–308.

32. Burgoon, J. K. (1978). Attributes of a newscaster's voice as predictors of his credibility. *Journalism Quarterly, 55,* 276–281.

33. Street, & Brady, Speech rate acceptance ranges as a function of evaluative domain, pp. 290–308.

34. Buller, & Aune, The effects of vocalics and nonverbal sensitivity on compliance, pp. 301–332.

35. Ray, Vocally cued personality prototypes, p. 273.

36. Berry, D. S. (1992, Spring). Vocal types and stereotypes of vocal attractiveness and vocal maturity on person perception. *Journal of Nonverbal Behavior, 16*(1), 41–54.

37. Burgoon, Buller, & Woodall, *Nonverbal communication,* p. 33.

38. Ekman, P., & W. V. Friesen. (1969). The repertoire of nonverbal behavior: Categories, origins, usages, and coding. *Semiotica, 1,* 49–98.

39. Benton, D. A. (2003). *Executive charisma.* New York: McGraw-Hill, p. 90.

40. Burgoon, Buller, & Woodall, *Nonverbal communication,* p. 42.

41. Ibid.

42. Ekman, P., & W. V. Friesen (1975). *Unmasking the face: A field guide to recognizing emotions from facial clues.* Englewood Cliffs, NJ: Prentice-Hall. Also see, Ekman, P., W. V. Friesen, & P. Ellsworth (1972). *Emotion in the human face: Guidelines for research and integration of findings.* New York: Pergamon Press.

43. Guerrero, L. K., P. A. Andersen, & M. Trost (1998). Communication and emotion: Basic concepts and approaches. In P. A. Andersen & L. K. Guerrero (Eds.), *Handbook of communication and emotion: Research theory, applications, and contexts* (pp. 3–28). San Diego, CA. Academic Press.

44. Jones, Del. (2008, February 25). It's written all over their faces. *USA Today,* p. 1B.

45. Smythe, M-J., & J. A. Hess (2005, April). Are student self-reports a valid method for measuring teacher nonverbal immediacy? *Communication Education, 54*(2), 170–179.

46. Paul, Annie Murphy. (2007, September/October). Mind reading. *Psychology Today,* pp. 72–79.

47. Andersen, P. A. (1999). *Nonverbal communication: Forms and functions.* Mountain View, CA: Mayfield, p. 40.

48. Kendon, A. (1967). Some functions of gaze direction in social interaction. *Acta Psychologica, 26,* 22–63; Exline, R. V., S. L. Ellyson, & B. Long. (1975). Visual behavior as an aspect of power role relationships. In P. Pliner, L. Drames, & T. Alloway (eds.), *Nonverbal communication of aggression.* New York: Plenum, Vol. 2, pp. 21–52; Fehr, B. J., & R. V. Exline. (1987). Social visual interaction: A conceptual and literature review. In A. W. Siegman & S. Feldstein (eds.), *Nonverbal behavior and communication* (2nd ed.). Hillsdale, NJ: Erlbaum, pp. 225–236; Andersen, P. A. (1985). Nonverbal immediacy in interpersonal communication. In A. W. Siegman & S. Feldstein (eds.), *Multichannel integrations of nonverbal behavior.* Hillsdale, NJ: Erlbaum, pp. 1–36; Silver, C. A., & B. H. Spitzberg. (1992, July). *Flirtation as social intercourse: Developing a measure of flirtatious behavior.* Paper presented at the Sixth International Conference on Personal Relationships, Orono, ME.

49. Gudykunst, W. B., & Y. Y. Kim. (1997). *Communicating with strangers: An approach to intercultural communication* (3rd ed.). New York: McGraw-Hill; Jensen, J. V. (1985). Perspective on nonverbal intercultural communication. In L. A. Samovar, & R. E. Porter (eds.), *Intercultural communication: A reader.* Belmont, CA: Wadsworth, pp. 256–272; Samovar, L. A., R. E. Porter, & N. C. Jain. (1981). *Understanding intercultural communication.* Belmont, CA: Wadsworth.

50. Richmond, Y., & P. Gestrin. (1998). *Into Africa: Intercultural insights.* Yarmouth, ME: Intercultural Press, p. 95.

51. Feingold, A. (1990). Gender differences in effects of physical attraction on romantic attraction: A comparison across five research paradigms. *Journal of Personality and Social Psychology, 59,* 981–993.

52. Andersen, *Nonverbal communication,* p. 113.

53. Andersen, P. A. (1998). Researching sex differences within sex similarities: The evolutionary consequences of reproductive differences. In D. J. Canary & K. Dindia (eds.), *Sex differences and similarities in communication.* Mahwah, NJ: Erlbaum, pp. 83–100; Berscheid, E., K. K. Dion, E. H. Walster, & G. W. Walster. (1971). Physical attractiveness and dating choice: Tests of the matching hypothesis. *Journal of Experimental Social Psychology, 7,* 173–189;

Berscheid, E., & E. H. Walster (1969, 1978). *Interpersonal attraction* (2nd ed.). Reading, MA: Addison-Wesley; [No author]. (1972, September). Beauty and the best. *Psychology Today, 5,* 42–46, 74; Berscheid, E., & E. H. Walster. (1974). Physical attractiveness. In L. Berkowitz (ed.), *Advances in experimental social psychology,* Vol. 7. New York: Academic Press, pp. 158–215; Brislin, R. W., & S. A. Lewis. (1968). Dating and physical attractiveness: Replication. *Psychological Reports, 22,* 976; Coombs, R. H., & W. F. Kenkel. (1966). Sex differences in dating aspirations and satisfaction with computer-selected partners. *Journal of Marriage and the Family, 28,* 62–66; Walster, E., V. Aronson, D. Abrahams, & L. Rottman. (1966). Importance of physical attractiveness in dating behavior. *Journal of Personality and Social Psychology, 4,* 508–516.

54. Dimitrius, J. E., & M. Mazzarella. (1998). *Reading people: How to understand people and predict their behavior—Anytime, anyplace.* New York: Random House, p. 31.

55. Schwartz, J. (1963). Men's clothing and the Negro. *Phylon, 24,* 224–231.

56. Kelly, J. (1969). *Dress as nonverbal communication.* Paper presented at the Annual Conference of the American Association for Public Opinion Research.

57. Thourlby, W. (1978). *You are what you wear.* New York: New American Library, pp. 143–151.

58. Marano, Hara Estroff. (2008, September/October). The style imperative. *Psychology Today,* 79–82.

59. Ibid., p. 82.

60. Stolzafus, L. (1998). *Traces of wisdom: Amish women and the pursuit of life's simple pleasures.* New York: Hyperion, pp. 134–135.

61. Joseph, N. (1986). *Uniforms and nonuniforms.* New York: Greenwood Press, pp. 2–3, 15.

62. Ibid., p. 143.

63. Morris, T. L., J. Gorham, S. H. Cohen, & D. Hoffman. (1996, April). Fashion in the classroom: Effects of attire on student perceptions of instructors in college classes. *Communication Education, 45,* 142–148.

64. Joseph, *Uniforms and nonuniforms,* pp. 168–169.

65. Brewer, Marilynn B. (1991). "The social self: On being the same and different at the same time." *Personality and Social Psychology Bulletin* 17:5: 475–82.

66. Hall, *The hidden dimension,* pp. 116–125.

67. Burgoon, J. K. (1978). A communication model of personal space violation: Explication and an initial test. *Human Communication Research, 4,* 129–142.

68. Heslin, R. (1974). *Steps toward a taxonomy of touching.* Paper presented at the Western Psychological Association Convention, Chicago, IL, 1974; Winter, R. (1976, March). How people react to your touch. *Science Digest, 84,* 46–56; Thayer, S. (1988). Touch encounters. *Psychology Today, 22,* 31–36.

69. Anastasi, A. (1958). *Differential psychology.* New York: Macmillan; Mehrabian, A. (1970). Some determinants of affiliation and conformity. *Psychological Reports, 27,* 19–29; Mehrabian, A. (1971). *Silent messages: Implicit communication of emotions and attitudes* (2nd ed.). Belmont, CA: Wadsworth.

70. Heslin, *Steps toward a taxonomy of touching;* Winter, R. How people react to your touch.

71. [No author]. (2007, September 24). To hug or not to hug depends on business. *The* (Toledo) *Blade* (from MarketWatch). p. 6B.

72. Ibid., p. 7B.

73. Ibid.

74. Birnbaum, Molly. (2009, July 1). Taking scent for granted. *USA Today,* p. 13A.

75. Ibid.

76. Andrews, Linda. (2007, November/December). The hidden force of fragrance. *Psychology Today,* pp. 57–58.

77. Ibid., p. 57.

78. Birnbaum, p. 13A.

79. Svoboda, Elizabeth. (2008, January/February). Scents & sensibility. *Psychology Today,* pp. 66–73.

80. Ibid., p. 70.

81. From: Robinson, Ken (with Lou Aronica). (2009). *The element: How finding your passion changes everything.* New York: Viking, pp. 32–33.

82. Burgoon, Buller, & Woodall, *Nonverbal communication,* pp. 127–128.

83. Sachs, A. (2007, January 29). Manners matter: Business-etiquette gurus are thriving. *Time,* pp. G7–10.

84. Sawdon, Martin. (2009). Remaining silent: Top 10 reasons for doing so. *Ezine@rticles.* Retrieved November 9, 2009, from http://ezinearticles.com/?Remaining-Silent—The-Top-10-Reasons-for-Doing-So&id=115919

85. Acheson, C. (2007). Silence in dispute. In C. S. Beck (ed.), *Communication yearbook31.* New York: Lawrence Erlbaum Associates, pp. 2–59.

86. As cited in Martin, Judith N., & Thomas K. Nakayama. (2010). Chapter 7: Nonverbal codes and cultural space. *Intercultural communication in contexts* (5th ed.). New York: McGraw-Hill, p. 281.

87. Carey, Benedict. (2009, May 12). Judging honesty by words not fidgets. *New York Times,* pp. D1 and D4.

88. Ibid., p. D1.

89. Ibid., p. D4.

90. Ritts, V., & J. R. Stein. Six ways to improve your nonverbal communications. Faculty Development Committee, Hawaii Community College. Retrieved January 2, 2005, from http://www.hcc.hawaii.edu/intrnet/committees/FacDevCom/guidebk/teachtip/commun-1.htm

Chapter 5

1. Thompson, K., & D. Dathe. (2001). *Moving students toward competent listening: The Thompson-Dathe integrative listening model (ILM).* Convention Paper Resource Center, International Listening Association (ILA). Retrieved December 6, 2004, from http://www.listen.org/pages/cprc_2001.html. The process of remembering has been added to the ILM framework as discussed in this chapter.

2. Friedman, P. G. (1978). *Listening processes: Attention, understanding, evaluation.* Washington, DC: National Education Association, p. 274.

3. Rubin, R. B., & C. V. Roberts. (1987, April). A comparative examination and analysis of three listening tests. *Communication Education, 36,* 142–153.

4. Youaver, J. B. III, & M. D. Kirtley. (1995). Listening styles and empathy. *Southern Communication Journal, 60*(2), 131–140.

5. Kiewitz, C., J. B. Weaver, H. B. Brosius, & G. Weimann. (1997, Autumn). Cultural differences in listening style preferences: A comparison of young adults in Germany, Israel, and the United States. *International Journal of Public Opinion Research, 9*(3), 233–247. Online abstract retrieved December 9, 2004, from http://www3.oup.co.uk/intpor/hdb/Volume_09/Issue_03/090233.sgm.abs.html

6. Ibid.

7. O'Brien, P. (1993, February). Why men don't listen . . . and what it costs women at work. *Working Women, 18*(2), 56–60.

8. Tannen, D. (1999, May 6). Listening to men, then and now. *New York Times Magazine,* 56ff.

9. O'Brien. Why men don't listen, pp. 56–60.

10. Ibid.

11. Srinivas, H. [no date]. *Information overload.* Retrieved July 21, 2007, from http://www.gdrc.org/icts/i-overload/infoload.html

12. Golen, S. (1990, Winter). A factor analysis of barriers to effective listening. *The Journal of Business Communication, 27,* 25–36.

13. Burton, J., & L. Burton. (1997). *Interpersonal skills for travel and tourism.* Essex: Addison-Wesley Longman.

14. Purdy, M. (2002). Listen up, move up: The listener wins. Monster Career Center. Retrieved December 9, 2004, from http://content.monster.com/listen/overview/. Copyright 2005—Monster Worldwide, Inc. All Rights Reserved. You may not copy, reproduce or distribute this article without the prior written permission of Monster Worldwide. This article first appeared on Monster, the leading online global network for careers. To see other career-related articles visit http://content.monster.com.

15. Nichols, M. P. (1995). *The lost art of listening.* New York: Guilford Press.

16. Steinberg, S. (2010, June 8). A change of heart for college students. *USA Today,* p. 7D

17. Greider, L. (2000, February). Talking back to your doctor works. *AARP Bulletin.*

Chapter 6

1. [No author]. (2010, December). "Connectedness and health." UC Berkeley Wellness Letter.

2. Goleman, D. (1995). *Emotional intelligence.* New York: Bantam, p. 178.

3. Locke, E. A. (2005). Why emotional intelligence is an invalid concept, *Journal of Organizational Behavior, 26*(4), 425–431.

4. Ibid., pp. 81–82.

5. Ibid., p. 193.

6. Goleman, D. (1998). *Working with emotional intelligence.* New York: Bantam, pp. 322–223; Covey, S. (1998). *7 habits of highly effective families.* New York: Golden Books, pp. 22–23, 238.

7. Ibid., pp. 86–90.

8. Ibid., pp. 106–110.

9. Ibid., pp. 111–126.

10. Fisher, H. (2007, May/June). The nature and chemistry of romantic love. *Psychology Today,* pp. 78–81.

11. Moalem, S. (2009) *How sex works: Why we look, smell, taste, feel, and the way we do.* New York: HarperCollins, p. 90.

12. Ibid., p. 14.

13. Kampe, K. K., C. D. Frith, R. J. Dolan U. Frith. (2001). "Reward value of attractiveness and gaze." *Nature, 413* (6856), 589.

14. Knut Kampe, quoted in H. Muir (2001). Beautiful people spark a brain reaction. *New Scientist* (October 10), p. 98.

15. Weinberg, G. (2002). *Why men won't commit: Getting what you both want without playing games.* New York: Atria Books, p. 30.

16. Svoboda, Elizabeth. (2008, January/February). Fast forces of attraction: The building blocks of sex appeal. *Psychology Today,* pp. 73–77.

17. Roberts, S. (2006, February 12). So many men, so few women. *The New York Times,* p. 3.

18. Ibid.

19. Ibid.

20. Karbo, K. (2006 November/December). Friendship: The laws of attraction. *Psychology Today,* p. 91.

21. Hatfield, E., & R. L. Rapson. (1992). Similarity and attraction in close relationship. *Communication Monographs, 39,* 209–212.

22. Rubin, R. B., E. M. Perse, & C. A. Barbato. (1998). Conceptualization and measurement of interpersonal communication motives. *Human Communication Research, 14,* 602–628.

23. Goleman, D. (1988, October 7). Feeling of control viewed as central in mental health. *The New York Times,* pp. C1, C11.

24. Ibid.

25. Wolfer, S. (2004, January/February). Save the date: Relationships ward off disease and stress. *Psychology Today, 37*(1), 32.

26. Cooper, Alvin, & Leda Sportolari. (2009). Romance in cyberspace: Understanding online attraction. In John Stewart (ed.), *Bridges not walls: A book about interpersonal communication* (10th ed.). New York: McGraw-Hill, pp. 365–374.

27. Marano, H. E. (1997, May 28). Rescuing marriages before they begin. *The New York Times,* p. C8.

28. Swartz, Jon. (2009, September 23). Gadgets: The glue that connects us. *USA Today,* pp. 1–2B.

29. Gottman, J. M., & J. DeClaire. (2001). *The relationship cure: A five-step guide for building better connections with family, friends, and lovers.* New York: Crown, p. 4.

30. Ibid., p. 25.

31. Ibid., p. 31.

32. Gordon, T. (1974). *T.E.T.—Teacher effectiveness training.* New York: Wyden.

33. Proctor, R. F. II. (1991). *An exploratory analysis of responses to owned messages in interpersonal communication.* Unpublished doctoral dissertation, Bowling Green State University, Bowling Green, OH, p. 11.

34. Weaver, R. L. II. (1996). *Understanding interpersonal communication* (7th ed.). New York: Harper/Collins, pp. 149–154.

35. Gordon, *T.E.T.,* p. 139.

36. See Baxter, L. A. (1988). A dialectical perspective of communication strategies in relationship development. In S. Duck. (ed.), *Handbook of personal relationships*. New York: Wiley, pp. 257–273. Also see Rawlins, William K. (1988). A dialectical analysis of the tensions, functions and strategic challenges of communication in young adult friendships. In James A. Anderson (ed.), *Communication Yearbook 12*. Newbury, CA: Sage, 157–189; Rawlins, William K. (1992). *Friendship matters: Communication, dialectics, and the life course*. Hawthorne, NY: Aldine de Gruyter.

37. Parks, M. R. (1985). Interpersonal communication and the quest for personal competence. In M. L. Knapp & G. R. Miller (eds.), *Handbook of interpersonal communication*. Thousand Oaks, CA: Sage, pp. 171–201.

38. Littlejohn, S. W. (1992). *Theories of human communication* (4th ed.). Belmont, CA: Wadsworth, p. 274.

39. Miller, G. R., & M. J. Sunnafrank. (1982). All is for one but one is not for all: A conceptual perspective of interpersonal communication. In F. E. X. Dance (ed.), *Human communication theory: Comparative essays*. New York: Harper & Row, pp. 222–223.

40. Luft, J. (1970). *Group process: An introduction to group dynamics* (2nd ed.). Palo Alto, CA: Science and Behavior Books.

41. From Falikowski, Anthony. (2002). Perception and the self *Mastering human relations*. (3rd ed.) Canada: Pearson Education. Retrieved December 20, 2009, from http://webhome.idirect.com/˜kehamilt/ipsyperc.html

42. Miller Sunnafrank. All is for one but one is not for all.

43. Falikowski, Perception and the self.

44. Taylor, D. & I. Altman, (1975). Self-disclosure as a function of reward-cost outcomes. *Sociometry, 38,* 18–31.

45. Cadden, Mary, & Suzy Parker. (2007, June 11), What matters most. *USA Today*, p. 1A. (Source: InsightExpress online survey of 1,001 married adults for *Reader's Digest* February 10–24, 2006. Margin of error, plus or minus 3 percentage points. Respondents could answer more than one.)

46. Dindia, K., M. A. Fitzpatrick, & D. A. Kenny. (1997, March). Self-disclosure in spouse and stranger interaction: A social relationships analysis. *Human Communication, 23*(3), 388.

47. Barbor, C. (2001, January/February). Finding real love. *Psychology Today*, 42–49.

48. Kimura, D. (1999, Summer). Sex differences in the brain. *Scientific American Presents, 10*(Special Issue, no. 2), 26; Hedges, L. V., & A. Nowell. (1995, July 7). Sex differences in mental test scores, variability, and numbers of high-scoring individuals. *Science, 269,* 41–45; Halpern, D. F. (1992). *Sex differences in cognitive ability* (2nd ed.). Hillsdale, NJ: Erlbaum; Blum, D. (1997). *Sex on the brain: The biological differences between men and women*. New York: Viking Press.

49. Gottman & DeClaire, *The relationship cure*, pp. 65–87.

50. Sommers, C. H. (2000). *The war against boys: How misguided feminism is harming our young men*. New York: Simon & Schuster, p. 87.

51. Goleman, *Emotional intelligence*, p. 131.

52. Wood, J. T. (1997). But I thought you meant. . . . Misunderstandings in human communication. Mountain View, CA: Mayfield, p. 69. In D. Vaughan, *Uncoupling: How relationships come apart*. New York: Random House.

53. Sommers, *The war against boys,* p. 151.

54. Levin, J., & A. Arluke. (1985). An exploratory analysis of sex differences in gossip. *Sex Roles, 12,* 281–285.

55. Ibid.

56. McGuinness, D., & J. Symonds. (1977). Sex differences in choice behaviour: The object-person dimension. *Perception, 6*(6), 691–694.

57. Sommers, *The war against boys;* Brody, L. R., & J. A. Hall. (1993). Gender and emotion. In M. Lewis & J. Haviland (eds.), *Handbook of emotions*. New York: Guilford Press, pp. 447–460.

58. Wood, But I thought you meant . . . , p. 69. In Vaughan, *Uncoupling*.

59. Ibid.

60. Ibid.

61. Ibid.

62. Axtell, R. (1997). *Do's and taboos around the world for women in business*. New York: John Wiley, pp. 161–162.

63. Boteach, S. (2000). *Dating secrets of the ten commandments*. New York: Doubleday, p. 165.

64. Fein, E., & S. Schneider. (2001). *The rules for marriage: Time-tested secrets for making your marriage work*. New York: Warner Books, pp. 187–188.

65. Boone, M. E. (2001). *Managing inter@ctively: Executing business strategy, improving communication, and creating a knowledge-sharing culture*. New York: McGraw-Hill, p. 223.

66. Falikowski, Perception and the self.

67. Mottet, T. P., & V. P. Richmond. (1998). An inductive analysis of verbal immediacy: Alternative conceptualization of relational verbal approach/avoidance strategies. *Communication Quarterly, 46*(1), 25–40.

68. Burgess, A. (2002, January 26). I vow to thee. *Guardian*. Retrieved March 24, 2003, from http://www.guardian.co.uk/Archive/Article/0,4273,4342138,00.html

69. Real, T. (2002). *How can I get through to you? Reconnecting men and women*. New York: Scribner's, p. 198.

70. Homans, George C. (1958). Social behavior as exchange. *American Journal of Sociology 63* (6): 597–606.

71. Thibaut, J. W., & H. H. Kelley. (1959). *The social psychology of groups*. New York: Wiley.

Chapter 7

1. Jayson, Sharon. (2008, November 17). Proof's in the brain scan: Romance can last. *USA Today*, p. 6D.

2. Ibid.

3. Knapp, M., & A. Vangelisti. (1995). *Interpersonal communication and human relationships* (3rd ed.). Boston: Allyn & Bacon.

4. Avtgis, T. A., D. V. West, & R. L. Anderson. (1998, Summer). Relationship stages: An inductive analysis identifying cognitive, affective, and behavioral dimensions of Knapp's relational stages model. *Communication Research Reports, 15*(3), 281.

5. Avtgis, West, & Anderson, Relationship stages, pp. 280–287.

6. Ibid., p. 283.

7. [No author]. (2008, February 14). Study gives more than lip service to kissing. *The* (Toledo) *Blade*, p. 1 and p. 5.

8. Avtgis, West, & Anderson, Relationship stages.

9. Ibid.

10. Ibid.

11. Saxbe, Darby. (2009, November/December). 10 ways to perk up a relationship. *Psychology Today*, pp. 80–85.

12. Casto, M. L. (2004). *The 7 stages of a romantic relationship*. The All I Need. Retrieved January 11, 2005, from http://www.theallineed.com/ad-self-help-2/self-help-010.htm. This article is adapted from the book: Casto, M. L. (2000). *Get smart! About modern romantic relationships: Your personal guide to finding right and real love*. Cincinnati, OH: Get Smart! Publishing.

13. Avtgis, West, & Anderson, Relationship stages, p. 284.

14. Ibid.

15. Ibid., p. 285.

16. Ibid.

17. Ibid.

18. Ibid.

19. Ibid.

20. Flora, Carlin, (2007, November/December). *Psychology Today*, pp. 71–76.

21. Knapp, M. L., R. P. Hart, G. W. Friedrich, & G. M. Shulman. (1973). The rhetoric of goodbye: Verbal and nonverbal correlates of human leave-taking. *Speech Monographs, 40*, 182–198.

22. Banks, S. P., D. M. Altendorf, J. O. Greene, & M. J. Cody. (1987). An examination of relationship disengagement perceptions: Breakout strategies and outcomes. *Western Journal of Speech Communication, 51*, 19–41.

23. Mauchline, P. (2000). *Evaluating whether a potential partner may be the one for you*. The Art of Loving. Retrieved January 8, 2005, from http://aboutyourbreakup.com/potential.html. Mauchline lists five questions only. Some of the information here is taken directly from his website.

24. Littlejohn, S. W. (1992). *Theories of human communication* (4th ed.). Belmont, CA: Wadsworth, p. 274.

25. Kirshenbaum, M. (1996). *Too good to leave, too bad to stay*. New York: Dutton, p. 94.

26. [No author]. (no date). *Competition and feeling superior to others*. Retrieved January 9, 2005, from http://mentalhelp.net/psyhelp/chap9/chap9q.htm. The questions and comments in this section have been taken from this source.

27. Ibid.

28. Lerner, H. (2001). *The dance of connection: How to talk to someone when you're mad, hurt, scared, frustrated, insulted, betrayed, or desperate*. New York: HarperCollins.

29. Infante, D. A. (1995, January). Teaching students to understand and control verbal aggression. *Communication Education, 44*(1), 51.

30. Guerrero, L. K. (1994, Winter). I'm so mad I could scream: The effects of anger expression on relational satisfaction and communication competence. *Southern Communication Journal, 59*(2), 125–141.

31. Kantrowitz, B., & P. Wingert. (1999, April 19). The science of a good marriage. *Newsweek*, 52–57.

32. [No author]. (1993, September–October). The rat in the spat. *Psychology Today*, 12.

33. Tracy, K., D. Van Duesen, & S. Robinson. (1987). "Good" and "bad" criticism: A descriptive analysis. *Journal of Communication, 37*, 46–59.

34. Ibid., p. 48.

35. Alberts, J. K., & G. Driscoll. (1992). Containment versus escalation: The trajectory of couples' conversational complaints. *Western Journal of Speech Communication, 56*, 394–412.

36. Cline, R. J., & B. M. Johnson. (1976). The verbal stare: Focus on attention in conversation. *Communication Monographs, 43*, 1–10.

37. Ibid.

Chapter 9

1. Wilmot, W. W., & J. L. Hocker. (2007). *Interpersonal conflict*. Boston: McGraw-Hill, p. 27.

2. Ibid., p. 53.

3. Ibid.

4. Drew, Naomi. (2002) Six steps for resolving conflicts. *Learning Peace*. Retrieved November 25, 2009, from: http://www.learningpeace.com/pages/LP_o4.htm

5. Wilmot & Hocker. *Interpersonal conflict*, p. 96.

6. Wieder-Hatfield, D. (1981). A unit in conflict management education skills. *Communication Education, 30*, 265–273.

7. Kantrowicz, B., & P. Wingert. (1999, April 19). The science of a good marriage. *Newsweek*, 52–57.

8. Waite, L. J., D. Browning, W. J. Doherty, M. Gallaher, Y. Luo, & S. M. Stanley. (2002, July 11). *Does divorce make people happy? Findings from a study of unhappy marriage*. The Institute for American Values. Retrieved January 11, 2005, from http://www.americanvalues.org/html/r-unhappyii.html

9. Ibid.

10. Munro, Kali. (2002). Conflict in cyberspace: How to resolve conflict online. *The Psychology of Cyberspace*. Retrieved November 25, 2009, from http://www-usr.rider.edu/~suler/psycyber/conflict.html

11. Ibid.

12. Gibb, J. (1961). Defensive communication. *Journal of Communication, 11*, 141–148.

13. Tymson, C. (no date). *Business communication: Bridging the gender gap*. Retrieved January 16, 2005, from http://www.tymson. com.au/pdf/gendergap.pdf

14. Sieler, A. (1999). *Leadership and change*. Observing Differently, Newfield, Australia. Retrieved January 20, 2005, from http://www.newfieldaus.com.au/Articles/leadership&change.htm

15. [No author]. (no date). How to resolve conflicts—without offending anyone. *ManagementParadise.com*. Retrieved November 25, 2009, from http://www.managementparadise.com/forums/articles/23700-how-resolve-conflicts-without-offending-anyone.html

16. Goleman, D. (1990, December 25). The group and the self: New focus on a cultural rift. *The New York Times*, pp. 37, 41.

17. Brownstein, R. (2007). *The second civil war: How extreme partisanship has paralyzed Washington and polarized America.* Dania Beach, FL: Penguin Press.

18. Deutsch, M. (1973). *The resolution of conflict: Constructive and destructive processes.* New Haven, CT: Yale University Press; Johnson, D. W. (1970). *Social psychology of education.* Edina, MN: Interaction Book Company; Johnson, D. W., & F. Johnson. (1994). *Joining together: Group theory and group skills* (5th ed). Boston, MA: Allyn & Bacon; Johnson, D. W., & R. T. Johnson. (1995). *Teaching students to be peacemakers* (3rd ed.). Edina, MN: Interaction Book Company.

Chapter 10

1. This story was originally published on Carol's blog, American Bedu. As quoted above, the story is from: "My Partner is a Foreigner." (2009, May). Pocket Cultures (the world in your pocket). Retrieved November 1, 2009, from http://pocketcultures.com/mypartnerisaforeigner/

2. Nieto, S. (1999, Fall). Affirming diversity: The sociopolitical context of multicultural education. In F. Yeo, The barriers of diversity: Multicultural education & rural schools. *Multicultural education,* 2–7; also in F. Schultz (ed.). (2001). *Multicultural education* (8th ed.). Guilford, CT: McGraw-Hill/Dushkin.

3. Harris, M. (1983). *Cultural anthropology.* New York: Harper & Row.

4. Carnes, J. (1999). A conversation with Carlos Cortes: Searching for patterns. In Schultz, *Multicultural education,* pp. 50–53. From Cortes, C. (1999, Fall). *Teaching tolerance,* 10–15.

5. Beamer, L., & I. Varney. (2001). *Intercultural communication in the global workplace* (2nd ed). Boston: McGraw-Hill/Irwin, p. 3.

6. Rosaldo, R. (1989). *Culture and truth: The remaking of social analysis.* Boston: Beacon Press.

7. Samovar, L. A., & R. E. Porter. (2001). *Communication between cultures* (4th ed.). Belmont, CA: Wadsworth, pp. 2, 46.

8. Martin, J. N., & T. K. Nakayama. (2001). *Experiencing intercultural communication: An introduction.* Boston: McGraw-Hill.

9. Aseel, M. Q. (2003). *Torn between two cultures: An Afghan-American woman speaks out.* Sterling, VA: Capital Books, p. 67.

10. Schultz, F. (2001). Identity and personal development: A multicultural focus. In Schultz, *Multicultural education.*

11. Martin & Nakayama, *Experiencing intercultural communication,* p. 185.

12. Cruz-Janzen, From our readers; Howard, G. R. (1999). *We can't teach what we don't know: White teachers, multiracial schools.* New York: Teachers College Press.

13. Carnes, A conversation with Carlos Cortes.

14. Takaki, R. (2008). *A different mirror: A history of multicultural america* (Revised Edition). New York: Back Bay Books (Little, Brown and Company), p. 20.

15. Martin & Nakayama, *Experiencing intercultural communication,* p. 8.

16. Liu, Jun. (2001). *Asian students' classroom communication patterns in U.S. universities: An emic perspective.* Westport, CT: Ablex. As reviewed by Mary M. Meares, Book Reviews. (2004). *Communication Education, 53*(1), 123.

17. Martin & Nakayama, *Experiencing intercultural communication.*

18. Triandis, H. (1990). Theoretical concepts that are applicable to the analysis of ethnocentrism. In R. Brislin (ed.), *Applied cross-cultural psychology.* Newbury Park, CA: Sage.

19. [No author]. (no date). Intercultural communication via the Internet: Receiving the message and sending a response. Educational Portal of the Americas. Retrieved November 1, 2009, from http://www.educoas.org/Portal/en/tema/tinteres/temaint29.aspx?culture=en&navid=36

20. Sabah, Z. (2006, October 13). Parents disapprove, but Internet romance a big hit. *USA Today,* p. 7A.

21. Ibid.

22. [No author]. (2001). *Dimensions of culture.* Retrieved December 2, 2004, from http://cwis.kub.nl/˜fsw2iric/vms.htm

23. Hall, E. T. (1976). *Beyond culture.* New York: Harper & Row, 1983; Hall, E. T. (1994). Context and meaning. In Samovar & Porter (eds.), *Intercultural communication.*

24. Ibid.

25. Chang, I. (2003). *The Chinese in America: A narrative history.* New York: Viking Press, p. xiii.

26. Hofstede, G. (2001). *Culture consequences: International differences in work-related values* (2nd ed.). Beverly Hills, CA: Sage.

27. Hall, *Beyond culture;* Hall, Context and meaning.

28. Martin & Nakayama. (2001). *Experiencing intercultural communication,* p. 44.

29. Ibid.

30. Orbe, M. P. (1998). *Constructing cocultural theory: An explication of culture, power, and communication.* Thousand Oaks, CA: Sage.

31. Adair, N., & C. Adair. (1978). *Word is out.* New York: Dell.

32. Raybon, P. (1996). *My first white friend.* New York: Viking Press.

33. Fadiman, A. (1997). *The spirit catches you and you fall down.* New York: Farrar, Straus & Giroux, p. 182.

34. Raybon, *My first white friend,* pp. 1–2.

35. DuPraw, M. E., & M. Axner. (1997). *Working on common cross-cultural communication challenges: Toward a more perfect union in an age of diversity.* Study Circles Resource Center—AMPU. Retrieved December 2, 2004, from http://www.wwed.org/action/ampu/crosscult.html

36. Carnes, A conversation with Carlos Cortes.

37. Langer, E. J., & M. Moloveanu. (2000, Spring). The construct of mindfulness. *Journal of Social Issues, 56*(1), 1–9. Also see, Langer, E. J., & M. Moloveanu. (2000, Spring). Mindfulness research and the future. *Journal of Social Issues, 56*(1), 129–139.

38. Pool, K. (2002, February). Valuing diversity. *Personal Excellence,* 13.

39. Cruz-Janzen, From our readers.

40. DuPraw & Axner, *Working on common cross-cultural communication challenges.*

41. Ibid.

42. Gudykunst, W. B., & Y. Y. Kim. (2002). *Communicating with strangers: An approach to intercultural communication* (4th ed.). Boston: McGraw-Hill.

43. Karim, A. U. (2001, April). *Intercultural competence: Moving beyond appreciation and celebration of difference.* Interculturally Speaking, Kansas State University Counseling Services' Human Relations Newsletter, I(1). Retrieved December 2, 2004, from http://www.ksu.edu/counseling/ispeak/people_to_people.htm

44. Taylor, R. (2001). *Are you culturally competent? (intercultural communication).* Springhouse Corporation. Retrieved December 2, 2004, from http://www.findarticles.com/cf0/m3231/431/74091624/print.jhtml. This World Wide Web article was excerpted and adapted from Taylor, R. (2000). Check your cultural competence. *CriticalCareChoices.* Springhouse, PA: Springhouse Corporation.

45. Maruyama, M. (1970). *Toward a cultural futurology.* Paper presented at the annual meeting of the American Anthropological Association, published by the Training Center for Community Programs, University of Minnesota, Minneapolis, MN. In Martin & Nakayama, *Intercultural communication in context.*

46. Martin & Nakayama, *Experiencing intercultural communication,* p. 320.

47. Hwang, J., L. Chase, & C. Kelly. (1980). An intercultural examination of communication competence. *Communication, 9,* 70–79.

48. Gudykunst & Kim, *Communicating with strangers.*

49. Takaki, Ronald. (2008). *A different mirror: A history of multicultural America* (Revised Edition). New York: Back Bay Books (Little, Brown and Company), p. 437.

Chapter 11

1. Research on the effectiveness of group work versus individual effort began in 1928, and a summary of it can be found in: Shaw, Marvin E. (1961). *Group dynamics* (3rd ed.). New York: McGraw-Hill, pp. 57–64.

2. Shaw, M. E. (1980). *Group dynamics: The psychology of small group behavior* (3rd ed.). New York: McGraw-Hill, p. 8.

3. Galanes, G. J., & K. Adams. (2007). *Effective group discussion: Theory and practice.* Boston: McGraw-Hill, p. 9.

4. Beebe, S. A., & J. T. Masterson. (2002). *Communicating in small groups: Principles and practices* (7th ed.). Boston: Allyn & Bacon.

5. Whetten, D. A., & K. S. Cameron. (1984). *Developing management skills.* Glenview, IL: Scott, Foresman, p. 6.

6. Ibid.

7. Tubbs, S. L. (2003). *A systems approach to small group interaction* (8th ed.). New York: McGraw-Hill.

8. Rimer, S. (2007, May 10). Harvard task force calls for new focus on teaching and not just research. *The New York Times,* p. A17.

9. Svinicki, M. (no date). *Using small groups to promote learning: Section 5. Improving specific teaching techniques.* Center for Teaching Effectiveness, the University of Texas at Austin. Retrieved January 19, 2005, from http://www.utexas.edu/academic/cte/sourcebook/groups.pdf, p. 1.

10. Wilson, G. L. (2004). *Groups in context: Leadership and participation in small groups* (7th ed.). New York: McGraw-Hill.

11. Beebe & Masterson, *Communicating in small groups.*

12. Ibid.

13. Gahran, Amy (1999, June 20). The content of online discussion groups, Part 1: Introduction. *Contentious.* Retrieved May 11, 2004, from http://www.contentious.com/articles/V2/2-3/feature2-3a.html, p. 1.

14. Goleman, D. (1990, December 25). The group and the self: New focus on a cultural rift. *The New York Times,* pp. 37, 41.

15. [No author]. (no date). Types of group communication tools. University of Illinois. Retrieved March 24, 2003, from http://illinois.online,uillinois.edu/stovall/GroupTools/GT/index.html

16. Thelen, H. A. (1997, March). Group dynamics in instruction: Principle of least group size. *School Review, 57,* 142.

17. Lawren, B. (1989, September). Seating for success. *Psychology Today,* 16–20.

18. Beebe & Masterson, *Communicating in small groups,* p. 113.

19. Janis, I. L. (1972). *Victims of groupthink.* Boston: Houghton Mifflin, p. 9.

20. Ibid., p. 3.

21. Greenhalgh, L. (2001). *Managing strategic relationships: The key to business success.* New York: Free Press.

22. Ibid., p. 237.

23. Janis, *Victims of groupthink,* pp. 174–175.

24. [No author]. (no date). "FaciliTips: Quick Tips for Online Facilitation." Retrieved November 23, 2009, from http://www.fullcirc.com/community/facilitips.htm

25. Hersey, P., & K. H. Blanchard. (1982). *Management of organizational behavior: Utilizing human resources* (4th ed.). Englewood Cliffs, NJ: Prentice Hall.

26. Benne, K. D., & P. Sheats. (1948). Functional roles of group members. *Journal of Social Issues, 4,* 41–49.

27. Adapted from Uschan, Chris. (2009, October 14). The DOs and DON'Ts of participating in an online event community." The Conference Handouts: Omni Press. Retrieved December 9, 2009, from http://blog.omnipress.com/2009/10/08-dos-and-donts-of-participating-online-event-community/

28. Benne & Sheats, Functional roles of group members.

29. Arnold, H. J., & D. C. Feldman. (1986). *Organizational behavior.* New York: McGraw-Hill, pp. 120–121.

30. French, J. R., & B. H. Raven. (1959). The bases of social power. Cartwright, D. (Ed.). *Studies in social power.* Ann Arbor (University of Michigan), MI: Institute for Social Research, pp. 150–167.

31. Schrodt, P., P. L. Witt, & P. D. Turman (2007, July). Reconsidering the measurement of teacher power use in the college classroom. *Communication Education, 56*(3), 308–332.

32. Ibid., p. 310.

33. Ibid., pp. 310–311.

34. Ibid., p. 311.

35. Abrams, R. (1999). *Wear clean underwear: Business wisdom from mom.* New York: Villard Books, p. 36.

36. Cramer, R. J., & T. R. Jantz. (2005). *An examination of personality traits among student leaders and nonleaders.* PSI CHI. The National Honor Society in Psychology, Loyola College. Retrieved January 24, 2005, from http://www.psichi.org/pubs/articles/article_421.asp

37. Bennis, W. (1998). *Managing People Is Like Herding Cats.* London: Kogan Page.

38. Burbules, N. C. (1993). *Dialogue in teaching.* New York: Teachers College Press.

39. Doyle, M. E., & M. K. Smith. (2001, September 18). *Shared leadership.* Infed Encyclopedia—The Encyclopedia of Informal Education. Retrieved January 25, 2005, from http://www.infed.org/leadership/shared_leadership.htm

40. Zigarmi, P., D. Zigarmi, & K. H. Blanchard. (1985). *Leadership and the one minute manager: Increasing effectiveness through situational leadership.* New York: William Morrow.

41. Hargrove, R. (2001). *E-leader: Reinventing leadership in a connected economy.* Cambridge, MA: Perseus, p. 7.

42. Chang, H. K. (2003, March 14). *Sustainable leadership requires listening skills.* Graduate School of Business, Stanford University. Retrieved January 25, 2005, from http://www.gsb.stanford.edu/news/headlines/vftt_vanderveer.shtml

43. Simonton, B. (2003). *Leadership skills—Listening, the most important leadership skill—Don't shoot the messenger.* Retrieved January 25, 2005, from http://www.bensimonton.com/messenger-leadership-skills.htm

44. McCutchen, B., & Heller, Ehrman, White, & McAuliffe, LLP. (2003, September). Preserving diversity in higher education. *A Manual on Admissions Policies and Procedures After the University of Michigan Decisions.* Retrieved January 25, 2005, from http://www.bingham.com/bingham/webadmin/documents/radb5f5a.pdf.

45. Nelson, C. S. (2004). *What makes a great leader great?* ConcreteNetwork.com. Retrieved January 25, 2005, from http://www.concretenetwork.com/csn_archive/greatleader.html

46. Giuliani, R. W. (2002). *Leadership.* New York: Miramax Books, p. 184.

Chapter 12

1. Levasseur, D. G., K. W. Dean, & J. Pfaff, (2004, July). Speech pedagogy beyond the basics: A study of instructional methods in the advanced public speaking course. *Communication Education, 53*(3), p. 247.

2. [No author]. (no date). Speeches (handouts and links). *The Writing Center,* University of North Carolina–Chapel Hill. Retrieved November 29, 2009, from http://www.unc.edu/depts/wcweb/handouts/speeches.html

3. Chadwick, T. B. (2001, September 21). *How to conduct research on the Internet.* Infoquest! Information Services. Retrieved February 2, 2005, from http://www.tbchad.com/resrch.html

4. Ormondroyd. J., M. Engle, & T. Cosgrave. (2001, September 18). *How to critically analyze information services.* Olin Kroch, Uris Libraries, Research Services Division, Cornell University Library. Retrieved February 2, 2005, from http://www.library.cornell.edu/okuref/research/skill26.htm

5. [No author]. (2007, March 20). Scientists study trains of thought that derail. *The* (Toledo) *Blade,* p. 3.

6. Ibid.

7. Cuomo, M. (1998). Graduation speech at Iona College. In A. Albanese & B. Trissler (eds.), *Graduation day: The best of America's commencement speeches.* New York: Morrow, pp. 72–73.

8. Toppo, Greg. (2009, November 17). Students may drink, have sex more if in coed dorms. *USA Today,* p. 8D. Toppo cites a study in the *Journal of American College Health* which surveyed 510 students living on five college campuses. Most—442 or 87 percent—lived in coed dorms.

9. Oakley, Barbara. (2007, April 19). The killer in the lecture hall. *New York Times,* p. A27.

10. [No author]. (2004). *Trends Journal.* The Trends Research Institute. Rhinebeck, New York. Retrieved November 3, 2005, from http://www.trendsresearch.com/

11. Brody, Jane. (2008, January 1). No gimmicks: Eat less and exercise more. *The New York Times,* P. D7.

12. Franklin, W. E. (1998, September 15). Careers in international business: Five ideas or principles. *Vital Speeches of the Day, 64.*

13. St. John, Ron. (2002, January 16). Supporting a speech. University of Hawai'i Maui Community College Speech Department. Retrieved November 29, 2009, from http://www.hawaii.edu/mauispeech/html/supporting_materials.html

14. Ibid., p. 719.

15. Walters, F. M. (2000, December 15). We, the people: Prize and embrace what is America. *Vital Speeches of the Day, 67*(5), 144.

Chapter 13

1. Mann, W., & J. Lash. (2004). *Some facts psychologists know about: Test and performance anxiety.* Psychological Services Center and the Division of Student Affairs and Services, University of Cincinnati. Retrieved November 3, 2005, from http://www.psc.uc.edu, p. 3.

2. Probert, B. (2003). *Test anxiety.* University of Florida Counseling Center. Retrieved November 3, 2005, from http://www.counsel.ufl.edu/selfHelp/testAnxiety.asp

3. [No author]. (n.d.). *Health, exercise, diet, rest, self-image, motivation, and attitudes.* Learning Strategies Database, Center for Advancement of Learning, Muskingum College, Muskingum, MI. Retrieved November 3, 2005, from http://muskingum.edu/~cal/database/Physiopsyc.html

4. [No author]. (no date). *Dealing with test anxiety.* SUNY Potsdam Counseling Center. Retrieved November 3, 2005, from www.potsdam.edu/COUN/brochures/test.html

5. [No author]. (no date). *Study skills for college.* Pennsylvania State University. Retrieved November 3, 2005, from http://www.bmb.psy.edu/courses/psu16/troyan/studyskills/examprep.htm

6. *Dealing with test anxiety.*

7. Probert, *Test anxiety.*

8. Mann, & Lash, *Some facts psychologists know about*, p. 3.

9. [No author]. (2002). *Test-taking strategies.* Academic Services, Southwestern University. Retrieved November 3, 2005, from http://www.southwestern.edu/academic/acser-skills-terstr.html

10. Mann & Lash, *Some facts psychologists know*, p. 3.

11. [No author]. (2002, January 17). *Test anxiety.* Counseling Center, University of Illinois at Urbana. Retrieved November 3, 2005, from http://www.couns.uiuc.edu/brochures/testanx.htm

12. [No author]. (2001, August 31). *Test anxiety: Overcoming test anxiety.* Counseling Center, University of Florida. Retrieved November 3, 2005, from http://www.counsel.ufl.edu/selfHelp/testAnxiety.asp

13. Lamm, R. D. (2003, September 1). Sustainability: The limited use of history in the new world of public policy. *Vital Speeches of the Day, 69*(22), 678.

14. Kreahling, L. (2005, February 1). The perils of needles to the body. (Health & Fitness). *The New York Times*, p. D5.

15. Taflinger, Richard F. (1996). How to communicate. Mind at work. Retrieved December 3, 2009, from mindwork/mawint3.html

16. Gruner, C. B. (1985, April). Advice to the beginning speaker on using humor—What the research tells us. *Communication Education, 34*, 142.

17. Keillor, G. (1998). Commencement address—Gettysburg College. In A. Albanese & B. Triller (eds.), *Graduation day: The best of America's commencement speeches.* New York: Morrow, p. 181.

18. Dilenschneider, R. L. (2001, July 15). Heroes or losers: The choice is yours. *Vital Speeches of the Day, 67*(19), 605.

19. Shrader, R. W. (2009, January). Don't tell me the future: Resilence, not prophecy, is the greatest gift. *Vital Speeches of the Day, 75*(1), 43–45.

20. Ibid.

21. [No author]. (2008). Chapter 11. Guidelines in how to write a bibliography in MLA style. A research guide for students. Retrieved January 4, 2010, from http://www.aresearchguide.com/11guide.html

Chapter 14

1. Motley, M. T. (no date). *Overcoming your fear of public speaking.* Communication Resource Center for Students, Fundamentals of Communication, Faculty Services Center, Houghton Mifflin Company. Retrieved February 7, 2005, from http://college.hmco.com/communication/resources/students/fundamentals/fear.html

2. Ibid.

3. Ibid.

4. Schacter, D. L. (2001). *The seven sins of memory: How the mind forgets and remembers.* Boston: Houghton Mifflin.

5. Adapted from DeNoon, Daniel J. (2006, April 20). Fear of public speaking hardwired. WebMD. Retrieved December 4, 2009 from http://www.webmd.com/anxiety-panic/guide/20061101/fear-public-speaking

6. DeNoon, Fear of Public Speaking.

7. Weber, A. (2006, November 12). Like, um, can you break those bad, you know, speech habits? *The* (Toledo) *Blade*, pp. H1–H6.

8. Sellnow, D. D., & K. P. Treinen. (2004, July). The role of gender in perceived speaker competence: An analysis of student peer critiques. *Communication Education, 53*(3), 293.

9. Argyle, M. (1991). Intercultural communication. In L. A. Samovar & R. E. Porter (eds.), *Intercultural communication: A reader* (6th ed.). Belmont, CA: Wadsworth, p. 43.

10. Adapted from Bjorseth, Lillian D. (2006). What you say before you speak, part I. *Self-Improvement Goldmine.* Retrieved December 4, 2009, from http://www.20daypersuasion.com/appearance.htm

11. Hahner, J. C., M. A. Sokoloff, & S. Salisch. (2001). *Speaking clearly: Improving voice and diction* (6th ed.). New York: McGraw-Hill.

12. Robinson, Lori Ann. (2009, July 24). Vocal tone: How do you sound? LAR Consultants. Retrieved December 4, 2009, from http://www.larconsultantsblog.com/2009/07/vocal-tonehow-do-you-sound.html

13. Cyphert, D. (2007, April). Presentation technology in the age of electronic eloquence: From visual aid to visual rhetoric. *Communication Education, 56*(2), 168–192.

14. Banton, Mernoush. (2009, February 17). Guidelines for using audiovisual aids. Retrieved December 4, 2009, from http://2myprofessor.com/Common/guidelines_for_using_audiovisual.htm

15. [No author]. (2005). *How many online?* ComputerScope, Ltd., Scope Communications Group, Prospect House, 3 Prospect Road, Dublin 9, Ireland. Retrieved February 8, 2005, from http://www.nua.ie/surveys/how_many_online/, p. 1.

16. Ibid.

17. Adapted from Brinkmann, Tracy. (2009). "Steps to Easier Speech Writing." Ezine@rticles. Retrieved December 4, 2009, from http://ezinearticles.com/?Steps-to-Easier-Speech-Writing&id=79793

Chapter 15

1. Petersen, J. A. (1999, August 12). *Better families.* Quoted on the Christianity New home page, Preaching Resources. Copyright 1996 by *Christianity Today, Inc/LEADERSHIP, 17*(3), 69.

2. Steele, Jonathan. (2009). An informative speech: How to motivate an audience with an informative speech. speechmastery.com. Retrieved December 4, 2009, from http://www.speechmastery.com/an-informative-speech.html

3. Schrodt P., P. L. Witt, P. D. Turman, S. A. Myers, M. H. Barton, & K. A. Jernberg. (2009, July). Instructor credibility as a mediator of instructors' prosocial communication behaviors and students' learning outcomes. *Communication Education, 38* (3), 350–371.

4. Rzadkiewicz, Carol. (2009, October 1). How to begin and end a speech. suite101.com. Retrieved December 4, 2009, from http://trainingpd.suite101.com/article.cfm/how_to_begin_and_end_a_speech

5. Lamm, R. (1998, September 15). Unexamined assumptions: Destiny, political institutions, democracy, and population. *Vital Speeches of the Day, 64*(23), 712.

6. Ehrensberger, R. (1945). An experimental study of the relative effects of certain forms of emphasis in public speaking. *Speech Monographs, 12,* 94–111.

7. Luntz, F. (2007). *Words that work: It's not what you say, it's what people hear.* New York: Hyperion, p. 126.

8. [No author]. (2005, February 25). *Visual communication of ideas.* Presentation Helper. Retrieved March 8, 2005, from http://www.presentationhelper.co.uk/visual_communication.htm

9. This study was cited in Arredondo, L. (1994). *The McGraw-Hill 36-hour course: Business presentations.* New York: McGraw-Hill, p. 177. Also see Weaver, R. L. II. (2001). *Essentials of public speaking* (2nd ed.). Boston: Allyn & Bacon, p. 186.

10. Lemonick, M. D. (2007, January 29). The flavor of memories. *Time,* p. 101.

11. Knapp, M. L., & A. L. Vangelisti. (1996). *Interpersonal communication and human relationships* (3rd ed.). Boston: Allyn & Bacon.

12. Kluger, J. (2004, December 20). The buzz on caffeine. *Time,* 52.

13. Werkman, Doris. (2004, Fall). General types of informative speeches. *SP 111: Fundamentals of Speech.* Retrieved December 4, 2009, from http://spot.pcc.edu/˜dwerkman/syllabus111.html

14. Finerman, E. (1996, March 1). Humor and speeches: A standup history. *Vital Speeches of the Day, 62*(9), 313.

15. [No author]. (no date). Chapter 14: Speaking to inform. Retrieved December 4, 2009, from http://74.125.95.132/search?q=cache:uArdbgkAylkJ:commfaculty.fullerton.edu/jhayes/000-Web-HCOM100/005-Other%2520TA%27s%2520Work/INFORM.PPToutline_veit.ppt+strategies+for+informative+speeches%3F&cd=18&hl=en&ct=clnk&gl=us

16. Hanke, Stacey. (2009, April). S. P. A. R. K. your listeners' attention. The Planner. Retrieved December 4, 2009, from http://74.125.95.132/search?q=cache:YQK1JuY7mA4J:www.1stimpressionconsulting.com/communication/bm˜doc/hanke-april09.pdf+key+to+getting+listener+attention%3F&cd=l&hl=en&ct=clnk&gl=us

17. Rokeach, M. (1968). *Beliefs, attitudes, and values: A theory of organization and change.* San Francisco: Jossey-Bass, p. 124.

18. Mackay, H. (2008, August). Postgraduate life: What you should know. *Vital Speeches of the Day, 74*(8), 357–360.

19. Ibid., p. 357.

20. Haines, M. P. (2001, July 23). Facts change student drinking. *USA Today,* p. 15A.

21. Lane, T. (2001, December 3). Colleges develop better awareness of drinking risks. *The* (Toledo) *Blade,* p. 1A.

22. Ibid., p. 6A.

23. Kluger, J. (2001, June 18). How to manage teen drinking (the smart way). *Time,* 42–44.

24. Lane, Colleges develop better awareness of drinking risks, p. 1A.

25. Waldron, R. (2000, October 30). Students are dying: Colleges can do more. *Newsweek,* 16.

26. Morse, J. (2002, April 1). Women on a binge. *Time,* 56–61.

27. Ibid., p. 56.

28. Haines, M. P. (2001, July 23). Facts change student drinking. *USA Today,* p. 15A.

29. Ibid.

30. Kluger, How to manage teen drinking, p. 43.

31. Haines, Facts change student drinking, p. 15A.

32. Ibid.

33. Lane, Colleges develop better awareness of drinking risks, p. 1A.

34. Haines, Facts change student drinking, p. 15A.

35. For definitions and examples, see [No author]. (no date). Handouts and links: Fallacies. The writing center at University of North Carolina at Chapel Hill. Retrieved January 5, 2010, from http://www.unc.edu/depts/wcweb/handouts/fallacies.html

36. Bauer, J., & M. Levy. (2004). *How to persuade people who don't want to be persuaded.* New York: John Wiley, pp. 17–18. The study cited is Davenport, T., & J. Beck. (2000, September–October). Getting the attention you need. *Harvard Business Review.*

37. Ibid., pp. 17–18.

38. Maslow, A. H. (1970). *Motivation and personality* (2nd ed.). New York: Harper & Row.

39. Rieck, Dean. (2000). The emotional appeals that make people buy. Direct Creative. Retrieved December 5, 2009, from http://www.directcreative.com/the-emotional-appeals-that-make-people-buy.html

40. Tracy, L. (2005, March 1). Taming hostile audiences: Persuading those who would rather jeer than cheer. *Vital Speeches of the Day, 71*(10), 312.

41. Odden, L. R. (1999, March 1). Talk to your children about the tough stuff: We are all in this together. *Vital Speeches of the Day, 65*(10), 301.

42. Tracy, L. (2005, March 1). Taming hostile audiences: Persuading those who would rather jeer than cheer. *Vital Speeches of the Day, 71*(10), 312.

43. [No author]. (2004, February). Optimism and longevity: What's the connection? *University of California, Berkeley Wellness Letter, 20*(5), 1.

44. McKerrow, R. E., B. E. Gronbeck, D. Ehninger, & A. H. Monroe (2003). *Principles and types of speech communication* (15th ed.). Boston: Allyn & Bacon.

45. Adapted from [No author]. (no date). Monroe's motivated sequence. Retrieved December 5, 2009, from http:/inside.ridgewater.edu/green/121/monroes.htm

Photo Credits

Chapter 1

Opener: Lifesize/Getty Images
p. 9:   Thinkstock/Jupiterimages
p. 11(left):   Design Pics/Don Hammond
p. 11 (right): Purestock/SuperStock
p. 19:   © Comstock/PunchStock

Chapter 2

Opener: Kablonk!/Photolibrary
p. 37:   Juice Images/Getty Images
p. 48:   © Ryan McVay/Getty Images

Chapter 3

Opener: © Stockbroker/Purestock/SuperStock
p. 60:   © Erica Simone Leeds

Chapter 4

Opener: Tetra Images/Getty Images
p. 107:   © Clark Brennan/Alamy
p. 112 (left):   McGraw-Hill Education
p. 112 (right): © 2006 Glowimages, Inc. All Rights Reserved

Chapter 5

Opener: Somos RF/Getty Images
p. 139:   Purestock/SuperStock
p. 142:   © Stockdisc/PunchStock

Chapter 6

Opener: Arlene Sandler/Purestock/SuperStock
p. 155:   © Holger Hill/Getty Images
p. 167:   Ingram Publishing/SuperStock
p. 174:   © Comstock/PunchStock

Chapter 7

Opener: Purestock/SuperStock
p. 190:   Blend Images/Alamy
p. 201:   Design Pics/Kristy-Anne Glubish

Chapter 8

Opener: © LWA/Dann Tardif/Blend Images LLC
p. 211:   Purestock/SuperStock
p. 212:   David Lees/Getty Images
p. 213:   © Stockbyte/PictureQuest
p. 216:   JGI/Tom Grill/Getty Images

Chapter 9

Opener: Donna Day/Imagestate
p. 236:   © David R. Frazier Photolibrary, Inc.

Chapter 10

Opener: Design Pics/Don Hammond
p. 246:   dyamicgraphics/Jupiterimages
p. 253:   Ingram Publishing

Chapter 11

Opener: Rich Legg/Getty Images
p. 279:   Purestock/SuperStock
p. 289:   Purestock/SuperStock
p. 294:   © Getty Images

Chapter 12

Opener: Aaron Roeth Photoraphy
p. 316:   Mike Kemp/Rubberball/Corbis
p. 320:   Design Pics/Darren Greenwood
p. 320:   Purestock/SuperStock
p. 323:   Janis Christie/Getty Images
p. 330:   Digital Vision/Getty Images

Chapter 13

Opener: Pixtal/AGE Fotostock
p. 344:   Art Vandalay/Getty Images
p. 351:   © Hill Street Studios/Blend Images LLC

Chapter 14

Opener: © Image Source/Alamy
p. 373:   Uppercut RF/Getty Images

Chapter 15

Opener: McGraw-Hill Education
p. 394:   Pixtal/AGE Fotostock
p. 398:   Flying Colours Ltd. Getty Images
p. 401:   © The McGraw-Hill Companies, Inc./
               Jan L Saeger, photographer
p. 409:   Susan See Photography
p. 409:   © Erica Simone Leeds
p. 417:   Ingram Publishing
p. 421:   McGraw-Hill Companies, Inc./
               Gary He, photographer
p. 421:   Delphine Fawundu/Purestock/Superstock

Index

Meaning
  connotative, 64–65
  constructing, 126
  denotative, 64
  determination of, 68–69
  of messages, 7–8
Meaning of Meaning (Ogden and
    Richards), 63
Mehrabian, Albert, 9, 102, 104
Meinecke, Christine, 158
Memory
  effectiveness, 342
  with emotions, 396
  in listening process, 127
  speaking from, 374
Men
  attractiveness of, 105
  body language of, 99
  as communicators, 75
  conflict by, 225
  conversational encouragement by,
    173–174
  conversational focus of, 172–173
  emotion detecting by, 153
  emotional expressiveness of, 172
  listening by, 161
  masculinity, 254
  report-talk by, 77
  self-concept of, 39
  smell sensitivity of, 113
Mena, Sofia, 350
Meridian, 79
Messages
  channels for, 9
  eye, 104–105
  I-messages, 165
  meaning of, 7–8
  mixed, 98
  obstacles to, 10
  owned, 165, 202
Metamessage, 85–86
Mexico, 250
Micro-expressions, 104
Microphone, 377
Microsoft PowerPoint (PP), 384
A Mighty Heart (Pearl), 248
Miller, George A., 51
Miller, Gerald, 167
Miller, Sherod, 161
"Mind Reading" (Paul), 104–105
Mindfulness, 262
Mindset (Dweck), 40
Mindset, growth, 40
Miscommunications, 82
Mixed messages, 98
"Mixed Signals" (Gosling), 35
Moalem, Sharon, 156
Models
  communication, 62
  for visual support, 379

Molnar, Theresa, 113
Monotone, 377
Monroe, Alan H., 423
Monroe's Motivated Sequence, 423
Morreale, Sherry, 6
Motivated sequence, 423
Motivation, 43, 407
  for interpersonal communication,
    159–161
  for interpersonal contact, 155–161
  self-, 153
Mouton, Jane, 236
Multiculturalism, 249–250, 257–261
Multimedia, 383
Muñoz, Mauricio Raúl, 392
Munro, Kali, 228
Murnighan, J. Keith, 23, 131
My First White Friend (Raybon), 258

N

Naftali the Storyteller, 329
Names, in intercultural
    communication, 132
Nasser, Haya El, 245
National Communication
    Association's (NCA's) Credo
    for Ethical Communication,
    25
National communities, 250
Native architecture, 61–62
Navajo, 251
Navarro, Mireya, 247
NCA. *See* National Communication
    Association's Credo for
    Ethical Communication
Needs
  hierarchy of, 416–417
  interpersonal, 159–161
Negotiating, 225
Nelson, Marilyn Carlson, 79
Netherlands, 111
The New York Times, 97, 116, 134, 216,
    247, 331
The New Yorker, 115, 283
Newberg, Andrew, 61, 68, 75, 144,
    224–225, 386
News, international, 261
Newsweek, 107, 163, 216
Noise, 10
Nondominant culture, 257–261, 260
Nonelective characteristics, 105
Nonverbal communication (NVC)
  active open-mindedness, 109
  appropriateness, 117
  assessing yourself, 119
  attractiveness, 105–106
  body adornment, 108
  body language as, 97–98, 103–104,
    111–113, 117

in brain, 96–97
characteristics of, 97–100
clothing, 106–108
in conflict with verbal communica-
    tion, 98
as cultural, 97–98
definition of, 94
as element of communication,
    94–96
emotions in, 116
expectancy violation theory and, 101
facial expressions, 104
feelings, attitudes in, 99
functions of, 115–116
honesty in, 116
improving, 116–118
interpretation of, 99
love, 106
manners, 114
paralanguage, 101–103, 117
as percentage of communication,
    9, 94
power through, 100
reactions to, 117
sensitivity to, 173
silence, 115
smell, 113
space and distance in, 108–111,
    117–118
in strategic flexibility, 96
time, 114, 118
touch, 99, 111–113
types of, 101–115
as unconscious, 98
variation by gender, 99
verbal communication and, 96–97,
    98, 115–116
Nonverbal cues, 115–116
Nonverbal symbols, 9
Norgaard, Mette, 133
Norms, 275
Notes, 374
  for public speaking, 385
Note-taking, 129–130
Nova, Chevrolet, 79
Numbers, in informative speeches,
    400–401
NVC. *See* Nonverbal communication

O

Obama, Barack, 9
Objective reality, 52
Objectivity, 300
Objects, 379
  informative speeches about, 396
O'Brien, Patricia, 133
Obscene language, 217
Obscenity, 70
Observers, 290